HOSPITALS & HEALTH CARE
ORGANIZATIONS

Management Strategies, Operational Techniques,
Tools, Templates, and Case Studies

HOSPITALS & HEALTH CARE
ORGANIZATIONS

Management Strategies, Operational Techniques, Tools, Templates, and Case Studies

Edited by
Dr. David Edward Marcinko, MBA, CMP™
Prof. Hope Rachel Hetico, RN, MHA, CMP™

Foreword by James Winston Phillips, MD, MBA, JD, LLM

CRC Press
Taylor & Francis Group
Boca Raton   London   New York

CRC Press is an imprint of the
Taylor & Francis Group, an **informa** business

A PRODUCTIVITY PRESS BOOK

CRC Press
Taylor & Francis Group
6000 Broken Sound Parkway NW, Suite 300
Boca Raton, FL 33487-2742

© 2013 by iMBA, Inc.
CRC Press is an imprint of Taylor & Francis Group, an Informa business

No claim to original U.S. Government works

Printed in the United States of America on acid-free paper
Version Date: 20120611

International Standard Book Number: 978-1-4398-7990-0 (Hardback)

Visit the Taylor & Francis Web site at
http://www.taylorandfrancis.com

and the CRC Press Web site at
http://www.crcpress.com

It is an incredible privilege to edit Hospitals & Health Care Organizations: Management Strategies, Operational Techniques, Tools, Templates, and Case Studies. *One of the most rewarding aspects of my career has been the personal and professional growth acquired from interacting with protean professionals of all stripes. The mutual sharing and exchange of practice-management ideas stimulate the mind and fosters advancement at many levels.*

Creating this text was a significant effort that involved all members of our firm. Over the past year, we interfaced with numerous outside private and public companies—as well as the Internet blogosphere—to discuss its contents. Although impossible to list every person or company that played a role in its production, there are several people we wish to thank for their support and encouragement: Kristine Mednansky—Senior Editor, Business Improvement (Health Care Management); Karen Sober—Editorial Assistant, and Richard O'Hanley—Acquiring Editor, all of Taylor & Francis Group. Any accolades are because of them. All other defects are my own.

Of course, this text would not have been possible without the support of our families, whose daily advocacy encouraged all of us to completion. It is also dedicated to our clients and contributing authors, who crashed the development life cycle in order to produce time-sensitive material in an expedient manner. The satisfaction we enjoyed from working with them is immeasurable.

David Edward Marcinko

Contents

SECTION I Managerial Fundamentals

SECTION II Policy and Procedures

SECTION III   Strategies and Execution

Foreword

In the business of medicine, there are three ways to increase revenue: (1) charge more, (2) do more, and/or (3) do the work more efficiently. In the current health care market where reimbursements are decreasing in the face of increasing expenses, a systemized approach is needed to maximize revenue to remain viable in the current health care arena.

In their new book, *Hospitals & Health Care Organizations: Management Strategies, Operational Techniques, Tools, Templates, and Case Studies*, Dr. David Edward Marcinko and Professor Hope Rachel Hetico bring their vast health care experience along with additional national experts to provide a health care model-based framework to allow health care professionals to utilize the checklists and templates to evaluate their own systems, recognize where the weak links in the system are, and, by applying the well-illustrated principles, improve the efficiency of the system without sacrificing quality patient care.

I first became aware of Dr. Marcinko while doing research for the master's thesis in my postgraduate LLM program following graduation from law school. The topic of my thesis was the anatomy and psychology of physician investments. There was no shortage of literature about the psychology of investing. However, health care professionals in general and physicians in particular are more unique in the psychological forces that guide their investing. Dr. Marcinko's previous book, *Financial Planning Handbook for Physicians and Advisors*, provided the foundation of physician investing allowing me to add to the discussion by bringing the academic ivory tower discussion into the everyday clinical environment of the physician. Since that time, I have benefited from his websites, our correspondences, and our telephone conversations.

As nothing in a health care system is isolated unto itself, because everything is codependent upon a number of other departments in the system, maximizing efficiency across departments and among different types of health care workers may prove to be a task to which many have been called but at which few have succeeded. If the number of assets, such as hospital beds, operating rooms, and ICU suites, are fixed, then these units must be maximized by working more efficiently to allow these fixed assets to be utilized more within a calendar period, thus resulting in increased revenue generation.

My wife and I recently experienced a health care delivery system that could have been detailed as a case history in this book. She had a total knee arthroplasty done by the doctor's doctor in joint replacement in Florida. This physician does 1000 total joints a year, operating only 3 days a week. Doing the math, you can see he does, on average, 6 or more joints a day, 3 days a week, 52 weeks a year. The procedures take, on average, about 2 hours; his patients are up walking within 1 hour of arriving from the recovery room and spend two to three nights in the hospital. The surgeon makes rounds every morning at 5:00 a.m. with the head nurse, the head of physical therapy, the discharge planner, and his physician assistant to ensure that everything is done to maximize the patient's recovery while utilizing the hospital's resources efficiently. With an average surgeon's fee of $4550 per procedure, the billable yearly income for the surgeon is $4,550,000.00. Using a conservative multiplier for hospital billing of 10, the billable income for the hospital is $45,550,000.00. The list could go on about how the hospital and surgeon have combined their efforts to effectively deliver quality medical care while efficiently utilizing resources to maximize revenue.

As detailed in the book, a system like this could not have occurred overnight. You cannot just look at a single department in a hospital and expect that its maximization will deliver a similar system to the above example. Instead, you must look at every department with which the patient will come into contact, either directly or indirectly, and make sure to identify any processes that may delay, deter, or bottleneck the overall delivery system.

Hospitals & Health Care Organizations: Management Strategies, Operational Techniques, Tools, Templates, and Case Studies is divided into three sections: (I) Managerial Fundamentals, (II) Policy and Procedures, and (III) Strategies and Executions. From these essential topics come direction and guidance through the use and application of practical health care–centered discussions, templates, checklists, and clinical examples to provide the framework for building a clinically efficient system.

The health care delivery system is not an assembly line, but with persistence and time following the established guidelines offered in this book, quality patient care can be delivered efficiently and affordably while maintaining the financial viability of institutions and practices.

James Winston Phillips, MD, MBA, JD, LLM
Post Office Box #600284
St. Johns, FL 32260-0284
Ph: (904) 613-3062
http://theothermedicaleducation.com

Preface

Our book, *Hospitals & Health Care Organizations: Management Strategies, Operational Techniques, Tools, Templates, and Case Studies*, will shape the organizational, management, and operational landscape by following four important principles.

First, we have assembled a world-class editorial advisory board and independent team of contributors and reviewers and asked them to draw on their experiences in operations, leadership, and lean managerial decision-making in the health care industrial complex. Like many readers, each struggles mightily with decreasing revenues, increasing costs, and high consumer expectations in today's competitive health care marketplace. Moreover, their practical experience and applied operating vision are a source of objective information, informed opinion, and crucial information to all working in this field.

Second, our writing style allows us to condense a great deal of information into the book. We integrate prose, managerial applications, and regulatory policies and perspectives with real-world case studies, models, checklists, and reports, as well as charts, tables, and diagrams. The result is an integrated oeuvre of lean management and operation strategies vital to all health care facility administrators, comptrollers, physician executives, and consulting business advisors.

Third, as editors, we prefer engaged readers who demand compelling content. According to conventional wisdom, printed texts like this one should be a relic of the past, from an era before instant messaging and high-speed connectivity. Our experience shows just the opposite. Applied health care management and administration literature has grown exponentially in the past decade, and the plethora of Internet information makes updates that sort through the clutter and provide strategic analysis all the more valuable. Oh, it should provide some personality and wit, too! Do not forget: beneath the management theory and case models are patients, colleagues, and investors who depend on you.

Finally, it is important to note that this book will not review ideas on industrial production line management (e.g., the Toyota experience), as is the usual case in older texts like this. Why? Health care delivery is a professional service and not a production assembly line, sans durable medical equipment, etc. Proper leadership and culture are implied in modern health care management, and we present case models and studies directly from the health care space and not by indirect example from the automotive, shipping, textile, or other manufacturing industries. Health care operations and management are our core and only focus.

Therefore, rest assured that *Hospitals & Health Care Organizations: Management Strategies, Operational Techniques, Tools, Templates, and Case Studies* will become an important book for the advancement of the working knowledge and the dissemination of management information, operations, and best strategic practices in our field. In the years ahead, we trust that these principles will enhance utility and add value to your work. Most importantly, we hope to increase your return on investment.

If you have any comments or would like to contribute material or suggest topics for future editions, please contact me.

Professor Hope Rachel Hetico
Managing Editor

TARGET MARKET AND IDEAL READER

This book should be in the hands of all:

- Chief executive officers, chief operating officers, chief technology officers, and vice presidents from every type of hospital and health care organization including public, federal, state, Veteran's Administration, and Indian Health Services hospitals; district, rural, long-term care, and community hospitals; specialty, children's, and rehabilitation hospitals; diagnostic imaging centers and laboratories; private, religion-sponsored, and psychiatric institutions
- Physician hospital organizations (PHOs), management services organizations (MSOs), regional extension centers (RECs), independent practice associations (IPAs), accountable care organizations (ACOs), regional health information exchanges (RHIEs), group practices without walls (GPWWs), integrated delivery systems (IDSs), medical homes (MHs) and their administrators, and all health care organization managers, health attorneys, executives, consultants, and their strategic advisors
- Ambulatory care centers, hospices, and outpatient clinics; skilled nursing facilities, integrated networks, and group practices; academic medical centers, nurses, and physician executives; business schools and health administration students, and all economic decision-makers and directors of allopathic, dental, podiatric, and osteopathic health care organizations

Collectively known as emerging and mature health care organizations (EMHOs) because of the merger, acquisition, and consolidation fervor in the industry today, readers from all these entities should use this textbook in the following way:

First, read Chapter 1 for a good content overview and browse through the entire book. Next, slowly read those parts or chapters that are of specific interest to your professional efforts. Then, extrapolate portions that can be implemented in specific strategies helpful to your health care setting. Finally, use it as an actionable reference text to return to time and again … . Learn and enjoy.

ABOUT THE INSTITUTE OF MEDICAL BUSINESS ADVISORS, INC.

iMBA, Inc. is a leading practice-management, economics, and medical valuation consulting firm and focused provider of textbooks, CD-ROMs, handbooks, templates, tools, dictionaries, and on-site and distance education for the health care administration, financial management, and policy domains. The firm also serves as a national resource center and referral alliance providing financial stability and managerial peace-of-mind to struggling physician clients. As competition increases, iMBA, Inc. is positioned to meet the collaborative needs of medical colleagues and institutional clients, today and well into the disruptive Health 2.0 participatory future.

CORPORATE SUBSIDIARIES

Advisors: www.CertifiedMedicalPlanner.org
Blog: www.MedicalExecutivePost.com
Dictionaries: www.SpringerPub.com/Search/Marcinko
Management: www.BusinessofMedicalPractice.com
Physicians: www.MedicalBusinessAdvisors.com

Disclaimer

This publication is designed to provide information in regard to the subject matter covered. It is not intended to constitute business, insurance, financial, technological, legal, accounting, or managerial advice. It is sold with the understanding that the editors, authors, and publishers are not engaged in these or other professional services. Examples are generally descriptive and do not purport to be accurate in every regard. The health economics, organization, and strategic management space is evolving rapidly, and all information should be considered time sensitive. If advice or other assistance is required, the services of a competent professional person should be sought.

Modified from a *Declaration of Principles* jointly adopted by:

- Committee of the American Bar Association
- Committee of Publishers and Associations

FAIR USE NOTICE

Hospitals & Health Care Organizations: Management Strategies, Operational Techniques, Tools, Templates, and Case Studies contains URLs, blog snippets, links, and brief excerpts of material obtained from the Internet or public domain, the use of which has not always been specifically authorized by the copyright owner. We are making such material available to advance the understanding of related issues and for the general purpose of reporting and educating. We believe that this constitutes a 'fair use' of any copyrighted material as provided by section 107 of U.S. Copyright Law. In accordance with Title 17 U.S.C. Section 107, the material is distributed to those who have expressed an interest in text purchase. Moreover, all register, trade, service, and copyright marks are the intangible intellectual property assets of their respective owners. Mention of any specific product, service, Website domain, or company does not constitute endorsement. No compensation was obtained for including same.

ABOUT INTERNET CITATIONS

Hospitals & Health Care Organizations: Management Strategies, Operational Techniques, Tools, Templates, and Case Studies makes use of "Uniform Resource Locators"—URLs—to direct subscribers to useful Internet sites with additional references. However, host entities frequently reorganize and update sites; therefore, URLs can change rapidly. Citations for this text are, therefore, "live" when published, but we cannot guarantee how long they will remain so, despite our best efforts to keep them current.

Although sponsored by the Institute of Medical Business Advisors, Inc., we maintain an arm's-length relationship with the independent authors and firms who carried out research and prepared the book. The goal of iMBA, Inc. is to be unbiased to the extent possible and to promote protean professional perspectives and opinions.

Acknowledgments

Creating this interpretive text was a significant effort that involved all members of our firm. Over the past year, we interfaced with various public resources such as state governments, the federal government, Federal Register (FR), Centers for Disease Control and Prevention (CDC), the Centers for Medicare and Medicaid (CMS), Institute of Medicine (IOM), National Research Council (NRC), and the U.S. Department of Health and Human Services (DHHS), as well as numerous private firms and professionals to discuss its contents.

Thank you all for believing in *Hospitals & Health Care Organizations: Management Strategies, Operational Techniques, Tools, Templates, and Case Studies* and helping to make it a success.

David Edward Marcinko **Hope Rachel Hetico** **Mackenzie Hope Marcinko**	Institute of Medical Business Advisors, Inc. Peachtree Plantation—West Suite # 5901 Wilbanks Drive Norcross, GA 30092-1141 www.BusinessofMedicalPractice.com www.MedicalBusinessAdvisors.com www.CertifiedMedicalPlanner.org www.MedicalExecutivePost.com www.SpringerPub.com/Search/Marcinko

Editors

Dr. David Edward Marcinko, editor-in-chief, is a health care economist, managerial and technology futurist, and former board-certified surgeon from Temple University in Philadelphia. In the past, he has edited seven practice-management books, three medical texts in two languages, five financial planning books, dozens of interactive CD-ROMs, and three comprehensive administrative dictionaries for physicians, accountants, attorneys, medical management consultants, and health care business advisors. Internationally recognized for his work, he provides litigation support and expert witness testimony in state and federal courts, and has clinical publications archived in the Library of Congress and the Library of Medicine at the National Institutes of Health. His thoughtful leadership essays have been cited in journals such as *Managed Care Executives, Healthcare Informatics, Medical Interface, Plastic Surgery Products, Teaching and Learning in Medicine, Orthodontics Today, Chiropractic Products, Journal of the American Medical Association, Podiatry Today, Investment Advisor Magazine, Registered Representative, Financial Advisor Magazine, CFP Biz (Journal of Financial Planning), Journal of the American Medical Association* (JAMA.ama-assn.org), *The Business Journal for Physicians,* and *Physician's Money Digest*; by companies and professional organizations such as the Medical Group Management Association (MGMA), American College of Medical Practice Executives (ACMPE), American College of Physician Executives (ACPE), American College of Emergency Room Physicians (ACEP), Health Care Management Associates (HMA), and PhysiciansPractice.com; and by academic institutions such as the UCLA School of Medicine, Northern University College of Business, Creighton University, Medical College of Wisconsin, University of North Texas Health Science Center, Washington University School of Medicine, Emory University School of Medicine, and the Goizueta School of Business at Emory University, University of Pennsylvania Medical and Dental Libraries, Southern Illinois College of Medicine, University at Buffalo Health Sciences Library, University of Michigan Dental Library, and the University of Medicine and Dentistry of New Jersey, among many others. Dr. Marcinko also has numerous primary and secondary editorial and reviewing roles to his credit.

Dr. Marcinko received his undergraduate degree from Loyola University, Maryland, completed his internship and residency at Atlanta Hospital and Medical Center, is a Fellow of the American College of Foot and Ankle Surgeons, and earned his business degree from the Keller Graduate School of Management, Chicago, and his financial planning diploma from Oglethorpe University, Atlanta. He was a licensee of the Certified Financial Planner Board of Standards, Denver for a decade and holds the Certified Medical Planner designation (CMP). He earned Series #7 (general securities), Series #63 (uniform securities state law), and Series #65 (investment advisory) licenses from the National Association of Securities Dealers (NASD) and a life, health, disability, variable annuity, and property-casualty license from the State of Georgia. Dr. Marcinko was also a cofounder of an ambulatory surgery center that was sold to a public company and has been a Certified Professional in Healthcare Quality (CPHQ); a certified American Board of Quality Assurance and Utilization Review Physician (ABQAURP); a medical-staff vice president of a general hospital; an assistant residency director; the founder of a computer-based testing firm for doctors; and the president of a regional physician practice-management corporation in the Midwest. He was a member of the American Health

Information Management Association (AHIMA) and the Healthcare Information and Management Systems Society (HIMSS); a member of the Microsoft Professional Accountant's Network (MPAN); a website engineer and beta tester for Microsoft Office Live Essentials program and a Microsoft Health User's Group (MS-HUG) member; and a registered member of the U.S. Microsoft Partners Program (MPP). Moreover, as the president of a privately held physician practice-management corporation in 1998, he consolidated 95 solo medical practices with $50 million in revenues.

Currently, Dr. Marcinko is the chief executive officer for the Institute of Medical Business Advisors (MBA), Inc. The firm is headquartered in Atlanta, Georgia, and works with a diverse list of individual and corporate clients. It sponsors the professional Certified Medical Planner (CMP) charter designation program and counsels maverick physicians, health managers, and financial advisors transitioning to niche health care advisory careers. As a nationally recognized educational resource center and referral alliance, the MBA Institute and its network of independent professionals provide solutions and managerial peace-of-mind to physicians, health care organizations, and their consulting business advisors. A favorite on the lecture circuit, Dr. Marcinko is often quoted in the media and frequently speaks on related topics throughout this country and Europe in an entertaining and witty fashion. He is also a social media pioneer and publisher of the *Medical Executive Post*, an influential syndicated Health 2.0 interactive blog forum. Dr. Marcinko is available to colleagues, clients, and the press at his corporate office in Atlanta.

Hope Rachel Hetico, managing editor, received her nursing degree (RN) from Valpariso University and her Master of Science in healthcare administration (MSHA) from the University of St. Francis, in Joliette, Illinois. She has served as both a managing editor and a contributing author for a dozen major textbooks and is a nationally known expert in managed medical care, medical reimbursement, case management, health insurance, security and risk management, utilization review, National Association of Healthcare Quality (NAHQ), Health Education Data Information Set (HEDIS), and Joint Commission on Accreditation of Healthcare Organizations (JCAHO) rules and quality compliance regulations.

Prior to joining the Institute of Medical Business Advisors as chief operating officer, Ms. Hetico was a hospital executive, financial advisor, insurance agent, Certified Professional in Healthcare Quality (CPHQ), and distinguished visiting assistant professor of health care administration for the University of Phoenix Graduate School of Business and Management in Atlanta. She was also the national corporate director for medical quality improvement at Abbey, and then Apria Healthcare, a public company in Costa Mesa, California.

A devotee of health information technology and heutagogy, Ms. Hetico was also responsible for leading the website www.CertifiedMedicalPlanner.org to the top of the exploding adult educational marketplace, expanding the online and on-ground CMP charter designation program, and nurturing the company's rapidly growing list of medical colleagues and financial services industry clients.

Professor Hetico recently completed a project for Resurrection Health Care in Chicago, and is currently at Saint Joseph's Hospital in Atlanta, Georgia.

Mackenzie H. Marcinko, project manager, is a linguistic intern from the Marist School, Atlanta, Georgia.

Contributors

Robert James Cimasi is the president of Health Capital Consultants (HCC), a nationally recognized health care financial and economic consulting firm. Mr. Cimasi has over 25 years of experience serving clients in 49 states, with a professional focus on the financial and economic aspects of health care service sector entities including valuation consulting; business intermediary and capital formation services; health care industry transactions including joint ventures, sales, mergers, acquisitions, and divestitures; litigation support and expert testimony; and certificate-of-need and other regulatory and policy planning consulting. Mr. Cimasi holds a masters in health administration from the University of Maryland, the Accredited Senior Appraiser (ASA) designation in business valuation, as well as the Master Certified Business Appraiser (MCBA), Accredited Valuation Analyst (AVA), and the Certified Merger & Acquisition Advisor (CM&AA). He has been certified and has served as an expert witness on cases in numerous states and has provided testimony before federal and state legislative committees. In 2006, Mr. Cimasi was honored with the prestigious Shannon Pratt Award in Business Valuation conferred by the Institute of Business Appraisers. He is the author of five nationally published books and numerous chapters in legal and financial treatises. He has written articles published in both peer-reviewed journals and trade publications, has frequently served as conference faculty and academic visiting instructor, has presented research papers and case studies before national audiences, and is often quoted by health care industry professional publications and the general media. Mr. Cimasi is also a Certified Medical Planner.

Robert James Cimasi, MHA, ASA, CBA, AVA, FCBI, CM&A, MCBA, CMP
President, Health Capital Consultants, LLC
1143 Olivette Executive Parkway
St. Louis, Missouri 63132-3205
www.HealthCapital.com

Dragana Gough has worked with more than 75 health care facilities analyzing and improving processes in a clinical environment. She has extensive experience in the analysis of ancillary/support departments, where she worked to improve work flow and staff scheduling, and has designed tools to predict workloads and staffing. She also has consulting experience in a variety of other areas including emergency services, perioperative services, outpatient services, and radiology.

Dragana Gough, BS, MSCP
Soyring Consulting
880 21st Avenue North
St. Petersburg, Florida 33704
www.soyringconsulting.com

Adam Higman is a Soyring consultant with management and consulting experience at a variety of multinational health care companies and acute care medical facilities. His expertise includes leading cost-reduction initiatives, market research and analysis, strategic planning, and physician/staff communications. Adam developed and implemented cost-reduction strategies and communications initiatives from the departmental level to hospital-wide. He has analyzed staffing functions and coordinated implementation efforts with medical, clinical, and support staff members.

Adam Higman, BS, MS
Soyring Consulting
880 21st Avenue North
St. Petersburg, Florida 33704
www.soyringconsulting.com

Denice Soyring Higman is the founder and president of Soyring Consulting. She has held positions at various levels of hospital management, including vice president, assistant administrator, director, and supervisor. She has also served as a consultant for hospital administration since 1983 and has been the project manager/director for hundreds of consultant engagements in all areas of the hospital and outpatient facilities.

Denice Soyring Higman, RN, BSN, MSN
Soyring Consulting
880 21st Avenue North
St. Petersburg, Florida 33704
www.soyringconsulting.com

Dr. Mark Mathews came to Creative Healthcare with over 20 years of active clinical practice in the field of anesthesiology. Located in Scottsdale, Arizona, he has served on the management board of his large multispecialty anesthesiology group in the Phoenix area as well as various committees within the Scottsdale Healthcare System. As such, he brings specialized expertise in hospital and outpatient surgical site management to CHC. Past projects with Creative Healthcare include development of operating room efficiency models and the application of Six Sigma analysis to medical billing. Currently, he is developing simulation models mimicking various medical inpatient and outpatient processes with an emphasis on improving patient safety through the application of Lean and Six Sigma analysis. After receiving his bachelor of science and medical degrees from the University of Arizona, Dr. Mathews completed his residency training in anesthesiology at the University of Minnesota. Subsequently, he received specialized fellowship training in neuroanesthesiology from the Barrow Neurological Institute in Phoenix. Currently, he is a diplomat of the American Board of Anesthesiology and maintains numerous memberships in professional medical societies. Dr. Mathews has professional practice experience with the Mayo Clinic Scottsdale, Barrow Neurological Institute, and the Scottsdale Healthcare System including clinical practice, clinical research, and resident teaching activities. In addition, Dr. Mathews also serves as a clinical neuroanesthetic consultant to Aspect Medical Systems in Boston, Massachusetts.

Dr. Mark Matthews
Managing Partner, Creative Healthcare
7033 E. Greenway Parkway
Suite 180
Scottsdale, Arizona 85254
www.creative-healthcare.com

Dr. Brent A. Metfessel is currently a senior medical informaticist in clinical analytics at United Healthcare, where he designs physician measurement algorithms and statistical methods and leads the application of risk adjustment methodologies to various health care quality and cost-efficiency measurement initiatives. His prior corporate positions have included clinical research coordinator at Anthem Blue Cross/Blue Shield and senior medical informaticist for Crossroads Technology Solutions. Dr. Metfessel has created and enhanced evidence-based medical policy as well as client reporting and analytic technologies using episode of care methodologies. He also designed custom-built primary care and specialist provider profiling systems and is a visionary in the application of the industry-leading clinical episode of care methodology to health care databases. Dr. Metfessel also has a decade of experience in general computer science, statistical analysis, artificial intelligence, and computational biology. He received his masters of science degree in health informatics from the University of Minnesota and his medical doctorate from the University of California, San Diego. He also holds a professional certificate in management for physicians from the University of St. Thomas.

Dr. Brent A. Metfessel, MS
Senior Medical Informaticist in Clinical Analytics
United Healthcare
Bloomington, Minnesota 55425
BrentMet@aol.com

Carol S. Miller has an extensive health care background in operations, business development, and capture in both the public and private sectors. Over the last 10 years, she has provided management support to projects in the Department of Health and Human Services, Veterans Affairs, and Department of Defense medical programs. In most recent years, Carol has served as vice president and senior account executive for NCI Information Systems, Inc., assistant vice president at SAIC, and program manager at MITRE. She has led the successful capture of large IDIQ/GWAC programs, managed the operations of multiple government contracts, interacted with many government key executives, and increased the new account portfolios for each firm she supported. She earned her MBA degree from Marymount University; BS degree in business from Saint Joseph's College, and BS degree in nursing from the University of Pittsburgh. She is a Certified PMI Project Management Professional (PMI PMP) and a Certified HIPAA Professional (CHP), with top secret security clearance issued by the DoD in 2006. Ms. Miller is also a HIMSS Fellow, past president and current board member, and an ACT/IAC Fellow.

Carol S. Miller, BSN, MBA, PMP
Managing Partner, Mackson Consulting
1818 Library Street
Suite 500
Reston, Virginia 20191
www.macksonconsulting.com

David J. Piasecki is the founder and operator of Inventory Operations Consulting LLC, a firm providing services related to hospital inventory management, material handling, and warehouse operations for manufacturers and equipment and other supply distributors in Southeast Wisconsin and Northeast Illinois. He has 15 years' experience in inventory operations accuracy and analysis, cycle counting, order picking, shipping, and receiving, and is a respected writer and industry expert. Mr. Piasecki is certified in Production and Inventory Management (CPIM) by the Association for Operations Management, in Alexandria, Virginia.

David J. Piasecki, CPIM
Inventory Operations Consulting, LLC
3929-80th Street
Suite #B
Kenosha, Wisconsin 53142

Dr. Eugene Schmuckler was a coordinator of behavioral science at the Georgia Public Safety Training Center and is a licensed psychologist. He is on the board of directors of the Association of Traumatic Stress Specialists and is a certified trauma specialist. Dr. Schmuckler is an international speaker and author, with publications translated into Dutch and Russian. He is the director of mentoring, coaching, and behavioral finance, and the dean of admissions for the Virtual Campus online Certified Medical Planner professional designation program from the Institute of Medical Business Advisors, Inc.

Eugene Schmuckler, PhD, MBA, CTS
Academic Dean, iMBA, Inc.
Peachtree Plantation–West
Suite # 5901 Wilbanks Drive
Norcross, Georgia 30092-1141
770-448-0769
www.MedicalBusinessAdvisors.com

Jennifer Tomasik is a principal at CFAR, a strategy and organizational change consulting firm serving clients worldwide from offices in Philadelphia, Pennsylvania, and Cambridge, Massachusetts. Jennifer leads CFAR's Healthcare practice area and is a founding member of CFAR's strategy and collaboration groups. She has been instrumental in designing many of CFAR's strategy tools and has broad experience and skill in developing strategy for health care organizations. Jennifer works with her clients to solve complex strategic and organizational challenges. Her approach to consulting emphasizes communication and collaboration, supported by a blend of quantitative and qualitative analytics. Jennifer has worked in the health care sector for nearly 15 years, with expertise in public health, clinical quality measurement, strategic management, and organizational change. Her clients include some of the most prestigious hospitals, health systems, and academic medical centers in the country.

Jennifer is a member of the American College of Healthcare Executives; a board member of ACHE Rhode Island; chair, Program and Education Committee, ACHE Rhode Island; and a member, ACHE Healthcare Consultants Committee. Jennifer's work on strategy and collaboration for health care organizations has been published broadly, including articles in *Healthcare Executive* and *American Journal of Medicine*, and chapters in two books—*Population Health* (2008) and

The Business of Medical Practice (2010 and 2011). She holds a master's degree in health policy and management from the Harvard University School of Public Health.

Jennifer Tomasik, MS
Principal, Center for Applied Research (CFAR)
Four Penn Center
1600 John F. Kennedy Blvd.
Suite 600
Philadelphia, Pennsylvania 19103
www.CFAR.com

Dr. Karen White has 20 years of management leadership experience in the health care industry. Her expertise is revenue cycle improvement with an emphasis on patient access and health information management/medical records. In her current position with Superior Consultant Company, her role as client engagement and project manager has encompassed strategic planning, revenue cycle reengineering and improvement, and business process redesign. She has overseen revenue cycle improvements resulting in an average of a 12% increase in cash by the end of the first quarter; an average of $1 million in additional reimbursable revenue; and business process redesign projects yielding an average of $1.5 million in savings. Dr. White is a trustee for a large health care integrated delivery network in the Midwest, serving on the executive committee as treasurer. She is a member of the National Association of Healthcare Access Management, Healthcare Financial Management Association, Medical Group Management Association, and the American Health Information Management Association.

Karen White, PhD, MSE
ACS—A Xerox Company
130 South First Street
Ann Arbor, Michigan 48104

Calvin W. Wiese is a senior-level finance executive with more than 10 years of CFO experience preceded by controllership and Big 4 audit experience in the health care industry. He is a visionary change agent recognized for his complex problem-solving ability and for consistently improving bottom-line financial results through benchmarking, effective budgeting processes, and inspiring staff toward top performance. Mr. Wiese has comprehensive, in-depth experience across all corporate finance, accounting, and treasury functions. He pioneered sophisticated capital finance, treasury, and investment management innovations recognized by Wall Street as the cutting edge of health care finance. His educational credentials include a master of business administration, a bachelor of science in accounting, and a bachelor of science in computer science. He is both a certified public accountant and certified managerial accountant.

Calvin W. Wiese, MBA, CPA, CMA
ACS—A Xerox Company
130 South First Street
Ann Arbor, Michigan 48104

Section I

Managerial Fundamentals

1 Overview of Operations in Health Care Organizations Today
Understanding Trends and Management Objectives

David Edward Marcinko and Hope Rachel Hetico

CONTENTS

INTRODUCTION

Since the middle of the 1980s, hospitals and other health care organizations have operated in an extremely competitive environment. During this period, hospitals have been under increasing pressure to improve quality and reduce costs. Furthermore, health care has come to be viewed as less of a human service and more of a commercial service, especially as new trends open up different approaches to medicine in 2012 and beyond.

In responding to this dynamic situation, health care managers have adopted management techniques from other industries in an effort to improve quality and reduce costs. Perhaps this transfer of ideas is most apparent in the functional area of operations management that traditionally deals with facility location, capacity, supply chain management, inventory systems, scheduling, layout, and quality management.

This chapter examines the leading trends, and then reviews some of the most promising avenues for improving hospital operations, including data management, process management, and development of human resources. It also highlights the importance of noneconomic performance measures. This chapter serves as an overview of this book and concludes with a discussion of strategic planning and leadership.

Our goal is to present emerging managerial concepts and trends that show how hospitals and health care organizations can use operations management to improve their competitiveness by exhibiting greater flexibility and higher quality, and as a result achieve better performance and outcomes.

COMPETITIVE BUSINESS MODELS, TRENDS, AND HEALTH CARE POLICIES

Several trends are affecting the health care industry, and these trends are, in turn, having an impact on financial performance. The ability of the industry to respond to these trends is determined by willingness to adapt, ability to retrain, and overall flexibility. Central, of course, is the level of leadership in making the changes.

First, this chapter examines the trends, and then gives an overview of the way health care managers are responding to these trends.

PATIENT-FOCUSED HEALTH CARE

One competitive trend is patient-focused and holistic health care, which centers on patient needs and attempts to humanize patient care. Patient-focused health care therefore incorporates the following components:

1. Patient education
2. Active participation of the patient
3. Involvement of the family
4. Nutrition
5. Art
6. Music

These are thought to improve patient outcomes. Furthermore, some think that patients will benefit from learning how to cope with health care processes before they enter into those processes and that this knowledge will result in better outcomes. An example of this would be classes to prepare couples for childbirth. These classes teach prospective parents the different stages of labor and strategies for dealing with the challenges associated with each stage. They cover options for pain management such as breathing and relaxation techniques and/or analgesics. The classes also provide education about clinical options such as induced labor and cesarian sections, and they cover practical issues such as what to wear and what kind of car seat to buy to transport the newborn home. We know from personal experience that this type of education is enormously beneficial in reducing stress and improving the decision-making ability of patients who are involved in health care processes.

As a result of this movement, some health care organizations have tried to reengineer the processes by which care is delivered in order to make it more patient focused. This is accomplished, in large part, by bringing the therapy to the patient rather than bringing the patient to the therapy. For example, storing more supplies and equipment in the patient's hospital room means that more services can be performed in the room. Obviously, this trend has significant implications for the operations management function in health care organizations in the areas of layout and human resources management. Supplies and equipment may be arranged differently to facilitate patient-focused care. Considerable staffing changes and cross-training may be in order to provide this type of service. Changes in facility layout to implement patient-focused care and reduce nonproductive movement of patients and personnel should be considered, especially when a facility is contemplating expansion or renovation of facilities.

IMPLEMENTATION OF THE DEFICIT REDUCTION ACT

The Deficit Reduction Act (DRA), S. 1932, was signed by President George W. Bush on February 8, 2006, and became Public Law No. 109-171. Implementation of the act included these provisions:

Subtitle A—Provisions Relating to Medicare Part A
  1. Hospital quality improvement (Section 5001)
  2. Improvements to Medicare-dependent hospital (MDH) programs (Section 5003)
  3. Reduction in payments to skilled nursing facilities (SNFs; Section 5004)
  4. Phase-in of inpatient rehabilitation facility classification criteria (Section 5005)

5. Development of a strategic plan regarding investment in specialty hospitals (Section 5006)
6. Demonstration projects to permit gain-sharing arrangements (Section 5007)
7. Post-acute care payment reform demonstration programs (Section 5008)

Subtitle B—Provisions Relating to Medicare Part B

1. Title transfer of certain durable medical equipment (DME) to patients after a 13-month rental (Section 5101)
2. Adjustments in payment for imaging services (Section 5102)
3. Limitations on payments for procedures in ambulatory surgical centers (ASCs; Section 5103)
4. Minimum updates for physician services (Section 5104)
5. Three-year extension of hold-harmless provisions for small rural hospitals and sole community hospitals (Section 5105)
6. Updates on composite rate components of basic case-mix adjusted prospective payment systems (PPSs) for dialysis services (Section 5106)
7. Accelerated implementation of income-related reductions in Part B premium subsidy (Section 5111)
8. Medicare coverage of ultrasound screening for abdominal aortic aneurysms; National Educational and Information Campaign (Section 5112)
9. Improvements to patient access and utilization of colorectal cancer screening under Medicare (Section 5113)
10. Delivery of services at federally qualified health centers (FQHCs) (Section 5114)
11. Waiver of Part B Late Enrollment Penalty for certain international volunteers (Section 5115)

Subtitle C—Provisions Relating to Parts A and B

1. Home health payments (Section 5201)
2. Revision of period for providing payment for claims that are not submitted electronically (Section 5202)
3. Timeframe for Part A and B payments (Section 5203)
4. Medicare Integrity Program (MIP) funding (Section 5204)

Subtitle D—Provisions Relating to Part C

1. Phase-out of risk adjustment budget neutrality in determining payments to Medicare Advantage organizations (Section 5301)
2. Rural PACE Provider Grant Programs (Section 5302)

The goal of the Act was to save nearly $40 billion over 5 years from mandatory spending programs through slowing the growth in spending for Medicare and Medicaid.

IDENTIFICATION OF "NEVER EVENTS"

As part of the DRA and its ongoing effort to pay for better care, not just more services and higher costs, the Centers for Medicare & Medicaid Services (CMS) is investigating ways to reduce or eliminate the occurrence of "never events"—serious and costly errors in the provision of health care services that should never happen. These events are characterized as

1. Unambiguous—clearly identifiable and measurable, and thus feasible to include in a reporting system
2. Usually preventable—recognizing that some events are not always avoidable, given the complexity of health care
3. Serious—resulting in death or loss of a body part, disability, or more than transient loss of a body function

4. Any of the following:
   a. Adverse
   b. Indicative of a problem in a health care facility's safety systems
   c. Important for public credibility or public accountability

Examples of never events include

Surgical events:
1. Surgery performed on the wrong body part
2. Surgery performed on the wrong patient
3. Wrong surgical procedure on a patient
4. Retention of a foreign object after surgery or other procedure
5. Intraoperative or immediately postoperative death in a normal healthy patient (Class 1 American Society of Anesthesiologists)

Product or device events:
1. Death or disability associated with contaminated drugs, devices, or biologics provided by the health care facility
2. Death or serious disability associated with a device used for functions other than the intended treatment
3. Death or serious disability associated with intravascular air embolism

Patient protection events:
1. Infant discharged to the wrong person
2. Death or serious disability associated with patient disappearance (elopement) for more than 4 hours
3. Suicide or attempts resulting in serious disability

Care management events:
1. Death or serious disability associated with a medication error (e.g., wrong drug, wrong dose, wrong patient, wrong time, wrong rate, wrong preparation, or wrong route of administration)
2. Death or serious disability associated with a hemolytic reaction due to the administration of ABO-incompatible blood or blood products
3. Maternal death or serious disability associated with labor or delivery on a low-risk pregnancy
4. Death or serious disability associated with onset hypoglycemia
5. Death or serious disability (kernicterus) associated with failure to identify and treat hyperbilirubinemia in neonates
6. Stage 3 or 4 pressure ulcers acquired after admission
7. Death or serious disability due to spinal manipulative therapy

Environmental events:
1. Death or serious disability associated with an electric shock
2. Any incident in which a line designated for oxygen or other gas contains the wrong gas or is contaminated by toxic substances
3. Death or serious disability associated with a burn incurred from any source
4. Death associated with a fall
5. Death or serious disability associated with the use of restraints or bedrails

Criminal events:
1. Any instance of care ordered or provided by a person impersonating a physician, nurse, pharmacist, or other medical personnel
2. Abduction of a patient of any age
3. Sexual assault
4. Death or significant injury from a physical assault

While the exact number of never events is not known, they add significantly to Medicare hospital payments, ranging from an average of an additional $700 per case to treat decubitus ulcers to $9000 per case to treat postoperative sepsis. Eighteen types of medical events may account for 2.4 million extra hospital days, $9.3 billion in excess charges (for all payers), and 32,600 deaths. Thus, paying for never events is not consistent with the goals of DRA or Medicare payment reform. Reducing or eliminating payments for never events means more resources can be directed toward preventing these events rather than paying more when they occur.

Legislatively, Minnesota and New Jersey mandate disclosure to the state and patients' families. Connecticut adopted a mix of state-specific reportable events for hospitals and outpatient surgical facilities. An Illinois law passed in 2005 required hospitals and ASCs to report 24 never events beginning in 2008. Several other states have considered or are currently considering never event reporting laws.

PAY-FOR-PERFORMANCE INITIATIVES

The concept of pay-for-performance (P4P) is an unproven trend, according to the Congressional Research Service, an arm of the Library of Congress. Initial studies suggest that P4P programs might change performance on quality measures that are used for the basis of bonus payments. Claims that P4P programs are cost saving in the long run are largely speculative, however, because determining whether a certain health care practice produces good results usually requires controlled studies rarely possible for a social policy. Moreover, physician pay is contingent on them believing that goals are fair, measures appropriate, performance accurately tallied, and incentives worthwhile.

HIERARCHICAL CONDITION CATEGORY MANAGEMENT

Hierarchical Condition Category Management (HCCM) is an emerging health care management trend designed to accurately reflect the health status of Medicare Advantage plan members and to help them remain financially viable in Part D of the system. Because the Medicare risk adjustment payment system uses clinical coding information to calculate risk premiums for Medicare Managed Care Organizations (MMCOs), HCCM seems best to address the following:

1. CMS risk adjustment system
2. Strategic and financial implications for Medicare plans
3. The initiatives required to effectively manage care under a risk adjustment payment system, and the key success factors associated with these initiatives

CONSUMER-DIRECTED HEALTH CARE PLANS

Another trend is consumer-directed health care (CDH) as patients become more knowledgeable consumers and more demanding about the quality of medical care they receive. Benefits managers in particular are proponents of CDH. They argue that employers should focus on which plans create the most value, go with quality, get employees to pay more, and move to a defined contribution approach. The concept of CDH is being implemented in employer strategies to change participant and provider strategies. This trend stimulates competition among providers based on both price and quality and forces providers to offer more information about cost and quality. Providers who successfully differentiate their strategies to respond to this trend may benefit financially.

CDH will have major ramifications for the operations management function in hospitals. In order for hospitals to compete on both price and quality, they will need to develop greater flexibility in order to differentiate their service offerings. Such flexibility is not likely to occur without sophisticated information systems that allow for data integration. Considerable staffing and training changes may be in order to provide this type of service.

Perhaps the best example of a CDH plan (CDHP) is the Health (Medical) Savings Account (HSA). An HSA is set up in conjunction with a traditional health insurance account, enabling the employer or employee to contribute tax-deferred money into a savings account to be used at a later time for a variety of health care costs.

1. *2012 HSA limits for contributions*: The 2012 maximum annual amount that can be contributed to an HSA is *$3100 for an individual*, up $50 from $3050 in 2011.
2. *2012 HSA limits for family coverage*: The 2012 maximum annual amount that can be contributed to an HSA is *$6250 for families*, up $100 from $6150 in 2011.
3. *2012 HSA limits for catch-up contributions*: Persons over age 55 are entitled to an additional annual *catch-up contribution of $1000 in 2012*—a number that remains unchanged from 2011.

The money in an HSA is used to pay an employee's deductible and co-pays as well as a number of other health insurance costs not normally covered under traditional heath insurance plans. Other benefits include the possibility of lower insurance premiums, additional fringe benefits without out-of-pocket costs, and the transfer of unused money after age 59½ for additional benefits. Employer contributions cease once enough money is deferred to cover deductibles, thereby significantly decreasing the annual HSA premium expenses.

TELEHEALTH AND MEDICARE

According to Richard S. Bakalar, MD, immediate past president of the American Telemedicine Association, many physicians think that telehealth is a wave of the future for Medicare, but so far the program has been slow to embrace technology. Congressional legislation in 1997 and 2000 largely established the telehealth component of Medicare, yet in 2006, the program spent only $2 million on medical services conducted electronically out of more than $400 billion in total spending. Remote patient visits, consultations, and other care can generate payment only if they fall under a handful of Medicare payment codes approved for telehealth applications, while the patient must be physically present with a health professional at the originating call site located outside of a metropolitan area. Some types of facilities are not approved to get paid for these services, and Medicare will only pay for home telehealth devices and care as part of an approved pilot project. A major factor in Medicare's cautious stance is concern that a large expansion would strain the system's finances by opening the doors for physicians and others to bill for a whole host of costly and potentially unnecessary telehealth services. For further discussion, see www.atmeda.org.

HOSPITAL, MEDICAL CLINIC, AND PHYSICIAN PRICING TRANSPARENCY

In 2007, federal and state legislatures called for hospitals across the country to make their prices "transparent." The term was defined as the full, accurate, and timely disclosure of hospital charges to consumers of health care, as well as the process employed to arrive at those fees. Moreover, transparency does not merely involve publishing a list of prices and fees. Essentially, hospital chief executive officers must be able to present their prices in a manner that is understandable to the general public and they must be prepared to explain the rationale behind their charges.

Currently, at least 33 states have already proposed or passed legislation regarding publication of hospital charges. For example, the average cost for a hip, knee, or ankle joint replacement is $38,443, while a heart valve operation is $124,561 and a back fusion is $60,406. Torrance California-based

Health Care Partners now notes on its Web site that it charges $15 for flu vaccines and $61 for a chest X-ray, while a colonoscopy costs $424.

Such initiatives demonstrate increased industry competition and advancing patient empowerment with CDHPs.

EVIDENCE-BASED MEDICINE

The next trend in health care is evidence-based medicine (EBM) that offers the promise of improving the quality of clinical services. EBM may be defined as the use of any techniques from science, engineering, and statistics (such as meta-analysis of medical literature, risk-benefit analysis, and randomized controlled trials) in order to aim for the ideal that health care professionals should make "conscientious, explicit, and judicious use of current best evidence" in everyday clinical practice.

Some argue that EBM is a trend that will prevail for the foreseeable future. In the past, standards of care were often set by panels of experts. Today, however, there is a greater demand for empirical evidence to establish the efficacy of clinical protocols. EBM can directly affect financial performance because it facilitates the elimination of therapies that cannot be demonstrated to be effective.

EBM can reduce a hospital's prescription drug costs. Evidence-based medicine may also affect operations management if it shows that multiple approaches to treatment can be efficacious. Of course, in order to accommodate different modalities of treatment, hospitals will need more sophisticated information systems that allow for data integration.

EBM may also be used to support another trend—the development of alternative and complementary medicine.

RISE OF RETAIL MEDICINE AND CONVENIENT CARE CENTERS

The retail medicine movement is gaining traction as convenient care center popularity grows. For example, CVS's purchase of MinuteClinics, and Walgreen's acquisition of Take Care Health Systems responded to the need for accessible, affordable, and quality health care. Convenient care centers, typically based in pharmacies and retail outlets, deliver basic needs to uninsured patients and serve as a competitive test for private physicians, clinics, and hospitals. Office of Technology Assessment studies by Hansen-Turton and Lin and O'Connell during the past two decades find the quality of care delivered by nurse practitioners and physicians to be equivalent.

ALTERNATIVE AND COMPLEMENTARY MEDICINE

The term "alternative medicine" refers to alternatives to Western medicine, such as herbal medicine, massage therapy, mind–body techniques, neurofeedback, nutritional therapy, chiropractic, Chinese medicine, or acupuncture. The term "complementary medicine" refers to the use of alternative medicine as supportive therapy in conjunction with traditional medicine. The use of alternative or complementary medicine cannot be dismissed as a fad and is already accounting for a significant volume of domestic health care business exceeding $22 billion per year. Complementary medicine is being accepted as adjunctive therapy to treat allergies, anxiety, back pain, cluster headaches, depression, digestive problems, sprains, and strains. More than 50 U.S. medical schools now teach some sort of alternative medicine as part of their standard medical curriculum. Managed care organizations (MCOs), such as Oxford Health Plans in Norwalk, Connecticut, Health Care Plan in Buffalo, New York, HealthEast in St. Paul, Minnesota, and Excellus BC/BS in Syracuse, New York all have panels of nontraditional health care providers.

Once again, greater flexibility will be required in all aspects of operations management in health care organizations to accommodate different modalities of treatment and thereby increase market share and revenues.

DEVELOPMENT OF SOCIAL HEALTH MAINTENANCE ORGANIZATIONS

A social health maintenance organization (HMO) offers extended coverage for some of the unconventional expenses associated with senior health care such as transportation and in-home day care not covered by traditional managed insurance or managed care plans. Social HMOs are not to be confused with the proliferation of "silent," "faux," or "mirror" HMOs, which are simply an intermediary attempt to negotiate reimbursement fees downward by promising a higher volume of patients in exchange for a discounted fee structure and pocketing the difference. According to the American Association of Health Plans (AAHP), social HMOs provide coordinated services by uniting federal and state funds and services to benefit the growing elderly domestic population. For further discussion, see www.aahp.org.

USE OF HOSPITALISTS (HOSPITAL-BASED MEDICAL GROUPS) AND ON-SITE MEDICAL GROUP STAFFING

The usual role of inpatient care in this country saw hospitalized patients cared for by their primary care or admitting physician. Although this model has the advantage of continuity, and perhaps personalization, it often suffered because of the limited knowledge base of the physician, as well as the physician's lack of familiarity with the available internal and external resources of the hospital. Furthermore, the limited time spent with each individual patient prevented the physician from becoming the quality leader in this setting. These shortcomings have led hundreds of hospitals around the country to turn to hospitalists as dedicated inpatient specialists. The National Association of Inpatient Physicians (NAIP), which changed its name to Society of Hospital Medicine (SHM) in 2003, estimates that this rapidly growing medical specialty could result in up to 60,000 hospitalists by 2013.

The term "hospitalist" was coined by Dr. Robert M. Wachter of the University of California at San Francisco (personal communication). It denotes a specialist in inpatient medicine. At its center is the concept of low-cost and comprehensive broad-based care in the hospital, hospice, or even extended care setting. Well-designed, hospitalist programs can offer benefits beyond the often-cited inpatient efficiencies they bring (personal communication). For further discussion, see www.hospitalmedicine.org.

Similarly, a related competitive integration model is on-site medical staffing, or physician employee affiliations (temporary to direct hire, direct placement, consulting, and on-site management) that represent an adjustment of the hospitalist concept. Benefits with this model include

1. Highly qualified applicants for all positions within the medical/health care environment
2. Reduction in direct costs with hourly rate charges for each employee-patient treated
3. Avoidance of physician employee fringe benefits, such as compensation for vacations, holidays, personal or sick leaves, worker's compensation, unemployment, Social Security, FICA, state and local taxes, administrative costs, and other benefits

This redeployment of existing MDs into the workplace (factory, police station, office building) or retail setting (Walmart, Intel Corp., Microsoft, IBM) is another exciting competitive challenge in health care today. The keys to success are thoughtful implementation and a commitment to measure the results of change and use the data to produce even more managerial innovation. For further discussion, see www.onsitemedicalstaffing.com.

GROWTH OF BOUTIQUE (CONCIERGE) MEDICAL PRACTICES

The boutique or concierge medical practice business model requires an annual fee for personalized treatment that includes amenities far beyond those offered in the typical practice or suggested by physician medical unions. Patients pay annual out-of-pocket fees for top tier service, but also use traditional health insurance to cover allowable expenses such as inpatient hospital stays, outpatient diagnostics and care, and basic tests and physician exams. Typical annual fees can range from $1500 to $5000 per patient, to family fees that top $25,000 a year or more. The concept, initially developed for busy corporate executives, has now made its way to others desiring such service.

GOVERNMENT-ENABLED PATIENT "BOUNTY HUNTERS"

Under the Health Insurance Portability Accountability Act (HIPAA), the U.S. Department of Health and Human Service (HHS) has operated an Incentive Program for Fraud and Abuse Information. In this program, HHS pays $100 to $1000 to Medicare recipients who report abuse in the program. To assist patients in spotting fraud, HHS has published examples of potential fraud, which include

1. Medical services not provided
2. Duplicated services or procedures
3. More expenses, services, or procedures claimed for than provided (upcoding/billing)
4. Misused Medicare cards and numbers
5. Medical telemarketing scams
6. Nonmedical necessity

There is no question that real fraud exists. The Office of the Inspector General of HHS saved American taxpayers a record $32 billion in 2006, according to Inspector General Glenn A. Fine. Savings were achieved through an intensive and continuing crackdown on waste, fraud, and abuse in Medicare and over 300 other HHS programs. To discourage flagrant allegations, regulations require that reported information directly contribute to monetary recovery for activities not already under investigation. For the DRA in 2009, this includes the following:

1. Encouraging the enactment of state False Claims Acts (Section 6032)
2. Employee education about false claims recovery (Section 6033)
3. Medicaid Integrity Program (Section 6034)
4. Enhancing third party recovery (Section 6035)

Nevertheless, expect a further erosion of patient confidence as they begin to take a "bounty hunter" view of health care providers.

PATIENT-FOCUSED HEALTH INFORMATION TECHNOLOGY

Fortunately, advances in patient-focused information technology are making possible greater flexibility in the delivery of health care services. For instance, telemedicine is facilitating remote delivery of health care services from hospitals, as is Internet-based medical imagery. In addition, Microsoft is starting its long-anticipated drive into the consumer health care market by offering free personal health records on the Web. The move, called HealthVault, comes after 2 years spent building its team, expertise, and technology, while managers have met with many potential partners including hospitals, disease-prevention organizations, and health care companies. Organizations that have signed up for HealthVault projects with Microsoft include the American Heart Association, Johnson & Johnson LifeScan, New York-Presbyterian Hospital, the Mayo Clinic, and MedStar Health, a network of seven hospitals in the Baltimore–Washington region. The company's consumer health offering includes a personal health record as well as an Internet search tailored for health queries, under the name Microsoft HealthVault (see www.healthvault.com).

A similar initiative named Revolution Health was also started in 2007 by Steve Case of AOL as an online assistant, advocate, and place to turn for reliable medical information. In midyear, it acquired CarePages, a leading social network for health and emotional support. The initiative provided invaluable emotional support for families when a loved one was hospitalized or receiving care. However, it was aborted last year. The medical director of Revolution Health was Dr. Jeffery

Gruen, MBA—a pioneer of information technology (IT)-driven health care consumerism (see www.revolutionhealth.com).

The "Medical Home" Concept

As the nation works to reinvigorate primary care in 2012, much is riding on the medical home concept. Some see it as an answer to a fragmented health care system that is not responsive to patients' needs for coordinated, comprehensive care. Others have invested in it as a vehicle to improve both the quality of care and control costs.

Basically, the medical home model allows more time with patients who really need to see a doctor and helps remove the pattern of seeing a new patient every 15 minutes. Instead, physicians block time to allow for several 30-minute appointments during the day for patients with complex cases. It is these types of patients—such as those with multiple chronic diseases or noncompliant patients—who can truly benefit from the extra time and are more vulnerable to having what has been called a "medical misadventure."

Medical homes and other practices have also moved toward team-based care where nurse clinicians, physician assistants, and other personnel with well-defined clinical skills can practice at the top of their license. This allows physicians to utilize the training of their entire staff, instead of trying to do it all, and focus on the care that only a licensed physician can provide (personal communication, Robert Graham, MD).

Accountable [Health] Care Organizations

An accountable health care organization (ACO) is a health system model with the ability to provide and manage patients in the continuum of care across different institutional settings, including at least ambulatory (outpatient) and inpatient hospital care and possibly post-acute care in some cases. Payment is consolidated rather than à la carte, and generally considered cost-effective and "bundled." Furthermore, ACOs have the capability of planning budgets and resources and are of sufficient size to support comprehensive, valid, and reliable performance measurements. The ACO model is one of the latest designs for managing health care costs and especially Medicare costs, and is gaining traction among policymakers desperate to control costs and boost quality in health care.

Patient Protection and Affordable Care Act

March 2011 marked the first anniversary of the Patient Protection and Affordable Care Act (PP-ACA or ACA), which was signed into law by President Barack Obama on March 22, 2010. Almost 2 years into the new era of health care reform, it is clear that Americans remain divided in their views on the ACA. Depending on the source, polls show the public remains confused about many aspects of the law, with mixed support for several provisions and strong opposition to the individual mandate and other parts of the ACA. However, with lawsuits challenging the constitutionality of the ACA, governors and state legislators vowing to refuse funding to implement certain ACA programs, and Congress poised to revise or repeal some or all of the law, opponents of the ACA are hopeful that they will have the chance to go back to the drawing board to craft reform legislation more to their liking, before full implementation in 2014. Meanwhile, supporters are pointing to widespread public approval of many of the insurance reforms in the law and claiming that once the health exchanges and other major components of the ACA take effect, public support will continue to grow.

Patient Choice Act

Austin Frakt, PhD, of the *Incidental Economist*, opined that many of the policy attributes, mechanisms, and challenges facing the ACA are similar to those of the Ryan–Rivlin Plan (also known as the Ryan–Coburn Plan). Ryan–Coburn was the Patient Choice Act (PCA) that was introduced into the last Congress, and may be the most comprehensive Republican health reform proposal put into bill form to date.

RECOVERY ASSET CONTRACTOR PROGRAM

In 2008, under the beta version of the Recovery Asset Contractor (RAC) program, CMS paid auditors a fee based on the amount of improper payments discovered. Hospital officials worried that this "bounty hunter" approach—the second for CMS after medical practice audits—creates a bias in auditors to focus only on collecting government overpayments. Other hospitals point to a pilot audit program in New York, Florida, South Carolina, and California, which found $357.2 million in overpayments and just $14.3 million in underpayments. Medicare estimates its error rate at 3.9% in 2007, down from 9.8% in 2003, but still totaling $10.8 billion in improper payments. RAC auditors were working in every state by 2010–2011.

AMERICAN RECOVERY AND REINVESTMENT ACT

On February 17, 2009, President Obama signed into law the American Recovery and Reinvestment Act (ARRA). The 1100-page document, the most sweeping economic legislation in the history of the United States, provides funding for health information technology initiatives for physicians, clinics, hospitals, and health care organizations. At about $20 billion, there has never been such an investment in health information technology (HIT) at one time. Some money will flow into the current calendar year, some dollars will flow in subsequent years, and some funding will be available until spent.

According to Steve Lieber, President of the Health Information Management Systems Society (HIMSS.org), these nine health care administration areas received HIT funding in 2009:

1. The Office of National Coordinator of HIT (ONCHIT) received $2 billion to fund HIT initiatives. Medicare and Medicaid funded HIT initiatives to physicians and hospitals beginning in 2011.
2. $1.1 billion allocated to the Agency for Health Care Research and Quality (AHRQ) for clinical practice effectiveness research.
3. The Indian Health Service (IHS) received unknown funding.
4. Construction funds to the Health Resources and Services Administration (HRSA) for community health centers.
5. $500 million allocated to the Social Security Administration (SSA) to upgrade HIT systems.
6. The Veterans Administration (VA) funded, in part, from the ARRA.
7. The Department of Agriculture received money for distance learning and broadband health applications.
8. $4.7 billion to the National Telecommunications Administration (NTA) for telemedicine diffusion.

Of course, time is of the essence if physicians and hospitals are to receive the full incentive payment for HIT adoption beginning in 2011. The monies are significant for physicians as full payment between 2011 and 2015 will range between $44,000 and $75,000. For each year a physician is not in the program, the incentive payments decline by 1% each year. The ultimate calculation of payments to physicians is based on Medicare patient volume.

For doctors and hospitals, the incentive payment began at $2 million in 2011, with additional payments based on Medicare volumes. The physician incentives stop in 2015. In 2015, there will be penalties for providers not participating in the program. Thus, ARRA is not only an economic stimulus bill, but an HIT stimulus bill for early adoption by medical providers.

HEALTH INFORMATION TECHNOLOGY FOR ECONOMIC AND CLINICAL HEALTH (HITECH) ACT

According to some, ARRA provided an opportunity to transform health care in the United States by providing $19 billion in HIT funding to ensure widespread adoption and use of interoperable HIT systems. President Obama's signing of the HITECH Act (a portion of the ARRA stimulus package) recognized the importance of HIT as the foundation for health care reform and cost savings. However, to others, it may become an economic black hole with an estimated cost to physicians of $35 to $75,000 each. Nevertheless, this initiative effectively launched the modern Health 2.0 and Health 3.0 collaborative scenes.

Among other groups taking a related leap with personal health records (PHRs) are Microsoft and Google. Both have launched products called personal health records in recent years. Both Microsoft's HealthVault and Google Health allow patients to store their own personal health histories online. Like all of their other apps, both are free to consumers. Unfortunately, Google Health is now defunct.

NEW-WAVE MEDICAL SPECIALISTS

What drives new-wave medical specialists? The answer, of course, is the next generation of physicians and their emerging new medical business and practice models, which include

1. *Ambulists* are doctors who travel locally and have no or only a sparse physical office presence of their own. They sporadically provide services that are additive to traditional practice models (e.g., an endocrinologist in a large family medical office with many diabetics).
2. *In situ* physicians regularly provide services that are complimentary to existing traditional practice models (e.g., dentists or podiatrists in a medical practice).
3. *Laborists* are obstetricians who do not wish to be on call. First begun in Cape Cod and other Massachusetts hospitals, such obstetricians work regular shifts for the sole purpose of delivering babies.
4. *Locum tenens* doctors travel around the country as itinerants (e.g., cruise ships) as temporary substitutes for another of the same specialty.
5. *Officists* remain in their own physical practice, and rarely see patients in the hospital, nursing home, patient home, outpatient facility, or elsewhere.
6. Finally, *dayhawk physicians* mimic the *nighthawk physician* model where radiologists in remote locations read films in the middle of the night as cash-strapped hospitals often find it cheaper to outsource to vendor of choice and in doing so may also get better private service in this country or overseas and more timely interpretations in many cases.

EMERGENCE OF COLLABORATIVE HEALTH 2.0

According to Susannah Fox, of the Pew Internet & American Life Project, more than half of the entire adult population in the United States used the Internet to get involved in the 2008 political process (pewinternet.org). Blogs, social networking sites, video clips, and plain old e-mail were all used to gather and share political information by what Lee Rainie, Director of the Pew Internet & American Life Project, dubbed a new "participatory class." By 2010, this participatory class had transitioned to reading medical blogs, listening to health care podcasts, updating their social network profile, watching surgical videos, and posting comments. Technology is not an end, but a means to accelerate the pace of discovery, widen social networks, and sharpen the questions someone might ask when they do get to talk to a health professional. GenY and GenX Internet users are the most likely groups to be turning up the network volume in health care, but no connected patient of any age is going back in the box. Ever since the term Web 2.0 was first used in 2004, there has been an inordinate amount of chatter about what it really is and its true impact. No one has really defined it clearly, but we believe the Web evolution relative to health care essentially falls into two generations:

Health 1.0

Health 1.0 is the traditional health care system. Information is communicated from a doctor (medical practice or hospital) to patients (individuals or customers). This is the basic business-to-consumer (B2C) Web site. The Internet became one big encyclopedia of information by aggregating information silos and knowledge repositories. Doctors, clinics, and hospitals aggressively launched Web sites for an Internet presence beyond their brick-and-mortar virtual establishments.

Health 2.0

According to Matthew Holt of The Health Care Blog (THCB), Health 2.0 may be defined as

A rapidly developing and powerful new business approach in the health care industry that uses the Web to collect, refine and share information. It is transforming how patients, professionals, and organizations interact with each other and the larger health system. The foundation of health care 2.0 is information exchange plus technology. It employs user-generated content, social networks, and decision support tools to address the problems of inaccessible, fragmentary, or unusable health care information. Health care 2.0 connects users to new kinds of information, fundamentally changing the consumer experience (e.g., buying insurance or deciding on/managing treatment), clinical decision-making (e.g., risk identification or use of best practices), and business processes (e.g., supply-chain management or business analytics).

Medical and related administrative information is communicated between clinic, practice, and individual patients, and collaboratively between and among all involved individuals. Therefore, if Health 1.0 was a book, Health 2.0 is a live discussion.

Micro Medical Practices

A micro medical practice is a low-overhead, high-tech and Health 2.0 enabled, labor-reduced, and often mobile office model that allows more physician control and patient face time. This concept can be extended to those patients who want or need to pay cash for their health care, high deductible health insurance, health insurance with high co-pays and residuals, and so forth (Figure 1.1).

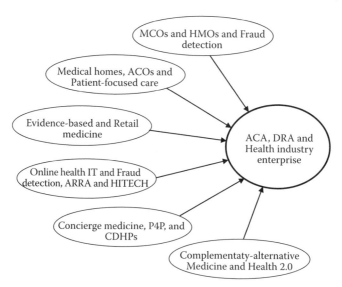

FIGURE 1.1   Competitive trends affecting the health care industry.

In summary, the effect of several competitive management and operational trends has changed the very nature of health care from a fairly narrow set of human services to a varied and complex set of commercial services. The expanded variety of health care services requires much greater flexibility in the delivery of health care services if a hospital is to compete effectively. Although advances in information technology are making it possible for health care organizations to be more flexible, the challenge for health care managers is to adapt the operations management approaches used in other service industries to deliver a greater variety of health care services with higher quality and lower prices.

INFORMATION AND ANALYSIS

Improvement of financial performance must start with improvement of operations management. One way for hospitals to improve operations management is to re-evaluate their information needs and the way that they analyze operations management data.

LENGTH-OF-STAY (LOS) FORECASTING

Substantial day-to-day variation in hospital occupancy leads to increases in costs. Hospitals may be able to improve their financial efficiency by preparing more accurate forecasts of length of stay and thus of their utilization of capacity. For instance, the accuracy of predicted length of stay can be improved by using multiple regressions. The patient's characteristics (age, gender, ethnicity, marital status, admission type, and admission source) and clinical indicators for their diagnosis-related groups are significant predictors of length of stay.

The effectiveness of interventions is often measured by length of stay. For example, the average length of stay for patients on the medical service of the University of California, San Francisco's Moffitt–Long Hospital fell by 15% in 1 year, compared to concurrent and historical controls adjusted for case mix. There was no reported decrease in patient satisfaction or clinical outcomes. However, this is a crude measure that is contaminated by the inclusion of all days in the hospital even if they were not preceded by some type of intervention. An approach that views only the slice of time after a medical intervention to measure the effect of the intervention on length of stay in a more precise manner can improve the accuracy of forecasting.

COLLABORATION AMONG ORGANIZATIONS

Another way to improve the health care operations management function is to obtain better information by collaborating with other organizations in gathering information. Most operational failures result from breakdowns in the supply of materials and information across organizational boundaries. Better capacity decisions can often be made in collaboration with other institutions.

For example, emergency rooms often take collaborative approaches and use Internet technology to regulate ambulance traffic to emergency rooms. Some metropolitan areas share information concerning accessibility and efficiency of care on a regular basis. The sharing of information facilitates benchmarking that leads to improved performance for the community.

Hospitals can benefit from involvement in community-based quality improvement initiatives. For example, community hospitals can collaborate with their competitors and members of the business community to share information that leads to the identification of opportunities to improve performance, the delivery of root cause analysis, and the development of process measures that facilitate change. Working with other organizations and employers in the community can not only lower costs, but also improve population health.

MEASURES OF PERFORMANCE AND SIX SIGMA

Still another way to improve performance is to use more meaningful measures of performance. Financial measures of performance provide only part of the information needed for decision making. Meaningful medical performance measures must also include the following:

1. Quality of clinical outcomes
2. Retention of expert clinical care providers
3. Patient satisfaction
4. Retention of staff and physicians
5. Volume and market share growth
6. Revenues and operating costs

Inclusion of these dimensions provides a more balanced scorecard, which then becomes an instrument that can be used to measure the attainment of strategic objectives.

In the same vein, the balanced scorecard approach can be modified to what has been termed a "dashboard" approach to accounting. The dashboard approach avoids information overload by benchmarking critical dimensions of performance. The performance of the health care organization on any dimension is compared to the industry average and the average of competitors. The dashboard approach also condenses information but allows for drill down from aggregate accounting measures to more detailed accounting measures when more specific information is required. For example, poor performance on return on investment may be traced down to poor return on assets and low asset turnover.

Six Sigma, on the other hand, is "a performance improvement methodology using statistical analysis to reveal the root cause of defects in products and performance. Long used in manufacturing, its principles and techniques have been introduced into the health care, service, education, and other sectors with impressive results" (Jack Welch, CEO of General Electric).

In Six Sigma performance analysis for health care, the statistician's bell-shaped curve becomes a representative of accounting and/or medical variation. It measures to the upper standard limits of 99.99966% as a rigorous systematic discipline that demands the use of various problem-solving tools and a particular methodology to measure performance and drive process improvement. In fact, more health care organizations are using the measurable feedback data provided by Six Sigma to augment other ongoing quality initiatives, like the balanced scorecard (dashboard). By validating the impact of care defects and medical improvements, as well as the use of small-scale experiments, reaching the optimal solution to a performance or outcome problem makes implementing a change more believable to the hospital or health care organization.

5S PROCESS MANUFACTURING

5S manufacturing is the name of a more recent workplace organization methodology that uses a list of five Japanese words (seiri, seiton, seiso, seiketsu, and shitsuke). This list describes how items, like durable medical equipment, are stored and how the new order is maintained. The decision-making process usually comes from a dialogue about standardization that builds a clear understanding among employees of how work should be done. It also instills ownership of the process in each employee. There are five primary phases of 5S: sorting, straightening, systematic cleaning, standardizing, and sustaining. Additionally, there are three other newer or secondary phases sometimes included: safety, security, and satisfaction. The concept, like lean Six Sigma, is gaining traction in the health care operational ecosystem.

PROCESS MANAGEMENT

Another way to improve financial performance is with improved process management. For example, hospitals can use a project management approach to improve their financial reporting processes.

Cost Management, Medical Activity-Based Costing, and Economic Order Quantity Cost Analysis

The process by which costs are determined may be improved. For instance, evidence-based management research concerning costs can lead to more accurate costing. Such research can provide evidence as to what services cost, what organizational activities are successful in controlling costs, and what impact cost control has on quality and patient outcomes.

Medical activity-based costing (MABC), on the other hand, is a systematic cause-and-effect method of assigning the cost of activities to medical products, health services, patients, or any cost object. MABC is based on the principle that medical products and health care services consume economic activities. Traditional cost systems allocate costs based on direct labor, material cost, revenue, or other simplistic methods. As a result, traditional systems tend to overcost high-volume products, services, and patients, and undercost low-volume items.

Economic order quantity cost (EOQC) analysis is an accounting method for minimizing hospital inventory such as DME. EOQC analysis measures costs by making three key assumptions:

1. Revenues (inventory depletion) are constant
2. Costs per order are stable
3. Just-in-time inventory delivery allows the placement of orders so that new orders arrive when inventory approaches zero

Health Information Technology Management

Yet another method of improving performance beyond electronic medical records (EMRs) is through better use of information technology in some clinical areas. Health management technology is being designed to improve patient safety in several ways. For example, information technology facilitates the collection and analysis of data so that therapies that cannot be demonstrated to be effective can be eliminated. This is part of the trend to evidence-based medicine discussed in the next chapter on "Market Competition in Modern Health Care Management (Surveying the Current Ecosystem)." Information technology also allows facilities to use bar coding or radio frequency identification devices (RFIDs) to ensure that inventory and supplies are accurately identified and inventories are maintained at the appropriate levels. By maintaining the lowest level of inventory consistent with good service, a facility can lower the amount of funds required to finance the inventory. Furthermore, information technology allows facilities to use drug databases and electronic prescribing with computerized physician order entry (CPOE) systems. These approaches prevent losses that may occur due to medication errors. Finally, information technology is vital for decision support systems that reduce the incidence of human error in decision making.

Better information technology can also improve financial management by facilitating the development of better databases with accurate and up-to-date information on products and prices to improve supply chain management. Some firms have developed information technology that allows them to offer data cleaning services to hospitals designed to improve the efficiency of supply chain management. In some instances, it may be cost-effective to purchase data cleaning services to eliminate out-of-date information on the products and services of vendors.

Supply Chain Management

Improved management of the supply chain has long been a focus in many industries; it is now having an impact on the health care industry. For instance, we have observed that hospitals in the United States have been more successful than hospitals in France and Finland in reducing levels of supplies inventory.

Just-in-time approaches to inventory management can improve financial performance. Improved supply chain management can reduce costs by eliminating unnecessary delays and eliminating defects in health care supplies.

Current competitive trends will likely make supply chain management more important. The emergence of complementary medicine has implications for the supply function in hospitals, as these therapies require supplies of rather exotic items such as acupuncture needles, herbs, beads, and so forth. Thus, improvements in patient care often require concomitant improvements in operations management processes.

Improving the quality of care using patient-focused care can also improve the financial performance of a facility. Patient-focused care not only refers to a holistic approach to care, but it also refers to the reengineering of processes to facilitate patient care. This reengineering may lead to increased efficiency of health care providers that result in lower costs. For example, in an effort to provide patient-focused care, a hospital may conduct job analyses leading to cross-training of personnel and the elimination of the duplication of performance of tasks.

OPERATIONS MANAGEMENT

The implementation of patient-focused care has implications for operations management.

For example, patient-focused care may require adjustments in materials management. The storage of more supplies and equipment in the rooms of patients might require the maintenance of higher levels of inventory and assets, and necessitate ordering supplies and equipment in different sizes.

Furthermore, some alterations in hospital design might have to be made to accommodate patient-focused care. Rooms for patients may need to be larger to accommodate more cabinets and drawers for storage of supplies and equipment, for example. Once again, improvements in patient care often require concomitant improvements in operations management processes.

SCHEDULING (ACCESS) MANAGEMENT

Better management of scheduling, or health care admissions access, can improve financial performance. There is some evidence that scheduling can be improved by giving schedulers more latitude to use their professional judgment and thereby avoid bottlenecks that occur over the use of critical resources. Moreover, improvements in outpatient scheduling can decrease patient waiting times, nurse staffing, and physician overtime.

Hospitals and health care organizations should also take a comprehensive approach to scheduling and consider how each component fits in with overall optimization.

In short, scheduling systems that provide flexibility and simplify decision making are likely to confer strategic advantage in the current competitive environment.

HUMAN RESOURCES DEVELOPMENT

The accounting system maps the economic reality of organizational performance. A key factor in organizational performance, however, is the effectiveness and efficiency of human resources. Hospitals can improve organizational performance by increasing the performance of human resources. Investment in human resources development activities is therefore one way to improve the efficiency and effectiveness of human resources and thus of overall organizational performance.

EMPLOYEE DEVELOPMENT

Investments in employee development can improve capability and enhance performance. For example, one way to improve customer satisfaction is to offer employee development in service encounter management.

Still another model for improving performance is to use employee development to ensure that employees fully utilize the capability of equipment. For example, some employees do not recognize and take full advantage of the capabilities of the systems and software available to them. As a result, many hospitals do not have full control over the inventory of supplies for their operating rooms. Moreover, employees sometimes do not use system capabilities to monitor inventory levels and reorder points even though the system has features capable of performing these functions. Human resources development could remedy such shortcomings.

HOSPITAL PERSONNEL, PHYSICIAN RECRUITMENT, AND PROFESSIONAL EMPLOYER ORGANIZATIONS

Still another way to improve human resources is to recruit physicians and hospital personnel who bring in expertise and disseminate it to other employees. Hospitals are increasingly hiring materials managers from other industries to upgrade their materials management capabilities.

Hospitals and related health care entities often lag far behind other industries with regard to professional human resource supply chain management. Hospitals can hire personnel with experience in other settings in order to gain new perspectives in supply chain management. With these new perspectives, agreements with suppliers can be renegotiated to make a hospital more competitive.

Internally, for example, improving the financial performance of any health care organization is a skillful balance between cinching the belt and investing in the right growth strategies. Whether that strategy calls for expanding a clinic, moving into a key market, or adding a new clinical program, recruiting the right physicians and medical personnel becomes all important in achieving economic goals. Without physicians and ancillary personnel, there are no patients. Indeed, doctors, nurses, and providers are key drivers in any health care organization's growth strategy. Simply put, finding and hiring the right medical professionals is a surefire prescription for success. A winning centralized operational process includes needs and criteria determinations, materials for sales, marketing, and recruiting, interviews and on-site visits, and the correct reimbursements package with employment contract.

External recruitment, on the other hand, may involve use of a professional employer organization (PEO) as hospitals and health care entities may find that employee leasing, also referred to as co-employment, can be an effective strategy to combat the spiraling costs of having a professional recruitment and clerical support staff. PEOs can offer financial and administrative benefits to hospitals, which, in turn, can increase staff loyalty and reduce turnover. Office-based physicians will find that the personnel services of an employee leasing company will give them more time to address the efficiency of their practices and the quality of care they provide for patients. Simply put, instead of the health care organizations, clinic, hospital, or practitioner being the *employer of record* of the workplace employees, this responsibility is *outsourced* to an off-site PEO that specializes in hiring, retention, labor management, and cost control. The organization retains functional control of the employees, and the PEO handles the human resources (HR) management issues. The PEO can provide these HR services *more cost-effectively* by combining employee groups and servicing their needs along with the employees of the many other health care organizations they already serve. Outsourcing becomes a matter of simple economics.

CULTURAL TRANSFORMATIONS

Lastly, human resource development can be used to effect cultural transformations. Consumer-driven health care may transform the culture of a health care facility into one where the patient and his or her family are active participants in the process of delivery of care and contributors to improvement in safety and quality.

Human resource development can transform the culture of the workforce to one that supports consumer-driven health care. It may also help create a safety culture.

STRATEGIC PLANNING

Financial performance may be constrained by poor decisions in the strategic planning process. If you want to enjoy good financial performance, you need to make good strategic decisions concerning the operations management function.

Many decisions made in the strategic planning process have a profound effect on operations management. There has been little integration of these issues, and there is considerable room for research in this area because operations management offers the potential to improve quality and lower costs.

Thus, hospitals and health care organizations can likely improve performance by integrating operations management into their strategic planning. Decisions concerning location and size obviously set the stage for good or bad performance. For example, a hospital that is located in an area that is underserved is more likely to enjoy good financial performance. However, the same location could suffer poor performance if there are problems with highway access or the location is not convenient to safe and affordable housing for the personnel who would staff the facility. Thus, intermediate infrastructure decisions significantly affect hospital cost, quality, and financial performance.

One option in the strategic planning process is to adopt the plant-within-a-plant or hospital-within-a-hospital approach. There has been an increase in the number of physician-owned specialty hospitals, and these facilities have the potential to serve as focused factories that lower costs and increase quality.

CAPACITY WORKFORCE MANAGEMENT

Other strategic decisions are concerned with capacity and workforce.

Capacity management decisions concerning equipment choices and workforce decisions affect the cost and quality of services. For example, a significant percentage of emergency room visits can be handled by staffing with nurse practitioners.

ACCOUNTING MANAGEMENT

Some accounting choices can greatly improve strategic control.

The use of the balanced scorecard approach—using a variety of measures to make an assessment—in a health care organization enhances strategic control of an organization, increases the knowledge of key stakeholders, and facilitates optimum organizational performance. By using a balanced scorecard approach, for instance, Duke Children's Hospital and Health Center in Durham, North Carolina, reduced costs by $30 million, increased total margin by $15 million, while improving clinical outcomes and staff satisfaction.

The balanced scorecard is also useful for employees in that it shows them what course of action to take in order to be consistent with the mission statement. The balanced scorecard for a health care organization can report information from a financial perspective (e.g., unit profitability), a customer perspective (e.g., patient satisfaction), an internal process perspective, (e.g., employee turnover rate), and a learning and growth perspective (e.g., training hours per caregiver).

LEADERSHIP

The organizational changes necessary for good operational performance rarely occur without some initiative on the part of management. If you want good financial performance, you need to assert the leadership necessary to design and implement needed changes in operations management.

But health care leadership today is not something that is done *to* people; it is something you do *with* them. Today's successful hospital executives must act more like leaders and mentors and less like administrators or managers. They must create trust and collaboration to empower their professional staff, volunteers, and employees. For some executives, this requires a fundamental shift in mindset. This new mentoring paradigm demands a holistic approach for the total health care organization so that the enterprise-wide environment assists everyone to realize their full potential. This maximization of performance is more than just a trendy business concept for leadership, and it is more than merely putting on a business suit and expecting results. It is a commitment to being a transparent, informed leader. One of the elements in this shift in mindset involves information communication. All relationships involve communication as an element of education, and health care leadership is no exception. In fact, what is really enabling is the dissemination of information to all stakeholders and peers. In essence, the leader takes on a more communicative role and thus empowers employees to their full potential. To successfully achieve this, the hospital executive must have a clear understanding of self and consider human values relative to the role of the health organization measurements and mission. This attention assists the executive to lead with self-confidence and to encourage differing opinions.

Leadership is the driver of all components, including information and analysis, strategic planning, human resource development and management, and process management.

OPERATIONS MANAGEMENT

One way to assert leadership is to make sure that the operations management function communicates to other executives the limits of their capabilities. For example, supply chain managers need to educate other administrators as to what supply chain managers can reasonably accomplish and what is beyond their control.

DECISION MAKING AND COMMUNICATIONS MANAGEMENT

Another way to promote good leadership is to be sure to include physicians and other stakeholders in the decision-making process. Physician involvement in strategic decision making has been shown to significantly improve hospital performance.

Still another method to show leadership is to have the requisite knowledge base and good communication skills. It is important to remember that managers recruited from other industries often lack the clinical expertise or interpersonal skills to communicate with personnel in the operating room. Thus, expertise from other industries is not always easily transferred to the hospital industry, so it is vital that channels of communication be created.

Good leadership is not limited to the boundaries of the organization. Those who work in operations management should also assert leadership within the community to improve the efficiency and effectiveness of the system as a whole. Managers of health care organizations are increasingly held accountable in the eyes of the public for the health status of the community. Accountability to the community is accomplished differently depending on whether a hospital is freestanding or a member of a system. Freestanding hospitals tend to be accountable through the compositional aspects of their boards. System-affiliated hospitals tend to be accountable through information monitoring and required reporting activities.

CONCLUSION

Powerful trends in the environment affect the way a hospital conducts its clinical and financial operations. Indeed, changes in clinical operations often cannot be made without concomitant changes in operations management.

In general, hospitals and health care organizations will be more competitive if they offer more variety, higher quality, and lower prices for services. Fortunately, new developments in information technology promise to improve the efficiency of clinical, strategic, and financial operations.

More importantly, the new information technology will not likely be effective unless hospitals also implement operations management techniques that are currently used in other industries under the same pressure to offer more variety, higher quality, and lower prices. Health care organizations should take a strategic approach to operations management by examining information and analysis, process management, human resources development, strategic planning, and leadership.

CASE MODEL 1.1: JUDE AND THE SURGI-PACKS

Jude was the COO of a suburban acute care hospital in Las Vegas. As he was driving home across town, he was caught in a traffic jam. He stared blankly at the advertisement on the back of a taxicab in front of him. The ad was a picture of one of the chorus lines in a typical show in Sin City. For some reason, the ad reminded him of a management team meeting that had taken place at the hospital earlier that day.

During the meeting, the CFO had complained that the hospital needed to improve its financial performance. When he asked for suggestions, Jude commented that many hospitals in the Las Vegas Valley were attempting to improve supply chain management by ordering prepacked surgical packs (surgi-packs) for the operating room. A vendor had offered to provide surgi-packs customized to suit the wishes of each surgeon. The CEO was puzzled. He wanted to know how customized surgi-packs could save money. He was under the impression that customization added costs. The CFO was more sanguine about the suggestion. He thought that it might reduce inventory levels and thus improve asset turnover ratios slightly. However, he felt that the biggest problems in the operating room were labor costs. He wanted to know if the surgi-packs would help reduce labor costs. The chief of nursing operations was not optimistic at all. She said that her major concern was how the surgi-packs would affect the quality of patient care. On that point, the CFO added that he thought that revenue generation was also a problem. He felt that real or perceived quality problems connected with the operating room had adversely affected the revenue generation of the hospital.

Jude responded that customization was not costly if the information technology was up-to-date. The proper software could provide customization with little or no additional cost. Jude added that the surgi-packs would likely decrease inventory levels. This would reduce the financing cost of inventory and possibly some holding costs as well. In financial terms, the lowering of inventory levels would increase current asset turnover and return on assets. Further, the reduction of assets would increase the equity multiplier and increase return on equity. With regard to labor costs, the surgi-packs would provide a savings because the surgi-packs would be assembled by unskilled labor at the vendor, and not by nurses in the operating room. However, Jude was unable to answer the concerns about quality and patient care.

Suddenly and belatedly, Jude realized in the traffic jam what he should have said to the chief of nursing operations and the CFO with regard to quality. First, he should have told the CNO that the surgi-packs would improve patient care because nurses in the operating room would have more time for patient care if they did not have to assemble the surgi-packs. Second, Jude realized that he should have argued that the surgi-packs might also alter the performance of the surgeons. If the surgeons had the opportunity to plan and establish their surgery profiles with the vendor, it might save time and reduce ordering errors.

KEY ISSUES

How should Jude prioritize the following in order to improve operations?

- Information technology issues
- Financial issues
- Patient care issues
- Communications issues

- Management issues
- Quality issues

Using the Malcolm Baldridge National Quality Award quality framework reflected in the checklists, consider what changes the hospital might implement to ensure that the hospital regularly makes good decisions on such issues as surgi-packs.

CHECKLIST 1: Health Care Business Model Options	YES	NO
Is your health care entity business model a		
Physician practice management corporation? (PPMC)	o	o
Publicly traded roll-up health care entity?	o	o
Sole proprietorship (Inc., Corp., P.A., or P.C.)?	o	o
C corporation (Inc., Corp., P.A., or P.C.)?	o	o
S corporation (Inc., Corp., P.A., or P.C.)?	o	o
Professional corporation (P.C.)?	o	o
Professional association (P.A.)?	o	o
Not-for-profit organization (NFP)?	o	o
General medical partnership (P)?	o	o
Limited partnership (LP)?	o	o
Limited Liability Corporation (LLC)?	o	o
Limited Liability Partnership (LLP)?	o	o
Master Limited Partnership (MLP)?	o	o

CHECKLIST 2: Publicly Traded Health Care Entity Benchmark Options	YES	NO
Where is your publicly traded health care entity listed or benchmarked:		
New York Stock Exchange listing (NYSE)?	o	o
American Stock Exchange listing (AMEX)?	o	o
Cain Brothers PPMC Index?	o	o
Over-the-Counter Listing (National Association of Securities Dealers)?	o	o
Master Limited Partnership Index?	o	o
Other listing?	o	o

CHECKLIST 3: Information and Analysis	YES	NO
Determine your information and analysis needs.		
Have you assembled the information—financial, nonfinancial, or clinical—that is needed for planning?	o	o
Is it on hand?	o	o
Would different forecasting techniques provide better results?	o	o
Would collaboration with competitors lead to better management of capacity?	o	o
Would sharing of information with competitors help in benchmarking performance?	o	o
Would collaboration with other organizations in the community improve health promotion and disease prevention?	o	o
Do reports show performance on clinical and nonfinancial dimensions?	o	o
Do reports avoid information overload but allow for drill down from aggregate to detailed data?	o	o

CHECKLIST 4: Process Management	YES	NO
Determine your process management requirements.		
Would a project approach improve any financial or analytical processes?	o	o
Could the reliability or validity of cost data be improved by cleaning the databases?	o	o
Could a just-in-time approach to inventory be implemented?	o	o
Could performance be improved by reengineering financial processes?	o	o
Could performance be improved by reengineering clinical processes?	o	o
Could staffing be improved by a new approach to scheduling?	o	o
Could service be improved by a new approach to scheduling patients?	o	o

CHECKLIST 5: Strategic Planning	YES	NO
Consider your options for strategic planning.		
Could operations management be better integrated into strategic planning?	o	o
Could changes in location, size, layout, design, and infrastructure improve performance?	o	o
Does the current delivery system provide sufficient flexibility to specialize in order to obtain or maintain a competitive advantage in delivering services?	o	o
Would changes in workforce and staffing be helpful?	o	o
Are there untapped resources in the community that could improve the performance of the hospital and improve the health status of the community?	o	o
Does the hospital financial reporting process keep it on track with its mission statement and strategy and follow a hierarchy that optimizes the performance of the hospital?	o	o

ACKNOWLEDGMENTS

Gregory O. Ginn, PhD, MBA, CPA, M.Ed., Certified Medical Planner™ (Hon), Assistant Professor University of Nevada–Las Vegas, Department of Health Care Administration and Policy, Las Vegas, NV.

BIBLIOGRAPHY

Alexander, J.A. and Weiner, B.J. Community accountability among hospitals affiliated with health care systems. *Milbank Quarterly*. 78:2 (2000): 157–184.

Aptel, O. and Pourjalati, H. Improving activities and decreasing costs of logistics in hospitals: A comparison of U.S. and French hospitals. *International Journal of Accounting*. 36:1 (2001): 65–90.

Baker, L.C., Phibbs, C.S., Guarino, C., Supina, D., and Reynolds, J.L. Within-year variation in hospital utilization, and its implications for hospital costs. *Journal of Health Economics*. 23:1 (2004): 191–211.

Barthell, E.N., Foldy, S.L., Pemble, K.R., Felton, C.W., Greischar, P.J., Pirallo, R.G., and Bazan, W.J. Assuring community emergency care capacity with collaboration Internet tools. *Journal of Public Health Management and Practice*. 9:1 (2003): 35–42.

Beauregard, T.R. Consumer-driven health care: Tangible employer actions. *Benefits Quarterly*. 20:2 (2004): 43–48.

Bellin, E. and Kalkut, G. Is time slice analysis superior to total hospital length of stay in demonstrating effectiveness of a month-long intensive effort on a Medicine service? *Quality Management in Health Care*. 13:2 (2004): 143–149.

Blair, R. Bells and whistles, RIP. *Health Management Technology*. 24:10 (2003): 4–6.

Blecher, M.B. and Douglass, K. Gold in goldenseal. *Hospitals and Health Networks*. 71:20 (1997): 50–52.

Bosch, P.M. and Dietz, D. Minimizing expected waiting in a medical appointment system. *IIE Transactions*. 32:9 (2000): 841–848.

Butler, T.W., Keong Leong, G., and Everett, L.N. The operations management role in hospital strategic planning. *Journal of Operations Management.* 14:2 (1996): 137–156.

Cayirli, T. and Veral, E. Outpatient scheduling in health care: A review of the literature. *Production and Operations Management.* 12:4 (2003): 519–549.

Cheang, B., Li, H., Lim, A., and Rodriguez, B. Nurse rostering problems—A bibliographic survey. *European Journal of Operational Research.* 151:3 (2003): 447–460.

Cleverly, W.O. Financial dashboard reporting for the hospital industry. *Journal of Health Care Finance.* 27:3 (2001): 30–40.

Côte, M.J. and Daugherty, C.R. Using project management to improve month-end reporting in a hospital. *Production and Inventory Management Journal.* 41:4 (2000): 17–22.

Douglass, K. No pain, big gain. *Hospitals and Health Networks.* 72:20 (1998): 38–39.

Finkler, S.A. and Ward, D.M. The case for the use of evidence-based management research for the control of hospital costs. *Health Care Management Review.* 28:4 (2003): 348–365.

Frase-Blunt, M. Telemedicine: Across the miles and right next door. *Hospital Topics.* 76:2 (1998): 9–13.

Garwood, D. Supply chain management: New paradigms for customers and suppliers. *Hospital Material Management Quarterly.* 20:3 (1999): 1–3.

Gemmel, P. and Van Dierdonck, R. Admission scheduling in acute care hospitals: Does the practice fit with the theory? *International Journal of Operations and Production Management.* 19:9/10 (1999): 863–878.

Ginn, G.O. and Hetico, H.R. In: *Healthcare Operations*, edited by D.E. Marcinko. [*Journal of Healthcare Organizations and Financial Management Strategies.* 2:1] iMBA Inc., Atlanta, GA, 2010.

Goldsmith, J. The new health-cost crisis. *Harvard Business Review.* 79:10 (2001): 20–21.

Goldstein, S.M. Employee development: An examination of service strategy in a high-contact service environment. *Production and Operations Management.* 12:2 (2003): 186–203.

Goldstein, S.M. and Ward, P.T. Performance effects of physicians' involvement in hospital strategic decisions. *Journal of Service Research.* 6:4 (2004): 361–372.

Gregerson, J. Rewriting the prescription for hospital design. *Building Design and Construction.* 36:6 (1995): 52–55.

Gumbus, A., Belthouse, D.E., and Lyons, B.E. A three-year journey to organizational and financial health using the balanced scorecard. *Journal of Business and Economic Studies.* 9:2 (2003): 54–64.

Johnson, D.E. Sell evidence-based medicine: Cut drug cost. *Health Care Strategic Management.* 22:2 (2004): 2–4.

Kowalski, J. Well-centered: Balancing materials and patient-focused care. *Materials Management in Health Care.* 4:10 (1995): 42–44.

Kremitske, D.L. and West, D.L. Patient-focused primary care: A model. *Hospital Topics.* 75:4 (1997): 22–28.

Lagoe, R.J. and Westert, G.P. Improving outcomes with community-wide distribution of health care data. *Health Care Management Review.* 29:1 (2004): 67–76.

Laird, S.P., Wong, J.S.K., Schaller, W.J., Erickson, B.J., and de Groen, P.C. Design and implementation of an Internet-based medical image viewing system. *Journal of Systems and Software.* 66:2 (2003): 167–181.

Li, L.X. and Benton, W.C. Hospital capacity management decisions: Emphasis on cost control and quality enhancement. *European Journal of Operational Research.* 146:3 (2003): 596–614.

Li, L.X., Benton, W.C., and Keong Leong, G. The impact of strategic operations management decision on community hospital performance. *Journal of Operations Management.* 20:4 (2002) 389–408.

Mang, A.L. Implementation strategies of patient-focused care. *Hospital and Health Services Administration.* 40:3 (1995): 426–525.

Marcinko, D.E. and Hetico, H.R. *Dictionary of Health Insurance and Managed Care.* Springer Publishing, New York, 2006.

Marcinko, D.E. and Hetico, H.R. *Dictionary of Health Information Technology and Security.* Springer Publishing, New York, 2007.

Marcinko, D.E. and Hetico, H.R. The revolving healthcare industrial complex. In: *The Business of Medical Practice*, edited by D.E. Marcinko. Springer Publishing, New York, 2011.

Moore, J.D. Looking for payoff from patient-focused care. *Modern Healthcare.* 28:7 (1998): 45.

Neil, R. Timing is everything. *Materials Management in Health Care.* 13:3 (2004): 12–15.

Omachonu, S., Suthummanon, S., Akcin, M., and Asfour, S. Predicting length of stay for Medicare patients at a teaching hospital. *Health Services Management Research.* 17:1 (2004): 1–11.

Pavia, L. Health care's top 10 trends that should ride into the next decade. *Health Care Strategic Management.* 17:4 (1999): 12–13.

Sandrick, K. A quest for the obscure. *Materials Management in Health Care.* 10:3 (2001): 16–18.

Schneider, J. Hospitals get alternative. *U.S. News and World Reports.* 133:3 (2002): 68–69.

Snow, R.J., Engler, D., and Krella, J.M. The GDAHA Hospital Performance Reports Project: A successful community-based quality improvement initiative. *Quality Management in Health Care*. 12:3 (2003): 151–158.

Tucker, A.L. The impact of operational failures on hospital nurses and their patients. *Journal of Operations Management*. 22:2 (2004): 151–159.

Whitson, D. Applying just-in-time systems in healthcare. *IIE Solutions*. 29:8 (1997): 32–37.

Whittington, J. and Cohen, H. OSF healthcare's journey in patient safety. *Quality Management in Health Care*. 13:1 (2004): 53–59.

2 Market Competition in Modern Health Care Management

Surveying the Current Ecosystem

Robert James Cimasi

CONTENTS

INTRODUCTION

The potential costs and benefits of free market competition within the health care field have been, and will continue to be, the focus of intense debate. Those who advocate market competition in health care stress numerous benefits, which include reduced costs, increased quality, improved efficiencies, and an incentive to innovate. Those who oppose competition in health care argue that distinct differences exist between hospital markets and other markets, thus cautioning against the use of basic economic models when drawing conclusions concerning improving the health care delivery system.

Nobel Laureate Kenneth Arrow broached one side of this debate in his 1963 article "Uncertainty and the Welfare of Medical Care," in which he argued that the market is incapable of insuring against uncertainties that an individual will likely face in the health care arena. Arrow concluded that "the laissez-faire solution for medicine is intolerable".[*] More recently, it has been argued that competition within the hospital market has created a commercialized environment that is incompatible with the needs of the community[†] and can further lead to a reduction in social welfare.[‡] For example, in the highly specialized area of organ transplants, competition may decrease a medical center's incentive to increase organ donation due to a likely possibility that the gains will be shared with their competitors.[§]

The opposing viewpoint argues that, without the existence of a competitive market, individuals lose their freedom to choose, or are allowed to consume medical care for "free"; therefore, the market cannot learn what an individual values most.[¶] An additional complication in the health care market is the prevalence of health insurance, which has resulted in price insensitivity in consumers leading to peripheral variables weighing more heavily on an individual's decision, rather than price and quality of service. This argument additionally states that to further exacerbate consumers' insensitivity to price, health insurance and fee-for-service systems create a moral hazard where service providers are compensated for performing more services regardless of whether the patient may benefit directly, and, conversely, the patient does not assume the costs of seeking out and receiving additional services regardless of need as they would in a free market. Free market economics argues that, when individuals are left to interact in an uninhibited way in a competitive market, producers are encouraged to provide higher quality goods at lower prices in an effort to attract the greatest number of consumers.

This debate is far more complex than simply a pro or con "competition in health care" stance. The multifaceted and layered structure of the health care system begs the question, "If competition is prudent, at what level within the health care sector will competition produce the largest overall utility for society?" One view is that competition should exist among integrated delivery systems such as Kaiser Permanente and HealthPartners, which is the optimal means to encourage high quality and efficiency.[**] A conflicting viewpoint is that the most advantageous level for competition to take place is at the individual provider level. It is at this level of prevention, diagnosis, and treatment

---

[*] Arrow, K. J. Uncertainty and the welfare economics of medical care. *The American Economic Review* 53: 5 (December 1963): 967.

[†] Relman, A. S. The problem of commercialism in medicine. *Cambridge Quarterly of Health Ethics* 16: (2007): 375.

[‡] Kessler, D. P. and McClellan, M. B. Is hospital competition socially wasteful? *The Quarterly Journal of Economics* 2: (May 2000): 577.

[§] Howard, D. Quality and consumer choice in health care: Evidence from kidney transplantation. *Topics in Economic Analysis & Policy* 5: 1 (2005): 18.

[¶] Cannon, M. and Tanner, M. Healthy competition. *What's Holding Back Health Care and How to Free It*. Washington, DC: Cato Institute (2005), p. 5.

[**] Enthoven, A. C. and Tollen, L. A. Competition in health care: It takes systems to pursue quality and efficiency. *Health Affairs* 9: (September 7, 2005): 420.

of individual health conditions that competition can drive improvements in efficiency and effectiveness, reduce errors, and spark innovation.*

The decade of the 1990s saw a massive restructuring of the U.S. health care delivery system. Technological advances made it possible for more procedures to be provided on an outpatient basis and hundreds of new provider arrangements and organizational structures were introduced. Emerging health care organizations (EHOs) were formed in response to increasingly competitive markets, where growing tension between competition and community benefits affected quality of care, patient satisfaction, profitability, and human resources, both positively and negatively. The managed care revolution and changes in reimbursement for Medicare services forced providers to look for more efficient ways to provide services. The last two decades have seen the accelerated transformation of U.S. health care professions into a service industry enterprise, whereby many believe that professional health services have been *unitized*, *protocolized*, and *homogenized*, in order to facilitate their "sale," as if they were just any other market commodity such as frozen orange juice, soy beans, or pork bellies. These changes have accelerated the *corporatization* of medicine as demonstrated by the increase in for-profit health care in hospitals, outpatient technical component providers (e.g., *independent diagnostic testing facilities* [IDTFs], *ambulatory surgery centers* [ASC]), and large for-profit health insurance payors.

The move toward specialized inpatient and outpatient facilities, often owned by physicians, is a more recent reaction to these significant changes. Rather than posing a threat to the health care delivery system, the development of specialty and niche providers represents innovations that allow health care services to be provided in a more cost-effective manner while also maintaining and improving quality and beneficial outcomes.

The continuing rise in the cost of health care services, representing a significant percentage of both government and business expenditures (not to mention a painfully increasing portion of the budgets of individuals and families), has become a regular news item. In our lifetimes, health care services seem to be resolutely unique in our market economy in that the demand for them has grown higher despite their growing costs, and, many believe, supply is actually driving demand. Increasing appeals for health care reform culminated in the passage of the Patient Protection and Affordable Care Act (ACA) and the Health Care and Education Reconciliation Act (Reconciliation Act), collectively referred to as "health care reform," in March 2010.

The ACA is a landmark piece of legislation that has impacted every aspect of health care delivery in the United States. While health care reform will impact market competition in new and different ways, competitive tensions continue to exist that may pose challenges to some of the ultimate goals of health care reform.

To gain a better understanding of these competitive tensions, Michael Porter's "Five Forces of Competition"† offers a model for analysis of market competition. Porter's work is considered by some to be seminal for an analysis of health care competition. This chapter is therefore divided into the following five major sections based on his Five Forces, and concludes with a case study. The accompanying analysis is designed to provide health care administrators with a more interdisciplinary approach to strategic planning and management.

1. *Barriers to free market competition in health care delivery*
   This section lists and briefly defines the major barriers to competition in health care.
2. *Growing tension in health care services markets*
   Examples illustrate competition in several different segments of the health care industry, physician professional practices, and other provider affiliations. This section includes an analysis of the challenges of competition for hospital systems.

---

* Porter, M. E. and Teisberg, E. O. Redefining competition in health care. *Harvard Business Review* 82: 6 (June 2004): 66.
† Porter, M. E. *Competitive Strategy: Techniques for Analyzing Industries and Competitors*. New York: The Free Press (1998).

3. *Competitive analysis*
   This section explores and analyzes market consolidation and evolution stemming from the introduction of managed care into the health care system.
4. *Implementing successful approaches from other industries*
   The analysis focuses on two aspects of the health care industry that differentiate it from other industries and represent barriers to the market's competitive controls. A range of competitive strategies employed successfully by specific companies in other industries is briefly examined.
5. *Lessons for emerging health care organizations*
   This section describes strategies and lessons that may be gleaned from competition and revisits the existing barriers to competition in health care to emphasize their impact on effective competitive strategies. It also considers the likely future of health care's competitive environment in light of the ACA and some general overall lessons for effective competition in today's health care markets.

The implementation of health care reform initiatives will drive changes in all aspects of the U.S. health care system, and will present an unpredictable landscape of new configurations, strategies, and tactics of increasing complexity in the health care marketplace. In light of the myriad changes proposed by the ACA, will some existing barriers to free competition in health care be removed? Will providers face a new competitive paradigm? In many respects, this may be the single most important question that those in health care planning and administration face today. The once well-defined, relatively stable business landscape of U.S. health care delivery now presents both challenges and opportunities in the competitive health care setting. For many health care executives, the issue may well be not so much that they do not yet have the right answers, it is that they have not yet asked the right questions.

BARRIERS TO FREE MARKET COMPETITION IN HEALTH CARE DELIVERY

Perfectly competitive markets exist only in economic theory. In reality, industries and markets have varying constraints on competition. The health care industry has often been characterized as unique with its many significant barriers to free market competition, such as market controls on price and quality.

There are three main reasons for these barriers in health care:

1. The nature of health care creates an unpredictable, urgent, and "infinite" level of demand.
2. The ubiquitous involvement of insurance companies, private and governmental, as intermediary organizations in the purchase of health care interferes with consumer motivations and, consequently, their choice of providers and services.
3. The difficulties in measuring health care quality and beneficial outcomes (both of quantifying and qualifying them) and the lack of information on the relative costs of health care providers and services also inhibit consumer selection, further removing incentives to providers to increase quality and lower costs.

Included among the many barriers to competition in health care delivery are the following:

1. Patients do not purchase services directly from providers.
2. Patients do not compare prices between providers.
3. The government is the largest purchaser of health care.
4. Private purchasers often lack market power.
5. Patients, purchasers, and providers lack information.
6. Occupational licensing.

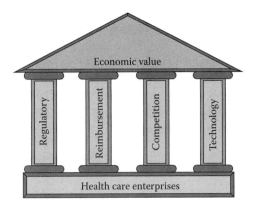

FIGURE 2.1 Four pillars of health care delivery.

7. Many providers have monopoly or near-monopoly power (yet antitrust laws prevent some potentially beneficial integration).
8. Providers are rewarded for increasing costs.
9. Capital investments are overly subsidized (Stigler argues that an industry will not use its power to collect money from the government unless the list of beneficiaries can be limited, due to the fact that the amount of subsidies will be divided among a growing number of rivals[*]).
10. Certificate of need (CON), regulation, and licensing laws are an entry barrier to competing and substitute providers and services.
11. Exit barriers protect low-quality providers.

Four Pillars of Health Care Economic Markets

In helping to frame the right questions that must be asked in order to analyze the current health care economic marketplace, health care planners and administrators should examine the health care competitive environment within the context of the *four pillars* of health care delivery, particularly the impact of regulation, reimbursement, and technology on health care competition (Figure 2.1).

Regulatory, Reimbursement, and Technological Environment as Major Considerations for Competitive Market Landscape

Continuing technological advances in diagnostic and therapeutic equipment may further increase competitive pressures between hospitals and physicians over technical component revenue streams. In addition, the regulatory environment is one of the primary drivers of competitive market forces. Competition over the technical component revenue streams and the regulatory uncertainty affecting physicians and hospitals intrinsically drive up the risk of participating in health care transactions involving these providers.

GROWING TENSION IN HEALTH CARE SERVICES MARKETS

The changes in reimbursement for Medicare services through the introduction of prospective payment systems and physician reimbursement cuts for professional services, as well as the increased focus on patient quality and transparency initiatives, have forced health care providers to look for

---

[*] Stigler, G. J. The theory of economic regulation. *The Bell Journal of Economics and Management Science* 2: 1 (Spring 1971): 5.

more efficient ways to provide services and additional sources of revenue and margin-producing business. Additionally, the rise of corporate health care provider networks and health systems, together with rising health care costs, suggests that competition among providers has become prevalent in the health care industry. Strict control of reimbursement costs from payors and consistent decreases in physician professional component fee reimbursement yield, reduction in traditional hospital inpatient use, and higher costs of capital have all contributed to the trend of physicians' investment in outpatient (and inpatient) specialty provider enterprises, which often compete with general acute care community hospital providers.

PRESSURES OF MARKET COMPETITION VERSUS COMMUNITY BENEFIT

Although the Federal Trade Commission (FTC) and the Department of Justice (DOJ) declared in 2004 that competition has positively affected health care quality and cost-effectiveness, skepticism persists. As a result, recommendations that would eliminate many of the barriers to competition that prevent the health care industry from fully benefiting consumers have not been instituted, despite the growing shift to consider consumers as "purchasers" of health care.

Shift from Defined Benefits to Defined Contributions

During the same time that changes in physician reimbursement for the professional fee component have occurred, there has been a change in the method of payment for health care services, with an accelerating movement from the traditional U.S. health coverage system of "defined benefits" (where employers provide a package of defined benefits to their employees) to a system of "defined contributions" (where employers contribute a set amount and then require employees to decide how much of their health benefit dollars to spend by selecting from a range of benefit plans). This shift is being driven by employers seeking to limit their exposure to what has become double-digit health insurance premium rate increases, and represents a fundamental shifting of the financial risk of health coverage from the employer to employees. Under this arrangement, employers can limit their contributions, while employees must contribute increasing amounts of their own money to pay for health insurance cost increases in attempting to maintain the same level and quality of health care.

Several provisions of the ACA were designed to overhaul these and other trends in the employer-based health insurance system, and the new changes may drastically affect how employers provide coverage to their employees. The ACA does not directly require large employers, which the ACA defines as those with 50 or more full-time employees (FTEs), to provide health insurance coverage to workers.[*] However, certain provisions in the ACA impose significant penalties on employers who decline to do so.[†]

Beginning January 1, 2014, large employers will be subject to penalties if they choose not to provide qualified coverage.[†] Some refer to this ACA provision as "pay or play".[*] Large employers who fail to provide *minimum essential coverage* and have at least one FTE that qualifies for a federal premium credit or cost-sharing reduction will be subject to a nondeductible federal tax penalty.

These employers will be assessed an annual fee of $2000 per FTE, excluding the first 30 employees from the assessment.[†] Employers with more than 50 employees that offer coverage but have at least one FTE receiving a premium tax credit will pay the lesser of $3000 annually for each employee receiving a premium credit or $2000 for each FTE.[†] Employers with more than 200 employees are required to automatically enroll employees into health insurance plans offered by

---

[*] The legislation defines full-time employees as employees who work, on average at least 30 hours of service per week. Pinheiro, B. M., J. C. Hemphill, C. J. Schoner, J. M. Calpas and K. R. Anderson. *Employers Guide to Health Care Reform.* Austin, TX: Aspen Publishers (2010), pp. 10-6–10-8.

[†] Patient Protection and Affordable Care Act. § 1513, Public Law 111-148, 124 Stat. 253, March 23, 2010.

the employer, and employers must provide employees with notice of automatic enrollment and a chance to opt out of enrollment.[*] The ACA considers coverage inadequate to meet the minimum essential standard "[if] the plan's share of the total cost of benefits is less than 60 percent, and it is unaffordable if the employee premium constitutes more than 9.5 percent of the employee's household income".[†]

Small employers, as defined in the ACA as those entities with at least one, but not more than 100 FTEs, are exempt from most of the above penalties. However, the ACA affords several tax credits to small businesses that provide coverage to their employees. For example, the ACA implements a federal tax credit for small businesses with 25 or fewer FTEs, which, depending on need, will offset up to half of insurance premiums.[‡] To qualify for the credits, an employer must pay at least half the premium for each employee. In 2011, more than 4 million companies were deemed eligible for the credit.[§]

Consumers as Purchasers of Health Care

While competition in the health care sector is generally considered to be resistant to market forces, it is still subject to some basic economic realities, particularly in the form of consumers as patients. In 2008, an estimated 46.3 million people in the United States—36 million of whom are U.S. citizens—were without health coverage. Another 10 million did not receive employer-based health coverage, purchasing it instead through the individual insurance market.[¶] The ACA's individual coverage mandate, which requires U.S. citizens and legal residents to maintain minimum amounts of health insurance coverage, will greatly alter the health care market landscape and is projected to increase the number of individuals with health coverage anywhere from 32 to 34[**] million individuals. Accordingly, the ACA may lead to both an increase in demand for health insurance as consumers comply with the mandate, which may in turn lead to an increase in demand for health care services because individuals will have more coverage and access to care. Patients will likely participate more directly in the health care purchase decision and payment continuum, presenting yet another layer of complexity and competitive marketplace challenges and opportunities.

Consumer-directed health care (CDHC) is a growing trend based on neoclassical economic theory and studies which have shown that insured individuals with higher deductibles tend to purchase less health care services than do insured individuals with low deductibles.[††] CDHC advocates promote the idea that consumers who pay for services directly are more likely to compare price to quality and demand higher quality care, a theory that supports the use of HSAs coupled with high-deductible health plans (HDHPs).[††] Generally, HSAs are personalized accounts into which an individual and/or his or her employer contribute, and then from which the individual may withdraw funds to cover health care expenses.[‡‡] HSAs put the purchasing power directly into the hands of the patient, who may use the funds tax-free to cover basic qualified medical expenses, including preventive

---

[*] Patient Protection and Affordable Care Act § 1511, Public Law 111-148, 124 Stat. 252, March 23, 2010.

[†] Pinheiro, B. M., J. C. Hemphill, C. J. Schoner, J. M. Calpas and K. R. Anderson. *Employers Guide to Health Care Reform*. Austin, TX: Aspen Publishers (2010), pp. 10-6–10-8.

[‡] Patient Protection and Affordable Care Act. Public Law 111-148, March 23, 2010.

[§] Cassidy, A. Small business tax credits. The Affordable Care Act offers incentives so that more of these companies will help provide their employees with health insurance. *Health Affairs* 4: (January 14, 2011).

[¶] Cassidy, A. Near-term changes in health insurance. *Health Affairs* 3: (April 30, 2010): 1.

[**] Estimate of direct spending and revenue effects of H.R. 3590 and H.R. 4872. Congressional Budget Office, Letter to Nancy Pelosi, Speaker U.S. House of Representatives, March 20, 2010, p. 2. Foster, R. S. Estimated financial effects of the 'Patient Protection and Affordable Care Act' as amended. Centers for Medicare and Medicaid Studies, April 22, 2010.

[††] Schneider, J. E., R. L. Ohsfeldt and J. Benton. Economic and policy analysis of specialty hospitals. Health Economics Consulting Group (February 4, 2005), p. 14.

[‡‡] All about HSAs, U.S. Treasury Department, July 22, 2007, p. 2, http://www.treas.gov/offices/public-affairs/hsa/pdf/all-about-HSAs_072208.pdf (accessed July 1, 2009).

care and over-the-counter drugs.[*] HDHPs are then used in the traditional insurance context to pay the costs associated with catastrophic events such as trauma and chronic disease.[†]

Although proponents of CDHC argue that the use of HSAs and HDHPs will promote better analysis of cost and quality at the point of service[‡], skeptics argue that there is not enough evidence to demonstrate that CDHC leads to better informed choices based on quality.[§] Nonetheless, CDHC plans have the capacity to alter the traditional health care marketplace, which has become accustomed to the third-party payor system. The mere existence of CDHP may alter the health care industry landscape to look more like markets in other industries where consumers are the ones making purchasing decisions, tending to more carefully scrutinize what they are getting in return for their money. Additionally, by making consumers more aware of how much procedures actually cost, this trend may impact the ability of hospitals to cross-subsidize for costly care.[¶]

Pay-for-Performance

An emerging quality initiative is the trend to reimbursing physicians based on some predetermined "measure" of "quality" or "performance," referred to as "pay-for-performance" (P4P). Defined as "quality-based purchasing," P4P relies on the use of payment methods and other nonfinancial incentives to encourage quality improvement in the health care system. However, several fundamental health public policy questions have led to concerns regarding the basic fairness and the potential risks associated with this shift to physician P4P. For example:

1. Who decides what performance means, what outcomes are desirable to achieve through P4P initiatives, and who will determine what "performance metrics" are established?
2. More important, without an accurate, comprehensive, and uniform quality reporting system currently in place, will market oligopoly health care and insurance providers manipulate the currently voluntarily reported physician quality data in furthering their own market control and profit agendas, thereby further detracting from physician autonomy and eroding physician control over their own quality of care and treatment protocols?
3. Who defines the nature, structure, format, and application of efforts to collect data and promote "transparency" in disclosing complex health care data?[**]

Hospital Medical Errors and Resulting Transparency and Quality Initiatives

A 2010 study by the U.S. Agency for Health Care Research on quality of care in the United States revealed that errors related to nosocomial infections acquired in hospitals are common, with approximately 1.7 million patients infected and 100,000 deaths.[††] Deaths related to preventable adverse events exceed deaths attributable to motor vehicle accidents, breast cancer, or AIDS.[††] Over the last several years, reports from the IOM and others have increased public awareness of medical

---

[*] All about HSAs, U.S. Treasury Department, July 22, 2007, p. 2, http://www.treas.gov/offices/public-affairs/hsa/pdf/all-about-HSAs_072208.pdf (accessed August 1, 2009).

[†] Jost, T. S. Is health insurance a bad idea? The consumer-driven perspective, *Connecticut Insurance Law Journal* 14: (Spring 2008): 380.

[‡] Jost, T. S. Is health insurance a bad idea? The consumer-driven perspective. *Connecticut Insurance Law Journal* 14: (Spring 2008): 379–380.

[§] Jost, T. S. Is health insurance a bad idea? The consumer-driven perspective. *Connecticut Insurance Law Journal* 14: (Spring 2008): 383.

[¶] Altman, S. H., Shactman, D., and Eilat, E. Could U.S. hospitals go the way of U.S. airlines? *Health Affairs* 25: 1 (Jan/Feb 2006): 17.

[**] Nakashima, E. Doctors rated but can't get second opinion. *Washington Post* (July 25, 2007); Robertson, K. Heart surgeon disputes bad rating. *Sacramento Business Journal* (August 13, 2007).

[††] U.S. Department of Health and Human Services Agency for Health Care Research and Quality. National Health Care Quality Report, Rockville, MD (December 2003, March 2004), pp. 147, 136–137.

errors.* Transparency and full disclosure to the public regarding provider fees, quality, and other information related to safety and medical errors, will significantly impact the future of the health care delivery market.

Specialty and Niche Providers

Although specialty and niche providers are not new providers, the increase in their numbers has led to concerns that more and more providers will be able to "cherry-pick" and "cream-skim" the most profitable patients and procedures away from community hospitals. Specialty hospitals focus on providing only cost-effective and/or profitable services, and refuse to provide services that result in a net loss or treat patients who cannot pay.† Furthermore, the development of new technology has made it possible for physicians to perform, in their office or ASC, services traditionally provided by hospitals.‡ Specialty hospitals and ASCs have been able to compete better than community hospitals for more profitable patients by: (1) concentrating only on specific diagnosis-related groups (DRG), (2) treating far fewer costly Medicaid patients, and (3) opting out of emergency room facilities and services so as to forego the related regulatory requirements under laws such as the EMTALA related to the provision of care regardless of a patient's ability to pay.†

Specialty hospitals and ASCs treat some of the most profitable diseases in a predominantly outpatient setting. These facilities have grown due to the increased incidence of these diseases as well as changes in consumer demands and new technologies. "Specialty hospitals are also able to achieve economies of scale and scope by providing high volumes of a limited scope of services and lowering fixed costs by reengineering the care delivery process".§ This narrow focus helps achieve profitability and makes such facilities more competitive than more generalized providers, where "greater diversification into a wider array of activities has the potential to lead to diminished financial performance".§

The ability to provide services at a reduced cost is a double-edged sword for ASCs. Under the Medicare system, reimbursement rates for hospital outpatient departments (HOPDs) are substantially higher than reimbursement rates for the same procedures performed in an ASC or a physician's office.¶ For most services performed in an ASC, payment is made under a system that aligns ASC reimbursement rates at a percentage of the Outpatient Prospective Payment System (OPPS) rates.** Due to the need to ensure budget neutrality between the old ASC payment system and the revised system, the reimbursement rate for ASC procedures was set at 65% of the OPPS rate in 2008.†† Centers for Medicare and Medicaid Services (CMS) cut this rate again in 2009‡‡, with a zero

---

* New push after transplant tragedy—Hospitals search for ways to prevent errors, Help doctors learn from others. *DoctorQuality* (October 1, 2003).

† Altman, S. H., Shactman, D., and Eilat, E. Could U.S. hospitals go the way of U.S. airlines? *Health Affairs* 25: 1 (Jan/Feb 2006): 19.

‡ *Medicare Part B Imaging Services: Rapid Spending Growth and Shift to Physician Offices Indicate Need for CMS to Consider Additional Management Practices*, Government Accountability Office, June 2008, GAO-08-452. Arlington, S. and Farino, A. Biomarket trends: Pharmaceutical industry undergoing transformation. *Genetic Engineering and Biotechnology News* 27: 15 (September 1, 2007).

§ Schneider, J. E., R. L. Ohsfeldt and J. Benton. Economic and policy analysis of specialty hospitals. Health Economics Consulting Group (February 4, 2005), p. 14.

¶ Wynn, B. O., L. H. Hilborne, P. S. Hussey, E. M. Sloss and E. Murphy. Medicare payment differentials across ambulatory settings, RAND Health Working Paper (July 2008), http://www.rand.org/pubs/working_papers/2008/RAND_WR602.sum .pdf (accessed September 24, 2009).

** Ambulatory Surgical Centers Payment System, MedPAC Payment Basics (October 2008), p. 1, http://www.medpac.gov/ documents/MedPAC_Payment_Basics_08_ASC.pdf (accessed September 24, 2009); Fact Sheets: Final 2009 Policy, Payment Changes for Hospital Outpatient Departments and Ambulatory Surgery Centers, Centers for Medicare and Medicaid Services (October 30, 2008), http://www.cms.hhs.gov/apps/media/fact_sheets.asp (accessed September 24, 2009).

†† Ambulatory Surgical Centers Payment System, MedPAC Payment Basics (October 2008), p. 2, http://www.medpac.gov/ documents/MedPAC_Payment_Basics_08_ASC.pdf (accessed September 24, 2009).

‡‡ Ambulatory Surgical Center Fee Schedule: Payment System Fact Sheet Series, Centers for Medicare and Medicaid Services, Department of Health and Human Services (January 2009), http://www.cms.hhs.gov/MLNProducts/downloads/ AmbSurgCtrFeepymtfctsht508.pdf (accessed January 13, 2009).

percent adjustment for inflation[*], and only increased the conversion factor for payments to ASCs by 1.2% for 2010, despite an increase of 2.1% for HOPDs for the same year.[†] Because the CMS account for an average of 34% of ASC revenue, changes to CMS reimbursement rates greatly affect the ability of ASCs to provide quality patient care services.[‡]

Furthermore, physicians who provide outpatient services in their offices only receive the physician fee component reimbursement rate under the Medicare Physician Fee Schedule.[§] When procedures are performed in an HOPD, hospitals (in the absence of bundled payments) receive both the physician fee, with which they reimburse their doctors, and the facility fee reimbursed under the OPPS rate.[¶] Moreover, while the payment differential between HOPDs and ASCs is standardized for the most part, the payment differential between services provided in HOPDs or ASCs and services provided in physicians' offices varies substantially by payor and service.[§]

In the face of physician professional fee reimbursement challenges, there have been numerous legislative and regulatory efforts undertaken at the federal and state levels, in large part due to lobbying initiatives by hospitals and their trade associations, to reverse the trend of, and restrict physician ownership/investment in, ancillary service technical component (ASTC) revenue stream enterprises (e.g., ASCs, IDTFs, surgical/specialty hospitals, and physical therapy). These measures have served to relegate independent physicians in private practice to receiving only professional fee component revenues, or to acquiesce by accepting employee status under the substantial control of hospital systems or large corporate players. Consequently, market competition among these various health care enterprises has profoundly impacted quality of care, patient satisfaction, profitability, human resource management, and community perceptions. Examples of these initiatives will be discussed below.

ACA Physician Ownership Provisions

Before passage of the ACA, the "whole hospital exception" to the Stark law allowed physicians to have an ownership interest in a hospital to which they refer patients, provided the physician was invested in the whole hospital and not a subdivision of the hospital, with no limitations as to the amount or extent of physician ownership, on either an aggregate or individual basis.[**] The ACA completely prohibits physician-owned hospitals that were not Medicare certified by December 31, 2010.[††] The ACA allows hospitals with a provider agreement prior to December 31, 2010 to continue Medicare participation if they meet the following four criteria: (1) located in a county with a population growth rate of at least 150% of the state's population growth over the last 5 years; (2) have a Medicaid inpatient admission percentage of at least the average of all hospitals in the county; (3) located in a state with below-national-average bed capacity; and (4) have a bed occupancy rate

---

[*] Fact Sheets: Final 2009 Policy, Payment Changes for Hospital Outpatient Departments and Ambulatory Surgery Centers, Centers for Medicare and Medicaid Services (October 30, 2008), http://www.cms.hhs.gov/apps/media/fact_sheets.asp (accessed September 24, 2009).

[†] Medicare Program: Changes to the Hospital Outpatient Prospective Payment System and CY 2010 Payment Rates; Changes to the Ambulatory Surgical Center Payment System and CY 2010 Payment Rates; Final Rule with Comment Period, 74 Fed. Reg. 60629, 60663 (November 20, 2009).

[‡] Becker, S. 10 Interesting facts and statistics for ASCs, *Becker's ASC Review* (January 2008), http://www.beckersasc.com/ambulatory-surgery-center/surgery-center-education/10-interesting-facts-and-statistics-for ascs.html (accessed November 5, 2008).

[§] Wynn, B. O., L. H. Hilborne, P. S. Hussey, E. M. Sloss and E. Murphy. Medicare payment differentials across ambulatory settings, RAND Health Working Paper (July 2008), http://www.rand.org/pubs/working_papers/2008/RAND_WR602.sum.pdf (accessed September 24, 2009).

[¶] Ambulatory Surgical Centers Payment System, MedPAC Payment Basics (October 2008), p. 1, http://www.medpac.gov/documents/MedPAC_Payment_Basics_08_ASC.pdf (accessed September 24, 2009).

[**] The law actually three separate provisions, governs physician self-referral for Medicare and Medicaid patients.

[††] *Section-by-Section Analysis with Changes Made by Title X and Reconciliation Included within Titles I–IX*, Democratic Policy Committee, http://dpc.senate.gov/healthreformbill/healthbill96.pdf (accessed May 24, 2010).

greater than state average.* A very limited number of physician-owned hospitals existing in 2010 met or were close to meeting all four criteria.† The *Reconciliation Act* provided a limited exception to the ACA growth restrictions for grandfathered physician-owned hospitals that treat the highest percentage of Medicaid patients in their county (and are not the sole hospital in a county).* Based on these provisions, the 2010 health care reform legislation will likely have a considerable negative impact on physician-owned hospitals, in terms of impeding development of new hospitals and expansion of existing hospitals.

Having stymied similar restrictions in several other bills over the past decade or so, physician-owned specialty hospitals are now subject to heavy restrictions on the growth or expansion of existing specialty hospitals with physician ownership.‡ Not only do these provisions reduce the beneficial effects of health care provider competition and create a greater potential for hospital consolidation, practice roll-up, and health system monopolies, but they further sustain the two-pronged attack on niche providers.

New Jersey Codey Act Decision

On November 20, 2007, a New Jersey court handed down a decision in the matter of *Health Net of New Jersey, Inc. v. Wayne Surgical Center, LLC*, holding that physicians who refer their patients to an ASC in which they have an ownership interest violate the 1989 Codey Act self-referral prohibitions. In its ruling, the court distinguished the current case (in which the ASC was physician owned) from the situation that includes a hospital owner. This decision has critical implications for the ASC community in that the court not only held that an ASC is not an extension of a physician's office, but also rejected a widely relied upon 1997 New Jersey Board of Medical Examiners advisory opinion, which stated that a surgeon's referrals of his or her own patients to a surgery center of which he or she is an owner does not constitute an impermissible referral.§

Twenty years after the Codey Act was enacted, the New Jersey legislature significantly amended the Act so as to permit certain referrals in which the referring physician has a beneficial interest in the ASC. On February 5, 2009, New Jersey legislators passed Assembly Bill A1933 (identical to Senate Bill 787, passed in December 2008), which provided several safe harbors for physicians referring patients to certain ASCs.¶,** The Amendment permits New Jersey physicians to refer patients to ASCs in which the referring physician has a financial interest provided that the following conditions are met: the referring physician personally performs the procedure; the referring physician's remuneration is directly proportional to his or her ownership interest (and not to the value of referrals); all clinically related decisions at a facility owned in part by nonphysicians are made by physicians and are in the best interests of the patient; and the referring physicians must disclose to the patient—in writing, before the time the referral is made—that he or she has a beneficial interest in the ASC.¶

Because many ASCs provide services to patients referred by their physician-owners, approximately 250 ASCs in the state had the potential to face prosecution for fraud and abuse-related

---

* *Section-by-Section Analysis with Changes Made by Title X and Reconciliation Included within Titles I–IX*, Democratic Policy Committee, http://dpc.senate.gov/healthreformbill/healthbill96.pdf (accessed May 24, 2010).

† Becker, S., Page, L., and Kurtz, R. Health Care reform: A brief analysis on how it impacts ASCs and physician-owned hospitals—10 observations. *Becker's Hospital Review*, http://www.beckersorthopedic andspine.com/news-a-analysis/legal-a-regulatory/1193-healthcare-reform-abrief-analysis-on-how-it-impacts-ascs-and-physician-owned-hospitals-10-observations (accessed May 20, 2010).

‡ Patient Protection and Affordable Care Act. H.R. 3590, 111th Congress (March 23, 2010), http://thomas.loc.gov/cgi-bin/query/F?c111:7:./temp/~c111G8zJzI:e0 (accessed April 28, 2010).

§ Court finds referrals to ASCs violate Codey Act. *WolfBlock Health Law Alert Newsletter* (November 2007); Sorrel, A. L. New Jersey court sends blow to doctor-owned facilities. *AMNews* 1:1, 2008 (January 14, 2008).

¶ Litten, E. G. *New Jersey's New Codey Law—New Limits on Physician Ownership and Referrals*. Fox Rothschild, LLP, News and Publications, Philadelphia, PA (February 2009).

** *Senate Substitute for Senate, No. 787*, State of New Jersey Senate (November 24, 2008), pp. 3–4.

actions if the legislature failed to amend the Act.* While these ASCs appear to have been spared by this legislation, the state has made clear a desire to reduce the growth of ASCs and specialty hospitals by inserting into the bill provisions that limit the future growth of these types of facilities in an effort to allow more competition between hospitals and ASCs.* For example, the bill implemented a moratorium on the development of new ASCs in New Jersey, as well as heightened requirements for registration and accreditation.†

Self-Referral "Under Arrangement" Scrutiny and IDTF Prohibitions

In recent years, certain physician/hospital relationships referred to as "under arrangements" and "per-click" leasing ventures have come under increasing regulatory scrutiny. An under arrangement transaction occurs when the hospital contracts with a third party (typically a joint venture owned, at least in part, by physicians who may refer) to provide a hospital service, and the hospital then bills and is reimbursed by Medicare for those services and pays the supplier, or joint venture. As the "entity" to which the physicians refer patients is the hospital, not the joint venture (i.e., the entity is deemed to be the entity that submits the reimbursement claim to Medicare), this type of "arrangement" is permitted under Stark. Buried in the 2008 Medicare Physician Fee Schedule proposed rule, CMS proposed revisions to the Stark regulations that broaden the definition of entity to include the person or entity that performs the designated health services and would prohibit space and equipment lease arrangements where per-click payments are made to a physician lessor who refers patients to the lessee.‡ While the proposed changes to the term entity did not appear in the 2008 Final Rule, CMS passed the changes the following year, expanding the definition of entity to include the entity that actually performs the designated health services.§ Upon passing, physician-owners of a hospital who were previously exempt under arrangements relationships now find themselves in a "financial relationship" with a previously exempt entity, thus making these types of arrangements illegal under Stark.¶

Certificate of Need

As the Federal Specialty Hospital Moratorium has ended, many states are now moving forward with their own initiatives to prevent market entry of physician-owned facilities through state CON regulations. Despite the original purpose of CON being to control costs, in light of continued evidence refuting CON's ability to reduce health care costs, arguments are now being made to support the use of CON as a way of preventing physician self-referral and supporting the continued viability of community hospitals' "charity care" policies. In the April 2007 issue of *Health Affairs*, for example, Jean Mitchell released findings indicating that physician-owners exploit the exceptions in the Stark law to self-refer patients for diagnostic imaging.** Additionally in 2007, Kansas pursued efforts to reinstate CON for specialty hospitals while Montana extended CON for specialty hospitals, with both states citing physician self-referral concerns. However, not all states seek to use CON to stifle competition from specialty hospitals. For example, in 2009, West Virginia passed a legislation that provided several avenues for ambulatory health care facilities to bypass the state's CON requirements.††

---

* McCarthy, L. New Jersey legislature clears safe harbors for referrals to ambulatory surgical centers. *BNA's Health Law Reporter* (February 12, 2009) (accessed June 20, 2011).

† Litten, E. G. *New Jersey's New Codey Law—New Limits on Physician Ownership and Referrals*. Fox Rothschild, LLP, News and Publications, Philadelphia, PA (February 2009).

‡ Greeson, T. W. and Zimmerman, H. M. Potential impact of 2008 Medicare physician fee schedule proposed rules on imaging arrangements. Reed Smith LLP, *Health Lawyers Weekly*, www.reedsmith.com/_db/_documents/Potential_Impact_of_2008_Medicare_Physician_Fee_Schedule.pdf (accessed September 25, 2007).

§ 73 Fed. Reg. 48,751 (Aug. 19, 2008) (to be codified at 42 C.F.R. 411.351).

¶ 42 U.S.C. § 1395nn(a)(1).

** Mitchell, J. The prevalence of physician self-referral arrangements after Stark II: Evidence from advanced diagnostic imaging. *Health Affairs* 26: 3 (April 17, 2007): 415–424.

†† Committee Substitute for Senate Bill 312, West Virginia Legislature, March 13, 2009.

Consolidation of Managed Care Industry

Managed care organizations (MCOs) are beginning to push their way into smaller markets, offering broader provider networks in the process. While there is nothing new about mergers in the managed care arena, for years, providers have expressed concerns about the steady consolidation. According to an American Medical Association (AMA) report entitled "Competition in Health Insurance: A Comprehensive Study of U.S. Markets, 2010 Update," a single insurer dominates in most of the nation's markets.[*] An AMA study of metropolitan areas in 46 states found that in 96% of the metropolitan statistical areas (MSAs), a single health insurer holds at least a 30% share of the commercial market.[*] A 2008 Government Accounting Office (GAO) survey found that the median market share at the state level of the largest small group carrier had risen to 47%.[†] This same GAO survey also concluded that in 34 of the 39 states surveyed, the five largest carriers had a combined market share that was 75% or more, and in 23 of these states, the combined market share for the five largest carriers represented more than 90%.[†] This reduction of competing health plans has raised concerns among both physicians and patients because competition drives innovation and the efficiency that can result when there is not a lack of competition within the health care marketplace.[‡]

"Out-of-Network" Reimbursement Disparities

Many third-party payors have implemented restraints on payments to facilities not within their network of preferred (discounted) providers. In New Jersey, out-of-network (OON) ASCs have historically benefitted from profitable reimbursement levels, receiving on average three times the reimbursement for being OON than in-network. This differential payment has resulted in payors filing lawsuits against OON providers, pressuring in-network providers to avoid referring to OON facilities or risk termination of provider agreements, and attempting to require OON facilities to give disclosure statements to patients scheduled to receive services at OON facilities.[§] On December 9, 2010, a modified version of a New Jersey Senate Bill, known as the *Health Care Transparency and Disclosure Act*, was presented to the New Jersey Assembly Financial Institutions and Insurance Committee as a substitute to Assembly Bill No. 3378 introduced on October 7, 2010.[¶] The revised bill makes various changes to the administration of health benefits plans regarding OON payments.[**] Specifically, the bill establishes that OON providers (1) are required to make a good faith and timely effort to collect a patient's co-insurance, co-payment, or deductible, (2) may waive a patient's payment if the provider determines the patient has a "medical or financial hardship" subject to certain limitations, and (3) are required to inform patients whether the services they seek are in-network or OON as well as explain to the patient his or her financial responsibility, give the patient a description of nonemergency services, and provide an estimation of those costs. Additionally, the proposed bill would modify the assignment of benefits legislation by potentially excluding OON providers from the direct pay benefit of the AOB law for up to 1 year if a carrier or insurer determines that the provider committed a pattern of violations of the proposed good-faith requirements.[††] In what some

---

[*] *Competition in Health Insurance: A Comprehensive Study of U.S. Markets, 2010 Update*, American Medical Association (2010).

[†] *Private Health Insurance: 2008 Survey Results on Number and Market Share of Carriers in the Small Group Health Insurance Market*. Government Accounting Office (February 27, 2009), p. 2.

[‡] Dicken, J. E. Limited competition among health plans troubling for AMA. *The Executive Report on Managed Care* (May 2006), p. 4.

[§] Fields, R. 5 Issues affecting the future of New Jersey ASCs. *Becker's ASC Review* 7: 9 (September 29, 2010).

[¶] *New Jersey legislature—Bills*, http://www.njleg.state.nj.us/bills/BillView.asp (accessed April 27, 2011).

[**] *Statement to Assembly Committee Substitute for Assembly, No. 3378* (December 9, 2010), http://www.njleg.state.nj.us/2010/Bills/A3500/3378_S1.PDF (accessed April 27, 2011).

[††] *Statement to Assembly Committee Substitute for Assembly, No. 3378* (December 9, 2010), http://www.njleg.state.nj.us/2010/Bills/A3500/3378_S1.PDF (accessed April 27, 2011).

consider a favorable provision of the proposed legislation, carriers are barred from terminating the OON provider from a managed care panel on the basis that the provider referred to an OON.[*] As of May 15, 2012, the proposed bill had not yet been passed. To be enacted, the proposed bill will need to be considered by the Assembly, the Senate Committee Structure, the state Senate, and finally signed by the New Jersey Governor.

COMPETITIVE ANALYSIS

PORTER'S FIVE FORCES—DEFINITION AND APPLICATION TO HEALTH CARE

Michael Porter[†] is considered by many to be one of the world's leading authorities on competitive strategy and international competitiveness. In 1980, he published *Competitive Strategy: Techniques for Analyzing Industries and Competitors*[‡], in which he argues that all businesses must respond to five competitive forces. Porter stresses that the essence of developing a competitive business strategy is relating a particular company to the environment in which it operates. Competition therefore extends beyond the actions of a company's current competitors and is rooted in its underlying economic structure.[§] In attempting to understand competitors and select competitive strategies, a review of these five forces may be useful to understanding the underlying fundamentals of competition.

1. *Threat of new market entrants*—This force may be defined as the risk of a similar company entering your marketplace and taking current or potential business from you.
2. *Bargaining power of suppliers*—This force is the negotiating power of suppliers. *Suppliers* can be defined as any business you rely on to deliver your product, service, or outcome.
3. *Threats from substitute products or services*—This refers to substitute products or services that your customers will purchase instead of your product or service.
4. *Bargaining power of buyers*—This force is the degree of negotiating leverage of industry buyers or customers.
5. *Rivalry among existing firms*—This is ongoing rivalry between existing firms and is often assumed to be the sole expression of competition, without consideration of the other competitive forces that define industries.

PORTER'S GENERIC STRATEGIES

Porter recommends three generic strategies to out-perform competitors or maintain a market position against competition: overall cost leadership, differentiation, and market niche/segmentation (Figure 2.2).

---

[*] Kurtz, R. Revised New Jersey out-of-network bill released; NJAASC views changes as positive. *Beckers ASC Review* 12: 1 (December 16, 2011).

[†] A professor of business administration at the Harvard Business School, Michael Porter serves as an advisor to heads of state, governors, mayors, and CEOs throughout the world. The recipient of the Wells Prize in Economics, the Adam Smith Award, three McKinsey Awards, and honorary doctorates from the Stockholm School of Economics and six other universities, Porter is the author of 14 books, among them *Competitive Advantage*, *The Competitive Advantage of Nations*, and *Cases in Competitive Strategy*.

[‡] Porter, M. E. *Competitive Strategy: Techniques for Analyzing Industries and Competitors*. The Free Press, NY, 1980.

[§] *Ibid.*, p. 3.

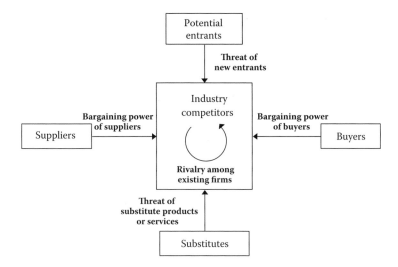

FIGURE 2.2 Michael Porter's five forces driving industry competition. (From Porter, M. E., *Competitive Strategy: Techniques for Analyzing Industries and Competitors*, p. 4, The Free Press, 1980. With permission.)

Overall Cost Leadership

Organizations focusing on this strategy seek to produce the same or better quality services at less cost than competitors, while attempting to earn greater profits through volume and/or increased efficiencies. During periods of strong price competition, organizations aim to merely stay in the market profitably through reduced prices.

This strategy may revolutionize a firm where industry competition has been weak. Competitors may be ill prepared, mentally, economically, or operationally, to minimize costs. Examples of industries that are characterized by this strategy include the steel, retail banking, and beer industries and it does occur occasionally in hospital inpatient care.

Differentiation

A differentiation strategy implies a focus on the production of a better or different product or service. This difference may be only one of perception or marketing. Quality imperatives demand a strategy equating the product with "desirable" quality standards. Differentiation can earn above-average profits even in slow growth or declining markets. With this strategy, cost is secondary but companies exist throughout the continuum between the pure theoretical strategies of cost, quality, and differentiation.

Market Niche/Segmentation

Companies utilizing this strategy focus on a section or group of buyers, a segment of a product line, or a specific area of a geographic market. The premise is that these companies, by focusing on a narrow target, can provide value to customers more effectively than rivals who compete more broadly. Low cost and differentiation are still competitive factors for any niche.

Porter's recommendation is to avoid being "caught in the middle," that is, being neither the lowest cost nor highest quality, or being insufficiently differentiated. While pursuing the chosen strategy as the company's primary strategic focus, a company should not lose sight of the two other strategies.

This strategy should not be evaluated in isolation. It must be integrated into as many short-term and long-term goals of the business and its market as possible.

APPLYING PORTER'S FIVE FORCES TO HOSPITALS AND PHYSICIAN GROUPS

Health care is often described as being different from other industries for a number of reasons, including

1. The large role of governmental regulation and reimbursement
2. The seemingly limitless demand for health care
3. The necessity of having local providers
4. The removal of consumers from the direct purchasing decisions because of employer-driven insurance purchasing
5. The difficulties in quantifying health and the quality and costs of care

Yet, these aspects may be found in other industries, and increasingly, these barriers to competition in health care are under pressure by, most notably, the FTC to be removed or diminished because of rising costs. Therefore, Porter's Five Forces model applies to health care just as with any other industry. In the *Harvard Business Review* article entitled "Making Competition in Health Care Work,"* Porter further explores the value of his model as a process or framework for use in examining competition in health care.

Porter's model applies to a company operating within a specific industry and so we must first define the health care industry, which contains numerous subsets interacting with each other, including hospitals, nursing homes, medical practices, home health agencies, subacute providers, ASCs, and urgent care centers. These facilities and providers, along with the administrators, equipment suppliers, pharmaceutical companies, and other support and managerial providers, all may be considered as part of the "health care industry" because they share the common goal of maximizing human health. This is not an easily quantifiable outcome, but it can be viewed as the common denominator among all the facets in the health care industry.

A hospital that does not acknowledge the local independent family medical practice or cardiology group working in the same industry as a competitor (as well as a "customer") may have missed the point. There is a complex relationship between the various subsets of the health care industry and any competitive evaluation should take several different perspectives on these relationships.

Threat of New Market Entrants

Historically, many hospitals and physicians have believed that there is a low risk (or even no risk) of new market competitors due to the entry barriers in their segments of the industry. Health care has been said to be a local business because providers must deliver services to patients in person.

However, technology and communications, as well as the ability to recruit providers nationally, are changing some aspects of the physician–patient relationship so that this is no longer universally or absolutely true. New entrants may no longer necessarily have to be based in their local market.

Overall, the threat from new entrants may be related to the size of the financial return in that particular segment of the industry. Health care differs from many industries as financial return does not always drive the decision process. The goals of charity, education, and community service make some decisions in the business of health care seem financially or economically irrational.

Bargaining Power of Suppliers

In health care, suppliers are primarily professional services providers, but they are also any person or organization involved in the provision of improved health for patients. Physicians are, in this sense, suppliers (if you do not directly employ them). Other suppliers may include medical supply companies, pharmaceutical companies, and outsourcers.

---

* Teisberg, E. O., M. E. Porter and G. B. Brown. Making competition in health care work. *Harvard Business Review* 3: 7 (July/August 1994): 1–3.

Suppliers can impact your business if they can raise your costs. Health care suppliers' prices are often controlled or influenced by the necessity of accepting what the government will pay for a product or service. The bargaining power of suppliers, besides those of service, is subject to increasing pressures.

It is significant, then, to note that health care is different from other industries in that the suppliers are often also the customers, as in hospital–physician relationships.

Rise of Urgent Care Walk-In Clinics

Recent trends suggest renewed interest in walk-in clinics, as the number of retail clinics across the United States has grown to nearly 1200 facilities at locations such as former urgent care centers, strip malls, and even in some grocery store chains.[*] Several factors drive this growing phenomenon, including more selective demographic targeting of plan members, greater cost control for the health plan, and a greater opportunity to market themselves to potential customers.[†] Retail clinics appeal to many individuals due to the clinics' flexible scheduling, extended hours, urgent care services, and other services not available at conventional physicians' offices. Retail clinics also appeal to insurers who are able to exercise higher levels of control over expenses in these business arrangements. By reducing administrative and other overhead costs, insurers may also be able to maximize profit margins and preserve their bottom lines, which may be threatened by new ACA mandates (e.g., limits on the percentage of premiums that insurers can spend on nonmedical costs).[‡] Under the ACA individual mandate, an estimated 50 million uninsured individuals will enter the health care marketplace in 2014.[§] By offering services in areas where individuals routinely travel for other purposes (e.g., strip malls and grocery stores), insurers may receive a large amount of commercial exposure among consumers.

Boutique–Concierge Medicine

Concierge, or boutique, medical practices began in 1996 in Seattle and are now in several major metropolitan areas. Concierge practices are concentrated principally on the east and west coasts, with most practices focused on providing primary care services.[¶] Concierge medicine is basically a "return to 'old-fashioned' medicine," where physicians limit their client base and devote more time to each patient. Patients can usually get in to see their physician within a day, and most have 24-hour access to their physician by pager or cell phone.[**] The current business model for concierge practices requires charging patients an annual retainer or membership fee in exchange for guaranteed access to standard health care services, as well as increased access to personalized physician services that are unique to the individual patient.[††] Physicians, tired of long hours, not having enough time with their patients, and dealing with overbooked caseloads, are turning to concierge medicine as a way of balancing their lives and providing quality care for their patients.[‡‡] Patients who have physicians in this type of practice appreciate the "perks" they get for paying a yearly fee—similar

---

[*] Weaver, C. Health insurers opening their own clinics to trim costs. *Kaiser Health News* (May 4, 2011), http://www.kaiser healthnews.org/Stories/2011/May/04/Insurers-Turn-To-Clinics-For-Cost Control.aspx (accessed May 31, 2011).

[†] Lewis, D. P. Insurer-owned clinics bid to offer more patient care. *American Medical News* (May 16, 2011), http://www .ama-assn.org/amednews/2011/05/16/bil20516.htm (accessed May 31, 2011).

[‡] Health insurance issuers implementing medical loss ratio (MLR) requirements under the patient protection and Affordable Care Act; Interim Final Rule. 45 CFD Part 158, Fed. Reg. 75: 230 (December 1, 2011): 74877–74878.

[§] *The Uninsured and the Difference Health Insurance Makes*. The Henry J. Kaiser Family Foundation, San Francisco, CA (September 2010); Patient Protection and Affordable Care Act. Public Law 111-148, Section 1501, 124 STAT 242 (March 23, 2010).

[¶] Physician services: Concierge care characteristics and considerations for Medicare. Report to Congressional Committees GAO-05-929. U.S. Government Accountability Office (August 2005), p. 3.

[**] Leidig, D. Concierge medicine: A new specialty? *The Reporter*: 2. Texas Medical Liability Trust (March–April 2005): 2.

[††] Linz, A. J., P. F. Haas, L. F. Fallon, Jr. and R. J. Metz. Impact of concierge care on health care and clinical practice. *Journal of the American Osteopathic Association* 105: 11 (November 2005): 515.

[‡‡] *Ibid.*, p. 518.

to "annual membership dues." These fees can range anywhere from $1000 per year to $10,000 per year depending on the patient's age, benefits received, area of the country, and practice.[*]

Amenities vary by practice, but some include more time with the physician (e.g., 30 min office visit), increased access to physicians, e-mailed "newsletters" or condition-specific information, physicians accompanying patients on visits to specialists, and house calls.[†]

Although concierge medicine may provide many benefits for patients, including more, and in some cases, nearly unlimited access to their physicians, it has been met with some scrutiny. For example, because Medicare beneficiaries cannot be charged more than 115% of the rate for services, many politicians have said that the annual fees patients pay for concierge medicine is a lot more than the Medicare rate and thus is illegal billing. Moreover, it is argued that this type of medicine is elitist, that it is available only to wealthy patients who can pay the annual fees. Many physicians report, however, that a bulk of their clients are middle-income people who are willing to pay more for this kind of care.[‡] Note that boutique medicine is not a substitute for traditional insurance. Patients will typically keep their traditional health insurance to pay for any tests or scans ordered by the physician.[§]

Hospital System and Physician Practice Realignment

Hospital Acquisition of Physician Practices   Hospitals have recently returned to the 1990s' trend of directly employing physicians and increasingly competing for physicians' time and loyalty as more physician-owned specialty hospitals open, allowing increasing numbers of physicians to refuse on-call emergency room duties and other traditional medical staff responsibilities.[¶] While hospitals primarily employed primary care physicians during the 1990s, the recent employment trend has seen a rise in the number of specialists employed by hospitals.[**] In a study undertaken by the Center for Studying Health System Change, it was reported that 30 out of 43 hospital systems had increased the number of employed physicians between 2005 and 2007, with a particularly notable increase in the incidence of employed specialists (83% of the systems).[††] A 2009 study by Medical Group Management Association (MGMA), entitled Physician Placement Starting Salary Survey: 2010 Report Based on 2009 Data, projected that, more than half (65%) of established physicians were placed in hospital-owned practices and that 495 of physicians hired out of residency or fellowship were placed within a hospital-owned practice.[‡‡]

Shortage of Supply of Physician Manpower   A widespread shortage of physicians is expected in the next 10–15 years. Recent reports have indicated that the United States will face a growing

---

[*] *Ibid.*, p. 515. See also Leidig, D. Concierge medicine: A new specialty? *The Reporter*: 3. Texas Medical Liability Trust (March–April 2005): 2.

[†] See Leidig, D. Concierge medicine: A new specialty? *The Reporter*: 3. Texas Medical Liability Trust (March-April 2005): 2. GAO. Physician services: Concierge care characteristics and considerations for Medicare. Report to Congressional Committees GAO-05-929 (August 2005), p. 15. Russano, J. Is boutique medicine a new threat to American health care or a logical way of revitalizing the doctor–patient relationship? *Washington University Journal of Law and Policy* 17: (2005): 313.

[‡] Freeman, L. Personal doctor: Specialty concierge medicine new area trend. *Naples Daily News* (February 16, 2008), www.naplesnews.com/news/2008/Feb/16/personal-doctor-specialty-concierge-medicine-new-t/ (accessed August 1, 2008).

[§] Hawryluk, M. Boutique medicine may run afoul of Medicare rules. amednews.com (April 8, 2002), www.ama-assn.org/amednews/2002/04/08/gvsb0408.htm (accessed August 1, 2008).

[¶] Lubell, J. Hospitals seen seeking closer doc partnerships. *Modern Health Care* (October 4, 2007).

[**] Beckham, D. New twist in employing physicians. *Hospitals and Health Networks*, www.hhnmag.com (accessed March 3, 2008). Harris, G. More doctors giving up private practices. *New York Times* 1: (March 25, 2010) 1–4, http://www.nytimes.com/2010/03/26/health/policy/26docs.html (accessed July 26, 2011).

[††] Christian, C. D. and Myre, T. T. Integration 2.0: Does health care reform signal the twilight of the private physician practice. *Valeo Online* (July 14, 2010), http://www.valeocommunications.com/2010/07/14/integration-20-does-health-care-reform-signal-the-twilight-of-the-private-physician-practice (accessed May 25, 2011).

[‡‡] MGMA Physician Placement Report: 65 Percent of Establishing Physicians Placed in Hospital-Owned Practices. Medical Group Management Association (June 3, 2010), http://www.mgma.com/press/default.aspx?id=33777 (accessed May 25, 2011).

physician manpower shortage, especially in primary care, in the coming years. This trend is driven by several factors, including the growth of an aging baby boomer population, which typically utilizes a greater proportion of health services than the nonelderly population.[*] Additionally, the number of practicing physicians in the United States is predicted to remain fairly stagnant over the next decade due to physician lifestyle changes, which have resulted in a reduction of the total number of work hours, and retirement of current physicians (approximately 99,000 of which were older than 65 in 2008).[†] It is estimated that a shortage of generalist physicians could reach anywhere from 35,000 to 44,000 by 2025, according to the American College of Physicians.[‡] By 2020, the Health Resources and Services Administration (HRSA) predicts a shortage of 21,400 general surgery physicians.[§] The HRSA also predicts deficits for such specialties as radiology, urology, and psychiatry by 2020.[§] The 2010 health care legislation responds to this projected shortage in physician manpower by increasing the number of graduate medical education training positions; giving priority to primary care and general surgery and to those states with the lowest resident physician-to-patient population; increasing workforce supply and support by training health professionals through scholarships and loans; promoting training in preventive medicine and public health; increasing the capacity for nurse education, support nurse training programs, providing loan repayment and retention grants, and creating a career ladder to nursing; and establishing a Prevention and Public Health Fund for prevention, wellness, and public health activities.[¶]

Joint Ventures between Community Hospitals and Niche Providers   The move toward specialized inpatient and outpatient facilities, often owned by physicians, is a natural reaction to the significant reimbursement, regulatory, and technological changes described above, and represents beneficial competition and innovations allowing health care services to be provided in a more cost-effective manner while also maintaining and improving quality and beneficial outcomes.[**] In an attempt to strengthen relationships and align economic incentives to enhance market position and financial success between physicians and hospitals, many specialty providers, such as orthopedic surgeons and cardiologists, are entering into joint ventures with one another.[††] As competition over ASTC revenue streams between physicians and hospitals remains intense, new forms of joint ventures and revenue sharing options are developing in an attempt to repair their recently contemptuous relationship, and to offer patients increased quality services and access.[‡‡] FutureScan predicts that the relationship between hospitals and physicians will stabilize within the next 10 years, resulting in more physicians investing with hospitals and both parties being involved in management decisions. The economic benefits of a physician and hospital joint venture relationship are significant. Collaboration between physicians and hospitals creates an economy of scale

---

[*] The Complexities of Physician Supply and Demand: Projections Through 2025: Executive Summary. Center for Workforce Studies of the Association of American Medical Colleges, http://www.aamc.org/workforce (accessed May 6, 2010).

[†] Kane, G. C. et al. The anticipated physician shortage: Meeting the nation's need for physician services. *American Journal of Medicine* 122: 12 (December 2009): 1159.

[‡] Aston, G. Calling all docs: Primary care shortage looms large. *Hospitals and Health Networks* (February 2011), http://www.hhnmag.com/hhnmag_app/jsp/articledisplay.jsp?dcrpath=HHNMAG/Article/data/02FEB2011/0211HHN_Inbox_physicians&domain=HHNMAG (accessed May 27, 2011).

[§] Harris, S. Physician shortage spreads across specialty lines. *Association of American Medical Colleges* (October 2010), https://www.aamc.org/newsroom/reporter/oct10/152090/physician_shortage_spreads_across_specialty_lines.html (accessed May 27, 2011).

[¶] *Summary of New Health Reform Law*. Kaiser Family Foundation (April 21, 2010), http://www.kff.org/healthreform/upload/8061.pdf (accessed May 6, 2010).

[**] Intellimarker: Ambulatory Surgery Centers Financial & Operational Benchmarking Study 2006. *Informed Health Care Media* (August 2006): 9.

[††] Financing the Future II Report 4: Joint Ventures with Physicians and Other Partners. Health Care Financial Management Association (February 2006), p. 3.

[‡‡] Hurley, R. E. et al. A Widening rift in access and quality: Growing evidence of economic disparities. *Health Affairs* (December 6, 2005): W5–567.

that will not be achieved if each continues to operate independently, thereby increasing hospital and health system interest.[*]

According to Jay Klarsfeld, MD, there are many advantages to a hospital-physician joint venture. Because hospitals make most of their money from inpatient services, opening a separate outpatient surgery center is not economically feasible. Because ASCs perform outpatient procedures economically and safely, it behooves the hospital to form a business relationship with the physician-owners. When the hospital sends patients to the surgery center, they share in the profit. Additionally, when physicians have influence over the design process and ownership of an outpatient facility, things run smoother and more efficiently. Studies have shown that when "physicians have an economic stake [they] show up on time, don't waste minutes in the OR, and make smarter purchasing decisions".[†] There are advantages for the physician as well. Most hospitals have a reputation in the community as being safe and reliable, and the physician-owner shares this good reputation in a joint venture. This makes the ASC more credible. A physician also has exposure to hospital vendors, and the association with the hospital can be helpful in purchasing.[†]

Co-Management Arrangements   Alignment, integration, and engagement of physicians is another key strategy for health systems seeking to create high-performing, high-quality, and high-efficiency organizations. Yet aligning physicians' interests with those of hospitals and health systems has been an ongoing struggle, particularly since the shift from small, physician/provider-owned, independent private practices to captive practices within larger integrated health systems (i.e., *the corporatization of the practice of medicine*). Successful hospital enterprises have understood that "to effectively respond to the economic incentives of reform, a hospital must achieve a deeper level of integration with the physicians that practice there".[‡] One way by which physicians and hospitals are trying to achieve this common goal is through co-management arrangements, which have reemerged in recent years as an alternative to joint ventures or strict employment arrangements between hospitals and physicians, who share mutual interests to lower costs, increase efficiency, and improve quality.[§]

Under the new co-management model, a hospital may enter into a management agreement with an organization that is either jointly owned or wholly owned by a physician to provide the daily management services for the inpatient and/or outpatient components of a medical specialty service line.[¶] A co-management arrangement incentivizes physicians for the development, management, and improvement of quality and efficiency, as well as for making the service line more competitive in the target market.[¶]

Co-management arrangements may result in health care entities that are value driven and provide physicians and hospitals an opportunity to achieve safety, quality, patient satisfaction, and cost efficiency, which ultimately result in improvement in the delivery of patient care.

Threats from Substitute Products or Services

Nontraditional health care providers are increasingly competing with traditional health care. Alternative providers such as chiropractors have taken a larger market share and some health care

---

[*] Financing the Future II Report 4: Joint Ventures with Physicians and Other Partners. Health Care Financial Management Association (February 2006), p. 4.

[†] Klarsfeld, J. The perils and payoffs of hospital joint ventures. *Outpatient Surgery Magazine* (January 2007): 18–19.

[‡] Achieving physician integration with the co-management model. Health Care Financial Management Association, http://www.hfma.org/Templates/Print.aspx?id=20619 (accessed July 19, 2010).

[§] Evans, M. Co-management emerges as alternative to joint ventures, employment by hospitals. *Modern Physician* (May 10, 2010), http://www.modernphysician.com/apps/pbcs.dll/article?AID=/20100510/MODERNPHYSI# (accessed July 21, 2010).

[¶] Danello, P. F. Clinical co-management: Hospitals and oncologists working together. *Journal of Oncology Practice* 2: 1 (January 2006).

systems and MCOs have embraced the changes in patient preferences for alternative medicine and developed networks of these providers.

Technology has fueled the entry of new competitors in many other industries, and health care is no exception. Patients are accessing medical advice and information through the Internet and becoming more informed about care and treatment options. With advances in medical imaging communication, radiologists in remote locations can outsource X-ray film readings for hospitals at lower prices. The role of the pharmacy and pharmacist is also changing and may become a threat to some portion of the service/advice/monitoring business of medical offices.

In short, competition can come in many forms and affect many subsets of health care services. Planning and analyzing potential substitute products and services requires creative thinking as well as thorough research. Health care's primary difference from other industries in this area may well be its regulation of medical professionals, treatments, and drugs, which may delay or prohibit the development of substitutes, therefore discouraging innovation—the "fundamental driver" of quality improvement and the "underlying dynamic" of a company's ability to compete.

"Purple Pill"

Increasingly, drugs offer an alternative treatment, often at a lower cost, reducing hospital stays or the need for costly surgeries or procedures. For example, the introduction of Prilosec, which became widely recognized as the Purple Pill (Nexium® for acid reflux disease), revolutionized the treatment of bleeding ulcer patients. The use of a proton pump inhibitor such as Prilosec (omeprazole) prior to endoscopy reduced the need for the procedure, and stopped bleeding faster than in patients taking a placebo, thereby reducing both the need for surgery as well as the length of hospital stays.[*]

Battle Lines among Providers

Competition exists not only among hospitals and physician-owned facilities, but also among health care professional providers themselves (e.g., ophthalmologists versus optometrists, anesthesiologists versus certified registered nurse anesthetists, and OB-GYNs versus certified nurse midwives). One of the most prevalent areas of competition is related to providers of imaging services. The issue of in-office ancillary imaging pits radiologists against other physicians. Increasingly, radiologists face competition from referring physicians.[†] A study funded by the Radiological Society of North America (RSNA) and presented in 2004 claimed that self-referral leads to increased utilization of diagnostic imaging. The study recommended that the radiologist professional community lobby the federal government to enact regulations making self-referrals more difficult. According to the chief researcher, Dr. David C. Levin, "Orthopedic surgeons really don't belong in the business of owning MR (magnetic imaging) scanners".[‡]

The result of such efforts was reflected in the passage of the *Medicare Improvements for Patients and Providers Act of 2008 (MIPPA)*.[§] After the *American College of Radiology (ACR)* announced plans to lobby for legislation requiring Medicare to define standards for physicians performing diagnostic imaging, and the *Medicare Payment Advisory Commission (MedPAC)* staff members stated "it's important for CMS to set national standards for each imaging modality…," Congress included in the MIPPA a provision requiring accreditation of physicians who provide the technical component for advanced diagnostic imaging services (e.g., magnetic resonance imaging [MRI], computed

---

[*] Gardner, A. Prilosec helps control bleeding in ulcer patients. *HealthDay Reporter*, U.S. Department of Health and Human Services (April 18, 2007), www.healthfinder.gov/news/newsstory.asp?docid=603797 (accessed March 31, 2008). Javid, G. et al. Omeprazole as adjuvant therapy to endoscopic combination injection sclerotherapy for treating bleeding peptic ulcer. *The American Journal of Medicine* 111: 4 (September 2001): 280–284.

[†] Thompson, T. L. Self-referral issue isolates radiology in multispecialty forum. AuntMinnie (October 7, 2004), www.auntminnie.com/index.asp?Sec=sup&Sub=imc&Pag=dis&ItemID=63177 (accessed February 18, 2005).

[‡] Volkin, L. and Dargan, R. S. Self-referral drives increase in diagnostic imaging among nonradiologists. American Society of Radiologic Technologists (December 10, 2004), www.asrt.org/content/News/IndustryNewsBrief/GenRes/Selfreferr041210.aspx (accessed February 18, 2005).

[§] Medicare Improvements for Patients and Providers Act of 2008, Public Law 110-275, 122 Stat. 2494 (July 15, 2008).

tomography [CT], and nuclear medicine/positron emission tomography [PET]) for which payment is made under the *Medicare Physician Fee Schedule (MPFS)*.* After the Secretary of Health and Human Services designates accreditation organizations in 2010, all suppliers of the technical component of advanced diagnostic imaging services will need to be accredited by January 2012.†

Competition has been increased somewhat by the ACA's revision of the "in-office ancillary services" exception to the Stark self-referral law.‡ This exception—once relied on by physicians in group practices to refer patients to the group—has now been stifled to an extent by some disclosures required by the ACA. Section 6003 of the ACA requires that for any referral for MRI, PET, CT or other radiology service, the referring physician must (1) inform the patient in writing (before any referral is made) that the patient may obtain these same services elsewhere, and (2) provide the patient with a written list of other nearby providers who offer the same or similar services.§ This will likely lead to far fewer physicians referring patients within their own group practices, and will allow patients to more freely seek out other providers should they choose to do so.

Bargaining Power of Buyers

Most health care is paid for by insurance organizations, whether private or governmental. Most private health insurance is purchased through employers who, to a great degree, make most of the buying decisions. Employer coalitions have emerged, but most command leverage on price rather than quality or value. This often leaves health care providers as the only advocates for consumers. Despite the fact that businesses bear less of the total U.S. health care premium dollar (approximately 25%¶) than government or individuals, corporate buyers have asserted substantial, if disproportionate, influence over health care companies, but not necessarily always in the best interests of the consumers or the community at large.

Health care is different from other industries in several respects. It is characterized by

1. More than one class of buyers—patients, family (proxies), insurance companies, and employers, each with different objectives
2. A divide between consumer and payor
3. An unequal balance of information between consumers and providers, which works to the detriment of the payor
4. A single largest payor—the government

Perhaps the most significant aspect of the ACA is the proposed establishment of American Health Benefit Exchanges (Exchanges).** Exchanges refer to new, transparent, and competitive private health insurance markets that aim to allow individuals and small businesses to purchase affordable qualified health plans.†† With implementation set to begin in 2014, state-run health insurance Exchanges aim to facilitate the purchase of qualified health plans, increase transparency of pricing

---

* Brice, J. ACR pursues designated physician imager legislation. Diagnostic Imaging Online (January 10, 2005), www .diagnosticimagingonline/showNews.jhtml?articleID=577700160 (accessed February 18, 2005). Public Meeting, Medicare Payment Advisory Commission (December 9, 2004), pp. 295–296. Medicare Improvements for Patients and Providers Act of 2008. Public Law 110-275, 122 Stat. 2494, Sec. 135(a) (July 15, 2008).

† Medicare Improvements for Patients and Providers Act of 2008. Public Law 110-275, 122 Stat. 2494, Sec. 135(a) (July 15, 2008).

‡ Brice, J. ACR pursues designated physician imager legislation. Diagnostic Imaging Online (January 10, 2005), www .diagnosticimagingonline/showNews.jhtml?articleID=577700160 (accessed February 18, 2005). Patient Protection and Affordable Care Act. § 6003, Public Law 111-148, 124 Stat. 697 (March 23, 2010).

§ Patient Protection and Affordable Care Act. § 6003, Public Law 111-148, 124 Stat. 697 (March 23, 2010).

¶ Iglehart, J. K. The American health care system—Expenditures. *New England Journal of Medicine* 340: 1 (January 7, 1999).

** Patient Protection and Affordable Care Act. § 6003, Public Law 111-148, 124 Stat. 697 (March 23, 2010).

†† Glossary: 'Exchange.' healthcare.gov, http://www.healthcare.gov/glossary/e/Exchange.html (accessed June 28, 2011).

and quality, and allow for more regulation of health insurance.* Health insurance Exchanges may be instrumental in assisting individuals and small businesses with making informed health insurance purchasing decisions, by enabling these consumers to compare health plan benefits, pricing, and quality, which is likely to change the competitive landscape among health care and health insurance providers.

Rivalry among Existing Firms

Integrated physician organizations and other types of EHOs may be viewed as new market entrants or simply as a group of existing providers reorganized in order to compete better. The number of these integrated provider organizations and EHOs grew tremendously during the 1990s through consolidation and mergers of traditional providers, but their effectiveness as competitors is in many ways still uncertain. Integration, affiliation, and collaboration among providers may, in some cases, be viewed as a means of circumventing competition unless the clinical benefits to patients can be demonstrated. The collapse of PPMCs, poor performance of hospital-managed physician practices including physician-hospital organizations (PHOs), the failure of capitated groups and independent physician associations (IPAs) in California, and the current trend toward divestiture of acquired practices would seem to indicate that EHOs have not been effective competitors. Nonetheless, the competitive forces that led to the formation of these integrated organizations still exist and these initial "failures" may have more to do with mismanagement and poor planning than the concept of physician integration itself.

The inherent mission of any health care organization is based on fostering human welfare. This mission is often deemed to be in conflict with the economic and financial goals of health care organizations, especially in the for-profit arena, as well as incompatible with the competitive forces that have been successful in other industries. These differences in basic values are deeply rooted. It is important to understand these differences when assessing the impact of intercompany rivalry on competition as a whole in stimulating quality and efficiency.

COMMUNITY BENEFIT—UNIQUE SIXTH FORCE?

If "community benefit" is defined as the "one true good" of health care, the question arises: Can a capitalist economy and for-profit health care system support this concept of community benefit? The debate between whether health care is a right or privilege has not yet been resolved in American society and puts health care in competition with other social goods for resources. Furthermore, due to the public health nature of many health care services, most health care services are influenced in some fashion by public opinion on matters related to health (i.e., the perception of community benefit), and society works on changing or accepting the health care system through many channels and several organizations including community organizations, political parties (independent of Medicare/Medicaid), civic organizations, and religious organizations. Thus, health care delivery—in a manner and to a degree that few other industries experience—may well be subject to this unique "sixth force."

Increased Scrutiny of Community Hospitals as Providers of Charity Care

In response to increased criticism that tax-exempt hospitals are not fulfilling their charitable missions, the ACA aims to increase transparency concerning the special benefits and incentives that tax-exempt hospitals receive by imposing additional requirements when qualifying for their 501(c)

---

* Kingsdale, J. and Bertko, J. Insurance exchange under health reform: Six design issues for the states. *Health Affairs* 29: 6 (June 2010): 1159.

(3) status.* In addition, the ACA requires tax-exempt hospitals to conduct a community health needs assessment (CHNA) every 3 years to better demonstrate that they are meeting the particular needs of the patient community they serve.† Tax-exempt hospitals will also be required under the ACA to establish a written financial assistance policy that would include, among other things: (1) the criteria for eligibility for financial assistance; (2) the basis for calculating amounts charged to patients; and (3) the steps to be taken in the event of nonpayment.† Other provisions in the ACA will require tax-exempt hospitals to increase their accountability for the quality of care provided to patients. Failure to comply with any requirement of the CHNA can result in a penalty of up to $50,000.†

To promote the goals of lowering health care costs and increasing the quality of patient care, two payment systems are being established with the goal to directly tie reimbursement to performance: value-based purchasing and bundled payments. Effective October 1, 2012, the ACA mandates a value-based purchasing model (first initiated by the CMS in 2007) for all hospitals.‡ Value-based purchasing (VBP) is a model whereby incentive payments are given to hospitals that meet or exceed certain performance benchmarks set by CMS.† In the past, hospitals were rewarded for simply reporting their performance in certain areas.§ Under the ACA and the (VBP) reimbursement model, such reporting is mandatory, with a percentage of Medicare reimbursement tied directly to quality.§ The benchmarks will take various aspects of care into consideration, including certain efficiency and patient satisfaction metrics.¶ Beginning in fiscal year (FY) 2013, the clinical measures for these incentive payments will include achieving certain quality metrics related to such clinical conditions as heart failure, pneumonia, and hospital-related infection, with more conditions to be considered after that time.†

Internal Revenue Service (IRS) Form 990 Disclosures

On February 14, 2008, the IRS posted information on its Web site concerning the governance of charitable organizations and related topics. The IRS also removed a previously posted preliminary staff discussion draft entitled *Good Governance Practices for 501(c)(3) Organizations* from its Web site. The IRS believes that its views on nonprofit governance are best reflected in the reporting required by the revised Form 990 and the governance components incorporated in the Life Cycle— an educational tool provided by the IRS.

The revision of Form 990 came in response to increasing scrutiny about how much charity care was actually being delivered at given hospitals. If one hospital in a community failed to provide their share of charity care, another hospital had to take those patients and ended up with a disproportionate number of unprofitable cases. The revision prompts hospitals to document their spending on charity care to verify that they are providing the amount of care they are claiming. Twenty-two states have laws that require disclosure on charity spending, and three states have a

---

* Marietta, C. S. PPACA's additional requirements imposed on tax-exempt hospitals will increase transparency and account-ability on fulfilling charitable missions. *Health Law Perspectives*. Health Law & Policy Institute, University of Houston Law Center (July 2010), p. 1. Patient Protection and Affordable Care Act. § 6003, Public Law 111-148, 124 Stat. 697 (March 23, 2010).

† Patient Protection and Affordable Care Act. § 6003, Public Law 111-148, 124 Stat. 697 (March 23, 2010).

‡ Anderson, J. and Slaw, H. New payment and delivery models under health reform require new relationships between physi-cians and hospitals. *BNA Health Law Reporter* (November 18, 2010): 2, http://news.bna.com/hlln/display/batch_print_display .adp (accessed November 23, 2010). See also Patient Protection and Affordable Care Act. § 6003, Public Law 111-148, 124 Stat. 697 (March 23, 2010).

§ Anderson, J. and Slaw, H. New payment and delivery models under health reform require new relationships between physi-cians and hospitals. *BNA Health Law Reporter* (November 18, 2010): 2, http://news.bna.com/hlln/display/batch_print_display .adp (accessed November 23, 2010).

¶ Heitin, L. Hospitals should plan now for value-based purchasing, which may be a game-changer. *AIS Health Business Daily* (August 11, 2010), http://www.aishealth.com/Bnow/hbd081110.html (accessed November 22, 2010).

minimum threshold.* Along with detailed disclosure of charity care, Form 990 will also require disclosure of governance policies and executive pay and perks. Hospitals will also be able to claim a share of bad debt and Medicare losses, but they must disclose the method used to estimate the losses.†

Increased Scrutiny of Nonprofit Organizations under the ACA

Nonprofit scrutiny was heightened even further in 2010 by the passage of the ACA. The health reform laws add many requirements that 501(c)(3) organizations must satisfy in order to maintain their status as a tax-exempt entity. The ACA adds to the Internal Revenue Code section 501(r), which sets out four new requirements that 501(c)(3) organizations that operate one or more hospital facilities must meet.‡ These requirements include (1) adopting and implementing written financial assistance and emergency medical care policies§, (2) limiting charges for emergency or other medically necessary care§, (3) refraining from taking "extraordinary collection actions" until making "*reasonable* efforts" to determine whether a patient qualifies for financial assistance§, and (4) requiring that each 501(c)(3) hospital organization conduct a CHNA at least once every 3 years in order to better demonstrate that the organization is meeting the particular needs of the patient community they serve.§ The CHNA requirement is effective for tax years beginning after March 23, 2012, and currently does not affect nonprofit hospital organizations.‡ Once in effect, failure to comply with any requirement of the CHNA can result in a penalty of up to $50,000.§

Antitrust Considerations

Antitrust law has traditionally been used to combat anticompetitive behavior arising from professional- and payer-imposed barriers to competition, as well as against consolidations (either by collaboration or merger) by provider groups and health systems.¶ However, at the beginning of this decade, strict antitrust enforcement in the health care sector tended to shift away from providers toward pharmaceuticals in a larger shift away from strict application of antitrust law to the health care sector generally.** During that time frame, antitrust jurisprudence began to shift to a significantly increased level of judicial deference to professionalism in health market transactions, which chilled the ability of federal antitrust authorities to bring effective enforcement actions against violators.†† Additionally, while federal enforcement agencies generally won cases against hospital mergers between the mid-1980s and the mid-1990s, those agencies lost all the hospital merger cases brought in federal court between 1995 and 2001.†† During this time frame, courts tended to take a purely economic look at elements of antitrust decisions such as a provider's market share and price, ignoring other elements germane to health care such as patients' personal and logistical considerations when choosing a provider.††

Promulgated by recent health care reform efforts, the *FTC* and the *DOJ* have expressed renewed concern regarding the adequacy of existing standards for horizontal mergers, maintaining that

---

* Blesch, G. Ohio readies charity standards. *Modern Health Care* (January 28, 2008), http://modernhealth care.com/apps/pbcs.dll/article?AID=/20080128/SUB/381946443 (accessed March 31, 2008).

† Evans, M. Scheduling challenges. *Modern Health Care* (January 7, 2008), http://modernhealthcare.com/apps/pbcs.dll/article?AID=/20080107/REG/911456645 (accessed March 31, 2008).

‡ *New Requirements for 501(c)(3) Hospitals Under the Affordable Care Act.* Internal Revenue Service, http://www.irs.gov/charities/charitable/article/0,,id=236275,00.html (accessed June 2, 2011).

§ Patient Protection and Affordable Care Act. § 6003, Public Law 111-148, 124 Stat. 697 (March 23, 2010).

¶ Chapter 4: Competition law: Hospitals. In: *Improving Health Care: A Dose of Competition.* The Federal Trade Commission and the Department of Justice (July 2004), pp. 1–3.

** Executive summary. In: *Improving Health Care: A Dose of Competition.* The Federal Trade Commission and the Department of Justice (July 2004), pp. 21–29. Industry snapshot and competition law: Pharmaceuticals. In: *Improving Health Care: A Dose of Competition.* The Federal Trade Commission and the Department of Justice (July 2004), p. 9.

†† Greaney, T. L. Whither antitrust? The uncertain future of Competition Law in health care. *Health Affairs* 21: 2 (March/April 2002): 185–186.

fortified measures of antitrust enforcement are crucial to cutting costs and improving quality of health care.[*] Most recently, the DOJ and FTC have focused their efforts on evaluating the impact of horizontal consolidation of certain health care organizations (e.g., pharmaceutical giants, payors, outpatient clinics, and hospitals) to determine whether their respective market sectors experience a decrease in competition as a result.[†]

As legislators continue to focus on reducing the cost of health care while improving quality and access, antitrust enforcement is likely to take on a larger role in the health care sector. With the promotion of a public option as part of health care reform legislation, more focus has been placed on the benefits of competition in the health care insurance marketplace, and the proposed repeal of the McCarran–Ferguson Act demonstrates how legislators will continue work to improve competition throughout the health care industry in an effort to reduce costs and improve quality.[†]

The FTC and DOJ have taken special interest in the impact of hospital consolidation on market competition. While most research conducted to date suggests a potential correlation between hospital consolidation and higher prices for hospital services, the magnitude of price increase estimated by these studies ranges from 5% to greater than 50%.[‡] While some dispute exists over the impact of consolidation on quality of care, studies utilizing methods perceived to be robust tend to show a reduced level of quality.[§] Surmising a sudden surge of hospital consolidation as a result of impending reform initiatives and continued technological growth, the FTC and DOJ may heighten the stringency of regulations and guidelines in order to ensure competitive veracity within the hospital sector.[¶]

IMPLEMENTING SUCCESSFUL APPROACHES FROM OTHER INDUSTRIES

Health care cannot be viewed in isolation from the market economy as a whole. Although there are significant differences between health care and other industries, many of the approaches used to compete in other industries can be applied successfully to the health care industry. By recognizing these differences, the spectrum of health care enterprises can begin to address the management challenges and obstacles facing the industry.

WHY HEALTH CARE MANAGEMENT APPEARS TO LAG BEHIND OTHER INDUSTRIES

Because of government regulation and traditional public beliefs about community good, health care has been shielded more than other industries have from the forces of competition and is now being forced to catch up quickly as cost pressures and demands for improved quality fueled by Internet-educated patients and health care reform increase. Health care may be well served by studying other

---

[*] The Importance of Competition and Antitrust Enforcement to Lower-Cost, Higher-Quality Health Care. Prepared Statement of the Federal Trade Commission before the U.S. Senate Subcommittee on Consumer Protection, Product Safety, and Insurance, Committee on Commerce, Science, and Transportation (July 16, 2009), pp. 1–2.

[†] FTC order restores competition lost through Schering-Plough's acquisition of Merck. Federal Trade Commission, Press Release (October 29, 2009), http://www.ftc.gov/opa/2009/10/merck.shtm (accessed November 11, 2009). FTC order prevents anticompetitive effects from Pfizer's acquisition of Wyeth. Federal Trade Commission, Press Release (October 14, 2009), http://www.ftc.gov/opa/2009/10/pfizer.shtm (accessed November 11, 2009). Commission order restores competition eliminated by Carilion Clinic's acquisition of two outpatient clinics. Federal Trade Commission, Press Release (October 7, 2009), http://www.ftc.gov/opa/2009/10/carilion.shtm (accessed November 11, 2009).

[‡] Williams, C. H., Vogt, W.B., and Town, R. How has hospital consolidation affected the price and quality of hospital care? Robert Wood Johnson Foundation, the Synthesis Project, Policy Brief No. 9 (February 2006). Vogt, W. B. Hospital market consolidation: Trends and consequences. *Expert Voices*. National Institute for Health Care Management (November 2009).

[§] Vogt, W. B. Hospital market consolidation: Trends and consequences. *Expert Voices*. National Institute for Health Care Management (November 2009). Williams, C. H., Vogt, W. B., and Town, R. How has hospital consolidation affected the price and quality of hospital care? Robert Wood Johnson Foundation, the Synthesis Project, Policy Brief No. 9 (February 2006).

[¶] Vogt, W. B. Hospital market consolidation: Trends and consequences. *Expert Voices*. National Institute for Health Care Management (November 2009).

industries in order to see what the nature and conduct of its future competitive environment is likely to be. The Case Model illustrates these issues by examining some strong performing companies and the environment in which they compete.

RECOGNIZING DIFFERENCES BETWEEN HEALTH CARE AND OTHER INDUSTRIES

Competition in health care is unique from competition in other sectors because traditional theories of economic forces do not always govern the choices made by professional practice enterprises within the health care industry. Unlike other markets, where competition is viewed positively as a necessary element of capitalism, competition in the health care sector is frequently considered to be resistant to the universal availability and accessibility of quality care.

While traditional notions of *supply* and *demand* and the inherent concept of competition have gained influence over health care professional practice enterprises in recent years, these factors were historically subjugated to a normative argument in favor of the mission-centered provision of services regardless of cost. This has led to the perception that health care demand is supply driven and operates within an inelastic pricing mechanism, the circumstances of which will be discussed later in this chapter.

As the relationship between price and quality of care is generally defined by providers rather than patients, consumers (i.e., patients) are less equipped to make informed purchase decisions than they are in other markets. Furthermore, the intensive regulation of medical professionals, new technologies and treatments, and evolving drug therapies may delay or disable the development of substitutes, and, therefore, stymie innovation, which is one of the fundamental drivers of quality improvement and the underlying dynamic of an organization's ability to compete.

Health care costs are not just rising, but are growing substantially in proportion to the cost of other goods and services in the U.S. economy.[*] The percentage of the gross domestic product (GDP) devoted to health care services has grown from 6% in 1965 to almost 18% today, and is projected to surpass 20% by 2018.[†] While there are many causes for this gap between growth in health care spending and growth in GDP, it should be noted that the impact of the economic recession which started in 2008 was more severe on GDP than it was on health care spending, though the growth rate of the latter did decline slightly.[*]

While some economists have cited the aging population as the reason for the increase in health care's share of the GDP, other voices assert that greed among health maintenance organizations (HMOs), pharmaceutical companies, hospitals, and medical providers such as doctors and nurses, is responsible.[‡] In reality, the rise in health care expenditures is, at least in large part, the result of a much deeper economic force. As economist William J. Baumol of New York University explained in a November 1993 *New Republic* article:

> …the relative increase in health care costs compared with the rest of the economy is inevitable and an ineradicable part of a developed economy. The attempt [to control relative costs] may be as foolhardy as it is impossible.[§]

---

[*] Sisko, A., Truffer, C., Smith, S., Keehan, S., Cylus, J., Poisal, J. A., Clemens, M. K., and Lizonitz, J. Health spending projections through 2018: Recession effects add uncertainty to the outlook. *Health Affairs* (February 24, 2009): w346.

[†] Fleenor, P. Three decades of government-financed health care in the United States. Tax Foundation (August 1994), http://www.taxfoundation.org/files/bd006ece1a4b8166023dbc913175b7b7.pdf (accessed November 11, 2009). Sisko, A., Truffer, C., Smith, S., Keehan, S., Cylus, J., Poisal, J. A., Clemens, M. K., and Lizonitz, J. Health spending projections through 2018: Recession effects add uncertainty to the outlook. *Health Affairs* (February 24, 2009): w347.

[‡] Stanton, M. W. The high concentration of U.S. health care expenditures. *Research in Action*, Issue 19, http://www.ahrq.gov/research/ria19/expendria.htm (accessed January 5, 2010); Why are health care costs so high? Planet Money Blog, National Public Radio (November 11, 2008), http://www.npr.org/blogs/money/2008/11/why_are_healthcare_costs_so_high.html (accessed January 6, 2010); Searcey, D. and Goldstein, J. Tangible and unseen health-care costs. *The Wall Street Journal* (September 3, 2009), http://online.wsj.com/article/SB125193312967181349.html (accessed January 6, 2010).

[§] Baumol, W. J. Do health care costs matter? *New Republic* (November 22, 1993): 16.

Baumol's observation is based on documented and significant differences in productivity growth between the health care sector of the economy and the economy as a whole.

Health care services have experienced significantly lower productivity growth rates than other industry sectors for three reasons:

1. Health care services are inherently resistant to automation. Innovation in the form of technological advancement has not made the same impact on health care productivity as it has in other industry sectors of the economy. The manufacturing process can be carried out on an assembly line where thousands of identical (or very similar) items can be produced under the supervision of a few humans utilizing robots and statistical sampling techniques (e.g., defects per 1000 units). The robot increases assembly line productivity by accelerating the process and reducing labor input. In medicine, most technology is still applied in a patient-by-patient manner—a labor-intensive process. Patients are cared for one at a time. Hospitals and physician offices cannot (and, most would agree, should not) try to operate as factories because patients are each unique and disease is widely variable.

2. Health care is local. Unlike other labor-intensive industries (e.g., shoemaking), health care services are essentially local in nature. They cannot regularly be delivered from Mexico, India, or Malaysia. They must be provided locally by local labor. Health care organizations must compete within a local community with low or no unemployment among skilled workers for high-quality and higher cost labor. While there have been significant advances in telemedicine in recent years, health care remains primarily a local industry.

3. Health care quality is—or is believed to be—correlated with the amount of labor expended. For example, a 30 min office visit with a physician is perceived to be of higher quality than a 10 min office visit. In mass production, the number of work hours per unit is not as important a predictor of product quality as the skills and talents of a small engineering team, which may quickly produce a single design element for thousands of products (e.g., a common car chassis).

Health care suffers a number of serious consequences when its productivity grows at a slower rate than other industries, the most serious being higher relative costs for health care services. The situation is an inevitable and ineradicable part of a developed economy. For example, as technological advancements increase productivity in the computer manufacturing industry, wages for computer industry labor likewise increase. However, the total cost per computer produced actually declines. But in health care (where technological advancements do not currently have the same impact on productivity), wage increases that would be consistent with other sectors of the economy yield a problem—the cost per unit of health care produced increases. Thus, the bad news is that health care's relative share of the GDP grows.

The good news, as Baumol states, may be that

> …productivity growth in the entire economy means we can afford more of everything. In an economy in which productivity is growing in almost every sector and declining in none…consumers can have more of every good and service; they simply have to transfer gains from the sector that's becoming more productive into the sector that's only becoming a little more productive.[*]

Therefore, if our society deems health to be important, then its employers and governments must be willing to adopt policies that share productivity gains in other sectors with health care providers. Businesses cannot take increasing profits and governments cannot take burgeoning taxes from a growing, technologically efficient economy and expect health care services to survive at acceptable levels of quality and access.

---

[*] Baumol, W. J. Do health care costs matter? *New Republic* (November 22, 1993): 18.

Innovation, whether based on technology or reorganization of processes, is necessary in health care delivery because innovation that produces quality and beneficial outcomes can reduce the burdens on society caused by disease and illness, including mortality, reduced quality of life, direct costs (e.g., for medications), and indirect costs (e.g., work absenteeism). However, in health care, innovation that results only in cost reduction at the expense of quality outcomes has not proven to be a bargain.

It is clear from the media and a growing public opinion that efforts to control medical expenses with "cost-effective care" have irritated patients, disrupted long-standing doctor/nurse–patient relationships, and created conditions that lower the quality of medical care. Proponents of cost-effective medicine are raising extremely contentious issues as they question, for instance, the expenditure of hundreds of thousands of dollars on one premature birth when thousands of children lack immunizations, or spending 30% of the Medicare budget on people in their last year of life when nearly 50 million Americans are uninsured or underinsured. Cost containment approaches by HMOs (e.g., gatekeepers and precertification) have spawned lawsuits and cries for legislation, and appear to be fueling a growing consumer revolution and political mandate for patient choice, quality standards, and allowing physicians, nurses, and other providers to act as patient advocates.

A system of health care that provides the highest quality medical service and the most successful, beneficial outcomes at the lowest appropriate cost requires open access to information and a balanced dialogue among government, businesses, and providers. Rather than pointing fingers, the entire health care community needs to commit itself to ensuring that hospital administrators and independent physicians and nurses, acting on behalf of their patients, have an active role in restructuring the community's health care delivery system rather than abdicating the responsibility to government or insurance companies.

Patients, providers, payors, and government leaders seeking to contain costs need to seek partnerships with others who understand the true underlying economics of the realities of rising health care costs, as discussed above, as well as the requirements of ethical patient care, and who are motivated to collaborate to improve the health of communities, rather than attempting to curb short-term medical expenditures at any cost.

INDUSTRY IN CONFLICT—EXCESS CAPACITY AND CERTIFICATE OF NEED LAWS

Fear of duplication stems from a misguided and misinformed assertion that societal costs increase in a competitive market when there are "too many" providers of the same health services—a situation paradoxically labeled as "excess capacity."

Excess capacity is a value-laden term, not an absolute standard. In an article published in *Health Services Research*, Carolyn Madden summarized a number of studies of excess capacity saying, "Without a clear statement of this standard [e.g., the correct number of hospital beds], we cannot determine what constitutes too many. The research literature provides no clear statement".[*] That is the trouble with duplication—everyone seems to be against it, but nobody knows what it means.

New market entrants are often called "cherry-pickers" because they focus on a specialized group of patients or procedures alleged to be more profitable than average. The implication is that these new competitors are greedy, and their business goals are inconsistent with maximizing community health. This view dismisses the importance of patient choice and proceeds with a one-dimensional focus on establishing a market monopoly. The ideal health care delivery system seeks value by considering all important components: access, quality, beneficial outcomes, appropriate cost, and patient choice. Monopoly is not one of them.

---

[*] Madden, C. W. Excess capacity: Markets, regulation, and values. *Health Services Research* 33: 6 (February 1999): 1652. Dr. Madden is a professor of Economics a professor at the University of Washington School of Public Health and Community Medicine.

For patient choice to exist, there must be more than one service provider because choice, by definition, involves alternatives. Duplication, by definition, is the existence of more than one service provider. Patient choice cannot exist without duplication. Arguments against duplication are arguments against patient choice. Health care decisions are deeply personal and based on individual and family experiences. The right of every person to make these decisions merits choice. Furthermore, like any other business, the medical business needs competition to keep it working efficiently and cost-effectively.

CON, or a similar program, is one in which government determines where, when, and how capital expenditures will be made for public health care facilities and major equipment. Professor Michael Morrisey of the University of Alabama–Birmingham Lister Hill Center for Health Policy[*] suggests that CON laws are resurfacing in some states to protect existing hospitals from competition, and in turn are easing pressure to reduce capacity and prices.[†] When that happens, incentives to improve quality decrease as well. The fundamental, yet flawed, idea of the CON was simple—lower costs by reducing duplication. From a market economy perspective, CON laws have been a miserable failure and have failed to lower health care costs. In an article reviewing the CON law and its application to modern markets, Patrick J. McGinley wrote, "In searching the scholarly journals, one cannot find a single article that asserts that CON laws succeed in lowering health care costs".[‡]

According to Professor Madden, "there is…agreement across all perspectives of [health economics theory] on one issue: the negative consequences of too much concentration of economic power".[†] Hospitals in more competitive markets have average costs below those of less competitive markets.[§] Healthy competition gives economic power to patients by creating choices for consumers and raising quality standards as providers compete for patient loyalty. When patient choice is diminished, decisions about access, quality, and beneficial outcomes become the sole purview of elite groups of decision makers who, in the absence of healthy competition, are free to ignore patient demands and needs.

Similarly, on May 24, 2005, the FTC delivered a statement before the Subcommittee on Federal Financial Management, Government Information, and International Security of the Committee on Homeland Security and Governmental Affairs, U.S. Senate on New Entry Into Hospital Competition. The FTC stated that

> …vigorous competition can have important benefits in the hospital arena, just as in the multitude of markets in the U.S. economy that rely on competition to maximize the welfare of consumers. Competitive pressures can lead hospitals to lower costs, improve quality and compete more efficiently. Competitive pressures also may spur new types of competition. In hospital markets, some new entrants specialize and prove only a limited portion of the in-patient and out-patient services that general hospitals tend to provide.[¶]

Specifically, the FTC testimony emphasized that

> Overall, testimony at the FTC/DOJ Hearings identified a number of benefits that SSHs [single specialty hospitals] may offer to consumers, with no significant controversy about the potential for SSHs to provide those benefits. Rather, as discussed in more detail below, debate about SSHs generally centered on how they may affect the functioning of general hospitals.[**]

---

[*] See www.soph.uab.edu/default.aspx?id=653&action=detail&fsid=3324 (accessed June 7, 2005).

[†] Madden, C. W. Excess capacity: Markets, regulation, and values. *Health Services Research* 33: 6 (February 1999): 1652. Dr. Madden is a professor of Economics a professor at the University of Washington School of Public Health and Community Medicine.

[‡] McGinley, P J. Beyond health care reform: Reconsidering certificate of need laws in a managed care competition system. *Florida State University Law Review* (1995).

[§] Zwanziger, J., Melnick, G., and Bamezai, A. California providers adjust to increasing price controls. In: *Health Policy Reform: Competition and Controls*, edited by R. Helms. Washington, DC: AEI Press (1993), pp. 241–258.

[¶] Prepared Statement of the Federal Trade Commission Before the Subcommittee on Federal Financial Management, Government Information, and International Security of the Committee on Homeland Security and Governmental Affairs, U.S. Senate on New Entry Into Hospital Competition (May 24, 2005), p. 3.

[**] *Ibid.*, p. 8.

Ultimately, the FTC testimony related to the efficacy of CON concluded that

> The Commission believes that CON programs generally are not successful in containing health care costs, and that they can pose anticompetitive risk. As noted above, CON programs risk entrenching oligopolists and eroding consumer welfare. The aim of controlling costs is laudable, but there appear to be other, more effective means of achieving this goal that do not pose anticompetitive risks. Indeed, competition itself is often the most effective method of controlling costs. A similar analysis applies to the use of CON programs to enhance health care quality and access.[*]

LESSONS FOR EMERGING HEALTH CARE ORGANIZATIONS

Many of the barriers to competition in health care are beginning to be dismantled, as information on health care quality and costs are better quantified and made available to buyers and patients. Recent political developments demonstrate that public opinion has turned against further cuts in access to and quality of health care. In many ways, the delivery of health care may be approaching the "crisis point" that is sometimes required to force change in a large system.

ACCOUNTABLE CARE ORGANIZATIONS

With the passage of the ACA, health care professionals are looking for new ways to increase efficiency and value, while decreasing the cost of providing health care services. One "solution" proposed by the reform legislation is the creation of accountable care organizations (ACOs). ACOs are health care organizations in which a set of providers, usually physicians and hospitals, are held accountable for the cost and quality of care delivered to a specific local patient population.[†] The two main objectives of ACOs are to increase the quality of health care while at the same time decreasing the cost. What distinguishes ACOs from other integrated health systems is the degree of autonomy given to physicians and the flexibility afforded to physician groups, hospitals, and other providers for the implementation of ACOs.[‡] Because hospitals and physicians are jointly responsible for the quality of care delivered to patients, they are jointly eligible for sharing in any of the cost savings achieved through clinical and operational efficiencies.[§] As part of the "shared savings program" put forth by the ACA, ACOs are scheduled to begin operation no later than January 1, 2012.

MEDICAL HOME MODELS

In recent years, provider interest in primary care has been on the decline. Low payments, heavy work demands, advances in technology, and a trend toward specialization have led medical students to choose careers other than primary care.[¶] Yet, research has shown that patient's utilization of primary care services can lower the total cost and improve the quality of health care—some of the main objectives of health care reform. Rapidly emerging interest in the patient-centered medical home (PCMH) model is one byproduct of health care reform's attempt to revitalize coordinated care and primary care.[¶] The Agency for Health Care Research and Quality (AHRQ)

---

[*] Prepared Statement of the Federal Trade Commission Before the Subcommittee on Federal Financial Management, Government Information, and International Security of the Committee on Homeland Security and Governmental Affairs, U.S. Senate on New Entry Into Hospital Competition (May 24, 2005), p. 18.

[†] Devers, K. and Berenson, R. Can accountable care organizations improve the value of health care by solving the cost and quality quandaries? *Urban Institute* (October 2009): 1.

[‡] Keckley, P. H. et al. Accountable care organizations: A new model for sustainable innovation. *Deloitte Center for Health Solutions* (2010): 11.

[§] Cys, J. Accountable care organizations: A new idea for managing Medicare. *American Medical News* (August 31, 2009), www.ama-assn.org/amednews/2009/08/31/gvsa0831.htm (accessed June 2, 2011).

[¶] Moreno, L., Peikes, D., and Krilla A. Necessary but not sufficient: The HITECH Act and health information technology's potential to build medical homes. Report for the Agency for Health Care Research and Quality, Rockville, MD (June 2010), p. 1.

defines a medical home as a model that organizes providers into homes to deliver the core functions of primary health care.* The main advocates of PCMH see it as a means of providing coordinated care through an individual's, and when appropriate, their family's, life-long relationship with a primary care provider.† A medical home is centered on the following five basic principles: (1) patient-centered care, (2) comprehensive team-based care, (3) coordinated care, (4) superb access to care, and (5) a system-based approach to quality and safety.* As with most primary care, providers take a holistic approach when diagnosing problems, while emphasizing prevention and overall health.* The Agency for Health Care Research and Quality (AHRQ) defines a medical home as a model which organizes providers into homes to deliver the core functions of primary health care.* The main advocates of PCMH see it as a means of providing coordinated care through an individual's, and when appropriate their family's, life-long relationship with a primary care provider.† A medical home is centered on the following five basic principles: (1) patient-centered care; (2) comprehensive team-based care; (3) coordinated care; (4) superb access to care; and, (5) a system-based approach to quality and safety.*

BARRIERS TO COMPETITION

This chapter has discussed aspects of how competition appears to manifest itself in the health care industry and has described some of the barriers to competition. Providers balance the desire for profits and the need to satisfy a value-based mission. The following list identifies significant barriers to competition in health care and efforts to make changes.

1. *Many patients do not purchase services directly from providers*

   There are a number of examples of employers and patient groups successfully contracting directly with providers for the provision of health care services.

   The creation of provider-sponsored organizations (PSOs) to allow provider organizations to contract directly with Medicare for the provision of all the health needs of a population demonstrated the government's interest in this approach, even though initial provider interest has been low.

2. *Patients do not compare prices between providers*

   Patients are paying an increasing portion of the premiums for their health care coverage and thereby feeling the impact of cost increases more directly.

   Increasing numbers of employers are providing employees with a range of options for health insurance coverage between insurers and differently priced types of coverage. Although this does not represent patients buying services directly from providers, it does remove one barrier to the informed selection of plan types and costs.

   MCOs do compare prices from providers and although any savings that result do not generally flow directly to the consumer, they represent a continuing market pressure on fees and charges for providers.

3. *The government is the largest purchaser of health care*

   Although the government faces immense pressure to control health care costs, it also faces pressure to expend additional funds in order to achieve its ostensible primary mission in its involvement in health care, that is, to improve public health. In many ways, the government has led the way for cost control through its development of resource-based reimbursement, prospective payment systems, and budget

* Patient centered medical home: What is the PCMH? Patient Centered Medical Home Resource Center of the Agency for Health Care Research and Quality, http://www.pcmh.ahrq.gov/portal/server.pt/community/pcmh__home/1483/what_is_pcmh_ (accessed August 12, 2010).

† Joint Principles of the Patient-Centered Medical Home. American Academy of Family Physicians (March 7, 2007), http://www.aafp.org/online/etc/medialib/aafp_org/documents/policy/fed/jointprinciplespcmh0207.Par.0001.File.dat/022107medicalhome.pdf (accessed August 10, 2010).

limitations. However, its conflicting goals have led it to approach these controls in a hesitant and piecemeal manner rather than effecting bold, comprehensive reforms. Consider, for example, the lack of government intervention in the face of mounting pressure to remove some of the barriers preventing a reduction in U.S. pharmaceutical costs.

4. *Private purchasers often lack market power*

The fact that most health care services must be provided locally hinders industry-wide competition in many service areas and may also restrict the potential market power of purchasers to local organizations. The Internet and other communications innovations may alter this situation somewhat.

As most health insurance is purchased by employees through their employers, individuals' choice of providers is limited both by the plans offered by their employer and by the panel of providers contracted with by the health insurer.

Employers, especially small companies, have been ineffective at organizing to gain market leverage in the negotiation of health benefits with insurers.

5. *Patients, purchasers, and providers lack information*

Improved methods for the measurement of medical outcomes and the delivery of medical treatments are being developed.

The communication of both clinical and provider-related health care information to patients/consumers is rapidly expanding with the explosive rise of Internet Web-page knowledge bases and chat room communities.

The government, employers, and other purchasers of health services and insurance are demanding and have progressed in their ability to receive meaningful information on quality from providers and insurers. Providers are improving their data collection techniques and capabilities in response to these pressures and in order to gain leverage in managed care contracting.

6. *Many providers have monopoly or near-monopoly power yet antitrust laws prevent some potentially beneficial integration*

Antitrust laws are being applied using a "rule of reason" on the basis of local market benefit rather than an absolute standard of monopoly that exists for health care facilities in many local markets.

Health care providers that convert from not-for-profit to for-profit operations are coming under increasing governmental antitrust scrutiny in many areas of the country.

7. *Providers are rewarded for increasing costs*

Governmental reimbursement systems continue to move away from reimbursement incentives for excessive care and costs through resource-based and prospective payment systems.

The absence of information on quality has led some consumers to base provider selection on cost, inferring that the two are necessarily related. Better information on quality will expose excessive costs.

8. *Capital investments are overly subsidized*

As the U.S. health care delivery infrastructure was being developed, the government provided incentives for capital investment in health care facilities and equipment in order to improve public health and access. Such artificial subsidies that have now been largely removed as the focus of regulation have turned to economic considerations and cost controls. The result may be a rise in the need for capital planning based on competitive cost benefit analysis.

9. *Certificate of need, regulation, and licensing laws are entry barriers to competing and substitute providers and services*

CON laws have been removed by many states, with Montana and other states currently reexamining their CON laws.

Allied health professionals and alternative medicine are increasingly being accepted and recognized by payors and patients as a legitimate alternative to traditional providers and services.

10. *Exit barriers protect low-quality providers*

Health care facilities, organizations, and providers have often been viewed by communities as a universal good and numerous market exit barriers to financial failure have been created, thereby restricting the likelihood that low-quality health care providers will leave the market. The transition to for-profit hospitals and other health care organizations makes the removal of such financial subsidies and other exit barriers increasingly probable.

INTEGRATION AS A COMPETITIVE STRATEGY IN HEALTH CARE

Several potential benefits are associated with the integration of companies in the same or related industries. These synergistic benefits depend on the type of companies and their integration strategies, as well as whether the anticipated transaction is a manifestation of horizontal consolidation or vertical integration.

Horizontal consolidation is "the acquisition and consolidation of like organizations or business ventures under a single corporate management, in order to produce synergy, reduce redundancies and duplication of efforts or products, and achieve economies of scale while increasing market share."*

Vertical integration involves the joining of organizations that are fundamentally different in their product and/or services offerings, that is, "the aggregation of dissimilar but related business units, companies, or organizations under a single ownership or management in order to provide a full range of related products and services."*

As health care is essentially a local business, horizontal integration within the local market has been limited by antitrust laws. Therefore, in order to control greater market share, a hospital's strategy has required vertical integration. Health care providers and organizations have placed much emphasis on the benefits of vertical system integration in the last 10 or more years, whereby a single health care organization owns all of the elements needed to provide a continuum of care for all the needs of a given patient population. Much of this effect has stemmed from the desire to be able to provide a "continuum of care" (i.e., to be able to single-source contract for the health care needs of a patient population and to profit from implementing preventative health care and utilization management measures). The relative economic benefits of this type of vertical integration versus horizontal integration strategies remain the subject of great debate in academia and among the strategic managers of other industries. One lesson that may be drawn from other industries is that neither of these forms of integration is universally applicable or beneficial to every organization and market. There are also great costs to integration, which must be outweighed by the benefits. Each specific benefit should be identified and researched when examining the probable effects of integration, consolidation, mergers, or divestitures as a competitive strategy.

During the rapid consolidation and integration of health care providers, insurers, and purchasers, in recent years, there was much discussion of a concept termed "managed competition." This term appears to have been an outgrowth of the term "managed care" and was viewed by many as the logical result of the integration of health care markets nationally. The concept of managed competition is apparently related to an idealized vision of competition between very large, integrated providers (organized into integrated delivery systems), large, national managed care payors,

---

* Boland, P. *The Capitation Sourcebook*. Boland Health Care (1996), p. 618.

and purchasing group coalitions that could achieve a balance of power between these interacting groups. However, many believe that the result of such an arrangement would more likely be a reduction in competition between members of each of these three groups and the creation of powerful bureaucratic and intractable organizations. Furthermore, this scenario does not appear to effectively remove any of the existing barriers to competition and, therefore, does not introduce any additional incentives for innovation to produce value for consumers, which, of course, is the *sine qua non* of competition.

The disadvantages of integration are becoming apparent, including

1. The loss of autonomy
2. Increased bureaucracy
3. Difficulty in aligning incentives
4. Other failed expectations

Many organizations that sought strategic advantage through integration are ending those arrangements and now divesting acquired organizations.

In other industries, specialized providers of goods and services are increasingly able to offer customers a full range of services through affiliation and affinity with other independent specialists, made more seamless through the use of increasingly sophisticated communications and computing technologies. However, this move to "dis-integration" must also be carefully considered if organizations are not to make further costly organizational changes inspired by a rushed judgment of general market trends.

Michael Porter et al. wrote in the *Harvard Business Review*:

> In industry after industry, the underlying dynamic is the same: competition compels companies to deliver increasing value to customers. The fundamental driver of this continuous quality improvement and cost reduction is innovation. Without incentives to sustain innovation in health care, short-term cost savings will soon be overwhelmed by the desire to widen access, the growing health needs of an aging population, and the unwillingness of Americans to settle for anything less than the best treatments available. Inevitably, the failure to promote innovation will lead to lower quality or more rationing of care—two equally undesirable results.[*]

If the emerging health care industry is to respond successfully to market pressure to reduce costs, then the health care market must first create incentives for innovation. The barriers to competition cannot include barriers to innovation as many do now. Health care purchasers, managers, and legislators must ensure that innovation takes the forefront of any reform if it is to be effective.

Michael Porter and Elizabeth Omstead Teisberg stated in their book, *Redefining Health Care*, that limiting competition is not the solution, but rather, "The only way to truly reform health care is to reform the nature of competition itself."[†] The offer that this reform should be focused around "value-based competition over the care cycle at the medical condition level."[‡] Porter explains that

> Because of the lack of effective competition at the condition level, the actual organization and structure of care delivery by most providers is not aligned with patient value. Lack of value-based competition on results has allowed care of a patient to be fractured across numerous specialties, hospital departments, and physician practices, each of which focuses on its discrete intervention. Nobody integrates care for

---

[*] Porter, M. E. et al. Making competition in health care work. *Harvard Business Review* (July/August 1994): 131.

[†] Porter, M. E. et al. *Redefining Health Care*. Boston: Harvard Business School Press (2006), p. 4.

[‡] *Ibid.*, p. 6.

the medical conditions as a whole and across the full care cycle, including early detection, treatment, rehabilitation, and long-term management.[*]

This is in sharp contrast to proponents of a universal health coverage system. As advocated by Arnold Relman, MD, in his recent book, *A Second Opinion: Rescuing America's Health Care*, "The present control of medical practice by market economies does not serve the health care needs of patients very well and is not compatible with a strong, ethically based profession…I urge physicians not only to support the development of a single-payer insurance system, but to help devise the reforms in the delivery system that must accompany a single-payor insurance, if inflation in medical costs is to be controlled and quality of care improved. The key to this new delivery system should be the development of prepaid multi-specialty medical groups in which physicians are paid largely by salary."[†]

Love Everyone, Trust No One, and Paddle Your Own Canoe

At the end of the day, it may be helpful for health care managers, in determining a response to market competition, to consider the old adage:

1. *Love everyone.* A consistent commitment to improving patient care, quality, and outcomes as well as keeping the needs of each of the constituencies of patients, payors, staff, and the greater community as part of the entire process, will most probably, given time, result in a sustainable competitive advantage.
2. *Trust no one.* Do not trust in the "kindness of strangers." A healthy skepticism of proposed strategies and solutions regarding alliances, partnerships, and joint ventures is indicated. The competition is, has been, and will continue to be fierce, with monopolistic motivations being exhibited by health care organizations integrating with other organizations and providers both horizontally and vertically, attempting to create effective patient care delivery models and secure business arrangements.
3. *Paddle your own canoe.* Assess your options and act on them. Although a long-term approach must be taken in strategic planning, today's successful health care organizations must continue to adapt in a timely manner to market pressures and cannot wait for a "white knight" to assist them. Be wary of weak forms of integration and half-hearted measures. Do not overly rely on outside sources for the foundation of financial or management capital to assist in competing against other providers in your market.

CASE MODEL 2.1: MANAGED HEALTH CARE IN CAPITOL CITY

BACKGROUND AND OVERVIEW

Capitol City is a medium-sized, upper-Midwestern city. Although managed care has significantly affected the delivery of health care in surrounding markets, and nationally for several years, only recently has its influence begun to affect the local delivery system. In many ways, Capitol City was the Brigadoon of health care, impervious to any challenge to its traditional fee-for-service reimbursement environment. The incursion of managed care into this market represents the introduction of competition for both local providers and purchasers.

[*] Porter, M. E. et al. *Redefining Health Care.* Boston: Harvard Business School Press (2006), p. 45.
[†] Relman, A. *A Second Opinion: Rescuing America's Health Care.* The Century Foundation (2007), p. 15.

PLAYERS

Hospitals

There are three hospitals located within the city:

1. Memorial Hospital, a 150-bed hospital, owned-controlled by a local board
2. St. Joseph's Hospital, a 300-bed Catholic hospital
3. St. Elizabeth's Hospital, a 100-bed Catholic hospital

Both St. Joseph's Hospital and St. Elizabeth's Hospital are owned and operated by a large Catholic system headquartered in another state. Memorial Hospital and St. Joseph's Hospital are located next door to each other on the north side of town, whereas St. Elizabeth's Hospital is located on the south side of town. In an effort to reduce costs and improve the health of the community, Memorial Hospital and St. Joseph's Hospital have had a long-standing agreement to avoid duplication of costly services in the community (e.g., St. Elizabeth's Hospital operates the only local emergency room, Memorial Hospital has the only invasive heart surgery program, and all three hospitals collectively own the only MRI center).

Another large hospital system (the Regional Health System) has hospitals in most of the surrounding communities, and would like to enter Capitol City's market.

Physicians

In response to the incursion of managed care, specifically the "gatekeeper" system, the area hospitals and Regional Health System have purchased nearly all of the primary care physician practices (FP, IM, and OB-GYN), and employed these physicians.

The specialists and surgeons have remained mostly independent in single-specialty groups of generally two to five physicians. The St. Joseph's Hospital and St. Elizabeth's Hospital's physician organization, Healthy Physicians, includes a few employed surgeons and specialists.

Outpatient Centers

There are two ambulatory surgery centers (ASCs) in the community:

- Riverside ASC is located in a medical office building next to St. Joseph's Hospital and Memorial Hospital and is owned by several independent surgeons and specialists (OB-GYN and plastic and general surgeons).
- Goodcare ASC is a freestanding ASC located on the south side of town. Goodcare ASC is owned by a large group of ophthalmologists who handle about 90% of the cases.

Managed Care Plans

The third-party payors in Capitol City have traditionally been large indemnity insurers. Two years ago, some insurers began offering a care plan similar to a preferred provider plan, with the panel open to all providers and reimbursement on a discounted fee-for-service basis.

Next, a managed care plan called HealthNet, owned and operated by hospitals and physicians in a neighboring community for several years, decided to enter the Capitol City market. Competition began to heat up as HealthNet offered partial ownership of their new Capitol City product to Memorial Hospital. HealthNet negotiated for drastic discounts of physician's usual charges, averaging 40%–80% discounts plus 20% withholds and onerous utilization management and case management controls in return for participation on their panels. Managed care had hit Capitol City.

APPLICATION OF PORTER'S FIVE FORCES TO CAPITOL CITY

Threat of New Market Entrants

Hospitals

For many years, Memorial Hospital, St. Joseph's Hospital, and St. Elizabeth's Hospital alone had served Capitol City. Now, Regional Health System was threatening to enter the market by purchasing primary care practices and opening walk-in clinics. In response to Regional Health System's threat, Memorial Hospital, lacking the capital of the Catholic hospitals, decided to enter into preliminary affiliation/merger discussions with Regional Health System as a defensive measure.

Physicians

The hospitals threatened to recruit physicians from other communities if they could not control the loyalties of local physicians through purchase, employment, or restricted managed care panels with drastic reductions in reimbursement. Once the local hospitals had purchased almost all of the primary care practices in the area, the specialists in small, independent practices felt it would only be a matter of time before the hospitals would "divide and conquer" the remaining independent area physicians. In response to these threats, a large portion of the specialists affiliated to form a large physician-owned and -driven management services organization, "Physician Net."

Outpatient Centers

In order to compete with the freestanding ASCs, hospitals were closing inpatient operating rooms (ORs) and reclassifying them as outpatient ORs. Both freestanding ASCs sought to strengthen their support and financial positions. Riverside ASC actively sought offers from the hospitals to be purchased while Goodcare ASC offered ownership shares to a larger base of surgeons and specialists in the community.

Managed Care Plans

Because of its undeveloped managed care system and low market penetration, national managed care companies began to identify Capitol City as a potentially lucrative market. To attract area physicians to participate in its panel, HealthNet increased its proposed provider reimbursement. Meanwhile, the Healthy Physicians organization developed its own health plan in partnership with a national insurance company and the two hospitals with which it was affiliated.

Application to Case Model Analysis

New entrants into a market are a threat to existing organizations because they intensify competition for customers. The level of the threat from the entry of new competitors into a market depends on the strength of entry barriers to the market. The Capitol City health care market was very fragmented, without any clearly defined delivery system, leaving it very susceptible to the threat of new market entrants. The barriers to entry that normally protect existing organizations serving a market were low, specifically

- High existing provider service costs and prices are easily matched or undercut.
- The state does not require a CON to build or develop additional health care products or services.
- The managed care penetration is only 8% of the Capitol City health care market, and most plans had open panels (if providers were willing to accept the terms they offered).

The Bargaining Power of Suppliers

Hospitals

The hospitals were purchasing Capitol City physician practices and threatened to recruit physicians from other communities to be employees in their respective health systems. The hospitals utilized their employed primary care physicians, under the gatekeeper managed care plans, as a bargaining chip in negotiations with the specialists and surgeons, who traditionally relied on the PCPs for many of their referrals.

Physicians

The hospitals rely on the specialists and surgeons, whose services comprise the majority of their admissions and utilization in their ORs. In response to the hospitals' control of the PCPs, the specialists and surgeons network recruited the membership of the independent emergency physicians who were under contract with St. Joseph's Hospital's Emergency Room and served as a patient access mechanism into their network of services.

Outpatient Centers

The outpatient centers were able to offer the same product as the hospitals, at a lower price, with higher physician and patient satisfaction. Even with the low cost of their services compared to their competition, the outpatient centers offered discounts to managed care plans in order to participate on their panels.

Managed Care Plans

The managed care plans control the access to covered lives and, therefore, the distribution of medical premium dollars. Physicians who wanted to participate in their preferred provider organization (PPO) products (which provided for better physician reimbursement, and, at that time, had the majority share of the Capitol City market) were required to participate in their health maintenance organization (HMO) products as well (which included deep discounts and withholds of physician fees). The managed care plans then began to offer equity ownership to area physicians in their Capitol City-based products.

Application to Case Model Analysis

Suppliers affect competition through their control of prices and the quality of the products and services they supply. In health care, it is very difficult to measure differences in the quality of physicians, procedures, or hospitals. What information is available is owned by the hospitals and managed care companies who do not readily share it with the community or their provider panels. In Capitol City, there were large discrepancies between the fee schedules of competing physicians and the hospitals (as much as a 75% difference for some services). These issues prevented patients and purchasers of these services from making informed decisions based on price or quality. In the health care industry, as in most service industries, labor is the primary cost. Because of the low unemployment rate in Capitol City, the competition among health care organizations to attract and retain quality workers was high.

Threats from Substitute Products and Services

Hospitals

More and more invasive surgeries are requiring less, if any, inpatient admissions. The outpatient centers became licensed for 23 hour stays, which enabled them to perform procedures that they could not perform as recently as 5 years prior (e.g., lumbar laminectomies and anterior cruciate ligament [ACL] repairs). The hospitals were opposed to physicians participating in any revenue stream other than their professional fees (e.g., ASCs, physical therapy, and other ancillary service technical component [ASTC] revenues). With their relationships with local leaders and media, the hospitals portrayed the physicians as "skimming the cream" from health care through their development of ASCs and other ASTC services that the charitable, not-for-profit hospitals rely upon in serving their mission in the community.

Physicians

The emergence of allied health professionals such as nurse practitioners, physician assistants, and chiropractors as an increasingly accepted alternative to some types of physician care has happened in Capitol City as well as nationwide. In response to this development and the need to control their own "access mechanisms," Physician Net developed a telephone triage system that was staffed 24 hours a day by registered nurses who referred patients to the network of specialists.

Outpatient Centers

Both the local hospitals and physicians began to aggressively pursue the development of outpatient centers, with the hospitals converting inpatient surgical units to outpatient operating rooms and physicians exploring the option of placing surgical suites within their medical offices. The outpatient centers made it more attractive for physicians to perform surgeries at their centers (e.g., block scheduling, advertising [Internet, television, and radio] to include medical staff, and forming committees of the medical staff to involve them in decision making). The convenience and patient-friendliness of the freestanding outpatient centers was a substantial competitive advantage.

Managed Care Plans

The independent providers began to negotiate with national managed care companies to jointly develop a specialty-driven point-of-service (POS) product for Capitol City. The managed care plans responded by offering equity ownership in their Capitol City products to area physicians in exchange for their exclusive participation on their panels.

Application to Case Analysis

By definition, substitute products and services perform the same or similar functions and provide equivalent utility and benefit as existing, established products and services. Technology has affected the health care industry as much, if not more, than most other industries and has provided both substitutes for traditional health services and new services, which in turn require more specialized devices and labor. Substitute products and services that evolved in the Capitol City market over the past few years include

- Outpatient surgery centers as a substitute for inpatient surgery and overnight stays.
- Managed care as a substitute for indemnity, fee-for-service insurance.
- Allied health professionals (nurse practitioners, physician extenders, and chiropractors), as a preferred alternative to primary care physicians in some delivery systems.
- Other specialists and providers who traditionally provided noninvasive services (podiatrists, optometrists, etc.) are being licensed to perform surgeries.
- Telephone triage and urgent care walk-in clinics provided a substitute to primary care and emergency room visits.

Bargaining Power of Buyers

In addition to the players discussed below, the description of buyers must include patients and employers. Patients in Capitol City have had little or no information on the quality of competing providers and no organization to provide leverage in negotiating managed care contracts except for the employer purchasing of health insurance. The local employers were largely in the same situation, without information or organization. An employer coalition had been formed but its close ties with the hospitals and lack of strong leadership prevented it from effectively commanding power or leverage on behalf of local employer members.

Hospitals

The development of the outpatient centers diluted the hospitals' power as suppliers and meant managed care plan "buyers" had another "supplier." In response to the physician ownership of outpatient centers, the Healthy Physicians system continued to recruit and employ specialists and surgeons, while Memorial Hospital and Regional Health System worked to foster a formal relationship with the independent surgeons and specialists. This competition between the hospitals with their employed physicians, and the specialists with their outpatient centers, was for both physician services and outpatient services and provided the managed care buyers with greater choice as consumers. Thus, the competition in suppliers increases the power of buyers, who are then able to play one organization against the other and turn to a substitute provider if the usual supplier is uncooperative about meeting their needs.

Physicians

The managed care company payors controlled not only the expenditure of premium dollars, but also the selection of which doctors had access to treat their plan members. In response, the independent surgeons and specialists of Physician Net further integrated into a single contracting medical group and were then able to finalize a deal with a national managed care plan to partner with them in the development of a POS plan in Capitol City.

Outpatient Centers

The opening of outpatient surgical suites within the hospitals gave local surgeons a choice of where to bring their patients (as long as their insurance covered the service). Goodcare ASC sold its ownership to the new Physician Net, the consolidated medical group of surgeons and specialists, who took the name Goodcare. Goodcare then designed and began construction of another identical outpatient center on the other side of town, to further cultivate its physician ownership's loyalty.

Managed Care Plans

Despite the creation of a health care "coalition" by employers in the community to educate their employees and leverage better pricing and service, the managed care plan still retained significant market power. Healthy Physicians, with subsidization from the deep pockets of its affiliated large hospital system, was able to price its product at an artificially low rate. They also were able to attract the employers in the community through their long-cultivated, close ties with the existing leadership of the employer coalition. HealthNet continued to try to build closer ties with physicians by offering them ownership investments at a low price.

Application to Case Model Analysis

Like powerful suppliers, buyers can affect the intensity of competition through their attempts to obtain the lowest price possible while demanding high quality and better service. The hospitals and outpatient centers have different customers (physicians and their referrals) than do the physicians and managed care plans (employers and patients). By forming an MSO, the specialists and surgeons of Goodcare were able to exert their bargaining power more effectively than the employers and patients who were not so tightly organized. The leverage a buyer can exert increases if they

- Purchase in large volumes through the merger or affiliation of smaller or fragmented buyers. The employer coalition that was formed exerted little leverage as each member employer continued to make its own independent decisions regarding the purchase of health insurance services.
- Have low switching costs. In the case of Capitol City, if patients change managed care plans, they most likely have to change their physicians.
- Have enough information to make informed purchasing decisions. Only the suppliers in Capitol City (hospitals and managed care companies) had the information necessary to support those decisions.

Rivalry among Existing Firms

Hospitals

Rivalry among existing firms led to strategic discussions, in some form, between almost all interested parties. When affiliation discussions between Memorial Hospital and Regional Health System broke off, Regional Health System, still interested in the market, entered into discussions with Goodcare. An affiliation was then formed for the development of a new hospital and ownership in Goodcare's outpatient centers. Healthy Physicians continued to build their system by purchasing the practices of the few independents that did not merge with Goodcare. By this point, almost all local providers had aligned with one of the health systems and the market had fully consolidated.

Physicians

With this market consolidation, rivalry among individual practices escalated to rivalry among health systems. Most of the remaining independent physicians either sold their practices or moved out of town.

Outpatient Centers

Goodcare's affiliation with Regional Health System meant that they had, in effect, entered the hospital business and would be competing as a direct rival with the inpatient hospital and their systems. The last independent outpatient center, Riverside ASC, and its physicians merged with Healthy Physicians at this time.

Managed Care Plans

This competition and resulting "shake-out" resulted in three major managed care payors operating in the market:

- Healthy Physicians
- HealthNet (coventure with Memorial Hospital)
- Goodcare (coventure with a national managed care company)

Response

The response of the providers to competition was consolidation and integration into three competing health systems. The informal but long-standing agreement for coordination of services for community benefit had ended. Memorial Hospital's invasive cardiology program, the only one in the area, now came under competition. Healthy Physicians recruited a cardiac surgeon and opened a high-end cardiac program within St. Joseph's Hospital. Healthy Physicians also closed the majority of the inpatient operating rooms at St. Elizabeth's Hospital for the construction of outpatient surgical suites. Meanwhile, Memorial Hospital converted its 40 h per week walk-in clinic to a 24-hour emergency unit. Goodcare and Regional Health System broke ground on a 150-bed tertiary care hospital—the first new competition for inpatient hospital services that Capitol City had seen in many years, and the first for-profit hospital venture in the state.

Application to Case Analysis

The strategy of one organization within an industry affects and is dependent on the strategy of the others, resulting in rivalry between competitors striving to improve their position (market share). Typically, an action by one competitor results in reactions from the others. The following are illustrations of the intensive rivalry among competitors in the Capitol City example:

- Each of the three health care systems committed to competing in the local market by investing large amounts of capital into building their respective delivery systems. Their reluctance to abandon a project after making such a high investment is a notable internal exit barrier.
- Each managed care plan, co-owned and sponsored by a hospital system, required exclusivity for both hospital and physician providers contracting for inclusion on their panels. This resulted in "splitting" families when some family members were forced to choose a different insurance plan than others.

Health care, like most service industries, is heavily reliant on labor, which is typically a fixed cost. High fixed costs increase the difficulties in competing based on cost differentiation.

Where agreements once existed between systems to allot responsibility for, rather than duplicate, expensive services (e.g., MRI, high-end cardiac programs and Level III certified trauma emergency rooms), the market began to develop three independent, full-service integrated delivery systems.

CONCLUSION

This case model illustrates how the rapid incursion of managed care into a medium-sized community can dramatically affect competition. As has occurred in markets throughout the country, the market matured very rapidly with the development of increased competition in one area, spurring competition in others. The incursion of managed care acted as a catalyst for the consolidation of physicians' services, which in turn led to the development of additional outpatient centers, ASCs, and eventually a new hospital that increased competition for hospital services. This gave the managed care organizations increased bargaining power, fueling the cycle of competition anew. Where once there was an "infinite" amount of revenue to be shared (through fee-for-service indemnity payors) collaboration and cooperation existed between competitors. Now, there is intense rivalry between systems for a finite amount of premium revenue because of managed care competition and capitated reimbursement.

KEY ISSUES

Who benefited most from the increase in competition:

— Hospitals?
— Physicians?
— HMOs?
— Insurance companies?
— Patients?

What were the disadvantages of increased competition?

CHECKLIST 1: Barriers to Competition Analysis	YES	NO
Patients Do Not Purchase Services Directly from Providers		
Has the emerging health care organizations (EHOs) considered the impact of the role of insurance as an intermediary on hospital competition?	o	o
Patients Do Not Compare Prices between Providers		
Has the EHO examined the fact that patients paying an increasing portion of the premiums for their health care coverage and increasing numbers of employers providing employees with a range of options for health insurance coverage may have a significant effect on competition?	o	o
The Government Is the Largest Purchaser of Health Care		
Has the role of the government in cost control through the development of resource-based reimbursement, prospective payment systems, and budget limitations been analyzed as it relates to competition?	o	o
Private Purchasers Often Lack Market Power		
Does the EHO's analysis of competition include the impact of managed care's restriction of patient selection of providers and facilities?	o	o
Patients, Purchasers, and Providers Lack Information		
Is the changing availability of information on medical outcomes and quality of providers incorporated into the EHO's competitive strategy?	o	o
Many Providers Have Monopoly or Near-Monopoly Power Yet Antitrust Laws Prevent Some Potentially Beneficial Integration		
Has the application of antitrust laws been evaluated in the competitive assessment of the local market?	o	o
Providers Are Rewarded for Increasing Costs		
Has the EHO considered the role of cost in the competitive environment?	o	o
Capital Investments Are Overly Subsidized		
Has the need for a cost benefit analysis of capital investment based on competitive factors been evaluated?	o	o
CON, Regulation, and Licensing Laws Are Entry Barriers to Competing and Substitute Providers and Services		
Have certificate of need laws and other barrier to market entry been reviewed as part of the competitive analysis?	o	o
Exit Barriers Protect Low-Quality Providers		
Has the EHO included exit barriers to financial failure in its analysis of competition?	o	o

APPENDIX: LIST OF PHYSICIAN RECRUITMENT AGENCIES

Action Medical Search—Recruitment firm offering physician placement throughout the United States. Includes job-searching strategies.

Advent Associates, Inc.—Provides physician recruitment services across the United States in all medical specialties with particular expertise in oncology, cardiology, and radiology.

Agent.MD—Recruiting, consulting, and representation of physicians on all compensation and contract negotiation issues for new health care practice opportunities at hospitals or groups.

Alliance Physician and Associates—A physician recruiting firm specializing in opportunities in Washington, Oregon, Idaho, and Alaska.

American Medical Consultants, Inc.—Physician recruitment company offering practice opportunities, listed at the site, throughout the United States.

APC Medical Resources—A recruitment firm offering both locum and permanent placement of physicians. Searchable database of jobs with call ratio and some details of practice opportunity.

ApolloMD—A physician staffing firm that focuses on providing quality services to all components of the emergency room—hospitals, physicians, and patients.

Cornerstone Physician Consulting—A recruitment firm specializing in physician employment and search nationwide.

Daniel Stern & Associates—A physician recruitment firm specializing in the field of emergency medicine. Conducts and makes available an annual National Salary Survey for emergency medicine physicians.

EHL Ecare Health Ltd.—A consulting firm offering recruitment, retention, and training for health care facilities.

Emergency Staffing Solutions—Provides emergency department and emergency physician staffing.

Enterprise Medical Services—A physician recruiter placing Canadian doctors in the United States. New positions are listed regularly.

Eva Page and Associates—A recruitment firm that specializes in employment for physicians in the Pacific Northwest and Alaska.

Farr Health Care—Recruiting physicians for jobs nationwide. Searchable database of opportunities at site.

Geneva Health International—A recruitment and staffing consultancy catering exclusively to the nursing and medical sectors internationally.

Global Medical Search, Inc.—A national physician search firm with its jobs listed in a text-based directory.

Gutermuth Medical Services—A contingency-based physician recruiter for clients who have multiple recruiting needs and a "guaranteed retainer" program for need-to-fill searches.

Hayman Daugherty Associates—Successful permanent placements of physicians with clients all across the United States.

Health Search USA—A nationwide physician recruitment agency. Search hundreds of employment opportunities in an on-line searchable database. Services include developing plans for retention programs, compensation, and succession.

Health Care Transitions—Physician recruitment firm with searchable database of opportunities and an FAQ for physicians interviewing for employment.

The HealthField Alliance, Inc.—Works on both a contingency and retainer basis, depending on clients' needs. Provides assistance and input in critical areas including compensation, contract interpretation, contract negotiations, income guarantees, and visit/interview plans.

HealthMatch Services—Physician recruitment firm with listings of current openings.

J and C Nationwide—A recruitment firm placing physicians in temporary locum tenens jobs and permanent practice.

Jackson and Harris—Offering permanent search, placement services, and salary survey for physicians.

K Group Online.com—A physician recruiter showing its list of nationwide job opportunities and applicants.

Kay Martin Associates—A contingency placement firm exclusively recruiting physicians. Site includes references from clients.

LAM Associates—Employer-paid physician recruiting agency placing full-time and locum tenens positions in Hawaii and the U.S. mainland.

Latter Associates—A physician recruiting company with a regional focus. Job search of database allows for customization of results for each applicant.

Locumotion—Medical recruitment and education services company education and career planning service for health professionals for the United Kingdom, Australia, New Zealand, and South Africa.

Marsh Group—Provides physician recruitment services for health care profession opportunities throughout the United States.

MDR Associates—A national permanent placement physician search firm. Member of The National Association of Physician Recruiters.

Med2020—Multispecialty physicians' jobs and resources site. Contains positions searchable by specialty and location.

Medical Placement and Search—A contingency radiology search firm offering references and a searchable database of jobs for applicants.

Medical Search Consultants—A recruitment firm specializing in the placement of orthopedic surgeons and physicians nationwide. Offering either contingency or retained fees searches.

Medicorp, Inc.—A recruitment firm offering physician recruitment and retention services. A physician compensation survey is available at site.

Medipro—An American company with offices in Central Europe that provides English-speaking, trained medical staff to hospitals in the United States.

Medstaff National Medical Staffing, Inc.—A physician locum tenens that focuses on physicians who specialize in emergency medicine, pediatrics, obstetrics and gynecology, and primary care.

MedSuccess—Physician placement services with individual attention given to physicians seeking new employment opportunities. CVs presented, with permission, to client base after complete job opportunity discussion.

National Physician Associates—Physician recruitment firm based in Arizona specializing in full-time and permanent part-time physician placement and the sale of medical practices.

Nephrology Resource Group—Physician recruitment and placement agency focusing on renal physicians.

NephrologyRecruiters.com—Dedicated nephrology physician placement service. Offers qualified candidates a convenient and confidential job placement resource.

Office of Celeste Tabriz—A physician consulting firm specializing in helping J-1 and H-1 physicians obtain the waiver positions that they are seeking.

The O'Kane Group—Physician recruitment and placement specialists for the Northwest United States. Includes company background, list of services, and contact information.

Olesky Associates, Inc.—Physician employment recruiters for both permanent and locum positions for all specialties nationwide.

Physician Employment Advocacy Services—A physician and health care executive recruitment firm.

Physician Finders—Employment agency for physicians. Directory of job openings at site.

Physician Recruitment Solutions—Otolaryngology recruiting and placement services on a nationwide basis.

Physician Solutions, Inc.—National locum tenens and permanent placement of physicians and health care professionals.

Physicianfit.com—Recruitment firm for physician practice opportunities, employment, and recruitment.

PhysicianRecruiting—Physician recruitment firm offering information and opportunity descriptions for employment in numerous fields of medicine.

Physicians Search—A recruitment firm offering practice opportunities of hospitals, medical groups, and health care systems, plus job search information and tips.

Pinnacle Health Group—Hundreds of physician opportunities throughout the country. Resources include employment articles at the site and e-mail newsletters for clients and physicians.

Placement USA—Physician placement and medical staffing. Jobs for medical professionals.

Radiologix, Inc.—Recruiting for radiology, magnetic resonance imaging, computed axial tomography, and positron emission tomography opportunities.

RDS Medical Recruiting—Specializing in the recruitment of physicians of all medical specialties for permanent placement.

Rock Medical, Ltd.—A physician placement that provides customized employment arrangements between health care facilities and qualified physicians.

Southeast Physician Search—A physician recruiting service working to build bridges between opportunities and physicians, whether you are a resident, a seasoned practitioner, or a medical facility.

Southeastern Physician Placement—Provides physicians with position placement opportunities.

St. John Associates—A national physician placement firm representing practice opportunities in all specialties, including psychiatry, neurology, orthopedic surgery, urology, neurosurgery, cardiology, and internal medicine subspecialties.

Team Health—A firm providing hospitalists for physician management and staffing in emergency medicine, radiology, anesthesia, critical care, hospitalist programs, and pediatrics.

United Search Associates—Physician recruitment firm with searchable database of opportunities.

Ursula Thomas and Associates—Professional physician search firm offering quality placement services to physicians nationwide. Free service to physician candidate.

U.S. Physician Resources International Inc.—Includes description of the recruiting process, job opportunities listed by specialty, and blind curricula vitae.

BIBLIOGRAPHY

Abraham, J., Gaynor, M., and Vogt, W. B. Entry and competition in local hospital markets (preliminary rough draft).

Anderson, G. F. and Poullier, J.-P. Health spending, access, and outcomes. Trends in industrialized countries. *Health Affairs* 18: 3 (May/June 1999): 178–192.

Anderson, T. Operating in a competitive environment. As health plans offer patients more choices, the latest technology can be just the image a hospital needs. *Washington Business Journal* (November 21, 2003).

Arnould, R. et. al. Does managed care change the mission of nonprofit hospitals? Evidence from the managerial labor market. National Bureau of Economic Research (NBER), NBER Working Paper Series (September 2000): 1–43.

Barlow, R. D. Surgical hospitals vie for surgery center business. Who says inpatient care is on the outs? *Repertoire*, www.medicaldistribution.com/rep/Rep_2003_May/Rep_52220031351172.htm (accessed May 2003).

Barrell, J. Managed care. Myth, real about market evolution. *Infusion* (August 1999): 14–19.

Bassing, T. Playing state's CON game. Does process benefit the public—Or stifle competition. *Birmingham Business Journal*, http://birmingham.bizjournals.com/birmingham/stories/2002/12/23/story1.html?t= printable (accessed December 23, 2002).

Baumol, W. J. Do health care costs matter? *The New Republic* (November 22, 1993): 16–18.

Baumol, W. J. Social wants and dismal science. The curious case of the climbing costs of health and teaching. *Proceedings of the American Philosophical Society* 137: 4 (1993): 612–637.

Becker, S. Bracing for a Medicare clampdown on specialty hospitals. *Outpatient Surgery* (August 2003).

Becker, S. and Werling, K. Rough stuff. Tired of competition from surgery centers, community hospitals are toughening their tactics—And ASCs are fighting fire with fire, www2.rosshardies.com/publication .cfm?publication_id=267&pf=1 (accessed October 2, 2003).

Bell, J. Key health system prepared to revoke doctors' credentials. *Business First of Columbus*, www.bizjournals .com/columbus/stories/2003/12/08/story1.html?t=printable (December 5, 2003).

Berlin, W. E., Grimes, O. K., and Shriver, P. C. Improving health care: A dose of competition. The July 2004 Joint DOJ/FTC Antitrust in Health Care Report's Practical Implications for Hospitals and Physicians. *Health Lawyers News* 24–30.

Bernstein, A. B. and Gauthier, A. K. Defining competition in markets. Why and how? *HSR: Health Services Research* 33: 5 (December 1998): 1421–1438.

Blair, J. D. and Buesseler, J. A. Competitive forces in the medical group industry. A stakeholder perspective. *Health Care Management Review* 23: 2 (March 22, 1998): 7–30.

Brubaker, B. Medicare deal likely to spark more health care competition. *Washington Post* (November 15, 2003), www.washingtonpost.com/ac2/wp-dyn/A46747-2003Nov15?language=printer, online edition.

Buchmueller, T. C. and Feldstein, P. J. The effect of price on switching among health plans. *Journal of Health Economics* 16: (April 1997): 231–247.

Burda, D. Raining on competition. Florida's specialty hospital ban is a bad idea for patients. *Modern Health Care* (July 12, 2004): 1.

Business reality meets political imperative. Competition loses. *Health Affairs* 23: 2.

Butler, S. M. A new policy framework for health care markets. Markets never go away; They simply adapt to the environment created for them. *Health Affairs* 23: 2 (March/April 2004): 22–24.

Cimasi, R. J. Improving health care. A dose of competition. *Health Care Consultant*, www.ftc.gov/opa/2004/07/ healthcarerpt.html.

Cimasi, R. J. The realities of rising health care costs. *Green Bay Press-Gazette* (January 19, 1999).

Cirillo, A. The hospital's strategic advantage in a consumer-driven marketplace. *Health Leaders*, www.health leaders.com/news/print.php?contetid=52819 (February 27, 2004).

Conn, J. Physician owners to fight back against OhioHealth. *Modern Physician*, www.modernphsician.com/ printout/printwindow.cms?newsId=1716&pageType=news (January 21, 2004).

Cunningham, P. J. Reduced charity care and research funding reflect pressures of managed care and competitive markets. Physicians more heavily involved with managed care plans tend to provide less charity care. *American Medical Association*, www.ama-assn.org/sci-pubs/sci-news/1999/snr0324.htm.

Cunningham, P. J., Grossman, J. M., St. Peter, R. F., and Lesser, C. S. Managed care and physicians' provision of charity care. *Journal of the American Medical Association* (March 24/31, 1999).

Dobson, A. A comparative study of patient severity, quality of care and community impact at MedCath heart hospitals. Executive Summary—September 2002. *The Lewin Group* 1–3.

Does Ambulatory Surgery Center Development Cause Hospital Closures? *Outpatient Surgery* (October 1997).

Dranove, D. and Ludwick, R. Competition and pricing by nonprofit hospitals. A reassessment of Lynk's analysis. *Journal of Health Economics* 18 (November 1999): 87–98.

Eddy, D. M. Performance measurement. Problems and solutions. *Health Affairs* (July/August 1998): 7–25.

Ellis, R. P. Creaming, skimping and dumping. Provider competition on the intensive and extensive margins. *Journal of Health Economics* 17 (1998): 537–555.

Enthoven, A. C. Employment-based health insurance is failing: Now what? A strategy, based on managed competition, to free employers from the health care cost spiral and produce effective managed care. *Health Affairs* W3-237–W3-249.

FASA Presentation. FTC/DOJ Hearings on Health Care and Competition Law and Policy. Federated Ambulatory Surgery Association, www.fasa.org/FTCStatement.doc (March 26, 2003): 1–3.

Federal Hearings on Health Care Competition Law and Policy Set (February 20, 2003).

Feldman, R. D., Wholey, D. R., and Christianson, J. B. HMO consolidations. How national mergers affect local markets. *Health Affairs* 18: 4 (July/August 1999): 96–104.

Fletcher, R. H. Who is responsible for the common good in a competitive market. *Journal of the American Medical Association* (March 24/31, 1999).

Friedman, B. Commentary. Excess capacity, a commentary on markets, regulation, and values. *HSR: Health Services Research* 33: 6 (February 1999): 1669–1682.

From Regulation to Competition. How Some Providers in New York Responded. New York State Department of Health. *Health Care Financing & Organization*. Findings Brief 4: 2.

FTC and DOJ Issue Report on Competition and Health Care, www.ftc.gov/opa/2004/7/healthcarerpt.html.

FTC Chairman Announces Public Hearings on Health Care and Competition Law and Policy to Begin in February 2003. Federal Trade Commission and Competition in the Delivery of Health Care, www.ftc.gov/opa/2002/11/murishealthcare.html.

FTC DOJ Hearings on Health Care and Competition—MedCath Presentation.

Galloro, V. Behavioral modification. Researchers continue to study the reverberations of a for-profit's entry into a hospital market. The findings are definitely mixed. *Modern Health Care* 32–36.

Gal-Or, E. The profitability of vertical mergers between hospitals and physician practices. *Journal of Health Economics* 18 (1999): 623–654.

Gee, P. Are you ready for 'big box' health care? *Health Leaders*, www.healthleaders.com/news/print.php?contentid=58603 (September 27, 2004).

Gerson, S. M. FCC v. Butterworth. Positive economic effects of hospital merger trump antitrust theory. *Health Law Digest* 24: 11 (November 1996): 3–7.

Ginsburg, P. B. Competition from specialty facilities: Is it a positive for health care? Presentation to Council on Health Economics and Policy.

Gold, M. Can managed care and competition control Medicare costs? It will take more than managed care and competitive options to ensure that Medicare can meet its obligations in the future. *Health Affairs* W3: 176–188.

Gordon, J. Crisis or competition? Hospital officials voice concern that specialty centers erode profits. *Business First*, http://louisville.bizjournals.com/louisville/stories/2003/09/08/story2.html (accessed September 8, 2003).

Gowrisankaran, G. and Town, R. J. Competition, payers, and hospital quality. *HSR: Health Services Research* 38: 6 (December 2003): 1403–1421.

Graham, J. The Federal Trade Commission and physician practice. *Medical Practice Management* (March/April 2005): 259–262.

Greenberg, W. Marshfield Clinic, physician networks, and the exercise of monopoly power. *Health Services Research* 33: 5 (December 1998): 1461–1476.

Gresenz, C. R., Rogowski, J., and Escare, J. J. Updated variable-radius measures of hospital competition. *Health Services Research* 32: 2: 417–430.

Gruber, J. The effect of competitive pressure on charity. Hospital responses to price shopping in California. *Journal of Health Economics* 38 (July 1, 1994): 183–212.

Guadagnino, C. Cancer center competition intensifies, www.physiciansnews.com/cover/302wp.html.

Haas-Wilson, D. and Gaynor, M. Increasing consolidation in health care markets. What are the antitrust policy implications? *Health Services Research* 33: 5 (December 1, 1998): 1403–1419.

Halvorson, G. C. Health plans' strategic responses to a changing marketplace. *Health Affairs* 18: 2 (1999): 28–29.

Hill, S. C. and Wolfe, B. L. Testing the HMO competitive strategy. An analysis of its impact on medical care resources. *Journal of Health Economics* 16 (June 1, 1997): 261–286.

Hirth, R. A., Chernew, M. E., and Orzol S. M. Ownership, competition, and the adoption of new technologies and cost-saving practices in a fixed-price environment. *Inquiry* 37: 3 (Fall 2000): 282–294.

Hospital competition can be good for your health. *Business Wire*.

Hospital litigation. More hospitals sue other hospitals, claim antitrust breaches, network exclusion. *Health Law Reporter* 10: 14 (April 5, 2001): 529–531.

Hospital Responses to Physician Competition. Horty Springer Whitepaper, Horty Springer Publications (2003).

Hospitals voice concerns at FTC–DOJ hearing on competition. *AHA News* (March 26, 2003).

Iglehart, J. K. Business reality meets political imperative. Competition loses. *Health Affairs* 23: 2 (March/April 2004): 7.

Iglehart, J. K. Physicians as agents of social control. The thoughts of Victor Fuchs. *Health Affairs* 17: 1 (January/February 1998): 90–96.

Innovation, Competition stifled by hospital group purchasing schemes. FTC, Justice Department Urged to Curb 'Continuing Marketplace Abuse.' Medical Device Manufacturers Association, www.medicaldevices.org/public/news/releases/pr030929.asp (September 29, 2003).

Jacobi, J. V. Competition law's role in health care quality. *Annals of Health Law*, http://80-web.lexis-nexis.com.

Kahn, C. N. and Cohen, J. Adverse effect of physician-owned limited service facilities. Healthy competition depends on level playing field. Council on Health Care Economic and Policy Conference on Specialty Hospitals, Ambulatory Surgery Centers and General Hospitals.

Keeler, E. B., Melnick, G., and Zwanziger, J. The changing effects of competition on non-profit and for-profit hospital pricing behavior. *Journal of Health Economics* 18 (November, 1999): 69–86.

Kronick, R. and Gilmer, T. Explaining the decline in health insurance coverage, 1979–1995. *Health Affairs* 18:2 (1999): 30–47.

Lave, J. R., Peele, P. B., Black, J. T., Evans, J. H., III, and Amersbach, G. Changing the employer-sponsored health plan system. The views of employees in large firms. *Health Affairs* 18: 4 (July/August 1999): 112–117.

Long, S. H. and Marquis, M. S. Pooled purchasing. Who are the players? *Health Affairs* 18: 4 (July/August 1999): 105–111.

Lynk, W. J. and Longley, C. S. The effect of physician-owned surgicenters on hospital outpatient surgery. What can happen when a hospital's staff physicians become its business rivals. *Health Affairs* 21: 4 (July/August 2002): 215–221.

Lynk, W. J. and Neumann, L. R. Price and profit. *Journal of Health Economics* 18 (November, 1999): 99–116.

Lynn, G. Perspectives on competition policy and the health care marketplace. Single specialty hospitals (March 27, 2003), www.hospitalconnect.com/aha/key_issues/niche/advocacy/index.html (accessed October 2, 2003).

Lynn, G. Perspectives on competition policy and the health care marketplace. Single specialty hospitals. Statement of the American Hospital Association before the Department of Justice and Federal Trade Commission Hearing (March 27, 2003).

Madden, C. W. Excess capacity. Markets, regulation, and values. *HSR: Health Services Research* 33: 6 (February 1999): 1651–1667.

Mallon, T. Competition between hospitals and ASCs. Is the playing field level? Presentation to Council on Health Care Economics and Policy, September 10, 2004.

Managed care industry profits to soar 60% in 2000. But not-for-profit HMOs struggle with big losses. *PR Newswire*, www.individual.com.

Managed care reducing charity work, study finds. Center for Studying Health System Change, AAHP. *Medical Industry Today*, www.medicaldata.com/members/MIT/detail.asp?Art=03259913.

Marnhar, B. B., Lewin, L. S., and Lewin and Associates, Inc. Physician supply and distribution. Issues and options for state policy makers. Prepared for The National Center for Health Services Research, Office of the Assistant Secretary for Health, U.S. Department of Health and Human Services (September 15, 2003): 2.8–2.31.

MedPAC: Specialty hospital competition doesn't harm community hospitals. American Surgical Hospital Association Press Release, November 18, 2004.

Melnick, G., Keeler, E., and Zwanziger, J. Market power and hospital pricing. Are nonprofits different? *Health Affairs* 18: 3 (May/June 1999): 167–173.

Morrisey, M. A. Competition in hospital and health insurance markets: A review and research agenda. Analysis information of both industries. *Health Services Research* (April 2001).

Most people uncomfortable with profit motive in health care. Many Americans favor government-run insurance and health care services provided by non-profits or government. *The Wall Street Journal Online* 2: 12 (December 4, 2003).

New bond deals could align physicians and hospitals, reduce competition. *Finance Watch* (May 23, 2003).

Needleman, J., Lamphere, J., and Chollet, D. Uncompensated care and hospital conversions in Florida. What does it mean for communities when hospitals convert? *Health Affairs* 18: 4 (July/August 1999): 125–133.

Nichols, L. M., Ginsburg, P. B., Berenson, R. A., Christianson, J., and Hurley, R. E. Are market forces strong enough to deliver efficient health care systems? Confidence is waning. Many health care market participants are now willing to consider strong governmental intervention to repair the health system. *Health Affairs* 23: 2 (March/April 2004): 8–21.

O'Conner, D. Is the sky falling on physician-owners. Emboldened by their success in harassing physician-owned surgical hospitals, hospital lobbyists are now lining up physician-owned ASCs in their crosshairs. *Outpatient Surgery Magazine* (April 2004).

OhioHealth pulls staff privileges from group of physicians. *Business First of Columbus*, www.bizjournals.com/columbus/stories/2003/12/15/daily34.html?t=printable (December 19, 2003).

O'Neil, B. Surgery centers and surgical hospitals. Make hay while the sun shines. *Today's Surgicenter* (February 2004): 24–25.

Ozgen, H. A national study of efficiency for dialysis centers. An examination of market competition and facility characteristics for production of multiple dialysis outputs. *Health Services Research* (June 2002): 1–20.

Page, L. Report: Hospital CEOs expect rising competition from ASCs, others, www.modernphysician.com/printwindow.cms?newsId=1080&pageType=news (accessed August 4, 2003).

Pauly, M. V. Managed care, market power, and monopsony. *Health Services Research* 33: 5 (December 1998): 1439–1460.

Perspectives on competition policy and the health care marketplace, www.hospitalconnect.com/aha/advocacy-grassroots/advocacy/testimony/2003/ (February 27, 2004).

Physician ownership of hospitals. Conflict or solution? *ASHA News*, www.surgicalhospital.org/images/news/paper_04.html (May 1, 2003).

Pierrot, A. H. The surgical hospital debate continues. *Surgicenteronline*, www.surgicenteronline.com/articles/341feat7.html (accessed September 21, 2003).

Piper, T. R. Specialty hospitals. Competition or cream-skimming? Missouri Certificate of Need Program and American Health Planning Association. Presentation Before the National Academy of State Health Policy. 17th Annual State Health Policy Conference. August 1–3, 2004.

Pope, C. The innovators. Competitive pressures inspire creativity in clinical operations. *MGMA Connexion* (February 2004): 40–45.

Porter, M. E. and Teisberg, E. O. Redefining competition in health care. *Harvard Business Review* (June 2004).

Public Citizen Health Research Group. Hidden rip-off in U.S. health care is unmasked. *Health Letter* 15: 9 (September 1999): 1–3.

Public Hearings. Federal Trade Commission and Department of Justice Hearings on Health Care and Competition Law and Policy. Federal Trade Commission.

Public Hearings. Health Care and Competition Law and Policy. Federal Trade Commission.

Public not served by threat to pull hospital privileges. *Business First of Columbus*, www.bizjournals.com/columbus/stories/2003/12/15/editorial1.html?t=printable (December 12, 2003).

Pryor, R. Competition and costs. *Modern Health Care* (June 24, 2002): 21.

Pyrek, K. M. The Medicare Bill aftermath. Surgical hospitals pick up the pieces and plan their strategy. *Today's Surgicenter* (January 2004): 21, 27–28.

Pyrek, K. M. Surgical-hospital model powered by quality of care, cost savings, ambience. *Surgicenteronline*, www.surgicenteronline.com/articles/331feat4.html (accessed September 21, 2003).

Reichard, J. Breaux—Specialty facilities threaten the survival of community hospitals. *Washington HealthBeat* (September 16, 2003): 1.

Rex-Waller, J. G. Federal Trade Commission and U.S. Department of Justice joint hearing on health care and competition law and policy.

Robinson, J. C. Consolidation and the transformation of competition in health insurance. *Health Affairs* 23: 6 (2004): 15.

Robinson, J. C. Financial capital and intellectual capital in physician practice management. *Health Affairs* (July/August 1998): 53–74.

Robinson, J. C. The future of managed care organization. *Health Affairs* (March/April 1999): 7–24.

Rogers, C. Specialty hospitals vs. general hospitals. Healthy competition or an uneven playing field. *AAOS Bulletin*, www.aaos.org/wordhtml/bulletin/oct03/feature1.htm (October 2003).

Rogers, D. Medicare battle enters new arena. Split emerges on payments as doctor-owned chains rival community hospitals. *The Wall Street Journal*, www.online.wsj.com/article/0,,SB106843132238462500,00.html (November 10, 2003).

Sage, W. M. Protecting competition and consumers. A conversation with Timothy J. Muris. *Health Affairs* 22: 6: 101–110.

Sage, W. M., Hyman, D. A., and Greenberg, W. Why competition law matters to health care quality. Competition law is a bellwether for changes in the way health care quality has been understood over the years. *Health Affairs* 22: 2 (March/April 2003): 31–44.

Schneck, L. H. Urgent care centers: Are they competition or opportunity. *MGMA Connexion*, www3.mgma.com (accessed April 3, 2006).

Schneck, L. H. Urgent care centers: Physician practices respond to competition. *Medical Group Management* 40: 8 (April 15, 2001).

Shalala, D. E. and Reinhardt Uwe, E. Viewing the U.S. health care system from within. Candid talk from HHS. *Health Affairs* 18: 3 (May/June 1999): 47–55.

Shanbhag, P. Confronting specialty competition. Hospitals should consider both strategic and facility design approaches. *Health Care Executive* (January/February 2004): 38–39.

Shortell, S. M., Morrison, E. M., Hughes, S. L., Friedman, B., Coverdill, J., and Berg, L. The effects of hospital ownership on nontraditional services. *Health Affairs* (Winter 1986): 97–111.

Siebenmark, J. MedPAC specialty hospital report won't silence competition debate. *Witchita Business Journal*, www.bizjournals.com/industries/health_care/industry_regulation/2005/03/28/witchita (accessed March 28, 2005).

Silverman, E. M., Skinner, J. S., and Fisher, E. S. The association between for-profit hospital ownership and increased Medicare spending. *New England Journal of Medicine* 341: 6 (August 1999).

Simon, C. J., Dranove, D., and White, W. D. The effect of managed care on the incomes of primary care and specialty physicians. *HSR: Health Services Research* 33: 3 (August 1, 1998): 549–569.

Smith, S., Heffler, S., and Freeland, M. The National Health Expenditures Projection Team. The next decade of health spending. A new outlook. *Health Affairs* 18: 4 (July/August 1999): 86–95.

Smith, S., Freeland, M., Heffler, S., and McKusick, D. The Next ten years of health spending. What does the future hold? *Health Affairs* 17: 5 (September/October 1998): 128–140.

Specialty hospital building boom threatens general hospitals. Competition heats up for profitable cardiac and orthopedic services. Center for Studying Health System Change, www.hschange.com/CONTENT/554/ (accessed July 29, 2003).

System drops doc investors in specialty hospital. *Cincinnati Business Courier*: www.bizjournals.com/cincinnati/ stories/2004/01/19/daily19.html?t=printable (January 21, 2004).

Taylor, M. Striking back at doc investors. OhioHealth pulls hospital privileges for physicians in largest revocation to date. *Modern Health Care* (January 26, 2004): 10.

Teisberg, E. O., Porter, M. E., and Brown, G. B. Making competition in health care work. *Harvard Business Review* 3: 7 (July/August 1994): 1–3.

The level playing field. *ASHA News*, www.surgicalhospital.org/images/news/paper_02.html (May 1, 2003).

The origins of the specialty hospital and reasons for its rise. *ASHA News*, www.surgicalhospital.org/images/ news/paper_03.html (May 1, 2003).

The structural analysis of industries. *Competitive Strategy* 3–33.

Tuohy, C. H. Dynamics of a changing health sphere. The United States, Britain, and Canada. *Health Affairs* 18: 3 (May/June 1999): 114–134.

Van de Ven, W. P. M. M. and Van Vliet, R. C. J. A. Consumer information surplus and adverse selection in competitive health insurance markets. An empirical study. *Journal of Health Economics* 14 (1995): 149–169.

Weissman, J. S., Saglam, D., Campbell, E. G., Causino, N., and Blumenthal, D. Market forces and unsponsored research in academic health centers. *Journal of the American Medical Association* (March 24/31, 1999).

Woolhandler, S. and Himmelstein, D. U. When money is the mission. The high costs of investor-owned care. *New England Journal of Medicine* 341: 6: 444–446.

Wrenn, B. Contribution to hospital performance: Market orientation vs. marketing effort and lack of competition. *Journal of Hospital Marketing & Public Relations* 14: 1 (2002): 3–13.

Wysocki, B., Jr. Regulation or competition? States battle over how to get reasonable, quality health care. *The Wall Street Journal* A4: (Tuesday, May 7, 2002).

3 Capital Formation Techniques for Hospitals

Institutional Types, Essentiality, and Governance

David Edward Marcinko and Calvin W. Wiese

CONTENTS

INTRODUCTION

Hospitals are capital-intensive businesses. Hospital buildings are unique structures that require large amounts of capital to construct and maintain. Inside these buildings are pieces of expensive equipment that have fairly short lives. Technological innovations continually drive demand for new and more expensive equipment and facilities. The ability to continually generate capital is the life-blood of hospitals. In order to compete and succeed, it is imperative for hospitals to continually invest in large amounts of capital equipment and expensive facilities.

Capital investment is fueled by profit. In order to continually make the necessary capital investments, hospitals must be profitable. Hospitals unable to generate sufficient profit will fail to make important capital investments, weakening their ability to compete and survive.

Hospital managers bear important responsibility in choosing which capital investments to make. There are always more capital opportunities than capital capacity. In many cases, capital opportunities not taken by hospitals create openings for others with capital capacity to fill the vacuum. By not taking such opportunities, hospitals are weakened, and their operating risk increases.

Stewardship, like governance, is a term that aptly describes the responsibility borne by hospital managers in making capital investments. The New Testament parable of the talents describes this kind of stewardship. In this story, a merchant entrusted three managers with money to invest. One manager was given five units, another two, and a third one. At the end of the investment period, the managers given five units and two units reported a 100% return. The manager given one unit reported zero return—he was fired and his unit was given to the first manager.

This is stewardship—and hospital managers are stewards of their organizations' assets. Too often, not-for-profit hospital managers hold an erroneous view of the returns expected of them. Like the third manager in the parable, they think zero return on equity is acceptable. They understand capital investment funded by debt needs to cover the interest on the debt, but they view capital investments funded by equity as having no cost associated with the equity. From an accounting perspective, they are right. From a stewardship perspective, they are dead wrong—just like the third manager in the parable.

Here is why—as stewards, they are responsible for managing the entrusted assets. Either that they can put those assets at risk themselves, or they can put those assets in the market and let other managers put them at risk. If they choose to put them at risk themselves, they then have the mandate of creating as much value from putting them at risk as they would realize if they put them in the market for other managers to put at risk. They have the duty to realize returns that are equivalent to the returns they could realize in the market; otherwise, they should just put them in the market. They can either invest in hospital assets or work the assets themselves, or they can invest in financial market assets so others can work the assets. When they choose to invest in hospital assets, the required return is not zero. That is the return they get fired for. The required return is equivalent to market returns.

Thus, when evaluating performance of hospital management teams, the minimum acceptable performance level is return on equity that is equivalent to the return that could be realized by investing the hospital assets in the market. Moreover, when evaluating a capital investment opportunity, it is important to apply a capital charge equivalent to the hospital's weighted cost of capital—a measure that imputes an appropriate cost to the equity portion of the capital along with the stated interest rate for the debt portion of the capital structure.

STRATEGIC CONSIDERATIONS IN CAPITAL FORMATION

RISK

Capital investments create risk. Risk is the uncertainty of future events. When hospitals make capital investments, they commit to costs that affect future periods. Those costs are known and relatively fixed. What are unknown are the benefits to be realized by those capital investments. For capital investments, risk is the certainty of future costs coupled with the uncertainty of future benefits. In some cases, while the future benefits are uncertain, there is a high degree of certainty that the benefits will exceed the costs. In these cases, risk can be very low. Risk may be better defined as the degree to which the uncertainty of unknown benefits will exceed the known and committed costs.

When capital assets are purchased, both the burdens and the benefits of ownership are transferred to the owner. The burdens are primarily the costs associated with acquisition and installation. The benefits are primarily the revenues generated by operating the capital assets. Risk of ownership is created to the degree that the benefits are uncertain.

Hospital managers need to be skilled at putting hospital assets at risk. Without clear knowledge and understanding of the benefits and the burdens, hospitals can quickly find themselves at unacceptably high levels of risk. Risk must be continually assessed and evaluated in order to successfully put hospital assets at risk. Hospitals require many varied capital investments; their capital investments represent a risk portfolio. An effective combination of risky assets can often create risk that is less than the sum of the risk of each asset.

Of course, financial managers have known this for years as a basic principle of Modern Portfolio Theory (MPT), first introduced by Harry Markowitz, PhD, with the paper "Portfolio Selection," which appeared in the 1952 *Journal of Finance*. Thirty-eight years later, he shared a Nobel Prize with Merton Miller, PhD, and William Sharpe, PhD, for what has become a broad theory for securities asset selection. Hospital assets may be viewed in much the same way. Prior to Markowitz's work, investors focused on assessing the rewards and risks of individual securities in constructing a portfolio. Standard advice was to identify those that offered the best opportunities for gain with the least risk and then construct a portfolio from them. Following this advice, a hospital administrator might conclude that a positron emission tomography (PET) scanning machine offered good risk-reward characteristics, and pursue a strategy to compile a network of them in a given geographic area. Intuitively, this would be foolish. Markowitz formalized this intuition. Detailing the mathematics of diversity, he proposed that investors focus on selecting portfolios based on their overall risk-reward characteristics instead of merely compiling portfolios of securities or capital assets that each individually has attractive risk-reward characteristics. In a nutshell, just as investors should select portfolios and not individual securities, hospital administrators should select a wide spectrum of radiology services and not merely machines.

Savvy hospital managers will mitigate ownership risk by constructing their portfolio of risky assets in a manner that lowers overall risk.

CAPITAL CAPACITY

Capital capacity is about risk. Because capital investments have risk associated with them, capital capacity is a measurement of how much risk a hospital can bear. Capital capacity is not simple to determine. Capital investments introduce varying levels of risk, depending on the relative uncertainty of the benefits to be derived. One million dollars invested in an MRI at a hospital that has a 2-month backlog for scheduling MRIs has a much lower risk than $1 million invested in a new service like a PET scanner.

Profit margins affect capital capacity. Larger profit margins create larger capacity for uncertainty, which implies more risk and that means more capital capacity. Higher liquidity means more capital capacity. Lower debt leverage means more capital capacity. Both liquidity and leverage are balance sheet ratios. Both imply capacity to absorb uncertain outcomes; both affect capital capacity.

Determining capital capacity is more art than science because of the variability in risk presented by various capital investments and the subjectivity associated with trying to measure that uncertainty.

That having been said, it is important to build models that estimate capital capacity. Most capital capacity models ignore the variability in risk presented by capital investments. They are typically built from published rating agency financial ratio medians. These models are based on the view that financial ratios of similar rating categories represent equivalent risks. This is a simplistic view; it suggests that credit analysts simply categorize risk on the basis of financial ratios. That is not the case. Published medians are the result of credit analysis, not the basis for credit analysis. Importantly, what is not usually published is the range or distribution around these medians.

Models that estimate risk need to differentiate among risks presented by capital investments. Capital investments with little risk should consume less capital capacity than capital investments with a lot of risk.

COST OF CAPITAL

It is critical to understand and to measure the total cost of capital. Lack of understanding and appreciation of the total cost of capital is widespread, particularly among not-for-profit hospital executives. The capital structure includes long-term debt and equity; total capital is the sum of these two. Each of these components has cost associated with it. For the long-term debt portion, this cost is explicit—it is the interest rate plus associated costs of placement and servicing.

For the equity portion, the cost is not explicit and is widely misunderstood. In many cases, hospital capital structures include significant amounts of equity that has accumulated over many years of favorable operations. Too many executives wrongly attribute zero cost to the equity portion of their capital structure. Although it is correct that generally accepted accounting principles continue to assign a zero cost to equity, there is opportunity cost associated with equity that needs to be considered. This cost is the opportunity available to utilize that capital in alternative ways.

In general, the cost attributed to equity is the return expected by the equity markets on hospital equity. This can be observed by evaluating the equity prices of hospital companies whose equity is traded on public stock exchanges. Usually, the equity prices will imply cost of equity in the range of 10%–14%.

Almost always, the cost of equity implied by hospital equity prices traded on public stock exchanges will substantially exceed the cost of long-term debt. Thus, while many hospital executives will view the cost of equity to be substantially less than the cost of debt (i.e., to be zero) in nearly all cases, the appropriate cost of equity will be substantially greater than the cost of debt.

Hospitals need to measure their weighted average cost of capital (WACC). WACC is the cost of long-term debt multiplied by the ratio of long-term debt to total capital plus the cost of equity multiplied by the ratio of equity to total capital (where total capital is the sum of long-term debt and equity).

WACC is then used as the basis for capital charges associated with all capital investments. Capital investments should be expected to generate positive returns after applying this capital charge based on the WACC. Capital investments that do not generate returns exceeding the WACC consume enterprise value; those that generate returns exceeding WACC increase enterprise value. Hospital executives need to be rewarded for increasing enterprise value.

SOURCES OF CAPITAL

In general, hospitals have three sources of capital: equity from earnings, equity from donations, and long-term debt.

Earnings generate cash, and a portion of that cash is available to fund capital investments. Besides funding capital investments, cash generated from earnings is used to fund working capital. As operations grow, more working capital is required to fund the difference between the operating receivables and operating payables because days of revenue in receivables tend to be a good deal higher than days of expense in payables. Additionally, cash on hand should increase as operations grow so that days of cash remain constant or increase. Once working capital has been adequately funded, any remaining cash generated from earnings is available to invest in capital.

Most not-for-profit hospitals engage in active fundraising to generate donations. Donations are a good source of capital in certain markets. Often, fundraising initiatives are less useful than they appear due to the costs expended in the fundraising activities. It is important to ensure that all the costs incurred in fundraising activities are properly attributed.

Borrowing long-term debt has been and will continue to be an important source of capital for hospitals. Debt is particularly attractive due to the low cost associated with borrowing on a tax-exempt basis. Long-term debt, borrowed on a tax-exempt basis, is probably the lowest cost form of capital available to hospitals. Tax-exempt borrowing is fairly complex due to the tax regulations affecting it. Because of its complexity, the costs associated with these transactions are quite high, making it less practical for small borrowings.

Tax-exempt borrowing transactions require many lawyers and high-priced investment bankers. Credit rating agencies and credit enhancers are also typically involved. Accessing the tax-exempt markets requires a good bit of sophistication and expertise. Despite these requirements, this capital is highly attractive to hospitals and should be used whenever possible.

CREDIT RATINGS

The market looks to rating agencies to develop and publish information about the degree of certainty the market should attach to promises and commitments made by a company concerning capital instruments. This information is rationalized into a credit rating. There are several companies engaged in the development and communication of credit ratings. These include Standard & Poor's, Moody's, and Fitch. Each of these is actively engaged in the analysis and publishing of credit for not-for-profit hospitals. The views of these rating agencies are very important to hospitals. They have a great deal of impact on hospitals' access to capital. Hospitals need to be actively engaged in influencing the opinion of these analysts.

Rating agencies express their opinion about hospital credits in the form of credit ratings. Table 3.1 describes the ratings published by Standard & Poor's and Moody's.

Ratings are associated with securities—usually bond issues. They are not specifically associated with hospitals. It is possible that a single hospital may have different ratings for different securities. This would be the case in the event that the different securities provide differing credit or security provisions. These may be explicit in the case of senior and subordinate securities, or they may be implicit in the structure of the security interests provided.

Ratings are subjective determinations made by credit analysts at the rating agencies. That having been said, there tend to be similarities in the financial ratios of hospitals within rating categories. The rating agencies publish the medians in each rating category for common financial ratio. Table 3.2 shows the 2007 medians published by Standard & Poor's. This table shows only the medians; importantly, the distributions around these medians are not provided. It is wrong to assume that ratings can be determined on the basis of these medians. Ratings are subjective determinations made by expert credit analysts.

Credit ratings are not permanent. Rating agencies can change them at any time, and it is not uncommon for ratings to be changed (upgrades and downgrades). In fact, rating agencies have an obligation to adjust their ratings as appropriate; they are in the business of providing information to the market. This information affects pricing decisions being made every day by the market. It needs to be as accurate and up-to-date as possible to prevent mispricings, especially the post 2008–2009 time period.

If a rating is too high, a buyer of the security could buy it at too high a price. When the rating is downgraded, the buyer would take a loss primarily created by the wrong rating. Conversely, if a rating is too low, a seller might sell at a price that is lower than it should be, realizing a loss because of the wrong rating. Thus, rating agencies endeavor to keep their ratings consistent with the credit state of the security.

Rating agencies get paid by issuers of securities when the securities are issued. Once issued, usually issuers do not make further payments to the rating agencies, especially in the case of hospitals.

TABLE 3.1
Ratings Published by Standard & Poor's and Moody's

Standard & Poor's		Moody's	
AAA	The obligor's capacity to meet its financial commitment on the obligation is extremely strong.	Aaa	Obligations are judged to be of the highest quality, with minimal credit risk.
AA	The obligor's capacity to meet its financial commitment on the obligation is very strong.	Aa	Obligations are judged to be of high quality and are subject to very low credit risk.
A	The obligor's capacity to meet its financial commitment on the obligation is strong.	A	Obligations are considered upper-medium grade and are subject to low credit risk.
BBB	Obligation exhibits adequate protection parameters. However, adverse economic conditions or changing circumstances are more likely to lead to a weakened capacity of the obligor to meet its financial commitment on the obligation.	Baa	Obligations are subject to moderate credit risk. They are considered medium grade and as such may possess certain speculative characteristics.
BB	The obligor faces major ongoing uncertainties or exposure to adverse business, financial, or economic conditions, which could lead to the obligor's inadequate capacity to meet its financial commitment on the obligation.	Ba	Obligations are judged to have speculative elements and are subject to substantial credit risk.
B	The obligor currently has the capacity to meet its financial commitment on the obligation. Adverse business, financial, or economic conditions will likely impair the obligor's capacity or willingness to meet its financial commitment on the obligation.	B	Obligations are considered speculative and are subject to high credit risk.
CCC	The obligor is currently vulnerable to nonpayment and is dependent upon favorable business, financial, and economic conditions for the obligor to meet its financial commitment on the obligation. In the event of adverse business, financial, or economic conditions, the obligor is not likely to have the capacity to meet its financial commitment on the obligation.	Caa	Obligations are judged to be of poor standing and are subject to very high credit risk.
CC	The obligation is currently highly vulnerable to nonpayment.	Ca	Obligations are highly speculative and are likely in, or very near, default, with some prospect of recovery of principal and interest.
C	A bankruptcy petition has been filed or similar action has been taken, but payments on this obligation are being continued.	C	Obligations are the lowest rated class of bonds and are typically in default, with little prospect for recovery of principal or interest.
D	The obligation is in payment default.		
+, −	The ratings from "AA" to "CCC" may be modified by the addition of a plus or minus sign to show relative standing within the major rating categories.	1, 2, 3	Moody's appends numerical modifiers 1, 2, and 3 to each generic rating classification from Aa through Caa. The modifier 1 indicates that the obligation ranks in the higher end of its generic rating category, the modifier 2 indicates a midrange ranking, and the modifier 3 indicates a ranking in the lower end of that generic rating category.

TABLE 3.2
2007 Medians Published by Standard & Poor's

	AA	A	BBB	NIG[a]
Net patient revenue	713,572	262,996	102,495	115,620
Maximum debt service coverage	4.1	3.5	2.5	1.5
Operating margin	3.1%	3.5%	1.2%	−1.3%
Profit margin	4.5%	3.2%	1.9%	−0.4%
Days cash on hand	211	159	110	50
Cash to debt	155.9	103.8	71.0	33.4
Debt to total capital	32.8	37.3	44.3	65.3
Days of revenue in accounts receivable	53.8	53.8	55.3	53.5
Capital expenditures to depreciation expense	159.9	147.8	119.6	

[a] Not investment grade.

An important decision hospitals need to make is what credit rating to target. Do they want to be an AA credit? An A credit? Or a BBB credit? This decision will drive a lot of dynamics of access to credit in the capital markets.

What credit rating to target is neither straightforward nor intuitive? If you ask most hospital executives what credit rating they are targeting, the answer will be A. When you ask why, the answers become less certain. In general, A and sometimes AA are considered the gold standards that hospitals should achieve. A feels right.

What many hospitals do not consider is the implication of their credit rating. What difference does it make to a hospital if they have an A rating versus a BBB rating? In general, the higher the credit rating, the more attractive are the debt instruments sold by hospitals. The higher the credit rating, the more certainty there is that the hospital will perform according to the promises made in the debt indenture. Accordingly, the interest will be lower because there is considered less risk. Credit risk is low.

Higher credit ratings are not always better. In general, so long as hospitals have an investment-grade credit rating, the lower the rating, the greater amount of capital it can access. Higher credit ratings require stronger balance sheets. Stronger balance sheets mean greater liquidity and lower leverage. Greater liquidity means higher cash balances, leaving less cash available for capital investments.

Lower leverage means less debt, reducing the amount of debt available to fund capital investments.

Higher credit ratings throttle growth. They limit the amount of capital hospitals can access. That is not necessarily bad, but hospitals need to consider that when targeting a credit rating. If hospitals need greater access to capital, they should target lower credit ratings. Lower credit ratings are not bad.

That is not to say lower credit ratings are better than higher credit ratings. However, neither are higher credit ratings better than lower credit ratings. What is important is how well the target credit rating matches hospital strategy. If a high credit rating results in starving a hospital's access to capital so that it loses important market opportunities, the high credit rating has probably not served the hospital well.

ANALYSIS OF HOSPITAL CREDITS

Hospital credit analysis evaluates the capacity of a hospital to perform on its commitments. In its current state, hospital credit analysis stands to improve its credibility.

Hospital credit analysis has had some spectacular failures both in overrating and in underrating. The ones that get the most attention are the overratings, like the Allegheny Health, Education and Research Foundation, whose criminal case ended in November 2002 as its former CEO,

Sherif Abdelhak, was sentenced to a prison term of up to 23 months for misusing charitable endowments to bolster the failing health care system. Abdelhak pleaded no contest to one count of misapplication of entrusted property, a second-degree misdemeanor that carried a maximum penalty of 24 months in prison.

However, underratings are prevalent too. Both overratings as well as underratings contribute to investor losses. Hospital credit analysis is about assessing uncertainty—specifically, the uncertainty associated with performing on commitments.

What are the most important factors that determine how likely it is that a hospital will perform its commitments?

GROWTH

Perhaps the most important factor in hospital credit analysis is growth. The dynamics of running hospitals almost always require growth. It is a rare hospital management team that can succeed without year-over-year admission growth.

Why is growth so important? Hospital pricing dynamics. Hospital prices are always under pressure. As technologies advance, populations become more affluent, and as people become older, the demand for health care increases. This upward demand requires an increasing portion of overall economic activity. That creates stress on the entire system and this stress is most manifest in pressures to limit rate increases.

Pressure to limit rate increases is coupled with expense rate increases that move up faster. The cost of labor is driven by normal supply and demand; with demand outstripping supply, prices move higher. Technology advancement creates more cost pressure; more technology investments are required and the technology costs increase more.

These factors converge on hospitals and result in prices for hospital services moving up less rapidly than the costs of labor and technology, resulting in decreasing profit margins. The solution for decreasing profit margins is to increase productivity. Increasing productivity is a lot easier when volumes are growing. It is very hard to increase productivity unless volumes are growing (i.e., managers are more capable of finding ways to limit the growth in personnel than they are in cutting personnel). With growing volumes, productivity increases when volume growth exceeds personnel growth. With stable or declining volumes, productivity can only be increased when personnel are reduced, and it is very hard to make that happen.

One of the most important factors in evaluating hospital credit is certainty of volume growth. Volume growth is largely driven by market dynamics. The most important market dynamic is population growth. Is there reason to believe that the population in the hospital's primary market will grow in the future? Census reports tell if population has grown in the past. Census forecasts suggest what might happen in the future. It is important to analyze the dynamics in a market that could affect population changes. Economic conditions, retirement patterns, and type of population can provide insights into future population trends.

Beyond population growth, market capture dynamics need analysis. Market capture is about how well a hospital captures its share of market growth. Ideally, hospitals will capture their share of market growth if market share remains reasonably constant or grows slightly. Balance among the market participants affects shared market growth. Balance is about sustainability of hospital operations with existing market positions. If there are hospitals in the market that are not sustainable with their current market positions, market instability can be expected in the future. Because most hospitals have many community stakeholders, hospitals do not die very often. Thus, it is hard to assume that a hospital that lacks sufficient market position to sustain itself will die or shut down. More likely, that hospital with its stakeholders will take drastic actions to attain the market position needed to sustain itself.

A balanced market environment is more important than absolute market position. Hospitals with large market shares in unbalanced or unstable markets are less certain to grow sufficiently than hospitals with small market shares in balanced, stable markets. This is somewhat counter to accepted wisdom among hospital credit analysts. Large market shares tend to be viewed by hospital credit analysts in a highly positive manner. Market balance does not typically get as much weight as absolute market share.

The important market dynamics that most affect growth are market population growth combined with balance among hospitals in the market. Hospital volume growth is more likely in these kinds of markets. That is not to say that absolute market share is irrelevant. Clearly, higher absolute market share is more attractive than lower absolute market share, but it is not as important as balance among hospitals in the market. The ideal hospital, then, is one that is positioned in a growing market that has balance among the hospitals in the market, and then, the higher the absolute market share, the better.

MARKET POSITION

In addition to market balance, market position is one of the most important factors in credit analysis. Historically, the measure most often used is market share—admissions to the hospital as a percentage of all admissions within the primary service area. Primary service area is commonly defined by the service areas (typically ZIP codes) that account for 80% of the total hospital admissions.

Although a critical measure, the typical market share calculation can miss important dynamics of market position that need to be considered. Hospitals with similar market shares can have very different market positions. The typical methods used can create inconsistent results when the relative concentrations of admissions among zip codes vary significantly.

Market dominance is a metric that expresses important information about market position. Market dominance is a measurement of the percentage of admissions drawn from service areas in which the hospital dominates. Admissions for the hospital and each competing hospital are determined for each service area. If the hospital admissions exceed the admissions from each of the competing hospitals by 1.5 times, the hospital dominates the service area and the admissions from that service area are included in the count of dominant admissions.

Tables 3.3 and 3.4 demonstrate how market share and market dominance describe market position. Both tables describe the same market—there is the same number of admissions in each ZIP code. Both tables describe the same hospital admissions—there is the same number of admissions for each hospital. The total columns and the total rows are the same in both tables. The

---

TABLE 3.3

Market Share and Market Dominance—Hospital A Dominates in One ZIP Code

Hospital	ZIP Code 1	ZIP Code 2	ZIP Code 3	ZIP Code 4	ZIP Code 5	ZIP Code 6	ZIP Code 7	ZIP Code 8	ZIP Code 9	Total
A	435	324	87	425	243	546	435	476	645	3643
B	123	300	54	523	225	435	324	546	765	3295
C	201	124	65	321	354	678	345	254	546	2888
D	198	90	32	123	211	232	123	65	23	1097
E	90	125	14	231	134	212	111	34	54	1005
F	85	231	88	50	154	134	143	78	76	1048
Total	1132	1194	340	1700	1321	2237	1481	1462	2109	12,976
Market share										28.1%
Market dominance										11.9%

TABLE 3.4

Market Share and Market Dominance—Hospital A Dominates in Four ZIP Codes

Hospital	ZIP Code 1	ZIP Code 2	ZIP Code 3	ZIP Code 4	ZIP Code 5	ZIP Code 6	ZIP Code 7	ZIP Code 8	ZIP Code 9	Total
A	335	474	37	752	93	896	135	51	870	3643
B	273	200	54	323	375	385	433	846	406	3295
C	151	99	65	321	354	428	654	404	421	2888
D	98	90	32	23	211	232	123	65	223	1097
E	90	125	14	231	134	162	111	34	104	1005
F	185	206	138	50	154	134	34	62	85	1048
Total	1132	1194	340	1700	1321	2237	1481	1462	2109	12976
Market share										28.1%
Market dominance										82.1%

difference between these tables is the distribution of admissions among the hospitals. Market share for Hospital A is 28.1% in both tables because the hospitals have the same number of admissions in each table. Market dominance for Hospital A is 11.9% in Table 3.3 and 82.1% in Table 3.4. In Table 3.3, Hospital A only dominates in one ZIP code, while it dominates four ZIP codes in Table 3.4. Clearly, the market position for Hospital A in Table 3.4 is stronger than it is in Table 3.3.

Market share is an important measure of market position. So is market dominance. Both should be used in making valid credit analysis. In most cases, market dominance is more important than market share. Attractiveness ranking for possible combinations of market share and market dominance is shown in the following.

Rank	Market Share	Market Dominance
1.	Strong	Strong
2.	Weak	Strong
3.	Strong	Weak
4.	Weak	Weak

Table 3.5 presents these market metrics for a randomly selected group of hospitals in California based on 2008 data.

MARKET DEFINITIONS

The definition of hospital "market" is often nebulous, with some entities defined by terms as ambiguous as "acute care inpatient hospitals," "specialty hospitals," or "anchor hospitals." This ambiguity occurs because health care is increasingly provided on an outpatient basis, and general inpatient hospitals face competition from a range of allied health care providers for the medical services they deliver.

For example, none other than the U.S. Supreme Court has explained that the determination of relevant hospital product and geographic markets is "a necessary predicate" to deciding whether a hospital merger contravenes the Clayton Act (antitrust). *United States v. Marine Ban Corporation Inc.*, 418 U.S. 602, 618 (1974) (citing *United States v. E.I. Du Pont De Nemours & Co.*), 353 U.S. 586, 593 (1957); *Brown Shoe Co. v. United States*, 370 U.S. 294, 324 (1962).

TABLE 3.5
Market Metrics in Randomly Selected California Hospitals

	Market Share (%)	Market Dominance (%)
Alameda County Medical Centers	13.3	0.0
Alameda Hospital	17.4	76.6
Arrowhead Regional Medical Center	10.9	0.0
California Hospital Medical Center–Los Angeles	8.2	19.0
Cedars Sinai Medical Center	9.5	36.5
Corona Regional Medical Centers	27.3	69.3
Eisenhower Memorial Hospital	33.5	48.1
El Camino Hospital	20.7	53.6
Enloe Hospital	47.3	59.8
Feather River Hospital	41.1	76.1
Glendale Adventist Medical Center	9.8	25.3
Glendale Memorial Hospital & Health Center	9.8	20.4
Good Samaritan Hospital–Los Angeles	2.7	3.2
Hoag Medical Center	18.5	51.7
John F. Kennedy Memorial Hospital	56.0	74.4
Loma Linda University Medical Centers	8.2	7.0
Marin General Hospital	42.7	52.9
Paradise Valley Hospital	12.5	32.4
Pomona Valley Hospital Medical Center	26.3	47.9
Queen of Angels/Hollywood Presbyterian Medical Center	9.7	42.3
Redding Medical Center	27.1	0.0
Redlands Community Hospital	16.4	46.7
Riverside County Regional Medical Center	10.0	0.0
San Joaquin General Hospital	17.1	0.0
Scripps Mercy Hospital	10.8	21.3
Selma Community Hospital	10.0	37.0
Simi Valley Medical Center	37.3	73.3
St. Helena Medical Center	7.5	34.1
Stanford Hospital	3.0	10.7
Sutter Memorial Hospital	9.5	0.0
Torrance Memorial Medical Center	23.4	29.0
UCLA Medical Center	1.9	0.0
USCF Medical Center	3.1	0.3
Ukiah Medical Center	60.7	73.0
White Memorial Medical Center	6.6	26.1

Hospital Competitive Markets

Hospital product markets also differ in several important respects from other markets, and appropriate capital formation analysis must take these differences into account. Because only a fraction of most hospitals' business is price sensitive, a restrictive market definition may harm patients or increase capital acquisition costs, or excessively enrich institutions. Moreover, capital formation in hospital mergers typically presents a greater potential for positive efficiencies than mergers in other industries.

Research suggests that simply increasing the number of competitors does not necessarily decrease prices or raise quality and may even have the opposite effect. As Rashi Fein, the Harvard health care economist observed, "[i]n health care, the invisible hand of Adam Smith is all thumbs" (Lee and Lamm 1993).

Since then, however, most studies suggest that there is no real correlation between higher market concentration and higher costs and prices. The reason for this counterintuitive result is because price sensitivity is less important and potential efficiencies and scale economics are greater.

Moreover, many hospitals are affiliating in role-based access control (RBAC) networks by controlling which patients, medical providers, or health plans have access based on the needs of patients, payors, physicians, or insurers. User, doctor, and patient rights and services are then grouped by name, and access to medical resources is restricted to only those authorized.

For example, when an RBAC network system is used by a hospital, each individual who is allowed access to the hospital's network would have a predefined role (doctor, nurse, lab technician, administrator, patient, etc.). If someone is defined as having the role of doctor, for example, then that user can access only resources of the health care network that the role of doctor has been allowed access to (e.g., electronic medical records). If another user has access as a diabetic patient, then that user cannot access unapproved health services such as OB-GYN. Each user is assigned one or more roles, and each role is assigned one or more privileges for users in that role.

Therefore, correctly defining the relevant hospital product market is crucial to correctly analyzing hospital capital formation, growth, merger, sale, and acquisition strategies. The establishment of a consistent, predictable, and economically sound standard for market definitions is also important to state, regional, and federal public policy makers. Hence, it is useful to review the definitional elements of proper hospital product types.

Hospital Types

Acute Care Inpatient Hospital

An acute care inpatient hospital is a health care organization or "anchor hospital" in which a patient is treated for an acute (immediate and severe) episode of illness or the subsequent treatment of injuries related to an accident or trauma, or during recovery from surgery. Specialized personnel using complex and sophisticated technical equipment and materials usually render acute professional care in a hospital setting. Unlike chronic care, acute care is often necessary for only a short time. Measures of acute health care utilization are represented by three separate rates:

1. Rate of admissions per 1000 patients
2. Average length of stay per admission
3. Total days of care per 1000 patients

Psychiatric Hospital

A psychiatric hospital (behavioral health, mental hospital, or asylum) specializes in the treatment of patients with mental illness or drug-related illness or dependencies. Psychiatric wards differ only in that they are a unit of a larger hospital.

Specialty Hospital

A specialty hospital is a type of health care organization that has a limited focus to provide treatment for only certain illnesses such as cardiac care, orthopedic or plastic surgery, elder care, radiology/oncology services, neurological care, or pain management cases. These organizations are often owned by physicians who refer patients to them. In recent years, single-specialty hospitals have emerged in various locations in the United States. Instead of offering a full range of inpatient services, these hospitals focus on providing services relating to a single medical specialty or cluster of specialties.

Long-Term Care Hospital

A long-term care hospital is an entity that provides assistance and patient care for the activities of daily living (ADLs), including reminders and standby help for those with physical, mental, or emotional problems. This includes physical disability or other medical problems for 3 months or more (90 days). The criteria of five ADLs may also be used to determine the need for help with the following: meal preparation, shopping, light housework, money management, and telephoning. Other important considerations include taking medications, doing laundry, and getting around outside.

Rural Hospital

The parameters of a rural hospital are determined based on distance. A rural hospital is defined as a hospital serving a geographic area 10 or more miles from the nexus of a population center of 30,000 or more. More specifically, a rural hospital means an entity characterized by one of the following:

1. *Type A* rural hospital—small and remote, has fewer than 50 beds, and is more than 30 miles from the nearest hospital
2. *Type B* rural hospital—small and rural, has fewer than 50 beds, and is 30 miles or less from the nearest hospital
3. *Type C* rural hospital—considered rural and has 50 or more beds

ESSENTIALITY

An important component of hospital credit analysis is essentiality. Hospitals are unusual businesses that many times possess some form of essentiality to their communities. Health care is important to the economic vitality of every community. Many hospitals have served their communities for many years; it is not uncommon to find hospitals that have been continuously operating for more than 100 years in the same community.

Most hospitals are not-for-profit. In not-for-profit hospitals, no private party actually "owns" the hospital; control is vested in various boards, but no one explicitly owns a not-for-profit hospital. In a broad sense, communities own not-for-profit hospitals. They are considered "charities" with a "charitable purpose." Though a not-for-profit hospital may not have owners, it has many "stakeholders," parties that have vested interests in the continuing success of the hospital.

Many hospitals have broad and vast webs of stakeholders. Stakeholders are why hospitals rarely close or are shut down. Too many stakeholders have interests in the continuing successful operation of hospitals.

Hospital stakeholder relationships need to be considered in the analysis of essentiality. How strong are these relations? How many are there? How important is the continuing success of this hospital to these stakeholders?

Another dimension of the essentiality analysis is service analysis. How significant are the hospital's services? If the hospital shuts down, what population segments would suffer? How significant is the population that would suffer? How much would they suffer?

Analysis of hospital's stakeholders and services should provide a credible view of the degree of essentiality associated with a hospital. Higher degrees of essentiality suggest higher likelihoods that hospitals, one way or another, will meet their commitments, particularly their payment commitments.

FINANCIAL RATIO ANALYSIS

Financial ratio analysis is routinely used as a part of credit analysis. The ratios focused on fall into two categories: performance and protection. Performance ratios express how well the hospital is operating. Profit margins and returns dominate the performance analysis. Protection ratios express the capacity to protect from unexpected downturns in operations. Protection ratios include liquidity ratios, coverage ratios, and leverage ratios.

What is more important, performance or protection? It depends on your outlook. If your outlook is long term, performance is more important. If it is shorter term, then protection dominates. It is like a car—performance is the engine, protection is the seat belt. If you are just driving around the block, you're less concerned about performance, but more concerned about how well the seat belt works. If you are taking a long trip, the performance of the engine is your top concern.

Credit analysts have different objectives. Bond insurers are really concerned about the hospital making its payments over a very long term, many times as long as 30 years. Rating agencies are more concerned about the shorter term; their job is to inform the market of relevant information that affects current trading. It is not surprising, then, to find that rating agency ratings tend to be more correlated with protection ratios than with performance metrics. Bond insurers, on the other hand, should have more interest in performance than protection, particularly at the time of underwriting.

Several performance metrics are typically analyzed. The most common are operating margin and profit margin. Operating margin is operating income divided by operating revenue; profit margin is net income divided by operating revenue. Neither of these is very good in comparing one hospital to another because they both incorporate capital structures that vary widely among hospitals. Some hospitals have very little debt in their capital structures, whereas other hospitals carry large amounts of debt. Because interest expense associated with this debt is included in both operating income and net income, these ratios are distorted by differences in capital structures making operating comparisons.

Another measure that is sometimes used is EBDIT margin—earnings before depreciation, interest, and tax divided by operating revenue. This measure is an improvement over both operating margin and profit margin, but it too is flawed. It excludes depreciation. Depreciation is the consumption of capital assets, and it is hard to assume that an effective performance measure should not carry the burden of capital asset consumption.

A better metric is operations before interest margin—operating income plus interest divided by operating revenue. This appropriately minimizes the distortion caused by various capital structures while properly including charges for consumption of capital assets. It should be reasonably comparable among hospitals and represents a good basis to evaluate performance.

Another performance measure that deserves attention in credit analysis is return on total capital—profit plus interest expense divided by debt plus equity. The common metric analyzed is return on equity (profit divided by equity), but it can be widely distorted by differences in capital structure. Return on total capital consistently measures across hospitals how well capital put at risk is performing.

Debt service coverage is a very important measure. It expresses the balance (or imbalance) between the size of debt and the size of the operation by relating net income available to cover debt service to debt service. It is calculated by dividing debt service (principal payments plus interest payments) by net income available for debt service (net income plus interest expense plus depreciation expense).

There are several permutations of this measure:

1. Historical (immediately prior year debt service with immediately prior year income available for debt service)
2. Maximum (highest debt service for any future year with immediately prior year income available for debt service)
3. Pro forma (highest debt service for any future year including debt service on proposed issue with immediately prior year income available for debt service)
4. Pro forma projected (highest debt service for any future year including debt service on proposed issue with projected income available for debt service)

Of these, pro forma is the best. It ensures that any new debt can be adequately covered by the existing business without the support of the new business the new debt will presumably create.

Liquidity is typically measured in terms of days of expenses covered by cash on hand. It is computed by dividing cash on hand by cash expense per day (typically computed by dividing operating expense minus depreciation by number of calendar days). It expresses how long the operation could be funded in the event that cash collections ceased—in no way a likely scenario, but a good way to compare relative amounts of cash among hospitals. It is a sound expression of the capacity of the balance sheet to absorb operating blips and downturns—the capacity to deal with future uncertain events.

Leverage is typically expressed by the debt to total capital ratio (long-term debt including current portion divided by long-term debt including current portion plus equity). Leverage is widely viewed as a measure of risk, but it is not a very good indicator of risk. Although higher leverage does indicate more risk than lower leverage for a given hospital, it does not necessarily mean higher risk when comparing among hospitals. It is one of the poorer ways to evaluate risk among different hospitals.

GOVERNANCE

Larry Scanlon, executive director of The Hunter Group, says, "I've never seen a distressed organization that could not be traced back to ineffective governance" (personal communication). Credit analysis needs to pay attention to governance issues. Governance makes a difference in long-term credit judgments.

Issues important in governance credit analysis include how the board functions, terms of board members, how board members are selected, and how senior management is chosen. These all have important impacts on the future course of the hospital.

Many times, the most important decision affecting a hospital's future is the choice of the CEO. Credit analysts need to know how the next CEO will be chosen and that the board members are qualified to be actively engaged in governing.

All these governance matters can be spelled out in corporate bylaws and articles of incorporation. Moreover, in the case of bond insurers, covenants can be reasonably given to ensure that these important matters are not changed.

Critical credit issues in governance are

Effective management oversight. Many hospital boards are not effective. Not-for-profit hospital boards tend be composed of upstanding community people who have little expertise in health care or the management of hospitals. Too often this results in a complacent board that readily accepts what management tells them. The board trusts management's judgment and follows management without a rigorous, informed debate. This works fine as long as management does the right thing. It is a disaster when management makes poor judgments.

Outside expert advisor. Given that many community hospital board members are not health care experts, alternative expert voices, independent of management, are needed. Boards should engage independent expert advisors to routinely review hospital data and provide counsel and analysis to the board.

Qualified board members. Qualifications for board members need to be credible and explicit. Requirements for continuing education need to be explicit. Members lacking health care experience need introductory education.

Board membership turnover. Turnover of board membership is important. Terms need to be staggered and the number of terms needs to be limited. Adequate turnover avoids perpetuation of unhealthy power relationships between boards and management.

Succession planning. Perhaps the most critical decisions boards make are appointments of senior executives, particularly the CEO and CFO. For these appointments, boards should engage nationally recognized search firms to lead an appropriate process and make recommendations to the board. Appointments should not be made without the positive recommendation of the nationally recognized search firm.

CAPITAL INVESTMENT

Capital investments affect hospitals' futures. How much capital is invested makes a difference and where it is invested makes a difference. Capital investments shape the future. Credit analysts are driven by polar-opposite concerns. On the one hand, they are concerned about adequacy of capital investment—Is enough capital being invested to ensure that market opportunities are not lost? On the other hand, they are concerned that higher capital means higher risk in the form of committed cost versus uncertain returns. Balancing these two concerns requires good business judgment.

Beyond the amount of capital invested, credit analysis needs to address how capital projects are chosen. Every hospital deals with the problem of capital investment opportunities exceeding capital capacity, many times by wide margins. How they choose which projects to fund and which to pass up is important.

Given the trade-offs faced in choosing capital investments, rejuvenation and replacement projects tend to get passed up more than they should. Usually, these do not create new revenue; they just preserve existing revenue. Preservation of existing revenue is important, and it must be adequately funded. In most cases, the amount invested in rejuvenation and replacement projects should bear some relationship to depreciation expense, because depreciation expense represents capital asset consumption during the period.

The remaining capital, after rejuvenation and replacement is funded, should be directed toward revenue growth. In picking these projects, strategy is more important than return. Every hospital needs a well-understood growth strategy. Most of them will be heavily dependent on capital investment, so the growth strategy should be evident by what capital investments are chosen. Credit analysts should explore how congruent the capital investments being made are to this strategy.

CAPITAL FORMATION PROCESS

MANAGING CREDIT RELATIONSHIPS

Every hospital needs to manage their credit relationships. Rating agencies and credit providers need to be targeted by hospitals for development and maintenance of credit relationships. Credit relationships are an ongoing process. They need to be fed and nurtured. Hospitals should make sure that they cultivate their relationships with credit analysts even during times when they are not seeking credit.

Too often, hospitals work on credit relationships only when they need capital financing. That is the wrong time. Relationships need to be in place before they need financing. Credit relationships should not be transaction-based, but instead formed and nurtured on an ongoing basis, resulting in better, more optimal transaction results.

Credit relationships are fed and nurtured through communication. Communication strategies need to be multifaceted—quarterly reporting, annual face-to-face reviews, and ad hoc telephone conversations. Reporting needs to go beyond just what is required by the covenants. Covenanted reporting should be viewed as the minimum.

Perhaps the most important component of nurturing credit relationships is the annual meeting. Annual meetings should be set up and conducted at the offices of the credit analysts. The meeting should review the past year and describe the plans for the future. An important component of the annual review is the financial forecast. Credibility is established by presenting a 3- to 5-year financial forecast each year. Variances from the forecast should be discussed and whether they are favorable or unfavorable should be explained. Candor about the good and especially the bad creates understanding and trust, which are critical components in credibility.

Financial forecasts are inherently uncertain. The future is unknown, and in most cases, unknowable. A financial forecast is not so much a prediction of the future, but a description of a management team's view of the future. That view encompasses both external factors that are largely out of the control of management, and internal factors that are controllable. The forecast describes the management's strategies of dealing with that environment. As such, the financial forecast creates the context for a very profitable discussion between management and analysts. The view of the external environment can be compared and contrasted and challenged by the analysts. It is important for them to develop a comfort level with management's view of the external environment. Given that environment, analysts can then evaluate management's strategies for successfully leading the hospital through that environment.

Presenting updated forecasts each year provides additional dimensions for useful dialogue. Changes in environmental views can be highlighted and discussed. Implications to hospital strategy can then be usefully identified and debated. Failures and successes in meeting the assumptions presented in prior forecasts highlight strengths and weaknesses of management in dealing with the uncertainties of its environment.

Tax-Exempt Debt

Tax-exempt debt has become an important means of external financing for hospitals, primarily because its cost is very attractive. Interest rates on tax-exempt financing are lower than interest rates on financing that is not tax-exempt because the interest income earned by the holders is exempt from federal income tax. In some states, it is also exempt from state income tax, and in some cities, it is also exempt from city income tax. Thus, the holders of these debt instruments (usually bonds) are willing to accept lower rates of interest.

Hospitals themselves are not capable of issuing tax-exempt debt. Only state and local governments are. A state or local government issues tax-exempt debt for hospitals and then loans the proceeds to hospitals. This is called "conduit" financing—the state or local government acts as a conduit through which hospitals can access tax-exempt debt markets. State and local governments are authorized to loan proceeds of their bond issues to hospitals through state statutes, and each state statute is different. Some states authorize any state or local government to issue bonds to loan to hospitals. Other states restrict such power to special-purpose governmental entities only. Moreover, some states restrict this power to a single governmental entity that is specially formed for the sole purpose of issuing tax-exempt bonds on behalf of hospitals.

The Internal Revenue Service (IRS) regulates the issuance of tax-exempt financing. While the IRS code nominally provides that debt instruments issued by state and local governments are exempt from federal income tax, it imposes special rules on conduit issues. Thus, tax-exempt issues whose proceeds are loaned to hospitals must comply with special IRS rules. Although very complex, these rules primarily regulate the use of proceeds, restricting the use of tax-exempt proceeds to the acquisition of property, plant components, and equipment.

Given state statutes, IRS code, and applicable security laws (both state and federal), issuing tax-exempt bonds is legally complex. Many lawyers get paid handsome fees every time tax-exempt debt is issued. The quarterback of the legal team is the bond counsel who represents the interests of the bondholders; the bond counsel issues the critical tax opinion that investors rely upon to claim tax exemption on the interest from these instruments. Everything revolves around getting this opinion.

Given its critical nature, only highly qualified lawyers are accepted by the market to provide this opinion. Underwriter's counsel represents the interests of the investment bankers; their primary concern is compliance with security laws. Issuer's counsel represents the interests of the state or local government, and hospital counsel represents the interests of the hospital; both have relatively minor roles. In the event credit enhancement is involved, credit enhancement counsel represents their interests and has significant influence on the process.

Another unique party to most tax-exempt bond issues is the bond trustee. The bond trustee is usually a bank that performs a fiduciary duty on behalf of the bond holders throughout the life of the bonds. The face of the faceless bond holders, they act on their behalf. Moreover, they, too, are represented by counsel in the bond issuance process.

State or local government typically appoints bond counsel. In many cases, they work with only a single firm. Not unusually, these relationships are quite cozy, and often result in fees being paid that are well in excess of what otherwise would be paid.

An excess of documents is involved in most tax-exempt financings. The heart of the documents is the indenture, which is the agreement between the bond trustee (on behalf of the bond holders) and the state or local government issuer. It contains the promises made to the bond holders, and it describes the work of the bond trustee. The bond trustee will only perform actions on behalf of bond holders that are explicitly set forth in the bond indenture. The bond indenture is the security given to the bond holders, describing all their recourses.

The bond indenture is typically supported by the loan agreement between the state or local government that issues the bonds and the hospital to which the proceeds are loaned. Its terms complement the terms of the bond indenture, which together form the conduit.

Bond Insurers and Credit Enhancement

Credit enhancement is commonly used when issuing tax-exempt bonds. Credit providers guarantee the payments promised by the bonds, essentially co-signing. As a party with recognized credibility in the market, the bond provider agrees to make payments on behalf of the obligor in the event the obligor fails to make payments. The effect of this is that the credit rating on the credit-enhanced instruments is higher than the underlying credit rating of the hospital obligor.

Credit enhancement is primarily provided by bond insurers and commercial banks. Bond insurers issue insurance policies that cover the payments of principal and interest over the life of the bonds, usually up to 30 years. For this policy, the bond insurer is paid an up-front premium; typically in the range of 40–300 basis points (hundredths of 1%) applied to the total principal and interest payments. Effectively, the credit rating of the insured bonds becomes the credit rating of the bond insurer, typically AAA or AA, instead of the underlying rating of the hospital obligor. The credit-enhanced bonds then are priced on the basis of the bond insurer's credit rating, resulting in lower interest rates. The difference between the interest rate based on the hospital obligor's underlying credit rating and the bond insurer's credit rating is the savings in interest payments derived by the insurance. The premium paid to the bond insurer is usually about two-thirds of the present value of this interest savings.

Commercial banks issue letters of credit to enhance hospital obligations. Letters of credit basically provide that the issuing bank will make any principal or interest payments that the hospital obligor fails to make. Usually, letters of credit are issued for 3 to 5 years with "evergreen" provisions.

Evergreen provisions provide the mechanism whereby the letter of credit can be extended for an additional year at each anniversary upon the agreement of the parties (not automatically). An important difference between bond insurance and letters of credit is the term—bond insurance covers the entire term of the bonds, whereas letters of credit cover less than the entire term (casting uncertainty on the credit enhancement provided by a letter of credit). Another important difference is the fee structure—letters of credit fees are paid on a quarterly basis, whereas bond insurance premiums are paid up-front.

Due to its short term, the letter of credit has to provide a "takeout" mechanism that is exercised in the event the letter of credit is not renewed. This takeout mechanism converts the underlying instrument into a bank loan with a short amortization—usually 5–7 years—and a "prime plus" rate of interest.

Letters of credit are most commonly used to support variable rate tax-exempt instruments. These instruments are usually auctioned once a week and a new interest set for the next week. The interest rates are extremely low and make very favorable forms of financing. They do introduce interest rate uncertainty. Although the rates are low, there is no certainty that they will remain low despite the current economic malaise of 2011–2012, although they have never traded above about 6% in the 20 or so years they have been in the market. Because of this uncertainty, they are typically limited to something less than half the debt of a hospital.

SECURITY AND COVENANTS

Almost every bond issue has security provisions. Usually, the security for bond holders is described in the bond indenture. Security for credit enhancers typically is greater than that provided bond holders and is spelled out in the agreements between the credit enhancers and the hospital obligor. Covenants are promises made between the parties and are used to describe the security provisions.

Mortgages on properties are not common security provisions. Mortgages, reserved for poorer credits, are considered somewhat arcane. More in favor are covenants not to encumber. The idea is to ensure that no property has a superior security interest to the interests of the bond holders. This form is less restrictive and provides more flexibility to the hospital obligor. Almost all bond issues will provide either a covenant not to encumber or a mortgage on almost all property as security for the promise to make payments.

Covenants based on debt service coverage are fairly common. Debt service coverage is a metric that expresses how much cash is being generated relative to the debt service of the hospital. It is, as a rule, calculated as net income available for debt services divided by annual debt service. Net income available for debt service is net income plus depreciation expense plus interest expense. Debt service is the principal and interest payments for all long-term debt. Sometimes, maximum annual debt service is used; debt service is scheduled out for each year into the future and the year with the highest amount is used. Debt service coverage is used as a trigger for various covenants. If debt service coverage falls below specified level, then provisions of covenants kick in.

The most common covenant is the rate covenant—hospital covenants to set rates sufficiently high to ensure that debt service coverage is at least X (typically 1.10). If the specified coverage is not maintained, then the hospital promises to hire a consultant to do a study and determine what changes need to be made to achieve the specified debt service coverage.

Perhaps the most confusing covenants deal with additional long-term borrowing. Usually, additional long-term debt can only be borrowed when the pro forma debt service coverage (debt service coverage including the additional long-term debt) is higher than a specified level. This limits the amount of long-term debt hospitals can borrow.

Covenants made to bond holders are very rigid. Because there can be many bond holders, and many of them may be fairly unsophisticated, there is almost no way to get relief from them. If they are too tight, about the only means to gain relief from them is to refund the bonds. Thus, great care must be used in making covenants to bond holders. Covenants with credit enhancers can be more flexible because credit enhancers can waive covenants—if relief is needed, hospitals have the option of requesting waivers from the credit enhancers who are usually quite sophisticated and may very well find it in their interest to waive.

CAPITAL STRATEGY

Capital investment is one of the most important strategies affecting the future of hospitals. Hospital executives need to be highly skilled at capital formation and capital allocation. Many hospitals are capital deficient; they lack adequate access to capital and they do not allocate capital to the investments that have the greatest impact on their future position. Hospitals that can access appropriate amounts of capital and know how to discern the most important investments will strengthen their market positions and ensure continued success. They will invest in a manner that makes their market an unattractive market for others to invest in, by understanding metrics such as

1. Market size and growth rate/stage in life cycle
2. Scope of competitive rivalry
3. Number of competitors and relative sizes
4. Prevalence of backward/forward integration
5. Entry/exit barriers
6. Nature and pace of medical technological change
7. Product and patient characteristics
8. Scale economies and experience curve effects
9. Capacity utilization and capital requirements
10. Health and hospital industry profitability and dominant economic traits
11. Competitive forces at work in the industry and strength
12. Drivers of change in the health care and hospital industry
13. Medical practices in strongest/weakest competitive positions
14. Competitive moves of rivals
15. Key factors determining competitive success or failure in industry
16. Attractiveness of industry

They will also invest in a manner that continues to capture the business that belongs to their franchise.

NOT-FOR-PROFIT HOSPITALS

U.S. not-for-profit hospitals undertook unprecedented amounts of debt in the late 1990s to early 2000s. This happened because corporate finance theory—and the modicum of economic literature on hospital financing and capital formation and structure at the time—suggested that debt constrained hospitals' capacity to deliver uncompensated care.

Yet, few health economists empirically evaluated the potential association of debt financing with uncompensated medical care. Of the first perhaps was Stephen A. Magnus, PhD, MS, Assistant Professor, Department of Health Policy and Management, University of Kansas School of Medicine; Dean G. Smith, PhD, Professor and Chair, Department of Health Management and Policy, University of Michigan School of Public Health; and John R. C. Wheeler, PhD, Professor, Department of Health Management and Policy, University of Michigan School of Public Health (personal communication).

In one of the first statistical analyses of a multistate sample of audited hospital financial statements in 1997—and ultimately published in the *Journal of Health Care Finance* in 2004—the researchers found that hospital debt levels predict higher levels of uncompensated care.

As further studies yielded similar results over time, hospital boards, policy makers, and regulators concerned with the provision of uncompensated care encouraged hospitals to issue more debt. This encouragement was provided through explicit flexibility, such as removing requirements for hospitals to issue tax-exempt bonds through state finance authorities and/or removing the project financing constraint. Likewise, hospital CFOs and physician executives who managed their organizations' financial risk benefited from a realization that optimizing the sources of financing did not impede mission-related objectives.

Up until the recent financial meltdown and credit market freeze, even current studies still seemed to offer no evidence to support concerns that debt had a negative impact on uncompensated care. However, hospitals filing bankruptcy in the fourth quarter of 2008 included a two-hospital system in Honolulu, one in Pontiac, Michigan, Trinity Hospital in Erin, Tennessee, Century City Doctors Hospital in Beverly Hills, California, Lincoln Park Hospital in Chicago, Illinois, and a four-hospital system (Hospital Partners of America), in Charlotte, North Carolina.

On the other hand, research results simply may have reflected the unusual economic and stock market conditions prevailing in the mid-2000s that are different today.

CURRENT MALAISE

Many for-profit, if not most not-for-profit hospitals, are seeing the effects of the economic downturn that has continued into 2012. For example, more than 30% of respondents to the most recent American Hospital Association (AHA) survey reported a significant decline in patients seeking elective care and 40% reporting a drop in admissions overall. The majority of hospitals also noted an increase in patients unable to pay for care.

DATABANK RESULTS

The report is based on survey results from 736 hospitals and information from DataBank, a Web-based reporting system used in 30 states to track key hospital trends:

1. Falling profit margins to (–) 1.6 percent—from (+) 6.1% year-over-year
2. Medicare and Medicaid patient care is growing
3. Reducing administrative costs (60%), staff (53%), and services (27%)
4. Borrowing for facility and technology improvements has decreased

Capital investments are also being postponed or delayed:

1. 56% delayed plans to increase capacity
2. 45% delayed purchase of clinical technology or equipment
3. 39% delayed investments in new information technology

The report was based on data from two major sources. A survey, The Economic Crisis: Impact on Hospitals, provides data from 736 hospitals from late October 2009 through November 10, 2009. DATABANK figures represent early results from 557 hospitals reporting data for July through September 2008 and 2009 as of January 2010.

ASSESSMENT

Relationships between all hospital operations (for-profit and not-for-profit entities) and capital structure formation represent a fruitful area for future investigations. A key issue to explore is the possibility of intertemporal trade-offs. For example, higher levels of debt may initially help to fund public services such as uncompensated medical care, but debt repayment eventually could limit a hospital's ability to provide core community benefits.

CONCLUSION

Because of the current economic ecosystem (post the 2008–2009 "flash-crash" and 2011–2012 stock market swoon), hospitals will have limited access to capital in 2013 and beyond, and so must find unique strategies to increase their capital formation opportunities. If they do not, others will take positions in their markets that will diminish their capacity to sustain the vital services that hospitals must provide. When traditional sources of capital are inadequate, hospitals need to seek out ways to develop alternative sources of capital.

Above all, capital is driven by operating profits. Capital sources become greater as operating profits increase. Hospitals must maintain, therefore, unrelenting focus on profit in order to continue expanding their capital investment opportunities.

CASE MODEL 3.1: CAPITAL FORMATION FOR
THE VALLEY MEDICAL CENTER

Nestled in the foothills of a western state, on the outskirts of its largest city is a bedroom community that is blossoming with accelerated growth and vigorous opportunity. The Valley Medical Center, the only hospital in the vibrant community of Alpha, is preparing to meta-morphose from the 50-year-old small rural 50-bed hospital into a modern, suburban 70-bed medical center needed to support this community's new growth.

This is an unusual market opportunity where the business has already achieved sufficient size to cover the debt service related to the replacement facility by more than 1.7 times. Over the past 2 years, admissions have grown an average of 6.3% each year and outpatient visits have grown an average of 7.9% each year. This growth is driven by close proximity to the large city's international airport. It is the closest hospital and its market is bounded to the east by the airport. The economic impact of this massive airport is doing much to transform Alpha from a sleepy cow town to an upscale suburban community.

PROTECTED MARKET

The hospital is positioned in a market with unusual boundaries that provide unique protec-tions from competition. The east border is bounded by the international airport. To the west, the river basin forms a natural barrier that separates the community from the adjacent town of Beta. A mountain with a national wildlife refuge is a barrier bounding the south. To the north are sparsely populated rural areas.

The primary market from which 80% of the hospital admissions originate is comprised of seven zip codes. There are no other hospitals in this area. The hospital holds a dominant posi-tion in five of these zip codes and 67.5 percent of all admissions originate in these dominant zip codes. Overall market share amounted to 58.5% during 2003.

Patient Origin	Admissions	Market Share	Dominant	Population 2000 Census
80601	1320		4	22,050
80602	55		4	6203
80603	201		4	5803
80621	481		4	12,248
80640	71			2076
80642	104		4	2734
80622	336			28,190
Total	2568	58.5%		79,305

MARKET GROWTH

The city of Alpha (primarily zip codes 80601, 80602, and 80603) projects its population growth to average 8.2% annually from 2003 to 2010. Gamma, another community in the ser-vice area (primarily zip code 80022), projects its population growth to average 11.5% annu-ally from 2003 to 2010. The remaining areas in the primary market are more rural and are expected to grow at 1%–2% annually. Overall, the primary market is expected to grow at about 6.8% annually through 2010. The primary market's population at the 2000 census was 79,320; by 2010, it is projected to reach 147,425, an increase of 86% in 10 years!

ESSENTIALITY

The Valley Medical Center provides essential services for at least 38,000 people. For its immediate market—the community, a town of over 27,000 people—the nearest alternative hospital is a 26 min drive (14.9 miles). For Delta, a rural town with population of 7500, the drive to the next closest hospital is 37 min (21.7 miles); for Epsilon, population 1600, the nearest hospital after Valley Medical Center is a 33 min drive (25.6 miles); and for the residents of Zeta, population 3000, the next hospital is a 27 min drive (19.7 miles). For these towns, the services of Valley Medical Center are very important. For some of the 18,379 patients who made emergency visits during 2003, Valley Medical Center was essential. The additional drive time would have meant death instead of life.

For the community of Alpha, the replacement of Valley Medical Center is an especially important ingredient fueling its growth. The construction of a new, modern medical center is a highly visible, dramatic symbol of the transformation taking place in Alpha. As a major symbol of growth and prosperity in Alpha, it becomes pretty much unthinkable that this new, modern center for health care will do anything but grow and prosper.

STRONG OPERATION

By almost any measure of operating performance, Valley Medical Center ranks high. It has an attractive payor mix. It is well managed and experiences growing volume. Its operating margins consistently exceed any and all benchmarks. Its percentage of labor cost to operating revenue is 43.5% over the past 5 years. Its Medicare margin percentage is positive compared to 59% of all hospitals in 2003 that had negative Medicare margins (i.e., paid less than the cost of caring for Medicare patients). Medicare margins have dropped every year since 1998, as the Medicare Payment Advisory Commission (MedPAC) correctly predicted continued margin compression with an estimated overall Medicare margin of negative 1.5% through 2005–2006.

Its mix of surgical to total admissions is also very attractive at 32%. It is hard to find anything unattractive about this hospital's operation. Operating performance this good and this consistent over this long a period is rarely seen. Every one of these operating metrics exceeds the maximum for every hospital rated by Moody's for 2003 and for the last 5-year average. There is no other hospital rated by Moody's that has achieved these operating metrics.

			Moody's Investors Service			
	2003	5-Year Average	Maximum	Aa Median	A Median	Baa Median
Operating margin	14.5%	14.4%	12.4%	3.3%	2.2%	0.0%
Excess margin	17.2%	16.9%	14.5%	7.3%	4.5%	1.7%
Operating cash flow margin	23.6%	23.2%	19.2%	11.2%	9.5%	7.1%

Payor Mix		
Medicare	25.7%	23.9%
Medicaid	16.4%	15.3%
Managed care	39.7%	42.2%
Commercial	2.7%	4.0%
Self-pay	15.5%	14.5%

Valley Medical Center holds a strong managed care position. Most managed care contracts are favorable discounts from charges ranging from 3% to 12%. The hospital contracts with every major managed care payor in the market except Kaiser. The hospital avoids contracting with Kaiser for strategic purposes. No single managed care contract dominates; the highest volume managed care contract contributes only 7.6% of total hospital revenue.

Top 10 Managed Care Contracts	Percentage of Revenue	Discount
United Healthcare	7.6%	10%
Cigna	5.2%	7%
PacifiCare	4.7%	20%
Blue Cross National	4.0%	DRG
Sloan's Lake	3.6%	10%
Aetna	1.9%	12%
Blue Cross HMO	1.7%	12%
Blue Cross PPO	1.6%	DRG
Great West/One Health	1.0%	7%
PHCS	0.8%	3%

COMMITTED MEDICAL STAFF

Valley Medical Center maintains a unique medical staff model that requires physician commitment to the hospital and creates unusually high physician loyalty. This commitment is demonstrated in several ways; most significantly, physicians cannot take patients from the primary market to any other hospital. The commitments physicians make to the hospital seek to align the benefits of staff privileges with the needs of the community and the hospital. At present, this unusual model is serving the hospital well; it is currently set to sunset in 10 years.

GOOD GOVERNANCE

The hospital is supported by a governance structure tied to the community. The membership of its nonprofit corporation is composed of state residents who have contributed at least $10,000 to the hospital's foundation and the board of directors. The board of directors is composed of 14 members—six appointed by the membership, six appointed by the board of directors, and two ex officio (medical staff president and hospital president). Board members are appointed for 6-year terms. This distribution of governance powers has served the hospital well, keeping it focused on the needs of the community, keeping a strong management team in place, and avoiding distracting entanglements with other interests.

HIGHER LEVERAGE

When the proposed bonds are issued, leverage, expressed in terms of debt to total capital, will be about 62%. Debt to total capital of 62% is within the range of credits in the A and Baa Moody's rating categories; it is 1.99 standard deviations above the mean for A rated credits and 0.67 standard deviations above the mean for Baa credits. Thus, while the initial debt to total capital ratio will exceed the median for investment-grade credits, it is well within the observed range for investment-grade credits; it would not even be considered an outlier in the Baa rating category.

Studies show no correlation between debt service coverage and leverage. Higher leverage may be associated with higher risk when debt service coverage is also low. However, when the hospital's leverage is expected to be highest, at 62%, debt service coverage is projected at 10.6 times. The lowest forecast debt service coverage is 3.4 times when debt to total capital is forecast to be about 51%. Investment grade ranges for debt service coverage are from 0.4 to 16.7 for the A category and from 5.4 to 11.2 for the Baa category. When this debt is issued, Platte

Valley Medical Center's leverage and coverage fit comfortably in the Baa rating category and are not outside the ranges observed in the A rating category.

UNDER 100 BEDS

Hospitals under 100 beds are not commonly rated in the investment-grade categories. Moody's expresses the view that smaller providers "tend to be more vulnerable to unexpected operating challenges, such as key physician departures, shifts in demographics, and competitive threats." Valley Medical Center has unique protections from these threats. Its committed medical staff model makes it less vulnerable to key physician departures because it is less likely that the patients of a departing physician will be moved to a competing hospital. For the foreseeable future, shifts in demographics are driven by the economic development around the international airport and they are overwhelmingly positive. Competitive threats are minimized by the unique natural market protections along with the committed medical staff model.

The profile commonly typifying hospitals under 100 beds is rural with little or no growth. The profile for Valley Medical Center is exactly the opposite.

NOT A SYSTEM

Valley Medical Center is a stand-alone hospital, not affiliated with a hospital system. As such, the credit risk is not spread to any other markets; it is concentrated on the international airport market. In the event this market becomes inadequate to meet debt service requirements, the hospital will almost certainly become an attractive acquisition candidate for most any of the hospital systems in the big city. Its market position would be highly complementary to any of these hospital systems.

LOTS OF CASH

Valley Medical Center has accumulated a great deal of cash. Cash balances amounted to $49.4 million at December 31, 2003 and represented 480 days of expenses. This compares to the Standard & Poor's medians of 211 days for AA hospital credits, 159 days for A hospital credits, and 110 days for BBB hospital credits. These cash balances, coupled with the project debt service reserve fund, represent unusual levels of protection against any downturns in operating performance.

FORECAST

Valley Medical Center has developed a 5-year financial forecast that encompasses the proposed project. Key ratios include

	2004	2005	2006	2007	2008
Admission growth	8.5%	3.6%	3.7%	3.8%	6.0%
Operating margin	10.7%	10.1%	12.2%	4.3%	5.5%
Net margin	12.6%	16.9%	21.3%	10.1%	10.1%
Earnings before interest 11.8%		11.4%	13.3%	12.2%	12.6%
EBID margin	20.1%	19.6%	21.1%	23.4%	22.9%
Debt service coverage	10.7	11.7	14.6	3.4	3.5%
Days of cash on hand	517	567	485	468	491
Debt to total capital	61.7%	58.0%	53.9%	51.3%	48.8%

NOT SPECULATIVE

This project is not speculative; current revenues are adequate to provide more than 1.7 times coverage of pro forma maximum annual debt service. This coverage does not count on the future growth driven by development around the international airport or market share growth driven by the more favorable location in the market, the additional bed capacity, and a modern facility. All of these factors are solid and significant and will positively affect the revenues of Valley Medical Center.

Further, liquidity is high and is forecast to remain at high levels—the lowest forecast level for cash is 468 days of cash in 2007. This high level of liquidity along with the debt service reserve fund provides good protection against possible future blips.

Strengths:
Strong market growth
Dominant market position
Protected market position
Strong operating performance
Strong managed care position
Physician loyalty
Lots of cash
Weaknesses:
Under 100 beds
Not a system

SOLUTION CONSIDERATIONS FOR THE VALLEY MEDICAL CENTER

Sources	
Equity	$17,000
Fixed rate tax-exempt bonds	76,075
Variable rate tax-exempt bonds	11,415
Original issue discount	−804
Earnings on construction fund	1532
Total	$105,218

Uses	
Hospital project	$89,570
Medical office building project	7470
Debt service reserve fund	7358
Issuance costs	825
Total	$105,218

KEY ISSUES

How important to hospital capital structure and formation are the following:

Source of assets?
Use of assets?
Credit ratings?
Market share?
Market metrics and benchmarking?

What additional issues should a hospital team consider in order to successfully transform a 50-bed hospital into a 70-bed medical center?

Hospital Product Markets

- What, if any, are the impacts of terminology vagaries on the definition of a hospital product market?
- What are the definitional impacts on competition for medical services provided by hospitals?
- What developments have there been in economic theory with regard to defining hospital product markets?
- How do payors (including employers) define hospital product markets?
- What data are available to assist in the formulation of an appropriate hospital product market?
- How do patients and physicians define hospital product markets?
- What developments have there been in economic theory with regard to defining hospital geographic markets?
- Assuming definitional stability, what data are available to assist in the formulation of an appropriate geographic hospital market?
- Do hospitals in more concentrated markets charge higher prices?
- Does the structure and performance relationship differ for not-for-profit and proprietary hospitals?

Acute Care Hospitals

- What correlation is there between fiscal capital formation efficiency measures and the actual measures that are implemented in an acute care hospital?
- Have discounts secured from acute care hospitals by managed care payors resulted in higher prices for other payors or for capital acquisition?
- What evidence is there that acute care hospitals in concentrated markets lead to higher prices?
- What evidence is there that ease of capital acquisition and formation in concentrated acute care hospital markets have led to changes in the breadth and quality of medical services?
- What evidence is there that concentrated acute care hospital markets have slowed the rate of managed care penetration?

Specialty Hospitals

- What factors drive the unbundling of inpatient acute care hospital medical and/or surgical services in specialty hospitals?
- What have been the effects of unbundling medical services for specialty focused hospitals?
- Has quality of medical care been enhanced as "focused specialty hospital factories" have emerged?
- Have costs and access increased or decreased in specialty hospitals?
- How has competition been affected by general inpatient acute care hospitals, the single-specialty hospital, and for services provided only by the general inpatient hospital?
- Is the development of a general acute care hospital any different than the emergence of specialized hospitals for children, rehabilitation, psychiatry, or the elderly?

- What actions have general inpatient hospitals taken in response to the emergence of competition from single-specialty hospitals?
- Do any of these actions involve anticompetitive conduct or capital formation compression?

Hospital Networks

- How prevalent are local geographic hospital networks or RBACs?
- What does competitive economic theory indicate about the circumstances under which hospital networks are likely to emerge?
- When are hospital network arrangements likely to be procompetitive and when are they likely to be anticompetitive?
- How do traditional antitrust concepts address the forms of anticompetitive conduct potentially likely to emerge in a health care setting?
- What implications for merger and acquisition potential does the existence of such network conduct have?

CHECKLIST 1: Credit Scoring

In order to decide if the timing is right for a hospital capital investment, consider the following issues to determine whether the competitive market is favorable or unfavorable.

	YES	NO	Favorable	Unfavorable
Is the market favorable?	o	o		
Location and ease of transportation access			o	o
Population and population growth; growing, stable, or declining			o	o
Sociodemographic profile (age mix, wealth indicators)			o	o
Business environment			o	o
Is it growing?	o	o		
Market share			o	o
Is it growing?	·o	o		
Is product line market share growing?	o	o		
Market dominance			o	o
Epidemiological information			o	o
Sources of competition			o	o
Are there freestanding physician-owned hospitals in the area?	o	o		
Are there ambulatory surgery centers in the area?	o	o		
Are there other outpatient services in the area?	o	o		
Out-migration			o	o
Competition and characteristics of competitors			o	o
CON			o	o
Rate regulation			o	o
Disproportionate share pools (net payor/receiver)			o	o
Use rates			o	o
Is the payor environment favorable?	o	o		
Payor dominance			o	o
Fractured payor market			o	o
Financial performance of payors			o	o
Provider-sponsored managed care organizations			o	o

Exclusive contracting		o	o
Payor methodology		o	o
Rate increases		o	o
Payor relations		o	o
Payor mix and payor mix trends		o	o
Profitability by payor		o	o
Is the medical staff situation favorable?	o	o	
Size and breadth of medical staff		o	o
Turnover of medical staff		o	o
Average age of total and active medical staff		o	o
Number and growth of active physicians		o	o
Top 10 admitters and percentage of admissions		o	o
Loyalty of medical staff (percentage of splitters)		o	o
Physician supply		o	o
Are the quality considerations favorable?	o	o	
Mortality indicators (product line, if available)		o	o
CMI adjusted ALOS		o	o
JCAHO scores		o	o
NCQA scores for provider-sponsored HMO		o	o
Patient satisfaction scores		o	o
Medical errors prevention programs		o	o
Clinical resource utilization		o	o
Formulary standardization		o	o
Clinical pathways		o	o
Is the financial performance favorable?	o	o	
Revenue growth		o	o
Operating margin		o	o
Earnings before interest margin		o	o
Profit margin		o	o
Return on equity		o	o
Return on capital		o	o
Return on assets		o	o
Salaries and benefits percent of operating revenue		o	o
Bad debt percentage of operating revenue		o	o
Pro forma maximum annual debt service coverage		o	o
Maximum annual debt service coverage		o	o
Annual debt service coverage		o	o
Pro forma maximum annual debt service to operating revenue		o	o
Maximum annual debt service to operating revenue		o	o
Is the balance sheet strength favorable?	o	o	
Days of cash on hand		o	o
Cash to debt		o	o
Days of revenue in accounts receivable		o	o
Average payment period		o	o
Debt to total capital		o	o
Debt to total assets		o	o
Pro forma debt to total assets		o	o
Debt to cash flow		o	o
Pro forma debt to cash flow		o	o
Average age of plant		o	o

BIBLIOGRAPHY

Beckham, D. How hospital leaders can harness luck. *Health and Health Care Networks*. Health Forum Inc. of the American Hospital Association, Chicago, September 2011.

Combes, J. Hospital governance at a cross roads. *Health and Health Care Networks*. Health Forum Inc. of the American Hospital Association, Chicago, October 2011.

DeWeert, F. *Bank and Insurance Capital Management*. John Wiley & Sons, New York, 2010.

DeWeert, F. *Essentials of Corporate and Capital Formation*. John Wiley & Sons, New York, 2010.

Halley, M.D. Engaging physicians in operational governance. *Hospitals & Health Networks*, pp. 1–2, July 11, 2011.

Lee, P.R. and Lamm, R.D. Europe's medical model. *N.Y. Times*, March 1, 1993.

Marcinko, D.E. and Hetico, H.R. *Dictionary of Health Economics and Finance*. Springer Publishing, New York, 2007.

Marcinko, D. (Editor). *Journal of Health Care Organizations and Financial Management Strategies*. iMBA Inc., Atlanta, GA, 2010.

4 Understanding Cash Flows and Medical Accounts Receivable

Monitoring, Management, and Improvement

David Edward Marcinko and Karen White

CONTENTS

Although providing high-quality care with improved health outcomes remains the primary concern of hospitals and medical entities of all sizes, geography, and demographics…money matters. The maxim "no margin, no mission" applies.

INTRODUCTION

It has been said that cash flows and accounts receivable (AR) are the lifeblood of any health care entity. Cash is the net amount of revenue generated by the health care organization during a particular period of time or "accounting interval." Cash flow analysis summarizes the effects of operating activities on cash balances during the accounting interval. In periods of rapid growth, increases in revenue may actually result in less cash and potential threats to corporate survival. This can occur upon acceptance of certain managed care or insurance contracts. On the other hand, compared to

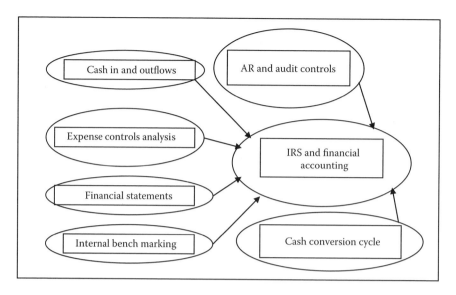

FIGURE 4.1   The hospital cash flow and AR accounting ecosystem.

other business sectors, health care organizations often have greater amounts of funds available to invest and, therefore, have different cash and AR management needs.

Accurate analysis of cash and AR allows the financial manager, hospital administrator, CXO, or physician executive to understand the effects of past strategic business decisions in quantitative form. The purpose of cash and AR analysis is to answer important questions such as

1. How much cash was generated by the health care entity?
2. How can a cash account be overdrawn when the accounting department said the clinic or hospital service segment was profitable?
3. How much was spent for new equipment and supplies, and where was the cash for the expenditures acquired?

Moreover, among other things, cash is used to

1. Generate positive future net cash flows and remain a viable economic health care entity
2. Meet hospital and health entity financial obligations
3. Generate hospital and medical entity profits and dividends

Most importantly, cash flow is then used to review past fiscal decisions and make a predictive leap into the economic future concerning—for example—the acceptance of Medicare, private health insurance, and various other managed care contract arrangements, or performing contingent account management, financial ratio analysis and benchmarking, AR management, new equipment purchases and staffing, or considering risky new service segments or servicing—The Affordable Care Act (ACA) of 2010.

The strategic managerial tool of cash flow and AR analysis allows the health care executive to evaluate revenues and more effortlessly make the translation to fixed reimbursement contractual remuneration and corporate health care. Figure 4.1 illustrates the components of AR and cash flow analysis.

Cash Flows and AR

Cash flow and AR analysis begins with financial statement analysis. Financial statements account for and report practice, clinic, or hospital economic activity for a specific accounting period through horizontal or linear analysis. Showing changes in this fashion forms a perspective for variances that have taken place. Yet, financial statements are, at best, only an approximation of economic reality because of the selective reporting of economic events by the accounting system, compounded by alternative accounting methods and estimates. The tendency to delay accounting recognition of some transactions and valuation changes means that financial statements tend to lag behind reality as well.

CONSOLIDATE FINANCIAL STATEMENTS

There are four financial statements:

1. *Net income statement (NIS)*, also known as the *statement of revenues and expenses* or the *statement of profit and loss*, reflects patient revenues and those medical expenses considered general overhead over a period of time. Smaller health care entities and medical practices may report income and expenses on a "cash accounting" basis, reflecting income actually received and expenses actually *paid*. However, in these practices, CPAs generally use "tax basis," which is a hybrid method of cash that adds depreciation as required by the IRS. The accrual method of accounting records expenses when they are *incurred* and income when *earned*, not when paid or received as in the cash method. The cash method is easier, but the accrual method is more accurate and most surgical practices use this method.

2. *Balance sheet (BS)* or *statement of financial position* reports fixed assets such as furniture, instruments, durable medical equipment (DME), and property. Current assets include those that can be converted into cash within a short period of time, such as AR, checking accounts, and money funds. Intangible assets include goodwill. Longer term assets are those that cannot be converted into cash so quickly. Accounts payable (AP) and current liabilities are short-term debts and notes, whereas long-term liabilities are loans repaid over many years. The last category reflects ownership in the form of retained earnings or equity and represents the difference between total assets and total unit liabilities unit.

   Net working capital of the balance sheet is the difference between current assets and current liabilities. The lower the net working capital, the more economically efficient the care provided. Some important ratios include those below:

   a. *Days sales outstanding* = AR/(net sales/365). Year-end receivables net of allowances for doubtful accounts, plus financial receivables divided by net sales per day. A decrease in days sales outstanding (DSO) represents an improvement in cash flows, whereas an increase represents deterioration. The hospital industry average is about 35 days.

   b. *Days payable outstanding* = AP/(total expenses [less depreciation and amortization]/365). Year-end payables divided by expenses per day. An increase in days payable outstanding (DPO) is an improvement, whereas a decrease is not. Payables exclude accrued expenses. Hospital industry average is about 24 days.

   c. *Days inventory outstanding* = Inventory/(net sales/365). Year-end inventories divided by sales per day. A decrease in days inventory outstanding (DIO) is an improvement, whereas an increase may be a sales deterioration. Hospital industry average is about 6 days.

d. *Days working capital* = (AR + inventory − AP)/(net sales/365). Year-end net working capital (service receivables plus inventory, minus AP) divided by sales per day. The lower the better. The hospital industry average is about 15 days.

3. *Statement of cash flows (SCFs)* summarizes the effects of cash on three activities:

a. *Operating* activities include cash inflows (receipts, interest, and dividends) and outflows (inventory, supplies, and loans).

b. *Investing* activities include the disposal or acquisition of noncurrent assets such as equipment, loans, or marketable securities.

c. *Financial* activities generally include the cash inflow or outflow effects of transactions and other events such as issuing capital stock or notes involving creditors and physician owners.

The SCF concerns liquidity, as opposed to profitability, and may have accompanying schedules that help explain the aggregated figures in the primary document.

4. *Statement of shareholder equity* is also known as the *statement of changes in unrestricted net assets* for the year (public health care entities).

Hospitals, clinics, and medical practices may produce these financial accounting statements for individual employees, physicians, and/or hospitalists, the Securities and Exchange Commission (SEC), banks, venture capitalists, and governmental or other related regulatory entities. However, cash flow and revenue analysis is generally an internal matter.

HEALTH CARE CASH CONVERSION CYCLE (CCC)

The manager of a medical practice, clinic, or hospital's net working capital strives to optimize the amount of cash on hand to ensure daily operations. Too much cash generates little return, whereas too little may jeopardize the health care enterprise, incur borrowing costs, or cause missed investment opportunities. Moreover, the extent to which current assets cover current liabilities determines whether the entity is considered liquid and thus able to meet its payment obligations on time.

When faced with the management of current assets and current liabilities, the alternative with the highest net present value (NPV) and internal rate of return (IRR) is typically selected. This is often a difficult balancing act because providing health care services generates little immediate cash, and then cash receipts are variable depending upon payors or other third parties. Yet, each hospital or entity distribution transaction requires immediate liquid cash for employees, vendors, debt holders, and investors in the form of dividend payouts or retained earning disbursements.

The CCC length measured in days is composed of two ratios. The first is the *average inventory holding period* (ending inventory divided by revenues per day), and the second is the *collection period* (ending AR divided by revenue per day). For both ratios, faster is better.

Sample CCC for an industry-average hospital (49 days is about average for nonelectronic claims submission):

1. Hospital admission to patient discharge (about 6 days)
2. Patient discharge to hospital bill completion (about 6 days)
3. Hospital bill completion to insurance (third-party administrator [TPA]) payor receipt (about 5 days)
4. Receipt by TPA to mailing of hospital payment (about 26 days)
5. Payment mailed to receipt by hospital (about 3 days)
6. Payment receipt by hospital to bank deposit (about 3 days)

Naturally, health care managers, administrators, and hospital executives should be interested in motivating changes in the behavior of staff such that processes within the control of the enterprise can be streamlined and completed in less time. For example, a day or two of reductions in the amount of time it takes from patient discharge to hospital bill completion, as achieved with the use of electronic charts and medical records systems, can significantly increase cash flow. Likewise, the use of electronic funds transfers and/or lockbox collection mechanisms can reduce the amount of time it takes for an AR to make it into the bank.

CASH FLOW MANAGEMENT ISSUES

Cash flow management in a health care organization is the process of reviewing and chart-order writing and documentation, providing medical services, coding, billing, analyzing, posting, invoicing, health claims denial analysis, resubmitting claims, receiving, monitoring, and adjusting cash flows.

For any health care organization, a most important aspect of cash flow management is avoiding extended shortages caused by having too great a gap between cash inflows and outflows, steeply discounted insurance receipts, or variable managed care reimbursement contract information. A health care entity will not be able to stay in business if bills and liabilities are left unpaid for any extended length of time.

Therefore, cash flow analysis needs to be done on a regular, almost daily basis, and used for future forecasting so that steps can be taken to head off cash flow problems. Many legacy computer software accounting and enterprise resource planning (ERP) programs, have built-in reporting features that make cash flow analysis for health care entities increasingly automated, typically using applications from Perot Systems, McKesson, Per-Se Technologies, Lawson, Citrix Systems, HEALTHsuites®, Ross Enterprise ERP, FACTS Claims Encounters, SAP, and the like.

As an example of improved turnaround using the new Microsoft Dynamics GP health care application service, the Facey Medical Foundation—a California nonprofit health care system serving more than 160,000 patients annually—improved cash flows, inventory management, budgeting, and purchasing along its entire enterprise-wide business process. Similarly, the Talbert Medical Group, an independent, physician-owned primary care and multispecialty medical group in Costa Mesa, CA, improved cash flow reporting, streamlined its business processes, and reduced costs by 40%.

Moreover, these newer ERP accounting systems increasingly contain electronic signatures and audit trail features that not only speed cash flow, but reduce fraud and abuse potential as well.

- *Electronic signatures.* The electronic signature module helps health care organizations improve security and enhance data validation by providing the ability to enforce dual signature authorization in addition to the capture of preformatted reason code information and text comments during system transaction activity.
- *Audit trails.* Audit trail capabilities provide tracking, tracing, and reporting accountability capabilities. With audit trails, health care organizations can capture and archive changes to all electronic data and documents required for maintaining regulatory compliance through features including before and after transactional information, user ID, and time and date stamps.

The second step of cash flow management is to develop and use strategies that will maintain an adequate cash flow. A most useful strategy is to shorten the cash flow conversion cycle (from AR to cash) as much as possible so that cash turnaround is expeditious.

ACCOUNTS RECEIVABLE

Doctors generate a patient account or an AR at the same time as they send the patient a bill or the insurance company a claim. AR are treated as current assets (cash equivalents) on the health care entity balance sheet, and usually with a percentage markdown to reflect historic collectibles.

The *balance sheet* is a snapshot of a health care entity at a specific point in time. This contrasts with the *income statement* (profit and loss), which shows accounting data across a period of time. The balance sheet uses the accounting formula

Assets (what the entity owns) = Liabilities (what the entity owes) + Practice Equity (what is left over)

According to the *Dictionary of Health Economics and Finance* (Marcinko and Hetico 2007, 2008), an AR aging schedule is a periodic report (30, 60, 90, 180, or 360 days) showing all outstanding AR identified by patient or payor, and month due. The average duration of an AR is equal to total claims divided by AR. Faster is better, of course, but it is not unusual for a hospital to wait 6, 9, 12 months, or more, for payment.

Each of these measures seeks to answer two questions:

1. How many days of revenue are tied up in AR?
2. How long does it take to collect AR?

An important measure in the analysis of accounts receivable is the AR ratio, AR turnover rate, and average days receivables, expressed by these formulas:

1. *AR Ratio* = Current AR balance/Average monthly gross production (suggested between about 1–5 for hospitals)
2. *AR Turnover Rate* = AR balance/Average monthly receipts
3. *Average Days Receivable* = AR balance/Daily average charges (suggested <100 days for medical practices).

Other significant measures include

1. *Collection Period* = AR/Net patient revenue/365 days
2. *Gross Collection Percentage* = Clinic collections/Clinic production (suggested >45%– 85% for hospitals)
3. *Net Collection Percentage* = Clinic collections/Clinic production – (minus) Contractual adjustments (suggested >75%–79% for medical practices)
4. *Contractual Percentage* = Contractual adjustments/Gross production (suggested <45%– 55% for hospitals)

Often, older AR are often written off or charged back as *bad-debt expenses* and never collected at all.

TYPE OF HEALTH CARE AR

There are three general types of medical AR:

1. Mainstream
2. Non-mainstream
3. Those not acceptable for third-party financing or related asset protection strategies

Mainstream AR

Mainstream AR are those due from third-party payors, which include categories such as Medicare, Medicaid, commercial insurance, private insurance, HMO/PPO, and related managed care plans. The average time to collect for most of these AR ranges from 100 to 180 days.

Non-Mainstream AR

With non-mainstream AR, the payors are actually other health care facilities themselves, such as nursing homes or hospitals, where the provider client is contracting services to the health care facility. Related types of non-mainstream AR include personal injury, no-fault, and worker's compensation.

Not-Acceptable AR

Not-acceptable AR are owed by patients directly (self-pay, some retail and concierge practices). In addition, certain types of longer turning worker's compensation, personal injury, and no-fault AR are not useful for most third-party financing strategies.

AR as Exposed Financial Assets

Even though it is not unusual to have AR in the range of a hundred thousand dollars or more, they can be easily attached by creditors because AR are known as "exposed" assets. A judgment creditor pursuing a doctor for a claim may pursue the assets of the clinic, and AR and cash are the most vulnerable assets. AR are as good as cash to a creditor, who usually has to do no more than seize them and wait a few months to collect them. If a creditor seizes AR, the practice, medical clinic, or health care entity may be hard pressed to pay its bills as they become due. One must therefore be vigilant to protect AR assets from lawsuit creditors.

Proactive AR Monitoring

The best way to manage AR problems is to avoid them in the first place by implementing a good system of AR control. This may be done with a *patient payment expectation policy*. Expectations are an important element of any business. Physicians who set payment expectations tend to have more satisfied patients. The key is to make sure that the patients know the expectations beforehand as there are several elements to consider when adopting these types of payment policies.

1. Find out what will work for your specific health care entity setting. Is there an ATM nearby; should the patient pay at the end of the visit or before service is rendered; will there be any penalties for postponing a co-pay, etc.
2. If substantial debt is built up, will the patient still be seen? At what point is the patient turned over to collections?
3. Keep in mind legal and ethical issues (i.e., emergencies).
4. After policies are in place, make sure that the staff is aware and ready to keep up the standard.
5. The policies need to be clear to the patients through mailings, the practice's Web site, signs posted in the facility, etc.

Nevertheless, poor AR control occurs because the doctor and/or hospital is too busy treating patients, or the front office or administrative staff does not have or follow a good system of AR control. Answering the following questions may help upgrade a system of AR control:

1. Is an AR policy in place for the collection of self-pay accounts (de minimus/de maximus amounts, annual percentage rate [APR], terms, penalties, etc.)?

2. Do employees receive proper AR, bad debt, and follow-up training within legal guidelines?
3. Are AR exceptions approved by the doctor, office manager or insurance/accounting department, or do they require individual scrutiny?
4. Are AR policies in place for dealing with hardship cases, pro bono work, co-pay waivers, discounts, or no-charges?
5. Are collection procedures within legal guidelines?
6. Are AR policies in place for dealing with past due notices, telephone calls, dunning messages, collection agencies, small claims court, and other collection methods?
7. Are guidelines in place for handling hospital, clinic, or medical practice consultations, unpaid claims, refiling of claims, and appealing claims?
8. Are office AR policies periodically revised and reviewed, with employee input?
9. Does the doctor, practice, clinic, or hospital agree with and support the guidelines?

THREE MODERN PATIENT ACCOUNT COLLECTIONS RULES

The following medical practice procedures will markedly increase up-front office collections and reduce AR:

1. Train staff to handle exceptions. What is your policy if the patient payment is significant? Will you allow 25% payments—one today and three over the next 3 months? Communicate your *patient payment expectation policy* to all staff. What will you do if a patient shows up without an insurance card? There will be other exceptions. Train employees to call the appropriate administrator, manager, or practice-management contact when an exception does not fit in the categories you provide and make sure those managers are responsive.
2. Understand that not everyone will shine in collections. The value of this new front-desk function should be reflected in job descriptions and wages. Track staff performance and hold employees accountable for collection goals. The most successful practices collect in the 90% range.
3. Provide professional signage that states your basic policy. "Payments are due at time of service." Avoid typewritten, lengthy explanations taped to walls or desks that look like clutter.

ASSESSMENT

As we have seen, cash flow and AR are the lifeblood of any health care entity and may come from patients, health insurance and third-party managed care contracts, the federal and state governments, Medicare, HMO business contracts, and other sources. Although there are several different types of cash flow and AR analysis, they all focus on the internal generation of funds available to owners, investors, and creditors.

CONCLUSION

The AR management and cash flow analysis techniques or the chapter can be used to make probability calculations and improve predictive business modeling, which is an important decision-making skill for all contemporary health care financial and managerial staff, physicians, and nurse-executives.

CASE MODEL 4.1: THE MACKENZIE HOSPITAL CLINIC

The Mackenzie Hospital Clinic was offered a private fixed-rate contract that would increase revenues by $50,000 for the next fiscal year. The clinic's 30% gross margin would not change because of the new business. However, $10,000 would be added to overhead expenses for another part-time assistant. More importantly, the AR collection time would be lengthened to 1 year, or paid at the end of the contract period.

The cost of services provided for the contract represents the amount of money needed to service the patients produced by the contract. Because gross margin is 30% of revenues, the cost of services is 70% or $35,000.

The financial manager had to decide whether there would be enough internally generated cash flow to accept the contract.

He knew that adding the extra overhead would result in $45,000 of new spending money (cash flow) needed to care for the patients. He had to further refine his calculations by dividing the $45,000 total by the number of days the contract extends (i.e., 365 days) to determine that the new contract would cost about $123.29 per day of cash flow. Now the financial manager had to ask—Where would the money come from?

He was reluctant to turn away any business for the clinic, so he decided he must develop other methods to generate the additional cash. He made the following suggestions:

- Extend AP timelines and reduce AR times
- Borrow with short-term bridge loans or a line of credit
- Discuss the situation with vendors for longer or more favorable terms
- Do not stop paying corporate taxes.

KEY ISSUES

1. Using the framework reflected in this chapter, consider what changes the Mackenzie Hospital Clinic might implement to ensure that it regularly makes good cash management, budgeting, and risk projection decisions.
2. If the Mackenzie Hospital Clinic is successful and attracts more long-term managed care fixed contracts, the serious nature of the cash flow problem becomes apparent. For instance, adding another nine contracts would multiply the above example tenfold. In other words, the clinic would increase revenues to $1 million with the same 70% cost of services and $100,000 increases in operating overhead expenses.
   - How much free cash flow would be required?
     (Using identical mathematical calculations, we determine that $450,000/365 days equals $1,232.88 per day of needed new cash flow.)
   - What happens if the contract only pays off at the end of the year?

CHECKLIST 1: Cash Flow Management Concepts	YES	NO
Determine if the following cash flow management concepts are appropriate for your health care organizations:		
Am I a cash flow manager?	o	o
If you answer NO—Is there a cash flow audit committee in place?	o	o
If you answer YES—Do I know my department's cash flow amount, timing, and recent changes?	o	o
Do I know how much working capital is available to my department?	o	o
– Are all significant department activities covered in my budget that affect working capital?	o	o
– Do I understand my department's working capital budget activities?	o	o
– Are cash management tools available to me?	o	o
– If so, do I use and understand them?	o	o
– Is the exposed working capital amount too much?	o	o
– Is the exposed working capital amount too little?	o	o
– Can I collect the cash accounts more efficiently?	o	o
Has my health care department evaluated its CCC in-house and complied with legal limitations?	o	o
If not, has the CCC been outsourced?	o	o
If it has been outsourced, do I have control over its turnover rate?	o	o
Am I aware of its cost?	o	o
Is the CCC electronic or traditional paper claims?	o	o
Are all CCCs transactions in compliance with generally accepted accounting principles (GAAP), and HIPAA privacy standards?	o	o
Is there a HIPAA business associate agreement in place for outsourced cash flow management duties?	o	o
If not, is an auditor or supervisor regularly informed of this privacy information?	o	o
Am I aware of the external sources available to me or my department for short-term financing?	o	o
Do I know the criteria used when investing the short-term cash of my department?	o	o
Am I in control of corporate/departmental cash?	o	o
Do I understand the importance of a cash budget?	o	o
Do I know why we need to hold or disperse cash?	o	o
Do I know where departmental cash is generated and/or spent?	o	o
Do I have cash budgeting authority?	o	o
Do I understand the best cash management strategy for my department or health care organization?	o	o
Have I evaluated my cash flow management fiduciary responsibilities to the company?	o	o
Do I know the cost of capital?	o	o

CHECKLIST 2: Operational Methods to Increase Cash Flow	YES	NO
Are collection policies prominent		
– For co-pays and deductibles, so patients know that payment is due at the time services are rendered?	o	o
– On vendor statements, so that they have a written copy of hospital policies with every invoice?	o	o
Does the health care entity have systems in place for the following:		
– Receiving payments through electronic funds transfers (EFT) or checks mailed into a lockbox?	o	o
– Checking scanners with direct bank deposit capability?	o	o
– Delaying all AP until due dates (stretch them but do not accelerate them)?	o	o
– Checking for penalties?	o	o
– Using banks in remote parts of the city to increase payment "float" time?	o	o
– Monitoring bank deposits and disbursement on a daily basis?	o	o
– Coordinating insurance benefits (because some patients do not immediately pay unless the facility collects the co-pay up front)?	o	o
– Maintaining credentialing files to flag patients covered by numerous insurance plans?	o	o
– Tracking plan, provider, and renewal status?	o	o

	YES	NO
– Creating separate accounts (especially in OB/GYN and pediatric cases because unwed birth provision and typical divorce judgments include provisions that hold both parents equally responsible for the health care bills of their children)?	o	o
– Reconciling claim submissions every day?	o	o
– Using electronic claims, computerized physician order entry, and other health care information technology systems to the extent possible?	o	o
– Regularly updating patient contact information according to HIPAA guidelines?		
Can we lengthen payroll periods for salary and wages?	o	o
Do I invoice patients		
– Daily?	o	o
– As soon as ancillary costs are recorded within the global surgical period?	o	o
– When they are released to the insurer?	o	o
Do we ever follow an individual patient's path to ensure that all charges have been filed?	o	o
Because a health care entity may lose up to 25% of revenues through improper coding, do I		
– Update ICD-9 or ICD-10 codes?	o	o
– Use a certified medical coder?	o	o
– Have the doctor or medical care provider directly provide the procedural code to the insurance staff?	o	o
Do we really know Medicare policy, rules, and regulations?	o	o
Do we have a copy of the most current *Medicare Provider Manual* (www.CMS.gov)?	o	o
Do I read the monthly *Medicare News*?	o	o
Do I understand the *CMS Correct Coding Initiative*?	o	o
Do we copy both sides of drivers' licenses and insurance cards for coverage verification and personal identification?	o	o

CHECKLIST 3: Accelerating the Cash Conversion Cycle	YES	NO
Do we use interim billing for long hospital admissions?	o	o
Do we use advanced deposits for elective or nonemergent admissions?	o	o
Do we obtain preadmission insurance verification?	o	o
Do we prepare bills during hospitalization and not at discharge?	o	o
Do we ensure physician completion of medical records in a timely fashion?	o	o
Do we deliver bills to postal authorities daily?	o	o
Do we use electronic billing where available?	o	o
Do we submit deductible and co-payment invoices at discharge?	o	o
Do we use discount programs for prompt payment?	o	o
Do we use dunning letters and telephone calls for collections?	o	o
Do we follow up quickly to TPA request for additional billing information?	o	o
Do we claim bad debt on Medicare deductibles and co-payments?	o	o

CHECKLIST 4: Financial Manager Knowledge Base	YES	NO
Am I confident of my knowledge of the following total organization margin percentages?		
– Operating margin	o	o
– Nonoperating margin	o	o
– Deductible ratio	o	o
– Markup ratio	o	o
– Return on total assets	o	o
Am I confident of my knowledge of the following liquidity ratios?		
– Current ratio	o	o
– Average payment period	o	o
– Days cash on hand	o	o
– Days in AR	o	o
Am I confident of my knowledge of the following capital structure ratios?		
– Equity financing	o	o
– Long-term debt to equity	o	o
– Fixed asset turnover	o	o
– Cash flow to debt	o	o
– Capital expenses	o	o
– Long-term debt per bed	o	o
– Times interest earned	o	o
Am I confident of my knowledge of the following asset efficiency indicators?		
– Total asset turnover	o	o
– Fixed asset turnover	o	o
– Current asset turnover	o	o
– Net fixed assets per bed	o	o
Am I confident of my knowledge of the following hospital volume indicators?		
– Beds	o	o
– Discharges	o	o
– Discharges per bed	o	o
– Patient days	o	o
– Occupancy rate	o	o
– Average length-of-stay (LOS)	o	o
– Medicare LOS	o	o
– Medicaid LOS	o	o
– Indemnity LOS	o	o
– Managed Care Organization LOS	o	o
– Payor mix	o	o
Am I confident of my knowledge of the following hospital pricing indicators?		
– Price per discharge	o	o
– Salaries per discharge	o	o
– Costs per discharge	o	o
– FTE staff per occupied bed	o	o
– Salary per FTE	o	o
– Facility wage index	o	o
Am I confident of my knowledge of the following profit indicators?		
– Profit per discharge	o	o
– Total margin	o	o
– Days cash on hand	o	o
– Long-term debt to equity	o	o
– Net price per discharge	o	o
– Capital cost per discharge	o	o

CHECKLIST 5: Financial Statements Knowledge Base	YES	NO
Am I confident of my knowledge of our hospital's balance sheet?		
– Fixed assets		
– Cash and equivalents	o	o
– Current assets	o	o
– AR	o	o
– Intangible assets	o	o
– Current liabilities	o	o
– AP	o	o
– Short-term liabilities	o	o
– Long-term liabilities	o	o
– Net working capital	o	o
– Hospital equity	o	o
Am I confident of my knowledge of our hospital's cash flow statement?		
– Operating activities	o	o
– Investing activities	o	o
– Financing activities	o	o
– Direct methodology	o	o
– Indirect methodology	o	o
– Profit margins	o	o
– Hospital efficiency	o	o
Am I confident of my knowledge of our hospital's net income statement?		
– Income sources and uses	o	o
– Expense sources and uses	o	o
– Adjustment to net income	o	o
– Accrual accounting method	o	o
– Cash accounting method	o	o
Am I confident of my knowledge of our hospital's statement of shareholder's equity?	o	o
Do I regularly read, review, and understand these financial statement entries?	o	o
– Footnotes		
– Management's Decision and Analysis of Financial Condition and Results of Operations (MD&A)	o	o

CASE MODEL 4.2: MEGA FEDERAL HOSPITAL CORPORATION

The MEGA Federal Hospital Corporation specializes in a certain type of high-risk heat coronary artery bypass graft surgery, with revenue as seen below

Description	GAAP	Tax
Capitation revenue received	$60,000,000	$60,000,000
Administrative costs (15%)	$9,000,000	$9,000,000
Net available to pay medical costs	$51,000,000	$51,000,000
Paid and reported claims at year end	$43,500,000	$43,500,000
Incurred but not reported (IBNR) claims	$7,500,000	$0
Profit/Income	**$0**	**$7,500,000**
Tax rate	35%	
Federal income tax due on IBNR	$2,625,000	

KEY ISSUES

Which of the following factors should have the greatest influence for MEGA Hospital Clinic in deciding whether to accept the contract?

- GAAP analysis
- IBNR deductions
- Pro forma estimates
- Reserve amounts
- Profit or loss
- Taxes refunded or due

SOLUTION

For a $60 million capitated contract, the MEGA Hospital did not profit and is responsible for a taxable income of $7,500,000. The $2,625,000 of taxes is payable to the Internal Revenue Service and is a direct reduction of the cash flow to the MEGA Hospital Corporation.

CHECKLIST 1: Balance Sheet AR Strategic Ratios	YES	NO
Are you aware of the following AR ratios for your health care entity?	o	o
If you answer YES:		
Do you know your entity's AR ratio?	o	o
Do you know your entity's AR turnover rate?	o	o
Do you know your entity's average days receivable length?	o	o
Do you know your entity's collection period length?	o	o
Do you know your entity's gross collection percentage rate?	o	o
Do you know your entity's net collection percentage rate?	o	o
Do you know your entity's contractual percentage rate?	o	o
Do you know your entity's bed-debt expense ratio?	o	o

CHECKLIST 2: PPMC Business Model Options	YES	NO
If a PPMC, what generational type of health care business entity is it?	o	o
First-generation national multispecialty entity?	o	o
Second-generation regional multispecialty entity?	o	o
Third-generation national single-specialty entity?	o	o
Fourth-generation regional single-specialty entity?	o	o
Fifth-generation Internet-enabled business-to-business (B2B) health care entity?	o	o
Sixth-generation Internet-enabled business-to-patient (B2P) health care entity?	o	o
Seventh-generation Internet-enabled business-to-consumer (B2C) health care entity?	o	o

CHECKLIST 3: AR Protection Strategies	YES	NO
Are you familiar with these AR protection strategies for your health care entity?	o	o
– Incorporation strategy	o	o
– Multiple corporation strategy	o	o
– Purchased AR strategy	o	o
– AR credit insurance strategy	o	o
– AR financing strategy	o	o
– AR factoring strategy	o	o
– AR leveraging strategy	o	o
– AR buy-in/buyout strategy	o	o

CHECKLIST 4: AR Credit Insurance	YES	NO
Does your health care entity have AR credit insurance?	o	o
If you answer YES:		
– Does it cover all the health care entity's AR?	o	o
– Does it cover a portion of the health care entity's AR?	o	o
– Does it cover the health care entity's designated AR only?	o	o
– Have you investigated the cost/benefits of AR credit insurance?	o	o
If you answer YES:		
– Is AR credit insurance helpful to the public investors of your health care entity?	o	o
– Is AR credit insurance helpful to the private investors of your health care entity?	o	o
– Is AR credit insurance helpful to your retail lenders or investment bankers?	o	o
– Is AR credit insurance dependent on the systemic/nonsystemic risks of your entity?	o	o
Have you identified your systemic health entity risks?	o	o
Have you identified your nonsystemic health entity risks?	o	o
Is AR insurance dependent on entity deductibles and premium?	o	o
Is AR credit insurance dependent on your health entity AR aging schedule?	o	o
Is there a limit or percentage amount of AR credit insurance for your health entity?	o	o
Is AR credit insurance premium cost dependent on your specific health care entity?	o	o
Is AR credit insurance premium cost dependent on systemic and nonsystemic risks?	o	o
Is AR credit insurance premium cost dependent on AR aging schedules?	o	o
Is AR credit insurance premium cost dependent on insurance amounts, etc.?	o	o

CHECKLIST 5: Internal AR Control	YES	NO
Do we check prenumbered patient encounter forms on a daily basis?	o	o
Should employees that post payments to AR open invoices?	o	o
Should employees who post payments to AR make bank deposit slips?	o	o
Do we reconcile patient sign-in sheets to the appointment book and either the daily report of charges or day sheet?	o	o
Do we review daily payment reports or the day sheet to detect any payments that may not have been posted?	o	o
Do we review contractual adjustments to make sure amounts appear reasonable after considering payor mix?	o	o
Do we track patient charge information on explanation of benefits to each ledger sheet and deposit slip?	o	o
Do we investigate any discrepancies?	o	o
Do we review patients' ledger cards for written-off balances?	o	o
Do we institute and police an account write-off bad-debt policy with signature authorization?	o	o
Do we issue a computer password to authorized personnel?	o	o
Are all entity employees bonded?	o	o
Is a manager authorized to sign checks?	o	o
Does an AR supervisor approve vendor invoices before signing checks?	o	o
Do we regularly review canceled-check endorsements and investigate irregularities?	o	o

CHECKLIST 6: AR Bad-Debt Expense Control	YES	NO
Do written AR collections guidelines exist for all third-party and self-pay accounts?	o	o
Are AR collection guidelines reviewed annually and revised periodically?	o	o
Are AR collection guidelines clearly detailed to serve as a reference to personnel?	o	o
Do clinic employees receive training on collection guidelines?	o	o
Do clinic employees receive training on collection guidelines after revisions?	o	o
Does management solicit suggestions for changes in policies and procedures?	o	o
Do AR guideline exceptions require the approval of management on a case-by-case basis?	o	o
Do self-pay AR guidelines allow monthly payments?	o	o
Do self-pay AR guidelines specify the maximum number of acceptable payments?	o	o
Do self-pay AR guidelines specify the minimum monthly acceptable payment?	o	o
Do AR collection guidelines specify actions taken if a patient or vendor misses a payment?	o	o
Does management support the AR collection guidelines, even with complaints?	o	o

CHECKLIST 7: Types of AR	YES	NO
Not all medical AR are appropriate for the various types of asset protection strategies. The following checklist will help determine appropriateness.		
Are you aware that "mainstream" AR are generated by health care service companies like the following third-party payors?	o	o
Medicare and Medicaid?	o	o
Commercial and private insurance?	o	o
HMOs, POSs, PPOs, and similar managed care plans?		
Are you aware that "non-mainstream" AR are generated by the following health care service company payors?	o	o
Hospitals, outpatient treatment centers, and health care facilities?	o	o
Medical clinics and ambulatory surgery centers?	o	o
Nursing homes and extended care centers?		
Are you aware that "not-acceptable" AR are generated from the following payor types?		
Self- and private-pay patients, retail clinics, and concierge medical practices?	o	o
Long-turnover worker's compensation, personal injury, and no-fault claims?	o	o

ACKNOWLEDGMENTS

To Dr. Gary L. Bode, CPA, MSA, CMP™, of the Institute of Medical Business Advisors, Inc., and Ross J. Fidler, of ACS—A Xerox Company—for technical assistance in the preparation of this chapter.

BIBLIOGRAPHY

Caffarini, K. Guidelines target safety of medical tourists. *American Medical News*. 51(25):19–20, 2008.

Dunn, R.T. Performance standards for coding professionals. Advance for Health Information Professionals. 2010. See http://health-information.advanceweb.com/common/editorial/editorial.aspx?CC=727.

Flareau, B. *Accountable Care Organizations*. Convurgent Publishing, New York, 2011.

H*Works (The Advisory Board). *Capturing Lost Revenues*. Advisory Board Company, Washington, D.C., 2001.

Marcinko, D.E. Cash flow analysis in medical practice. In: *The Business of Medical Practice*, edited by D.E. Marcinko. Springer Publishing, New York, 2011.

Marcinko, D.E. and Hetico, R.N. *Dictionary of Health Insurance and Managed Care*. Springer Publishing, New York, 2007.

Marcinko, D.E. and Hetico, R.N. *Dictionary of Health Economics and Finance*. Springer Publishing, New York, 2008.

Moore, N. F. Improving the revenue cycle process: Document imaging and shared access to scanned documents is essential to streamlined operations. (NAATP INSIGHTS) (Report): An article from *Behavioral Healthcare*. Vendome Group LLC, New York, 2010.

Petaschnick, J. Sr. (Editor). *HARA*. Aspen Publishers. (Fourth Quarter 2001). For further information, see www.advisoryboardcompany.com.

5 Appreciating the Impact of IBNR Claims on Hospital Revenue Cycles
Monitoring, Management, and Enhancement

David Edward Marcinko and Karen White

CONTENTS

The foundation of solid financial health for any medical entity lies in the effective management of the organization's incurred but not reported (IBNR) health care claims and revenue cycles (Figure 5.1). In practical terms, effective management means understanding the process and targeting the core of the revenue cycle in order to fine-tune and support fiscal health and business growth.

The particular IBNR health care claims control and revenue cycle management needs of any health care organizations arise for various reasons, including the following:

- Health care entities may self-insure professional liability risks to offset the current medical malpractice insurance crisis.
- Nonprofit health care entities must replace plants and equipment with cash or debt, not by issuing investor-owned equity funds.
- Hospital bonds and pension plans must be funded.
- Hospital donations, gifts, and endowment funds must be managed.

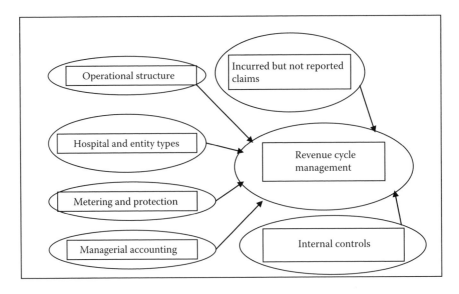

FIGURE 5.1   Hospital IBNR and revenue cycle accounting ecosystem.

THREE DOORS OF A HOSPITAL'S REVENUE CYCLE

Now that cash flows, financial statements, and accounts receivable (AR) have been reviewed in the preceding chapter, attention may be directed away from these financial accounting issues and focused more deeply on the managerial accounting issues of IBNRs and revenue cycle enhancement. Traditionally, the revenue cycle for a health care organization was divided into seven steps:

1. Patient eligibility and verification
2. Coinsurance payments and deductible capture
3. Billing, CPT® coding, and invoicing
4. Paper or e-claim submission
5. Remittance and/or explanation of benefits (EOB) advice
6. Patient billing statements
7. Patient payment options and mechanisms

Today, the processes of hospital revenue cycles are grouped into three areas corresponding to the journey of a patient through the system ("three doors"): the front door, the middle door, and the back door.

FRONT DOOR

Front-door processes are termed patient access functions and revolve around scheduling, registration, preadmission, and admissions. When these processes are streamlined and swift, the value is most evident to hospitals' customers, the patients, but it is also vital to the revenue maintenance (and enhancement) of the facility. The most effective and efficient time to accomplish patient access activities is when patients and their caregivers are together. Patient access needs to be handled by highly skilled and motivated employees who can accomplish a hospital's goals for information capture while carrying out customer service objectives. This is also the optimal stage for achieving denial management.

MIDDLE DOOR

Middle processes include case management (CM) and health information management (HIM). Those involved in the CM function act as gatekeepers to review the appropriateness of clinic referrals and ensure that financial clearance is established. CM also involves developing a plan for discharge and monitoring to ensure that it is timely and appropriate to the level of care. Another important focus of CM is the freeing up of acute care beds.

The HIM functions revolve around document management, coding, transcription, and charge capture. Financial performance can be significantly improved when CM and HIM activities are optimized by using information technologies that are integrated with process and workflow. The end result can be an increase in revenue and reduction in regulatory risk.

BACK DOOR

Back-door processes are termed patient financial services (PFSs) functions and revolve around billing, collections, follow-up, and resolution. These are the business office billing and administrative functions that support the front-line caregivers and that interface with external payers and patients to resolve outstanding AR. Back-door processes bring significant value to hospitals by reducing administrative costs, increasing collections levels, and dramatically lowering the percentage of aged receivables.

Hospitals seeking to improve their bottom lines through better-managed and enhanced revenue cycle operations in these three areas—front, middle, and back—usually encounter challenges with people, processes, and technology.

This chapter, therefore, examines ways of enhancing hospital revenues through the following managerial processes:

* Optimizing organizational structure
* Raising the bar through benchmarking
* Adopting technology

REVENUE ACCOUNTING RECOGNITION FOR HOSPITALS

Numerous generally accepted accounting principles (GAAP), the Financial Accounting Standards Board (FASB), the Government Accounting Standards Board (GASB), and Staff Accounting Bulletin (SAB) pronouncements from the Securities and Exchange Commission (SEC) control the hospital and health care industry. According to revenue recognition expert Harold S. Peckron, a distinction must be made as to whether the hospital is a for-profit, not-for-profit, or governmental entity. Examples follow.

FOR-PROFIT HOSPITALS

For-profit hospitals represent the smallest number in the health care industry (see www.aha.org).

If the hospital is a for-profit unit, it records revenues on the accrual basis and applies general for-profit GAAP guidelines under FASB Concepts Statement (CON) No. 5, *Recognition and Measurement in Financial Statements of Business Enterprises.*

If the for-profit hospital is publicly traded, certain provisions of SEC SAB No. 101, *Revenue Recognition in Financial Statements,* and SAB No. 104, *Revenue Recognition,* apply. SABs 101 and 104 discuss medical billings for third-party payers and reach the conclusion that collections must occur before revenue is recognized for the collection agent, not the hospital. For-profits may also be subject to the USA PATRIOT Act and the Sarbanes–Oxley Act, discussed in Chapter 7.

NOT-FOR-PROFIT HOSPITALS

Most hospitals in the health care industry are not for profit. Not-for-profits generate most of their revenues from patient services and, to a lesser degree, from grants or contributions. Such entities, unlike their for-profit cousins, use fund accounting since they report no shareholder equity but only the change in net assets.

FASB CON No. 4, *Objectives of Financial Reporting by Non-business Organizations,* FASB Statement No. 136, *Transfers of Assets to a Not-for-Profit Organization or Charitable Trust That Raises or Holds Contributions for Others* (dealing with pledges), and FASB Statement No. 117, *Financial Statements of Not-for-Profit Organizations,* assist in defining the revenue recognition basis, which, in large measure, is no different from the accrual basis of the for-profit hospital.

GOVERNMENTAL HOSPITALS

Many hospitals in the industry are military based (e.g., Walter Reed Army Medical Hospital in Washington, DC, or state hospitals) and are governed by the GASB. The GASB, under Statement No. 34, *Basic Financial Statements—and Management's Discussion and Analysis—for State and Local Governments* (amended by GASB Statements No. 35 and 37), recites the fund accounting aspects, including required supplementary information.

The GASB also allows the governmental hospital unit to apply *all* FASB pronouncements that are not in conflict with the GASB Statements.

GASB Statement 34 requires an expanded statement of revenues, expenses, and changes in net assets/equity and adopts the accrual basis in reporting revenues (GASB Statement No. 20, *Accounting and Financial Reporting for Proprietary Funds and Other Governmental Entities That Use Proprietary Fund Accounting*). Governmental hospitals must report revenues under GASB Statement 34 net of discounts and allowances by major source of revenue, with separate subtotals for operating revenues, expenses, and income or loss.

ALL HOSPITAL'S REVENUE SOURCES

Notwithstanding the above three-tiered classification scheme (for-profit, not-for-profit, or governmental) applied to hospital units, the primary revenue source is patient revenue. This revenue can be further viewed as routine service, premium service, resident service, and so forth, and is generally disclosed as operating revenue. To arrive at *net* patient revenue, all adjustments are then made, and third-party payers would be one such adjustment.

Revenue from third-party payers, even if the hospital uses a billing-collection agent (SABs 101 and 104), is realized and recognized revenue to the hospital notwithstanding the collection method. This is because of the adjustment that the third-party payer reimbursement makes, as an estimate, to the gross patient service revenue. Third-party payer revenue should be recognized at the time the service is rendered, at the hospital's customary adjusted rates.

REVENUE RECOGNITION FOR MEDICAL PRACTICES

As in any service business, cash flows, collections, and credit policy are paramount. Most medical practices report revenues upon tendering of the service, consistent with FASB CON No. 5, *Recognition and Measurement in Financial Statements of Business Enterprises*. However, despite this standard method of revenue recognition for both cash and third-party payer patients (which are similar to those in hospital accounting; see the discussion of hospital revenue recognition above), many dental, podiatric medical, osteopathic, and allopathic medical practices adopt the cash basis (not the accrual basis) for revenue recognition. This lends support to record keeping for tax preparation purposes, and the cash-basis records are generally converted to the accrual basis for loan or lease application purposes.

Medical practices treat third-party payers such as Medicaid and Medicare in much the same manner as do hospitals, with revenue recognition occurring at the time service is tendered, with an adjustment to revenues for experience with third-party payer payments and collectibility of direct billings to patients, resulting in net patient service revenue.

REVENUE CYCLE MANAGEMENT ISSUES

Any effective hospital revenue cycle management program should start by reviewing and negotiating automated third-party payer contracts to ensure adequate payment rates. Helpful health information technology system features include

- Patient registration and admitting systems that produce clean claims
- Effective management of patient documentation and accurate final code assignments
- Patient financial accounting systems that improve cash flows

MEDICARE REVENUE AUGMENTATION

Many hospitals have a Medicare utilization rate of 65% to 75% or higher for inpatient acute services and between 35% and 55% for outpatient services. Such levels of Medicare utilization underscore the revenue importance of having an effective Medicare payment program. Examples of measures that health care executives can take to reduce denials as well as improve and defend Medicare payments include

- Reviewing cost allocation statistics
- Requesting cost-finding changes
- Reviewing cost allocations to nonreimbursable cost centers
- Ensuring that all allowable costs that qualify for payment are claimed
- Identifying costs not allowed and excluding them
- Maintaining adequate documentation and controls
- Assigning costs to appropriate cost centers
- Capturing all qualifying Medicare bad-debt expenses

AVOIDING THE MEDICARE REVENUE FLOW CONUNDRUM

Hospital managers and administrators should closely monitor Medicare interim rates to identify factors that could indicate problems with Medicare revenue flow—particularly overpayments. This requires attentiveness to volume fluctuations, inpatient and outpatient shifts, price increases, cost increases and decreases, new cost centers, nonreimbursable cost centers, and so forth.

To effectively monitor Medicare revenue costs, hospital managers, Chief X Officers (CXOs), and nurse- or physician executives should

- Prepare interim cost reports
- Monitor interim rates on a monthly or quarterly basis
- Review financial statements for illogical or unreasonable trends

Unfortunately, hospitals and health care organizations that are overpaid may find it difficult to later repay Medicare program overpayments, thereby exacerbating the Medicare revenue flow conundrum.

OPTIMUM ORGANIZATIONAL STRUCTURE

The optimal organizational structure for hospital revenue cycle operations is one in which the leaders (or department managers) of the process areas—patient access, CM, HIM, and PFS—report to a director of revenue cycle management who in turn reports to the chief financial officer (CFO) of a hospital. It is important to have a single point of executive leadership in order to align the financial goals and objectives, as the annual Revenue Cycle Survey by the Healthcare Financial Management Association (HFMA) points out.

Results of this annual HFMA survey suggest that it is ideal to have a director of revenue cycle management (although this title varies among institutions). This structure does not increase the total number of direct reports for a CFO but provides a way to assemble the process areas of a hospital's revenue cycle under the finance arm. In smaller facilities (100 beds and under), the director of revenue cycle management may also fill one or more of the manager positions (patient access, CM, HIM, and PFS).

Financial bonus incentives for the director and managers should be based on meeting and exceeding revenue cycle goals and set and paid out yearly. If a member of this management team vacates the position prior to the end of the financial year, the bonus is not paid out.

FINANCIAL BENCHMARKING

As a general rule, comparison of results achieved incites the competitive nature of all human beings, not the least of whom are hospital employees. Add an opportunity for a financial incentive based on results, and a scenario for raising the bar materializes. Health care financial executives can access a number of sources for benchmarks throughout the industry: professional associations, the *Hospital Accounts Receivables Analysis (HARA)* report, vendors, hospital associations, and consulting firms, to name a few of the more robust sources.

For example, a 2008–2009 study by Solucient examined national performance benchmarks across four critical areas: quality of care, operational efficiency, financial performance, and adaptation to the environment.

The first step is to thoroughly assess each area of your hospital's revenue cycle in order to document the current baseline of performance (e.g., length of stay [LOS], facility admissions, patient days, outpatient visits, inpatient and outpatient surgeries, staffed beds).

Following that, comparison to the selected benchmark will indicate where performance sits relative to industry standards. For instance, one might use the following targets for different levels of coding expertise:

Type	Coding Specialist I	Coding Specialist II	Coder I	Coder II
Inpatient	>45 records daily	>32 records daily	>23 records daily	>15 records daily
Outpatients and ERs	2 min/chart or 250/day	2 min/chart or 250/day	3 min/chart or 160/day	4 min/chart or 120/day
Ambulatory surgery	3.5 min/chart or 130/day	4 min/chart or 120/day	6 min/chart or 80/day	8 min/chart or 60/day

Management, with active involvement by supervisory and frontline staff, then sets goals. Buy-in across revenue cycle operations is critical to acceptance by all those who will ensure that objectives are understood and that goals are reached and exceeded.

Because patient access encompasses the functional areas critical to "first-pass" success of the revenue cycle, it is prudent to focus on activities related to ensuring that all necessary patient information is collected up front accurately and—most important—only once.

Revenue Cycle Technology Adoption

Technology plays a key role across revenue cycle operations. By functional area, the following are key targets:

- *Patient (admissions) access management.* This is the front-end process of a hospital revenue cycle. It is made up of all the preregistration, registration, scheduling, preadmitting, and admitting functions. Enhancing revenue cycles in this area requires the following:
    - A call center environment with autodialing, faxing, e-mail, and Internet connectivity to quickly ensure and verify all pertinent information that is key to correct and timely payment for services rendered
    - Master Person Index software to eliminate duplicate medical record numbers and assist with achieving a unique identifier for all patients
    - Registration and admission software that scripts the admission process to assist employees in obtaining required elements and check that insurer-required referrals are documented
    - Claims denial management (CDM) definition, including focus on how to obtain all the correct patient information up front while the patient is in-house
    - Imaging of data up front
- *Patient CM.* This function is usually part of the middle process, similar to HIM. This area generally requires a CM information system.
- *Health information technology and management.* Another middle process of a hospital revenue cycle that is often still referred to as (electronic or paper) medical records. This

area is made up of chart processing, coding, transcription, correspondence, and chart completion. Better control of revenue cycles requires the following recommended technology:

- – Chart-tracking software to eliminate manual out-guides and decrease the number of lost charts
- – Encoding and grouping software to improve coding accuracy and speed and improve reimbursement
- – Autoprinting and autofaxing capabilities
- – Internet connectivity for release of information and related document management tasks
- – Electronic management of documents with electronic health records (EHRs) and so forth

• *PFS.* This is the back-end process of a hospital revenue cycle. The operations include all business office functions of billing, collecting, and follow-up post patient care. Recommended technology to optimize these functions includes the following:

- – Automated biller queues to improve and track the productivity of each biller
- – Claims-scrubbing software to ensure that necessary data are included on the claim prior to submission
- – Electronic claims and reimbursement processing to expedite the payment cycle

• *Selling or auctioning bad debt.* As a sign of the contracting economic times, some struggling hospitals are using a new method to collect revenue: the Internet. It has become a channel to cut write-offs and bad debt ratios, which lower stock prices if publicly held. Rather than simply hiring agencies to collect patient bills, hospitals have begun to put their AR up for sale or auction online. Bidders on the debt include the same agencies that serve the hospitals, some of which provide guaranteed payments to hospitals in exchange for access to the debt. The auctions are also attracting other companies that buy the debt outright.

One practice used to auction debt is for the hospital to determine the criteria they will utilize for selecting the debt that will be auctioned. The criteria generally focus on AR of a certain age, but demographic regions, legal accounts, and monthly payment accounts could also be considered.

Once the criteria are determined, a listing of accounts is generated and supplied to potential buyers along with a request for proposal that asks each potential buyer to provide information on their experience in servicing hospital-type AR, as well as details of their expertise, collection techniques, references, and price. Usually the winning bidder will pay a flat price for the entire AR. It is important for the hospital to understand that when auctioning AR, the winning bidder owns the accounts, and their collection tactics will not necessarily comply with the hospital's standards for collections.

Automation can lead to decreased paperwork, process standardization, increased productivity, and cleaner claims. In 2010, *Hospital & Health Network's* "Most Wired Survey" found that the 100 most wired hospitals—including three out of the four AA+ hospitals in the country—had better control of expenses, higher productivity, and efficient utilization management. Additionally, these top hospitals tend to be larger and have better access to capital. The positive return on investment in technology increases allocation of funding to technology. This correlation is important because it begins to link the investment in information technology with positive financial returns in all areas of a hospital's business, including the revenue cycle.

REVENUE CYCLE PERFORMANCE EVALUATION AND REVIEW

Health care organizations and physician practices today face an inordinate number of challenges. It is necessary to ensure that regulatory compliance is met; staff are highly skilled and competent and receive ongoing training; processes are effective; and resources are available to invest in the latest technology and tools.

Revenue cycle performance evaluations are designed for health care organizations and physician practices that are interested in measuring their intellectual capital (their staff), evaluating the effectiveness of their processes/workflows, and optimizing existing technology as well as potentially selecting and implementing new technology to enhance their business. The financial data analysis component of the evaluation will also help pinpoint problematic components of the revenue cycle. In addition, the evaluation should identify incremental net patient revenue and increased cash flow opportunities and make it possible to determine the operational changes necessary to achieve them.

The review should cover applicable aspects of the revenue cycle from scheduling and patient access through patient discharge and the coding/billing and account resolution/collection processes. The managers who report to the director of revenue cycle management should be involved in the revenue cycle performance evaluation process.

Performance evaluations should be designed to be minimally intrusive to the staff and business operations. Use a standard data request, such as the one used to collect financial data for state reporting. This will allow you to compare to industry standards, provide a variance report, and highlight areas where the organization is performing well and areas where there is opportunity for financial performance improvement. Interviews with client directors/managers should enable you to develop a gap analysis scorecard based on current versus optimal processes.

The following is an example list of who needs to be involved in the revenue cycle performance evaluation:

- CFO
- Chief information officer
- Director of revenue cycle management
- Director/manager(s) of PFS
- Director/manager(s) of patient access
- Director/manager(s) of HIM
- Director of CM
- Director of managed care
- Charge description master coordinator

The table below identifies the various departments and functions performed in the revenue cycle.

Revenue Cycle Department	Functional Area
Patient access	Scheduling
	Insurance verification
	Financial clearance
	Registration and admitting
	Financial counseling
	Eligibility
Health information management	Documentation flow, completeness, and timeliness
	Transcription timeliness
	Coding and abstracting accuracy timeliness
	Discharged not final billed (DNFB)
Charge description master (CDM)	Charge description master maintenance
	Charge capture

Case management	Observation
	Length of stay/avoidable days
	Continued stay authorizations
	Clinical appeals
Patient financial services	Claim accuracy and timeliness
	Accounts receivable follow-up
	Denials management
	Contract management (payment accuracy)
	Cash posting
	Bad debt collections
	Customer service
Information technology	Systems in place, versions

At the conclusion of the revenue cycle performance evaluation, an executive summary should be prepared that describes

- The current-state themes regarding people, process, and technology
- A review of your known opportunities
- A gap analysis scorecard based on current versus optimal processes
- A benchmark analysis
- A benefits forecast
- A prioritized list of the most appropriate solutions to consider for improvement of the financial position of the organization

HEALTH CLAIMS DENIAL MANAGEMENT

Typically, denied and rejected claims quickly surface as a source of multimillions in revenue leakage and unnecessary expense.

Payers have been struggling with increased costs. They thoroughly inspect claims for errors and have become adept at using their rules to deny and delay claims. Zimmerman* reports that the denied percentage of gross charges climbed from 4% in 1990 to 11% in 2001 to 15% to 16% today. In contrast, providers typically lack the tools to aggressively manage current denied claims and prevent future ones.

Without denial tracking, an organization may not recognize the heavy financial impact of denied claims. The *HARA* report indicates that bad debt and gross days are declining. However, a majority of providers write off denials as contractual allowance, distorting the numbers but not the resulting lower margins and reduced cash. H*Works of the Advisory Board Corporation reports that the typical 350-bed hospital loses between $4 million and $9 million each year in earned revenue from denials and underpayments (assume $103 million annual gross revenue and 40% contractual allowance). Recouping lost revenue from denials and underpayments will, according to H*Works, increase an organization's operating margin by 2.6%.

Industry estimates report that at least 50% of denials are recoverable and 90% are preventable with the appropriate workflow processes, management commitment, strong change leadership, and

---

* Bruce Nelson of Zimmerman and Associates, Hales Corner, Wisconsin 53151, in an article dated January 16, 2004, available at http://www.hhnmag.com/hhnmag_app/hospitalconnect/search/article.jsp?dcrpath=AHA/PubsNewsArticle/ data /0401HHN_InBox_Finances&domain=HHNMAG.

the correct technology. H*Works estimates that for a revenue capture of $3 million from denials and underpayments, the recovery infrastructure costs are only about 3%.

With all this in mind, better management of rejections and denials, as well as the information necessary to resolve and prevent them, surfaces as probably the best strategy to improving financials. By streamlining the revenue cycle, managing rejections and denials proves to be less expensive and to provide faster returns than initiating new services.

UNPAID BILLS AND DEBT LEVELS

According to Fitch Ratings, bad debt fell among for-profit hospitals during the first quarter of 2008. Nonetheless, for-profits still had a higher percentage of unpaid bills than nonprofit peers and physicians.

For example, bad debt levels as a percentage of revenue fell from 18.4% in the fourth quarter of 2007 to 17.7% in the first quarter of 2008. While declining debt is always a good sign, this stands in contrast to physician practices, whose bad debt level is typically in the 5% to 10% range. It is also higher than the debt faced by nonprofits, which had bad debt levels of 5.5% in 2006.

Fitch reported that bad debt fell among for-profit hospitals partly because of the lower number of uninsured patients being treated at such facilities, as well as more efforts by the hospitals to collect copayments up-front and improve internal and external collections efforts.

HEALTH CARE REFORM AND POLITICAL FIAT

Perhaps the newest opportunity for enhanced revenue cycle management is by political fiat as states are required to make "timely payments" to health care providers.

For example, a new law signed by Missouri governor Jay Nixon, on April 27, 2010 (H1498), was prompted by a 2009 report from the Missouri Department of Insurance that showed that almost 26% of claims at urban hospitals, and more than 37% of claims at rural hospitals, are past due by 90 days or more. The law requires insurers to either pay or deny claims within 45 days of receipt and eradicates the insurers' ability to "suspend" claims. Plans that do not pay claims within 45 days will pay a daily penalty to the provider of 1% of the outstanding claim.*

PROBLEM OF IBNR HEALTH CARE CLAIMS

An *IBNR claim* is a concept that signifies that health care services have been rendered but not invoiced or recorded by the health care provider, clinic, hospital, or organization; hence, no revenues have been received. Usually the result of a commercial prospective payment risk contract between managed care organizations and health care providers, an IBNR claim refers to the estimated cost of medical services for which a claim has not yet been filed or monitored by an IBNR collection systems or control sheet.

More formally, IBNRs are a financial accounting of all services that have been performed but, as a result of a short period of time or lag, have not been invoiced or recorded. The medical services that will not be collected should be accounted for using the following accrued but not recorded entry:

- *Debit*—accrued payments to medical providers or health care entity
- *Credit*—IBNR accrual account

---

* Robert Coughlin PayCor, Inc., Cincinnati, Ohio 45203, Health Plan Week Podcast, May 3, 2010.

An example of an IBNR is hospital coronary artery bypass graft surgery for a managed care plan member. Out of the capitated, global, accountable care organization or prospective payment funds, the surgeon and/or health care organization has to pay for all related physical and respiratory therapy and rehabilitation services, as well as ancillary providers, drugs, and durable medical equipment, as contractually obligated. This may also include complication diagnosis and extensive follow-up treatment.

Accordingly, the health plan will not be completely billed until several weeks, months, or quarters later or even further downstream in the reporting year after the patient is discharged. In order to accurately project the health plan's financial liability, however, the health plan and hospital must estimate the cost of care based on past expenses.

Since the identification and control of costs are paramount in financial health care management, an IBNR reserve fund (an interest-bearing account) must be set up for claims that reflect services already delivered but, for whatever reason, not yet reimbursed. From the accounting perspective, IBNR is accrued as an expense and is related as a short-term liability each fiscal month or accounting period. Otherwise, the organization may not be able to pay the claim, if the associated revenue has already been spent. The proper handling of these bills in the pipeline is crucial for proactive providers and health organizations that are exploring arrangements that put them in the role of adjudicating claims or operating in a subcapitated system. This is especially important with newer patients who may be sicker than prior norms.

Recoverables that hospitals post as part of their large reserve charges are also, in many cases, IBNR losses. They may be recorded as IBNR claims on their balance sheets. Once these losses start becoming actual losses, the hospital may look to the insurer to pay a part of the claim. This causes disputes between the payer, provider, and/or health care organization.

IBNR PROBLEMS FOR HEALTH CARE ORGANIZATIONS

IBNR claims represent one of the most contentious contract terms negotiated between health care organizations and managed care providers. Enactment of IBNR agreements requires major adjustments to the health care organization's calculation of financial surplus or deficit. Theoretically, the summation of IBNR should be based on quantifiable, actuarially sound principles. However, there is a high degree of flexibility in how final IBNR calculations are derived, hence the conundrum.

Among the contract variables influencing IBNR computations are the cutoff adjustment after the end of the contract year, the estimated amount of time necessary to submit a clean claim, and the quality of a health plan's claim processing. By default, IBNR places the health care provider or organization in a position of adjudicating claims. As a result, providers and organizations are forced into a position of advanced financial risk assumption.

In the extreme, a failure to keep expenses within the limits of associated revenues can cause losses that, if continued, will lead to distress, reorganization, bankruptcy, and closure. Likewise, failure to properly account for potential claims has the propensity to lead to poor financial decisions. Unfortunately, many health care providers and organizations lack organized and accessible historic information from which they can make educated decisions related to IBNR contract terms. This issue began to achieve critical mass relating to self-funded hospitals or health care employer plans that were effectively operating as an insurance company. The Internal Revenue Service (IRS) ruled that these self-funded employer groups could not deduct IBNRs because the deduction was based on estimates. Subsequent challenges to the IRS yielded some results for those expenditures that can be supported by valid receipts subsequent to year-end. However, the IRS still maintains that any reserve based on estimates that is reflected in the tax return of noninsurance company entities will be denied.

IBNR CLAIMS-MANAGEMENT VOLUME AND REVENUE CONSEQUENCES

Problem health care claims typically account for about 10% to 20% of claims volume, but they cost far more to process and take two to five times longer to pay. Problem IBNR claims can increase the average claims-payment time beyond regulatory standards, which can subject the organization to possible regulatory action and jeopardize client and vendor relationships. Ineffective claims management can result in a number of adverse revenue consequences, including

- Inadequate cash flow
- Reserve shortfalls and fiscal instability
- Inaccurate pricing
- Administrative cost increases
- Regulatory sanctions
- Jeopardized provider or client relationships
- Accreditation problems

Now, let us examine the revenue consequences of problem IBNR health care claims.

INADEQUATE CASH FLOWS

Both provider and payer organizations suffer when problem claims delay payments. Medical groups and hospitals increasingly resent payment delays due to problem claims. On the payer side, a sudden increase in the amount of money paid to providers upon the resolution of problem claims looks bad on financial reports and may require the payer organization to draw upon lines of credit if it has inadequate funds reserved to make payments. Such an increase also can trigger increased regulatory scrutiny.

RESERVE SHORTFALLS AND FISCAL INSTABILITY

In addition to the cash flow problems that arise from a high volume of problem claims, a payer organization may also experience a negative "tail" effect on reinsurance coverage if it fails to realize that it has met the reinsurer's stop-loss threshold or fails to file reinsurance claims within the reinsurer's time limit. Most reinsurance contracts are for a 1-year term plus a "tail" period of 3 to 6 months during which the payer organization can submit claims received after the contract ends for services provided during the contract term. If the payer organization has not booked all of the claims related to a particular member or to its aggregate level by the end of the reinsurance contract, it may not be able to receive reimbursement from the reinsurer for these claims.

INACCURATE PRICING

A payer organization's medical loss ratio is the largest component and thus the primary driver of the premium price. The medical loss ratio includes claims actually paid plus those IBNR claims. A high volume of problem claims means that IBNR claims are underreported, which frequently leads to an underestimation of costs and inadequate premium pricing. Providers that accept a large share of financial risk without collecting and analyzing cost data adequately also are likely to underestimate their medical costs when negotiating contracts and thus receive inadequate payments from payers.

Administrative Cost Increases

Problem claims repeatedly cycle through the payment system and cause administrative costs to rise. A claims examiner must review supporting documentation and records of actions for each problem claim and may need to request more information from the provider and consult with a supervisor or the utilization review department before taking action. The increased staff time required for these tasks may force the organization to hire more claims-processing and adjudication staff.

Regulatory Sanctions

Claims-payment criteria are mandated by the Centers for Medicare and Medicaid Services, the U.S. Department of Labor for self-insured plans, and state insurance or managed care departments for commercial products. Provider complaints or negative agency reviews can result in sanctions that increase both the organization's administrative dollar costs and the medical cost ratio. Sanctions include fines, more frequent government oversight of claims-payment processes, and mandated increases in claims-payment reserves and working capital. The ultimate sanction is assignment of state regulatory staff or retained consultants to manage the organization's claims operations. The affected organization must pay fees and expenses for retained consultants. Some leading managed care organizations recently have suffered downturns in financial performance as a result of mandated assignment of their claims operations to the state or consultants.

Potential Solutions to the IBNR Challenge

IBNRs pose a complex set of issues for health care providers before and after contractual terms are solidified with managed care organizations (MCOs). The establishment of a favorable IBNR framework is predicated on actuarial prowess, historical information, interpretation of contract terms, the ability to technically interoperate with managed care information technology systems, and simplification of contract terms and conditions to remove ambiguity.

Since IBNRs have a high degree of changeability in how final claims are derived, commercial capitation risk contracts should be reevaluated each year to determine whether they provide a viable option versus other alternatives. Additional variables that influence IBNR computations are the cutoff adjustment after the end of the contract year, the estimated amount of time necessary to submit a clean claim, and the quality of the MCOs' claim processing systems.

IBNR Calculations and Methodology

The following are three accepted methods for estimating IBNRs:

1. *Actuarial data analysis*
   IBNRs are calculated with demographic data, insurance reports, statistical and risk-dampening stochastic probabilities, utilization data, and past payment claims data to estimate IBNRs. This costly method is most appropriate for newer organizations without a significant claims history.
2. *Open referral analysis*
   This method estimates the cost of all open referral authorizations on file (in and out of network). Essentially, it assumes a traditional open referral accounting structure in a restricted gatekeeper-controlled environment. Then, the average cost per medical service segment is estimated and multiplied against the average cost per segment. In this manner, cost estimates are matched with medical service segments over time, and IBNR claims are mitigated.
3. *Historic cost analysis*
   This method of estimation is most appropriate for established organizations and is based on the actual number of past claims on a per-member/per-month basis (see Table 5.1).

TABLE 5.1

Forecasting IBNR Factors (Smith Model)

Months Delay	Number of Losses	% of Losses	Cumulative % of Losses	Actual Number of Losses 2000–2005	Adjusted Number of Losses 2000–2005
1	127	64.8	64.8	2	3
2	31	15.8	80.6	3	4
3	14	7.1	87.8	2	2
4	9	4.6	92.3	1	1
5	1	0.5	92.9	0	0
6	2	1.0	93.9	5	5
7	2	1.0	94.9	3	3
8	5	2.6	97.4	4	4
9	0	0.0	97.4	7	7
10	2	1.0	98.5	7	7
11	0	0.0	8.5	6	6
12	2	1.0	99.5		
13	0	0.0	99.5		
14	0	0.0	99.5		
15	0	0.0	99.5		
16	0	0.0	99.5		
17	0	0.0	99.5		
18	1	0.5	100		
Total	**196**			**40**	**43**

Results: Calculations: IBNR claims = 3 out of 43. Smith IBNR factor = 3/43 × 100 = 6.98%.

Note: Input needed: gross claim, date of loss, and date reported.

INTERNAL CONTROLS AND FRAUD REDUCTION

Employee theft in any medical entity is an often underreported business matter and may be a causative factor in reduced revenue situations. Opportunity is the main causative factor in embezzlement, and perceived need, rationalization, and opportunity compose the commonly accepted model used in ethics classes. Proactively setting up internal controls not only prevents some embezzlement but can also make honest employees feel more comfortable in that it is harder to be falsely suspected. Preventive internal controls include the following:

- Daily inspection of the entity's online checking, savings, and credit card accounts by the CXO or other appropriate administrator. This is the vital first line of defense against most embezzlement scenarios.
- Separation of duties in all financial matters. This makes embezzlement possible only with collusion of at least two employees. Only management should have check-signing privileges. Only preprinted checks should be used: avoid using check creation programs that allow printing of blank checks. Void checks and subsequent sequential numbering should be retained.
- Rotation of duties as most prolonged embezzlement schemes will be uncovered if a different person periodically performs the duty. The "perfect" office employee, who refuses to take a vacation, may in fact be hiding such a scheme. Rotation of duties has the side benefit of cross-training employees, an important factor in small- and medium-sized practices.

- Bonding of key employees. Bonding companies pursue criminal matters as a matter of policy, once you prove guilt. The fear of certain prosecution is sometimes a deterrent.
- Do not let the staff order anything with a practice credit card.
- Physical safeguards by locking up theft-prone items.
- Enable software audit trails. If your software tracks corrective entries and deletions, use it. In addition to documenting possible fraud, this allows examination of which procedures went wrong and how to, or how not to, fix them.
- Internal miniaudits and/or spot audits with frequent random checks of theft-prone systems can easily be set up and quickly performed.
- Security cameras.
- Computer monitoring programs that allow real-time, keystroking, password/fingerprint protection or logged inspection of employee computer screens.

COMMON EMBEZZLEMENT SCHEMES

Common medical practice and clinic embezzlement schemes include the following:

1. Pocketing cash "off the books." To the IRS, this is like embezzlement to intentionally defraud it out of tax money.
2. Employees pocketing cash from cash transactions.
3. Bookkeepers writing checks to themselves. This is easiest to do in flexible software programs like QuickBooks and Peachtree accounting and financial software (www.quickbooks .com, www.peachtree.com). It is one of the hardest schemes to detect.
4. Employees ordering personal items on practice credit cards.
5. Bookkeepers receiving patient checks and illegally depositing them in an unauthorized, pseudo-practice checking account they set up in a bank different from yours. They then withdraw funds at will. If this scheme uses only a few patients who are billed outside of the health care entity's accounting software, it is hard to detect.
6. Bookkeepers writing payroll checks to nonexistent employees. This scheme works well in larger practices and medical clinics with high seasonal turnover of employees and practices with multiple locations.
7. Bookkeepers writing inflated checks to existing employees, vendors, or subcontractors. Physician-owners should beware if romantic relationships between the bookkeeper and other practice-related parties develop.
8. Bookkeepers writing checks to false vendors. This is another low-profile, protracted scheme that exploits indifference to accounts payable.

NEGATIVE HOSPITAL REVENUE HEADWINDS GOING FORWARD

In a September 2011 report, "US Hospital Medians Show Resiliency against Industry Headwinds but Challenges Still Support Negative Outlook," Moody's said most U.S. hospitals struggled with weakening revenue growth in 2010 and 2011 but still maintained stable financial performance and achieved somewhat improved balance sheet positions.

And, in a significant trend, median growth rate of net patient revenues and total operating revenues slowed to just 4.1% and 4.0%, respectively, with continued pressure expected in FY 2011–2012. Median growth rate of inpatient admissions turned negative, −0.4%, in FY 2010, following no growth in FY 2009.

However, on the upside, Moody's reported that an intense focus on controlling operating spending led to improvement in key FY 2010–2011 operating measures and improved debt coverage ratios. Total cash and investments as well as liquidity metrics also showed improvement due to stock market gains (now likely tempered), lower capital spending, and moderately higher retained earnings.

CONCLUSION

For several years now, health care providers have been challenged to deliver quality patient care in an environment of shrinking profit margins. Total margins and operating margins have followed the same trend. Analysts report that an operating margin of less than 5% leaves an organization without the resources to invest in new technology and capital projects and will eventually force the facility to close or merge. With rising labor costs, a poorly performing economy, and an aging population, these numbers are not likely to improve soon.

Although the health care industry has seen an overall improvement in AR days and bad debt for an extended period, it appears that many facilities have reached their peak in addressing these areas, particularly given current demands to reduce staff and other operational costs after the 2008–2009 financial meltdown and impending implementation of the Patient Protection and Affordable Care Act in 2014.

So, where is the next major opportunity for reducing costs or maximizing revenue opportunities?

Revenue cycle improvement seems to be the most promising and popular area today. In fact, PriceWaterhouseCoopers lists five areas to reinvent the revenue cycle:

1. Organizational/accountability
2. Process/workflow improvements
3. Information systems/management reporting enhancements
4. Quality assurance mechanisms
5. Department and staff productivity measurements

Thus, to succeed in enhancing hospital or health care entity revenue streams, the topics addressed in this chapter should be explored and possibly implemented for better results. Beginning with patient access and IBNR analysis—and through the application of optimal organizational structure, benchmarking, and technology adoption—the outcome may be a faster performing revenue cycle and more profitable health care organization.

CASE MODEL 5.1: ST. JAMES OUT-PATIENT PHYSICAL THERAPY, INC.

St. James Out-Patient Physical Therapy Clinic recently received an invoice for durable medical equipment (DME) in the amount of $500,000, with terms of a 2% discount if paid within 10 days. Otherwise the entire amount would be due in 30 days (2–10, net 30). However, as the new department head of physical therapy, you are not sure if you can afford to pay early because of the recent financial meltdown and credit squeeze. You realize that understanding the percentage interest rate cost differential is important.

KEY ISSUES

You must make two financial decisions: a primary decision and an alternate decision.

1. What is the annual effective cost of interest on this invoice (primary)?
2. If the 2% discount could still be taken even if the invoice was not paid until the 20th day, what would the effective interest rate then be (alternate)?

SOLUTIONS

1. The 2% discount would be obtained for making payment 20 days before needed. The annual interest cost would be 36%, calculated in this manner:

$$2\% \times [360 \text{ days}/20 \text{ days}] = 36\%$$

2. The new effective interest rate would be 18% if payment was deferred until the 20th day.
3. The financial cost, amortized as an annual percentage rate (APR) for the difference, is calculated in this manner:

$$18\% \times \$500,000 = \$90,000$$

CHECKLIST 1: Mitigating IBNR Revenue Cycle Risks	YES	NO
Due to the various unknown factors that have the propensity to affect IBNR, the following checklist steps should be considered to help mitigate risk:		
Do I follow or have I developed standards related to managed medical care claims-processing systems?	o	o
Do I follow or have I developed policies and procedures for administrative staff designed to support IBNR terms and conditions?	o	o
Do I review historical information relevant to IBNR influencing variables?	o	o
Is my historic information actuarially sound?	o	o
Do I follow or have I developed policies and procedures related to better record keeping?	o	o
Do I solicit legal opinions for IBNR contract terms as needed?	o	o
Do I solicit accounting opinions for IBNR contracting terms as needed?	o	o
Do I utilize net present value (NPV) calculations to evaluate IBNR terms and ongoing participation?	o	o
Do I share IBNR-related information with critical staff members?	o	o
Do I consider credits and debits, accounting periods, and audit disputes?	o	o
Do I structure risk pool arrangements properly?	o	o

CHECKLIST 2: IBNR Claim Variables	YES	NO
Do I understand the following variables influencing IBNRs?		
Do I perform the computations and IBNR cutoff adjustments for the prospective medical reimbursement contract year?	o	o
Have I estimated the amount of time necessary to submit a clean medical claim?	o	o
Do I know the quality of a health plan's claim processing?	o	o
Do I want to adjudicate claims?	o	o
Do I have adjudication authority?	o	o
Do I have adjudication knowledge?	o	o
Am I in a position of advanced financial risk assumption for my claims department?	o	o

---

CHECKLIST 3: IBNR Claims-Management Volume	YES	NO
Do I understand the following claims management volume issues affecting IBNRs?		
Inadequate revenues, income, and cash flow?	o	o
Cash and reserve shortfalls or fiscal instability?	o	o
Inaccurate or noncompetitive medical service pricing?	o	o
Affects of licensure or accreditation problems?	o	o

CASE MODEL 5.2: IMPROVING REVENUE CYCLE AT A WEST COAST PUBLIC HOSPITAL

Mr. Johnson was the chief financial officer (CFO) of a 222-bed teaching hospital in southern California. Mr. Johnson recognized a lot of problems with the processes within the various revenue cycle departments he managed that impacted cash flow for the facility. Mr. Johnson met with the hospital chief executive officer (CEO) to express his concerns and the fact that he felt that his existing staff did not have the expertise to fix many of the problems they were facing.

Ms. Thomas, the hospital CEO, agreed with Mr. Johnson's evaluations and concerns, and the two prepared a package for the Board of Supervisors to submit a request for proposal to several revenue cycle improvement vendors. This request was approved by the Board and sent to several vendors with known successful track records in this area. During the next several weeks, the responses were evaluated and a final vendor selected.

It was determined through a revenue cycle performance evaluation completed by the vendor prior to the kickoff of the engagement that the largest opportunity for improved cash would be to address the bottlenecks in the cash flow, the excessive days in accounts receivable, the backlogged accounts in denied claims, and improved process through the entire revenue cycle at this public hospital.

When the engagement began, the net days in accounts receivable were 103, and the time from discharge to final bill was 33 days. The vendor was engaged for a 4-year period to provide cash acceleration and revenue cycle improvement on a pay-for-performance (P4P) fee structure. A historical review of the hospital's financial data determined an average monthly collection amount (baseline) the hospital was achieving each month prior to the start of this engagement. The P4P fee structure required the vendor to reach the baseline each month before the hospital was required to pay any profession fees for the services of the vendor.

KEY ISSUES

What could the hospital do to realize immediate benefits with regard to the following?

- Accelerated cash flow
- Reduced days in accounts receivables
- Streamlined revenue cycle processes
- Better trained existing staff
- Return on investment

SOLUTION

The methodology used by the vendor was to initiate process improvement that incorporated best practices within the hospital's billing, medical records, case management, and admissions/registration areas. The vendor brought in a project director to oversee all aspects of the revenue cycle; placed highly experienced revenue cycle consultants in interim management roles over patient accounting, patient access, clinical registration, and medical records; and added additional consultants to focus on areas such as denial management, charge capture, case management, information technology, and system integration.

Further, cross-training throughout the revenue cycle operations and a series of regularly scheduled meetings between the hospital department managers and the vendor staff improved the overall communications among the various hospital departments involved in the revenue cycle.

The documented results of the engagement and the efforts of the vendor provided an improvement of $1,740,182 in monthly average cash collections, which equated to a 19% increase in collections. In addition, unbilled accounts receivable decreased from $27 million to just over $5 million. Net days in accounts receivable were reduced to 39 days from 64, while the return on investment to the hospital was 564%, and the hospital's incremental cash improved $90,489,475 over the life of the engagement (see table below).

Return on Investment

Total cash collections over term of engagement	$366,489,475
Average monthly cash collections	$7,047,875
Total Engagement Incremental Cash	**$90,489,475**
Average monthly incremental cash	$1,740,182
Vendor performance fee rate	21%
Total engagement performance fee	$13,081,529
Average monthly performance fee	$251,568
Total management fee	$2,960,000
Total Cost to Client (Fees Plus Expenses)	**$16,041,529**
Client's Return on Investment	**$74,447,946**
Return on Investment, Percentage	**564%**

By forging a strong revenue cycle team with hospital staff and revenue cycle consultants while the hospital staff was being trained and developing improved billing and registration processes, the vendor guided the hospital to increased collections, better productivity, reduction in accounts receivable, a positive return on investment, and increased cash collections within a few months.

CHECKLIST 1: Revenue Cycle Organizational Structure	**YES**	**NO**
Determine the advantages of a centralized system.		
Is there more than one executive in charge of the areas of revenue cycle operations (defined as patient access, case management, health information management [HIM], and patient financial services [PFS]) at your hospital or health care facility? If yes, what are their names and titles?	o	o
_____		
_____		
Have you ever considered having the CFO as the executive in charge overall?	o	o
If yes, do you think this organizational structure would provide better results?	o	o
Are any other executives in charge overall, and/or do you report to them?	o	o

o   Chief information officer
o   Director of revenue cycle management
o   Director/manager(s) of PFS
o   Director/manager(s) of patient access
o   Director/manager(s) of HIM
o   Director of case management
o   Director of managed care
o   CDM coordinator

CHECKLIST 2: Benchmarking	YES	NO
Determine the benchmarks against which you will measure the performance of your hospital.		
Would application of industry standards improve processes?	o	o
Would processes improve through setting a baseline of current status performance levels?	o	o
Would performance be improved by reengineering front-end processes?	o	o
Would performance be improved by reengineering middle processes?	o	o
Would performance be improved by reengineering back-end processes?	o	o

CHECKLIST 3: Technology Adoption	YES	NO
Assess the level of technology adopted by your hospital.		
Would retraining in systems improve the perception of system quality by staff?	o	o
Do you have a call center environment?	o	o
Do you use the following software?	o	o
Master Person Index	o	o
Admission Process Scripting	o	o
Chart Tracking	o	o
Encoder	o	o
Claims Editing	o	o
Do you have automated biller queues for follow-up?	o	o
Do you utilize any imaging software in registration/admissions areas?	o	o
Do you issue claims to third-party payers and receive reimbursements electronically?	o	o

CHECKLIST 4: Revenue Cycle Performance Evaluation	YES	NO
Perform a revenue cycle performance evaluation with summaries.		
Are current-state themes regarding people, process, and technology included in your evaluation?	o	o
o A review of known opportunities and threats?		
o A gap analysis scorecard based on current versus optimal processes?		
o A benchmark analysis?		
o A benefits forecast?		
o A prioritized list of appropriate solutions to consider for improvement of the financial position of the organization?		
Are next-step recommendations for revenue cycle services implementations included?	o	o

ACKNOWLEDGMENTS

Thanks are due to Dr. Gary L. Bode, CPA, MSA, CMP, of the Institute of Medical Business Advisors, Inc., and Ross J. Fidler of ACS—A Xerox Company—for technical assistance in the preparation of this chapter.

BIBLIOGRAPHY

Bode, G. L. and Marcinko, D. E. *Internal Controls and Fraud Prevention. Business of Medical Practice*, Springer Publishing, New York, 2011.
Caffarini, Karen. A successful sabbatical can take years of planning. *AMNews* (July 7, 2008).

Dunn, Rose T. "Performance Standards for Coding Professionals." *Advance for Health Information Professionals* (2010). See http://health-information.advanceweb.com/common/editorial/editorial.aspx?CC=727.

Flareau, B. *Accountable Care Organizations,* Convurgent Publishing, New York, 2011.

H*Works (The Advisory Board). *Capturing Lost Revenues*. Washington, DC, 2001.

Moore, N. F. "Improving the Revenue Cycle Process: Document Imaging and Shared Access to Scanned Documents Is Essential to Streamlined Operations." (NAATP INSIGHTS)(Report): An article from Behavioral Healthcare. Vendome Group LLC, New York, 2010.

Marcinko, D. E. and Hetico, R. N. *Dictionary of Health Economics and Finance*. Springer Publishing, New York, 2008.

Marcinko, D. E. and Hetico, H. R. "IBNR Healthcare Claim Strategies." In Marcinko, D. E. (editor). *Financial Strategies in Healthcare Organizations*. iMBA Inc, Atlanta, GA, 2010.

Marcinko, D. E. and Hetico, H. R. "Understanding Hospital Revenue Cycle Management." In Marcinko, D. E. (editor). *Financial Strategies in Healthcare Organizations*. iMBA Inc, Atlanta, GA, 2010.

Petaschnick, J. Sr. Editor. *HARA*. Aspen Publishers. (Fourth Quarter 2001). For further information, see www.advisoryboardcompany.com.

PriceWaterhouseCoopers. *What's Hot and What's Not in Healthcare 2006*. Presentation at South Carolina HFMA conference, Hilton Head Island, SC, June 6, 2010.

See www.solucient.com. Also, Aventis Pharmaceuticals provides annual updates analyzing the managed care industry in its *HMO-PPPO/Medicare-MedicaidDigest* series, available in print and also online at www.managedcaredigest.com.

Zimmerman & Associates, LLC. *Best Practices of Denial Management*. Presentation at HFMA Annual Networking Institute (ANI) conference, Washington, DC, 2004.

Section II

Policy and Procedures

6 Health Care Workplace Violence Prevention

Strategies for Risk Reduction and Prevention

Eugene Schmuckler, David Edward Marcinko, and Hope Rachel Hetico

CONTENTS

Violence is a serious problem in many countries, and research by the World Health Organization indicates that violence in the health care workplace is actually a global phenomenon. Crossing borders, cultures, work settings, and occupational groups, violence in the health care workplace is at a very high level. New research shows that more than half of the health sector personnel surveyed had experienced at least one incident of physical or psychological violence in the year previous to the study.

INTRODUCTION

Domestically, the impact of workplace violence in the United States became widely exposed on November 6, 2009, when 39-year-old Army psychiatrist Maj. Nidal M. Hasan, MD, a 1997 graduate of Virginia Tech University who received a medical doctorate in psychiatry from the Uniformed Services University of the Health Sciences in Bethesda, Maryland, and served as an intern, resident, and fellow at the Walter Reed Army Medical Center in the District of Columbia, went on a savage 100-round shooting spree and rampage that killed 13 people and injured 32 others. In April 2010, he was transferred to Bell County Jail in Belton, Texas. An Article 32 hearing, which determined whether Hasan would be fit to stand trial at court martial, began on October 12, 2010. Hasan was subsequently deemed fit and was arraigned on July 20, 2011, and his trial was scheduled for March 2012, but reset for August, 2012.

DEFINITION OF HEALTH WORKPLACE VIOLENCE

Having established the reality of violence as an issue in the health care industry, Barry W. Nixon, MS, of workplaceviolence911.com, defines the meaning of workplace violence as "violent acts including assaults and threats which occur in, or are related to the workplace and entail a substantial risk of physical or emotional harm to individuals, or damage to an organizations resources or capabilities." More specifically, it includes

- Actual violence that causes or is intended to cause injury or harm to a person or property
- Threatening remarks and/or behavior in which intent to harm is stated or implied or indicates a lack of respect for the dignity and worth of an individual
- Verbal abuse
- Mobbing, bullying, or emotional abuse
- Possession of a weapon while working or on company property.

EFFECTS OF WORKPLACE VIOLENCE

The effects of workplace violence are pervasive, and the health care sector continues to lead all other industry sectors in incidents of nonfatal workplace assaults. For example, in 2000, 48% of all nonfatal injuries from violent acts against workers occurred in the health care sector. Nurses, nurses' aides, and orderlies suffer the highest proportion of these injuries. Nonfatal assaults on health care workers include assaults, bruises, lacerations, broken bones, and concussions. These reported incidents include only injuries severe enough to result in lost time from work. Of significance is that the median time away from work as a result of an assault or other violent act is 5 days. Almost 25% of these injuries result in longer than 20 days away from work. Obviously, this is quite costly to the facility as well as to the victim.

A study undertaken in Canada found that 46% of 8780 staff nurses experienced one or more types of violence in the last five shifts worked. Physical assault was defined as being spit on, bitten, hit, or pushed.

Both Canadian and U.S. researchers have described the prevalence of verbal threats and physical assaults in intensive care, emergency departments, and general wards. A study in Florida reported that 100% of emergency department nurses experience verbal threats and 82% reported being physically assaulted. Similar results were found in a study undertaken in a Canadian hospital. Possible reasons for the high incidence of violence in emergency departments include presence of weapons, frustration with long waits for medical care, dissatisfaction with hospital policies, and the levels of violence in the community served by the emergency department.

Similar findings have been reported in studies of mental health professionals, nursing home, and long-term care employees, as well as providers of service in home and community health.

Violence in hospitals usually results from patients, and occasionally family members, who feel frustrated, vulnerable, and out of control. Transporting patients, long waits for service, inadequate security, poor environmental design, and unrestricted movement of the public are associated with increased risk of assault in hospitals and may be significant factors in social services workplaces as well. Finally, lack of staff training and the absence of violence prevention programming are associated with elevated risk of assault in hospitals.

Although anyone working in a hospital may become a victim of violence, nurses and aides who have the most direct contact with patients are at higher risk. Other hospital personnel at increased risk of violence include emergency response personnel, hospital safety officers, and all health care providers. Personnel working in large medical practices fall into this category as well. Although no area is totally immune from acts of violence, it most frequently occurs in psychiatric wards, emergency rooms, waiting rooms, and geriatric settings.

Many medical facilities mistakenly focus on systems, operations, infrastructure, and public relations when planning for crisis management and emergency response; they tend to overlook the people. Obviously, no medical facility can operate without employees who are healthy enough to return to work and to be productive. Individuals who have been exposed to a violent incident need to be assured of their safety.

The costs associated with workplace violence crises are not limited to health care dollars, absenteeism rates, legal battles, or increased insurance rates. If mishandled, traumatic events can severely impair trust between patients, employees, their peers, and their managers. Without proper planning, an act of violence can disrupt normal group processes, interfere with the delivery of crucial information, and temporarily impair management effectiveness. It may also lead to other negative outcomes such as low employee morale, increased job stress, increased work turnover, reduced trust in management and coworkers, and a hostile working environment.

Data collected by the U.S. Department of Justice shows workplace violence to be the fastest growing category of murder in the country. Homicide, including domestic homicides, is the leading cause of on-the-job death for women and is the second leading cause for men. The National Institute for Occupational Safety and Health (NIOSH) found that an average of 20 workers are murdered each week in the United States. In addition, an estimated 1 million workers—28,000 per week—are victims of nonfatal workplace assaults each year.

Workplace attacks, threats, or harassment can include the following monetary costs:

- $13.5 billion in medical costs per year
- 500,000 employees missing 1,750,000 days of work per year
- 41% increase in stress levels with the concomitant related costs

UNDERSTANDING THE RISKS

More assaults occur in the health care and social services industries than in any other. In 2000, Bureau of Labor Statistics (BLS) data show that 48% of all nonfatal injuries from occupational assaults and violent acts occurred in health care and social services. In 1999, 637 nonfatal assaults on hospital workers occurred—a rate of 8.3 assaults per 10,000 workers—and NIOSH confirmed this ratio in April 2002, reporting that U.S. hospital workers suffer nonfatal assaults at more than four times the rate of overall private sector workers, which is 2 per 10,000 workers. Almost two-thirds of the nonfatal assaults occurred in nursing homes, hospitals, and establishments providing residential care and social services.

Several studies indicate that violence often takes place during times of high activity and interaction with patients, such as at meal times, during visiting hours, and during patient transportation. Assaults may occur when service is denied, when a patient is involuntarily admitted, or when a health care worker attempts to set limits on eating, drinking, or tobacco or alcohol use.

The issue of assaults against health professionals is not new. Between 1980 and 1990, 106 occupational violence-related deaths occurred among the following health care workers: 27 pharmacists, 26 physicians, 18 registered nurses, 17 nurses' aides, and 18 health care workers in other occupational categories. Using the National Traumatic Occupational Fatality database, the study reported that between 1983 and 1989, there were 69 registered nurses killed at work. Homicide was the leading cause of traumatic occupational death among employees in nursing homes and personal care facilities.

Of greater significance than these numbers is the likely underreporting of violence and a persistent perception within the health care industry that assaults are part of the job. Underreporting may reflect a lack of institutional reporting policies, employee beliefs that reporting will not benefit (and may actually harm) them, or employee fears that employers may deem assaults the result of employee negligence or poor job performance.

HOSPITAL RISKS

NIOSH summarizes the risk factors for occupational violence to hospital workers. These include

- Working directly with volatile people, especially if they are under the influence of drugs or alcohol or have a history of violence or certain psychotic diagnoses
- Working when understaffed—especially during meal times or visiting hours
- Transporting patients and long waits for service
- Overcrowded, uncomfortable waiting rooms
- Working alone
- Poor environmental design
- Inadequate and/or ineffective security
- Lack of staff training and policies for preventing or managing crises with potentially volatile patients
- Drug and alcohol abuse
- Access to firearms
- Unrestricted movement of the public
- Poorly lit corridors, rooms, parking lots, and other areas

Violence occurring in other occupational groups is most often related to robbery. In health care settings, however, acts of violence are most often perpetrated by patients or clients. Family members who feel frustrated, vulnerable, and out of control and colleagues of patients (especially when the patient is a gang member) are also identified as perpetrators of abuse.

However, the presence of coworkers has been identified as a potential deterrent to assault in health care.

Health care and social service workers face an increased risk of work-related assaults stemming from several factors, including the following:

- The prevalence of handgun and other weapon ownership—as high as 25% among patients, their families, and friends. Handguns are increasingly used by police and the criminal justice system for criminal holds and the care of acutely disturbed, violent individuals.

- The increasing number of acute and chronically mentally ill patients now being released from hospitals without follow-up care, who now have the right to refuse medicine and who can no longer be hospitalized involuntarily unless they pose an immediate threat to themselves or others.
- The availability of drugs or money at hospitals, clinics, and pharmacies, making staff and patients likely robbery targets.
- Situational and circumstantial factors such as
  - Unrestricted movement of the public in clinics and hospitals.
  - The increasing presence of gang members, drug or alcohol abusers, trauma patients, or distraught family members.
  - Long waits in emergency or clinic areas, leading to client frustration over an inability to obtain needed services promptly.
- Low staffing levels during times of specific increased activity such as meal times and visiting times, and when staff is transporting patients. This also includes isolated work with clients during examinations or treatment.
- Solo work, often in remote locations, particularly in high-crime settings, with no backup or means of obtaining assistance, such as communication devices or alarm systems.
- Lack of training of staff in recognizing and managing escalating hostile and assaultive behavior.
- Poorly lit parking areas.

The guidelines established by the Occupational Safety and Health Administration (OSHA) seek to set forth procedures leading to the elimination or reduction of worker exposure to conditions causing death or injury from violence by implementing effective security devices and administrative work practices, among other control measures. Health care professionals need to be aware that violence can occur anywhere and in any practice settings.

In hospitals and clinics, which are more likely to report incidents of violence than private offices, the most frequent sites are

- Psychiatric wards
- Acute care settings
- Critical care units
- Community health agencies
- Homes for special care
- Emergency rooms
- Waiting rooms and geriatric units

The impact of workplace violence is far-reaching and affects individual staff members, coworkers, patients/clients, and their families. Those who have been affected, directly or indirectly, by a workplace violence incident report a broad spectrum of responses—anger is the most common. There are also reports of

- Difficulty returning to work
- Decreased job performance
- Changes in relationships with coworkers
- Sleep pattern disturbance
- Helplessness and symptoms of posttraumatic stress disorders
- Fear of other patients
- Fear of returning to the scene of the assault

CONTRIBUTING RISK FACTORS

A number of factors may contribute to the risk of violence or potentially violent situations in the workplace, including but not limited to the following:

- *Characteristics of patients or clients:* History of aggressive or violent behavior; clinical conditions such as dementia, head trauma, hypoglycemia, or emotional disorders; or substance abuse.
- *Environmental factors:* Inflexible institutional culture, rules and policies, restrictions on activities, noise or lighting levels, busy or high-activity times, invasion of personal space, layout of or overcrowding in units or areas housing patients/clients (e.g., emergency department settings).
- *Staff characteristics:* Staff dynamics (i.e., conflict among staff members); staff attitudes, such as anxiety or ambivalence toward the prevention or management of aggression; and staff behavior (e.g., tone of voice, body language, or overt aggression).
- *Organizational policies and educational programs:* A lack of policies or programs aimed at preventing and reducing the incidence and impact of workplace violence can in fact lead to increased risks.

HADDON MATRIX FOR INJURY PREVENTION

An invaluable tool for prevention program establishment is the Haddon matrix. In 1968, William Haddon, Jr., a public health physician with the New York State Health Department, developed a matrix of categories to assist researchers trying to address injury prevention systematically. The idea was to look at injuries in terms of causal factors and contributing factors rather than just using a descriptive approach. It is only recently that this model has been put to use in the area of workplace violence.

The matrix (see Figure 6.1) is a framework designed to apply the traditional public health domains of host, agent, and disease to primary, secondary, and tertiary injury factors. When applied to workplace violence, the host is the victim of workplace violence, such as a nurse. The agent is a combination of the perpetrator and his or her weapon(s) and the force with which an assault occurs. The environment is divided into two subdomains: the physical and the social. The location of an assault, such as the ER, the street, an examining room, or a hospital ward, is as important as the social setting in patient interaction, presence of coworkers, and supervisor support.

Subsequent versions of the matrix (see Figure 6.2) divide the environment into physical environment and social, socioeconomic, or sociocultural environment. Each factor is then considered a preevent phase, an event phase, and a postevent phase.

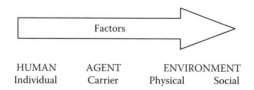

FIGURE 6.1 Haddon matrix.

Preevent	Are we psychologically prepared for the event?
Event	What is the level of exposure of the individuals?
Postevent	What will the outcome be?
Results	Distress responses, behavioral change, psychiatric illness

FIGURE 6.2 Workplace injury factors.

The Haddon matrix lends itself to a medical setting in that it uses a classical epidemiological framework to categorize preevent, event, and postevent activities according to the infectious disease vernacular, host (victim), vector (assailant or weapon), and environment. The strength of the Haddon matrix is that it includes the ability to assess preevents or precursors in order to develop primary preventive measures.

Figure 6.3 shows how the Haddon matrix categorizes the influence of

- Human or host behavior
- Agent or vehicle of situation
- Physical and sociocultural environment
- Preevent, event, and postevent
- Gaps and opportunities for improvement

From the perspective of administration, the Haddon matrix does not implicate policy. This means that the matrix does not necessarily guide policy. When implemented, the Haddon matrix can be a "politically" neutral, trans- or multidisciplinary objective tool that identifies opportunities for intervention. Furthermore, it outlines sensible targets of change for the physical and social environments.

Phases	Host	Agent	Physical Environment	Social Environment
Preevent (prior to assault)	Knowledge Self-efficacy Training	History of prior violence communicated	Assess objects that could become weapons, actual weapons, egress (means of escape)	Visit in pairs or with escort
Event (assault)	De-escalation Escape techniques Alarms/two-way phones	Reduce lethality of patient via increasing your distance	Egress, alarm, cell phone	Code and security procedures
Postevent (postassault)	Medical care/ counseling Post-event debriefing	Referral Law enforcement	Evaluate role of physical environment	All staff debrief and learn Modify plan if appropriate

FIGURE 6.3 Haddon matrix (social influence).

Phase	Affected Individual and Population	Agent Used	Environment
Preevent	Psychological first aid	Communicate efforts to limit action	Have plans in place detailing agency roles in prevention and detection
Event	Population uses skills	Mobilize trauma workers	Communicate that response systems are in place
Postevent	Assessment, triage, and psychological treatment	Communicate, establish outreach centers	Adjust risk communication
End results	Limit distress responses, negative behavior changes, and psychological illness	Minimize loss of life and impact of attack	Minimize disruption in daily routines

FIGURE 6.4   Haddon matrix environmental influence.

ESTABLISHING A VIOLENCE PREVENTION COMMITTEE FOR GUIDELINES

According to Nixon,* management must demonstrate a commitment by taking workplace violence seriously and appointing an influential manager to be responsible for the workplace violence prevention effort. This manager should establish a workplace violence prevention committee (also referred to as a threat management committee). Participants on the committee should include representatives from security, human resources, occupational health and safety, legal, finance, risk management, public relations, doctors, nurses, and union, if applicable. Smaller-sized firms that do not have these specific dedicated resources should designate an operations person to put together an appropriate team to address the issue using available resources.

ELIMINATE AT-RISK BEHAVIORS

The committee should focus on creating a violence-free work environment by eliminating at-risk behaviors on both an individual and organization level. One of the key responsibilities of the committee should also be to establish a workplace violence zero-incident policy (see model policies at (www.workplaceviolence911.com/ModelPolicies). Note that a zero-incident focus is a proactive approach that targets prevention and goes beyond zero tolerance that generally focuses more on reacting. An example of addressing an at-risk behavior in a medical center could be to have a procedure for flagging the charts of high-risk patients to give early alert to staff or remind them to check for weapons and to keep security on standby.

ESTABLISH A PREVENTION POLICY

A cornerstone of your program is to establish a clear workplace violence prevention policy that will set the framework and provide guidance to managers, doctors, nurses, and employees. The focus should be on violence prevention, with the ultimate goal being zero incidents. In addition, the policy should make the concept of treating people in a respectful manner and maintaining their dignity a central theme that is integrated into the policy and its communication (see www.workplace violence911.com for information on the ultimate workplace violence prevention policy).

---

* Nixon, Barry, W. Medical Workplace Violence Risks, in Marcinko, D.E. (Ed.), *Insurance and Risk Management Strategies*, Jones and Bartlett, Sudbury, MA, 2007.

No Weapons Policy

Incorporate a "no weapons policy" provision into your workplace violence prevention policy or establish a separate policy that clearly establishes that no weapons are allowed on the premises and that employees are prohibited from possessing a weapon while on duty. Medical centers and hospital emergency rooms should also conspicuously post signs clearly stating that all weapons are prohibited on the premises for the public and patients to see.

Define Entities at Risk

The workplace violence prevention committee should also research the nature of risk to the health care company associated with the health care industry. Ask questions like

- How does violence from the surrounding community have the potential to affect your workplace?
- What services that you offer have a history of being exposed to violence in the industry (e.g., trauma or acute psychiatric care)? If so, what kind of incidents, type of facilities, geographic characteristics, and so forth?
- How frequently are assaultive incidents, threats, and verbal abuse occurring, and where? Who is involved?

Where there are known hazards that exist within this type of business, industry, or geographic area, specific actions should be taken to mitigate and address the problems. This is essential because these are the signs that indicate the greatest potential for violence to occur and commensurately represent the highest potential liability.

Facility Assessments

Conduct periodic facility risk assessments to identify unsafe areas, hazards, or vulnerabilities that exist in your physical facilities that could contribute to significant risk. For example, are there access doors that have broken locks? Are effective access controls processes in place and enforced? Are there dimly lit stairwells or an external entrance door that is regularly propped open?

Organizational Assessments

Conduct periodic organizational violence assessments to identify management practices, employee behaviors, and perceptions that are not conducive to creating a violence-free workplace (e.g., terminating employees via e-mail, harassment of employees, and incongruent policies). The assessment should closely review safety records for a history of violent incidents and close calls. This data can help you determine trends, conditions, circumstances, and underlying causes of violence as well as identify cultural norms and behaviors. One such behavior is bullying, which often is endemic in a given firm, and this can substantially contribute to undue stress or conflict in the organization. This is of particular importance since studies are starting to show that bullying often precedes actual violence erupting. Therefore, it should be considered as a potential warning sign. Collect utilization data from the employee assistance program and analyze the results. This type of data can be key in identifying at-risk factors on the organization level. Also conduct a "dignity and respect" audit of all human resource, security, safety, and operational policies to ensure they are designed to treat employees in a sensitive and respectful manner.

The above point is particularly true for designing termination, layoff, and discipline procedures that are sensitive to ensuring fair, respectful, and dignified treatment of employees. According to *The Disposable Worker: Living in a Job-Loss Economy* (published by the Center for Workforce

Development at Rutgers University), the vast majority of employers are ignoring this advice. The study states that workers laid off from their jobs during the past 3 years received no advance notice, no severance pay, and no career counseling from their employers. This flies in the face of strong evidence that employers who are arrogant, abrupt, rude, stingy, or just plain gutless in their practices are courting aggression and violence. Dick Ault, PhD, a former FBI agent specializing in profiling, put it well by stating that special precautions should be taken when at-risk behaviors are present. His view that "you have to approach the firing of anyone with the utmost of dignity, even people who really don't deserve it" (personal correspondence), are words that employers should heed.

INDIVIDUAL THREAT ASSESSMENT

Identify external experts experienced and thoroughly trained in how to professionally assess the violent nature of an individual and the likelihood of an employee becoming violent. It is important to have a resource on contract prior to the need for their services.

ENHANCE PHYSICAL SECURITY

Enhance physical security measures and establish workplace violence audit team(s) to conduct ongoing assessments and effectiveness of security efforts. Some common security-sensitive areas are the following:

- Emergency department
- Pharmacy and medical records department
- Mother/infant care
- Cashiers and general outpatient clinics
- Specialized outpatient clinics (substance abuse, abortion, etc.)
- Animal research and mental health units

In addition, to harden targeted areas or improve control, use security prevention through environmental design engineering/architectural controls processes when building or retrofitting facilities to maximize crime prevention. For example, set up emergency rooms so that there are barriers (e.g., doors requiring key card access) to the public accessing areas where patients are being kept. Have intake personnel protected by bullet-resistant plastic barriers or an overly wide counter that cannot be easily reached over.

Provide nursing personnel with handheld alarms or noise devices and/or communication devices to be able to get help (e.g., cellular phones, pagers, whistles, or mobile alarms) to use while on duty, and establish processes for pinpointing their whereabouts using Global Positioning System technologies.

SYNCHRONIZE PERSONNEL, SECURITY, AND SAFETY POLICIES

Synchronize your personnel, security, and safety policies to ensure they create an integrated workplace violence prevention effort.

DEVELOP CRISIS RESPONSE PROCEDURES

Establish a crisis response team (specially trained to deal with crisis) and develop crisis response procedures to deal with an incident. Select members based on preestablished criteria, which should include their ability to remain calm during a crisis or pressure situations, special skills related to handling crisis or emergencies, as well as technical competency related to health care, knowledge of facilities, public relations, security, and so forth. The team should put a crisis communication and public relations plan in place before a crisis occurs. Additionally, preestablish a critical incident debriefing process and skilled counselors to be able to assist victims after an incident.

Keep in mind that the speed at which you are able to address the needs of employees who have experienced a traumatic event will dictate how fast you are able to return work levels to normal operations. Within the following few days of an incident, reactions such as fear, anxiety, exhaustion, as well as anger may surface. In the long run, lack of confidence, depression, and the development of posttraumatic stress disorder are possible outcomes.

EMERGENCY POLICE PROTOCOL

Create an emergency protocol with the police. This should include identifying the contact person at the police department when an incident needs to be reported. It is also important to identify a backup contact and make sure that contact knows who from your firm is responsible for getting in touch with them. You should also have the police visit your site and learn your facility layout. In addition, you should make your address and building numbers clearly visible. Where there are multiple buildings, make address numbers clearly visible on the front and top of each building.

ENHANCE HIRING PROCEDURES

Enhance hiring procedures to include health care organization employment-screening processes focused on screening out violence-prone applicants before they are hired. Use critical behavior traits to identify behavior-based interview questions. Screening tools can include

- Reference checking regarding previous employers
- Background checks (e.g., for a criminal background)
- Verification of identity
- Driving record and credit history
- Drug testing and psychological assessments
- Critical behavior traits

PROMOTE AN EMPLOYEE ASSISTANCE PROGRAM

Actively and regularly promote your employee assistance program and train supervisors on how to make an effective referral. If you are in a smaller organization that does not have an employee assistance program, establish a list of local service providers in your community that employees can be referred to.

TRAIN MANAGERS, SUPERVISORS, DOCTORS, NURSES, AND EMPLOYEES

Provide ongoing training for managers, supervisors, doctors, nurses, and employees. Training should be provided in the following areas:

- Implementation of workplace violence prevention policy
- How to identify early warning signs in patients, the public, and employees, and how to appropriately intervene
- Importance of reporting, taking threats seriously, and responding
- How to deescalate potentially hostile situations, including treating patients, the public, and employees in a respectful manner
- Effective ways to deal with domestic violence situations in the workplace
- If deemed appropriate for your setting, training in how to safely restrain patients

INVOLVE EMPLOYEES IN PREVENTION EFFORTS

Make sure all employees know that workplace violence prevention is everybody's business and help them understand the important role they can play in reducing violence. A truly effective prevention effort must maximize the participation of employees and their support. By encouraging the following practices, employers can enlist employee support, and they will contribute substantially to a successful effort to prevent violence at work:

- Reporting of threats, suspicious activities, or actions of violence regardless of whether you personally believe the threat is serious.
- Avoiding horseplay, practical jokes, harassment, or other risky behaviors that could lead to injury, creating animosity or shame or invoking angry reactions.
- Treating all employees, customers, and contractors with dignity and respect. *How* something is said is just as important as *what* is said.
- When feeling overly stressed, seeking help from an employee assistance program or other support services designed to act as relief valves for frustrations or problems (e.g., church, family, or friends).
- Actively following the firm's policy regarding workplace violence and the procedures for dealing with workplace threats and crisis.

Additional interventions that employers can use to focus on preventing workplace violence include

- Publishing a list of whom to call and resources available to assist with issues
- Using external resources as appropriate for the following:
  - Individual threat assessments
  - Legal
  - Facility risk assessment
  - Security protection firm
  - Employee assistance program support
  - Organizational threat assessment

ASSESSMENT

Physicians, advisors, nurse-executives, administrators, and many managers view workplace violence as the sole responsibility of a deranged, psychopathic, or troubled employee, while the truth is closer to the reality that an outbreak of violence in an organization is often the result of chronic unresolved conflict that should have been noticed and properly managed. Despite our best attempts to place the blame on the individual's behavior, the organization is not blameless. Violence is the tragic aberration of an organization's culture—the culmination of personal frustration that has built to a crescendo because of perceived injustice, humiliation, loss of dignity, shaming, and loss of value and control that ultimately explode into a desperate act.

Acts of health care organization workplace violence can be reduced, and the many human and financial costs that result can be avoided with forethought and strategic and progressive action. Attending to workplace conflict is not simply "soft-hearted" or humanitarian—it is prudent business and risk reduction planning.

Yesterday, organizations that ignored the quality challenge did not survive—recall American automobile manufacturers who faced the "quality invasion" of Japanese imports in the 1970s. Most companies responded well, hence Ford's slogan "Quality is Job 1." Today, product and service quality management initiatives such as total quality management, continuous improvement, and customer satisfaction programs are unquestioned requirements for business success.

For tomorrow, the competitive and leadership advantage of the 21st century for the industry may be strategic conflict management, and it may be the separating factor in determining who survives in the global competitive marketplace.

CONCLUSION

Violence in the hospital or medical workplace is an emerging safety and health issue. Its most extreme form, homicide, is the fourth-leading cause of fatal occupational injury in the United States, according to the BLS Census of Fatal Occupational Injuries.

CASE MODEL 6.1: BOULDER-CREST MEDICAL CENTER (BCMC)

NEWS FLASH! The news report comes in: Two employees at the Boulder-Crest Medical Center have been killed in the workplace, and two have been wounded. A witness has called 911, and the police as well as other emergency personnel are at the scene. The perpetrator (a former employee of the medical center) has been taken into custody, the victims are being treated, and the police are interviewing witnesses and gathering evidence.

In this situation, the medical center's crisis response plan called for the immediate involvement of an official from the public information office (PIO) in addition to the following BCMC employees:

1. A top management representative
2. A security officer
3. A human resources (HR) specialist
4. An employee assistance program (EAP) counselor

Top management representative: The deputy hospital administrator coordinated the response effort because she was the senior person on duty at the time. In addition to acting as coordinator, she remained available to police throughout the afternoon to make sure there were no impediments to the investigation.

She immediately called the families of the wounded and assigned two other senior managers to notify the families of the deceased. She also arranged for a friend of each of the deceased coworkers to accompany each of the managers. She took care of numerous administrative details, such as authorizing expenditures for additional resources, signing forms, and making decisions about such matters as granting leave to coworkers. It was necessary for the medical center to remain in operation, and it was impossible to allow all of the employees to go home for the rest of the day.

To ensure a coordinated response effort, she made sure that medical center personnel directly involved in the crisis had cell phones for internal communication while conducting their duties in various offices around the building.

Security staff: The security staff assisted the police with numerous activities including locating witnesses and preserving the crime scene.

HR representative: The HR specialist contacted the medical center's corporate office and alerted them to the situation so that they could immediately begin to monitor any criminal and other legal proceedings. He made a detailed written record of the incident but did not take statements from witnesses, because to do so might have impeded the criminal investigation and possible subsequent prosecution of the case. He also helped the HR supervisor with internal documentation related to the incident.

Employee assistance program (EAP) counselor: The medical center had only one EAP counselor available at the time of the incident. However, in prior planning for an emergency, the medical center had contracted with a local EAP provider to provide additional counselors on an as-needed basis. The one EAP counselor on duty called the contractor, and four additional counselors were at the medical center at the time. It was not possible to use the medical center's social workers, as one of the victims was a social worker. The counselors remained available near the scene of the incident to reassure and comfort the staff. Since they were not medical center staff, they wore readily visible identification badges.

Arrangements for postincident traumatic stress debriefings were scheduled to begin in 2 days. The EAP counselor also arranged for two contract EAP counselors to be at the medical center for the next week to walk around the center inquiring how the staff members were doing and to consult with supervisors about how to help the staff in their recovery efforts.

Public information officer: The PIO handled all aspects of press coverage. She maintained liaison with the media, provided an area for reporters to work, and maintained a schedule of frequent briefings.

KEY ISSUES

The community, patients, press corps, and employees of Boulder-Crest Medical Center realize there are no guarantees of personal safety and antiterrorism in the modern era. But BCMC was able to take lessons learned, boldly keep its commitment to safety and violence prevention in the medical workplace, and consider new solutions to the dilemma. Upon reviewing the situation at BCMC, consider the following questions:

1. How would your health care facility or hospital have obtained the services of additional EAP counselors?
2. How would or should employees be given information about this incident?
3. Who would clean up the crime scene?
4. Would you relocate employees who worked in the area of the crime scene?
5. What approach would you take regarding the granting of excused absence on the day of the incident and requests for leave in the days/weeks following the incident?
6. How would you advise BCMC management and administration to deal with work normally assigned to the victims?
7. What support would your organization provide to supervisors to get the affected work group(s) back to functioning?
8. What are the possible direct and indirect financial ramifications and recovery costs of the retroactive, crisis-prone approach to medical workplace violence used at BCMC?
9. What might have been the financial costs of using a more proactive, crisis-prepared approach to workplace violence at BCMC?
10. What might have been the financial cost savings at BCMC if a crisis-prepared approach to health care violence had been used?

POSSIBLE SOLUTIONS:

Financial and Economic Cost of BCMC Recovery*
(The Reactive Crisis-Prone Approach)

BCMC Incident (Medical Workplace Violence Event)	Costs
1. Incident debriefing with impacted employees (3 managers, 5 doctors, 10 nurses, and 27 employees working in impacted area)	$1,200.00
2. Center closed due to incident for 3½ days	$122,856.00
3. Revenue lost (assumes that for six weeks after the incident, there is a 25% productivity decline)	$1,724,694.00

4. Cleanup of incident area/crime scene	$2,000.00
5. Increase in annual health care premiums due to increased use of psychological services (20% of employees need counseling for 3 months, 10% for 6 months, and 1% for 12 months)	$5,000.00
6. Lawsuit settlement (assumed out-of-court settlement at 60% of the average settlement of $500,000.00)	$300,000.00
7. Public relations campaign, marketing, and communication strategy with stakeholders to counter negative press and restore confidence in company	$10,000.00
8. Replacement cost for 10% turnover of workforce (e.g., 25 managers and 75 employees; assumes 25% of salary replacement cost for managers and 10% for employees against national figures of 50% to 100% of salary for replacement cost)	$315,500.00
Total	**$2,481,250.00**

* Cost estimates based on workplace violence prevention software like that available from www.workplaceviolence911 .com.

Focus on Proactive Violence Prevention at BCMC*
(The Zero-Incident Crisis-Prepared Approach)

Prevention Actions	Cost
Programmatic Steps	
1. Establish a workplace violence prevention committee	$2,000.00
2. Focus on eliminating at-risk behaviors	Internal staff
3. Establish a comprehensive workplace violence prevention policy	*$500.00
4. Policy of no weapons in the workplace*	
5. Define the nature of the risk to the company	Internal staff
6. Facility risk assessments	$2,000.00
7. Organizational violence assessments	$6,000.00
8. Individual threat assessment	$1,000.00
9. Enhance physical security	(Capital Budget $60,000.00)
10. Synchronize your personnel, security, and safety policies	$2,000.00
11. Develop crisis response procedures	$4,000.00
12. Emergency protocol with police	Internal staff
13. Enhance hiring procedures	$7,500.00
14. Promote your employee assistance program	Internal staff
15. Training managers, doctors, nurses, and employees	$24,000.00
16. Involve employees in the prevention effort	Internal staff
Programmatic steps subtotal	$49,000.00
Insurance	
17. Employment practices liability insurance (assumes $100,000.00 deductible)	$35,000.00
Insurance subtotal	$35,000.00
Capital budget	$60,000.00
Capital budget subtotal	$60,000.00
Grand total	$144,770.00

* Cost estimates based on workplace violence prevention software like that available from www.workplaceviolence911 .com.

BCMC econometrics: $2,481,250.00 – $144,770.00 = $2,336,480.00 (retroactive costs) – (proactive costs)

Potential BCMC cost savings: $2,336,480.00 (zero-incident, crisis-prepared approach)

CHECKLIST 1: Medical Workplace Violence Risks	YES	NO

In preparation for the prevention and response to potential incidents of medical workplace violence, it is suggested that the following risk assessment areas be examined, within a total overview of the hospital facilities, clinic, and/or medical office needs, and capabilities:

	YES	NO
Is our facility vulnerable in any of the following ways or areas?	o	o
Physical health care facility layout and access controls. (Use counters to control traffic, initiate escort service for visitors, or consider the use of convex mirrors).	o	o
Personnel and visitor control access. (Are there some areas that need to be made nonpublic? Are badges needed?)	o	o
Preparedness of the hospital's, clinic's, or other health care facility's emergency response team.	o	o
Communication system and capabilities. (Panic alarms in reception areas, HR offices, social service offices; telephone connection with local law enforcement agency—can one get through to 911 directly, or does one have to dial 9 prior to getting an outside line? Make arrangements with the phone service provider to establish direct call 911. Modify phones so that when a 911 call comes in, it actually identifies the sector or telephone from which the call was placed.)	o	o
Provision for special needs (e.g., interpreters or employees with physical disabilities).	o	o
Is a policy established to require all employees to advise of threats heard?	o	o
Is a policy established to require employees to immediately notify human resources when a restraining order has been introduced?	o	o

CHECKLIST 2: Initial Assessment	YES	NO

Prior to the establishment of a comprehensive medical workplace violence policy, and as an integral part of the policy development, it is necessary to conduct a survey in a number of areas.

	YES	NO
Does your survey cover security procedures?	o	o
Employee/visitor/guest identification?	o	o
Access control?	o	o
Prohibited items on facility property?	o	o
Drugs and other illicit substances?	o	o
Inspection of cars and personal items?	o	o
Security capabilities?	o	o
Crisis management team/plans?	o	o
Does your survey cover human resources concerns?	o	o
Employment application screening?	o	o
Drug/alcohol testing policy?	o	o
Background investigations?	o	o
Psychological testing?	o	o
Minimum standards of conduct?	o	o
Sexual harassment?	o	o
Workplace violence?	o	o
Intolerance to infractions?	o	o
Disciplinary actions?	o	o
Termination procedures?	o	o
Posttermination monitoring?	o	o
Americans with Disabilities Act (ADA) compliance?	o	o

	YES	NO
Does your survey cover EAP programs?	o	o
Availability of counseling?	o	o
Stress management programs?	o	o
Alcohol/drug treatment programs?	o	o
Does your survey cover medical/first aid capabilities?		
In-house medical capabilities?	o	o
Private/public medical response capabilities?	o	o
Does your survey cover public/media relations responsibilities?	o	o
In-house capabilities?	o	o
Major incident/disaster response?	o	o
Does your survey cover legal requirements?	o	o
Review of and familiarity with issues involving workplace violence, negligent hiring, training, retention, termination, ADA, OSHA?	o	o

CHECKLIST 3: Crisis Plan	YES	NO
Have you determined:	o	o
Who calls 911?	o	o
Who is responsible (e.g., senior staff, person on duty at time of call)?	o	o
Who is in charge?		
Have you established procedures for calling:		
Family members?	o	o
The media?	o	o
Have you made certain that sprinklers, fire extinguishers, fire alarms, and first-aid kits are all operational and fully stocked?	o	o
Are local law enforcement officers familiar with layout of facility?	o	o
Have you identified staging areas:		
For emergency responders?	o	o
For employees to congregate?	o	o
For the press?	o	o

CHECKLIST 4: Training Programs	YES	NO
Have you trained all personnel to recognize "troubled" patients, family members, and fellow employees?	o	o
Have you provided training in the following:	o	o
Employee safety procedures for self-protection?	o	o
How to avoid becoming a victim?	o	o
How to escape?	o	o
How to respond if taken hostage?	o	o
Have you provided training in the following:	o	o
Conflict resolution?	o	o
How to recognize developing anger?	o	o
How to deal with difficult expressions of anger?	o	o

CHECKLIST 5: Training Program Topics	YES	NO
This list of training topics is geared primarily to hospital supervisors and clinic managers and focuses on internal employees as opposed to the general public or patients. For unit managers, head nurse, or nursing supervisor, it is recommended that personal safety issues also be included. Are the following topics covered in the training program?		
Does the training program cover the following?	o	o
Improving employee performance	o	o
How to conduct performance evaluations, including the proper way of	o	o
providing feedback data	o	o
How to document incidents—zero-tolerance for incidents of sexual harassment, stalking, or weapons on premises		
Understanding the policies and procedures of the practice, hospital, clinic, or other health care facility		
Have you trained personnel on the following?	o	o
Services and assistance available through the EAP	o	o
How to refer to EAP	o	o
Other resources available to employees		
Have you provided a comprehensive overview of the role of security, human resources, the medical department, and the crisis management team?	o	o
Does your training program cover indications of drug and alcohol use (including both legal and illegal substances)?	o	o
Does your training program include a complete overview of workplace violence, including a symptom recognition session?	o	o
In this area, it is important not to focus on any one profile as it is too general. Rather, the emphasis needs to be placed on the recognition of behavioral changes. Also to be included in this block is the need for the supervisor to refer the affected employee to the EAP.		
Does your training program include procedure guidelines on how to terminate employees?	o	o
Does your training program include stress awareness and management including anger and conflict resolution?	o	o

CHECKLIST 6: Threat Incident Report	YES	NO
Policy should require employees to report all threats or incidents of violent behavior that they observe or are informed about to the designated health care management representative (DHMR). The DHMR is to take the steps necessary to complete a threat incident report as quickly as possible, including private interviews of the victim(s) and witness(es). The report will be used by management to assess the safety of the workplace and to decide upon a course of action.		
Does your threat incident report include the following?	o	o
Name of the threat maker and his or her relationship to the health care facility (office or clinic) and to the recipient		
Name(s) of the victims or potential victims	o	o
When and where the incident occurred	o	o
What happened immediately prior to the incident	o	o

The specific language of the threat	o	o
Any physical conduct that would substantiate an intention to follow through on the threat	o	o
How the threat maker appeared (physically and emotionally)	o	o
Names of others who were directly involved and any actions they took	o	o
How the incident ended	o	o
Names of witnesses	o	o
What happened to the threat maker after the incident	o	o
Name of any supervisory staff involved and how they responded	o	o
What event(s) triggered the incident	o	o
Any history leading up to the incident	o	o
The steps that have been taken to ensure that the threat will not be carried out	o	o
Suggestions for future prevention	o	o

CHECKLIST 7: Protecting a Medical Office	**YES**	**NO**
Are doors and windows locked at the end of each day?	o	o
Are file cabinets locked and other open temptations to theft removed each day?	o	o
Are clients/patients under supervision at all times in the office?	o	o
Is there an adequate waiting area?	o	o
Does the office layout help control the flow of clients and the public?	o	o
Are there blind spots to hide or where someone could be concealed without others finding out?	o	o
Are there furnishings that block your exit in the event of an emergency or an attack?	o	o
Are there objects such as plants, lamps, and others that could be readily used as a weapon against you?	o	o
Do you have access to a shield for use in your defense in case of attack?	o	o
Could you immediately summon help if needed?	o	o
Do you have alarms or keywords signaling others of danger or that help is needed?	o	o
Does your office routinely discuss ways to improve security after potentially dangerous situations?	o	o

CHECKLIST 8: Ten Commonsense Ideas for Preventing Medical Workplace Violence Problems	**YES**	**NO**
Have you installed metal detectors to identify weapons?	o	o
Have you installed alarm systems or panic buttons?	o	o
Do you use bright and effective lighting systems?	o	o
Do you use curved mirrors at hallway intersections or concealed areas?	o	o
Have you ensured all areas have two exits?	o	o
Have you arranged furniture to prevent entrapment?	o	o
Have you established "time out" or seclusion rooms?	o	o
Do you provide for adequate staffing, particularly during times of increased patient activities and during restraint procedures?	o	o

Have you trained employees to identify hazardous situations, in managing agitated patients or family members, and appropriate responses in emergencies?	o	o
Have you established liaison with local police?	o	o
To protect staff, do you provide:	o	o
Enclosures?	o	o
Deep service counters?	o	o
Bullet-resistant glass?		

CHECKLIST 9: Safety Awareness	**YES**	**NO**
Are you familiar with the facility or office's evacuation plan?	o	o
Are you familiar with the exit to use to evacuate the work area?	o	o
Do you know the difference between the fire alarm for bomb threats versus other emergency alarms?	o	o
Do you know the location of fire extinguishers?	o	o
Do you know the location of first aid kits and what is to be done with them in case of an alarm?	o	o
Do you know who is responsible for contacting local authorities in the event of an emergency?	o	o
Do you know where you are to gather outside the building?	o	o
Do you know who is responsible for seeing that the office is cleared every time the alarm sounds?	o	o
Do you know the office procedures in the event of a telephone bomb threat?	o	o

CHECKLIST 10: Safety Tips for Hospital Workers	**YES**	**NO**
Have any of these signals, associated with impending violence, been exhibited?		
Verbally expressed anger and frustration	o	o
Body language such as threatening gestures	o	o
Signs of drug or alcohol use	o	o
Presence of a weapon	o	o
Do you demonstrate the following kinds of behavior to help defuse anger?		
Present a calm, caring attitude	o	o
Do not give orders	o	o
Acknowledge the person's feelings (for example, "I know that you are frustrated")	o	o
Avoid any behavior that may be interpreted as aggressive (for example, moving rapidly, getting too close, touching, or speaking loudly)	o	o
Do you:		
Evaluate each situation for potential violence when you enter a room or begin to relate to a patient or visitor?	o	o
Remain vigilant throughout the encounter?	o	o
Avoid isolating yourself with a potentially violent person?	o	o
Always keep an open path for exiting—don't let the potentially violent person stand between you and the door?	o	o
Do you take these steps if you can't defuse the situation quickly?		
Remove yourself from the situation	o	o
Call security for help	o	o
Report any violent incidents to your manager or management team	o	o

CHECKLIST 11: Safety Features	YES	NO
Have you installed surveillance cameras at the entrance to and inside high-risk areas like the emergency department? (Inside cameras should be very visible.)	o	o
Have you conspicuously posted a sign by the entrance to high-risk areas stating that weapons of any kind are prohibited on the premises and all people entering are being photographed for security purposes?	o	o
Have you installed street-level cameras (similar to those at traffic signals that send tickets for running a light) to record license plate numbers?	o	o
Have you installed metal detectors at the entrances to high-risk areas?	o	o
Have you installed monitors to show those entering high-risk areas?	o	o
Have you worked with local police to establish a substation in or near the emergency department?	o	o
Have you installed cameras at the access door to where patients are being housed?	o	o
Have you installed panic buttons in high-risk areas such as at the admissions desks and emergency department patient rooms?	o	o
Have you given ER personnel mobile units to be able to alert security?	o	o
Have you placed curved mirrors at hallway intersections or concealed areas?	o	o
Have we reconfigured all treatment rooms in high-risk areas to have two exits?	o	o

OSHA PUBLICATIONS

For a free copy of OSHA publications, send a self-addressed mailing label to this address: OSHA Publications Office, P.O. Box 37535, Washington, DC 20013-7535, or send a request by fax to (202) 693-2498 or phone (202) 693-1888. To file a complaint by phone, report an emergency, or get OSHA advice, assistance, or products, contact your nearest OSHA office under the "U.S. Department of Labor" listing in your phone book, or call (800) 321–OSHA (6742).

ACKNOWLEDGMENTS

Thanks are due to Barry W. Nixon, MS, of www.workplaceviolence911.com, for technical assistance in the preparation of this chapter.

BIBLIOGRAPHY

Bureau of Justice Statistics, http://www.ojp.usdoj.gov/bjs/.

Dana, D. *The Dana Measure of the Financial Cost of Organizational Conflict: An Interpretive Guide*. Dana Mediation Institute, Inc. 2001, www.mediationworks.com.

Distasio, C. A., "Protecting Yourself from Violence in the Workplace." *Nursing* 32:6 (2002).

"Fatal Choices." University of Washington Alumni Magazine. Seattle, September 2000. Available online at www.washington.edu.

Fatal Occupational Injuries by Event or Exposure, U.S. Department of Labor, Bureau of Labor Statistics, Census of Fatal Occupational Injuries, 1991–2002.

Gamble, R. H. "Apocalypse Maybe," *Controller Magazine*, June 1998.

Hoel, H., Sparks, K. and Cooper, C. L. *The Cost of Violence/Stress at work and the Benefits of a Violence/Stress-Free Working Environment*. Report Commissioned by the International Labour Organization (ILO), Geneva, Switzerland, January 1, 2001.

Jones, S. "Work Stress Taking Larger Financial Toll," August 9, 2000.

McKoy, Y. and Smith, M. H. "Legal Considerations of Workplace Violence in Healthcare Environments," *Nursing Forum* 36:1, January 2007, Wiley, NY.

Workplace Violence in Health Services, Joint ILO/ICN/WHO/PSI research, 2002.

FURTHER READING

Buba, V. "Sexual Harassment Risks in Medical Practice." In Marcinko, D. E. (editor). *Risk Management and Insurance Planning for Physicians and Advisors.* Sudbury, MA: Jones and Bartlett, 2006.

Colling, M. S. and Russell L. *Security—Keeping the Healthcare Environment Safe,* Joint Commission on Accreditation of Healthcare Organizations 1996.

Kerr, K. *Workplace Violence: Planning for Prevention and Response.* Butterworth-Heinemann, New York, 2010.

Levin, P. F., Beauchamp Hewitt, J. and Misner, S. T. "Insights of Nurses About Assault in Hospital-Based Emergency Departments." *The Journal of Nursing Scholarship.* 30:3 (1998): 249.

Marais, S., Van Der Spuy, E. and Rontsch, R. "Crime and Violence in the Workplace—Effect on Health Workers Part II." Crime, Violence & Injury Lead Programme, MRC, and Institute of Criminology, University of Cape Town, South Africa.

McNamara, S. A. "Behave Yourself"—Interview in Hospitals and Health Networks (H&HNS), page 14, January 2010.

McPhaul, K. M. and Lipscomb, J. A. "Workplace Violence in Healthcare: Recognized but Not Regulated." *Online Journal of Issues in Nursing.* 9:3 (2004): Manuscript 6.

Nixon, B. "Medical Office Workplace Violence Risks." In Marcinko, D. E. (editor). *Risk Management and Insurance Planning for Physicians and Advisors.* Sudbury, MA: Jones and Bartlett, 2007.

Privitera, A. "Workplace Violence in Mental and General Health Settings." Jones and Bartlett, Sudbury, MA, 2010.

Runyan, C. S., Zakocs, R. C. and Zwerling, C. "Administrative and Behavioral Interventions for Workplace Violence Prevention" *American Journal of Preventive Medicine* 18:4 Suppl. (2000): 116–127.

Schmuckler, E. "Bridging Financial Planning and Human Psychology." In Marcinko, D. E. (editor). *Financial Planning for Physicians and Advisors.* Sudbury, MA: Jones and Bartlett, 2004.

Schmuckler, E. "Workplace Violence in Healthcare—Case Reports." In Marcinko, D. (editor). *Healthcare Organizations.* iMBA Inc., Publishers, Atlanta, GA, 2010.

Schmuckler, E. "Professional Career Development," in Marcinko, D. E. (editor). *Financial Planning for Physicians and Healthcare Professionals.* New York: Aspen Publishers, 2003.

Special Report on Violence in the Workplace. Bureau of Justice Statistics, December 2001.

Violence—Occupational Hazards in Hospitals. DHHS (NIOSH) Publication No. 2002-101.

"Violence at Work: The Experience of UK Doctors." British Medical Association, Health Policy and Economic Research Unit, October 2003.

7 Implications of the USA PATRIOT and Sarbanes–Oxley Acts for Hospitals
Operational Policies for Affected Health Care Organizations

David Edward Marcinko and Hope Rachel Hetico

CONTENTS

INTRODUCTION

In the wake of the September 11, 2001, terrorist attacks against the United States, the U.S. Congress passed Public Law 107-56, whose short title is "Uniting and Strengthening America by Providing Appropriate Tools Required to Intercept and Obstruct Terrorism (USA PATRIOT Act) Act of 2001."

Also, because of well-publicized scandals involving Enron Corporation and its auditor, Arthur Andersen, the U.S. Congress passed Public Law 107-204, whose short title is "The Sarbanes–Oxley Act of 2002." Both the USA PATRIOT Act and the Sarbanes–Oxley Act contain sections that affect some hospitals and health care organizations.

The purpose of this chapter is to determine the financial and strategic management implications of the USA PATRIOT Act and the Sarbanes–Oxley Act for affected hospitals and health care organizations.

In order to accomplish this, we will focus on the legislation itself, the financial literature concerning the legislation, and the business literature concerning the impact of these two laws on the strategic management of hospitals.

THE USA PATRIOT ACT

The USA PATRIOT Act comprises sections covering a variety of topics. Much of the act revises or updates laws already in the United States Code (U.S.C.) in order to better coordinate efforts against terrorism. It is complemented by Executive Order #13224 and U.N. Security Council Resolution #1373, as monitored by the Office of Foreign Assets Control (OFAC) through its Specially Designated Nationals (SDN) list and Terror Exclusion List (TEL).

However, several other pieces of legislation applicable to hospitals and health care organizations have arisen because of the electronic age. For example, the Internet Spyware Prevention Act of 2005, H.R. 744 (I-SPY Act), passed by the U.S. House of Representatives on May 23, 2005, criminalizes unauthorized spyware, phishing, or other methods of obtaining sensitive personal health or other information without consent; it forbids the bringing of a civil action under the law of any state if such action was premised in whole or in part on the use of illegally obtained protected information.

As is the case with the Health Insurance Portability and Accountability Act of 1996 (HIPAA) and the USA PATRIOT Act, protected information defined in the I-SPY Act includes first and last names, home or other physical addresses, e-mail addresses, telephone numbers, Social Security numbers, tax identification numbers, driver's license numbers, passport numbers, other government-issued identification numbers, credit card numbers, bank account numbers, and passwords or access codes associated with credit card, insurance company, hospital, or bank accounts. The I-SPY Act does not apply to government agencies involved in national security operations and investigations.

President George W. Bush also signed the USA PATRIOT Improvement and Reauthorization Act into law on March 9, 2006. This legislation continued the authorization for intelligence and law enforcement officials to share information and use the same tools against terrorists that had been granted in the original Act. According to the President:

> The law…will improve our nation's security while we safeguard the civil liberties of our people. The legislation strengthens the Justice Department so it can better detect and disrupt terrorist threats. And the bill gives law enforcement new tools to combat threats to our citizens from international terrorists….*

In early 2007, Senator Mark Pryor introduced the Counter Spy Act to make it illegal to implant spyware on a personal computer (PC) without consent. Spyware allows one to duplicate Web sites, including financial, health care, or retail sites, where personal medical records or financial information such as credit card numbers and insurance information is stored. It is usually downloaded without user knowledge during another software download or by simply clicking on a link ("drive-by downloading"). Once downloaded, it is almost impossible to remove.

---

* Bush, George W. *Public Papers of the Presidents of the United States: George W. Bush, 2006, book I.* Page 428. Washington, D.C. Government Printing Office, 2006.

In fact, an AOL study revealed that 80% of all computers in its test group were infected and that 89% of the users of those computers were unaware of it. The Counter Spy Act of 2007 also provides that the Federal Trade Commission (FTC) enforce the law as if a violation was an unfair or deceptive practice. The agency would have authority to bring civil and criminal penalties (fines and/or imprisonment for up to 5 years) for violations.

In addition, late in 2007, the Committee on Energy and Commerce passed two additional bills designed to protect Americans from invasive Internet spyware and Social Security number theft. The first was H.R. 964, the Securely Protect Yourself Against Cyber Trespass Act (the Spy Act); the second was H.R. 948, the Social Security Number Protection Act of 2007.

The Spy Act shields Internet users, doctors, and patients from under-the-radar spyware programs that secretly invade PCs and monitor online activity. The Act requires software distributors and advertisers to notify and require consent from consumers and patients before programs can be downloaded from the Internet. Offenders could be assessed a fine of up to $3 million for each unfair or deceptive spyware act and up to $1 million for each violation relating to the collection of personal information without notice and consent.

The Social Security Number Protection Act is intended to protect patients and consumers from the ever-increasing problem of identity theft. The legislation restricts the sale, purchase, and use of Social Security numbers except in situations approved by the FTC, such as for law enforcement or health purposes. Violators would be fined $11,000 per infraction, up to $5 million.

At first blush, the USA PATRIOT Act and these legislative derivatives seem to have very little to do with hospitals, health care organizations, or the medical industrial complex; however, upon closer inspection, several sections appear to be relevant to the hospital and health care industry.

PREVENTION AND DETECTION OF MONEY LAUNDERING

Title III of the USA PATRIOT Act is entitled the "International Money Laundering Abatement and Anti-Terrorist Financing Act of 2001." The purposes of the act are "to prevent, detect, and prosecute money laundering and the financing of terrorism."

Once again, a casual reading does not suggest that this is relevant to the hospital industry. However, the definition of a financial institution is quite broad and may include some health insurance companies. The mergers, acquisitions, and restructuring that occur frequently in the health care industry have the potential to suddenly create anti-money laundering responsibilities for accountants since the responsibilities may apply across the entire organization. According to Title III:

Responsibilities in a money laundering program may include

- Internal policies, procedures, and controls
- The designation of a compliance officer
- Ongoing employee training programs
- An independent audit program to test the programs

Thus, hospital, physician, and nurse-executives should ascertain whether their organization has anti-money laundering responsibilities, and if so, identify a designated compliance officer and determine the exact nature of any responsibilities under the anti-money laundering program.

PREPAREDNESS FOR BIOLOGICAL AND CHEMICAL ATTACKS

Title X of the USA PATRIOT Act contains several calls for strengthening the public health system. Section 1013(a)(4) calls for "enhanced resources for public health officials to respond to potential bioterrorism attacks." Section 1013(a)(6) calls for "greater resources to increase the capacity of hospitals and local health care workers to respond to public health threats."

Prior to September 11, 2001, the capacity of hospitals to respond to biological and chemical attacks by terrorists was quite limited. A survey of 186 hospitals concluded that hospital emergency departments (EDs) are generally not prepared to respond to biological or chemical attacks. Further, a hospital must have a plan in order to develop the capacity to respond to biological and chemical attacks.

Strictly speaking, however, hospital, ED, and health care organizational preparedness plans are not as directly encumbered by the USA PATRIOT Act, the Department of Homeland Security's Chemicals of Concern (COC) List, or the various steps of its Section 550 Program as some other industries. The COC guidelines are particularly pertinent for the agricultural industry, which is a heavy user of noxious and explosive chemicals like chlorine, nitrates, sulfur, and organophosphates. If you are not sure whether a substance is potentially toxic or covered under Title X of the USA PATRIOT Act, contact EPA's Risk Management Profile hotline at 1-800-424-9346 or 703-412-9810. For further details, see www.EPA.gov.

Nevertheless, hospitals and health care organizations may have other sources of contaminants, such as those listed below

Mercury. Mercury is a heavy metal used in several products in hospitals, like thermometers, computers, batteries, and fluorescent lamps. The metal can be toxic to the nervous system and cause problems with memory, information processing, attention, language, and fine motor skills.

Dioxin. Dioxins are toxic chemical compounds formed during the burning of hospital waste. The chemicals are also found in products with polyvinyl chloride (PVC), a plastic polymer. Dioxin has been linked to the development of several kinds of cancer. In humans, dioxin exposure may cause changes in the immune system and in the levels of some hormones.

DEHP. Di (2-ethylhexyl) phthalate (DEHP) is a plasticizer added to PVC products to soften and increase flexibility of some medical devices (like intravenous [IV] bags and tubing). It does not bind well with the PVC and can leach out of the product and into the body. DEHP may be toxic to the liver, lungs, and developing male reproductive system.

Volatile organic compounds (VOCs). VOCs are chemicals emitted as gases from liquid or solid products. Some of the most common types of VOCs are in formaldehyde, pesticides, solvents, and cleaning agents. Exposure may cause irritation of the eyes, nose, or throat; breathing problems; headache; and nausea. VOCs may be toxic to the liver, kidneys, and central nervous system.

Glutaraldehyde. Glutaraldehyde is a colorless, oily liquid used to cold-sterilize medical instruments and some types of hospital equipment. It is also used in labs and in the processing of X-ray films. Exposure can irritate the airways and cause breathing problems, nosebleed, burning of the eyes, headache, or nausea. Contact with the skin can lead to a rash or hives.

For some time now, the Joint Commission (formerly the Joint Commission on Accreditation of Healthcare Organizations, known as JCAHO) has also required hospitals to have a disaster preparedness plan mimicking the USA PATRIOT Act. For example, before September 11, 2001, only one in five hospitals had a response plan specifically tailored for biochemical attacks. By February 2005, two out of three hospitals had response plans for biochemical attacks. Today, such disaster plans are almost uniformly present to one degree or another, although successful implementation may be suspect.

After the terrorist attacks of September 11, 2001, "disaster preparedness" evolved into something that could more accurately be described as "emergency preparedness." Experience in New York and Virginia has shown that there will be spillover outside the immediate geographic areas affected by a terrorist attack, which will affect suburban and rural hospitals. Thus, the emphasis in emergency preparedness is on the coordination and integration of organizations throughout the local system. Hospitals therefore need to revise existing plans for disaster preparedness to reflect the realities of potential terrorist threats.

Mitigation against risk is essential to safeguard the financial position of a hospital. Hospitals can mitigate risks by developing an emergency preparedness plan. The hospital should start by identifying possible disaster situations such as earthquakes and biological or chemical attacks that could affect the facility. Next, the hospital should identify the potential damages that could occur to structures, utilities, computer technology, and supplies. After that, the hospital should use resources currently available to safeguard assets and then budget to acquire any additional materials or alterations required to secure the facility. Using this approach, Olive View Medical Center in Los Angeles lowered recovery costs from $48 million after an earthquake in 1971 to $6.6 million after another earthquake in 1994.

Hospitals can take several steps to mitigate even in the absence of significant funding:

- First, hospitals can establish links with 'first responders' such as local law enforcement, fire departments, state and local government, other hospitals, emergency medical services, and local public health departments.
- Second, hospitals can establish training programs to educate hospital staff on how to deal with chemical and biological threats.
- Third, hospitals can make changes in their information technology to facilitate disease surveillance that might give warning that an attack has occurred. Information technology may be useful in identifying the occurrence syndromes such as headache or fevers that might not be noticed individually but in the aggregate would signal that a biological or chemical agent had been released.
- Fourth, hospitals may be able to acquire access to staff and equipment to respond to biological and chemical attack through resource-sharing arrangements in lieu of outright purchases.

In addition to preparedness for an attack within its catchment area, a hospital must be prepared for an attack on its own facility. Hospitals should assess the vulnerability of the heating, ventilation, and air conditioning (HVAC) systems to biological or chemical attack. The positioning of the air intake vents is especially important because intakes on roofs are fairly secure as compared to intakes on ground level.

One way to increase security is to restrict access to the facility. Some hospitals are using biometric screening to restrict access to their facilities. Biometric screening identifies people based on measurements of some body part such as a fingerprint, handprint, or retina. The advantage of this approach is that there are no problems with forgotten badges, and biometric features cannot be shared or lost like cards with personal identification numbers (PINs).

In preparing for a possible attack, hospitals should also examine the federal, state, and local laws that might affect their response to a biological or chemical attack. Unfortunately, there is no central source of legislation, and an extensive search of many sources might be required to determine the legal constraints.

Obviously, upgrading emergency preparedness plans costs money. Trustees and financial officers should always be alert to federal, state, or local funds that may come available to defray some of the costs of preparedness. Some good places to search for information would be the Department of Health and Human Services (DHHS) (see www.os.dhhs.gov) and the Centers for Disease Control and Prevention (see www.cdc.gov and www.govbenefits.gov/govbenefits_en.portal). Other private sources are www.patriotactresearch.com and patriotact.com.

PROTECTION OF CRITICAL INFRASTRUCTURES

Title X of the USA PATRIOT Act also contains Section 1016, entitled "The Critical Infrastructures Protection Act of 2001." It acknowledges that the defense of the United States is based on the functioning of many networks and that these networks must be defended against attacks of both a physical and a virtual nature. Section 1016 specifies that actions necessary to carry out policies designed to protect the infrastructure will be based on public and private partnerships between the government and corporate and nongovernmental agencies. Further, it specifies that these actions are designed to ensure the continuity of essential government functions under all circumstances. Toward this end, the act establishes a National Infrastructure Simulation and Analysis Center (NISAC) to support counterterrorism, threat assessment, and risk mitigation. NISAC will acquire data from governments and the private sector to model, simulate, and analyze critical infrastructures including cyber, telecommunications, and physical infrastructures.

Attacks on the Internet and attacks on the information systems of hospitals have already occurred in significant numbers and are likely to continue. As a result of the USA PATRIOT Act, agencies to combat information technology (IT) terrorism have been created, such as the Critical Infrastructure Protection Board and the Critical Infrastructure Assurance Office. An Information Sharing and Analysis Center (ISAC) has been created to gather, analyze, and distribute information on cyber threats and vulnerabilities, provide alerts, and develop response plans. An ISAC for health care that will compile industry best practices, develop security systems, and establish a governance structure to which health systems can turn is under development.

The increasingly complex relationships among layers of hardware and software mean that new avenues for exploitation appear on almost a daily basis. Also, increased connectivity among computers means that the effects of attacks can be far reaching. One interesting consequence of the USA PATRIOT Act is that some cyber attacks can now be defined as acts of terrorism. As a practical matter, legal recourse against most attacks is of no use since laws tend to apply only locally and cyber attacks can come from anywhere in the world. As a result, most organizations concentrate on technical defenses to protect their infrastructure. However, efforts to protect computer systems may not be entirely defensive. One mode of defense is to monitor for intrusions, trace the source of intrusions, and aggressively attack and shut down the server of an intruder.

FINANCIAL IMPLICATIONS OF USA PATRIOT ACT FOR HOSPITALS

The financial implications of the USA PATRIOT Act are summarized in Table 7.1.

HEALTH INSURANCE IMPLICATIONS OF THE USA PATRIOT ACT ON HOSPITALS

With the recent popularity and growth of health savings accounts (HSAs) and/or medical savings accounts (MSAs), compliance with the USA PATRIOT Act has become an important issue for these new, hybrid health insurance products that place financial services organizations into relationships with shared information institutions such as hospitals, health care organizations, medical clinics, and patient clients.

TABLE 7.1
Financial Implications of USA PATRIOT Act

Activities That May Require Increased Funding	Potential Return on Investments
Prevention of money laundering: —Training for staff —Detection software	Prevention or mitigation of financial losses and criminal liability
Preparedness for biological and chemical attack: —Training for staff —Software for monitoring, analysis, and reporting	Prevention or mitigation of losses due to lapses in emergency preparedness
Preparedness for cyber attack: —Training for staff —Protective and counterattack software	Prevention or mitigation of losses due to lapses in computer security affecting medical or financial information
Increased physical security for facility	Prevention or mitigation of losses due to lapses in physical security

This happens because many, perhaps even the majority of, HSAs, MSAs, and high-deductible health care plans are opened online, as patients and insurance company clients use Internet search engines to find the "best" policy type to meet their needs. Appropriately, banks, health care entities, and hospitals are working with insurance companies, trust companies, and broker-dealers to offer identity-compliant and integrated HSAs and MSAs. Verifications that these clients are who they claim to be are as paramount as monitoring their activity.

Health care organizations may meet these requirements of the USA PATRIOT Act by adhering to its Customer Identification Program (CIP) and anti-money laundering requirements. Section 314(b) of the Act permits financial institutions, upon providing notice to the United States Department of the Treasury, to share information with one another in order to identify and report to the federal government activities that may involve money laundering or terrorist activity. This USA PATRIOT Act derivative partially accomplishes this through three critical goals:

1. First, it gives investigators familiar tools to use against a new threat.
2. Second, it breaks down a wall that has prevented information sharing between agencies.
3. Third, it updates U.S. laws to respond to the current Internet environment.

On October 1, 2003, Section 326 (CIP) of the Act went fully into effect, requiring the implementation of reasonable procedures to verify the identity of new customers and certain existing customers opening a new account.

Section 3261 of the USA PATRIOT Act also requires banks, savings associations, hospital and medical union credit unions, and certain non-federally regulated banks to have the CIP fully implemented. Broker-dealers in securities are subject to similar but slightly different rules.

For additional compliance, the USA PATRIOT Act also amended the Bank Secrecy Act to give the federal government enhanced authority to identify, deter, and punish money laundering and terrorist financing activities.

The passage of the USA PATRIOT Act, and these important derivatives, means that hospitals must be more vigilant about laws concerning money laundering, reporting of disease and quarantine, and cyber attacks. This means that more funds may be needed in order to combat money laundering, biological and chemical attacks, and security of all kinds, particularly IT security. Furthermore, many of the changes necessary to improve preparedness can be made with fairly small outlays of funds, and more funding provided by the federal government may eventually materialize. Whatever outlays are required now may result in very large savings later if hospital assets are safeguarded against attacks of virtual or real assets.

USA PATRIOT Act's Impact Since Inception

Almost a decade after passage of the USA PATRIOT Act, little is known about how it is being used to track terrorists, health care organization activity, or innocent Americans.

For example, the Department of Justice (DOJ) foiled numerous attempts to learn how the Administration has deployed the new tools granted under the Act. Even Congressional hearings several years ago, during the tenure of Attorney General John D. Ashcroft, yielded virtually no new information about the number of times individuals' library records were sought or how many court orders were obtained to monitor someone's computer activities or conduct surveillances on U.S. citizens. DOJ officials claimed that even generic numbers are classified and are provided confidentially only to congressional intelligence committees.

Unfortunately, the terrorist incidents of July 2007 in the United Kingdom implicated eight medical workers (doctors, medical students, lab technicians) from a clandestine Al-Qaeda sleeper cell. Although the violence was successfully thwarted, the fact that all were tied to the British National Health Service (NHS) indicates the international nature of such threats and the need to carefully screen the foreign-trained physicians on whom we increasingly rely.

In 2009, Attorney General Eric Holder reauthorized the PATRIOT Act and reiterated his support for warrantless wiretapping:

> There are certain things that a president has the constitutional right that the legislative branch cannot impinge upon.*

PATRIOT ACT EXTENSION

In May 2011, President Barack Obama signed into law a 4-year extension for parts of the PA's controversial domestic surveillance law, just before the provisions were to expire. The three provisions that were extended allowed authorities to use roving wiretaps, conduct court-ordered searches of business records, and conduct surveillance of foreign nationals who may be acting alone in plotting attacks.

FREQUENTLY ASKED USA PATRIOT ACT QUESTIONS

Q: What is Executive Order 13224?
A: Signed by President George W. Bush in September 2001, the order authorizes the Executive Branch to block the property of, and prohibit transactions with, persons who commit, threaten to commit, or support terrorism.

Q: What is U.N. Security Council Resolution 1373?
A: U.N. Security Council Resolution 1373, adopted at the end of September 2001, declares that all states (or nations) shall prohibit their nationals or any persons and entities within their territories from making any funds available for terrorism. In the broad wording of Resolution 1373, financial assets, economic resources, or financial or other related services shall not be made available, directly or indirectly, for the benefit of persons who commit, attempt to commit, facilitate, or participate in the commission of terrorist acts.

Q: To whom do the USA PATRIOT Act laws apply?
A: All U.S. citizens, permanent resident aliens, and entities and organizations located in or out of the United States (including any subsidiary or foreign offices overseas) must comply with the USA PATRIOT Act, Executive Order 13224, and Office of Foreign Assets Control regulations. Further, U.N. Security Council Resolution 1373 and other resolutions have the force of international law binding on all member states.

Q: What is the Office of Foreign Assets Control (OFAC)?
A: OFAC is a division of the U.S. Department of the Treasury. It helps enforce sanctions against terrorist organizations, drug traffickers, money launderers, and noncooperative foreign countries.

Q: What is the OFAC-SDN list?
A: The OFAC Specially Designated Nationals (SDN) and blocked persons lists are U.S. government lists of individuals and organizations identified as terrorists or otherwise associated with terrorism, drug trafficking, and money laundering.

Q: What is the Terror Exclusion List (TEL)?
A: TEL is the U.S. Department of State's list of organizations identified as terrorists or otherwise associated with terrorism for immigration purposes.

Q: What sanctions do hospitals face if material support is given to watch-listed parties?
A: The health care organization faces the possibility of having its assets frozen and its tax-exempt status revoked, if it exists. There is also the potential for criminal and civil penalties. In addition, administrators, managers, and executives may face penalties.

Q: Do current USA PATRIOT Act laws define "material support?"
A: The Antiterrorism and Effective Death Penalty Act broadly defines *material support* as "currency or monetary instruments of financial securities, financial services, lodging, training, expert

---

* Senate Confirmation Hearings: Eric Holder, Day One. Washington, D.C., 2009. Transcript available at http://www .nytimes.com/2009/01/16/us/politics/16text-holder.html?pagewanted=28&_r%BC1&pagewanted%BCall.

advice or assistance, safe houses, false documentation or identification, communications, equipment, facilities, weapons, lethal substances, explosives, personnel transportation, and other physical assets, except medicine or religious materials."

Q: Should a health care entity amend funding support agreements to comply with the USA PATRIOT Act?

A: Yes, it is recommended that any grant or funding agreement include prohibitions against violence or terrorist activities.

THE SARBANES–OXLEY ACT

In response to the failure of public accounting firms to detect corporate fraud, the Sarbanes–Oxley Act requires rotation of auditors to maintain independence, increases accountability for corporate fraud, and prescribes changes in governance, internal controls, ethics, and disclosure.

Previously, the Treadway Commission Report (*Fraudulent Financial Reporting: 1987–1997—An Analysis of U.S. Public Companies*) was its equivalent, sponsored by The Committee of Sponsoring Organizations (COSO) to provide:

> … an analysis of financial statement fraud occurrences. While the work of the National Commission on Fraudulent Financial Reporting in the mid-1980s identified numerous causal factors believed to contribute to financial statement fraud, little empirical evidence existed about other factors related to instances of fraud prior to release of the 1987 report (NCFFR, 1987). Thus, COSO commissioned this research project to provide information that can be used to guide future efforts to combat the problem of financial statement fraud and to provide a better understanding of financial statement fraud cases.

In other words, the Treadway Commission Report first spelled out the whys and wherefores of internal control as the original de facto standard for defining such corporate controls.

Unfortunately, many leaders, including some hospital administrators and physician executives, still think that the Sarbanes–Oxley Act applies only to investor-owned or publicly traded health care organizations. While this is partially true, the legislation does contain some provisions that are applicable to nonprofit hospitals. Also, moral persuasion is increasing in the health care sector.

For example, provisions relating to the retaliation against hospital whistleblowers and to medical document retention and/or destruction are applicable to nonprofit health care entities as well as their for-profit counterparts. Moreover, nonprofit hospitals that issue tax-exempt bonds and/or rely on bond ratings from services such as Moody's and Fitch have to comply with Sarbanes–Oxley provisions to obtain and maintain those bond ratings.

In addition, Sarbanes–Oxley provisions do have some implications for all hospitals, regardless of ownership type.

GOVERNANCE

Title III, Section 302, is entitled "Corporate Responsibility for Financial Reports." This section requires that the principal officers and financial officers sign the financial report, certify that the report contains no false statements, and certify that the report is materially correct. They face stiff penalties if any of these certifications are found to be untrue.

The implications extend beyond just Centers for Medicare & Medicaid Services fraud, civil penalties, and imprisonment. Hospitals are now largely operated by public entities and thus file financial forecasts and financial statements. Periodic statutory financial reports are to include certifications that

- The signing officers have reviewed the report.
- The report does not contain material untrue statements or omissions considered misleading.

- The financial statements and related information fairly present the financial condition and the results in all material respects.
- The signing officers are responsible for internal controls, have evaluated these internal controls within the previous 90 days, and have reported on their findings.
- A list of all deficiencies in the internal controls is provided, as is information on any fraud that involves employees who are involved with internal activities.
- Any significant changes in internal controls or related factors that could have a negative impact on the internal controls are documented.

The Sarbanes–Oxley Act also establishes an independent governing commission, which is required to study and report on the extent of off-balance transactions. The commission is required to determine whether generally accepted accounting principles or other regulations result in open and meaningful reporting.

The Sarbanes–Oxley Act puts a new premium on the independence of board members and the importance of the audit, compensation, and nominating committees. As a result, boards will be more likely to compensate directors fairly in light of their increased responsibilities. Further, boards will likely pay more attention to the education of board members.

Boards and officers should seek to do more than just comply with the Sarbanes–Oxley Act. Compliance can lay the groundwork for "enterprise risk management," which identifies potential obstacles to accomplishing strategic objectives and thereby improves performance.

As a result of the Sarbanes–Oxley Act, even not-for-profit hospitals would do well to upgrade the membership of the board in terms of financial expertise and independence, update bylaws, and establish audit committees. Further, hospital boards should be making more sophisticated financial analyses examining revenue position, cost position, market strength, and the adequacy of capital. Last, hospital boards should be smaller and composed of people with more financial skill who are adequately compensated for their service.

INTERNAL CONTROLS

The Sarbanes–Oxley Act, Title III, Section 302(a)(4)(A)–(D), indicates that the officers signing the financial reports are responsible for

- Establishing and maintaining internal controls
- Designing the internal controls so that material information relating to the issuer is made known to the officers
- Evaluating the effectiveness of internal controls within 90 days
- Presenting in the report their conclusions about the effectiveness of internal controls

Title IV, Section 404, requires each annual report to contain an internal control report that states that it is the responsibility of management to establish and maintain an internal control structure and to provide an assessment of the effectiveness of that structure.

With regard to corporations in general, the compliance burden of these requirements for internal controls is quite substantial and will fundamentally change the way corporations do business internally and the way they do business with their auditors. Revenue recognition is a particularly important issue in the new internal controls, and corporations should consider forming a revenue recognition committee to serve as a primary tool of internal control. Organizations should consider purchasing internal control software that is robust and flexible so that compliance is sustainable even when business operations change significantly.

With regard to hospitals, the Sarbanes–Oxley Act will cause nearly all hospitals, regardless of ownership type, to institute internal controls to ensure the accuracy of financial reports, even though it is not currently mandatory for not-for-profit hospitals. However, most executives expect the requirements to become mandatory for not-for-profit hospitals, and many hospitals have already begun implementing internal controls to assure the accuracy of financial reports. Further, compliance programs in hospitals should be considered not optional but required. There will likely be an expansion of the functions of the compliance officer, and hospitals will be more likely to establish procedures for receiving complaints and tips from anonymous whistleblowers. New software for hospitals can provide continuous auditing to monitor for Sarbanes–Oxley Act violations.

ETHICS

Title IV of the Sarbanes–Oxley Act is entitled "Enhanced Financial Disclosures," and Section 406 is entitled "Code of Ethics for Senior Financial Officers." Section 406 calls for ethical handling of actual or apparent conflicts of interest, full disclosure in the financial reports, and compliance with government rules and regulations.

With regard to corporations in general, the ethics prescribed in the Sarbanes–Oxley Act cover the handling of conflicts of interest, accurate disclosure in reports, and compliance with laws and rules. The Sarbanes–Oxley Act requires publicly traded companies to disclose whether they have adopted a code of ethics for senior financial officers. The Sarbanes–Oxley Act may have the result of forcing financial officers to pay more attention to the accuracy of financial reporting and the evaluation of business risk. Further, it will force corporations to develop cultures that reinforce corporate values, to carefully assign responsibilities, and to reward employees who perform ethically and effectively.

With regard to hospitals, although most hospitals already have a Joint Commission code of ethics that addresses a different set of ethical issues for their board, they would also do well to upgrade their codes to reflect the Sarbanes–Oxley Act. There is some evidence that voluntary compliance with regard to the code of ethics has already taken place to ensure their access to funds by strengthening their reputation.

DISCLOSURE

Title IV, Section 409, is entitled "Real Time Issuer Disclosures." It requires disclosure to the public "on a rapid and current basis such additional information concerning material changes in the financial condition or operations of the issuer, in plain English, which may include trend and qualitative information and graphic presentations…(that) is necessary or useful for the protection of investors and in the public interest."

With regard to corporations in general, most rely too much on the annual budget as the only performance management tool. The problem is that few organizations are able to identify the cost of servicing a key customer and the revenue associated with that customer. Thus, most organizations and most financial officers would not easily be able to identify the impact of losing a key customer, and thus, they would not be likely to recognize and disclose a key loss. Organizations need to maintain records that show a high-level activity layer that shows the relationship between the revenues and costs for key customers.

Furthermore, financial statements published and disclosed by regulated health care entities are required to be accurate and presented in a manner that does not contain incorrect statements. These financial statements must include all material off-balance-sheet liabilities, obligations, or transactions. Regulated hospitals and health care organizations are required to publish information in their annual reports concerning the scope and adequacy of the internal control structure and procedures for financial reporting. This statement must assess the effectiveness of such internal controls and procedures.

A financial expert and/or registered accounting firm must in the same report attest to, disclose, and report on the assessment of the effectiveness of the internal control structure and procedures for financial reporting.

Regulated health care entities are required to disclose to the public, on an urgent basis, information on material changes in their financial condition or operations. These disclosures are to be presented in terms that are easy to understand, supported by graphic presentations of trend and qualitative information as appropriate.

With more specific regard to hospitals, the Sarbanes–Oxley Act could lead to voluntarily expanded disclosure in not-for-profit hospitals. Some hospitals have already voluntarily taken a stricter stance on disclosure.

Hospitals may be required to take stricter stances on disclosure by the attorney general of their respective states, if not directly by the Sarbanes–Oxley Act. Hospitals should do the following:

- Adopt a strict conflict of interest disclosure statement and policy.
- Develop an unambiguous definition of what constitutes conflict of interest.
- Develop and use solid criteria for selecting new board members.
- Treat prospective physician board members like all board members.

FINANCIAL IMPLICATIONS OF THE SARBANES–OXLEY ACT FOR HOSPITALS

Although the Sarbanes–Oxley Act was passed in response primarily to events that took place outside the health care industry, its passage has nevertheless affected the financial management of some hospitals. The effect of the Sarbanes–Oxley Act on the health care industry can be explained by the concept of "isomorphism." DiMaggio and Powell identify the concept of "mimetic isomorphism," whereby organizations adopt the form of other organizations in society to obtain legitimacy in the eyes of society.

Thus, although the letter of the law currently affects only publicly traded corporations, it creates social pressures that affect not-for-profit organizations such as hospitals.

This social pressure may soon metamorphose into legal pressure or "coercive isomorphism." States and their attorneys general may soon pass additional or more stringent legislation requiring not-for-profit hospitals to conform more exactly to the Sarbanes–Oxley standards. Some bond markets are also pressuring not-for-profit hospitals to adhere to Sarbanes–Oxley standards. Although insurers could penalize hospitals that do not comply with the Sarbanes–Oxley Act, there are as yet no examples of this happening.

The financial implications of the Sarbanes–Oxley Act are presented in Table 7.2.

On the one hand, the Sarbanes–Oxley Act creates a compliance burden for hospital executives. Some effort must be expended to recruit, retain, compensate, and educate more financially astute

TABLE 7.2
Financial Implications of the Sarbanes–Oxley Act

Activities That May Require Increased Funding	Potential Return on Investments
Compensation of board members	Increased safeguards against loss due to fraud or mismanagement
Education of board members	Better access to capital
Acquisition of software for more sophisticated financial analysis	Lower risk and lower cost of capital
Increased internal audit personnel	Better financial decisions due to decreased conflict of interest
Internal audit software	Better financial decisions due to increased financial acumen
Increased independent audit fees	Increased safeguards

board members to comply with the requirements for governance. Further, more time must be spent on the development of codes of ethics and cultures of compliance.

Yet something about Sarbanes–Oxley Act compliance must be working because nonprofit hospitals in North Carolina intend to voluntarily implement Sarbanes–Oxley–like internal controls, beginning in 2008. First reported by www.ManagedHealthcare.com and in the *Philanthropy Journal*, these North Carolina entities explain that they have a duty to be as transparent as possible and to demonstrate that they deserve public trust in managing contributions. No pressure for improved financial statements was cited, nor were concerns about fraud in the executive suite. To that end, the organizations require each chief executive officer (CEO) and chief financial officer (CFO) to sign off on financial statements. Audit committees also include a financial expert who is separate from the finance committee and who reports directly to the board of directors rather than to management.

Interestingly, these few are not the first nonprofit health entities to tackle Sarbanes–Oxley compliance. The University of Pittsburgh Medical Center, which is a public, nonprofit health care organization, proclaimed itself to be the first large health care system to voluntarily attain compliance with the Sarbanes–Oxley Act. Its outside auditors, Ernst & Young, certified full compliance in 2007.

Some capital outlay will probably be required to develop or acquire more sophisticated financial software that can show the relationships between revenues and costs for each major line of customers so that hospitals can comply with the higher levels of disclosure required. Further, considerable capital outlays may be required to upgrade the internal auditors' software and to pay for independent audits that will likely be more expensive due to the required rotation of auditors. Last, the requirements of the Sarbanes–Oxley Act may make some hospitals more economically risk averse, which could result in poorer financial performance.

For example, according to a report by a Sarbanes–Oxley research and compliance firm, Lord & Benoit, the average first-year cost for management assessment—with additional audit fees—was about $78,474 or nearly 14% less than the Securities and Exchange Commission (SEC) originally predicted for similar businesses.

On the other hand, there may be benefits that will accrue from the stricter burden of compliance. Stricter ethics may result in boards making decisions that are better for hospitals. Better disclosure may ultimately cause less risk to investors and provide better access to capital. More astute boards may actually make better financial decisions. Stronger internal controls may well help to avoid embarrassing and costly financial failures in hospitals.

PENALTIES

Sarbanes–Oxley imposes penalties of fines and/or up to 20 years' imprisonment for altering, destroying, mutilating, concealing, or falsifying records, documents, or tangible objects with the intent to obstruct, impede, or influence a legal investigation.

The legislation also imposes penalties of fines and/or imprisonment up to 10 years on any accountant who knowingly and willfully violates the requirements of maintenance of all audit or review papers for a period of 5 years.

Organizations may not attempt to avoid these requirements by reincorporating their activities or transferring their activities outside of the United States.

Example Fines

As part of a settlement arising from allegations of improper Medicare billing related to the Sarbanes–Oxley Act and others, Abraham Lincoln Memorial Hospital in Lincoln, Illinois, paid fines of $1.34 million in 2006 and entered into a 3-year corporate integrity agreement arrangement. It also agreed to maintain a compliance plan and provide information regarding the plan to the DHHS.

The settlement required no admission of wrongdoing as the hospital maintained it acted on the recommendation of outside consultants. Adequacy of patient care was not an issue in the investigation.

The Lincoln hospital case is the fourth settlement in 3 years arising from an investigation of for-profit hospital claims under the Sarbanes–Oxley Act, the False Claims Act, and/or its related derivative regulations.

Sarbanes–Oxley Act Impact Since Inception

Since enactment 10 years ago, Sarbanes–Oxley today is still perceived to have a limited, but growing, impact in driving improved corporate health care governance in 2012. There is also a belief in the nonprofit hospital industry that voluntary adoption of the Sarbanes–Oxley Act will keep Congress and state legislators at bay during a time of increased scrutiny of the tax-exempt status of hospitals.

Indeed, some nonprofit health care providers are adopting parts of the Sarbanes–Oxley Act to manage risk, achieve efficiencies, and improve performance with more effective internal controls and financial reporting methods. Additionally, board members who serve on both public company and tax-exempt boards are demanding the adoption of the Sarbanes–Oxley Act by tax-exempt health care providers. Of course, establishing a sound corporate governance environment can also result in much greater confidence in an organization, internally and externally.

A study done by FTI Consulting in 2008 showed that high-net-worth investors and financial advisors felt that corporate board members are still too closely aligned with the interests of executive management teams as opposed to shareholders. The survey of more than 200 high-net-worth investors and professional financial advisors, administered by independent research firm Affluent Dynamics, revealed that clear majorities (61% of financial advisors and 64% of high-net-worth individuals) say that boards operate in the interests of management rather than those of shareholders.

Slowly, but increasingly, hospitals, tax-exempt clinics, and other health care organizations are beginning to adopt portions of the Sarbanes–Oxley Act that affect their entities, albeit in a fragmented, "Sarbanes–Oxley Lite" approach that is becoming more substance than style. The Sarbanes–Oxley Act is also now on the radar screen of the *American Journal of Medical Quality.*

Based on such findings, for-profit health care organizations and related entities have significant work to do to reassure investors, medical executives, patients, and consultants about the effectiveness and quality of corporate governance practices and whether these practices are appropriately safeguarding hospital reputations, which both groups consider to be crucial in the creation of shareholder value.

However, in the words of former health care administrator and current industry and iMBA Inc. pundit Rachel Pentinmaki, RN, MHA, CMP™ (Hon) (personal communication, Atlanta, Georgia, September 2011):

> Although Sarbanes-Oxley has mimicked the slow start of HIPPA, but *[sic]* it has the potential to become even more important, onerous and costly to all affected hospitals and health care organizations.

Frequently Asked Sarbanes–Oxley Act Questions

Q: Who is a "financial expert?"
A: Anyone with education and experience as a public accountant, auditor, financial officer, comptroller or principal, and/or from a position involving similar functions.

Q: What is a "whistleblower?"

A: Any employee who provides information or assists in the investigation of any provision relating to fraud against shareholders.

Q: Are there materiality guidelines for complaints?

A: There are no materiality qualifiers in the Act. All complaints regarding accounting or internal controls or auditing reporting matters are covered.

Q: Is the audit committee required to review all complaints?

A: Yes, even though not stated specifically in the legislation.

Q: What level of complaint detail does the audit committee need to review?

A: This can vary as operational incidents may be summarized, while more serious incidents must be presented in detail for appropriate resolution.

Q: How is independence defined?

A: Independence has two definitions: (1) pertaining to an audit firm and (2) pertaining to a member of an audit committee.

Q: Can an audit firm perform a service that is a subject of the audit itself?

A: No, and audit committee members of the board cannot accept compensation or be affiliated with the issuer or a subsidiary.

Q: How should employees be notified of their ability to report Sarbanes–Oxley concerns?

A: Generally, entities should (1) post bulletin boards at all locations where other legal notices such as Worker's Compensation are posted and (2) place notices and links on company intranets or private Web sites.

Q: What else happens if an entity is not in compliance?

A: Depending on the section, noncompliance penalties range from the loss of stock exchange listing and loss of directors' and officers' (D&O) insurance to multimillion-dollar fines and imprisonment.

Tenth Anniversary of Sarbanes–Oxley

According to the 2011 Sarbanes–Oxley Compliance Survey by Protiviti, nearly 90% of respondents said the recession of 2008–2009 and the current economic malaise did not affect compliance, and half said that internal control over financial reporting has improved over the last year. This confirms a general sense that big companies especially have grown comfortable with their Sarbox processes.

Indeed, the costs of compliance continue to trend down. However, cost reductions have come over the course of 9 years. What does this mean for Dodd–Frank and other recent financial reform laws? It is hard to generalize, but part of the tremendously energetic response by the financial services and other industries—such as health care—to various pieces of Dodd–Frank legislation is driven in some part by the Sarbox experience.

CONCLUSION

In summary, both the USA PATRIOT Act and the Sarbanes–Oxley Act provide little indication in their titles that they will affect the management of hospitals or health care organizations. Nevertheless, both acts were intended to safeguard the nation and its economy. Since the health care industry is such a large and integral part of the economy, it necessarily follows that legislation designed to protect our nation and its economy will invariably have an effect on hospitals. Both acts require hospitals to analyze their activities and make capital outlays, but compliance with both acts can prevent or mitigate losses and very possibly improve financial performance.

CASE MODEL 7.1: EVAN AND THE USA PATRIOT ACT

Evan was the chief financial officer of a community hospital in San Marcos, Texas. His hospital had recently been acquired by an insurance company. As he left the hospital, he reflected on the events of the day. During a meeting of the management team, the issue of the USA PATRIOT Act had come up. Evan knew that it contained many diverse sections, and he was concerned that the legislation might affect his job duties. His grandfather, who lived in Las Vegas, had told him that some of the hospitals in Las Vegas had once been used for money laundering, and he knew that there was a money laundering section of the USA PATRIOT Act. When he asked the CEO if he thought the money laundering section might apply, the CEO laughed. He said that the money laundering in Las Vegas was concerned with illegal activities of the "Mob" and that the USA PATRIOT Act was aimed at terrorists. Besides, he added that the money laundering prevention and detection activities were designed for financial institutions, not hospitals.

Evan also asked about the section on bioterrorism and whether the community hospital had an emergency preparedness plan. The CEO responded that the hospital had a disaster preparedness plan that had been instituted after the disastrous floods that had occurred some years earlier. Further, the CEO said that the terrorists would most likely attack San Antonio because of its huge military bases or Austin because of its large population of narcissistic yuppies who could be easily terrorized. In any event, attacks on San Antonio or Austin would not likely affect San Marcos, so contingency plans were not needed.

Evan said nothing, but he felt uneasy. Instead of driving home to Buda, he drove to the library of the Texas State University and sought an authoritative interpretation of the USA PATRIOT Act from a private clearinghouse publication. He also spent some time doing a database search.

KEY ISSUES

Was the CEO correct with regard to the following assertions?

1. The USA PATRIOT Act money laundering detection and prevention sections do not apply to the hospital.
2. The USA PATRIOT Act sections on bioterrorism attacks have little relevance for the community hospital in San Marcos.

CHECKLIST 1: USA PATRIOT Act	YES	NO
Money Laundering		
Do the money laundering statutes apply to my health care organization?	o	o
Does the hospital have an anti-money laundering monitoring system?	o	o
Does the hospital have a suspicious financial activity detection system?	o	o
Does the hospital have a fraud control officer?	o	o
Does the hospital have the required internal financial controls?	o	o
Does the hospital have an independent audit program?	o	o
Does the hospital monitor and screen wire fund transfer payments?	o	o
Does the hospital have a watch list of potential offenders?	o	o
Does the hospital have and use suspicious activity reports?	o	o
Does the hospital have a new and ongoing employee training program?	o	o
Does the hospital have a supervisory policy?	o	o
Does the hospital review new vendor account documentation?	o	o
Does the hospital review and screen new corporate client accounts?	o	o

Bioterrorism

Is the emergency preparedness plan up to date?	o	o
Have all threat sources been identified?	o	o
Have potential damages been assessed?	o	o
Have appropriate safeguards been installed?	o	o
Does the budget reflect additional safeguards needed?	o	o
Has the hospital established links to first responders?	o	o
Has the hospital instituted staff training in response to bioterrorism?	o	o
Does the information technology recognize syndromes?	o	o
Has the hospital instituted resource-sharing arrangements?	o	o
Has the hospital evaluated the vulnerability of the HVAC systems?	o	o
Does the hospital have an aggregate pool of electronic storage where the data can be	o	o
easily secured, backed up, and retrieved?	o	o
If so, do you know where the data is stored and/or where it is outsourced?		
Has the hospital secured access to all parts of the facility?	o	o
Has the hospital reviewed pertinent federal, state, and local laws?	o	o
Have applications been made for available funding?	o	o

Critical Infrastructure

Do I monitor information available from the health care ISAC?	o	o
Have I provided backup records and alternate systems?	o	o
Have I evaluated software to prevent cyber attacks?	o	o

Financial Implications

Must your health care entity comply with the Bank Secrecy Act (BSA)?	o	o
Must your hospital comply with the customer identification program (CIP)?	o	o
Are you familiar with the Office of Foreign Assets Control (OFAC)?	o	o
Are you aware of the Specially Designated Nationals (SDNs) and Terror Exclusion	o	o
List (TEL)?		

Internet and Electronic Security

Are you aware of HR 744, the Internet Spyware Prevention Act of 2005 (known as I-SPY)?	o	o
Are you familiar with the Counter Spy Act of 2007?	o	o
Are you aware of HR 964, the Securely Protect Yourself Against Cyber Trespass Act?	o	o
Are you familiar with HR 948, the Social Security Number Protection Act of 2007?	o	o

CASE MODEL 7.2: CLARE AND THE SARBANES–OXLEY ACT

Clare had just graduated from the University of Texas at Austin. While taking classes in the McCombs College of Business, she had learned of the Sarbanes-Oxley Act. McCombs College instructors had paid special attention to the Sarbanes-Oxley Act since it was the financial collapse of Enron Corporation and the failure of its auditor, the Houston office of Arthur Anderson, that had led to the passage of the Sarbanes-Oxley Act.

Clare had recently gone to work for Saint Sebastian Catholic Hospital in Austin. She was uncertain whether the Sarbanes-Oxley Act applied to a not-for-profit Catholic hospital, so she asked her CEO a few questions. First, she asked if the hospital had a code of ethics that was reflective of the Sarbanes-Oxley Act. The CEO replied that they were required to have a code of ethics under JCAHO. He added that the code of ethics had been good enough for JCAHO at the last accreditation visit.

Next, Clare asked him some questions about the composition of the board of directors. In particular, she wanted to know how many of the board members had financial expertise. The CEO said that a majority of the board did not have financial backgrounds because other factors were deemed more important. He stated that there were three primary groups of board members. One group of the board members was composed of representatives of Catholic orders who had deep understanding of ethical issues. This was essential to keep the hospital from getting on the wrong side of the Vatican with regard to obstetrical and gynecological issues. Another large group of board members was composed of wealthy philanthropists who contributed to the hospital. However, they had inherited their wealth and did not necessarily know anything about managing wealth. Last, a large group of board members was physicians who practiced at the hospital. It was essential to have them on the board to ensure their cooperation.

Last, Clare asked the CEO if the hospital kept financial data organized in such a way that it could identify major sources of revenues and expenses by customer. The CEO replied that he could not imagine why they would want to do that because all that was necessary was that the hospital provide good health care and conduct itself in a way that was consistent with Roman Catholic beliefs and values.

KEY ISSUES

Clare mulled over the CEO's answers. After work, she stopped by the Perry–Castaneda Library to research the Sarbanes-Oxley Act.

1. What would Clare find about the code of ethics required for a hospital?
2. What would Clare find about requirements for the composition of a board?
3. What would Clare find about the relationship between managerial accounting and internal controls?

CHECKLIST 1: The Sarbanes-Oxley Act	YES	NO
Governance		
Is a Section 302 governance report in place for your regulated health care entity?	o	o
Do you regularly review current governing board structure?	o	o
Do the board members sign the financial reports?	o	o
Do the board members certify that there are no false statements in the financial reports?	o	o
Do the board members certify that the financial statements are materially correct?	o	o
Has your board established the following committees:		
– An audit committee?	o	o
– A compensation committee?	o	o
– A nominating committee?	o	o
Does the hospital compensate the members of the board of directors?	o	o
Does the hospital provide education for the board of directors?	o	o
Has the hospital increased the proportion of board members capable of financial analysis?	o	o
Has the board met with your directors' and officers' (D&O) insurance carrier?	o	o
Has your controller, CFO, CEO, and/or internal auditors read the Treadway Commission report?	o	o
Internal Controls		
Is a Section 404 internal control report in place and filed annually?	o	o
Do the board members certify that internal controls are adequate to detect material errors?	o	o
Do the board members certify that they have recently tested the adequacy of internal controls?	o	o

Do the board members report on their conclusions about the effectiveness of internal controls based on the tests?	o	o
Is the internal control software sufficiently robust and flexible that it will still work after significant changes in operations?	o	o
Has the hospital established channels for complaints or anonymous tips from whistleblowers?	o	o
Do you outsource whistleblower compliance and treatment?	o	o
Ethics		
Is a Section 406 ethics policy report in place?	o	o
Has the hospital updated its code of ethics to reflect the Sarbanes-Oxley Act?	o	o
Did you have someone independently review your corporate code of ethics?	o	o
Does the hospital take steps to develop and maintain a culture of compliance?	o	o
Do you maintain ethics and compliance coordination with your HR department?	o	o
Disclosure		
Does the hospital have a Section 409 policy on disclosure?	o	o
Does the policy require disclosure of material changes of financial position or operations?	o	o
Does the hospital scrutinize prospective board members for conflicts of interest?	o	o
Does the hospital treat physicians the same as other board members?	o	o
Do you have regular follow-up with outside and internal legal counsel?	o	o
Finance		
Are all revenue streams consistently documented and accounted for?	o	o
Is revenue being properly allocated?	o	o
Do you understand the civil and criminal penalties of noncompliance and fraud?	o	o

ACKNOWLEDGMENTS

The authors would like to thank Gregory O. Ginn, PhD, MBA, CPA, CMP (Hon), Associate Professor, Department Health Care Administration and Policy at the University of Nevada, for technical assistance in the preparation of this chapter.

BIBLIOGRAPHY

Adapted from: www.Mott.org.

Allen, K., Price, P. and Stevens, J. "Minimizing the Consequences of Disaster." *Healthcare Purchasing News* 27:4 (2003): 81–82.

Andrews, J. "It's Always Orange Alert for Health Facility Security." *Healthcare Purchasing News* 27:5 (2003): 14–15.

Barrett, R. "Disclosure: The Real Challenge of Sarbanes-Oxley." *The CPA Journal* 74:1 (2004): 11.

Beasley, M. S. and Hermanson, D. R. "Going Beyond Sarbanes-Oxley Compliance: Five Keys to Creating Value." *The CPA Journal* 74:6 (2004): 11–13.

Bloch, G. D. "Sarbanes-Oxley's Effect on Internal Controls for Revenue." *The CPA Journal* 73:4 (2003): 68–70.

Cutlip, K. "Strengthening the System: Joint Commission Standards and Building on What We Know." *Hospital Topics* 80:1 (2002): 24–28.

Daulerio, A. J. "Panelists: Nonprofits Should Brace for Sarbanes-Oxley Spillover." *The Bond Buyer* 36:31758 (2003): 4. (See also, Greene, J. "What Every Board Needs to Know." *Trustee* 57:6 (2004): 9–12.)

DiMaggio, P. J. and Powell, W. W. "The Iron Cage Revisited: Institutional Isomorphism and Collective Rationality in Organizational Fields." *American Sociological Review* 48:2 (1983): 147–160.

Frist, B. "A Time for Preparedness." *Modern Healthcare* 32:51 (2005): 19.

Gantner, J. J. "Executive Insights." *Healthcare Financial Management* 57:4 (2003): 32–36. (See also Jaklevic, M. C. "Conflict Resolution." *Modern Healthcare* 34:12 (2004): 22.)

Gerrish, J. C. "Ten New Commandments for Corporate Governance." *ABA Banking Journal* 94:11 (2002): 16–20.

Glabman, M. "Bioterrorism: The Silent Killer." *Trustee* 54:10 (2001): 30.

Grace, H. S. and Haupert, J. E. "Financial Officers' Code of Ethics: Help or Hindrance?" *The CPA Journal* 73:3 (2003): 65–66.

Grobmyer, J. E. and Reilly, G. "Good Governance: Ensuring the Financial Health of Your Hospital." *Trustee* 568 (2003): 32–33.

Harrington, C. "The New Accounting Environment." *Journal of Accountancy* 196:2 (2003): 28–33.

Haugh, R. "The Benefits of Transparency." *Hospitals and Health Networks* 77:10 (2003): 16.

Jaklevic, M. C. "Letting the Sunshine in." *Modern Healthcare* 33:12 (2003): 26–28.

Karnow, C. "Launch on Warning: Aggressive Defense of Computer Systems." *Journal of Internet Law* 7:1 (2003): 9–14.

Larson, R. K. and Herz, P. J. "Accountants, Corruption, and Money Laundering." *The CPA Journal* 73:6 (2003): 34–36.

Malz, A. "Code of Ethics in the Wake of Sarbanes-Oxley." *Trustee* 56:10 (2003): 31.

Marcinko, D. E. and Hetico, H. R. The US PATRIOT Act. In Marcinko, D. E. (editor). *The Business of Medical Practice.* Springer Publishing, New York, 2011.

Melnick, S. V. "Accountants' Anti-Money-Laundering Responsibilities." *The CPA Journal* 73:12 (2003): 50–51.

Messmer, M. "Sarbanes-Oxley Act: What Does It Mean To Me?" *Strategic Finance* 84:9 (2003): 13–14.

Moss, B. "Getting Personal: Biometric Security Devices Gain Access to Health Care Facilities." *Health Facilities Management* 15:9 (2002): 21–24.

Murphy, J. K. "After 9/11: Priority Focus Areas for Bioterrorism Preparedness in Hospitals." *Journal of Healthcare Management* 49:4 (2004): 227–235.

Myers, R. "Ensuring Ethical Effectiveness." *Journal of Accountancy* 195:2 (2003): 28–33.

Nelson, L. "Stepping into Continuous Audit." *Internal Auditor* 61:2 (2004): 27–29.

O'Hare, P. K. "Sarbanes-Oxley Raises Red Flag for Not-for-Profits." *Healthcare Financial Management* 56:10 (2002): 42–44.

Preimestberger, C. "Why Disaster Recovery Isn't Optional Anymore." *eWeek* 28:12 (July 2011).

Rosen, B. F. and Bresnick, M. L. Special to the *Daily Record.* January 18, 2008. See www.mddailyrecord.com/article.cfm?id=140707&type=Daily.

Royo, M. B. and Nash, D. B. "Sarbanes-Oxley and Not-for-Profit Hospitals: Current Issues and Future Prospects." *American Journal of Medical Quality* 23:1 (February 2008): 70–72. See http://ajm.sagepub.com/cgi/content/citation/23/1/70.

Sarbanes-Oxley Act § 404(a)(1)–(2).

Sarbanes-Oxley Act § 409.

See http://frwebgate.access.gpo.gov/cgi-in/getdoc.cgi?dbname=107_cong_public_laws&docid=f:publ056.107.pdf.

Steinberg, S. H. "What Does a Hospital Trustee Do?" *Physician's News Digest* (2005). (See http://physiciansnews.com/business/1005steinberg.html.)

Thallner, K. A. "High-Profile Cases Generate Interest in Corporate Responsibility: Exploring the Impact That Recent Events Will Have on Health Care." *Journal of Health Care Compliance* 4:5 (2002): 14–18.

Tyler, L. L. and Biggs, L. L. "Conflict of Interest: Strategies for Remaining Purer than Caesar's Wife." *Trustee.* 57:3 (2004): 24–26.

Unkovic, D. "A New Model for Health Care Boards." *Trustee* 57:1 (2004): 27–28.

U.S. Congress. The Sarbanes-Oxley Act of 2002. 107th Congress of the United States of America. H.R. 3763. 2002; http://Thomas.LOC.gov. Public Law 107-204.

U.S. Congress. Uniting and Strengthening America by Providing Appropriate Tools Required to Intercept and Obstruct Terrorism Act (USA PATRIOT Act) of 2001. 107th Congress of the United States of America. H.R. 3162. 2002; http://Thomas.LOC.gov. Pub. L. No. 107-56.

Wetter, D. C., Daniell, W. D. and Treser, C. D. "Hospital Preparedness for Victims of Chemical or Biological Terrorism." *American Journal of Public Health* 91 (2001): 710–716.

Winters, B. I. "Choose the Right Tools for Internal Control Reporting." *Journal of Accountancy* 197:2 (2004): 34–40.

8 Collaborating to Enhance Performance in a Changing Health Care Landscape
Opportunities for Widespread Policy and Outcomes Improvement

Jennifer Tomasik

CONTENTS

INTRODUCTION

On Friday, May 9, 2003, a 5-year-old boy was undergoing diagnostic testing for his epilepsy at Children's Hospital in Boston when he suffered a massive seizure. Two days later, on Mother's Day, he died. Despite the fact that he was in intensive care at one of the world's leading pediatric hospitals, none of the physicians caring for him ordered the treatment that could have saved his life.

The death was tragic, but even more troubling from an organizational perspective was the series of events that led up to it. The Massachusetts Department of Public Health investigated the death, and the *Boston Globe* reported on the results that, "the investigation portrays a situation where lines of authority were deeply tangled, and where no one person had accountability for the patient. Each of the doctors who initially worked on the case—two at the bedside and one consulting by phone—told investigators that they thought one of the others was in charge." In the end, no one was in charge.

This is a striking example of how even the most talented clinicians in one of the world's best hospitals can fail not only to provide adequate care but to save a savable life—all because the lines of authority were unclear. The lack of clarity resulted in this team's inability to collaborate effectively at a time when the stakes could not have been higher.

This story reflects just one of many difficult collaboration challenges in health care. In this chapter, we will focus on the increasing need for collaboration among physicians, clinicians, hospital executives, and administrative leaders in the dynamic, complex health care environment. We will look specifically at collaboration along three different dimensions, including

1. Interprofessional teams
2. Institution to institution
3. Physicians and administrators

In each instance, we will describe useful tools that can be applied to improve collaboration and overall institutional performance—all in the service of providing better patient care.

But first, let us discuss the case for collaboration: why, beyond this most obvious and tragic case, is it important for health care organizations to improve collaboration?

WHAT IS COLLABORATION ANYWAY?

Merriam-Webster defines *collaboration* as "to work jointly with others or together especially in an intellectual endeavor." While true, we find this definition insufficient for our purposes. Our colleagues at The Rhythm of Business, a consulting firm focused exclusively on collaboration, provide a more productive way to think about collaboration:

> Collaboration is a purposeful, strategic way of working that leverages the resources of each party for the benefit of all by coordinating activities and communicating information within an environment of trust and transparency [1].

We add to this definition one additional yet critical dimension. Collaboration also means working with, and through, differences. Any highly functioning team will, by its very nature, have differences—team members are ideally bringing innovative ideas that compete for "idea space" at the table. Effective collaboration requires that teams not only value differences but, in fact, also encourage them to surface. Viewed in this way, collaboration is not an event or an idea. It is not "agreeing to get along." Effective collaboration is an ongoing, systematic, strategic process. It is also, we believe, a business imperative—and nowhere more so than in health care.

Business Case for Collaboration

Getting along is nice, of course, but reaffirming our belief that collaboration is not about agreeing to get along, research focused on the impact of collaboration shows that *collaboration improves performance*. A recent IBM study suggests that companies that characterize themselves as effective in collaboration are also shown to be the most adaptable to change [2].

Furthermore, organizations that are more successful at executing strategy are also more effective at collaboration. Consider the results from *The Secrets to Successful Strategy Execution*, by Neilson, Martin, and Powers in 2008 [3]. The authors found that information sharing and clear decision rights—two pillars of effective collaboration—are by far the most important features of firms that successfully execute strategy. And there is additional research:

- A *McKinsey Quarterly* article reports that organizations whose employees collaborate more effectively are more productive and consistently outperform their competition (as

measured by higher returns using the earnings before interest, taxes, depreciation, and amortization (EBITDA) formula [4].
- Kenneth Cohn, author of *Collaborate for Success, Breakthrough Strategies for Engaging Physicians, Nurses and Hospital Executives*, finds that "effective collaboration is an under-utilized method to boost revenues, cut expenses, improve outcomes and use health care professionals' limited time more effectively" [5].
- Results of an American Nurses Credentialing Center study that looked at 14 Magnet hospitals and found a positive correlation between the quality of physician–nurse relationships (based on measures of collegiality and collaboration) and the quality of patient care outcomes [6].

WHY IS COLLABORATION IN HEALTH CARE PARTICULARLY IMPORTANT?

Tom Davenport, consultant, author, and teacher, has extensively studied knowledge workers (as we would argue most health care workers are) in terms of how they think, what motivates them, and how they accomplish tasks. In his book, *Thinking for a Living* [7], Davenport created a classification structure for knowledge-intensive processes. He looks at the complexity of work (from routine or structured tasks to those that are unstructured and require interpretation) and maps it against the level of required process interdependence (from individual workers or systems to collaborative groups). We have adapted this framework in the graphic below (Figure 8.1).

We have found that most organizations operate using a mixture of four types of processes, including

1. *Transactional processes*—largely focused on routine work that can be accomplished by individuals or systems
2. *Integrated processes*—still routine in nature but requiring greater collaboration among individuals or teams
3. *Expert processes*—focus on judgment-oriented work and depend on "star performers"
4. *Collaborative processes*—the most complex work that requires collaborative teams to partner on activities in addition to experienced individuals' interpretations and judgments

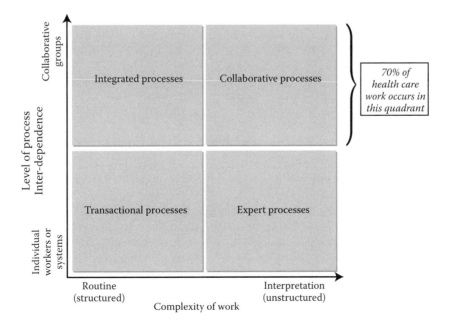

FIGURE 8.1   The knowledge-intensive worker.

Davenport estimates that 70% of health care work occurs in the collaborative quadrant. This percentage is not difficult to imagine given the complexity of patient care delivery and the systems and teams that must come together in the service of it.

But even if you agree that effective collaboration is important, and even if you agree that building your collaborative skills is imperative to future success—*how* do you actually get better at collaborating? Let us look at several opportunities to improve collaboration in health care settings.

IMPROVING THE EFFECTIVENESS AND PERFORMANCE OF INTERPROFESSIONAL TEAMS

The strength of the team is each individual member. The strength of each member is the team.

—Phil Jackson

An academic medical center (AMC) developed a strategic plan to differentiate itself in cancer care. The problem: the pillar of their cancer service was a poorly functioning Breast Care Center (BCC). The issues in the center showed up in a number of ways: patients were frustrated by wait times, clinicians were disengaged and demotivated, performance metrics were low, and leadership was not in agreement about what needed to be done to reorganize the center. The unifying goal that drove the team's work was, as the associate medical director phrased it, "My mother and my wife should actually want to come here for their breast care, and then want to stay once they're here."

An analysis of the BCC showed a significant lack of clarity around authority and accountability. This lack of clarity played out in a number of ways, leaving people confused and frustrated on a regular basis. Who does the director of the BCC report to? What is the authority of the chair of radiology within the BCC? These and other questions served as the focal point of the collaboration work to improve the performance of the leadership team and the BCC as a whole.

BUILDING A SHARED LANGUAGE

Teams are becoming more and more important in health care delivery. In diagnosing and treating patients, the strength of interprofessional teams results from a potent combination of individual areas of expertise (primary care, specialist, subspecialist, nurse, therapist, etc.) toward a collective end (coordinated, high-quality care). The same is true when you consider the interprofessional teams required to run a hospital or a physician group. Clinical, financial, and operational skills are all required to run an institution that functions as a whole that is greater than the sum of its individual parts.

Teams break down when it is unclear whether or how they should participate in such processes. Think back to the story of the team caring for the young boy at Children's Hospital. In complex situations, uncertainty about substance (what is clinically needed at this point?) can get mixed with uncertainty about process (whose patient is this?). In such situations, either politics dominate substance (I am not senior enough to call out the attending) or conflict is avoided and suboptimal choices are made. Teams become less competent because roles and responsibilities are unclear. In the Children's Hospital case, no one believed that they alone had the authority to make the patient "theirs" and to therefore take on the authority and accountability that implies.

Decision-making in any team setting can be complicated. The number of players, interests, and perspectives in any given health care situation makes decision-making that much more difficult. Given the challenge of making decisions in highly complex situations, what can be done to help individuals collaborate more effectively on interprofessional teams?

A Tool for Productive Collaboration: Decision Charting

Decision charting has been proven to exponentially improve team collaboration and performance. The process begins by laying out critical decisions for a team and assigning the following roles to the individuals that comprise the team. This mnemonic may be helpful:

A—Approve the decision.
R—Responsible for staffing the decision (make sure that A has what they need).
C—Consult to the decision before it is made.
I—Informed about the decision after it is made.

Team members complete decision charts independently, based on how they believe each team member is currently involved in a specific decision. The data are then used to evaluate agreements and discrepancies among team members. This process also establishes a common vocabulary for making decisions. It sharpens delegation, ensures accountability, and increases effective communication among individuals and team members [8].

The following chart is an example of two decisions and six stakeholders. Look specifically at the second decision, "The decision to hire a new cancer director." It is fairly clear who has the A, but no one has the R. (Note that the percentage is the percent of respondents who assigned that role to that stakeholder.)

	Enterprise Chief Nursing Officer	Dean of Finance	Hospital Chief Nursing Officer	EVP of Health Affairs	Department Chair	CCO
Continue or discontinue the Neuroscience Service Line	C 56%	C 63%	I 69%	A 100%	C 44%	R 63%
Hire a new Cancer Director	C 56%	C 69%	I 81%	A 81%	C 56%	C 50%

Decision charting was used to help build key interprofessional relationships and clarify roles for the entire center. The use of decision charting allowed the group to have the difficult conversations in ways that were concrete, transparent, and not taken as personal attacks. Part of the safety of decision charting is that roles, rather than names, can be used to encourage people to think about function rather than about individual personalities.

Simply put, the completion of the decision charting process improved both patient care and bottom-line performance for the BCC. Wait times for diagnostic mammogram appointments improved, decreasing the number of days to a visit by 89%. Outpatient revenue increased by 44%. More effective collaboration between and among the director, the chair, the administration, and the clinicians was credited for producing these results. The BCC is now a major contributor to the institution's success.

IMPROVING COLLABORATION BETWEEN AND AMONG INSTITUTIONS

Alone we can do so little; together we can do so much.

—Helen Keller

The board of a small community hospital handed down an edict to its CEO—put in place a memorandum of understanding to merge with a specific AMC, and bring it back to them within 2 months.

The hospital already had a relationship with this particular AMC, as well as others, but until this moment, the CEO had not been considering formal partnerships at all—never mind merging his hospital with another. When I asked the CEO what the board wanted to get out of the relationship with this particular center, he hesitantly responded, "Survival?"

Here is a situation where a seasoned hospital CEO, whose market position was admittedly beginning to crumble, had a board—which actually knew very little about health care or the complexities of this particular market—reacting out of fear. They presented an ultimatum that the CEO felt he had to respond to, even though he himself was not clear about the goal of the merger. Without feeling authorized to think clearly *with* the board members about what might be in the best interest for that institution, he was forced to move down a specific path.

This is a familiar story, especially given the turbulent health care market that has emerged following the passage of national reform in the Patient Protection and Affordable Care Act (PPACA). Few would argue that health care is experiencing a new wave of integration, and with this wave comes a series of challenges that we believe effective collaboration can address.

A WAVE OF INTEGRATION

Hospital merger and acquisition transaction volume has increased by over 300% between 2008 and 2010 [9]. The reasons for this dramatic rise include

- Health care reform (PPACA)
- Lack of access to capital
- The advent of accountable care organizations (ACOs)
- The need to gain leverage in negotiating with payers
- Increased participation from private equity in health care services
- Declining patient volumes
- Rising uninsured population
- Decreasing Medicare payments
- On average, declines in credit ratings [10]

Merger and acquisition activity is expected to continue for the next several years, as confirmed by a recent survey where 86% of hospital leaders said they expect to see increased acute care mergers and acquisitions [11].

ALLIANCE PARADOX

The rising tide of integration—as evidenced by increased merger, acquisition, and joint venture activity—brings a curious paradox. While organizations need to form a greater number of alliances than before, and even rely on them as a way to enhance competitiveness and growth (whether that be between or among physician organizations, acute care hospitals, rehabilitative services, etc.), leaders face considerable challenges in making these alliances and collaborative partnerships actually work.

Consider that somewhere between 30% and 70% of alliances fail, meaning that they do not meet the goals of the parent entities or that they do not deliver on promised operational or strategic benefits. Fully 50% of alliances terminate [12]. Given the high probability of failure, how do you improve collaboration to enhance performance and increase the chances of success?

GIVES AND GETS OF COLLABORATION

Collaboration is fundamentally built on agreements whereby each participating entity expects that together, they can do something greater than either partner could do on its own. If this is not the case, then collaboration should not be pursued. Each has something to "give" to the partnership, and each has something to "get" out of it. Overall, the end product should be greater than the sum of the individual parts.

Let us return to the earlier example of our community hospital CEO. In thinking about a merger partner with which to collaborate, the first two questions he should have asked his board were

1. What do we need from a partnership?
2. What can we offer in return?

In answering these questions, the CEO and his board will have a much clearer idea of what they need to get from a relationship and what they have to give in return. This fundamental step is often overlooked in the heat of discussions about alliances. We would argue that the first step to answering these questions is by inviting clinical and administrative staff to collaborate on developing an understanding of what we call the current state of the business.

The current state is an opportunity to test people's assumptions about what is driving the business against data that reveal what is actually happening. In one case, for example, we worked with a prestigious AMC that competed with many local community hospitals. Though they prided themselves on the tertiary and quaternary care they delivered, they realized through the development of a current state that nearly three quarters of their actual patient volume was considered secondary care—care that could reasonably and more cheaply be delivered at one of the community hospital competitors. At the same time, the revenues related to this care represented a substantial proportion of their operating margin. These insights revealed their vulnerability at a time when physician referrers were increasingly being pressured to send their patients to lower-cost settings.

This realization helped the AMC's clinical and administrative leaders develop clear strategies for how to reduce their cost structure. This included developing important collaborative relationships to secure critical referral lines for their more complex patients. In addition, the act of bringing physicians, nurses, and administrators together to do this work strengthened their relationships. Each understood the rationale for the strategies that were going to be required and had actively participated in the shaping of those strategies—something that research shows will inevitably increase the likelihood of effective implementation of the strategies.

IMPROVING COLLABORATION BETWEEN PHYSICIANS AND HOSPITAL ADMINISTRATORS

It is the long history of humankind (and animal kind, too) those who learned to collaborate and improvise most effectively have prevailed.

—Charles Darwin

Beyond institutional mergers and joint ventures, collaboration in health care is being driven by other factors; there is a need to move from a health care system driven by volume and characterized by fragmentation, waste, high cost, and inconsistent quality to a system where care is coordinated, costs are lower, and quality is higher.

Merger mania in the 1990s was driven by similar concerns, including the fear of for-profit competition and the rise of managed care. The results of this earlier round of mergers were unexpected. The 1990s "consolidation fever" raised hospital prices by at least 5% and did not measurably improve quality [13]. Hospitals purchased physician practices without a great deal of thought about expectations and mutual accountability, and many of those relationships failed—usually with significant financial implications.

Fearful of history repeating itself, savvy health care leaders are thinking differently about how to develop the collaborative relationships they need to succeed today. They see ACOs and global payments—where institutions will take on greater risk for the cost and quality of the services a patient requires—as an opportunity to get clear about how they can best position themselves across the full continuum of care. They believe that potential gains are not likely to show up simply as a result of mergers and acquisitions or consolidation per se. Rather than just integrating the bottom lines of their institutions, they are focused on ensuring that those individuals and teams who actually care for patients can productively collaborate with each other and that they understand the clear and compelling rationale for why that collaboration is necessary. Nowhere is this relationship more important than between hospital administrators and the medical staff.

Given the often difficult nature of relationships between hospital administrators and medical staff, how do you improve collaboration to increase productivity and performance?

DEVELOPING PHYSICIAN COMPACTS TO IMPROVE COLLABORATION AND PERFORMANCE

Not long ago, I was invited to help a very successful community hospital system improve its relationship with a large private practice of cardiologists. I had the opportunity to interview individuals from the hospital and in the physician practice to develop a point of view about the interests of each party and how the parties perceived each other. Of the many stories heard, there was one that epitomized the disconnection between intent and perception.

The hospital administrators described their deep commitment to the physician group and desire to help that group succeed. They listed investment upon investment that had been made to make it easier for those physicians to work on-site, including millions of dollars to renovate office space, build new catheter labs, and bring some dedicated hospitalists on site so the cardiologists would not have to be on call 24/7. When we spoke to the cardiologists, however, they had a very different point of view. One of the practice leaders explained, "These guys are just trying to build the facilities at the hospital so they can bypass us. They know we can refer our patients elsewhere. They are trying to build these facilities so they can control the referral stream and draw patients straight to the hospital." This story captures an age-old tension that has historically existed between administrators and physicians.

What rests underneath this tension is something that Jack Silversin, DMD, DrPH, and Mary Jane Kornacki, MS, refer to as the traditional "physician compact." The compact is an (often) unwritten, nonlegal agreement between physicians and administrators that reflects an understanding of what each party has to give and what each expects to get in return. Silversin and Kornacki write about the three foundational pillars of what physicians have often expected to get from administrators:

- *Autonomy:* The ability to take care of patients without interference and retain control over daily operations related to their practice
- *Protection:* A buffer from market forces and change in return for surrendering some of their independence
- *Entitlement:* Yearly increases in compensation, supportive staff, and internal referrals regardless of how one treats staff or behaves toward colleagues [14]

In the case of the cardiologists, each of these things was true. But today's tumultuous health care landscape is changing many of the traditional underpinnings of the physician compact. Consider that hospitals used to focus exclusively on inpatient business, leaving outpatient business to physicians. Today, hospitals and physicians often compete for what can be lucrative outpatient business, particularly with the rise of physician-owned ambulatory surgery centers. Many physician practices are grappling with these changing realities and are rethinking what they have to give and what they need to get from a new physician compact—in some cases between and among the physicians inside a group practice and in others between the physicians and the hospitals with which they work.

What Does a Physician Compact Look Like?

In the simplest of terms, a physician compact lays out an understanding of what each party expects from the other. Silversin and Kornacki worked with Virginia Mason Medical Center in Seattle, Washington, to reinvent and make visible its compact between administrators and physicians nearly a decade ago. It fits on a single page and clearly and simply describes the organization's responsibilities and the physician's responsibilities.

Virginia Mason Medical Center Physician Compact	
Organization's Responsibilities	*Physician's Responsibilities*
Foster Excellence	Focus on Patients
• Recruit and retain superior physicians and staff	• Practice state-of-the-art, quality medicine
• Support career development and professional satisfaction	• Encourage patient involvement in care and treatment decisions
• Acknowledge contributions to patient care and the organization	• Achieve and maintain optimal patient access
• Create opportunities to participate in or support research	• Insist on seamless service
Listen and Communicate	Collaborate on Care Delivery
• Share information regarding strategic intent, organizational priorities, and business decisions	• Include staff, physicians, and management on team
• Offer opportunities for constructive dialogue	• Treat all members with respect
• Provide regular, written evaluation and feedback	• Demonstrate the highest levels of ethical and professional conduct
	• Behave in a manner consistent with group goals
	• Participate in or support teaching
Educate	Listen and Communicate
• Support and facilitate teaching, GME, and CME	• Communicate clinical information in clear, timely manner
• Provide information and tools necessary to improve practice	• Request information, resources needed to provide care consistent with VM goals
	• Provide and accept feedback
Reward	Take Ownership
• Provide clear compensation with internal and market consistency, aligned with organizational goals	• Implement VM-accepted clinical standards of care
• Create an environment that supports teams and individuals	• Participate in and support group decisions
Lead	• Focus on the economic aspects of our practice
• Manage and lead organization with integrity and accountability	Change
	• Embrace innovation and continuous improvement
	• Participate in necessary organizational change

So How Do You Actually Create a Compact?

Silversin and Kornacki explain that, although the specific steps are likely to differ from group to group, the work generally unfolds in the following way:

1. *Decide if changing the compact is a must-do issue*—Both parties must be committed to the process and open to facing and working through what are likely to be difficult issues.
2. *Develop and sustain aligned sponsorship*—Having physician leaders sponsor change is critical to the work, in that they provide oversight, sanction the change that is required, and hold others accountable. These individuals participate in the creation of the compact, as well as ensuring that people live up to it.
3. *Implement a process with physicians*—Physician participation is imperative, although how and to what degree for different physicians can certainly change depending on the

situation. Overall, the physicians involved should feel some urgency to change and a sense of the strategic imperative to do so.

4. *Use available levers to reinforce the new compact*—The compact is nothing more than a sheet of paper if each party chooses not to live up to the expectations that they have negotiated. There are many levers that can help guide desired behaviors and hold each party accountable for the agreements they have made (e.g., compensation, incentives, measurement, and feedback).

The team that created a physician compact at Wheaton Franciscan Medical Group, a group of more than 320 primary care and specialty physicians in the Midwest, used some helpful criteria to frame their compact work:

1. Compacts need to have reciprocity with benefits to both leadership and physicians, where both receive benefits and believe that the exchange is equitable.
2. Compacts need to have a shared sense of strategic imperatives that balance individual autonomy with the medical group's best interest.
3. Compacts should be developed and supported for alignment within a changing environment of different cultures [15].

These principles nicely balance the rationale for change while recognizing the tension that will almost certainly exist in some way between individual and collective interests.

We cannot emphasize strongly enough that the process of getting to the compact is as important, if not more so, than the compact itself. Effective collaboration is built on a foundation of trust. The most compelling vision and the most committed partners will not matter a bit if the parties cannot develop and sustain trust. The cardiology group we described earlier did not trust the intentions of the hospital, and therefore, collaboration was very difficult. With a physician compact, the iterative process of discussing expectations, reiterating those expectations, and then acting in ways that put those expectations into practice enables both physicians and administrators to collaborate and hold each other accountable for the agreements they have made and, ultimately, to build and sustain trust.

CONCLUSION

This is a time of great change in health care. No one is certain how the future landscape will unfold, but it is clear that changes in regulation, reimbursement, technology, the economy, and science will significantly impact the work of those clinicians and administrators who dedicate their careers to improving patient care.

Experience has shown that better collaboration between and among the many different parts of the health care delivery system holds great potential to improve the quality of care and the relationships of those delivering it. It has also shown that the opportunities to improve collaboration are widespread. The focus in this chapter has been to introduce and share a selected set of tools that can be used to improve collaboration along several dimensions:

- Clarifying roles and authority through decision charting
- Understanding the give and the get needed to establish effective alliances through the current state
- Working jointly to establish and test a set of refined expectations through a physician–administrator compact

In the end, improved collaboration can help your institution with everything from interprofessional productivity to patient satisfaction to the most critical service of all: caring for patients and saving lives.

CASE MODEL 8.1: THE VALUE OF COLLABORATION

One of the nation's top teaching hospitals found that, despite its best attempts, their focus on quality of care remained what could be described as episodic: one quality issue would show up in their results, they would address that issue with vigor (typically with an "initiative"), the issue would subside, and they were on to the next issue.

In making a commitment to quality of care across the spectrum of care, the hospital understood that the closer to the patient the quality work happened, the better the results would be. They therefore established unit-based clinical leadership teams (UBCLs).

The UBCLs were leadership trios at the unit level—a physician leader paired with a nurse leader to manage the unit and joined by a project manager for quality. They started their collaboration journey with the basics—how to work together:

o   A weekly operations meeting to review metrics and plan ahead
o   Interdisciplinary rounding
o   Orienting house staff to the unit
o   Linking the work of the UBCLs to specific projects (they started with transitions in care from the hospital to the outpatient setting) and supporting the team to set targets

The UBCLs have been in place in every hospital unit throughout the system for several years now. The UBCL partnership provides a flexible accountability structure at the unit level that can serve many purposes.

The unit model is sustained by a physician–nurse partnership at the very top of the organization. The chief medical officers (CMOs) and chief nursing officers (CNOs) across the system banded together to design the UBCLs and to create the infrastructure and support for it. The CMOs and CNOs have focused from the beginning on institutionalizing the UBCLs and giving them staying power.

For example, the health system's chief learning officer has been involved from before the beginning—helping the organization learn from itself, project managing the overall initiative, and integrating it into other systemwide efforts. The project manager for quality (and supervisors) received Six Sigma training to boost their leadership and project management skills.

CHECKLIST 1: Interprofessional Teams	YES	NO
Are team members clear about the specific decision being addressed?	o	o
Are team members clear about their role in that decision?	o	o
Are all relevant roles represented in the decision-making process?	o	o
Is the person with the A taking up that authority fully?	o	o
Is the person with the R taking up that responsibility fully?	o	o
Are those with Cs being consulted before the decision is made?	o	o
Are those with Is being informed once the decision is made?	o	o

REFERENCES

1. Shuman, J. and Twombly, J. "The Real Power of Collaboration." *Effective Executive* XIII(04), 36–42 (2010).
2. IBM Business Services: "Unlocking the DNA of the Adaptable Workforce" *The Global Human Capital Study 2008 Chemicals and Petroleum Edition*, Bentley University, Waltham, MA, 2008.

3. Neilson, G. L., Martin, K. L. and Powers, E. *The Secrets to Successful Strategy Execution.* Harvard Business Press, Boston, 2008.

4. Beardsley, S. C., Johnson, B. C. and Manyika, J. "Competitive Advantage from Better Interactions." *McKinsey Quarterly* 53–68 (2006).

5. Cohn, K. H. *Collaborate for Success! Breakthrough Strategies for Engaging Physicians, Nurses, and Hospital Executives.* Health Administration Press, Chicago IL. 2006.

6. Lindeke, L. and Sieckert, A. "Nurse-Physician Workplace Collaboration" *Continuing Education and Online Journal of Issues in Nursing.* 10(1): 2 (2005).

7. Davenport, T. H. *Thinking for a Living: How to Get Better Performances and Results from Knowledge Workers.* Harvard Business Press, Boston, 2005.

8. Tomasik, J. "Building a Shared Language: How Administrative and Clinical Leaders Can Improve Performance and Productivity." *Healthcare Executive* May/June 2008.

9. Fishman, E., Neumann, P. and Owens, J. "Merger and Acquisition Activity in the Healthcare Sector: What's Hot and How Not to Get Burned." (PowerPoint slides) 2011, *www.healthlawyers.org/Events/.../ fishman_neumann_owens_slides.pdf.*

10. Grauman, D., Harris, J. and Martin, C. "Access to Capital: Implications for Hospital Consolidation." *Healthcare Financial Management* 64:4 (2010).

11. Minich-Pourshadi, K. "Hospital Mergers & Acquisitions: Opportunities and Challenges." *HealthLeaders Media* 50–54 (November 15, 2010).

12. Kale, P. and Singh, H. "Managing Strategic Alliances: What Do We Know Now and Where Do We Go From Here?" *Academy of Management Perspectives* 45–62 (2009).

13. Vogt, W. B and Town, R. "How Has Hospital Consolidation Affected the Price and Quality of Hospital Care?" *Robert Wood Johnson Foundation: Policy Brief No. 9.* 2006.

14. Silversin, J. and Kornacki, M. J. "Creating a Physician Compact That Drives Group Success." *MGM Journal* 47(3): 54–62 (2000).

15. Shukla, S., Meyer, L. and Stingl, D. "Physician Compact: A Tool for Enhancing Physician Satisfaction and Improving Communication." *American College of Physician Executives* 35:1 (2009).

9 Tracking Medical Procedures with Outcomes Reporting
Techniques of Benchmarking and Improvement

Brent A. Metfessel

CONTENTS

INTRODUCTION

In the last two decades, physician performance measurement has gained increasing importance and visibility. Given the rising cost of health care, as well as increasing patient responsibility for and control over health care spending, physician practice pattern assessment has become important to multiple stakeholders, including consumers and consumer groups, health care providers, federal and state governments, and health plans. Many health plans use some type of physician measurement methodology and typically evaluate the quality and cost of care using computerized information systems and large health care databases, which can contain many millions of records.

Thus, physicians need clear awareness of the methods used to track their practice patterns, whether the tracking includes the cost of the practice, the quality of care (such as the frequency of preventive services that a physician provides), or outcomes monitoring. Using information systems for such purposes is part of *medical informatics*, which is at the intersection of information technology, computer science, and health care. Given this definition, the field is clearly very broad and dynamic. For the purposes of physician performance measurement and the tracking of care processes, medical informatics can be defined as the applied science at the junction of the disciplines of medicine, business, and information technology that supports the health care delivery process and promotes measurable improvements in both the quality of care and cost-effectiveness (Medical College of Wisconsin).

PROFILING CARE PROCESSES WITH DATA CATEGORIES

Having the correct data to support the measures used in physician performance measurement is key to accurate reporting. The data must be "clean" and as free from errors as possible. Errors in the data may occur due to a number of factors, such as poor diagnosis or procedure coding as well as the miskeying of data fields such as cost values. In addition, the category of data used needs to match the desired measures that one hopes to obtain and analyze.

For example, if a person or organization wants to look at the effect of a congestive heart failure treatment regimen on exercise tolerance, claims data would not be the appropriate source. Functional status data would need to be collected as well. The following five data categories are of greatest interest in care profiling: 1) claims, encounter, and other administrative data; 2) functional status data; 3) patient satisfaction data; 4) clinical and medical record data; and 5) health risk assessment (HRA) data.

CLAIMS, ENCOUNTERS, AND OTHER ADMINISTRATIVE DATA

This data category is the most readily available and the most abundant. Basically all health plans have access to such data, which include member demographic information such as age and gender, International Classification of Diseases (ICD-9 and ICD-10) codes for diagnoses, Current Procedural Terminology (CPT) codes for procedures, physician information, including medical specialty, National Drug Codes to identify drugs, various cost fields, and other information. Claims databases can become quite large and, for major health plans, often include millions of records. Basic quality and cost-efficiency performance measurement are usually done using claims and administrative data. Quality measures obtainable from claims data include the frequency of preventive and disease monitoring services (such as the frequency of hemoglobin A1c [HbA1c] tests to monitor diabetes), certain complications of care such as surgical site infections, and proxies for outcomes such as whether a treatment for a chronic condition leads to a decrease in emergency room (ER) visits and hospital admissions. The Centers for Medicare and Medicaid Services (CMS), the National Committee for Quality Assurance (NCQA), which publishes the Healthcare Effectiveness Data and Information Set (HEDIS), and the American Medical Association Physician Consortium for Performance Improvement (AMA PCPI) are examples of national organizations that work to develop the algorithms applied to claims data to evaluate adherence to evidence-based medicine and the related evidence-based quality-of-care measures. Other national organizations, such as the National Quality Forum (NQF) and the AQA Alliance (formerly known as the Ambulatory Care Quality Alliance), do not create new measure algorithms but have standard processes for reviewing and endorsing quality measure algorithms submitted from other organizations such as the above. Measure algorithms receiving endorsement from these organizations have been subsequently widely adapted in health plan performance measurement systems. Other examples of performance measures include the appropriateness of drug treatment for specific conditions (such as coronary artery disease, diabetes, and pediatric pharyngitis), patient safety measures (such as tracking patient falls), and infection control (such as the rate of central line catheter-associated infection).

FUNCTIONAL STATUS DATA

This category includes subjective data gathered from the patient in terms of his/her view of the illness and the impact of the illness on activities of living, such as whether a congestive heart failure patient has the ability to walk up a flight of stairs without significant shortness of breath. The effect of a treatment regimen on such parameters can be performed to determine whether there is improvement in the patient's view and whether side effects or complications are creating new difficulties for the patient. The SF-36 (QualityMetric, Inc.), a functional status survey with 36 query items, includes a scale that assesses eight health concepts:

- Limitations in physical activities because of health problems
- Limitations in social activities because of physical or emotional problems
- Limitations in usual role activities because of physical health problems
- Bodily pain
- General mental health (psychological distress and well-being)
- Limitations in usual role activities because of emotional problems
- Vitality (energy and fatigue)
- General health perceptions

Functional status data can be an excellent way of measuring specific health outcomes in the patient's view, but because collecting this information requires surveys of individual patients, collection and analysis can be resource intensive and expensive, and thus, functional status data are less abundant than claims and administrative data.

PATIENT SATISFACTION DATA

This is a subjective measure of what the patient perceives in terms of the level of service quality and care provided by the clinician. Many health plans consider patient satisfaction an important measure of physician quality. Many researchers link patient satisfaction to clinical outcomes, although it is not a direct measure of clinical quality. These data, however, are also resource intensive to collect and require commitment on the part of the patient to fill out the forms and return them through mail or online. Selection bias may also occur in terms of patient satisfaction data, because patients who choose to fill out and return the forms may, in some cases, not be representative of the overall patient population for a physician. More recently, the field has moved from measuring "satisfaction" to elucidating a more validated and specific "patient experience of care." The Consumer Assessment of Healthcare Providers and Systems (CAHPS), funded and administered by the Agency for Healthcare and Research Quality (AHRQ), is part of a national initiative to measure, report on, and improve health care quality from the viewpoint of patients and other consumers. Separate surveys are used for evaluating ambulatory care and facility or hospital care. In addition, the National CAHPS Benchmarking Database contains more than 10 years of CAHPS survey data from commercial and Medicaid plans and is designed to facilitate comparative analysis of individual CAHPS survey results with benchmarks, including national or regional averages. The CAHPS program works closely with other public and private research agencies, known collectively as the CAHPS Consortium, for continued review and enhancement of the survey tools.

CLINICAL AND MEDICAL RECORDS DATA

This category includes laboratory values and radiology results, along with other aspects of the medical record. With the advent of government initiatives and mandates to increase the use of electronic health records, numerous companies that develop software for electronic health records now exist, and the competition is intense. Nevertheless, some health plans and vendors that perform information reporting for health plans do collect (or intend to collect in the near future) data such as laboratory results. The proper use of such data, although again very resource intensive to collect and analyze, can provide a much clearer picture of outcomes and treatment progress. Using diabetes as an example, claims data can provide information such as the frequency of performance of HbA1c tests, but a separate laboratory result data feed can give the actual value of HbA1c, and thus, the level of control of the diabetes over the past 3–4 months can be assessed as an outcome measure. In an effort to make laboratory values more abundant, the recent creation of CPT Category II (CPT II) codes attempts to create a hybrid between claims data and laboratory results. For example, HbA1c or low-density lipoprotein results can be coded as to whether a particular laboratory target or threshold is met (e.g., low-density lipoprotein cholesterol levels less than 100 mg/dl). Although not as granular as actual laboratory results, CPT II codes can significantly increase the abundance of at least basic laboratory data. As claims-based quality measures are refined and enhanced in the future, CPT II codes may increase in importance in an effort to better collect actual outcomes data, and physicians well versed in the use of the codes could have a distinct advantage in terms of quality performance measurement. Some national standard measures, such as the percentage of diabetics with controlled HbA1c (less than 8.0%) and controlled blood pressure (less than 140/90), allow the use of CPT II codes to measure compliance to such measures.

HRA DATA

Although health risk assessment (HRA) data are not generally used to profile care processes *per se*, such data help determine which members are at the highest risk for chronic illness in the future, such as heart disease. Patients usually fill out such surveys directly, and many Internet sites now include free HRAs and calculation of risk scores. Included in HRA surveys are smoking history, dietary habits, general health questions, level of energy, emotional health, driving habits, and other parameters. Physicians can use such results as guides to ascertain which members need the most intensive intervention and thus help prevent poor future outcomes.

CONVERTING INFORMATION AND DATA TO VALUE AND KNOWLEDGE

Data streams such as claims inputs are difficult to use in their raw form. Such streams may contain 50 fields (data items) or more per record and thus need further processing in order to be useful in reporting and evaluating physician practice patterns. The following depict the six major steps in converting raw data to usable information that leads to action that benefits organizations (such as health plans) and physicians.

DATA COLLECTION

This involves inputting the data into the computer, which may range from a large mainframe to a personal workstation, depending on the size of the database. In the past, data often came in the form of a tape and had to be read into the mainframe computer disk storage. More recently, physicians' offices have been able to directly send the claims data electronically into the health plan system. In this scenario, claims data are the data source, along with membership data (containing member demographics and eligibility information), physician identifying information, and pharmacy claims, which contain National Drug Codes, fill dates, fill amount, cost data, and other fields (Figure 9.1). Conveyance of health care data always occurs securely and in compliance with applicable laws and regulations, and only among those permitted to receive and send data consistent with such laws and regulations.

DATA INTEGRATION AND MAPPING

In the managed care industry, many different claims systems exist. National managed care organizations and third-party vendors of reporting software generally have to integrate the disparate systems together into a common format. This involves standardizing the data fields so that the same data items appear in the same location in the record and have a specified number of characters or digits. Thus, numeric fields such as cost will have the same number of digits no matter what claims system the values originally came from, and text fields such as physician specialty will have "mappings" so that the different specialty codes from the various systems that refer to the same specialty will be mapped to a single code in the final database. Such data standardization and mapping are critical to the accurate reporting of physician practice patterns, since the input into the reporting programs needs to enter the system in a single standard format.

PROCESSING OF DATA AUDITS

Items in the database records are audited to check whether they meet basic criteria, and this process is also known as data cleansing. Usually, the health plan either develops its own software to conduct

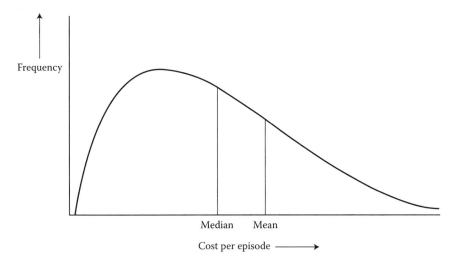

FIGURE 9.1 Illustration of a typical distribution for cost per episode data.

the checks or purchases the software from a third party. Some examples of basic audits include the following:

- Age–procedure mismatch, such as pediatric procedures performed on adults
- Gender–diagnosis or gender–procedure mismatch, such as gynecology surgery in males
- Notation of missing data or fields
- Invalid values such as an invalid physician specialty
- ICD-CPT mismatch, such as a bunion procedure where the only diagnosis code is asthma
- Data with out-of-range values, such as a claims record with a cost field value of $1,000,000

In many cases, records with errors or audit flags are output as exception reports. In those cases, the health plan would decide whether to keep the record, modify it, or throw it out prior to input into the reporting system.

When a health plan brings a new group of physicians into its network, physicians and their office staff need to keep in mind that the initial mapping of the physician group's data may increase the chance for data errors, and thus, diligence is needed on the physician side to ensure a smooth, error-free transition to the new database system.

DATA GROUPING FOR CASE-MIX ADJUSTMENT

Proper risk adjustment or case-mix adjustment of the data is a necessary component of physician performance measurement. Such algorithms help level the playing field among physicians or facilities (such as hospitals) that are being compared. Without such adjustment, a physician who receives a complaint from a health plan that his/her practice is too costly could argue that his/her patients are sicker, which may be true in some cases. To adjust for case mix, the data need to be fed into a grouper that clusters the data into clinical classes or risk groups. The class in which a data record belongs can then be added to the claims record as an additional field. These fields are then input into the reporting system along with the rest of the record in order to calculate case-mix or risk-adjusted "expected" or target values for physicians or other comparative groups. The cost of practice is a commonly used value that is adjusted by case mix, but other metrics can undergo adjustment as well, such as visit rates and procedure utilization.

INFORMATION REPORTING

In this step, the case mix–adjusted data are run through the reporting software systems to generate reports that provide information on practice pattern performance. Such reports may be displayed in a variety of formats, ranging from simple spreadsheets to secure, online reporting platforms that integrate sophisticated graphical displays, and statistical analysis. Furthermore, many health plans have developed their own reporting platforms for tables and displays. Hard-copy reports are often mailed out to physicians, but increasingly, health plans have physician performance reports accessible on the Web so that physicians and in some cases plan members can readily view the reports online. There is speculation that online reporting that is accessible to present and prospective patients increases the stakes resulting from physician performance reporting, because performance results can then directly affect patient traffic for a physician or physician group and thus have economic impact to the practice. On the other hand, however, consumers are calling for clearer and more transparent information for consumers so that they can inform themselves about these statistical quality and efficiency markers, as well as more intangible markers such as a friend or loved one's experience.

Items commonly reported, both online and in hard-copy format, include the total cost of practice, cost by service category (such as laboratory costs, specialist professional costs, and facility costs), visit rates, preventive services rates (such as mammography screening), complication rates, and case mix–adjusted performance ratios (actual/expected cost) or cost variance (actual – expected cost). Many of the numeric measures on a report can undergo case-mix adjustment and the physician given a performance statistic such as a cost-efficiency ratio or a ratio of proportion of quality rules fulfilled for the physician or practice compared to a reference group of peers. A performance ratio of 1.0 means the physician is practicing at the norm for the comparison group, and practice pattern variation can be investigated further through other reports or discussion with the physician if the performance ratio deviates significantly from that number. Typically, reports are distributed quarterly to physicians and generally cover 1–3 years of experience. Online and hard-copy reports are required to be secure and compliant with all privacy regulations.

VALUE OF INFORMATION

Both physicians and health plans can benefit from information reporting. Such reporting can open up discussion with peers in practice or with health plan medical directors and can result in the wider dissemination of best practices (Figure 9.2). It is thought that adherence to evidence-based standards of care and decreased practice variation around those standards, as a result of methodologically sound reporting, should improve both the quality and cost-effectiveness of care, given

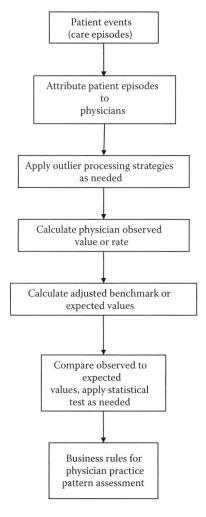

FIGURE 9.2 Typical health plan process for physician cost-efficiency evaluation.

that high quality of care can lead to lower cost, especially in the long term (e.g., savings in ER usage, unplanned hospitalizations, and resource use from complications), although quantifying this effect remains an active area of research. Thus, both the physician and the health plan can benefit.

PHYSICIAN MEASUREMENT, CASE-MIX ADJUSTMENT, AND PROFILING ISSUES

It is difficult to construct an adequate practice pattern profile without case-mix or risk adjustment. There needs to be an algorithm that adjusts for the mix of clinical conditions encountered in a physician's patient panel. Case-mix adjustment can be made for disease class and, in some cases, severity within disease class, specialty of practice, benefit plan (such as whether there is a pharmacy benefit), and other features of the data that may affect reported results. Comparing a tertiary care center in New York City to a community hospital outside the city is problematic without adjusted data. The tertiary care center may use more resources and thus cost more than the community hospital no matter how exemplary the tertiary care center is. In addition, it is difficult to compare a cardiologist to a family practitioner, because in general the cardiologist will see patients of greater severity even within the same illness class. Many health plans can and do address questions that arise about case-mix adjustment through educational literature or their provider relations staffs.

ALGORITHMS FOR CASE-MIX ADJUSTMENT

A wide variety of methodologies that are useful for case-mix, risk, and severity of illness adjustment exist. There are also a number of third-party vendors, as well as national and government-supported organizations, that sell software groupers for case-mix categorization. Since each methodology has different strengths, some health plans have purchased more than one software package. There is no such thing as a "perfect" adjuster, since no data system can ever actually "see" a patient to get a complete clinical picture. Nonetheless, existing case-mix adjustment algorithms can be divided into the following three basic categories: 1) clinical quality rule adjusters; 2) episode-based case-mix adjusters; and 3) population- or patient-based case-mix adjusters.

Clinical Quality Rule Adjusters

An example of a clinical quality rule is "diabetics who received two or more HbA1c tests annually." Some quality rule software systems have up to several hundred clinical quality rules, derived from clinical care guidelines and from national standards, such as the National Quality Forum (NQF)-Endorsed standards. Some of these organizations represent collaborative efforts between physician specialty organizations, health plans, and governmental agencies working together for the common goal of quality improvement. Usually, each rule in clinical quality measurement systems is adjusted for clinical condition. For example, there may be separate rules for lipid testing for diabetics and lipid testing for coronary artery disease patients. In addition, quality rules have clinical adjusters for excluding patients with more severe instances or confounding clinical situations. As another example, patients who are already blind would be excluded from diabetic retinopathy exam measures, and patients with polycystic ovary syndrome would be excluded from diabetes measure denominators when they were only identified by metformin use.

Episode-Based Case-Mix Adjusters

These adjusters are also called condition- or process-based adjusters. These data groupers typically classify the claims records into episodes of care that track the progress of an acute illness from onset to resolution and include related diagnoses and treatments. Some groupers track illness conditions for specified windows of time, regardless of whether the illness "resolved" within that time, while others track illnesses for variable time periods, depending on the level of clinical activity for the condition, and use this activity level to infer onset and resolution of the condition. One commonly used commercial grouper incorporates a hybrid of the two methods, with variable time periods for acute conditions, and fixed time periods (typically 1 year) for chronic conditions without a clear onset and resolution). The purpose of these adjusters is to capture the longitudinal process of care for a single condition. A member or patient can and often does have more than one episode of care category or instance during a reporting period. Categories of episodes, roughly paralleling illness classes, may vary from a couple hundred to nearly 1000 distinct categories. There is a trade-off between the granularity of classes (more classes can more precisely define illness categories) and cell sizes (more classes may reduce the number of instances in each illness category, leading to less statistical stability in performance measurement).

Population- or Patient-Based Case-Mix Adjusters

These adjusters utilize complex algorithms to create risk-based categories based on individual episodes of care, but with a compositing algorithm at the final step, which leads to a single illness burden or risk level for a patient. Thus, each patient falls into one category, unlike in process-based adjusters, where a patient can fit into more than one category. Patients with more complex or major chronic illnesses are given more severe categories than patients with only minor acute illnesses or those who do not access the health care system at all during the period (usually, these members are still given a base age–gender risk category). These systems have the advantage of being able to readily identify patients with multiple complex conditions. Typically, there are fewer categories with these adjusters, and they range from about 20 distinct risk categories to about 200 categories. Some health plans use population-based adjusters for actuarial purposes, to set case rates or capitation payments, or for predictive modeling, where advanced statistical algorithms, such as multiple regression analysis, are used to predict which patients are likely to use the most health care resources in the future based on their utilization in the past. Health plan case- or disease-management resources can then be targeted to the highest risk patients in an effort to increase patient quality of life while decreasing the total resource utilization and cost of care, including decreasing ER use, hospital admissions, sentinel events, and expensive third- or fourth-line medications. The ability of a case-mix adjuster to explain variation in resource utilization is determined by the square of the correlation coefficient (R^2), with the case-mix categories or risk score being the independent variables and a measure of resource use (such as cost) being the dependent variable. Age–gender models have an explanatory power of only about 3%–7%, while publications on proprietary adjusters have generally shown that they explain about 30%–60% of the variation for retrospective analysis. Prospective explanatory power is somewhat less, usually around 15%–30%.

CALCULATION OF EXPECTED VALUES

The purpose of a case-mix adjustment algorithm is to calculate the expected value of a measure for a physician or facility. The expected value is what a physician "should" obtain based on normative values for the individual case-mix or risk groups. To calculate the value, a weighted average is usually performed, where the normative cost, such as a plan average, for each case-mix unit or group is weighted according to the physician's individual experience. Thus, for a physician who saw 50 cases of an expensive disease and 20 cases of an inexpensive disease, the expected value will be much more weighted toward the more resource-intensive illness, since more cases were seen.

One limitation of the above expected value calculation methodology is that it is a "parametric" algorithm; that is, it assumes a normal (bell-shaped) distribution of costs. However, it is well known that medical costs are not normally distributed but skewed toward the high cost side (positively skewed or skewed right). This is because the lower bound of costs is at zero cost, but there is theoretically no upper bound. Many systems have outlier exclusion algorithms or methodologies where outliers are capped at a certain cost level; for example, episode or patient costs greater than $25,000 are capped at $25,000, and this value is used for reporting. Other systems may completely exclude outliers, such as excluding the top 5% and lowest 5% of costs from the performance rating calculations. The theory is that outliers are statistical anomalies or catastrophic conditions in which a physician may have less complete control over resource use. The development of more advanced statistical techniques for measurement is an active research area but runs into difficulty if the techniques become too complex to explain to external stakeholders.

A variety of statistical methodologies have been used to determine whether the deviation from the expected value is statistically significant. One method is the use of a 95% confidence interval, which is calculated based on a physician's case mix–adjusted cost. In this method, if the lower bound of the physician's 95% confidence interval is above a cost-efficiency ratio of 1.0, then the physician is considered statistically significant in terms of having a higher than expected cost of practice.

CASE-MIX INDICES

Once an expected value is calculated for a physician or facility, comparison of the physician's actual practice patterns to the expected value(s) can take place. In reporting, the following three basic measures utilize expected values.

Ratio of Actual to Expected

This measure is termed "performance ratio" or "efficiency ratio." A value of about 1.0 would mean that physician practice patterns are close to the expected target or plan average. For cost comparisons, a value of slightly below 1.0 might even be more ideal, as long as this occurs where high-quality care is maintained. For quality-of-care reporting, a performance ratio can be used to compare the proportion of rules fulfilled (or showing compliance with the measure) compared to a peer group with a similar rule mix. Since rule compliance is typically a "yes–no" value, different statistics based on a binomial distribution or chi-square test are utilized rather than those described for cost of care, which is based on a continuous variable.

Difference between Actual and Expected Values

This measure is termed "cost variance" and is very useful for looking at the cost impact of practice variation. An additional advantage of this measure is its approximately normal distribution, unlike performance ratios, which are skewed toward the high end. This means that relatively simple statistics can be used to isolate physicians or facilities with high positive cost variances for further analysis. Oftentimes, a z-score (number of standard deviations from the mean) of +2 or more is used as the approximate criteria for overly high utilization, although other criteria can also be used. It should be noted that a highly negative cost variance can point to care problems as well, particularly problems with patient access to care or underutilization of services; hence, the reasons for very low cost variances also need to be discovered. The quality score is important in this context as well, as physicians with negative cost variances coupled with low quality scores would point to a high likelihood of underutilization. One property of the cost variance is that the value gives higher weight to more expensive episodes. Thus, physicians who treat more expensive disease conditions may show higher cost variances, even though their performance ratios do not show a strong deviation from unity. Thus, it is recommended that a cost variance value is not reported alone but a performance ratio is also taken into account in reporting results.

Ratio of Expected Value to Unadjusted Plan Average (Expected/Average)

This measure is the "illness burden" of the physician practice or the level of illness in the physician's patient panel. A high illness burden means that the physician or facility treats patients who are more ill compared to the average physician or facility. A physician with a high illness burden and yet a reasonable performance ratio suggests that the physician is highly effective with complex patients. Health plans could decide to give special attention to such physicians to keep them as active as possible in the network.

OTHER CONSIDERATIONS IN ANALYZING CASE-MIX METHODOLOGIES

It is important that physicians understand the basics behind case-mix methodologies, at least for one or two methods mostly used for their practice performance reports. Such education may consist of readings provided with the distributed performance reports that explain the case-mix adjustment algorithms as well as evidence for the algorithms' validity. There are further considerations that are relevant to physicians when dealing with case-mix-adjusted reports.

Are the Reported Performance Measures Adjusted by Specialty?

The rationale for the additional adjustment comes from the fact that, even though a number of specialties may treat congestive heart failure, for example, an internist or family practitioner generally treats less severe cases than would a cardiologist. Thus, even if a report is case mix adjusted by illness class, the adjuster may not fully account for the differences in patient acuity within the illness class. Adjusting by specialty will enable a more "apples to apples" comparison, thus resulting in more meaningful information for the physicians themselves. However, for less common illnesses, the additional specialty adjustment may cause the cell sizes to become too small, causing the adjustment to lose meaning, since there would not be enough patients in some cells for meaningful comparisons. Currently, health plans typically adjust for specialty for most conditions. Specialty adjustment is most applicable to economic or cost measures. This is because, for most quality measures, any physician treating a patient for a given condition should be able to comply with the measures, and thus, specialty should not be a valid reason for variance. As an example, a primary care physician can follow recommendations for the testing of HbA1c in a diabetic just as often as an endocrinologist can.

What Are the Exclusion Criteria?

After the case-mix adjustment is performed, it is important that there exist criteria for dealing with outliers prior to reporting. Without such criteria, there is a much greater chance that a good clinician may perform poorly on a performance report, since a few high-cost outliers, which may occur due to no fault of the clinician, can strongly skew the case-mix indices and lead to artificially high cost variances and performance ratios, particularly for measurement methods relying on mean averages (parametric methods). Some methodologies exclude general catastrophic cases, such as members with costs above $25,000, or there may be a calculation where catastrophic members are included in the reporting information but their claim costs are truncated to a specified maximum amount. Low outliers may be dealt with in a similar fashion, as very low costs (such as an episode of care costing less than $30) may be due to data anomalies. Dealing with high and low outliers in this manner is known in statistical circles as Winsorization. Thus, for example, if a patient has costs of $50,000, the costs will be truncated to $25,000 prior to reporting. This has the advantage of including all patients but the disadvantage of not knowing the actual cost of the patient panel. Another way of excluding outliers involves excluding them at the case-mix class level. This means that illnesses that generally use less resources will have different criteria—in this case, a lower exclusion boundary for high-cost outliers—than would an illness class that typically has high resource use. As discussed previously, if cost is used as the measure of interest, the distribution curve of cost for a particular illness is skewed to the high side and thus does not look like the bell-shaped normal distribution. This makes developing proper exclusion criteria more complex. For greater accuracy, a "nonparametric" or "distribution-free" outlier test is useful. One such test was developed in 1993 by Sprent and consists of the following equation:

$$(|X_i - M|/\text{MAD}) > \text{Max},$$

where X_i represents any value being evaluated for outlier status, M represents the median (the value for which 50% of sample values are above, 50% below) of the sample (such as all cases in a disease class), and MAD is the median absolute deviation. To calculate the MAD value, first obtain the absolute value of the difference between each value and the sample median. Then, sort the difference scores in ascending order. The median of the difference scores is the MAD value. Max is then the criteria point for excluding outliers. A reasonable value of Max would be 5. Both low and high outliers would be excluded based on this equation.

Outliers may still have useful information in themselves. Consequently, after excluding them from the comparative analysis, it may still be useful to report on them separately, since such patients, particularly high outliers, may in some cases be steered to case management protocols.

Is There a Statistical Test?

The significance of performance ratios (outcome/expected outcome [O/E] ratios) depends on data considerations; therefore, statistical tests are often necessary to evaluate the likelihood that variations in physician performance measures are due to true variation or random factors (Table 9.1). For example, a physician with a patient panel of 30 or less (which is relatively common, since health plans typically measure physicians based only on patients from the health plan doing the measuring) who has an O/E ratio of 1.3 is more likely to be affected by random factors than a physician with a patient panel of 1000. In addition, this ratio is more likely due to random factors when the physician has patients in highly variable conditions with a wide spread of costs. One example is pneumonia, the treatment of which can range from a few visits and plain X-rays to long hospitalizations and expensive medications. Alternatively, a ratio of 1.3 is less likely due to random factors for a physician treating fairly homogeneous conditions such as pharyngitis. A statistical test takes these factors into account when determining statistical significance. A typical method is the use of a 95% confidence interval, as previously described. If the confidence interval does not include an O/E ratio of 1.0, then the physician is statistically different from his/her peers (statistically lower cost if the entire interval is below 1.0 and statistically higher cost if the entire interval is above 1.0).

Other statistical techniques, known as nonparametric statistics, are not as sensitive to outliers as techniques based on mean averages and, thus, may not need outlier exclusions. This is because these techniques use the median (50th percentile) rather than mean averages as the measure of central tendency. The use of these methods as they relate to physician performance measurement is an active area of research.

TABLE 9.1
Example of a Quality-of-Care O/E Ratio Calculation for a Physician Practice

Quality-of-Care Rule or Standard	Eligible Patients	Actual Done	Not Done	Expected Done	Expected Not Done
HbA1c testing for diabetics	45	40	5	39	6
Eye exam for diabetics	42	22	20	25	17
Lipid-lowering therapy for coronary artery disease	20	16	4	18	2
Strep test before antibiotic for pharyngitis in children	60	49	11	54	6
Total	*167*	*127*	*40*	*136*	*31*

Composite rule adherence rate	
Physician	76.00%
Expected	81.40%
O:E ratio	*0.93*

Note: Higher O/E ratios indicate better adherence.

PERFORMANCE REPORTS AND MEDICAL PRACTICE PATTERN PROFILES

This section deals with the kind of measures and information that a physician may see in a performance report or may be displayed in reports internal to the health plan. Physicians need a strong knowledge base about commonly used metrics in reporting so that the physician can intelligently discuss the report content with his/her peers when needed as well as with the health plan that delivered the reports.

QUALITY REPORTING

Typically, good quality care may lead to reduced costs, at least in the long run, since stable patients have fewer unplanned visits, less ER usage, and a reduced frequency of hospital admissions, all of which save money.

The Healthcare Effectiveness Data and Information Set (HEDIS) contains measures obtainable from claims, survey, physician, membership, and medical record data. HEDIS was developed in conjunction with the National Committee for Quality Assurance (NCQA), and HEDIS measures are widely accepted. Consumers, managed care organizations, and accrediting bodies have a high level of interest in the HEDIS results. The measures included in HEDIS are updated annually and include the use of preventive services, access to care, level of utilization of key procedures, quality measures for acute and chronic illness care, other physician data such as residency completed, board certification, physician turnover for a health plan, health plan membership statistics, and survey data such as member satisfaction. Although HEDIS was formerly developed for performance measurement at the health plan level, many measures have also been adapted for use at the physician level.

Most of the quality-of-care measures discussed so far are process-of-care measures. However, outcome measures are an important component of quality reporting. There are a number of ways of using data to measure outcomes.

Outcomes Obtained from Claims Data

Claims data have clear limitations for outcomes analysis, as the data mainly deal with the process of care and do not have information directly pertaining to outcomes except where specified in the ICD-9 codes. However, since the advent of CPT II codes, intermediate outcomes, such as whether a laboratory result is above or below a certain threshold, are now available in claims data. However, CPT II codes are still used relatively infrequently, presenting challenges in their systematic use. Thus, one must rely in many cases on *proxy* measures for outcomes. Proxy measures are process-of-care metrics that can imply certain outcomes, such as the length of an illness episode. The following are some ways of ascertaining outcomes of care using claims data:

- *Complications of care.* ICD-9 codes directly contain language for denoting outcomes. There exist codes for wound infection and dehiscence, miscarriage in pregnancy, and general surgical complications. The coding of a major infection in a cancer patient on chemotherapy is another example of complications-based outcomes obtainable through claims data.
- *Procedure reperformances.* Two coronary artery stent procedures within a period of 6 months to 1 year may imply failure of the first stent. However, a medical record check may ultimately be needed, since it could also be a stent placed in a new vessel. Returns to the operating room within a few days of a surgical operation or an outpatient procedure that turns into an inpatient stay within a few days also implies poor outcomes.
- *Readmission rates.* Two or more hospitalizations for the same episode of care within 30–60 days also imply poor outcomes.
- *Episode length analysis.* The length that an episode of care lasts can be compared between physicians. Shorter episodes for acute illnesses imply better outcomes, unless it is due to the expiration of a patient or poor access to care.

- *Medication prescribing patterns.* In some conditions, the drugs prescribed may imply certain outcomes. A rheumatoid arthritis patient who needs REMICADE® probably has a more severe form of the illness.
- *ER and hospital utilization.* Frequent ER use or hospitalizations for chronic conditions such as asthma or congestive heart failure imply a poor outcome from outpatient treatment.

Outcomes Obtained from Nonclaims Data

Outcomes from nonclaims data are described as follows:

- Patient satisfaction data may be an indicator of outcomes, since patient satisfaction or experience of care (see the previous discussion of the CAHPS survey initiative) often relates directly to how well a patient has progressed with respect to his/her illness.
- Functional status survey data provide a direct subjective account of the severity of illness or outcome of treatment, depending on when the survey was given. A congestive heart failure patient who reports in a survey that he/she cannot walk up a flight of stairs may show nonresponsiveness to treatment, which needs to be addressed.
- Clinical data analysis is becoming important as much more organizations are adding clinical data to claims, such as laboratory values. HbA1c values, for example, hold the key to how well controlled a diabetic is over the long term.

The difficulty with nonclaims data is that the collection of such data can be resource intensive and costly, depending on the sophistication of the information systems available.

ECONOMIC REPORTING

This type of practice pattern measurement system emphasizes the economic impact of practice variation. Usually, a cost data field is used as the measure of interest, and variation from the norm is often determined through case-mix indices, as discussed previously. Costs may also be broken down into service categories, such as laboratory, surgical, radiology, and professional costs (evaluation and management [E&M] costs), facility, and drug. Each of these service categories should also be case mix adjusted so that a performance index, cost variance, or other measures can be provided for each one.

Areas that can be profiled in economic and resource utilization profiling include the following:

- Consulting, specialty, and subspecialty referral practices
- Prescription habits, including the use of brand-name drugs and generic equivalents, especially for chronic conditions such as hypertension and Type II diabetes
- The use of invasive and interventional tests such as angiograms, intravenous pyelograms, bone scans, and certain biopsies
- The use of noninvasive procedures and tests such as computed tomography (CT) and magnetic resonance imaging (MRI) scans, cardiovascular stress tests, chest X-rays, and ultrasounds
- Average length of hospital stay, surgical operating times, the use of assistant surgeons, and other utilization parameters

DRILL-DOWN ANALYSIS

If a physician receives a report that points to significant practice variation, the question comes up as to what factor(s) caused the variation. This is where the capability of "drill-down" analysis becomes important. In this method, an area of variation is pinpointed, and reports are brought up in greater detail, specifically concerning the area of variation. For example, if a physician shows a high cost variance for migraine headache, a drill-down analysis into the disease state may show that the physician uses CT and MRI scans of the head significantly more frequently than his/her peers.

The physician can then be educated about the clinically appropriate use of such scans, only reserving them for cases having a high index of suspicion for an anatomical abnormality such as a tumor. Another method of drill-down analysis, used in a published report by a large independent practice association in upstate New York, involved dividing physicians into quintiles depending on adjusted costs, with the lowest quintile (bottom 20%) being the least expensive and the highest quintile (top 20%) being the most expensive. This was done for patients with hypertension and separately for ear, nose, and throat (ENT) patients with nonsurgical tonsillitis, adenoiditis, and pharyngitis. Strong differences in prescribing patterns, such as lower use of generic drugs, were found in drill-down analysis between physicians in the highest quintile and those in the lower quintiles for hypertension and a higher utilization of fiberoptic laryngoscopy for physicians in the higher quartiles for the ENT patients. Such methods have the advantage of being able to quickly identify the likely causes of practice variation and are less influenced by outliers, which may complicate a drill-down analysis. The above algorithm is an example of a nonparametric analysis, since the division into quintiles does not depend on a normal distribution.

Episodes of care case-mix adjustment are naturally suited to this kind of analysis, but other population-based groupers also allow drill-down if the clinical categories that are precursors to the assignment of a risk score are used. The idea behind drill-down is to obtain much greater detail on an area of interest. Thus, if a physician is found to have a high overall cost variance or performance ratio, a user can select the physician and drill down into ER usage, hospitalization frequency, types of illnesses seen, or procedures performed. Case mix is useful even for the more detailed reports, since if, for example, ER use or the utilization of specified procedures is not adjusted for illness burden, the "my patients are sicker" argument may hold. However, if the procedures are related to illness classes, physicians can be compared to their peers on procedures used for that illness class, as discussed above.

As an example, consider the following scenario. Dr. Jones is a family practitioner who had a high patient load from a single large health plan. These patients under his care had a total of 450 episodes over a 2-year period. His case mix–adjusted performance ratio was 2.28, and his cost variance was $157,400. Dr. Jones requested a drill-down analysis to determine why his practice patterns showed such a high variance from the norm. The health plan data analysts found that one area that had high variance was patients he saw with tendinitis of the lower extremity. He saw 30 episodes of care for this condition, having a total performance ratio of 6.0 for the illness class and a cost variance of $25,300. On further drill-down, the analysts found that the major cost center included the frequency of MRI scans of the lower extremity for the tendinitis patients. His scan rate was 0.4, which means an average of 4 out of 10 episodes received scans, making a total of 12 scans in all. His peers of the same specialty showed 0.1 scans per episode of tendinitis of the lower extremity. Dr. Jones showed a performance ratio of 3.0 and a cost variance of $10,800 for scan use. On learning this information, Dr. Jones decided to alter his referral patterns so that his scan rate was brought closer to the norm.

Trending may be useful in physician measurement to look at practice patterns over time. Trending is also a good way of looking at response to quality improvement initiatives as well. Although trending, as discussed above, has value, it presents a number of challenges in terms of implementing in a practical fashion. Few health plans have readily available long-term data (covering 4–5 years or more) required to create usable trend analysis. If episodes of care are used for practice pattern analysis, using short date intervals (such as quarterly intervals) so that there can be more points on the trend chart may lead to statistical instability, because care activity can legitimately vary significantly from quarter to quarter for a single episode of care, particularly for long-term or chronic illnesses. Another alternative would be to include the results from rolling quarterly reports, with each report resulting in a single data point. Including the results of quarterly reports in the trend chart would mean that the data lack independence between points, since each quarterly report is based on rolling date intervals and may include 1 or 2 years' worth of data. Nonparametric analysis, such as dividing physicians into quintiles based on cost or quality results as discussed previously, are less influenced by outliers, and thus, performance on physician measures may be more stable over time.

TABLE 9.2

Example of a Cost-Efficiency O/E Ratio Calculation for a Physician Practice

Episode of Care Type	Number of Episodes (A)	Observed Mean Cost per Episode (B)	Total Observed Cost (B*A)	Expected Cost per Episode (C)	O:E Ratio per Episode (B/C)	Total Expected Cost (D*A)
Diabetes, low severity	40	$1966	$78,640	$1751	1.12	$70,040
Diabetes, high severity	12	$6770	$81,240	$6844	0.99	$82,128
Pharyngitis	120	$188	$22,560	$168	1.12	$20,160
Esophagitis	24	$1220	$29,280	$1014	1.20	$24,336
Total	**196**		**$211,720**			**$196,664**

Composite cost-efficiency analysis

Physician total observed costs	$211,720
Physician total expected costs	$196,664
O/E ratio	**1.08**

DEALING WITH UNCERTAINTY IN PHYSICIAN PERFORMANCE MEASUREMENT

Due to high-profile concerns in terms of the variation in quality of care as well as its affordability, physician practice pattern measurement is here to stay. Until further advances in this area are created, physicians with unexpectedly poor performance ratios, especially in the area of cost-efficiency, should review their data to determine if there are opportunities to improve as well as potential outlier cases contributing to an aberrant value and should look at the health plan methodology for statistical analysis and outlier exclusions (Table 9.2). It is important for the physician or other provider being measured to communicate any issues to health plan personnel where possible. Physicians need to remember that practice pattern analysis is a continually evolving field. Given the state of the art, physicians, specialty societies, and other advocacy groups have a responsibility to work with health plans and other physician performance measurement agencies to ensure that quality improvement is at the forefront, they are active in giving feedback on health plan physician measurement methods, and, as much as possible, a collaborative approach is used in working with health plans and other measurement organizations.

CONCLUSION

Many stakeholders, including health plans, various government agencies and accrediting organizations, consumers and consumer groups, and health care providers themselves, are increasingly asking for more detailed information on physician and facility practice patterns. Not only must quality and adherence to evidence-based medicine be a primary concern but, as we have discussed, there are also important statistical issues when evaluating quality and adherence to evidence-based medicine, including appropriate drill-down methodologies to help determine the reason for practice pattern variation. Furthermore, even if quality of care meets standards, it is relevant to inquire into cost-efficiency, but in doing so, one must use case-mix adjusters and additional drill-down methodologies to help determine the reason for practice pattern variation. If possible, longitudinal trending should be analyzed as well. The methodology should incorporate appropriate statistical testing to aid in the detection of true variation in care as opposed to random variation. The algorithms and methodology used should be transparent and explainable. Where possible, supplementation with member satisfaction data, functional status surveys, and clinical values such as laboratory results may lead to better information on quality and outcomes of practice patterns. This is a continually evolving field, and we can look forward to further advances that make quality and cost-efficiency measurement more accurate in the near future, with further collaboration between physicians, health plans, and government agencies toward the common goal of quality improvement while working together to increase affordability and access to quality care.

CASE MODEL 9.1: SEEKING DIRECTOR OF MEDICAL QUALITY IMPROVEMENT

The director of quality improvement will direct the hospital-wide organizational performance improvement program reporting to the service line director of quality. The director of quality improvement will be responsible, either personally or through delegation, for coordinating those systems necessary for the identification and resolution of known or suspected problems and opportunities to improve the dimensions of performance in health care. He/She will be responsible for ensuring hospital-wide compliance with all accreditation and licensure standards and will provide guidance and education to facility leadership, clinical personnel, board of trustees, and medical staff members related to performance improvement.

POSITION REQUIREMENTS:

Education:

- At a minimum: Graduate of an accredited school of nursing with a baccalaureate degree in nursing
- Masters degree in a health care discipline highly preferred

Experience:

- Minimum of 5 years of current clinical experience in an acute care facility required as a director of quality management
- Supervisory and/or management experience required

Special Qualifications:

- Comfortable and skilled at working with physicians, health care providers, and other stakeholders in the organization
- Capable of gaining immediate credibility with individuals through experience, presentation, communication skills, empathy, and compassion
- Analytical skills, including working knowledge of basic statistics and statistical analysis methodologies
- Knowledge of PC-based computer software (i.e., Word, Excel, Access, and/or similar systems) preferred
- Ability to work independently and interdependently
- Knowledge of health-care-related regulatory and accreditation requirements

CONTACT:

National Management Recruiter
USR Healthcare
(615) 445-3035 Office
(800) 826-8127 Toll Free
http://www.usrhealthcare.com

CHECKLIST 1: Physician Practice Pattern Assessment Reports	YES	NO	OTHER	OTHER
In order to help understand a physician practice pattern assessment report, the following questions can act as a guide:				
Is there an assessment on the quality of care?	o	o		
Is there an assessment of the cost-efficiency of care?	o	o		
How can the reports be accessed?			Web o	Hard copy o
Who can you discuss the reports with?			Colleagues o	Health plan staff o
If there is a cost-efficiency assessment, are the reports adjusted by specialty?	o	o		
For cost-efficiency reports, what type of case-mix adjuster is there?			Population based o	Episode based o
Is there a test for statistical significance?	o	o		
Is there outcomes reporting, such as complications of care and procedure reperformances?	o	o		
Is there a drill-down analysis available?	o	o		
Is there a process for dealing with high or low outliers?	o	o		
Is there a way of attributing episodes or quality rules to physicians?	o	o		

BIBLIOGRAPHY

Adams, J. L., E. A. McGlynn, J. W. Thomas, and A. Mehrotra. 2010. Incorporating statistical uncertainty in the use of physician cost profiles. *BMC Health Services Research* 10: 57–63.

Agency for Healthcare Research and Quality (AHRQ). 2008. CAHPS®: Assessing Health Care Quality from the Patient's Perspective (Program Brief). Available at: https://www.cahps.ahrq.gov/content/cahpsOverview/07-P016.pdf (accessed on September 6, 2011).

American Academy of Family Physicians (AAFP). 2007. Performance Measures Criteria. Available at: http://www.aafp.org/online/en/home/policy/policies/p/performancemeasures.html (accessed on September 6, 2011).

Bottle A., and P. Aylin. 2008. Intelligent information: A national system for monitoring clinical performance. *Health Services Research* 43(1 Part 1): 10–31.

Goldfield, N., and P. Boland. 1996. *Physician Profiling and Risk Adjustment*. Aspen Publishers, Inc.

Greene, R. A., H. B. Beckman, and T. Mahoney. 2008. Beyond the efficiency index: Finding a better way to reduce overuse and increase efficiency in physician care. *Health Affairs* 20(4): w250–w259.

Hussey, P. S., H. de Vries, J. Romley, M. C. Wang, S. S. Chen, P. G. Shekelle, and E. A. McGlynn. 2009. A systematic review of health care efficiency measures. *Health Services Research* 44(3): 784–805.

Kelley, D. L. 1999. *How to Use Control Charts for Healthcare*. Milwaukee, WI: American Society for Quality, pp. 1–34.

Marcinko, D. E. 2010. Healthcare organizations. *Journal of Financial Management Strategies* 2(1): 1–20.

Metfessel, B. 1998. Specialist profiling using claims and administrative databases. *American Journal of Integrated Healthcare* 1(4) Fall: 168–174.

Metfessel, B. 2011. Using health information technology to track medical care. In: D. E. Marcinko (ed.), *The Business of Medical Practice*, 3rd edition. New York: Springer Publishers.

National Quality Forum. NQF-Endorsed® Standards. 2011. Available at: http://www.qualityforum.org/ Measures_List.aspx (accessed on September 12, 2011).

Patel, P. H., D. Siemons, and M. C. Shields. 2007. Proven methods to achieve high payment for performance. *Journal of Medical Practice Management* 23(1): 5–11.

Sachdeva, R. C., and S. Jain. 2009. Making the case to improve quality and reduce costs in pediatric health care. *Pediatric Clinics of North America* 56(4): 731–743.

Sheshkin, David J. 2007. *Handbook of Parametric and Nonparametric Statistical Procedures*. Boca Raton, FL: Chapman & Hall/CRC.

Vasilevskis, E. E., D. Meltzer, J. Schnipper, P. Kaboli, T. Wetterneck, D. Gonzales, V. Arora, J. Zhang, and A. D. Auerbach. 2008. Quality of care for decompensated heart failure: Comparable performance between academic hospitalists and nonhospitalists. *Journal of General Internal Medicine* 23(9): 1399–1406.

10 Health Information Technology Security and Privacy

Rules, Regulations, Penalties, and Recovery Efforts

Carol S. Miller

CONTENTS

INTRODUCTION AND OVERVIEW

Health care organizations are entrusted with the most private information of their patients and employees. Security and privacy will continue to impact the health care data exchange. The following are several examples of where security and privacy regulations will be tested:

1. The Department of Health and Human Services (DHHS) has set a goal for health care facilities by 2015 to transition from the use of paper files and forms to the use of electronic health records (EHRs). Each facility will need to ensure that all the security and privacy requirements are in place.
2. President Barack Obama created the Health Information Technology Regional Extension Centers, which will play a major role in implementing a nationwide system of health information networks. According to the DHHS, these centers need to ensure that hospitals comply with regulatory and legal requirements to protect the patient's health information.
3. Industry experts estimate that the amount of health data stored online measures in terabytes and will substantially grow in the next couple of years. New vulnerabilities such as physician mobility, wireless networking, health information exchange (HIE), cloud computing, connectivity of data to personal home computers, and lack of sophisticated controls will impact security and privacy.

Health information technology (HIT) is a common element of nearly every health reform proposal. HIT can decrease costs, improve health outcomes, be utilized in the coordination of care, and improve public health care services and follow up. Electronic HIEs and the rise of consumer-focused health management tools can improve the flow of information necessary for good health care as well as help individuals take a greater role in improving their own health, that is, with the increased utilization of personal health records (PHRs). Throughout the United States, providers and hospitals are taking great strides to digitize all patient information, which in turn raises the concern about the security and privacy protection of medical information. With larger volumes of data stored electronically, there is a greater potential for sophisticated malware attacks that target applications and/or cause personal identity theft. As the health care industry increasingly relies on technology as a means of storing and providing care, security needs to mean more than basic guidelines on a password or a set of "shelved" policies and procedures. This growing reliance on technology exposes the health care industry to new threats that go beyond those that have traditionally been a concern to health care in the past decade.

This chapter addresses the security and privacy regulations, laws, and requirements, continuity of operation (COOP) and disaster recovery (DR), risks and mitigation steps in evaluating security and privacy, and helpful hints to consider in protecting organization functions in case of security and/or privacy breaches. The following section addresses EHRs, PHRs, wireless medical devices and data exchanges, and medical center kiosks as they relate to the health care environment and security and privacy.

LAWS, RULES, AND ACTS IMPACTING SECURITY, PRIVACY, AND ELECTRONIC DATA TRANSMISSION

There are several older laws and regulations that initially started the privacy and security scrutiny related to patient medical information. The originals are still in effect, but subsequent laws have been enacted to clarify and modernize the original rules. In addition, there are also well-established standards for controlling security. Below is a summary of the major laws, regulations, and standards impacting security and privacy. Further reading for each of the rules and regulations are listed at the end of this chapter.

Health Insurance Portability and Accountability Act of 1996

The Health Insurance Portability and Accountability Act of 1996 (HIPAA) includes provisions related to insurance, privacy, security, transactions, and code sets. HIPAA became a law on August 21, 1996. It was designed to improve the efficiency and effectiveness of the health care system by "facilitating the electronic exchange of information with respect to certain financial and administrative transactions carried out by health plans, health care clearinghouses, and health care providers who transmit information electronically in connection with such transactions." (www.hhs.gov)

HIPAA's intent was to protect people who had an existing or chronic illness that made it difficult for them to change employers and still have good medical insurance. Physicians originally saw HIPAA as a bureaucratic intrusion, full of ambiguous requirements that necessitated more paper trails, and many still feeling the same currently. To implement the provisions of the act, DHHS was required to adopt a suite of uniform, national standards for transactions, unique health identifiers, code sets for the data elements of the transactions, security of health information, and electronic signature. Congress also recognized the challenges to the confidentiality of health information presented by the increasing complexity of the health care industry, by advances in the health information systems technology and communications, and through required promulgation of standards for the privacy of individually identifiable health information. It is clear from all the discussions and written comments that legislators regard privacy as of paramount importance for most people and privacy in a health care setting particularly so. The challenge for the HIT specialist in that setting is to find ways of safeguarding it.

HIPAA Privacy Regulations

The HIPAA Privacy Rule establishes national standards to protect individuals' medical records and other personal health information and applies to health plans, health care clearinghouses, and those health care providers that conduct health care transactions electronically. The rule requires safeguards to protect the privacy of information and sets limits and conditions on uses and disclosure that may be made without patient authorization. The rule also gives patient rights over their health information, including rights to examine or obtain a copy of a health record and to request corrections.

Privacy protections under HIPAA extend to every patient whose information is collected, used, linked to, or disclosed by covered entities. HIPAA imposes responsibilities on the entire workforce of a covered entity—including all employees and volunteers—in order to secure those rights. It imposes the following privacy-related requirements on health care organizations:

1. Develop and implement explicit written privacy policies and procedures and document its enforcement
2. Establish boundaries and limit purposes for disclosure
3. Establish security protections against deliberate misuse or disclosure
4. Develop a system for consumer control that enables patients to see records, obtain a copy, and know who else has seen them
5. Meet obligations for public responsibility by balancing claims to privacy with use of information for important, socially useful purposes (with appropriate protection)
6. Develop and implement procedures for individuals to submit complaints and designate a privacy official to handle any complaints
7. Develop a training plan and train the workforce on the policies and procedures related to privacy with patient health information

States have many laws and regulations that address health information for privacy protection. In most cases, where state requirements are stricter, they remain in force preempting HIPAA, but if the state laws are less strict, HIPAA requirements prevail.

HIPAA Notice of Privacy Practices

As of March 30, 2011, HIPAA requires that plan participants of employer-sponsored health plans receive a Notice of Privacy Practices (NPP). The requirement applies to health plans such as medical, dental, vision, prescription drug, Section 125 health flexible spending account (HFSA), and health reimbursement arrangements (HRA). HIPAA required that an NPP be provided to health plan participants at the time the plan was first subject to the HIPAA Privacy Rule. It is required that a notice of the availability of the NPP be sent to plan participants at least once every 3 years. The reminder must tell participants how to obtain a copy of the NPP for the plan. The reminder, or an actual NPP, does not need to be sent to the plan participant's home. Plans can include the notice in other benefit materials sent to participants or distributed at work.

Many insurance companies and employers include the NPP with the plan's annual open enrollment materials. If the actual NPP is distributed more often than every 3 years, the notice requirement has been satisfied, and a reminder does not need to be sent. If the employer's insurance carrier sends an NPP to plan participants, the employer is not required to send a separate notice. Most carriers provide an NPP annually to participants of fully insured health plans.

An employer can distribute one NPP that covers all of their plans subject to HIPAA. It is not necessary to create a separate NPP for every plan. However, to do this, the employer must draft an employer-specific notice that correctly refers to all employer-sponsored plans subject to HIPAA.

The NPP specifies the patient's rights to the following:

1. Right to see and obtain a copy of their own health record
2. Request corrections of errors or add information that has been omitted that the patient finds
3. Receive an accounting of how their information has been used
4. Request limits on access to and additional protections for particularly sensitive information
5. Request confidential communications for particularly sensitive information
6. Pursue the complaint with the DHHS Office for Civil Rights if problems are not satisfactorily resolved—www.hhs.gov/ocr
7. Right to receive an NPP of any health care provider, health care clearinghouse, or health plan

HIPAA requires no other documentation from the patient in order for information to be used or disclosed for basic functions, such as treatment and payment, or for a broad range of other core health care operations.

Supplemental Authorization

HIPAA does require that patients sign a supplemental authorization before information can be used for certain "extra" purposes such as research or certain kinds of marketing and fund-raising. HIPAA extends extra protections for especially sensitive information such as psychotherapy notes, communicable diseases such as human immunodeficiency virus (HIV) and acquired immune deficiency syndrome (AIDS), substance or alcohol abuse, mental health disorders, or other information categories.

HIPAA Administrative Simplification Rule

The entire purpose of the HIPAA Administrative Simplification Rule was to simplify the electronic submission of claims and to decrease the associated costs with paying for health care services. In 2009, the policies and regulations related to privacy, security, and electronic data interchange (EDI) standards for transactions, code sets, and identifiers were put into place with the goal of encouraging the adoption of national standards and EDI in preference to paper processing and to increase interoperability and real-time exchange of administrative, clinical, and financial health information.

HIPAA administrative simplification regulations now include the following, which will be elaborated upon later in this chapter:

1. Electronic health care transaction and code sets
2. Health information privacy
3. Unique identifiers for employers
4. Security requirements
5. Unique identifiers for providers
6. Enforcement procedures
7. Standards for Electronic Health Care Claims Attachments
8. Unique identifier for health plans
9. Modifications to the HIPAA Electronic Transaction Standards (upgrade to versions 5010 and National Council for Prescription Drug Programs [NCPDP] D.0 and 3.0)
10. HIPAA Administrative Simplification—Modifications to medical data code set standards to adopt the ICD-10-CM and ICD-10-PCS

The HIPAA Administrative Simplification Rule does not require health care providers to submit claims electronically; however, if claims are submitted electronically, they need to use a software or health care clearinghouse to convert information and data into the required standardized formats in order to be HIPAA compliant. In addition, the rule does not require data to be stored by the provider in any standardized format, as long as the data can be translated into the standard transaction format when data are transmitted electronically. Even though the rule does not require electronic submission, insurers, both private and public, are encouraging providers to convert to EHRs and EDI submissions.

Covered Entity under HIPAA

Individuals, organizations, and agencies that meet the definition of a covered entity under HIPAA must comply with the rule's requirements to protect the privacy and security of HIE of data and must provide individuals with certain rights with respect to their health information. If an entity is not covered, it does not have to comply with the Privacy or the Security Rule.

There are three different covered entities:

1. A health care provider that renders health care service, bills or transmits these services in electronic format and is paid by an insurer. This includes doctors, clinical psychologists, dentists, chiropractors, nursing homes, and pharmacies.
2. An individual or group health plan that provides or pays the cost of medical care. This includes health insurance companies, health maintenance organizations (HMOs), company health plans, and government programs such as Medicare, Medicaid, veteran health programs, military health programs, and Indian Health Services.
3. A health care clearinghouse. This includes entities that process nonstandard health information that they receive from another entity into a standard (i.e., standard electronic format or data content), or vice versa.

As part of HIPAA, covered entities must comply with administrative, physical, and technical safeguards. Administrative safeguards include the following:

1. Adoption of a written set of privacy procedures and the designation of a privacy officer to be responsible for developing and implementing all required policies and procedures.
2. Reference to management oversight and organizational buy-in to the security rules within the policies and procedures.
3. Listing of employees and classes of employees who will have access to electronic protected health information (PHI).

4. Procedure for addressing access authorization, establishment, modification, and termination.
5. For covered entities outsourcing their business processes, a framework must be in place for the third party to comply with the HIPAA requirements.
6. Covered entities must show the documentation of ongoing training programs regarding the handling of PHI.
7. Contingency plans must be in place for backing up their data and having a DR procedure in place.
8. Procedures should document the scope, frequency, and process of audits.
9. Procedures should address instructions for addressing and responding to security breaches.
10. Risk analysis and risk management processes need to be included to demonstrate reasonable precautions in place and mitigation actions to prevent PHI from being used for non-health purposes.
11. Documentation needs to be included for all configuration management changes.
12. Covered entities must make their documentation of HIPAA practices available to the government.

For physical safeguards, controls must be in place to add or remove hardware and software from the network so that personal health data are not compromised and protection is in place to prevent inappropriate access. In addition, access to equipment containing health data should be controlled and monitored; hardware and software access and proper workstation policies regarding access or visibility need to be established.

Technical safeguards for controlling access to computer systems and enabling data to be protected in transmission need to be established to prevent interception by anyone other than the intended recipient. This includes protecting information systems housing personal health data from intrusion, and data that have not been compromised or erased in an unauthorized manner. Data corroboration needs to be put into place to include such items as message authentication, digital signatures, or double-keying. Finally, covered entities are responsible for authenticating entities with which they communicate—the entity who it claims to be. The safeguards might include password systems, telephone verification, or callbacks.

Business Associates under HIPAA

HIPAA requires the use of business associate agreements to safeguard external party practices that will have some access to PHI. Because safeguarding patient information can apply to external vendors and internal tracking and monitoring practices may not always work, these separate agreements and procedures for external staff need to be put into place.

A "business associate" is a person or entity that is employed by, is exposed to, performs certain functions or activities that involve the use or disclosure of PHI on behalf of, or provides services to a covered entity. This can include medical data that are either in hard copy or electronic format of the medical record. Business associate functions and activities include claims processing or administration; data analysis, processing, or administration; utilization review; quality assurance; billing; benefit management; practice management; and repricing. Examples include a third-party administrator that assists a health plan with claims processing, an attorney who provides legal services to a health plan that has access to PHI, a consultant performing utilization review for a hospital, a health care clearinghouse that translates claims from one format to a standard transaction on behalf of the providers, or even a transcriptionist who provides transcription services for a provider.

As of February 18, 2010, all business associates must abide by at least the following rules:

1. Comply with the HIPAA Security Rule—Implement specific policies, procedures, and physical, administrative, and technical safeguards to protect medical data.
2. Follow the HIPAA Privacy Rule—Protect medical data from misuse and follow the terms of new or existing business associate contracts.

3. Train all employees on HIPAA and the business associate requirements—Train employees to provide the strongest protections to medical data.
4. Provide "Breach Notifications" if medical data are compromised or lost—Promptly notify medical entity partners and, in some cases, patients if medical data in the business associate's possession are compromised or lost.

ADMINISTRATIVE SIMPLIFICATION COMPLIANCE ACT

The Administrative Simplification Compliance Act (ASCA) amended the HIPAA and required that all claims submitted to Medicare on October 16, 2003 and beyond be done so electronically, except for certain circumstances.

GENETIC INFORMATION NONDISCRIMINATION ACT OF 2008

The Genetic Information Nondiscrimination Act of 2008 prohibits the use of genetic information to make health insurance coverage determinations and in employment-related decisions. This law supports a patient's privacy. Forty states have enacted legislation related to genetic discrimination in health insurance, and 31 states have adopted laws regarding genetic discrimination in the workplace according to the National Human Genome Research Institute (www.genome.gov).

AMERICAN RECOVERY AND REINVESTMENT ACT OF 2009

The American Recovery and Reinvestment Act of 2009 (ARRA) includes improvements for privacy and security standards for health information. This act provided substantive changes to HIPAA statute and privacy and security regulations, enforcement, and provisions to address health information held by entities not covered by HIPAA. Under ARRA, business associates are required to directly comply with most of the HIPAA security rules, must comply with the privacy rules that are made applicable to them by their contract with the covered entity, and must comply with any changes to privacy rules that were part of ARRA, regardless of whether those provisions are in their contracts with covered entities. In addition, business associates can now be held directly accountable by federal or state authorities for any failure to comply with HIPAA as amended by ARRA or applicable regulations. ARRA clarifies that entities that transmit or process data on behalf of covered entities such as HIEs or e-Prescribing Gateways are business associates for purposes of HIPAA. Even vendors who contract with a covered entity to offer PHRs to patients as part of its EHR must also enter into a business associate agreement.

ARRA specifically requires that covered entities provide notification to individuals and to the Secretary if their health information has been breached, and then, the covered entity must notify the individual per the requirements. The breach notification only relates to breaches of "unsecured health information." Information that is unusable, unreadable, or indecipherable to unauthorized individuals does not trigger the notification requirement.

Under the Privacy Rule, covered entities are required to access, use, and disclose only the *minimum necessary* amount of patient health information (PHI) needed to satisfy the purpose for which the data were acquired, used, or disclosed. Entities must identify who needs access to information to carry out job duties, categories or types of patient health information, and conditions appropriate to gain access to patient information. ARRA takes it a step further in establishing guidance and definitions on what constitutes the minimum necessary. In addition, under the Privacy Rule, covered entities must provide an individual an accounting of disclosures of PHI made from the individual's medical record for the previous 6 years with a number of disclosures for treatment, payment, and health care operations that are exempted from these requirements, where ARRA modifies that to only the previous 3 years, but eliminates the exemptions. For the latter provision (entities adopting

EHRs by January 1, 2009), these new provisions apply on January 1, 2014, and for those adopting EHRs on or after January 1, 2009, they applied as of January 1, 2011.

ARRA establishes a new advisory committee infrastructure with a new HIT Policy Committee and a new HIT Standards Committee. The HIT Policy Committee is required to make recommendations with respect to technologies that protect privacy and promote security in an EHR, including those that allow for the segregation of sensitive health information and the use of limited data sets. The Policy Committee's recommendation must prioritize the development of standards to facilitate the new accounting for disclosure requirements for HIPAA-covered entities and business associates.

HEALTH INFORMATION TECHNOLOGY FOR ECONOMIC AND CLINICAL HEALTH ACT

The Health Information Technology for Economic and Clinical Health (HITECH) Act, enacted as part of the ARRA, was signed into law on February 17, 2009 to promote the adoption of Meaningful Use standards for HIT. Subtitle D of the HITECH Act addresses the privacy and security concerns associated with the electronic transmission of health information, in part, through several provisions that strengthen the civil and criminal enforcement of the HIPAA rules. In addition, this act establishes payment incentives under Medicare Part B for eligible professionals who adopt and meaningfully use certified EHR technology. To be considered a meaningful EHR provider, at least 50% of the encounters during the EHR reporting period during the payment year must occur with a practice/location equipped with certified EHR technology. Specifics related to this act will be described later on in this chapter. Additional and more specific information can be obtained at www.hipaasurvivalguide.com.

Other Impacts of the HITECH Act

The HITECH law included several other changes that affected both the privacy and security regulations for EHR exchange:

1. Previously, under HIPAA regulations, only covered entities could be held liable for HIPAA violations; however, with the HITECH law, both individuals (physicians, nurses, and other staff) and covered entities will be held liable.
2. HITECH allows the State Attorney General to file federal civil actions on behalf of residents in the state who they believe were adversely affected by an HIPAA violation.
3. HITECH requires the DHHS Secretary to provide periodic audits to ensure that covered entities and their business associates comply with HIPAA security provisions.
4. HITECH expands privacy requirements in which the physician's office, hospital, or other health care organization using EHR technology provide a patient with a 3-year history of personal health information (PHI) disclosures, including any disclosures previously considered exempt such as laboratory work or payment purposes.
5. The law requires that organizations that keep patient data in electronic format must provide an electronic copy if the patient requests it in that format.
6. HITECH also included new breach notification requirements on covered entities, business associates, vendors of personal health records (PHRs), and related entities if a breach of unsecured PHI occurs. The DHHS Rule was published on August 24, 2009, and the Federal Trade Commission (FTC) Rule was published on August 25, 2009.
7. HITECH also extends current accounting for disclosure requirements to information used to carry out treatment, payment, and health care operations when an organization uses EDI. HITECH also limits the time frame to 3 years instead of 6 years. For organizations implementing EHRs from January 2009 to January 2011, this rule will be effective on January 2011, and for organizations who had implemented EHRs prior to January 2009, it will be effective on January 2013.

8. The most far-ranging change under HITECH is the extension of HIPAA's provisions to business associates. Effective February 17, 2010, companies that provide services such as claims processing and billing and handle PHI for health care providers are directly covered by the HIPAA security rule. This doubly impacts firms such as an insurance business that is both a covered entity working with vendors that handle PHI and a business associate in cases where it operates as a third-party administrator for clients who fully insure their workforce and must verify all business associate compliance.

In addition, the Office of the National Coordinator (ONC) released an interim rule for the provision related to HITECH, Meaningful Use Section for EHR technology, that specifies standards and certification criteria for EHR technology, which include baseline for security controls such as encryption and authentication, but the Meaningful Use documents only cite the need for security risk assessment. Furthermore, in order to comply with the HITECH requirements, offices, hospitals, and others are being requested to document security and privacy procedures, workforce training procedures, implementing physical safeguards, and restrict discrepancies of PHI to minimum necessary information.

Patient Protection and Affordable Care Act

Administrative simplification provisions build upon the HIPAA with new and expanded provisions, including a requirement to adopt operating rules for each of the HIPAA transactions; a unique, standard health plan identifier; and standards for electronic funds transfer (EFT) and electronic health care claims attachments. The Affordable Care Act (ACA) requires that health plans certify their compliance with the standards and operating rules and provides penalties for noncompliance. The law was enacted on March 23, 2010.

International Organization for Standardization

The International Organization for Standardization (ISO) is the world's largest developer of standards. Although ISO's principal activity is the development of technical standards, ISO standards also have important economic and social repercussions. Medical organizations can easily adapt to ISO security practices. ISO 27799-2008 is an information security standard to provide health care organizations and other holders of personal health information on how to protect such information via the implementation of ISO/EC 27002. It is a comprehensive set of controls comprising best practices in information security. Details on the 10-step ISO approach is addressed in the section "COOP, DR, and Security Evaluations" in this chapter.

National Institutes for Standards and Technology

Special Publications (SP) provide a series of security-related documents related to IT security. The most relevant is the National Institutes for Standards and Technology (NIST) SP 800-35—Guide to Information Technology Security Services. This guide sets out the following phases of the security life cycle to include

1. *Phase 1: Initiation*—The organization evaluates whether implementing an IT security service might improve the effectiveness of the organization's IT security program.
2. *Phase 2: Assessment*—The organization determines the security posture of the current environment using metrics and identifies the requirements and viable solution.
3. *Phase 3: Solution*—The decision makers evaluate potential solutions, develop the business case, and specify the attributes of an acceptable service arrangement solution.

4. *Phase 4: Implementation*—The organization selects and engages the service provider, develops a service arrangement, and implements the solution.
5. *Phase 5: Operations*—The organization ensures operational success by consistently monitoring service provider and organization security performance against identified requirements, periodically evaluating changes in risks and threats.
6. *Phase 6: Close out*—The organization ensures a smooth transition as the service ends or is discontinued.

Other relevant NIST documents are the following:

1. NIST SP 800-27—Engineering Principles for IT Security: A Baseline for Achieving Security
2. NIST SP 800-30—Risk Management Guide for IT Systems
3. NIST SP 800-33—Underlying Technical Models for IT Security
4. NIST SP 800-36—Selecting Security Products
5. NIST SP 800-41—Introduction to Firewalls and Firewall Policy
6. NIST SP 800-55—Security Metrics Guide
7. NIST SP 800-64—Security Considerations in the Information System Development Life Cycle

For more specific details, go to the NIST web site at www.nist.gov.

PENALTIES FOR HIPAA VIOLATIONS

Security and privacy regulations are long and complex. Many of their requirements are clear and specific, and many need to be interpreted along the way. There are civil and criminal fines for noncompliance and organizations and regulations responsible for enforcing various parts of the HIPAA regulations. They include the following:

1. The Office for Civil Rights (OCR) with DHHS, which regulates the privacy rules
2. The Centers for Medicare and Medicaid Services (CMS), which regulates security and EDI

Previously, penalties under HIPAA were for general noncompliance and specific noncompliance and could be violation charges, fines, and/or imprisonment, depending on the degree of breaches. This could range from a $100 violation up to $250,000 per year and from 5 to 10 years of imprisonment, with the latter being related to the intent to sell, transfer, or use the information for commercial advantage, personal gain, or malicious harm.

Other risks of noncompliance include the following:

1. Exposure to lawsuits for breach of confidentiality
2. Loss of accreditation
3. Audits by CMS leading to damage to business interests and reputation, loss of reputation, and loss of patients or members

Developing appropriate methodologies and protocols will help decrease the risk of noncompliance by improving the understanding of these regulations and improving communication and HIPAA training among health care IT users. Failure to do so would, at the very least, open institutions up to fines and negative press coverage. It can also open companies up to serious litigation from people whose information is compromised.

With the introduction into law of the 2009 ARRA Act, which includes the HITECH Act, penalties for HIPAA violations have increased. There is now a tiered system of civil monetary penalties based on the level of knowledge of noncompliance and corrective actions. They are

1. For reasonable cause and not willful—$1000 for each violation.
2. For willful neglect and not corrected—$50,000 per violation, with a maximum fine of $1,500,000 for all such violations in a year.
3. In addition, HIPAA still includes criminal penalty fines of up to $250,000 and up to 10 years in prison for disclosing or obtaining health information with the intent of selling, personal gain, or malicious purpose.

ELECTRONIC DATA INTERCHANGE

EDI is the transfer of data between different companies using networks, such as the Internet. In other words, EDI is the structured transmission of data between organizations by electronic means through agreed message standards with minimum human intervention. In common usage, EDI is understood to mean specific interchange methods agreed upon by national or international standards bodies, with one typical application being the automated purchase of goods and services. As much more companies are connected to the Internet, EDI is becoming increasingly important as an easy mechanism for companies to buy, sell, and trade information.

Organizations have adopted EDI for the same reasons that they have embraced much of today's modern technology—enhanced efficiency and increased profits. Benefits of EDI include the following:

1. Secure and reliable interchange
2. Reduced cycle time
3. Better inventory management to include better storing and manipulation of data electronically
4. Increased productivity
5. Reduced cost (especially with the Internet) by decreasing human interaction and materials such as faxes and paper
6. Improved accuracy and decrease in errors
7. Improved business relationships
8. Enhanced customer service
9. Increased efficiency
10. Increased sales
11. Speed of transferring information electronically
12. Minimized paper use and storage
13. Increased cash flow
14. Auditable trail
15. Absence of a dedicated IT person to manage any software installations such as WEB EDI
16. Accessibility anywhere in the world, such as WEB EDI

Paper-based claims usually lack information; therefore, third-party administrators will not reimburse, leading to any inquiry on the claim. EDI has the potential to reduce such inquiries and the attendant delays in time and productivity.

Those who send and receive these documents are called *trading partners*. They agree on the specified information to be transmitted and how it should be used. This is done in human-readable specifications called Message Implementation Guidelines. Trading partners can use any method for the transmission of documents. The most common is a bisync modem through a value-added network (VAN), referred to more commonly as a (go-between) clearinghouse. VAN providers use their communication protocols to ensure that EDI is transmitted securely. The most popular examples of EDI via the Internet (WEB EDI) are the File Transfer Protocol Secure (FTPS), Hyper Text Transfer Protocol Secure (HTTPS), and Applicability Statement 2 (AS2). AS2 firms communicate EDI or business-to-business data such as XL over the Internet using the Hypertext Transfer

Protocol (HTTP), a standard by the World Wide Web. AS2 provides security for the transportation of data through digital signatures and data encryption and ensures reliable, nonreputable delivery through the use of receipts. Other connections are modem-to-modem connections, Bulletin Board Systems (BBS), and embedding EDI documents in Extensible Markup Language (XML). All of these Internet protocols seamlessly transform data into EDI format and quickly transmit them to the trading partner. The only identified downside to using EDI is the associated cost in time and money to initially set up the EDI communication pathway—the implementation, customization, and training and the business process charge for transmission.

DATA STANDARDS

The American National Standards Institute (ANSI) utilizes the approved set of EDI standards known as X12 standards, which include prescribed formats, character sets, and data elements for the exchange of business documents and forms. The Accredited Standards Committee (ASC) was chartered by ANSI in 1979 to develop and continually maintain the EDI standards and related documentation for national and global markets. ASC X12 enhances business processes, reduces cost, and expands the organization's reach. Currently, ANSI ASC X12 Standard, Version 4010 is being utilized for all transactions, except for retail pharmacy transactions, that continue to use the standard maintained by the NCPDP, because it is already in widespread use. Effective January 1, 2012, the newest X12 Version 5010 Standard for HIPAA transactions becomes effective, replacing Version 4010. This will allow for larger field sizes to accommodate ICD-10-CM diagnosis coding and have improved functionality, better meet the current business needs, and incorporate corrections into the original standard that users have identified. The standards are designed to work across industry and company boundaries. In addition, effective January 1, 2012, with the approval of DHHS, retail pharmacies can use either NCPDP Telecommunication Standard Version D.0 or Version 5010 for billing pharmacy supplies and professional services. This will enable some pharmacies to use the NCPDP standard for billing medication therapy management services because the services are part of the prescription, while others will use the X12 Standard for billing these services as part of the "professional services" requiring the use of the professional claim.

A Designated Standard Maintenance Organization (DSMO) has been established and named by the DHHS Secretary under HIPAA to maintain standards adopted under HIPAA and to receive and process requests to adopt new standards or modify those existing. Members of the DSMO include the ASC X12, Dental Content Committee of the American Dental Association (DeCC), Health Level Seven (HL7), NCPDP, National Uniform Billing Committee (NUBC), and National Uniform Claims Committee (NUCC).

The following table provides a list of the current electronic transaction claim formats approved under HIPAA. In addition, transaction sets are required by HIPAA for enrollment or disenrollment in a health plan and for all coordination of benefits (COB) involving dental, professional, institutional, and retail pharmacy drugs. All provider transmissions for the latter, COB, need to be in compliance with the HIPAA Privacy Rule.

Transaction	Description	EDI Message Type
EDI Health Care Claim Transaction Set	• Used to submit health care claim billing information, encounter information, or both, except for retail pharmacy claims • Can be sent from providers to payers directly or through a clearinghouse • Can be used to send claims information between payers for COB	837

EDI Retail Pharmacy Claim Transaction	• Used to submit retail pharmacy claims to payers from providers who dispense medications • Can be sent from providers directly or through a clearinghouse • Can be used for COB between two insurers and between payers and regulatory agencies to monitor rendering, billing, and/or payment of pharmacy services	NCPDP (Telecommunications and Batch) Standard Version 5.1 and/or NCPDP D.0 NCPDP 3.0 for Medicaid pharmacy subrogation (batch standards)
EDI Health Care Claim Payment or Advice Transaction Set	• Used to make a payment by sending an explanation of benefits (EOB) or remittance advice or both only from a health insurer to a health care provider directly or via a financial institution	835
EDI Enrollment and Maintenance Set	• Used by employers, unions, government agencies, associations, or insurance agencies to enroll members to a payer such as an insurance company, HMO, preferred provider organization (PPO), government agencies (Medicare, Medicaid, etc.), or others	834
EDI Payroll Deducted and Other Group Premium Payment for Insurance Products	• Used to make a premium payment for insurance products • Can be used to order a financial institution to make a payment to a payee	820
EDI Health Care Eligibility/Benefit Inquiry	• Used to inquire about the health care benefits and eligibility associated with a subscriber or dependent	270
EDI Health Care Eligibility/Benefit Response	• Used to respond to a request or inquiry about health care benefits and eligibility associated with a subscriber or dependent	271
EDI Health Care Claim Status Request	• Used by a provider, recipient of health care products or services, or an authorized agent to request the status of a health care claim • Health level 7 (HL7) specifications are used for content and format of the attachment	276
EDI Health Care Claim Status Notification	• Used by a health care payer or authorized agent to notify a provider, recipient, or authorized agent regarding the status of a health care claim or encounter or to request additional information from the provider • *Note*: This transaction set does not replace 835	277
EDI Health Care Service Review Information— Certification and Authorization	• Used to transmit health care service information such as subscriber, patient, demographic, diagnosis, or treatment data for the purpose of request for review, certification, notification, or reporting the outcome of a health care services review	278
EDI Functional Acknowledgement Transaction	• Used to define the control structure for a set of acknowledgments to indicate the results of syntactical analysis of the electronically encoded documents • Encoded documents are the transaction sets, which are grouped in functional groups, used in defining transactions for business data interchange • *Note*: This transaction set is not named in the HIPAA Legislation or Final Rule but is necessary for X12 transaction set processing	997

Source: www.edibasics.co.uk.

NATIONAL PROVIDER IDENTIFIER

The National Provider Identifier (NPI) is a HIPAA Administrative Simplification Standard that provides a unique identification for covered health care providers, all health plans, and health care clearinghouses. The NPI must be used in administrative and financial transactions adopted under HIPAA, and with one identifying number, it will simplify security and allow greater protection or encryption of the provider number. The NPI can be used to identify the health care provider on prescriptions, COB between health care plans, inpatient medical record systems, program integrity files, and other areas. Depending on his/her practice, a provider can obtain an individual or group NPI; however, there are situations where an individual NPI number is required such as with the submission of pharmacy and laboratory claims. The NPI remains with the provider, regardless of job or location change. NPI will eventually be the standard identifier for all e-prescribing under Medicare Part D.

The NPI is a 10-digit, intelligence-free numeric identifier with a check digit in the last position to help detect keying errors. If there is a security breach, the number in itself cannot identify the protected health organization. The use of one identifier with a check digit simplifies the encryption of this number when transmitted electronically, thereby enhancing security.

HIPAA also requires that employers have standard national numbers that identify them on standard transactions. The employer identification number (EIN), issued by the Internal Revenue Service (IRS), was selected as the identifier for employers. This number is used as a federal tax identification number for the means of identifying any business entity and for the purpose of reporting employment taxes. The EIN should be protected as a social security number is.

Both the Information Technology Laboratory (ITL) and the NIST are involved in the development of technical, physical, administrative, and management standards and guidelines for cost-effective security and privacy of sensitive unclassified information in federal computer systems. These standards and guidelines can be applied to the management of medical IT.

Additional reference material for NPI can be found at www.cms.gov/nationalprovidentstand.

ICD-10

ICD-10 is a coding of diseases, signs and symptoms, abnormal findings, complaints, social circumstances, and external causes of injury or diseases, as classified by the World Health Organization (WHO). The code set allows more than 14,400 different codes and permits the tracking of many new diagnoses. These codes are three to seven characters in length and 68,000 in total number, whereas ICD-9-CM diagnosis codes are three to five digits in length and over 14,000 in number. ICD-10-PCS procedure codes are alphanumeric, seven characters in length, and total approximately 87,000, whereas ICD-9-CM procedure codes are only three to four numbers in length and total approximately 4000 codes.

Moving to ICD-10 is expected to impact all physicians. Due to the increased number of codes, the change in the number of characters per code, and increased code specificity, this transition will require significant planning, training, and software/system upgrades/replacements, as well as other investments.

On January 1, 2012, standards for electronic health care transactions changed from Version 4010/4010A1 to Version 5010. These electronic health care transactions include functions such as claims, eligibility, inquiries, and remittance advices. Unlike the current Version 4010/4010A1, Version 5010 accommodates the ICD-10 codes and must be in place first before the changeover to ICD-10.

ICD-10 codes must be used on all HIPAA transactions, including outpatient claims with dates of service and inpatient claims with dates of discharge on and after October 1, 2014. Otherwise, claims and other transactions may be rejected, and claims will need to be redone and resubmitted with the correct ICD-10 codes. This could result in delays and may impact your reimbursements; therefore, early preparation is necessary.

COOP, DR, and Security Evaluations

COOP and DR are two separate disciplines. COOP refers to the processes, policies, and procedures related to recovering or continuing essential day-to-day functions in the event of a natural disaster or human-induced security breach. DR, in turn, is the process by which an organization resumes business after a disruptive event.

An effective IT COOP plan must first classify each IT process and resource as it relates to the operations. Is it critical, important, or marginal? Second, an appropriate level of risk needs to be established by the business owners of the practice or facility based on the business impact of a failure to a system or process. There are systems for which any interruption would represent a significant loss. Others, although critical, could still recover from a small delay during a switch to a backup server. In other words, there are systems that we must protect from ever failing and systems that we must be able to recover. The challenge is less in identifying what is critical, but rather in knowing how to protect it. Certain applications may have built-in resiliency to certain types of failure. However, protection for many systems must be manually designed and implemented. Even with the most well-engineered and executed COOP plan, outages can occur.

DR is the way we support recovery from a loss. Disasters come in many forms—natural, accidental, and malicious. Therefore, recovery plans are often developed with multiple layers of protection. Most recovery strategies rely on the use of diverse resources—either logical or physical. Recovery techniques and strategies are as varied as the types of disasters they are designed to mitigate. New solutions continue to help reduce risk and improve recovery times.

A disruption on activity to any type of network event can have a real impact on operations to include compromised patient information, lack of confidence in the IT system, and decreased revenue through the loss of patient trust and subsequent loss of patients and/or cost associated with a security consultation. In today's global information age, the business continuity takes on a higher level of complexity and urgency than ever before. Security breaches, whether by natural disaster, security intrusions, or acts of terrorism, can cripple operations and limit a practice of a facility's ability to deliver services to their patient population. Without a solid plan, an untimely event could put entire operations and even patients in jeopardy.

Because no set of prevention measures is perfect, it is necessary to both detect security breaches and take actions to reduce their impact. The first step is to evaluate the existing environment and identify where the organization is at risk. This includes a thorough assessment of current systems and data and performing checks such as real-time intrusion testing, validation of data audit trails, firewall testing, and remediation when gaps or failed systems are exposed. Any business, whether a health care practice, health care facility, or any other public or private firm, must efficiently plan for and be able to quickly recover from any event that may diminish or impact day-to-day operations and/or patient information.

Those involved with overseeing security should have a working knowledge of federal regulations and of the following security mechanisms:

1. Vulnerability assessment
2. Security policy, procedure and plan development, and/or assessment of existing plan
3. Risk management
4. Assessment of environmental factors
5. Firewall, router (especially a filtering router that examines the IP address and header information in every packet coming into the network), and server assessment
6. Security application assessment
7. Incident response and recovery assessment
8. Authentication and authorization systems
9. Security products
10. Firewall implementation—A means of the first line of defense

11. Public key infrastructure (PKI) design
12. Virtual private network (VPN) design and implementation
13. Intrusion detection systems
14. Penetration testing and information sensitivity assessment
15. Security awareness training and compliance program
16. Evaluation of system architecture and components
17. Documented system inventory
18. List of threats with severity of impact
19. List of safeguards for controlling
20. Level of residual risk that would remain after recommended changes are made
21. Development and/or assessment of DR plan
22. Storage and archiving of health information
23. Developing and implementing data access control procedures
24. Sign or amend contracts with business associates to protect the confidentiality of protected patient data exchanges conducted electronically
25. Implementing technical mechanisms to prevent unauthorized access
26. Establishing a reporting and response system for confidentiality violations
27. Developing a sanctions policy for the discipline of violations by employees, agents, and contractors
28. An audit trail record all related to a single person, account, or entity
29. Assessment of virus-checking software

Contingency plans must be developed and tested to determine their effectiveness. All risks or vulnerabilities addressed need to be prioritized with action plans to mitigate the risk. There are four controls for vulnerabilities: (1) deterrent controls, which reduce the likelihood of a deliberate attack; (2) preventative controls, which protect vulnerabilities and reduce or prevent impact; (3) corrective controls, which reduce the effect of an attack; and (4) defective controls, which discover attacks and develop preventive or corrective controls. In order to determine whether the integrity of the system security has been compromised, the ability must exist to detect when information or system state is potentially corrupted.

Evaluation of information security and DR plans is an ongoing process of discovering, correcting, and preventing security problems. This continual process is designed to provide appropriate levels of security to all aspects of the system. Assessments and related documentation are integral parts of compliance with HIPAA security standards.

As referenced previously in this chapter, ISO offers a 10-step approach that addresses the security management needs of the health sector. They are

Business continuity planning—It is vitally important that IT security mechanisms, policies, and procedures address the continuity of health care business functions. Systems must be in place to ensure the continuity of health care flow despite system outages and during DR. Workarounds need to be developed and tested to include even a manual paper process.

System access control—This requires that the system curtail how much information each user can access using minimal PHI as required by an employee's job description. System access control granted by the system administrator allows end-user application access as well as data access. Each end user should traditionally be given a role, and then, the administrator programs the system, which will allow the end user access only to the minimal amount of information needed. Access controls ensure that all access to resources is authorized where necessary. These controls also protect the confidentiality and integrity of patient data. These measures provide assurances that sufficient management, operational, and technical controls are in place to protect sensitive data and system or network components. The access control mechanisms can be user-centric (based on credentials or access rights associated with a user), resource-centric (based on access control lists that detail the access rights of various users on a particular information resource), or role-based access (associated with groups of individuals). Any health care organization can help protect data by controlling who can use an application, database, record, or file. Particular attention should be paid to controlling who is allowed to enable or disable the security features or to change user privileges. Every access control process should include knowing who is attempting to access, mediating access according to some processing rule, auditing user actions, and managing where or how data are sent.

System development and maintenance—Clinical systems, application systems, system files, and development and support processes all have security requirements as well as a need for cryptographic control. Information security features in systems refer to specific functions that can be incorporated into or are integral to the information system. All operational systems must have security safeguards to minimize loss, modification, or misuse of user data in application systems. These include regular backups verifying data security in each record. Protecting the confidentiality, authenticity, and integrity of information will require coordination of all staff. Each user needs to acknowledge use and/or possession of data. The hardware structure needs to be maintained, especially in a health care system that operates 24/7. Security needs to be maintained at the operating system level, network, and application levels.

Physical and environmental security—Access to clinical workstations and mobile devices should be controlled so that access is available only to authorized personnel. An inventory record and maintenance schedule should be established for all IT equipment, including warranties and maintenance contracts. All staff should be required to report an unauthorized access that is observed. All workstations should be secured to prevent loss, damage, theft, duplication, or compromise of assets after working hours. Finally, all staff should keep secure tracking records of personnel equipment inventories.

Compliance—This involves legal requirements, security policy, technical compliance, and system audit considerations. All of the ISO requirements can be downloaded from the ISO site.

Personnel security—The greatest harm/disruption to a clinical system comes from the actions of individuals, both intentional and unintentional. Intentional actions are those intending to disrupt security, but sometimes, unintentional actions, such as a programming error, could jeopardize security. Several personnel security measures should be considered:

1. Review all positions for sensitivity level.
2. State whether individuals have received the background screening appropriate for the position to which they are assigned. If individuals are permitted system access prior to the completion of an appropriate background screening, the conditions and controls should be documented.
3. Critical functions need to be divided among different individuals to ensure that no individual has all the necessary authority or information that could result in fraudulent activity.
4. Establish a process for requesting, establishing, issuing, and closing user accounts.
5. Establish termination procedures.

Security organization—A management framework for information security and for access by third parties should be established and controlled. Information security should be added to all contracts with third parties, whether consultants, billing agents, maintenance staff, or others.

Communication and operations management—To ensure a secure operating environment, the IT staff should utilize a help desk for support and troubleshooting to replicate the IT physical architecture as a mirror to the existing server in case the system goes down; fully integrate and document machine maintenance replication and backups; protect integrity of software and data; provide manual inspections of power supplies, line connections, hubs, and routers; and document policies to ensure the safety of information networks.

Asset classification and control—All technology assets need to receive an appropriate level of protection. Asset and inventory control as well as unauthorized duplication of data should be addressed.

Security policy—The development and continual reviews and updates of the security policy should be ongoing. This policy needs to be reviewed with all staff.

SECURITY RISK MANAGEMENT AND PROCESSES FOR HEALTH CARE SYSTEMS

IT security risks are risks to data and systems. Many of these security threats or risks also directly impact the protection of privacy. As a best practice, patient and operator safety risk management and IT security risk management processes should be separate but linked and should be assessed separately. The same basic methodology and process for assessing and mitigating risk can and should be applied by health care facilities when combining equipment of different vendors as a health care delivery network, when adding new equipment to an existing network, or when significantly changing the configuration of an existing network. Remember that the protection of security and privacy are quite different in a health care facility that, depending on the type, may need to remain open 24 hours a day. Operation under adverse conditions will still be essential in treating current patients and maintaining and/or restoring health care services to optimal usage.

The skills of the risk management team members require specific elaboration. People with general IT knowledge as a background often are not aware of the health care–specific issues that may lead to impractical measures at the end. The security risk analysis team should be multidisciplinary with the following attributes:

1. Represents both business and technical aspects of the systems (including IT knowledge)
2. Understands both clinical processes and manufacturers' development processes
3. Understands the health care–specific requirements (safety and security)
4. Includes a member familiar with the safety risk management process for products

In addition, the team should be supplemented in an ad hoc manner by visiting experts who can help with any related network issues, IT security details, vulnerability tool assessments, and other specialized issues as they arise in the risk assessment project.

The IT security risk assessment will answer the following basic questions:

1. What are the valuable assets that fall under the intended use of the system?
2. What are the security-related requirements for the assets under consideration?
3. Who will perform a potential attack (human and nonhuman actors)?
4. What are the possible threat paths?
5. What are the possible impacts of a successful attack?
6. What is the score of the initial risk?
7. What actions may mitigate the risk?
8. What is the score of the residual risk?

The process of IT security risk management includes the following:

Listing the assets under consideration and understanding their intended use—This should include a typical but not exhaustive list of assets, including hardware and software used for processing medical information and key data elements, and include different kinds of data such as

1. Specific components/medical application systems such as image-creating modalities, components, and others of the IT infrastructure
2. Unspecific components/medical application systems of the IT infrastructure
3. Medical applications software
4. Data about the configuration of hardware and software
5. Personal data of a specific patient
6. Personal data of staff and other persons
7. Health care procedure support information, including the history of use and operator/user details

The list of assets needs to be detailed enough to begin the assignment of direct threats to each of them and to be able to identify and implement appropriate risk mitigation measures. For example, simply listing the hospital information system as one asset would not provide enough specificity to detail a realistic, specific threat. In general, a network diagram (even if it was an agreed-upon "typical network") allows a systematic overview of the IT architecture of the developed equipment or the whole network. It eases the identification of identical systems used at multiple locations in the same installation (or by the same health care provider) that are exposed to the same risks and that need the implementation of the same risk mitigation measures. By properly using such an overall network approach, a single risk management team can broaden the potential mitigations to account for system use in a wide variety of network implementations.

Collection of security-related requirements for the assets—The assessment team should collect all materials that detail the system requirements for security, including specifics for all assets on the levels of confidentiality, integrity, availability, accountability, and other items. This requirement collection can be a specific document collection or be realized as a set of explicit references that are detailed, one by one, and documented as part of the risk management process. Input requirements typically would come from the following:

1. Regulatory requirements such as HIPAA
2. Customer requirements such as from government agencies
3. Secure platform configuration guides such as NIST
4. Internal security/privacy policy documents
5. Industry "best practices" white papers
6. Requirements from correction actions based on prior experience.

Documentation of potential threats and applying them to systems to determine vulnerabilities, including actors, threat paths, and possible outcomes—With the lists of assets and security-related requirements, the risk assessment team brainstorms, develops, and documents all possible threats for each asset. When a general threat may be exploited in a particular system, it becomes known as systems vulnerability. Each asset should be documented with the chain of identification access paths, actors, motives, and outcomes.

A wide variety of human and nonhuman actors that are involved in security threats include the following:

1. Authorized persons who are insiders with valid account access but are not authorized to perform a specific task. These could include accidental attacks, insiders

who are paid to be initiators, and insiders who are motivated by personal profit or revenge.

2. Persons who are not authorized to access the network and have no account but find an access route. This would include vandals, paid individuals to perform nonapproved access, journalists seeking stories on VIPs, visitors, patients, and terrorists.

3. Nonhuman events that happen on an unpredictable basis without direct human influence such as local infrastructure failure, major industrial accidents, or natural disasters.

Pathways to access the target network vary. They are different in their ability to be detected—some are viewable by persons, whereas others are not. Examples of physical access include sitting at a medical system console with a means to compromise security; equipment without proper physical security that can be stolen; or the use of removable media (CD, DVD, USB, etc.). Other nonviewable access could be through an IP network or a telephone connection.

The impact of access can be a single diagnostic or monitoring event, a single patient, a single diagnostic or monitoring system, or an entire deployed set of systems under a particular software version number. The larger the number of systems impacted, the larger the severity. However, it is important to keep in mind that even a single patient privacy event can be of extreme severity. The irreversible disclosure of damaging private health information, such as certain diseases and conditions, may be financially devastating to individuals, especially when applied to well-known public figures.

Scoring of the risks—The scoring for a risk assigned to an identified vulnerability is a combination of the likelihood of a successful attack and the severity of the resulting impact on the assets. The goal of this analysis is to arrive at a reasonable categorization of the risk so that mitigation activities can be prioritized. This does not require a fine-grained numerical evaluation. Three levels are sufficient: (1) high; (2) medium; and (3) low. The team needs to be careful about any speculation regarding any possible scenarios. When assessing the likelihood or the probability of a security breach, the motivation behind the attack or breach is a key factor, because it usually determines the resources and effort that will be expended by the violator. Violators can be indiscriminate attackers that occur by the lack of clear security policies or procedures or the lack of training or deliberate attackers done through targeted terrorism, for financial gain, or through revenge.

The severity of a security event can be described in terms of loss or degradation of confidentiality, integrity, and availability.

Loss of integrity—System and data integrity refers to the requirement that information is protected from improper modification. Integrity is lost if unauthorized changes are made to the data or system by either deliberate or accidental acts. If the loss of system or data integrity is not corrected, continued use of the compromised system or corrupted data could result in inaccuracy, fraud, or impact safety.

Loss of availability—If a system is unavailable to its end users, the medical facility or provider's office mission may be affected. Loss of system functionality and operational effectiveness may introduce safety concerns and/or reduce the quantity and quality of care.

Loss of confidentiality—System and data confidentiality refers to the protection of information from unauthorized disclosure. This could violate many of the regulatory directives, cause firms to violate the contractual business associate agreements, and potentially lead providers to violate HIPAA regulations.

The scoring of a risk is determined by combining the likelihood and severity of a security violation or attack. It also determines the ranking of the risk mitigation measures. An example of sample risk scores derived from likelihood and severity is listed in the table below.

		Severity	
Threat Likelihood	Low	Medium	High
High	Low	High	High
Medium	Low	Medium	High
Low	Low	Low	Medium

To take this a step further, the table shows the sample description of the risk scores. It represents the score of a risk to which an asset might be exposed if a given vulnerability was exploited and the corresponding need for corrective measures.

Risk Score	**Necessary Actions**
High	Strong need for corrective measures. An existing system may continue to operate, but a corrective action plan or other risk mitigation measure must be put into place as soon as possible.
Medium	Corrective actions are needed, and a plan must be developed to incorporate these actions within a reasonable period of time.
Low	The system's owner must determine whether corrective actions are still required or decide to accept the risk.

Proposing and implementing mitigations for vulnerabilities appropriate to the health care domain—After the aforementioned steps, the provider or facility now has the relevant data available to define necessary risk mitigation measures. The goal is to develop measures that will best reduce the risk to an acceptable score for a specific system or for a specific health care provider. If new risks appear, then the process should be repeated. Note that risk mitigation can include system internal technical controls (such as network port closure), system external technical controls (such as firewall appropriately configured), or process description and training for key staff. In general, mitigation plans span technology, processes, and people.

Summarizing residual risks along with the system's role in advancing the health care mission—During the final stages of risk assessment and review, a summary of the residual risks and subsequent mitigation plans should also be developed.

CONCLUSIONS

Regulations and policies are in place to protect the security of systems and applications, health care delivery processes involving diagnosis and treatment, and the privacy of patient personal data. It is important to maintain a good partnership and working relationship with all stakeholders including staff, contractors, government review agencies, patients, and others, thus ensuring both the effective mitigation of security risks while advancing the health care mission.

Security and privacy risks will continue as systems integrate, and more electronic mobile devices become the prevalent method of recording and referencing patient information. Providers and hospitals need to continue to monitor security and privacy risks and develop action plans to mitigate each risk situation. Patient data are and will continue to be vulnerable to cyber attacks that will be subject to more sophisticated approaches and access as these individuals develop more technical capabilities. Hopefully, the vendors will keep this in mind as they improve not only the capabilities of EHRs but also its security and privacy monitoring regulators.

CASE MODEL 10.1: THE SEARCH FOR A CHIEF SECURITY OFFICER

The Mighty-Soft Hospital is a futuristic 1500-bed fortress-like facility that operates with a state-of-the-art dual wired–wireless infrastructure complete with computerized physician order entry system, radio frequency inventory device control tags, and integrated electronic medical records—the envy of its competitors and vendors—and offers a formidable strategic competitive advantage in the marketplace.

Now, imagine the potential liability, PR disaster, and chagrin when its *enfant terrible* CEO is told of a massive security breach similar to the ChoicePoint and Lexis-Nexis fiascos. The ID theft involves the release of critically protected health care financial, employment, clinical, and contact information for all of its patients, employees, physicians, business associates, and affiliated medical personnel.

Suddenly, senior management is charged with the task of establishing the new position of Chief Security Officer (CSO) for Mighty-Soft and navigating a crisis management dilemma never previously faced by the formerly Health Insurance Portability and Accountability Act of 1996 (HIPAA)-compliant electronic giant.

The CSO is to be a senior-level management position responsible for championing institutional security. Awareness of electronic and HIPAA policy and procedure developments while working to ensure compliance with internal and external standards related to information security is vital. The CSO is to report directly to the CEO and the chief information officer (CIO).

The Search Committee developed the following list of CSO duties and responsibilities:

- Chair the hospital's *information security and privacy committee* in its policy development efforts to maintain the security and integrity of information assets in compliance with state and federal laws, and accreditation standards
- Provide project management and operational responsibility for the administration, coordination, and implementation of *information security policies* and procedures across the enterprise-wide hospital system
- Perform periodic *information security risk assessments* including disaster recovery and contingency planning, and coordinate internal audits to ensure that appropriate access to information assets is maintained
- Work with the financial division to coordinate a *business recovery plan*
- Serve as a *central repository* for information security-related issues and performance indicators. Research security or database software for implementing the central repository, and note that a server-based system could be useful for a wide area network, so that this information can be shared with the enterprise-wide hospital system. Develop, implement, and administer a coordinated process for response to such issues
- Function when necessary as an approval authority for platform and/or application security and coordinate efforts to *educate* the hospital community in good information security practices
- Maintain a broad understanding of *federal and state laws* relating to information security and privacy, security policies, industry best practices, exposures, and their application to the health care information technology environment
- Make recommendations for short- and long-range security planning in response to future systems, new technology, and new organizational challenges
- Act as an advocate for security and privacy on internal and external committees as necessary

- Develop, maintain, and administer the security budget required to fulfill organizational information security expectations
- Demonstrate effectiveness with consensus building, policy development, and verbal and written communication skills
- Possess the clear ability to explain information technology concepts to audiences outside the field
- Become the public face for the Mighty-Soft Hospital's legacy security system

Minimum Qualifications:

- Bachelor's degree in Computer Science or related field or equivalent experience
- Three or more years of experience in the health care industry
- Five or more years of experience in information security
- Eight or more years of experience in information technology
- In-depth understanding of network and system security technology and practices across all major computing areas (mainframe, client/server, personal computer/local area network, telephony) with a special emphasis on Internet-related technology

Preferred Qualifications:

- Experience with electronic medical devices
- Specific experiences in the health care industry
- Familiarity with legislation and standards for PHI and patient privacy
- Demonstrated successful project management expertise
- Professional certification, for example, CISSP, CISA, PMP
- Experience with student record/higher education laws

Key Issues:

- What is your IT hardware infrastructure and how are security-related devices deployed?
- What security requirements are imposed by federal and state authorities on your institution?
- What would you consider the most important criterion for choosing a CSO?
- What relationship will the CSO have with the CIO, CMIO, and CEO?
- What level of security education/training do you consider necessary for your hospital community?
- What are the key security issues that your CSU will have to address?
- What are the key privacy issues?
- What are the key risk management issues?
- What are the pros and cons of EHRs for your institution?
- What do you see as the EHR priorities for your CSO?
- What are the security issues of EHRs for your institution?

CHECKLIST 1: Health Information Security	YES	NO
Do you have an information security officer?	o	o
Have you taken steps to ensure the security of the electronic health records in your care? Have you protected	o	o
• Confidentiality?		
• Possession?		
• Data integrity?		
• Authenticity?		
• Availability?		
• Utility?		
Do you have a list of all of the security features in your system(s)?	o	o
Of these features, have you tested them all, *that is*, penetration testing?	o	o
Have you evaluated how adequately these features are being used?	o	o
Have you considered the role of ethics in your information security policy?	o	o
Have you done a security risk assessment?	o	o
Do you have a business continuity program?	o	o
Do you have a disaster recovery plan in place?	o	o

CHECKLIST 2: HIPAA Compliance	YES	NO
Have you reviewed HIPAA's requirements, including the following?	o	o
• Title I: Health Care Access, Portability, and Renewability		
• Title II: Preventing Health Care Fraud and Abuse		
• Administrative Simplification		
• Medical Liability Reform		
• The Privacy Rule		
• The Transactions and Code Sets Rule		
• The Enforcement Rule		
• The National Provider Identifier		
Have you accommodated all required and any necessary optional data elements in the nine HIPAA transactions you send/receive electronically?	o	o
Do you know what an electronic data interchange (EDI) clearinghouse is and how it can be beneficial?	o	o
Have you prepared to accommodate an electronic implementation of any of the nine HIPAA transactions you still handle manually (i.e., on paper, via phone, etc.), but cannot send/receive electronically?	o	o
Are you aware of the use or substitution of the following HIPAA-mandated requirements?	o	o
• Required code set structures		
• Health Identifier Standards		
• National Provider Identifier		
• Health Plan Identifier		
• Employer Identifier		
If you are transmitting or receiving electronic transactions directly or through a value-added network (VAN), have you checked with your system vendor or Management Information System (MIS) department to ensure that they are aware of HIPAA and are prepared to implement (or have implemented) HIPAA standards with your trading partner(s)?	o	o
Have you set up a system for consistent mapping and ongoing maintenance of the standard (e.g., by using Translation Software)?	o	o
Have you checked with your system vendor or MIS department to see if the cross-reference tables for the provider and health plan (PAYERID) national identifiers can be used to automatically upload these IDs into your system?	o	o

	o	o
Have you done an internal security evaluation for patient-identifiable information that is both at rest (e.g., in databases, on media, etc.) and in motion (e.g., transmission files, dial-up systems, remote sites, etc.)?	o	o
Have you made a list of all of the security features in your system(s) from your system vendor or MIS department?	o	o
Have you evaluated how adequately the security features are in use today?	o	o
Have you determined what features need to be put into place and made sure your vendor or MIS department is geared to do so?	o	o
Are you currently in compliance?	o	o

Transaction 270 Health Care Eligibility, Coverage, or Benefit Inquiry   o   o

This is used by providers to request details of health care eligibility and benefit information or to determine if an information source organization has a particular subscriber or dependent on file. Do you normally use this one first?

Transaction 271 Health Care Eligibility, Coverage, or Benefit Response   o   o

This is used by the payer to respond to 270 requests. Have you tracked how long it takes for the response?

Transaction 276 Health Care Claim Status Request   o   o

This is used by providers to request the status of health care claims. Have you established a time frame for how long after positive eligibility you send this transaction?

Transaction 277 Health Care Claim Status Notification   o   o

This is used by the payer to respond to 276 requests. Do you know the different types of claim statuses?

Transaction 278 Health Care Services Review Information—Request and Response   o   o

Health care providers use *request* transactions to request information on admission certifications, referrals, service certifications, extended certifications, certification appeals, and other related information.

Review entities use *response* transactions to respond to inquiries regarding admission certifications, referrals, service certifications, extended certifications, certification appeals, and other related information.

Do you understand these transactions?

Transaction 820 Payment Order/Remittance Advice   o   o

Insurance companies, third-party administrators, payroll service providers, and internal payroll departments use this to transmit premium payment information. Will you typically use this?

Transaction 834 Benefit Enrollment and Maintenance   o   o

Benefit plan sponsors and administrators use this to transmit enrollment and benefits information between each other. Will you typically use this?

Transaction 835 Health Care Claim Payment/Advice   o   o

This is used by the payer and the provider to make payments on a claim, send an explanation of benefits (EOB) remittance advice, or to send both the payment and EOB in the same transaction. Do you have a system for checking if the reimbursement was correct?

Transaction 837 Health Care Claim   o   o

There are three separate Implementation Guides for 837 Health Care Claims:

- Dental
- Institutional
- Professional

Have you determined when you would use these?

Have you checked whether your vendor or MIS department can accommodate the HIPAA standards for these transactions?   o   o

If you are transmitting or receiving electronic transactions directly or through a VAN, have you checked with your system vendor or MIS department to ensure that they are aware of HIPAA and are prepared to implement (or have implemented) HIPAA standards with your trading partner(s)?   o   o

	YES	NO
Have you set up a system for consistent mapping and ongoing maintenance of the standard (e.g., by using Translation Software)?	o	o
Have you checked with your system vendor or MIS department to see if the cross-reference tables for the provider and health plan (PAYERID) national identifiers can be used to automatically upload these IDs into your system?	o	o
Have you done an internal security evaluation for patient-identifiable information that is both at rest (e.g., in databases, on media, etc.) and in motion (e.g., transmission files, dial-up systems, remote sites, etc.)?	o	o
Have you made a list of all of the security features in your system(s) from your system vendor or MIS department?	o	o
Have you evaluated how adequately the security features are in use today?	o	o
Have you determined what features need to be put into place and made sure your vendor or MIS department is geared to do so?	o	o
Are you currently in compliance?	o	o
Do you have contracts with clients for the following:	o	o
• Clearinghouse services?		
• EDI enrollment procedures?		
• Trading partner agreements?		
• Customer service procedures?		
• Services you outsource?		
Have you instituted the security mechanisms required by HIPAA?	o	o
Do you have HIPAA-compliant security protections, such as	o	o
• Means of identification, authorization, and authentication?		
• Firewall(s)?		
• Data encryption?		
• Digital signature?		
• Periodic virus checking?		
• Access control measures (password, token, etc.)?		
• Audit trail analysis?		
• Security escalation procedures?		
• Sanctions?		
• Physical security?		
• Disaster recovery plan?		
• Reevaluate existing security and confidentiality policies?		
Do you periodically revise existing security and confidentiality policies to meet HIPAA criteria?	o	o
Do you have an explicit privacy policy?	o	o
Do you have the Notice of Privacy Practices posted for public access?		
Do you provide patients with a Notice of Privacy Practices?	o	o
Do you have a Privacy Officer?	o	o
Are your patients able to see records, get a copy, correct errors, and know who else has seen them?	o	o
Do you have a Security Officer?	o	o
Do you have a policy on workstation use?	o	o
Do you have a policy on storage and archiving of health information?	o	o

CHECKLIST 3: ISO 17799	YES	NO
Is your organization ISO 17799 compliant?	o	o
Have you addressed business continuity planning?	o	o
Do you have the following access control systems in place:	o	o
• System access and use monitoring?		
• Application and operating system access management?		
Do you have formal processes in place for developing and maintaining your security system?	o	o

Do you have the following physical and environmental security controls in place?	o	o

- Secure areas that restrict access to authorized personnel
- Secure locations for equipment
- Inventory of equipment
- Security training for all personnel

Have you restricted user access to data files?	o	o
Have you separated duties to reduce the possibility of fraudulent activity?	o	o
Do you have systems in place to control third-party access?	o	o
Do you have systems in place to control information and software exchanges with other organizations?	o	o
Have you written policies and procedures that are clear and concise?	o	o

- Have you ensured that the policies and procedures have management support?
- Have you communicated the policies and procedures to the staff and business partners?

Do you have processes in place to handle audits, security responsibilities, and authorizations?	o	o

- Have you determined who should define and enforce these processes?
- Have you developed an executive security forum with representatives from information technology (IT) and your business units?
- Have you considered third-party partners and requirements for outsourcers in your decisions?

Have you taken an inventory of your critical assets?	o	o

- Have you classified, labeled, and assigned an owner to these assets?
- Have you built an inventory database?
- Do you periodically review the inventory for changes and make modifications as needed to meet the requirements of the business?

Have you protected your organization from internal threats?	o	o

- Do you complete background checks and screen all personnel to ensure that each person has clearance appropriate to the job requirements?
- Do you have a policy for terminated employee IT accounts?
- Are you keeping key information confidential?
- Do you require nondisclosure agreements?
- Have you established procedures for reporting security incidents and threats?

Have you secured your office borders?	o	o

- Do you have card access, guard gatekeeper, and other entry controls?
- Do you have a secure guest account for third-party guests to control access to secure sites, such as conference rooms?
- Have you cabled securely?
- Have you locked critical server areas?
- Do you regularly maintain equipment?
- Are desktops locked when not in use?

Do you have appropriate operational procedures to help prevent security failures?	o	o

- Have you developed an incident response team?
- Have you segregated duties to minimize opportunity for system misuse?
- Have you ensured that licensing contract requirements are followed?

Have you developed and documented an access control procedure?	o	o

If yes, have you included:

- Allocation of privileges?
- Users' responsibility for their password and desktop?
- Access to the network?
- Options for secure remote connectivity?

Do you have a strong disaster recovery plan?	o	o

- Have you assigned roles?
- Have you tested the plan?
- Do you have a regular schedule for updating the plan?

Do you have a solid business continuity plan to get the organization back on track and functioning?   o   o
  • Have you assigned roles?
  • Have you tested the plan?
  • Do you have a regular schedule for updating the plan?

CHECKLIST 4: National Institutes for Standards and Technology	YES	NO
Have you reviewed the National Institutes for Standards and Technology (NIST) web site to keep current with industry changes?	o	o
Have you reviewed the six phases of the IT Security Life Cycle to determine your organization's status?	o	o
• Initiation		
• Assessment		
• Solution		
• Implementation		
• Operations		
• Closeouts		
Can you explain each phase?	o	o
Have you reviewed the appendices attached to this chapter to ensure that your IT security meets NIST recommendations?	o	o
Have you reviewed the latest NIST Draft Special Publications to acquaint yourself with new directions?	o	o

---

CHECKLIST 5: Setting Up Your Security System—A Review	YES	NO
Have you set up a business continuity project?	o	o
Have you assessed your business risk?	o	o
Do you have an emergency preparedness plan?	o	o
Do you have a disaster recovery plan?	o	o
Do you have a business recovery plan?	o	o
Have you tested your business recovery procedures?	o	o
Have you trained your staff?	o	o
Do you have a process for keeping your business continuity plan current?	o	o
Have you reviewed your security model?	o	o
Do you have a risk management process?	o	o
Do you have policies for mitigating risk?	o	o

CASE MODEL 10.2: THE WASHINGTON HOSPITAL

The Washington Hospital is interested in implementing an electronic health record (EHR) for its major clinic areas. The flagship hospital currently utilizes a legacy-based system and several of the clinics have independently purchased software programs to provide a more inclusive electronic database particular to that clinic.

In addition, each of the software programs purchased in specific clinics has been modified to serve their own needs. The other satellite hospitals and clinics are not linked to the flagship hospital and have independent systems, applications, and software in place.

The hospital is interested in obtaining one EHR system that can be used in a standardized and uniform methodology and process throughout all of its hospitals and clinics.

KEY ISSUES:

Should the Washington Hospital do any of the following?

1. Abandon the clinic's software programs in lieu of a more centralized EHR.
2. Assess various EHR systems for health care providers available in the marketplace, comparing a series of hospital- and clinic-developed requirements against vendor capabilities.
3. Obtain an EHR product that provides interface to the existing clinic software products.
4. Assess whether the EHR vendors totally comply with the Health Insurance Portability and Accountability Act of 1996 (HIPAA) and privacy regulations as well as update their systems automatically with HIPAA changes.
5. Have the vendors assess the existing system/applications/software programs currently in use at each of the hospitals and clinics and determine the best application configuration.
6. Utilize the internal information technology staff to develop an interface solution.

SOLUTION:

There are multiple ways to find a solution for the hospital. The best selections are Nos. 2, 3, 4, and 5. It is always advisable to select an EHR package that meets the needs of the hospital(s). However, it would behoove each hospital to develop a detailed requirements list and a list of HIPAA-related security and privacy questions as a guide in reviewing the vendors. The hospital should establish an evaluation team comprised of information technology (IT) security, IT chief information officer, privacy advocate or officer, clinical staff, operations staff, and others to be part of the review and evaluation team. This will ensure that all questions are addressed; all issues are responded to by the vendor; and that all staff is assured of what the final product will accomplish.

CHECKLIST 1: Mitigating HIPAA Risks	YES	NO
Is my health care organization a HIPAA-covered entity by virtue of being a medical office, clinic, outpatient care center, or hospital?	o	o
Is my health care organization a HIPAA-covered entity by virtue of being a nursing home, extended care facility, or skilled nursing facility?	o	o
Is my health care organization a HIPAA-covered entity by virtue of being an insurance company, health maintenance organization, managed care organization, independent physician association, physician–hospital organization, or similar intermediary or third-party payor?	o	o
Is the system in my health care entity protected health information (PHI) compatible?	o	o
Am I aware what is the permitted use and disclosure for PHI in my health care entity?	o	o
Is the PHI system public key informatics protected?	o	o
Is the PHI system private key informatics protected?	o	o
Do I know when systems entry authorization is needed?	o	o
Do I have a designated Privacy Officer who routinely audits HIPAA compliance?	o	o
Does the hospital have a detailed work and project plan to review action items?	o	o
Is there an assigned committee to address HIPAA-related issues?	o	o
Are regular meetings scheduled to discuss HIPAA-related issues, status, and/or resolutions?	o	o
Is there a contingency data backup plan, a disaster plan, or an emergency operation plan?	o	o
Has the backup plan or disaster plan been tested?	o	o

Is there a specific individual or organization assigned to oversee responsibility for security?	o	o
Does the hospital have a security configuration management plan?	o	o
Is there a security incident procedure and management plan?	o	o
Does the hospital utilize pre-programmed internal audits in their system to monitor security?	o	o
Is there a defined process to assure integrity for personnel security?	o	o
Is staff cleared for access on a need-to-know basis?	o	o
Do job descriptions define specific access needs?	o	o
Does the hospital routinely monitor each individual's access and compare it to the job description?	o	o
Does the hospital have a mandatory training program for all personnel including management?	o	o
Does the hospital provide information or training to staff on handling virus protection?	o	o
Are all virus protection software programs installed and routinely updated?	o	o
Is there a process for equipment control?	o	o
Is there a process for maintaining records?	o	o
Is there a process for visitor sign-in or escort?	o	o
Is there a process for testing and revision?	o	o
Is there a policy or guideline on proper workstation usage?	o	o
Are the workstations, monitors, and/or thin-clients secure?	o	o
Is there a technical security service?	o	o
Is there an audit control of system activity to identify potential suspected data access?	o	o
Is there an entity authentication process, such as user identification, personal identification number, password, or callback verification?	o	o
Is there a standard for electronic signature that is HIPAA compliant?	o	o
Does the hospital have a liability protection plan?	o	o
Can files be transferred via the Internet in a secure manner?	o	o
Is a protection process in place with wireless products to assure confidentiality and privacy?	o	o
Does the staff discuss protected health information with the patient within earshot of other patients, such as on the phone, in a reception area, or at the registration desk?	o	o
Has the staff left sensitive patient information on the answering machine?	o	o
Were faxes that included medical record data being forwarded to the correct recipient?	o	o
Does the staff make announcements in the waiting room that potentially include protected health information?	o	o
Is patient information being listed on whiteboards, X-ray boxes, computer screens, or other areas that would have been visible to the public or others who do not need access to that information?	o	o
Are computer screens visible to the patient and are security measures in place to restrict access if the user walked away from the computer?	o	o
Is physical access to areas where medical records are kept restricted?	o	o
Is there a termination procedure and process to ensure individuals are removed from the access list, shared passwords, or user accounts?	o	o
Is there a process where all computers, laptops, or building cards are returned by a terminating employee?	o	o
Is there a procedure in place to ensure this process will be accomplished in a consistent manner?	o	o
Are new employees trained on HIPAA as part of their orientation?	o	o
Is a process in place for identifying the "correct" patient?	o	o
Do the patients ever carry their medical record from one location to another in the hospital?	o	o
Is it possible for a single person to breach security?	o	o
Are there internal security assessments on all networking devices?	o	o
Are there external security assessments on public facing systems?	o	o
Are all devices encrypted or do they have firewalls?	o	o
Is there "help desk" support for HIPAA?	o	o
Does anyone else, within the hospital, have access to and use of any employee's computer?	o	o

Can employees load personal compact discs/digital versatile discs onto their laptops?	o	o
Is there a system for monitoring private use of laptops?	o	o
Is a checklist for HIPAA included in the hospital's policies and procedures?	o	o
Does the computer system automatically log off if the desktop is unoccupied?	o	o
Do employees have a log-off process when leaving their desktop?	o	o

ACKNOWLEDGMENT

The author would like to thank Richard Mata, MD, MS-MI, MS-CIS, for his technical assistance in the preparation of this chapter.

APPENDIX: SAMPLE NOTICE OF PRIVACY PRACTICES

[*Insert Name of Practice, Hospital, or Environmental Health Officer*]_____

NOTICE OF PRIVACY PRACTICES

This notice describes how medical information about you may be used and disclosed and how you can get access to this information. Please review it carefully. If you have any questions about this Notice, please contact: our Privacy Officer who is [*Insert Name of Privacy Officer*]_____

This Notice of Privacy Practices describes how we may use and disclose your protected health information to carry out treatment, payment, or health care operations and for other purposes that are permitted or required by law. It also describes your rights to access and control your protected health information. "Protected health information" is information about you, including demographic information, which may identify you and which relates to your past, present, or future physical or mental health or condition and related health care services.

We are required to abide by the terms of this Notice of Privacy Practices. We may change the terms of our notice, at any time. The new notice will be effective for all protected health information that we maintain at that time. Upon your request, we will provide you with any revised Notice of Privacy Practices by accessing our web site (Insert Physician Practice web site address), calling the office, and requesting that a revised copy be sent to you in the mail or asking for one at the time of your next appointment.

1. USES AND DISCLOSURES OF PROTECTED HEALTH INFORMATION

Uses and Disclosures of Protected Health Information Based upon Your Written Consent

You will be asked by your physician to sign a consent form. Once you have consented to use and disclosure of your protected health information for treatment, payment, and health care operations by signing the consent form, your physician will use or disclose your protected health information as described in this section. Your protected health information may be used and disclosed by your physician, our office staff, and others outside of our office that are involved in your care and treatment for the purpose of providing health care services to you. Your protected health information may also be used and disclosed to pay your health care bills and to support the operation of the physician's practice.

Following are examples of the types of uses and disclosures of your protected health care information that the physician's office is permitted to make once you have signed our consent form.

These examples are not meant to be exhaustive, but to describe the types of uses and disclosures that may be made by our office once you have provided consent.

Treatment—We will use and disclose your protected health information to provide, coordinate, or manage your health care and any related services. This includes the coordination or management of your health care with a third party that has already obtained your permission to have access to your protected health information. For example, we would disclose your protected health information, as necessary, to a home health agency that provides care to you. We will also disclose protected health information to other physicians who may be treating you when we have the necessary permission from you to disclose your protected health information. For example, your protected health information may be provided to a physician to whom you have been referred to ensure that the physician has the necessary information to diagnose or treat you.

In addition, we may disclose your protected health information from time-to-time to another physician or health care provider (e.g., a specialist or laboratory) who, at the request of your physician, becomes involved in your care by providing assistance with your health care diagnosis or treatment by your physician.

Payment—Your protected health information will be used, as needed, to obtain payment for your health care services. This may include certain activities that your health insurance plan may undertake before it approves or pays for the health care services we recommend for you such as making a determination of eligibility or coverage for insurance benefits, reviewing services provided to you for medical necessity, and undertaking utilization review activities. For example, obtaining approval for a hospital stay may require that your relevant protected health information be disclosed to the health plan to obtain approval for the hospital admission.

Health Care Operations—We may use or disclose, as needed, your protected health information in order to support the business activities of your physician's practice. These activities include, but are not limited to, quality assessment activities, employee review activities, training of medical students, licensing, marketing and fund-raising activities, and conducting or arranging for other business activities.

For example, we may disclose your protected health information to medical school students that see patients at our office. In addition, we may use a sign-in sheet at the registration desk where you will be asked to sign your name and indicate your physician. We may also call you by name in the waiting room when your physician is ready to see you. We may use or disclose your protected health information, as necessary, to contact you to remind you of your appointment.

We will share your protected health information with third-party "business associates" that perform various activities (e.g., billing, transcription services) for the practice. Whenever an arrangement between our office and a business associate involves the use or disclosure of your protected health information, we will have a written contract that contains terms that will protect the privacy of your protected health information.

We may use or disclose your protected health information, as necessary, to provide you with information about treatment alternatives or other health-related benefits and services that may be of interest to you. We may also use and disclose your protected health information for other marketing activities. For example, your name and address may be used to send you a newsletter about our practice and the services we offer. We may also send you information about products or services that we believe may be beneficial to you. You may contact our Privacy Contact to request that these materials not be sent to you.

We may use or disclose your demographic information and the dates that you received treatment from your physician, as necessary, in order to contact you for fund-raising activities supported by our office. If you do not want to receive these materials, please contact our Privacy Contact and request that these fund-raising materials not be sent to you.

Use and Disclosure of Protected Health Information with Written Authorization—Other uses and disclosures of your protected health information will be made only with your written authorization, unless otherwise permitted or required by law as described below. You may revoke this authorization, at any time, in writing, except to the extent that your physician or the physician's practice has taken an action in reliance on the use or disclosure indicated in the authorization.

Other Permitted and Required Uses and Disclosures That May Be Made with Your Consent, Authorization, or Opportunity to Object

We may use and disclose your protected health information in the following instances. You have the opportunity to agree or object to the use or disclosure of all or part of your protected health information. If you are not present or able to agree or object to the use or disclosure of the protected health information, then your physician may, using professional judgment, determine whether the disclosure is in your best interest. In this case, only the protected health information that is relevant to your health care will be disclosed.

Facility Directories—Unless you object, we will use and disclose in our facility directory your name, the location at which you are receiving care, your condition (in general terms), and your religious affiliation. All of this information, except religious affiliation, will be disclosed to people that ask for you by name. Members of the clergy will be told your religious affiliation. [*This section will only be applicable to larger practices or those practices that operate facilities.*]

Others Involved in Your Health Care—Unless you object, we may disclose to a member of your family, a relative, a close friend, or any other person you identify, your protected health information that directly relates to that person's involvement in your health care. If you are unable to agree or object to such a disclosure, we may disclose such information as necessary if we determine that it is in your best interest based on our professional judgment. We may use or disclose protected health information to notify or assist in notifying a family member, personal representative, or any other person that is responsible for your care of your location, general condition, or death. Finally, we may use or disclose your protected health information to an authorized public or private entity to assist in disaster relief efforts and to coordinate uses and disclosures to family or other individuals involved in your health care.

Emergencies—We may use or disclose your protected health information in an emergency treatment situation. If this happens, your physician shall try to obtain your consent as soon as reasonably practicable after the delivery of treatment. If your physician or another physician in the practice is required by law to treat you and the physician has attempted to obtain your consent, but is unable to obtain your consent, he or she may still use or disclose your protected health information to treat you.

Communication Barriers—We may use and disclose your protected health information if your physician or another physician in the practice attempts to obtain consent from you, but is unable to do so due to substantial communication barriers, and the physician determines, using professional judgment, that you intend to consent to use or disclosure under the circumstances.

Other Permitted and Required Uses and Disclosures That May Be Made without Your Consent, Authorization, or Opportunity to Object

We may use or disclose your protected health information in the following situations without your consent or authorization. These situations include

Required by Law—We may use or disclose your protected health information to the extent that law requires the use or disclosure. The use or disclosure will be made in compliance with the law and will be limited to the relevant requirements of the law. You will be notified, as required by law, of any such uses or disclosures.

Public Health—We may disclose your protected health information for public health activities and purposes to a public health authority that is permitted by law to collect or receive the information. The disclosure will be made for controlling disease, injury, or disability. We may also disclose your protected health information, if directed by the public health authority, to a foreign government agency that is collaborating with the public health authority.

Communicable Diseases—We may disclose your protected health information, if authorized by law, to a person who may have been exposed to a communicable disease or may otherwise be at risk of contracting or spreading the disease or condition.

Health Oversight—We may disclose protected health information to a health oversight agency for activities authorized by law, such as audits, investigations, and inspections. Oversight agencies seeking this information include government agencies that oversee the health care system, government benefit programs, other government regulatory programs, and civil rights laws.

Abuse or Neglect—We may disclose your protected health information to a public health authority that is authorized by law to receive reports of child abuse or neglect. In addition, we may disclose your protected health information if we believe that you have been a victim of abuse, neglect, or domestic violence to the governmental entity or agency authorized to receive such information. In this case, the disclosure will be made consistent with the requirements of applicable federal and state laws.

Food and Drug Administration—We may disclose your protected health information to a person or company required by the Food and Drug Administration to report adverse events, product defects or problems, biologic product deviations, track products; to enable product recalls; to make repairs or replacements, or to conduct post-marketing surveillance, as required.

Legal Proceedings—We may disclose protected health information in the course of any judicial or administrative proceeding, in response to an order of a court or administrative tribunal (to the extent such disclosure is expressly authorized), in certain conditions in response to a subpoena, discovery request, or other lawful process.

Law Enforcement—We may also disclose protected health information, so long as applicable legal requirements are met, for law enforcement purposes. These law enforcement purposes include (1) legal processes and otherwise required by law, (2) limited information requests for identification and location purposes, (3) pertaining to victims of a crime, (4) suspicion that death has occurred as a result of criminal conduct, (5) in the event that a crime occurs on the premises of the practice, and (6) medical emergency (not on the Practice's premises) and it is likely that a crime has occurred.

Coroners, Funeral Directors, and Organ Donation—We may disclose protected health information to a coroner or medical examiner for identification purposes, determining cause of death or for the coroner or medical examiner to perform other duties authorized by law. We may also disclose protected health information to a funeral director, as authorized by law, in order to permit the funeral director to carry out their duties. We may disclose such information in reasonable anticipation of death. Protected health information may be used and disclosed for cadaveric organ, eye, or tissue donation purposes.

Research—We may disclose your protected health information to researchers when an institutional review board that has reviewed the research proposal and established protocols to ensure that the privacy of your protected health information has approved their research.

Criminal Activity—Consistent with applicable federal and state laws, we may disclose your protected health information, if we believe that the use or disclosure is necessary to prevent or lessen a serious and imminent threat to the health or safety of a person or the public. We may also disclose protected health information if it is necessary for law enforcement authorities to identify or apprehend an individual.

Military Activity and National Security—When the appropriate conditions apply, we may use or disclose protected health information of individuals who are Armed Forces personnel (1) for activities deemed necessary by appropriate military command authorities; (2) for the purpose of a determination by the Department of Veterans Affairs of your eligibility for benefits, or (3) to foreign military authority if you are a member of that foreign military services. We may also disclose your protected health information to authorized federal officials for conducting national security and intelligence activities, including for the provision of protective services to the President or others legally authorized.

Workers' Compensation—We may disclose your protected health information as authorized to comply with workers' compensation laws and other similar legally established programs.

Inmates—We may use or disclose your protected health information if you are an inmate of a correctional facility and your physician created or received your protected health information in the course of providing care to you.

Required Uses and Disclosures—Under the law, we must make disclosures to you and when required by the Secretary of the Department of Health and Human Services to investigate or determine our compliance with the requirements of Section 164.500 *et. seq.*

2. YOUR RIGHTS

Following is a statement of your rights with respect to your protected health information and a brief description of how you may exercise these rights.

You have the right to inspect and copy your protected health information. This means you may inspect and obtain a copy of protected health information about you that is contained in a designated record set for as long as we maintain the protected health information. A "designated record set" contains medical and billing records and any other records that your physician and the practice use for making decisions about you.

Under federal law, however, you may not inspect or copy the following records—psychotherapy notes; information compiled in reasonable anticipation of, or use in, a civil, criminal, or administrative action or proceeding; and protected health information that is subject to law that prohibits access to protected health information. Depending on the circumstances, a decision to deny access may be reviewable. In some circumstances, you may have a right to have this decision reviewed. Please contact our Privacy Contact if you have questions about access to your medical record.

You have the right to request a restriction of your protected health information. This means you may ask us not to use or disclose any part of your protected health information for the purposes of treatment, payment, or health care operations. You may also request that any part of your protected health information not be disclosed to family members or friends who may be involved in your care or for notification purposes as described in this Notice of Privacy Practices. Your request must state the specific restriction requested and to whom you want the restriction to apply.

Your physician is not required to agree to a restriction that you may request. If physician believes it is in your best interest to permit use and disclosure of your protected health information, your protected health information will not be restricted. If your physician does agree to the requested restriction, we may not use or disclose your protected health information in violation of that restriction unless it is needed to provide emergency treatment. With this in mind, please discuss any restriction you wish to request with your physician. You may request a restriction by [describe how patient may obtain a restriction].

You have the right to request to receive confidential communications from us by alternative means or at an alternative location. We will accommodate reasonable requests. We may also condition this accommodation by asking you for information as to how payment will be handled or specification of an alternative address or other method of contact. We will not request an explanation from you as to the basis for the request. Please make this request in writing to our Privacy Contact.

You may have the right to have your physician amend your protected health information. This means you may request an amendment of protected health information about you in a designated record set for as long as we maintain this information. In certain cases, we may deny your request for an amendment. If we deny your request for amendment, you have the right to file a statement of disagreement with us and we may prepare a rebuttal to your statement and will provide you with a copy of any such rebuttal. Please contact our Privacy Contact to determine if you have questions about amending your medical record.

You have the right to receive an accounting of certain disclosures we have made, if any, of your protected health information. This right applies to disclosures for purposes other than treatment, payment, or health care operations as described in this Notice of Privacy Practices. It excludes disclosures we may have made to you, for a facility directory, to family members or friends involved in your care, or for notification purposes. You have the right to receive specific information regarding these disclosures that occurred after April 14, 2003. You may request a shorter time frame. The right to receive this information is subject to certain exceptions, restrictions, and limitations.

You have the right to obtain a paper copy of this notice from us, upon request, even if you have agreed to accept this notice electronically.

3. COMPLAINTS

You may complain to us or to the Secretary of Health and Human Services if you believe your privacy rights have been violated by us. You may file a complaint with us by notifying our Privacy Contact of your complaint. We will not retaliate against you for filing a complaint.

You may contact our Privacy Contact [*Insert Name of Privacy Contact*] at (_____)____-_____ or [*Insert e-mail address of Privacy Contact*] _____ for further information about the complaint process.

This notice was published and becomes effective on (*complete with a date which should be no later than [insert day and month], 20-*).

FURTHER READING

Dems power stimulus bill through Congress. Associated Press. February 14, 2009. http://www.msnbc.msn .com/id/29179041/.

American Health Information Management Association (AHiMA). Defining and Disclosing the Designated Record Set and the Legal Health Record. May 3, 2011.

HIPAA Compliance, Creative Marking Program, 2010–2011.

Information Security Risk Management for Healthcare Systems, Joint MITA-NEMA/COCIR/JIRA SPC Paper, October 17, 2007.

World Health Organization (WHO). International Classification of Diseases (ICD). http://www.who.int/ classifications/icd/en/.

Modifications to HIPAA Transactions, Government Affairs, Issue Brief, American Pharmacists Association, March 2009.

National Institute of Standards and Technology, Computer Security Division, Computer Security Resource Center, NIST Special Publications, http://csrc.nist.gov.

NIST SP 800-35—Guide to Information Technology Security Services

NIST SP 800-27—Engineering Principles for IT Security: A Baseline for Achieving Security

NIST SP 800-30—Risk Management Guide for IT Systems

NIST SP 800-33—Underlying Technical Models for IT Security

NIST SP 800-36—Selecting Security Products

NIST SP 800-41—Introduction to Firewalls and Firewall Policy

NIST SP 800-55—Security Metrics Guide

NIST SP 800-64—Security Considerations in the Information System Development Life Cycle

Summary of Health Privacy Provisions in the 2009 Economic Stimulus Legislation, Center for Democracy Technology, April 29, 2009.

Section III

Strategies and Execution

11 Health Information Technology Execution and Use
Exchanging Patient Data— Benefits and Rewards

Carol S. Miller

CONTENTS

INTRODUCTION AND OVERVIEW

To operate a provider's office or a health care facility, personal health data are the essential base of any record or interaction with a patient and are vital for an organization to perform effectively. However, along with utilizing the information technology (IT) systems and electronic information highway, security and privacy must be addressed through risk assessments, policies, procedures, training, and continual monitoring.

Storing and transmitting health information in electronic form exposes it to risks that are different from the risks associated with storing and sending information in paper format. For example, although both paper-based and electronic systems need protection from fire, water, wear, and tear, electronic data are also vulnerable to hardware or software malfunctions that can make data inaccessible, corrupted, and vulnerable to illegal access. In addition, cyber crimes and unauthorized intrusions from both internal and external users are increasing dramatically every year, costing companies millions of dollars. Nonetheless, electronic health records (EHRs) and personal health records (PHRs) are usually considered more secure than paper patient charts, because paper records lack an audit trail and can be more easily lost, and many times, provider handwriting is illegible.

Risk is inherent in the delivery of health care and has substantially increased as direct (network) and indirect (media) connectivity has increased. Threats can range from a failed computer system, electrical outage, and widespread disaster such as an earthquake, volcano, fire, or even man-made causes related to terror to an indiscriminate or targeted malicious attack to the software. Threats can also occur from personal revenge, originating in an angry or vengeful person such as an employee or a patient. Just as easily, threats or the release of important and confidential patient data can occur from a careless employee who might misplace a laptop or is irresponsible with security codes and passwords. An August 2010 survey by Imprivata, Inc. (www.imprivata.com) stated that 76% of organizations claim "breach of confidential information or unauthorized access to clinical applications" as their greatest security concern, and yet 38% of those who reported state they cannot track the inappropriate access. Many health care facilities and provider offices are just not equipped with either the know-how or the time to deal with security breaches when they occur. They may lack security budgets and resources, have insufficient training, and/or utilize outdated security and privacy policies and procedures. If jeopardized, providers and hospitals face damage to brand and reputation, loss of patient goodwill, and revenue.

Health care organizations must take the new risks seriously, for health care information is a vital business asset and protecting it preserves the value of this asset. In addition, securing patients' information protects their privacy and enhances the organizations' reputation for professionalism, patient well-being, and trustworthiness.

There are six attributes of information that need to be protected by information security measures.

1. *Confidentiality*—The protection and ethics of guarding personal information, for example, being cognizant of verbal communication leaks beyond conversation with associated health care colleagues.
2. *Possession*—The ownership or control of information, as distinct from confidentiality. For example, a database of protected health information (PHI) belongs to the patients.
3. *Data integrity*—The process of retaining the original intention of the definition of the data by an authorized user. This is achieved by preventing accidental or deliverable but unauthorized insertion, modification, or destruction of data in a database. A course of action would be to make frequent backups of data to compare with other versions for changes made.
4. *Authenticity*—The correct attribution of origin. This includes the authorship of an e-mail message or the correct description of information such as a data field that is properly named. Authenticity may require encryption.
5. *Availability*—The accessibility of a system resource in a timely manner, for example, the measurement of a system's uptime. Is the intranet available?
6. *Utility*—Usefulness, fitness for a particular use. For example, if data are encrypted and the decryption key is unavailable, the breach of security is the lack of utility of the data (they are still confidential, possessed, integral, authentic, and available).

As personal health data become increasingly involved and part of the electronic data interchange (EDI), the information aspects of privacy, security, and ethics also become ever more critical. All doctors take an ethical oath to protect the patient, and the obligation to uphold this oath extends to health data management, even for employees who do not take an oath.

Complicating and implicating security is the fact that IT has many and varied uses in the health care field. There are community hospitals, hospital-wide systems, university medical centers, research facilities, clinics, surgical centers, free-standing facilities, government facilities (Veterans Health, Military Medical facilities, and Indian Health hospitals and clinics), provider offices, rural and urban sites, and many others. In addition, today, we have other technological interfaces that further complicate the security and privacy implications. Some of these include

1. The transition of all hard copy records to various EHR formats, systems, and security controls
2. The ease and availability of using health care application service providers (ASPs) via Internet portals and cloud computing
3. Speech recognition systems replacing dictation systems
4. Health care local area networks (LANs), wide area networks (WANs), personal area networks (PANs), voice-over Internet protocol (IP) networks, Web, and ATM file servers that are being used
5. The use of barcodes to monitor pharmaceuticals to decrease medication errors and warn providers of potential adverse reactions
6. Telemedicine and other real-time interactive systems for multiple viewings of magnetic resonance imaging (MRI) scans or other diagnostic tests from multiple locations
7. Personal digital assistant (PDA), iPads, smartphones, and other wireless connectivity devices that rely on digital or broadband technology, including satellites and radiowave communications, are increasingly being used
8. The use of wireless technology with at-home or rural medical device monitoring, including wireless telemetry, radio-frequency identification (RFID), and Wi-Fi
9. Multiple personal health systems with varying degrees of access and control
10. Clinics and medical centers using kiosks with connectivity to patient data clinical systems
11. Personal access to insurance claim records that include personal health information, procedures, diagnoses, and other related information, especially during the payment and appeals process

This chapter addresses EHRs, PHRs, wireless mobile devices, and kiosks as they relate to benefits and potential barriers/issues, the impact of the new regulation on Meaningful Use and EHRs, the Federal Health IT Strategic Plan, and the security and privacy impacts related to each [1].

BENEFITS OF EHRS

There are still providers and some hospitals, clinics, and free-standing facilities that have been slow to convert to EHRs, but there is an increasing impetus of all providers of care to convert to an EHR product and system to comply with federal regulations [2]. As stated by Dr. Dave Koeller, "the EHR as part of a Clinical Information System (CIS) is a powerful tool which ties together documentation of the patient visit (clinical information), coding (diagnosis and treatment procedures), which then translates into more accurate billing processes, reduces reprocessing of medical claims, and that translates into increased customer satisfaction with a provider" (www.ameda.com). Compiled from many articles written on EHRs, the perceived and demonstrated advantages of an EHR system include the following:

1. *Meet the requirements of legal and regulatory agencies such as the Joint Commission on Accreditation of Healthcare Organizations (JCAHO) or the National Committee on Quality Assurance (NCQA), and/or other accreditation standards.* There is a drive and need to join the National Health Information Network (NHIN)—the interoperable network

for exchanging health data and medical information between the government (Indian Health, Department of Defense [DoD], Veteran Affairs) and the private sector facilities across the United States. Clinicians can connect and exchange health information using advanced and secure electronic communications.

2. *Obtain better access to patient records.* Electronic records provide quicker access to needed information in a more timely manner and provide clinicians a secure access. The availability of a prior history, a laboratory test result, an allergy, or other data instantaneously, especially in an emergency situation, will lead to improved health outcomes for patients. Unlike the time-consuming and complicated task of copying, faxing, and transporting paper records to different locations, EHRs allow information to be shared more easily among doctors' offices, hospitals, and across health systems, leading to better coordination of care. With paper records, too often, care had to wait, because the chart was in one place and needed in another.

3. *Improved documentation of patient medical records.* Typed records, besides being clearer and easier to read, do provide a more detailed accountability of medical information obtained during the visit, especially if the clinician is entering the information during the visit with the patient. With this detail in place, it provides a more detailed description of the visit, thereby improving coding levels. Paper records tend to be incomplete, fragmented, hard to read, and sometimes even hard to find.

4. *Improved quality and legibility.* Information may have been forgotten from the time the provider saw the patient and documented written notes in their office. Previously documented lab levels or blood pressure readings are quicker to obtain from preestablished areas organized by sections within the EHR or graphically charted showing trends, leading to improved decision making. Access to patient data, regardless of the location or provider of care, can more quickly be visualized electronically, which in turn improves the quality of services rendered, especially during an emergency situation. Said another way, the EHR provides a single, shareable, up-to-date, rapidly retrievable source of information, potentially available anywhere at any time. Electronic records help with the standardization of forms, terminology and abbreviations, and input of data. Digitization of forms facilitates the collection of data for epidemiology and clinical studies, quality improvement, resource management, and public health communicable disease surveillance. Physicians will more easily be able to review the "complete" medical record information that comprised decision support information, electronic prescribing results, electronic referrals requests and responses, radiology, laboratory ordering and results, and other data instantaneously for a more in-depth picture of the patient. In addition, "alerts and notices" or "event monitoring" can be configured into the EHR system to help health care providers incorporate best practices into patient treatments. These can be used to predict, detect, and potentially prevent adverse events and can include discharge/transfer orders, pharmacy orders, radiology results, laboratory results, and any other data from ancillary services or provider notes. EHRs bring a patient's total health information together to support better health care decisions and assist the providers of care in reducing medical errors.

5. *Provide administrative cost savings.* Initially, there is a cost for the purchase of the EHR system and associated training of staff; however, subsequently, there is a cost savings where administrative staff remove manual paper tasks such as manually placing information into the chart or refiling charts and instead utilize more sophisticated processes for entering data, such as scanning and direct data entry.

6. *Reduced cost of care.* Even with an initial cost (a barrier to many providers), ultimately, the cost of care is reduced by more efficient record keeping and abilities to quickly assess prior and current health data. Billing staff will more readily convert all documented procedures and services into correct codes, improving insurance reimbursement. Poorly documented or mislabeled information will be more efficiently captured. Cost would decrease

for transcription services, resources such as clerical medical record staff, and drug, lab, and X-rays. Many malpractice insurers are also adjusting their rates for providers who utilize EHRs, thereby decreasing insurance cost.

7. *Improved efficiency.* Staff will improve in efficiency in entering data when the system process is learned. Built-in tracking and reminder processes are continually alerting staff and providers of required follow-ups, preventive care, next appointments, chemotherapy protocols, and much more. With an EHR in place, providers can easily avoid a duplicative test or unnecessary test by doing a quick search to determine if a prior one was done and was sufficient. These systems offer the potential for automating, structuring, and stream-lining clinical workflow. As an example, there would be a decrease in chart pulls and chart filings, and further efficiencies are gained in time, enabling providers to see more patients in a given day and/or spend more valuable time with the patient themselves.

8. *Security of patient records.* The EHR system is more secure than paper records. Encryption, log-on procedures, access authorities, audit trails, and other controls greatly improve the security and privacy of patient data. Only those who have a need to know have access. Paper records require secure housing against fire, rain, age, and other hazards.

9. *Patient safety.* Bar coding in pharmacy systems has improved patient safety, having a computer-based system with built-in algorithms that can assist a clinician with one or more steps or reminders for the diagnostic and therapeutic processes, and likewise supports patient safety. EHRs reduce decision errors through improved documentation and access.

10. *Patient empowerment.* EHRs will help empower patients to take a more active role in their health and in the health of their families. Patients can receive electronic copies of their medical records and share their health information securely over the Internet with their families.

11. *Improved patient and provider convenience.* Patients can have their prescriptions ordered and ready even before they leave the provider's office, and insurance claims can be filed immediately from the provider's office as well.

12. *Need for storage is dramatically reduced.* Paper or film records must be held for a minimum of 7 years and require significant storage space. Electronic records require less storage space, and the costs of storage media is significantly less. Regardless, it is important to note that electronic medical records, like medical records, must be kept in unaltered form and authenticated by the creator. The physical medical records are the property of the medical provider or facility that prepares them. This includes films and tracings from diagnostic imaging procedures such as X-rays, CT, PET scan, MRI, ultrasound, and others.

CONTINUED BARRIERS AND ISSUES WITH EHRS

Even though many providers of care are moving forward with electronic documentation of medical information, there are still perceived and real barriers impacting some providers of care in moving forward with this process [3].

1. High start-up cost is probably the foremost barrier or concern of providers. The EHR product, hardware, initial and annual software license, training both initially during implementation and ongoing, other peripherals, and the follow-on module updates, maintenance, and/or replacements are all associated with a cost that can be quite an expensive proposition, especially to a small provider practice.

2. The loss of productivity does occur as the staff and providers learn the new system and associated process changes in day-to-day operation.

3. There are many EHR products in the marketplace. Providers are faced with decision points on which vendor system to purchase and the degree of modules needed to successfully support the clinical work within that practice. In general, technical integration such as the uncertain quality of the system purchased, functionality issues, the lack of integration with other applications, and other similar issues can impact a smooth transition to EHRs and actually create more problems and cost than the existing process in place. In addition, incompatibility between systems (user interface, system architecture, and functionality) can vary between suppliers' products.

4. Certification, security, ethical matters, privacy, and confidentiality issues are still a high concern. The increased portability and accessibility of electronic medical records may increase the ease with which they can be accessed and stolen by unauthorized persons or unscrupulous users. Even today, large-scale breaches in confidential records occur, and others can easily happen when a more integrated connectivity exists between systems, providers, hospitals, and wireless devices. Continued concerns about security contributing to the widespread adoption of EHRs are still pervasive in the provider community. Still lingering is the privacy concern and the adequate protection of individual records being managed electronically. As an example, with an electronic record in a hospital setting, there can easily be over 100 individuals from doctors, nurses, technicians, admissions, quality control, billing staffing, and many more who have access to at least part of a patient's record during an average hospital stay. In addition, there are multiple individuals at payers, clearinghouses, research firms, and others that have access to patient information at any given time.

FEDERAL HEALTH IT STRATEGIC PLAN

On 25 March 2011, the Office of the National Coordinator for Health Information Technology (ONCHIT) released the Federal Health IT Strategic Plan for 2011–2015. There are five goals in the plan clearly tied to EHRs. Below is a summary of those elements related specifically to EHRs.

GOAL I: ACHIEVE ADOPTION AND INFORMATION EXCHANGE THROUGH THE MEANINGFUL USE OF HEALTH IT

A. Accelerate adoption of EHRs.
  1. Provide financial incentive payments for the adoption and meaningful use of certified EHR technology.
  2. Provide implementation support to health care providers to help them adopt, implement, and use certified EHR technology.
  3. Support the development of a trained workforce to implement and use health IT.
  4. Encourage the inclusion of Meaningful Use in professional certification and medical education.
  5. Establish criteria and a process to certify EHR technology that can support Meaningful Use criteria.
  6. Communicate the value of EHRs and the benefits of achieving Meaningful Use.
  7. Align federal programs and services with the adoption and meaningful use of certified EHR technology.
  8. Work with private sector payers and provider groups to encourage providers to achieve Meaningful Use.
  9. Encourage and facilitate improved usability of EHR technology.

B. Facilitate information exchange to support the meaningful use of EHRs.
   1. Foster business models that create health information exchange (HIE).
   2. Monitor HIE options and fill the gaps for providers that do not have viable options.
   3. Ensure that HIE takes place across individual exchange models and advance health systems and data interoperability.
C. Support health IT adoption and information exchange for public health and populations with unique needs.
   1. Ensure that public health agencies are able to receive and share information with providers using certified EHR technology.
   2. Track health disparities and promote health IT that reduces them.
   3. Support health IT adoption and information exchange in long-term/postacute, behavioral health, and emergency care settings.

GOAL II: IMPROVE CARE, IMPROVE POPULATION HEALTH, AND REDUCE HEALTH CARE COSTS THROUGH THE USE OF HEALTH IT

A. Support more sophisticated uses of EHRs and other health IT to improve health system performance.
   1. Identify and implement best practices that use EHRs and other health IT to improve care, efficiency, and population health.
   2. Create administrative efficiencies to reduce cost and burden for providers, payers, and government health programs.
B. Better manage care, efficiency, and population health through EHR-generated reporting measures.
   1. Identify specific measures that align with the National Health Care Quality Strategy and Plan.
   2. Establish standards, specifications, and certification criteria for collecting and reporting measures through certified EHR technology.
C. Demonstrate health IT–enabled reform of payment structures, clinical practices, and population health management.
D. Support new approaches to the use of health IT in research, public and population health, and national health security.
   1. Establish new approaches to and identify ways health IT can support national prevention, health promotion, public health, and national health security.
   2. Invest in health IT infrastructure to support the National Prevention and Health Promotion Strategy.
   3. Ensure a mechanism for information in support of research and the translation of research findings back into clinical practice.

GOAL III: INSPIRE CONFIDENCE AND TRUST IN HEALTH IT

A. Protect confidentiality, integrity, and availability of health information.
   1. Promulgate appropriate and enforceable federal policies to protect the privacy and security of health information.
   2. Enforce existing federal privacy and security laws and maintain consistency with federal confidentiality policy.

    3. Encourage the incorporation of privacy and security functionality into health IT.

    4. Identify health IT system security vulnerabilities and develop strategic solutions.

    5. Identify health IT privacy and security requirements and best practices, and communicate them through health IT programs.

B. Inform individuals of their rights and increase transparency regarding the uses of PHI.

    1. Inform individuals about their privacy and security rights and how their information may be used and shared.

    2. Increase transparency regarding the development of policies and standards related to uses and sharing of PHI.

    3. Require easy-to-understand reporting of breach notifications.

C. Improve safety and effectiveness of health IT.

GOAL IV: EMPOWER INDIVIDUALS WITH HEALTH IT TO IMPROVE THEIR HEALTH AND THE HEALTH CARE SYSTEM

A. Engage individuals with health IT.

B. Accelerate individual and caregiver access to their electronic health information in a format they can use and reuse.

    1. Through Medicare and Medicaid EHR Incentive Programs, encourage providers to give patients access to their health information in an electronic format.

C. Integrate patient-generated health information and consumer health IT with clinical applications to support patient-centered care.

    1. Support the development of standards and tools that make EHR technology capable of interacting with consumer health IT and build these requirements for the use of standards and tools into EHR certification.

    2. Solicit and integrate patient-generated health information into EHRs and quality measurements.

    3. Encourage the use of consumer health IT to move toward patient-centered care.

GOAL V: ACHIEVE RAPID LEARNING AND TECHNOLOGICAL ADVANCEMENT

It was interesting to note that ICD-10 was only mentioned once in the Federal Health IT Strategic Plan. The ICD-10 code sets would enable a more granular understanding of health care treatments and outcomes and more complete analyses of treatment costs, ultimately allowing for better disease management and more efficient health care delivery.

In summary, the Federal Health IT Strategic Plan merges Meaningful Use, certification, HIE, and the Institute of Medicine work on creating a learning health care system.

MEANINGFUL USE AND ITS IMPACT ON EHRS

The American Recovery and Reinvestment Act of 2009 (ARRA) introduced the "Meaningful Use" requirement for EHR systems with three main components: (1) the use of a certified EHR in a meaningful manner, such as e-prescribing; (2) the use of a certified EHR technology for electronic exchange of health information to improve quality of health care; and (3) the use of a certified EHR technology to submit clinical quality and other measures. Meaningful Use refers to a set of 15 criteria that medical providers must meet in order to prove that they are using their EHRs as an effective tool in their practice. There are also 10 additional criteria that are considered a la carte, from which only five need to be demonstrated by the medical provider. In total, 20 Meaningful Use criteria must be used within the EHR to qualify for stimulus payments during Stage One of the EHR incentive program. Each of the criteria was developed and further reviewed by the Office of the National Coordinator with public input.

The 15 core criteria required by the provider are (referenced in ARRA, Meaningful Use document) listed in the following table:

Demographics (50%)	Computerized physician order entry (CPOE; 30% including a medication)
Vitals—Blood pressure and body mass index (50%)	Drug–drug and drug–allergy interactions (functionality enabled)
Problem list ICD-9-CM or SNOWMED (80%)	Exchange critical information (perform test)
Active medication list (80%)	Security risk analysis
Smoking status (50%)	Report clinical quality—Blood pressure, body mass index, smoke plus three others
Patient clinical visit summary (50% within 3 days)	Medication allergies (80%)
Hospital discharge instructions (50%) or patient with electronic copy (50% within 3 days)	Clinical decision support (one rule)
e-Prescribing (80%)	

The additional 10 criteria, five of which must be selected, are (referenced in ARRA, Meaningful Use document) listed in the following table:

Drug-formulary checks (one report)	Feed immunization registries (perform at least one test)
Lab results (40%)	Hospital advance medical directives (50% for >65 years and older)
Patients by condition (one report)	Send reminders to patient for preventative and follow-up care (20% for >65 and <5 years)
Medication reconciliation (50%)	Patient electronic access to labs, problems, meds, and allergies (10% in 4 days)
Summary care record at transitions (50%)	Send patient-specific education (10%)

Meaningful Use will be measured in stages over 5 years. Each stage represents a level of adoption. Many certified EHRs will allow providers to complete all Meaningful Use criteria, whereas others will only certify what is required in the early stages and modify at a later date with any new criteria. The three stages are the following:

Stage One. Essentially, Stage One is using the major functionality of a certified EHR. This includes documenting set percentages of visits, diagnoses, prescriptions, immunizations, and other relevant health information electronically; using the clinical support tools (warnings and reminders that will be included in a certified EHR); and sharing patient information. Providers and hospitals must report quality measures and public health information. For providers, they must report on six clinical quality measures: three required core measures and three additional measures selected from a set of 38 clinical quality measures. Eligible hospitals and Critical Access Hospitals (CAHs) must report on all 15 of the clinical quality measures. Stage One is required in years 2011 and 2012.

Stage Two. In addition to continuing to use all functionality from Stage One, physicians will be required to use EHRs to send and receive information such as lab orders and results. Other criteria may be added. Stage Two is expected to be implemented in 2013 but has recently been postponed.

Stage Three. This stage will continue fulfilling the criteria from Stages One and Two and will include clinical decisions support for national high-priority conditions, e-mailing patients in a PHR, accessing comprehensive patient data, and improving population health. Stage Three criteria have not been developed to date, and the implementation is not expected until 2015.

Centers for Medicare and Medicaid Services (CMS) payment penalties for noncompliance to the Meaningful Use regulations will begin in 2016, with an initial 1% penalty that could escalate to 5% 5 years later. Therefore, with these criteria in place, we are likely to see virtually all hospitals' attempt to meet the Meaningful Use criteria to avoid penalty cost.

INCENTIVE PROGRAM FOR EHRs

Issued by the CMS, this final rule defines the minimum requirements that providers must meet through their use of certified EHR technology in order to qualify for payments. For Medicare, eligible professionals, eligible hospitals, and CAHs must successfully demonstrate meaningful use of certified EHR technology every year they participate in the program. For Medicaid, eligible professionals and eligible hospitals may qualify for incentive payments if they adopt, implement, upgrade, or demonstrate Meaningful Use in their first year of participation. They must also successfully demonstrate Meaningful Use for subsequent participation years.

STANDARDS AND CERTIFICATION CRITERIA FOR EHRs

Issued by the ONCHIT, this rule identifies the standards and certification criteria for the certification of EHR technology, so eligible professionals and hospitals may be assured that the systems they adopt are capable of performing the required functions. In addition, the American National Standards Institute (ANSI) has received approval from the Office of the National Coordinator to become the sole approved accreditor under its permanent EHR certification program, which will begin in 2012. They will verify EHRs to ensure that the EHRs are able to perform functions required by health care providers to meet the Meaningful Use requirement and qualify for the Medicare and Medicaid incentives.

BEACON COMMUNITY COOPERATIVE AGREEMENT PROGRAM

Through the ONCHIT, an innovative program called the Beacon Community Program was developed to accelerate and demonstrate the ability of health IT to support the local health care systems. The Beacon communities will receive $220 million in ARRA awards to help lay the groundwork for emerging health IT development. This funding was given to 17 selected communities throughout the United States that have already made inroads in the development of secure, private, and accurate systems of EHR adoption and HIE. The program will support these communities to build and strengthen their health IT infrastructure, including strong privacy and security measures for data exchange, which will improve care coordination, increase the quality, safety, efficiency, and population health care, and slow the growth of health care spending. The resulting experience will inform efforts throughout the United States to support the meaningful use of EHRs, the primary goal of the federal government's new health IT initiative [4].

REGIONAL EXTENSION CENTERS

Under the Health Information Technology for Economic and Clinical Health (HITECH) Act, as described in the previous chapter, Regional Extension Centers (RECs) will support and serve health care providers to help them quickly become adept and meaningful users of EHRs. The RECs will provide training and support services to assist doctors and other providers in adopting EHRs, offer information and guidance to help with EHR implementation, and provide technical assistance as needed. The goal of these centers is to provide outreach and support services to primary care providers in the next couple of years. The government via the RECs is encouraging providers to register for the incentive program and seek support as they adopt health IT.

The Extension Program will also establish a Health Information Technology Research Center (HITRC), funded separately, to gather relevant information on effective practices and help the regional centers collaborate with one another and with relevant stakeholders to identify and share best practices in EHR adoption, effective use, and provider support.

PERSONAL HEALTH RECORDS

The Healthcare Information and Management Systems Society (HIMSS) defines an electronic personal health record (ePHR) as follows (www.himss.org/phrs):

> An electronic Personal Health Record ("ePHR") is a universally accessible, layperson comprehensible, lifelong tool for managing relevant health information, promoting health maintenance and assisting with chronic disease management via an interactive, common data set of electronic health information and e-health tools. The ePHR is owned, managed, and shared by the individual or his or her legal proxy(s) and must be secure to protect the privacy and confidentiality of the health information it contains. It is not a legal record unless so defined and is subject to various legal limitations.

As stated, a PHR is a health record that is initiated and maintained by an individual, that is, the patient. This record would include a complete summary of the health and medical history including allergies and adverse drug reactions, listing of chronic diseases, family history, illnesses and hospitalizations, imaging reports, immunization records, laboratory test results, medications and dosing, including over-the-counter medications, surgeries, and other procedures, vaccinations, and other information of the individual by the individual gathering and inputting data from many sources. It is important to note that PHRs that are not part of a provider's EHR are not considered to be legal records and, therefore, are not covered entities under the Health Insurance Portability and Accountability Act of 1996 (HIPAA). In addition, PHRs and EHRs are not the same. There is no legal mandate that compels a consumer or patient to store her personal health information in a PHR, like a provider is required with an EHR.

PHRs are not easy to define. The highly fragmented technology can consist of a stand-alone, personal computer (PC)-based system in which a patient inputs his/her medical history, or it can consist of a Web-based system that allows people to set up personal accounts and pull data from other applications and information sources. Revolution Health (defunct), Google Health (defunct), Microsoft HealthVault, WebMD, Keas.com, No More Clipboard, and other products in the market provide PHR capabilities and services. Most personal health information is recorded and stored in personal computer-based software that may have the capability to print, backup, encrypt, and import data from other sources. This software could provide sophisticated features such as data encryption, data importation, and data sharing with health care providers and is subject to physical loss and damage of the personal computer.

PHRs can be beneficial in improving interactions with patients and provide appeal to patients, because they promise individuals greater control over their personal medical data and the potential of protecting and promoting public health. However, ever since they emerged to the public a decade ago, by most accounts, there is no widespread public acceptance, adoption, and usage. The challenge is still the integration with EHR technology, burdens on cost and/or time, and the perceived added value to the practice of medicine. In addition, industry executives say a number of shortcomings have discouraged adoption, such as PHRs tend to lack interactive features that would make them more compelling, such as the ability to schedule appointments or contact doctors. The number of online records also inhibits usage. Finally, the modest growth of EHRs limits the amount of data a PHR can draw on. As stated by Jason Fortin, Senior Research Analyst at the CSC's Emerging Practices Group, "With a robust EHR, there is no way to feed a PHR." These findings come at a time when other technologies such as EHRs, mobile health devices, e-prescriptions, and other technologies are seeing accelerated rates of adoption as health care delivery organizations implement systems to manage patient data.

However, prospects might be brightening. The federal government has had an early stake in PHRs. The Veterans Affairs Department (VA) started dabbling with them as early as 2003, with its My HealtheVet Program. The CMS launched its first PHR pilot program in 2006. This program and associated tools were available through the Internet, enabling individuals to track their health care services and better communicate with their providers. The type of PHR CMS has been testing is populated with health information from Medicare claims data. In the future, these records may be able to get information from a provider's EHR system directly and immediately.

The DoD is rolling out a global EHR program that will be used by its providers in its medical centers and will allow access by VA with bidirectional HIE in real time. The multiagency Blue Button initiative announced by President Barack Obama in August 2010 (www.va.gov/bluebutton) offers users the ability to download electronic information via My HealtheVet and CMS' MyMedicare.gov. In addition, the Department of Health and Human Services (DHHS) Direct Project promises easier data exchanges among providers and record applications that could boost PHR usage. PHRs might also get a lift from the government's Meaningful Use program, which offers financial incentives for doctors and other medical providers to adopt EHRs. Stage Two, set to begin in 2013, will challenge providers to expand patients' access to health records.

A report entitled "Vendor Assessment: When Will PHR Platforms Gain Consumer Acceptance?" was based on an online survey of 1200 consumers between 18 and 23 February 2011 to gauge their interest in PHRs and to compare the numbers with a similar report conducted in 2006. Published last month, the survey found that widespread consumer adoption of PHRs remains elusive despite numerous PHR options offered by providers, health plans, and employers as well as third-party vendors such as Dossia and Microsoft HealthVault.

In addition, according to the IDC Health Insights' survey, only 7% of the respondents in 2011 reported ever having used a PHR, and less than half of these respondents (47.6%) are still using one to manage their family's health. Furthermore, the majority of respondents (50.6%) said the reason that they had not used the online technology was that they were not familiar with the concept of a PHR. These results were similar to a 2006 IDC Health Insights study that showed that approximately 7% of respondents indicated that they used a PC- or Web-based PHR, and a little more than half (51.9%) were unaware of PHRs.

WIRELESS CONNECTIVITY MODALITIES

Mobile and wireless technologies are playing a vital role in the health care industry and will be a driving force behind EHR adoption. From bedside patient care and medication administration, check-in/out applications, chronic pain management, medical diagnostic device monitoring, and medical management to laboratory management, records management, and telehealth, the opportunities for mobile solutions are far reaching. Moreover, patient safety concerns and a plethora of compliance mandates act as viable investment drivers. As a result, health care organizations—hospitals, clinics, home health care, free-standing facilities, emergency rooms, providers, long-term health care facilities, and others—are increasing their mobile computing and communication devices now and more so in the future. These wireless products lend themselves to improved workforce productivity, reduced overhead and associated operating cost, increased efficiency and accuracy, and quick distribution of critical client and process information. In the United States, the usage of EHRs is projected to dramatically increase in the next couple of years due to the ARRA. Ultimately, this can and will project a significant savings to many health care facilities. However, one of the key issues to date is that many current EHR solutions lack the next-generation user interface technologies such as multi-touch and gesturing and continue to rely almost exclusively on image scanning and typing for data capture.

Growing emphasis has been placed on tablet/iPad solutions from Blackberry's Research in Motion (RIM), General Electric, Apple, and others. These devices are purpose-built for health care settings (rugged and disinfectable design). Although the capabilities and form factors of many consumer-oriented mobile devices are appealing to health care end users, many fall short in supporting full-shift applications or are designed to withstand the potentially inclement conditions of health care environments. Reported by CNBC Reporter Berta Coombs in her March 23, 2011 article entitled "The iPad Is Tops with Doctors," she said "Analysts at Chilmark Research estimate 22 percent of doctors in the U.S. were using iPads by the end of 2010. In February, four out of five doctors surveyed by the health marketing company Aptilon said they planned to buy an iPad this year." "For doctors who will have to input much of that data, a lightweight, portable table that can be used at a patient's bedside fits the bill."

However, one of the biggest questions hanging over the adoption of tablets for health care is what the Food and Drug Administration (FDA) Medical Device Data Systems (MDDS) regulations affecting health care providers will do about apps used in patient care, as well as using features like the camera on the iPad2 for diagnostic purposes. By May 18, 2011, a provider must register their MDDS with the FDA. If the system qualifies as an MDDS, compliance to the regulations must be completed by February 18, 2012. If compliance is not attained, the provider could be subject to financial penalties. The biggest question is, if an error is introduced because of a software mistake, how do providers make sure that it is reported and where is the oversight? So far, the FDA has cleared a handful of apps for the iPhone and iPad for remote monitoring and radiology.

Mobile and wireless developments in the health care industry are not only improving patient safety but are also maximizing the efficiency and reliability of health care professionals. The advancements in mobile and wireless technologies and underlying health care information infrastructure continue to facilitate enhanced care in a timely manner.

The scope of wireless and/or mobile computing is expanding daily. As an example, the use of wireless-enabled devices is happening in hospitals across the country and according to a report from ABI Research, "this multibillion-dollar market is poised for even faster growth as more and more medical equipment is shipped Wi-Fi-enabled" (www.cnbc.com). Everyone securing wireless technology needs to be aware of the wireless architecture, wireless standards, special security needs for wireless devices, growing range of application choices, and the unique support and maintenance requirements needed to support the wireless systems and users. The use of wireless in hospitals, clinics, provider offices, free-standing facilities, long-term care, and even home care is becoming well established. Each of these health care entities is seeing the immediate benefits and results that wireless offers, which can include improved clinical decision making, strengthening the continuity of care that patients receive from alternative or remote sites or other providers, accessing medical records or diagnostic tests, checking for adverse events, and others. However, with all the benefits from wireless technology comes the need to further address the issues of privacy and security. Becoming more knowledgeable about privacy and security risks, balanced with an understanding of the effective benefits of the wireless systems development, is essential before a health care organization takes any major steps forward toward acquiring and implementing wireless solutions.

Wireless communications fall into two categories: (1) wireless voice such as cordless/cellular telephones and mobile phones and (2) wireless data such as cellular digital packet data and wireless local area networks (WLAN). As good as today's wireless capabilities are, tomorrow, these wireless products will be obsolete and another generation will appear. The biggest question is not whether wireless is here to stay but, rather, the extent to which we have the foresight to fully exploit it while preserving the privacy and security of the individual's health information.

Most technology tools available to physicians today are complicated and cumbersome and do not fit easily into the patient and staff workflow process. New generations of technologies are coming out, are more readily being used by hospitals and providers, are changing the way they practice medicine, and are improving practice efficiency and accuracy. For example, physicians today can acquire a mobile practice companion or PDA device that offers immediate and secure access to critical clinical information no matter where or when physicians need it to assist with patient care. Coordinating care for complex public health issues or emergency situations requires collaborative planning and defined protocols of communication and information. The wireless handheld device has become the crucial tool linking care teams, again regardless of location. Clinical reminders and health alerts can be streamed in real time over a wireless application to keep providers well-informed about any care technique.

VA has been leading the way with virtual visits and remote patient monitoring, which could save the U.S. health care system billions of dollars, especially if it is used to manage patients with chronic diseases.

Linking the wireless to the organization's main computer system can yield the following benefits:

1. Convenient access to patient data
2. Accurate and timely entry of data
3. More efficient utilization of provider time
4. Reduced medical errors
5. Elimination of duplicate data entry
6. Improved patient care
7. Decreased cost
8. Improved workflow
9. Decreased patient and clinician wait times
10. Saving of time and cost—as an example, if a doctor can check a patient's vitals via his BlackBerry, he can avoid bringing the patient in to do the exact same thing

Why do providers and hospitals want to use wireless technology? There are several drivers:

1. Need for faster, decentralized decision making
2. Need to be closer to beneficiary population
3. Increased responsiveness to beneficiary service needs
4. Need for real-time medical decision making
5. Ability to collaborate with patients in real time, search, publish/subscribe, or even obtain personal information
6. Need to decrease medical errors
7. Need for bedside standardized protocol
8. Increase industry pressure for better data quality and efficiency

High-speed Internet and portal technologies will be accessed by computers, wireless devices, and telephones using voice recognition and speech synthesis applications. This process has already started and will continue to evolve as mobile computing vendors provide deeper and broader functionality.

IMPLEMENTING WIRELESS TECHNOLOGY

During implementation and utilization, security issues and concerns must remain visible and must be addressed as to how the device will maintain the security integrity for the provider's office or the hospital enterprise. As hospitals and providers elect to use mobile devices, they should consider the following suggestions:

1. Standardize wireless devices and application solutions whenever possible.
2. Maintain a comprehensive security protocol.

3. Enable connectivity to the intranet and legacy systems.
4. Deploy wireless systems management tools in the beginning.
5. Begin to build key skills prior to deployment.
6. Document procedures for testing and designing of the wireless infrastructure and applications.
7. Ensure that a help desk or assigned IT person can respond to wireless questions.
8. Implement a very detailed and required personnel training program for all staff to help them transition to the wireless concept and understand the security and privacy implications.

In preparing for the implementation of wireless computing, each provider's office, hospital system, or other health care entity need to properly plan what they will need for now and the immediate future. It is not only purchasing the wireless service and connectivity; it is looking at the way we need to change the existing business process to more adequately accommodate the wireless capabilities. Vendors should be interviewed to determine their capabilities and support to the provider's office or hospital system. In addition, each facility should conduct a detailed on-site analysis of critical physical and clinical problems to determine if wireless computing offers the right answers, and most importantly, data need to be secured internally and externally regardless of when, where, or how they are created, stored, processed, or transmitted.

EXAMPLES OF WIRELESS BEING USED

A well-demonstrated example of wireless capabilities is seen within the DoD. The U.S. military's tactical EHRs applications could become available using mobile device applications such as the iPad, iPod touch, iPhone, and other modalities. The testing comes as part of several projects being run by medical commands in Afghanistan and Iraq involving their hands-free EHR Pilot and the Tele-behavioral health initiative.

Another example is the Post-Traumatic Stress Disorder (PTSD) Coach. This application can help users learn about and manage symptoms that commonly occur after trauma. Any data created by the user of this app are only as secure as the phone/device itself. Users are free to share data, but as the self-monitoring data belong to each user, HIPAA concerns do not apply while the data are stored or shared. If the user were to transmit or share data with a health care provider, the provider must then comply with HIPAA rules.

The VA developed the Blue Button capability, which allows VA patients to download their personal health information through their VA MyHealtheVet account to share with medical providers. A complementary application was created, which gives veterans the ability to access their personal EHRs stored in MyHealtheVet on their mobile device.

This application is currently available on both Apple's iOS and Google's Android platform. The application allows veterans to view their personal information and medications at the touch of a button.

As the process to convert and integrate EMRs to mobile devices begins, the CMIO magazine stated a few expectations from providers in several of their articles. The author of the January 3, 2011 article entitled "Mobile Devices: EMR Integration Is Beginning," Jeff Byer said, "About 72 percent of the U.S. physicians are currently using smartphones—up from 2009's 64 percent—and the percentage should reach 81 percent by 2012, according to Manhattan Research's 2010 'Taking Pulse' report. No wonder a no-holds, all-out war among vendors is on in the mobile technology market space. The prize: clinicians' workflow—and thus purchasing—loyalty."

In another CMIO magazine article, the following comments were made. Mobile devices may work well for consultation but are too small to be used for routine primary diagnosis. Security and calibration issues remain unsettled, and the FDA has not yet decided how to handle these devices, David Hirschorn, MD, said on November 29, 2010 during a presentation at the 96th Annual Meeting of the Radiological Society of North America. Because the iPhone and iTouch are net-enabled, "there is a world of potential for their use. But, how do you know whether your device is operating within the correct parameters and that it is OK to use?" Hirschorn asked. In addition, the agency said that the mobile devices raise safety and effectiveness questions and must undergo a more in-depth premarket approval (PMA) process in order to gain market clearance to be used effectively for diagnostic purposes. To appropriately diagnose a chest X-ray or bone work, a display screen size of 20 in. is necessary. "Anything less than that [is] like a postage stamp," says Hirschorn. "There is just not enough real estate to work with." The iPod is only 3.5 inches, while the iPad is 9.7 inches, not significant enough in size to ensure a proper clinical diagnosis, he noted (www.cio.net, EMR Integration Is Just the Beginning).

In the same article, Henry J. Feldman, MD, chief information architect, Division of Clinical Informatics at Harvard Medical Faculty Physicians, and a hospitalist with the Division of General Internal Medicine at Beth Israel Deaconess Medical Center (BIDMC) at Harvard Medical School in Boston says he uses an internally built, Web-based EMR platform from his iPad to engage patients at the bedside via devices such as electronic anatomy textbooks to show and compare reference images to a patient's X-ray. As a hospitalist, Feldman appreciates that the technology allows him to become familiar with patients within minutes by accessing records quickly. Feldman typically writes 85% of an admission note on a desktop computer because "iPads aren't great for writing big documents," he says. However, the other 15% of input is done on iPads because it is easy to clarify the patient's story/history and reconcile data on the iPad at the bedside.

Finally again, in this same article, Andrew Barbash, MD, medical director of neurosciences and virtual care services at Holy Cross Hospital, Silver Spring, says "Practitioners must make sure their EHR applications are flexible enough to be pushed out to any mobile devices. It's best to assume clinicians will be able to pick whatever mobile device they need moving forward with clinical care, but what they will be able to do on that EMR is dependent upon how that EMR is structured and whether it was created specifically for someone to interact with it in a mobile manner" [personal communication].

KIOSK

A kiosk is basically a computer that is set up in a public area so that patients can access or input information. Most medical kiosks in hospital or clinic settings provide HIPAA-compliant security and privacy for clinically accurate blood pressure, heart rate and weight, health risk assessment measurements, and a PHR management system that keeps all of your health information secure, organized, and readily accessible.

In addition to the diagnostic capabilities, most medical kiosks provide a variety of authentication techniques (including biometrics) to ensure data privacy, security, and integrity. Security can include any combination of authentication including a magnetic stripe card, at least a four-digit PIN, thumbprint, photo ID, and signature. Any data captured at the medical kiosk including demographics, medical history, personal health information, and vital signs can be archived to any PHR system.

According to most hospitals, all information is maintained in a secure environment that meets or exceeds all applicable HIPAA standards for data security and privacy. Their architecture provides a robust, scalable, enterprise-class architecture for centralizing application development, Web services (SOAP or XML over HTTPS), and deep integration with existing administrative and clinical systems. The result is the ability to leverage existing skill sets and applications within and beyond the client organization, to receive maximum functionality, value, and return on investment for the kiosk vendor.

Some clinicians may have serious privacy concerns with a patient filling out information in a public setting, but can simply put up a visual barrier so that others cannot see the computer screen or simply place the kiosk in a separate room. Most information accessed from their health record through the kiosk will have all of the associate security precautions in place—a personal identification number or password will be used to log into the kiosk and another access number will be used to log into your medical records, and a timed sequence will occur that will automatically disconnect the access if not used in a pre-established timeframe. Some systems offer an electronic privacy curtain providing for discrete encounters at the device. The FDA mandates that, if private health information or engagement with a medical professional is to occur from a device in a public place, a privacy measure is mandatory.

Paul Craig provides a slightly different picture by stating that kiosks do not provide the safety and security they are supposed to. He stated and then demonstrated how easily he could subvert the security of different kiosks by being able to get a command shell, install arbitrary software, and change security settings.*

In addition, because of the large and embarrassing leak of state department documents by WiKiLeaks, this has recharged the debate over EHRs, raising concerns that the government may not be capable of safeguarding America's most intimate health information. What WiKiLeaks shows is how security information is all about the integrity of individuals. Once you have the information of any kind in electronic format, it is easy to take, access, share, and download.

SECURITY AND PRIVACY WITH EHRS, PHRS, AND WIRELESS MODALITIES

Providers and hospitals have a legal, moral, and ethical duty to protect all clinical and research information by ensuring that security and privacy safeguards are in place. A higher degree of control is necessary to prevent unauthorized access to especially sensitive information. All health care entities, especially those involved in high-risk groups need to assess whether electronic systems include features and functionality that may increase risk of inappropriate use and disclosures or offer additional layers of protections for sensitive information. Highly sensitive health data involve certain conditions, tests, and records of vulnerable or high-profile patients and minors. Implementing security features for such categories can present challenges in EHRs because specific functionality may not be present in all systems or be fully evolved.

Consistent and reliable methods for authenticating patient identity and link patients to their records warrant specialty security because they are essential to delivering quality care and improving patient safety. There is great variability and incompatibility of patient identification systems in health care facilities, making it difficult to uniquely identify patients within one facility or between entities. A system of identifying patients between entities must exist for interoperability to occur. Safeguarding patient information is critical to preventing identify theft, medical identity theft, fraud, and abuse and may be addressed through improved physical and logical access control systems and constant vigilance. All providers of care should require strict policies and procedures governing the use of physical media and portable devices to prevent loss or theft.

Special circumstances may arise in which patient identification or access to patient records may require anonymity or special precautions, such as in the case of celebrity or high-profile individuals, workplace privacy, domestic violence, child or vulnerable adult abuse, litigation, organ donors, and prisoners. EHRs should have the capability to use a "record hold" de-identification mechanism, access restriction, or alias to afford greater protection. In addition, special protection needs to be offered to patients with mental health disorders, HIV/AIDs and sexually transmitted diseases, substance abuse, and chemical dependency, and other similar types of diagnosis. Organizations must have the ability to segregate any records related to these treatments, especially as these treatments can and will encompass multiple medical specialties and multiple access points. EHR systems require continued development of functionality to manage security, add levels of security, block access to specific notes or lab results, track versioning, and mask sensitive entries for release of information.

---

* Ducklin, P., Internet kiosks harmful to your health. *Naked Security*, November 27, 2010. Available at http://nakedsecurity.com/2010/11/27/kiosksharmful-to-health/

As a separate issue, there is still controversy surrounding procedures, surgeries, and tests related to abortion, family planning, genetic testing, and cosmetic surgery. These services and procedures can relate to personal and religious beliefs and can impact insurance qualifications (health or life), employment discrimination, and any public figure image.

Consideration should be given to enabling core security features such as role-based access, passwords, and audit trails as well as aliases or alternative account numbers for those undergoing special procedures or tests.

In addition, issues of consent and custody may require the unique handling of health information if the patient is unable to consent to disclosures either permanently or temporarily due to health or legal status. Examples would include wards of state, incapacitated or incompetent individuals, inmates or detainees, minors, minors in a custody conflict, and parties involved in adoptions. Records of the deceased are also included in this category.

Data generated, collected, and reported in support of clinical trials by a clinical investigator at an investigative site are source data. This information can be found in progress notes, patient diaries, orders, EKGs, X-ray and lab results, and other ancillary test results that are part of a medical record. Analysis of the data by the clinical investigator and study sponsor may lead to decisions about specific treatment. These data elements, when captured and stored electronically, are subject to the FDA rules, specifically 21 CFR Part 11, which outlines security and electronic signature requirements for research records and research source documentation (www.fda.gov). In addition to the typical audit trails and role-based access, each organization should employ technical security features that identify, protect, and authenticate research records.

Several other helpful considerations for protecting data are

1. Limit access and provide screening controls to only those staff working directly with the patient or those with administrative responsibilities (such as risk management or legal).
2. Use a unique user identification to reliably maintain an audit trail navigation and documentation. This should include activities related to document viewing, manual printing, addendums, retract or restored documents, follow-up requests, and document creation along with date and time stamps.
3. Use of an EHR system that can map a record to a scanned copy of a release, power of attorney, or other legal documents.
4. Moving of a medical record into a "restricted area" when there is a sentinel event or other pending legal processes. This will immediately lock down access and restrict personnel from any reviews.

All providers and hospitals, entrusted with the protection of data, must ensure that a given EHR system includes functionality that will enable the organization to meet its regulatory and operational requirements. These individuals should identify security features that offer higher degrees of protection to protect sensitive patient information. Even when selecting an electronic system, organizations must evaluate the system independently and systematically and not rely on the vendor's interpretation of system functionality. If the system of choice requires implementation of additional security measures, the organization must determine if it will be able to do so without risking the security of, or access to, the data. Approaching system selection from the perspective of the regulatory and operational impact will no doubt prove invaluable in its future use to both the organization and the individuals whose information it contains.

SUMMARY

Both the providers and hospitals should partner with their IT counterparts and build a relationship of trust and teamwork, as both areas of expertise must join forces toward achieving the common goal of improving patient care through technology that includes all aspects of privacy and security protection. EHRs, PHRs, and a multitude of mobile devices will be used more readily in the near future as vendors adapt their technology, security, and capabilities to accommodate the health care marketplace. Its ease of use, its ability to quickly connect to apps, clinical patient data, and/or to record information at a remote site or bedside will give the provider a tool to better manage his patients and their associated outcomes.

There is a Presidential directive to have EHRs throughout the clinical environment for both the private and public sector facilities. Patients seem to be more eager to be involved in their health care status and treatment. Vendors are listening to the provider and hospital community and are adapting their systems and mobile devices to accommodate the provider's day-to-day operation. There is no question that a couple of years from now, this technology will be far more advanced than today, that patient's treatments and outcomes will dramatically improve, and that providers will rely on the electronic capabilities of multiple devices more heavily than they ever have.

CASE MODEL 11.1: MOUNTAIN MEDICAL CENTER'S EXPERIENCE WITH A COMPUTERIZED PHYSICIAN ORDER ENTRY SYSTEM

Mountain Medical Center is a 200-bed hospital in a large city in the Intermountain West area. In a discussion with a vendor representative of XYZ Solutions at the Hospital Quality of Care conference, the CEO and the CFO of Mountain Medical Center discussed their desire to improve quality of care at their hospital because medication error rates were increasing, including several recent deaths. The vendor suggested the XYZ Solutions system of registration, billing, and computerized physician order entry (CPOE) as a mechanism to capture medication errors before patients are affected. Desperate for a solution and anxious to join the technology bandwagon, the hospital scheduled a demonstration of the system at the hospital site. Impressed by the ease of use and functionality of the system, the hospital entered into negotiations for pricing. The final initial investment in the client-server system for hardware, software, training, and other CPOE implementation functions was determined to be $4,200,000. Although this investment was a sizeable portion of the total budget, the management staff remained committed to improving quality of care and, consequently, launched the project.

Various committees were set up to help with development and implementation. One group was a physician executive committee, brought together to obtain physician input into the functionality of the system. Nurses were represented by a separate committee. Along with the management team, these committees guided the selection of customized functions with the hope of streamlining workflows. After about a year of development and functionality testing, the system was nearly ready to "go live." Training on the system took place during an intensive 3-week period, after which it was mandated that the system be used for nearly all orders. The first week of system use went as planned, acknowledging the expected learning curve; but soon after, doctors and nurses began complaining that the system was difficult to use, and required going through two or three screens just to order a single drug. The response time was also slow, sometimes taking 5–10 s between screens. In addition, some orders would get lost in the system or inadvertently go to the wrong department. Frustration with the system was heard throughout the hospital, including concerns about patient safety and diminished time for patient care due to the excess time needed to enter orders. On knowing such problems, the vendor explained that the system was only in place at one other institution and that some features were not as yet field tested. As a result of these issues, Mountain Medical Center decided to pull the plug on the system 2 months after the go-live date.

The institution is now considering re-installing a similar system. During a meeting of the CEO, CFO, CIO, and several physician representatives, the next implementation will make the following changes:

- A workflow analysis will be done to see if any work processes can be made more efficient and error free, even before computerization, such as making sure anyone given a diagnostic test can be matched directly to an order. In the present system, sometimes patients would go for a test prior to the actual entry of the order, making patient–order matching difficult.
- The organization will provide a request for information to multiple vendors to create a vendor "short list." Vendors on the short list will demonstrate the systems to a wide variety of stakeholders including nurses, physicians, clerical personnel, and management.
- A "rapid prototyping" method of system development will be used rather than the previous linear, sequential model of development. Physicians, nurses, and other personnel will test system features in the early phases of development. Feedback can be incorporated into new modifications. This process can have several iterations before the "go-live" date.
- A longer period of training will take place, once again incorporating feedback.
- Management will be in continual close communication with stakeholders throughout system development and implementation.
- The team will look into implementation using a smaller budget (about $3 million) for the system.

KEY ISSUES:

Although the Mountain Medical Center realizes that there are no guarantees about the next implementation, the institution was able to take lessons learned and boldly keep their commitment to quality care and consider new solutions.

1. What pros and cons are likely to be encountered in implementing the following parts of the proposed new system implementation:
   - Technological issues?
   - Vendor selection issues?
   - Workflow change?
   - Organizational issues?
   - Cultural issues?
   - Project management issues?
   - Financial issues?
2. What additional areas need attention in order to prevent another unsuccessful implementation? How should those areas be handled?
3. What problems will the team face in attempting to meet their goals despite the smaller proposed budget?

CHECKLIST 1: Health IT Strategic Management Planning	Yes	No
Does your strategic plan call for an increase in attention to information technology, including a budgetary increase?	o	o
Are there plans in place to look into workflow improvements in preparation for automation?	o	o

	Yes	No
Is the rest of the management team on board with the technology component of the strategic vision?	o	o
Are there plans in place that will guide the organization in a build vs. buy decision?	o	o
Would further planning using outside resources as guidance be helpful for strategic planning?	o	o
Have methods to determine ROI of the system been put into place?	o	o
Does the team realize that ROI is a long-term rather than a short-term issue?	o	o
Would it help the process if key employees had parts of their bonuses tied into the successful implementation of the system?	o	o

CHECKLIST 2: Health IT Vendor Selection	Yes	No
Do the vendors have at least five to 10 existing clients?	o	o
Do the vendors have multiple medical informaticists that specialize in the applications being considered?	o	o
Is the vendor willing to negotiate a fair price?	o	o
Does the vendor permit contact of clients to verify satisfaction with the vendor?	o	o
Are the clients satisfied overall?	o	o
Are multiple stakeholders involved in the process of vendor selection?	o	o
Is the vendor willing to work within the strategic vision of the institution?	o	o

CHECKLIST 3: Organizational and Institutional Cultural Issues	Yes	No
Are plans in place to make clinicians (nurses, physicians) intimately involved with all parts of the process?	o	o
Are there any monetary or other incentives for clinicians to use the system?	o	o
Have new work processes been set in place to accommodate the new system?	o	o
Are these new work processes more efficient than the replaced processes?	o	o
Are super users involved to give help to peers when necessary?	o	o
Is there ongoing communication between management and other stakeholders concerning strategic goals involving the system?	o	o

CHECKLIST 4: Hospital Information System Administrative Functions	Yes	No
Can the existing hospital information system perform the following functions?		
Admission scheduling	o	o
Accounts payable and receivable	o	o
Patient and payer billing	o	o
Patient demographic information such as name, unique identifier, age, gender, reason for admission, and other data items	o	o
Staffing and staff scheduling	o	o
Pharmacy inventory	o	o
Internal finance, budgeting, and accounting	o	o
Patient census	o	o
Facility maintenance	o	o

CHECKLIST 5: Hospital Information System Clinical Functions	Yes	No
Are pharmacy information systems in place that include bar coding and drug interaction checking?	o	o
Does your computerized physician order entry (CPOE) system allow clinicians to directly order tests and treatments online?	o	o
If so, can these CPOE systems also be checked for selected appropriateness of care parameters?	o	o
Can other departmental information systems, such as laboratory information systems, radiology systems, and intensive care systems also be checked for clinical care appropriateness computing?	o	o
Are electronic medical records (EMRs) in place that allow physician orders, free text clinical notes, decision support, radiology images, and other areas to be nearly fully computerized, allowing a "paperless" medical institution?	o	o
Do EMRs allow secure password protection at multiple levels to ensure that access to personal health information (PHI) is restricted to those who need the information at that time?	o	o
Do EMRs allow appropriate encryption of data that is essential for transmission between systems in order to prevent data interception?	o	o

CHECKLIST 6: Clinical Guideline Implementation Functions	Yes	No
Do existing clinical guidelines implement the following functions?		
Point-of-care (POC) utility	o	o
Benchmarking and clinical performance tracking	o	o
Online electronic alerts	o	o
Regulatory rule changes reporting	o	o

ACKNOWLEDGMENT

To Richard Mata, MD, MS-MI, MS-CIS, for his technical assistance in the preparation of this chapter.

APPENDIX: DISASTER RECOVERY PLANNING*

Disaster recovery planning is the process of assessing risks that an organization faces, then developing procedures that enable it to return to normal operations as quickly as possible and minimize economic loss after a disaster. A small firm will have fewer resources, and may outsource this service.

No off-the-shelf disaster recovery plan can possibly meet the needs of all organizations.

An effective plan must account for an organization's size and other defining characteristics.

Understanding the basic principles of disaster recovery planning can keep team members from getting lost in the long process of developing a solid plan for their organization. As the team is assembled, all members should be briefed on the basic planning principles and the eight steps of developing a plan.

The disaster recovery function consists of the people, departments, and support organizations that implement the disaster recovery plan and facilitate recovery. How the function is organized

---

* From NIST SP 800-30; see http://csrc.nist.gov.

depends on the geographical dispersal of facilities, the type of facilities occupied, the number of employees, and other factors.

The first step in developing a disaster recovery plan is to establish a well-rounded team that represents all the functions of an organization. Next, the organization develops a business impact analysis to assess its risks, then establishes roles that each department, business partner, and outside service agency play in the plan. The organization then develops and documents disaster recovery policies and procedures.

After documenting policies and procedures, the organization implements its disaster recovery plan. During this step, the final plan is distributed to all departments, organizations, and employees involved in disaster response and recovery. Next, the plan must be tested and rehearsed, and eventually the organization should run a live simulation of a disaster.

The final step in disaster recovery planning is the maintenance phase, which includes continual assessment of new threats, adjustments for organizational changes, and determining the impact of new technology on recovery procedures.

Most organizations rely heavily on their computer systems and communications networks. Thus, the IT and network management staff have essential roles in disaster recovery planning and response as well as the database administrator.

One of the greatest frustrations for disaster recovery planners is the difficulty of gaining and maintaining support from upper-level managers. Executives need to be trained in disaster recovery planning and regularly briefed on the progress of the plan.

The disaster recovery planning coordinator should represent all corporate concerns for the plan and balance various department perspectives. The coordinator needs to be detail oriented without getting lost in the process, and be able to work diplomatically with all departments and external resources. In addition to the documents that the planning coordinator keeps, a team member needs to keep current logs of disaster recovery planning activities.

Every department in the organization needs to be represented on the disaster recovery planning team. Each department should have two representatives—a primary and an alternate. The primary department representative is a full member of the planning team, and the alternate department representative is a secondary member. The primary and alternate representatives are also co-leaders of their department's internal disaster recovery planning efforts.

To help determine the skills of planning team members, the coordinator should compile an inventory of their background and training. A skills inventory includes a list of corporate team members and those in departmental planning groups, along with an assessment of each team member's skills. The inventory should point out which employee skills are most helpful in disaster recovery planning, and which team members have prior experience in managing such plans. This information should be available to everyone on the team.

The major obstacle to disaster recovery training is getting all the team members together at one time and getting them to focus on the topic. Formal training sessions should be conducted away from organization facilities. Hotels and meeting centers are readily available and are not expensive.

The goal of an awareness campaign is to inform all the employees in an enterprise about the disaster recovery planning effort. The biggest obstacles to an effective awareness campaign are adequate funding and experienced communications staff to work on the campaign. Of course, the funding required for a successful campaign depends on the organization's size and geographical characteristics.

Organizations use one of two major models to establish a disaster recovery function—a centralized office or a part-time coordinator. Some organizations use a centralized office of disaster recovery planning, while others place the function in another department. The centralized office model requires a higher budget than a part-time planning coordinator. Regardless of the office structure for disaster recovery planning, salaries are usually the most expensive item in the budget.

When developing a disaster recovery plan, the team must recognize that organizations in many industries are required by law to have specific procedures in place. Managers often have trouble interpreting what action or standard a regulation requires, so an organization's legal counsel must research and interpret these requirements. Disaster recovery planners need the same type of legal assistance.

Once the planning team has completed all the tasks for organizing its disaster recovery plan, it should be ready to move to assessing risks in the enterprise.

REFERENCES

1. Office of the National Coordinator for Health Information Technology. Federal Health IT Strategic Plan, 2011–2015. http://www.healthit.hhs.gov.
2. The benefits of an Internet-based personal health record versus a paper-based personal health record is expected to grow rapidly within the next three years. Interview with CEO, Glen Tullman of Allscripts.
3. Rampersad, S., and Martin, L. 2011. Ending the paper chase in the operating room. In: Leading the Lean Healthcare Journal, edited by Wellman, J. and Hagan, P. New York: Productivity Press.
4. Ashish, K.J., DesRoches, C.M., Campbell, E.G., Donelan, K., Rao, S.R., Ferris, T.G., Shields, A., Rosenbaum, S., and Blumenthal, D. 2009. Use of electronic health records in U.S. hospitals. *New England Journal of Medicine* 360: 1628–1638. April 16, 2009.

FURTHER READING

CMS EHR Meaningful Use Overview, June 14, 2010.

Coombs, B., 2011. The iPad is Tops with Doctors, http://www.cnbc.com/id/42218296, March 23, 2011.

Doctors Say Electronic Health Record Goals are unrealistic.

Duclin, P., http://nakedsecurity.sophos.com/2010/11/27/kiosks-harmful-to-health, November 27, 2010.

EHR Meaningful Use Criteria.

Electronic Health Records, the New e-Security Worry, http://www.case.edu/magazine/springsummer2009/healthrecords.html.

Emerging Technologies.

Enrado, P. The Health Record Review, April 5, 2010.

Federal Health IT Strategic Plan, 2011–2015.

Groen, P. and Wine, M. Wireless Strategies for Healthcare Provider Organizations, Ambulatory Information Systems, http://himss.org, January 2009.

Halamka, J. Federal Health IT Strategic Plan: The Government's Five Goals, March 28, 2011.

Health information exchanges and your EMR selection process. *New England Journal of Medicine* January 25, 2011.

Health Information Technology Extension Program, http://www.healthit.hhs.gov/portal/server.pt/community/healthit_hhs-gov_rec_program.

HHS Secretary Sebelius Announces Plans to Establish Health IT "Beacon Communities," December 2, 2009.

HL7 Publishes Plan-to-Plan Personal Health Record (PHR) Data Transfer Implementation Guide, May 2, 2011.

Improving Health Through Health Information Technology, http://healthit.hhs.gov/portal/server.pt/community/healthit_hhs-gov-one_beacon_community.

Korkut, B. and Krebs, D. The Top 10 Health IT Trends for 2011, Mobility to Play a Larger Role in Health IT.

Lewis, N.B. Health IT Savings will be Bigger than Projected, May 6, 2010.

Meaningful Use Announcement, Electronic Health Records and Meaningful Use.

Moore, J. Has Government Set HER Goals Too High?, http://www.myemrstimulus.com/government-set-ehr-goals-high.

Obama's $80 Billion Exaggeration, Wall Street Journal, http://online.wsj.com/article/SB123681586452302125.html, Retrieved March 3, 2010.

Redling, B. Technology Survey 2010: Uncle Sam's EHR Incentives, http://www.physicianspractice.com/meaingful-use/content/article, August 24, 2010.

Steciw, A., http://searchhealthit.techtarget.com/healthitexchange/healthitpulse/meaningful-use-and-mobile-health, December 6, 2010.

The New Wireless Health-Care Market.

http://en.widipedia.org/wiki/American_recovery_and_reimbursement_act_of_2009.

http://en.wikipedia.org/wiki/electronic_medical_record, June 7, 2011.

http://en.wikipedia.org/wiki/personal_health_record.

http://healthit.hhs.gov/portal/server.pt/community/healthit_hhs_gov__onc_beacon_com munity_program__improving_health_through_health_it/1805.

http://www.cmio.net/index.php?option=com_articles&view=article&id=25475:rsna-ipadsiphones-not-quite-ready-for-prime-time.

http://www.fierceemr.com/story/unnecessary-tests-reduced-emr-alerts/2011-04-21.

http://www.hhs.gov.

http://www.hhs.gov/ocr/privacy/hipaa/understanding/special/healthit/phrs.pdf.

http://www.hhs.gov/recovery.

http://www.ieeeusa.org/volunteers/committees/mtpc/documents/ReportonWirelessandMobileTechnologiesfor HCMarch2010_000.pdf.

http://www.navyehr.org/index.php/tips-tricks-top-menu/tips-tricks-setting-up-a-patient-kiosk.

http://www.protouchblog.co.uk/2011/04/kiosk-security-breach-of-private-information, April 18, 2011.

http://www.providersedge.com/ehdocs/ehr_articles/EMR_Confidentiality_and_Information_Security.pdf.

http://www.techrepublic.com/blog/10things/10-ways-to-avoid-it-security-breaches/780.

www.imprivata.com.

www.internet2.edu/government/arra.html.

www.iom.edu.

www.rand.org.

12 Medical Supply Chain Inventory Management Strategies

Data Capture, Just-in-Time Strategies, and Economic Order Quantity Analysis

David J. Piasecki and David Edward Marcinko

CONTENTS

INTRODUCTION

Inventory cost accounting methods are seldom used by medical practitioners. After all, doctors, hospitals, and health care organizations provide a service, and generally do not sell things.

However, inventory is playing an increasingly important role in the financial viability of procedurally based practitioners, clinics, and hospitals. This occurs because these health care entities maintain, dispense, and use durable medical equipment (DME) more abundantly than ever before. Voice systems, radio-frequency identification (RFID), optical character recognition (OCR), pick-to-light and laser scanners, charge-coupled device (CCD) scanners, hand-held batch and radio-frequency (RF) terminals, vehicle-mounted computers, and wearable computers are now all part of the modern health care system inventory data collection and management picture.

Ironically, the financial challenge of hospital inventory management was first articulated in the *Efficient Healthcare Consumer Response Report* in 1996. The report identified $11.6 billion of cost-saving opportunities in the American health care system directly due to inefficient product movement and ineffective inventory control and materials management. Now, more than 15 years later, this situation has only grown worse. As material costs have increased, our overburdened health system cannot afford such inefficiency.

For example, DME stock-out emergencies are real and costly. Moreover, inventory models such as economic order quantity (EOQ) costing have been in existence long before modern data capture inventory costing methods, just-in-time (JIT) inventory controls, total quality management protocols, and the other supply chain inventory management (SCIM) initiatives often used to prevent them.

SCIM is a method of accounting that takes into consideration raw materials, the construction of useful products, and the distribution of those products. Physician proceduralists, medical dispensers, and hospitals must understand SCIM, because a health care entity's profitability will suffer if it has too much, or too little DME inventory on hand. DME can be a cost center or a revenue driver, depending on its management.

Perpetual or periodic inventory costing methods are the traditional ways to account for DME usage. With perpetual costing, a new unit price is recalculated with each order. With periodic costing, the cost of inventory is determined once, at the end of the period.

How can the health care entity determine the proper DME inventory level? One uncommonly used, but increasingly important, approach is the EOQ method.

Some astute clinic and hospital administrators are just now using EOQ to manage their DME inventory. They are increasing their financial benefits by determining the most cost-effective answers to the questions:

1. How much inventory should I order?
2. When should I order the inventory?
3. How can I increase efficiency and reduce channel costs?

In other words, how can a hospital or health care organization optimize inventory levels, reduce expenses, and still improve patient care and safety?

AUTOMATED DATA COLLECTION

Automated data collection (ADC), also known as automated data capture, automated identification (AutoID), or automated identification and data capture (AIDC), consists of many different technologies. Bar codes, voice systems, RFID, OCR, laser scanners, and vehicle-mounted and wearable computers are all part of ADC management and inventory activities.

However, the fear of six-figure project costs often prevents many small- to mid-sized hospitals and health care systems from taking advantage of these technologies. The key to implementing cost-effective ADC systems is to know what technologies are available and the amount of integration needed to implement them. Applying this processing knowledge in a health care organization will help in developing the scope of any project. Limiting projects to or prioritizing by those applications that have a high benefit/cost ratio allows these operational improvement technologies within a reasonable budget.

For example, adding a keyboard-wedge bar-code scanner to an existing personal computer (PC) or blade terminal in a nursing station is a very low-cost method for applying ADC to existing hospital reporting applications. This type of hardware is inexpensive and the only real programming required is to add a bar code to the proper form (work order, pick and delivery slip, etc.).

ADC TECHNOLOGIES

Some of the current hospital data capture technologies include the following:

BAR CODES

There are two major categories of bar codes: one dimensional (1D) and two dimensional (2D). 1D bar codes are the ones most familiar and consist of many different symbologies including universal product code (UPC), Code 128, Code 39, and Interleaved 2 of 5, just to name a few. The symbology used may be dictated by hospital or pharmaceutical supply chain partners through a standardized compliance label program or, if only used internally, can be chosen by the central supply manager based upon specific application.

2D bar-code symbologies are capable of storing more data than their 1D counterparts and require special scanners to read them. Although continued growth in the use of 2D bar codes is expected, most hospital and health care applications will continue to use 1D symbologies simply because the technology is less expensive and only enough data are needed in the bar code to access the associated records in an inventory system database.

BAR-CODE SCANNERS

Laser or CCD

There are primarily two technologies used to read bar codes. Laser scanners use a laser beam that moves back and forth across the bar code reading the light and dark spaces. Laser scanners have been in use for decades and are capable of scanning bar codes at significant distances. CCD scanners act like a small digital camera and take a digital image of the bar code, which is then decoded. CCD scanners offer a lower cost, but are limited to a shorter scan distance (usually within a few inches; however, the technology is advancing quickly and devices with longer scan distances are becoming available). Because of the scan distance limitations, users in a hospital storage or warehouse environment will likely find laser scanners to be their best choice. However, for applications where bar codes are read from documents—such as in a pharmacy production-reporting application—CCD scanners are acceptable.

Autodiscrimination

Autodiscrimination describes the functionality of a bar-code reader to recognize the bar-code symbology being scanned, thus allowing a reader to read several different symbologies consecutively. Most scanners come with this functionality and also allow reprogramming to read only certain symbologies (this prevents someone from scanning the wrong bar code when multiple bar codes are present).

Keyboard-Wedge Scanners

Keyboard-wedge scanners connect between a computer keyboard and the computer and send ASCII data to the computer as if the scanner were a keyboard. More simply put, the computer does not know that a scanner is attached and treats the data as though they were key strokes from the user. The advantage of this is that there is no need for special software or programming on the computer. In its simplest application, one hooks the scanner up, makes sure the cursor is in the correct field, scans a bar code containing the data (such as a work order number, an item number, or a location), and the data will immediately appear in the field on the screen. Keyboard-wedge scanners offer a low-cost entry into the world of ADC for hospitals and can provide increases in accuracy and productivity in many stationary data entry applications. There are also wireless versions of keyboard-wedge scanners available.

Fixed-Position Scanners

Fixed-position scanners are used where a bar code is moved in front of the scanner as opposed to the scanner being moved to the bar code. Applications include DME counters and automated pharmaceutical conveyor systems. Many fixed-position scanners are omni-directional, which means that the bar code does not have to be oriented any specific way to be read.

PORTABLE COMPUTERS

Portable computers come in a vast variety of designs with varying levels of functionality. However, there is a lack of progress in portable terminal design, especially with the hand-held units used in many health care settings. On the plus side, costs have come down over the years and evolving technologies are being developed for devices such as personal digital assistants (PDAs), smartphones, iPads, and computerized physician order entry (CPOE) systems that will soon make portable data collection and ordering terminals smaller, lighter, and more functional.

BATCH VERSUS RADIO FREQUENCY

Batch terminals are used to collect data into files on the device and are later connected to a computer to download the files. RF terminals use radio-frequency waves to communicate live with the host system or network. Batch devices were heavily used in the past, and still have viable hospital legacy applications today, but the introduction of wireless standards has made RF technology much more affordable and easier to maintain and implement.

HAND-HELD DEVICES

Hand-held terminals generally have very small liquid crystal display (LCD) that is usually difficult to read, as well as very small, with confusing keypads into which it is difficult to enter data. This does not mean that these cannot be valuable tools in a hospital operation, only that one must consider all the factors when implementing this type of technology. Hand-held devices often come with integrated bar-code scanners, but can be used without a scanner or with a separate scanner.

VEHICLE-MOUNTED DEVICES

Vehicle-mounted devices have several advantages over hand-held devices including larger screens and larger keypads similar to a standard keyboard on a portable computer. Generally, vehicle-mounted devices use a separate wired or wireless bar-code scanner to input data.

WEARABLE SYSTEMS

Wearable systems will likely have the most growth in the coming years. Currently, offerings in wearable systems are limited and include devices such as Symbol Technologies' WS Series that is strapped to the wrist/forearm and uses a small ring-type laser scanner for reading bar codes; or the Talkman from VoCollect that is designed for voice systems. Wearable systems provide the functionality of hand-held devices while still allowing workers to use both hands.

VOICE TECHNOLOGY

Voice technology (a.k.a. speech-based systems) has come of age in recent years and is now a very viable and desirable solution in hospital and DME warehouse ADC applications. Voice technology is really composed of two technologies: *voice directed*, which converts computer data into audible commands, and *speech recognition*, which allows user voice input to be converted into data. Portable voice systems consist of a headset with a microphone and a wearable computer.

The advantages of voice systems are hands-free and eyes-free operation that allows people to communicate with a computer the way people communicate with each other. Applications for voice systems include order picking, quality inspection, shipping, receiving, and cycle counting.

Speech-recognition capabilities have been gradually improving through better software and hardware, but it is not yet a perfected technology. To compensate for problems associated with speech recognition, one should limit the speech input to a fairly short list of keywords and phrases for commands, and primarily numeric characters for voice data input. Alpha characters would have to be spoken phonetically (Alpha, Bravo, Charlie, Delta, etc.) to maintain an acceptable level of accuracy.

OPTICAL CHARACTER RECOGNITION

For years, OCR has been used in mail sorting and document management, but has had very little application in hospital warehouse operations primarily because it is not as accurate as bar-code technology. As hardware and software improve, we may see this "old" technology make a comeback. The primary advantage of OCR is that it can read the same characters that a human can read, eliminating the need to have both a bar code and human readable text on labels, documents, and so on. It also provides the ability to input data from documents that do not include bar-coded information.

Light Systems

Although some may argue whether or not a pick-to-light system is an ADC technology, the fact is it accomplishes some of the same tasks.

For example, *pick-to-light systems* consist of lights and LED displays for each pick location. The system uses software to light the next pick and display the quantity to pick. Pick-to-light systems have the advantage of not only increasing accuracy, but also increasing productivity. Because hardware is required for each pick location, pick-to-light systems are easier to cost-justify, where very high picks per stock keeping unit (SKU) occur. Hospital chart flow racks and horizontal carousels are good applications for pick-to-light. In batch picking, pick-to-light is also incorporated into the cart or rack that holds the charts that are picking into (put-to-light).

INTEGRATION OF ADC TECHNOLOGIES

While hardware costs of ADC equipment continue to come down, the cost of integration will often prove to be the project buster. Software and integration costs will often be several times the cost of the hardware, especially in smaller health system operations where only a few devices will be used.

Integration of ADC technologies is also far from standardized. For example, when implementing an RF system with portable terminals, one integrator may create a program on the terminals that will write directly to the file on the host system, another may create programs on a separate server to do this, another may write or modify a program on your host system and use terminal emulation software, and another may use a screen mapping tool to reformat an existing program to be used on the portable device. Make sure to speak with several integrators to ensure the best solution. Moreover, make sure to participate heavily in equipment selection and program/process design (prompts, data input) to ensure a system that provides the highest levels of accuracy and productivity.

Real-Time Locator System

A real-time locator system (RTLS) uses RFID technology that provides the objects they are attached to the ability to transmit their current location. The system requires some type of RFID tag to be attached to each object that needs to be tracked, and RF transmitters/receivers located throughout the facility to determine the location and send information to a computerized tracking system. While it sounds like a great way to eliminate "lost" inventory, the systems are still too costly for most inventory tracking operations and are more likely to be used to track more valuable assets.

Screen Mapping/Screen Scraping

This software provides the functionality to change the arrangement of data fields on a computer screen that accesses a mainframe computer program. Screen mapping is frequently used in combination with terminal emulation software to "remap" data fields from a standard mainframe program to be used on the smaller screen of a portable hand-held device.

Speech-Based Technology

Speech-based technology, also known as voice technology, is really composed of two technologies: (1) *voice directed*, which converts computer data into audible commands, and (2) *speech recognition*, which allows user voice input to be converted into data. Portable voice systems consist of a headset with a microphone and a wearable computer.

TERMINAL EMULATION

Software used on desktop and portable computers is available and allows the computer to act like a terminal connected to a mainframe system. If you have a networked desktop PC and are accessing mainframe programs (green screen programs), you are using terminal emulation. Terminal emulation is also a common method used to connect portable computers (as in pharmacy bar-code ADC systems) to mainframe software.

WAREHOUSE MANAGEMENT SYSTEM

Computer software designed specifically for managing the movement and storage of materials throughout the health care system warehouse or chain of command generally controls the following three operations: (1) put-away, (2) replenishment, and (3) picking. The key to these systems is the logic to direct these operations to specific locations based on user-defined criteria. Warehouse management systems (WMSs) are often set up to integrate with ADC systems.

RADIO-FREQUENCY IDENTIFICATION

RFID refers to a device attached to an object that transmits data to an RFID receiver. A device can be a large piece of hardware the size of a small book like those attached to ocean containers, or a very small device inserted into a label on a package. RFID has advantages over bar codes such as the ability to hold more data, and to change the stored data as processing occurs. Moreover, it does not require line-of-sight to transfer data, and is very effective in harsh environments where bar-code labels will not work. RFID is not without its own problems, however, as RF signals can be compromised by materials such as metals and liquids.

Although RFID technology is receiving much current attention, it still tends to be cost-prohibitive for most hospital inventory tracking applications. As chip prices go down, there will be continued growth in the application of RFID, but, as in the case of 2D bar codes, many warehouse applications simply do not require this added functionality. The low-cost 1D bar code will likely continue to be the technology of choice for many hospital inventory tracking applications.

Smart labels are labels with integrated RFID chips. The idea is to produce labels (probably with bar codes) as well as programming the RFID chips embedded in the label. This would provide all current functionality (human- and machine-readable text and bar codes) as well as adding RFID functionality.

Slap-and-ship describes an approach to complying with vendor requirements for physical identification of shipped goods. Most recently, slap-and-ship has been used to describe complying with RFID requirements (such as those from large health care systems); however, it is also applicable to any compliance labeling requirement (such as compliance bar-code labels). Slap-and-ship implies meeting the customer's requirement by applying the bar-code labels or RFID tags, but not utilizing the technology internally.

Anti-skimming bills were recently approved by California and Washington State relative to RFID privacy and are focused on making it illegal for criminals or businesses (or criminal businesses) to read and use personal information from RFID-enabled items such as driver's licenses and credit cards without the owner's consent.

RFID COMPARISONS TO BAR CODES

Advantages:

1. *RFID technology does not require line-of-sight reading.* Unlike a bar code, an RFID tag can be read through other materials (though some materials may cause problems). Theoretically, this means one could take a pallet of mixed products, all of which contain

individual RFID tags, and have an RFID reader read all the tags within the palletized load without having to physically move any of the materials or open any cases.

2. *RFID tags can hold more data than bar codes.* The operative word here is "can." As the data-storage capacity of RFID tags increases, so does the cost of the tags. Therefore, many RFID tags will not hold any more data than a bar code.

3. *RFID tag data can be changed or added to as a tag passes through specific operations.* Once again, cost comes into play as read-only tags are much less expensive than read/write tags. Therefore, limited use of this functionality is seen.

4. *RFID tags are more effective in harsh environments where bar-code labels have problems.* RFID tags can be sealed within a plastic enclosure, eliminating many of the problems that plague bar codes in harsh environments where they are exposed to chemicals, heat, abrasion, dirt, and grease buildup.

5. *A large number of RFID tags can be read almost instantaneously.* Though it may seem as though the tags are all read at once, they are actually read sequentially (one at a time); however, this happens so fast that it is virtually imperceptible.

Disadvantages:

1. *Cost*—This is the biggest hurdle to RFID tags replacing bar codes for item-level tracking of low-cost health care products. A bar code can be produced on an item for less than 1 cent, yet the most optimistic proponents of RFID are still "hoping" for 4- or 6-cent RFID tags sometime in the future. Moreover, even if a 5-cent tag is achieved, it is still a significant cost to add to the manufactured cost of low-cost consumer goods. Even with higher cost products, the benefits of RFID must be greater than the additional cost.

2. *RFID signals may have problems with some materials.* Metals (oxygen canisters) and liquids (nitrous oxide) can cause problems when trying to read RFID tags. Tag placement is becoming a science in and of itself since—depending on the product—even a case-level RFID tag may have to be placed in a specific location on the case and cases stacked in a specific orientation to get a consistent read.

3. *Though RFID does not require a line-of-sight, it is also not restricted by it.* With the proper bar-code equipment, one can selectively read a single bar-coded case on a shelf more than 10 ft. away. This cannot be done with RFID because an RFID reader will read all tags within its range. Even though one can get directional RFID readers, they are still not as selective as a visual device (bar-code scanner). There are still many warehouse applications that require this line-of-sight capability.

4. *RFID tags can fail.* The unique issue with RFID failure is the automated nature of RFID optimized processes. If an RFID tag is damaged, how does one know that all the tags have not been read?

5. *RFID speed.* The smart label scenario (using labels with integrated RFID chips) appears to be the most likely one for mass RFID use for case and unit tracking of inventory. Unfortunately, it takes more time to print, program, and verify an RFID-enabled label than to simply print a bar-code label. In addition, RFID smart labels seem to have some serious quality problems. Failure rates (inability to properly program and read the tag) are anywhere from 10% to 30%. For automated print-and-apply applications, this could be a serious problem.

6. *RFID standards are still being developed.* No business entity would want to invest in an RFID system that is based on soon-to-be-obsolete specifications. Most RFID systems currently in place are based upon proprietary technology where the readers are designed to read only RFID tags from a specific manufacturer. Compare this to bar-code technology, where standards have been in place for decades. Most bar-code scanners are designed to read all standard bar-code symbologies.

ELECTRONIC PRODUCT CODE

Electronic product code (EPC) is an emerging RFID standard developed by the AutoID center. It is the RFID version of the UPC bar-code standard. Like UPC, EPC is intended to be used for specific product identification as well as case and pallet identification. However, EPC goes beyond UPC by not only identifying the product as an SKU, but also providing access to additional data (via the EPC network) about the origin and history of the specific units. The EPC tag itself identifies the manufacturer, product, version, and serial number. It is the serial number that takes EPC to the next-generation level by providing the key to data related to specific lots/batches/units. It potentially allows tracking of the specific unit's history as it moves through the supply chain. These unit-level data are stored somewhere else (the Internet or other network), but a standardized architecture allows access to the data much like one would access a Web page (though this would be happening automatically behind the scenes). This architecture is known as the EPC network.

EPC has become increasingly important because it is the standard being utilized by the Department of Defense (DoD) for the upcoming RFID standardization considerations.

SOME EPC MISCONCEPTIONS

1. *Misconception 1—EPC is strictly an RFID standard.* Granted, RFID is part of EPC, but there is a lot more to EPC. Most notably is the EPC network, which is where all the data related to EPC will exist. This is a significant change in item-based data management and should not be taken lightly.
2. *Misconception 2—The use of RFID for EPC tags will allow them to hold more data than bar codes.* This is simply not true. RFID tags could hold more data than a bar code, but under the EPC standard, they will not. The data in the EPC RFID tag simply act as an address to the rest of the data and work in a way that is similar to the way a URL provides access to a Web page. The EPC network essentially takes the concept of the Internet and applies it to inventory data. When an RFID reader reads a tag, it will pass this address to software that can then access the additional data residing on servers that could exist anywhere in the world. What kind of data will exist on the EPC network? Just about anything related to the DME item or container. For example, it might include detailed item information, such as description, ingredients, size, weight, cost; manufacturing information about the specific lot, such as when and where it was produced and expiration dates; and distribution information about where it has been, including addresses, dates, and times. The data could be as detailed as including environmental factors such as temperatures during manufacturing or storage. This data flexibility is accomplished through the use of a new computer language called physical markup language (PML) that is essentially a variation of the more commonly known extensible markup language (XML). The purpose of PML is to provide a standard vocabulary to represent and distribute information about AutoID-enabled objects.
3. *Misconception 3—Data in the tags will be changed as they pass through the supply chain.* Once again, RFID technology is capable of this functionality, but the EPC standard is not utilizing it. Data will only be written to the tag once under the EPC standard. Any changes in status or other update information will be written to the EPC network, not the tag.
4. *Misconception 4—The use of RFID for EPC tags will allow them be more durable than bar codes.* Probably not; while more expensive RFID tags encased in a plastic shell are more durable than bar codes in harsh environments, the lower cost, unprotected RFID circuits glued to a paper label that are more likely to be used do not share these durability characteristics.

RFID VERSUS WI-FI FOR HOSPITAL INVENTORY TRACKING SYSTEMS

The two wireless technologies currently competing to provide hospitals with better systems for managing equipment inventories are wireless-fidelity (Wi-Fi) and active RFID. Wi-Fi is the name of the popular wireless networking technology that uses radio waves to provide wireless high-speed Internet connections. The Wi-Fi Alliance is the non-profit organization that owns Wi-Fi (registered trademark) and the term specifically defines Wi-Fi as any "wireless local area network products that are based on the Institute of Electrical and Electronics Engineers' 802.11 standards." Yet, less than 5% of North American health care facilities are equipped with these real-time locating systems; therefore, the market is currently up for grabs.

The advantage of Wi-Fi-based RTLSs is that most hospitals already have Wi-Fi networks in place, and many medical devices are equipped with Wi-Fi functionality. Moreover, Wi-Fi vendors such as AeroScout, Ekahau, and PanGo market their products based on a standards-based non-proprietary functionality. The downside of Wi-Fi systems is that hospitals will need to install additional access points to bring the needed functionality to existing networks.

On the other hand, RFID vendors such as RF Code and Radianse point to the wide application of RFID for asset tracking, and to the technology's longevity in the industry. Still, RFID tags remain suspect because their ability to efficiently track DME may not be private or secure. Increasingly, Wi-Fi seems more ubiquitous than RFID.

Finally, of the three Wi-Fi major vendors, only Ekahau makes a point of stressing that its inventory system is based *only* on Wi-Fi and *not* RFID; therefore, the issue is not clear cut. Perhaps, it will take *both* technologies to deploy RTLSs for hospital emergency rooms, intensive care units, and operating rooms, etc. [1].

GENERAL RECOMMENDATIONS

As a general recommendation, RFID is not yet practical for most small- to mid-sized health care entities or medical clinics looking to automate their inventory-related transactions (though it does work for other applications such as with returnable containers and asset tracking).

Despite the hype over RFID, bar codes are not becoming obsolete and are still very effective at quickly and accurately identifying products, locations, and documents. Unless there exists an application where bar codes simply do not work, or where RFID offers a significant advantage over bar codes, use bar codes. Even if an application that cries out for RFID exists, hospital material management administrators may want to consider waiting (if possible) as the cost of the technology comes down.

According to Robert M. Wachter, MD, professor and chief of the Division of Hospital Medicine and associate chairman of the Department of Medicine, and Lynne and Marc Benioff, endowed chair in Hospital Medicine, University of California at San Francisco, and chief of the Medical Service at UCSF Medical Center [personal communication]:

> Ultimately, of course, we need both bar coding and RFIDs, and we need rigorous studies looking at what works and what doesn't. But, you have to start somewhere. Even though the evidence continues to trail, based on what I know today, if I was a hospital ready to get into the IT game, I'd go with bar coding first.

In the next few years, standards will be finalized, hardware prices will drop, software will become more readily available, and, more importantly, the bugs will be worked out of all these systems [2].

HEALTH CARE INVENTORY MANAGEMENT

Health care inventory is a term that describes medical items used in the delivery of health care services or for patient use and resale, and like DME, a certain safety margin of stock should always be available. Inventory ranges from normal administrative office supplies to highly specialized chemicals and reagents used in the clinical laboratory. It should be distinguished from *capital supplies* such as major equipment, instruments, and other items that are not used up faster than inventory or related inventory wastes [3].

Historically, asset utilization ratios provided information on how effectively the enterprise used its inventory assets to produce revenues, or deplete its cash. For example, the *inventory turnover ratio (ITR)* determines the total volume of inventory turnover (change) during a pre-determined accounting period (month or quarter). It is defined as cost of inventory purchased for the period, divided by average inventory (AI) at cost.

Dunn and Bradstreet, the supply chain management (SCM) and consulting company, does not provide exact comparatives for private health care ITR. Nonetheless, ITR is useful as an internal performance indicator of inventory turnover speed and cash flow enhancement. Currently, however, for public hospitals, 60–75 days is estimated to be the average time for inventory turnover.

The main problem with traditional ITR, similar analyses such as AI and ICP, and the usual inventory costing methods (e.g., last-in first-out [LIFO], first-in first-out [FIFO], specific identification, average costs), and even JIT inventory costing, is that they do not embrace SCIM. This occurs because sources of profit or loss are not recognized in the traditional inventory cost accounting equation

$$\text{Cost of goods sold} = \text{beginning inventory} + \text{net purchases} - \text{ending inventory}$$

INVENTORY METHODOLOGIES

A good SCIM system offers opportunities for improved efficiency in any health care organization. The following traditional methods of inventory cost accounting and management are useful when one is calculating the cost of supplies (as opposed to medical items for resale and DME).

LAST-IN FIRST-OUT

The LIFO inventory costing method means that the last items purchased are the first to be used (at least for cost calculations if the inventory consists of identical units). In times of rising prices, a lower total cost inventory is produced with a higher cost of goods sold. The last items purchased are most often the most expensive, and used first for the calculation. This happens because LIFO increases an expense (cost of goods sold) and decreases taxable income. Given the same revenue, higher expenses mean less profit. Deflation has the opposite effect.

FIRST-IN FIRST-OUT

The FIFO inventory costing method means that the first items purchased are the first to be used (at least for cost calculations if the inventory consists of identical units). In times of rising prices, a higher total cost inventory is produced with a lower cost of goods sold. This happens because FIFO decreases an expense (cost of goods sold) and increases taxable income. Deflation has the opposite effect.

SPECIFIC IDENTIFICATION

Specific identification is used for larger pieces of equipment, as it traces actual costs to an identifiable unit of product and is usually applied with an identification tag, serial plate, or RFID scanner. It does not involve flow-of-cost analysis. It does, however, permit the manipulation of income because health care entities state their cost of goods sold, and ending inventory, at the actual cost of specific units sold.

Average Cost

Average costing calculates ending inventory using a weighted average unit cost. When prices are rising, the cost of goods sold is less than under LIFO, but more than that under FIFO; hence, income manipulation is also possible.

JIT Management

Although technically not a costing technique, JIT inventory management means that inventory supplies like DME are delivered as soon as needed by the health care organization, the prescribing doctor, or the patient. In JIT, inventory is "pulled" through the flow process. This is contrasted to the "push" approach used by conventional SCIM. In the push system, DME is already on-site, with little regard to when it is actually needed. In the JIT "pull" system, the overriding concern is to keep a minimum cost inventory; so that means having a system in which inventory is obtained on an as-needed basis. The key elements of JIT consist of six parts:

1. A few dependable vendors or suppliers willing to ship with little advanced notice
2. Total sharing of demand information throughout the supply chain
3. More frequent orders
4. Smaller size of individual orders
5. Improved physical plant (hospital or clinic) layout to reduce travel flow distance
6. Use of a total quality control system to reduce flawed medical products

Using the JIT method, inventory is delivered when needed, rather than in advance, saving handling and storage costs. The health care entity never needs to stockpile inventory, and cash flow is enhanced. JIT is further characterized as follows:

1. Little or no work orders
2. Little or no tracing of materials
3. Fewer inventory accounts or accounts payables
4. Reduction or elimination of work-in-progress or handling activities
5. No tracing of overhead and direct labor costs

JIT requires a dependable working relationship with suppliers and the precise calculation of inventory needs, especially for the following:

1. Sterile surgical packs
2. Gastrointestinal and gastrourinary instrumentation
3. Orthopedic and OB-GYN inventory
4. Invasive heart and lung equipment
5. Radioisotopes and trace radiographic materials
6. Equipment for almost all pre-scheduled medical interventions and procedures

This means that, when JIT inventory monitoring is used, health care managers are better prepared with the proper inputs to control and reduce inventory, including when dramatic bursts or declines occur. This means a more rapid and higher cash flow balance, rather than inventory balance.

Each of these traditional methods of inventory cost accounting is adequate for most health care facilities, but as inventory orders and costs continue to increase, EOQ costing may be the most effective means of accounting for inventory in DME-intensive organizations.

ECONOMIC ORDER QUANTITY PROCESS

Economic order quantity costing is a determination of the number, amount, or quantity of DME orders that minimize total variable costs required to order and hold items as inventory [4]. Therefore, how does a health care organization determine current inventory costs and proceed to implement a SCIM policy, such as EOQ costing? The approach involves the following steps:

1. Perform an inventory of all DME in the clinic, hospital department, or ambulatory surgical center by physical, electronic, or other counting or inventory tracking means.
2. Analyze how much DME inventory quantity is on hand.
3. Determine associated inventory and ordering costs for the DME on hand.
4. Perform an EOQ cost analysis.

In-house staff or an external inventory management team can achieve these goals.

Therefore, why are some clinic managers, supply chain managers, central supply directors, and hospital administrators still not taking advantage of EOQ, a basic DME inventory process? A small part of the answer lies in the concept of economies of scale, as most medical office and clinics are still small businesses incapable of large-scale SCIM initiatives. This will change going forward, as the pace of industry mergers, consolidation, and acquisitions increases, and multiple offices and clinics form larger enterprise business units and hospital networks, which require more DME and improved inventory fiscal control.

Even with larger health care systems and hospital chains, a larger "part of the answer lies in the poor results sometimes received due to inaccurate EOQ processes input data. Accurate product costs, activity costs, forecasts, history, and lead times are crucial in developing DME inventory models that work."*

EOQ costing assumes

1. Constant demand rate
2. Constant lead time
3. Entire quantity is received at once
4. Constant unit costs
5. No limits on size of inventory

The mathematical formula for EOQ is the square root of $2SO/C$, where inputs S is the annual usage or purchases in units, O is the cost per order, and C is the annual carrying cost per unit.

$$\text{EOQ} = \sqrt{\frac{2(\text{Annual usage in units})(\text{Order cost})}{\text{Annual carrying cost per unit}}}$$

S = ANNUAL USAGE OR PURCHASE IN UNITS

Although typically annual purchases in units and cost per order are historically known, better management of inventory will benefit from forecasting and a reduction in lead times. This will allow a health care organization to operate with less safety stock and can also reduce inventory levels and annual use.

O = ORDER COST

Order cost is the sum of the fixed costs incurred each time an item is ordered. In the EOQ calculation, order cost is represented as a fixed dollar amount per purchase order (PO) line.

---

* Pentin-Maki, Rachel, RN MHA, iMBA Inc., Atlanta, GA (personal communication).

It is important to note that order costs are only the costs related to processing the purchasing transaction. Order cost may include costs associated with entering a requisition or PO, approval steps, expediting, processing the receipt, vendor invoice processing, and vendor payment. Any cost that changes based on the order quantity would not be considered part of order cost, which includes time spent unloading trailers and counting receipts.

Order cost can change based on the characteristics of the product being received. For example, when processing receipts of very small items delivered in parcels, the time spent unloading and opening the parcel and the time spent putting the product away may be included in order cost because the labor used is primarily due to the purchasing transaction. However, if processing multiple DME cartons or pallets of a product, most of the time spent unloading and putting the product away is actually due to the quantity ordered and, therefore, would not be included in order cost.

Sourcing activities such as processing vendor quotes would not be included in order costs unless this cost is incurred every time an order is placed. Though often difficult, a portion of freight costs can be included in order cost provided you can accurately calculate how much of the freight cost is fixed (due to the transaction) rather than variable (due to the quantity ordered).

C = Annual Carrying Cost per Unit

Carrying cost is the cost associated with having inventory. In the EOQ calculation, carrying cost is represented as the annual cost per average on-hand inventory unit. This is usually calculated as a percentage of unit cost. It would include interest costs on loans for inventory, insurance, and inventory storage costs. Though interest and insurance may be the same percentage for all items, storage costs may vary based upon the characteristics of the specific product.

You should only apply costs that change based on the quantity of inventory stored. In some cases, you may choose not to include any storage costs in the calculation. This is especially true if storage costs are fixed and changes in inventory levels do not actually change these costs.

Risk costs such as risk of obsolescence, damage, or spoilage may also be included in carrying costs. Like storage costs, these costs likely vary by product or product group.

Several primary components of carrying costs may represent a source of lost profits. These include rent, utilities, insurance, taxes, employee costs, and the interest rate and opportunity costs of having office space or capital tied up in DME. In fact, research by Jones suggests that hospitals and other companies do indeed understate carrying costs because only variable costs are considered while other costs like handling, accounting and administrative, and depreciation are not. Yet these costs may be more significant in the EOQ equation than the variable costs.

Example:

A large ambulatory surgery center performs orthopedic bone surgery and uses about 10,000 self-absorbing bone fixation pins every year. Historically, it is known that the cost per pin is $200, and the annual inventory carrying cost per pin is $10. Using the EOQ formula, we can determine when and how many bone fixation pins are required for the organization.

EOQ SOLUTION CALCULATION:

According to the above formula, the EOQ is 632, as follows

$$\sqrt{\frac{2(10,000)(\$200)}{\$10}}$$

2(10,000)($200)/$10 = $400,000
Square root of $400,000 = 632

This means that there are 16 orders per year or 10,000 divided by the 632 EOQ. The time between each order is 3.3 weeks or 52 weeks divided by the 16 orders. Therefore, the vital economic questions of when and how much DME to order have been answered.

The key to optimizing order quantities is getting the inputs to the calculation correct. These include accurate product costs, forecasted annual demand, order costs, and carrying costs. Most problems with EOQ outputs are the result of incorrect order cost and carrying cost inputs. To some extent, computer technology has actually contributed to problems with order quantity calculations by automating the process and hiding the key inputs (order costs and carrying costs) in secured system setup areas. In some cases, these inputs are simply "plugged in" during the initial system setup to get the system up and running and are never actually reviewed on a continual basis.

When implementing the EOQ calculation, it is also important to project the short-term and long-term effects the EOQ calculation will have on warehouse space, cash flow, and operations. This is accomplished by comparing the output of the EOQ calculation with your current ordering practices. If the EOQ output shows overall increases in order quantities, you may choose to "temporarily adjust the formula until arrangements can be made to handle the additional storage requirements and compensate for the effects on cash flow. If the projection shows inventory levels dropping and order frequency increasing, you may need to evaluate staffing, equipment, and process changes to handle the increased activity." For hospitals, medical offices, surgical centers, or emerging health care organizations with extensive inventories, a phased approach is highly recommended.

You should focus on cost reduction and not necessarily inventory reduction. Reducing order and re-order costs through process changes, e-procurement, vendor managed inventory, vendor certification programs, and technologies such as bar codes and RFID, will ultimately result in inventory cost reduction.

Re-Order Point

Once you have calculated the EOQ for the health care organization's inventory, you will need to figure out the re-order point (ROP) for new shipments. The ROP for new inventory orders is calculated as follows:

$$\text{ROP} = (\text{average use per unit of lead time} \times \text{lead time}) + \text{safety stock}$$

Example:

A hospital chain with lead time of 1 week uses 6400 delivery room birthing sets per 50-week year (6400/50) × 1 week + 0 = 128 ROP. If lead time and average use are certain, no safety stock (quantity zero) is needed.

If competition, a variable birth rate, or some other factor changes and now demands a safety stock of 150, the new ROP is 128 + 150 = 278.

Assessment of EOQ

EOQ may be a useful technique if there is an opportunity to change the current DME ordering policy of a medical office or clinic, or if the current policy is inadequate. Though it may appear that this technique would solidify purchase quantity, there are still other factors to consider because the EOQ equation makes these unrealistic assumptions:

1. Lead time is known
2. Demand is a fixed constant

3. No shortages occur
4. No quantity discounts are permitted

For example, a hospital or clinic still needs to review the likelihood of a stock out (quantity of an inventory item falling to zero), use of safety stock levels, the length of time DME is kept on hand, quantity discounts that vendors may offer, and product volume within the practice or health enterprise.

When a quantity discount is expected, this formula may be used:

$$\text{Total cost (Carrying Cost [CC] + Order Costing [OC] + Product Cost [PC])}$$
$$= C \times (Q/2) + Q \times (D/Q) + \text{PD}$$

where
$D =$ discount
$P =$ unit price
$Q =$ order quantity

A methodical approach in calculating EOQ with discounts may be summarized as follows:

1. Compare the EOQ when price discounts are ignored and costs are based on the new formula above. *Note*: EOQ = square root of $2OS/C$
2. Compute the cost for those amounts greater than the EOQ at which price reductions occur
3. Select the value of Q that results in the lowest total costs

Moreover, clinic and hospital goals and strategies may sometimes conflict with EOQ methodology. Measuring DME performance solely by inventory turnover is a mistake. Some health care entities have achieved aggressive goals in increasing inventory turns only to find that their bottom line has shrunk due to increased operational costs.

While EOQ may not apply to every DME inventory situation, some health care entities will find it beneficial in at least some aspect of their operations.

Whenever there is repetitive purchasing of DME, you should consider using the EOQ equation to determine appropriate order amounts.

The process here is to divide the year into the increments in which annualized sales are relatively constant (i.e., summer, spring, fall, and winter). Then, the EOQ model can be applied separately to each period. During the transition between seasons, DME inventories would either be run-down or built-up, with special seasonal orders. Though EOQ is most effective with stable demand, seasonal demand can be managed by using shorter time periods or converting the EOQ quantity into a period order quantity (stated in number of days of demand). However, if you plan to use the EOQ method, be sure that usage and carrying costs are based on the same time period.

HOSPITAL MATERIALS MANAGEMENT INFORMATION SYSTEMS

The singular focus of any Hospital Materials Management Information System (HMMIS) is to deliver significant improvements in the ability of hospital facilities, networks, and other health care organizations to accurately optimize the processes and workflows associated with materials management systems and reduce the costs related to inventory, DME, pharmaceuticals, and (SCM) [5].

Strategically, hospitals must exploit contemporary technologies and connectivity with suppliers and trading partners to

1. Improve patient care and safety
2. Increase efficiency
3. Drive down costs
4. Optimize inventory levels

SOFTWARE SELECTION

Software selection and implementation services have become big business for consulting firms as well as the software vendors themselves. Even with outside assistance, selecting the right software for hospital operations and having a successful implementation can be an extremely difficult undertaking. Horror stories of failed enterprise resource planning (ERP) system implementations are unfortunately very common. Anyone who frequently reads business publications have read stories where large health care corporations, posting smaller than forecasted profits, cite problems associated with the implementation of a new software system as one of the causes. Whether these claims are legitimate or not is up to debate. What is true is that hospitals are highly dependent on information systems, and failures in the selection and implementations of systems can result in anything from a minor nuisance to a complete operational shutdown.

Those unfamiliar with business inventory management software should be prepared to be bombarded with acronyms and buzz words. E-business, Web-enabled, e-procurement, e-fulfillment, e-manufacturing, collaborative, modular, and scalable are just a sampling of the terms used to describe (sell) hospital software inventory products.

Health care enterprise inventory tracking software with implementation ranges in price from a few thousand dollars to millions. In fact, up until recently, if you were a medical clinic with annual revenues of less than $200 million, many of the top enterprise software vendors did not even consider you a potential customer. Fortunately, this arrogance has been tempered recently due to economic conditions (primarily the software vendors' cash flow). Unlike 5 years ago, when the software vendors felt that they held all the cards, today, it is truly a buyer's market. No matter how big or small an entity, many vendors will be vying for software dollars. That is the good news. The bad news is that you must sift through all these products to find the one that best meets your business needs.

The most important part of the software selection process is defining the processes within your health organization and determining functionality that is critical to your medical operation. Many times clients get distracted by the bells and whistles and forget about their core health care business functions. As a health care entity in the DME distribution fulfillment business, focus on functionality related to order processing, as well as warehouse and transportation management. Be wary of the software vendor that claims that packages work equally well in all environments. Most software packages are initially designed with specific situations in mind; asking the vendor about their biggest customers will often give you an idea as to the type of operation the software was designed to work [6].

When you look at the detailed functionality of a product, it will be important to have listed detailed functionality requirements of your health care operation. This is where hospitals often make mistakes by emphasizing functionality that they currently do not have, but would like, and overlooking core health care processes that their current system handles well.

For example, if you are awestruck with functionality that allows remote access to a medical charting system from an Internet browser on an ambulatory device and, as a result, overlook critical functionality related to order entry or demand planning, you may end up with a system that provides great visibility to the fact that patient revenues are failing. Never assume a software package "must" be capable of handling something considered a standard function. Some examples of detailed functional requirements are as follows:

1. E-commerce capabilities
2. Multi-facility demand planning
3. Postponement and configure-to-order functionality
4. Forecasting and demand planning
5. Back-order processing
6. Lot or serial number tracking

7. Forward pick location replenishment
8. Batch or wave order picking
9. Returns processing
10. Back-flushing DME inventory
11. Co-product processing
12. Outsourcing specific operations
13. Multiple stocking units of measure
14. Product substitutions
15. Blanket orders
16. Shipment consolidation
17. Multi-carrier rate shopping and manifesting
18. First-in first-out processing

Do not settle for "yes, we can do that" responses from the software vendor. It is your responsibility to verify that not only can they do it, but also that they can do it to the level required. Ask detailed questions as to exactly how it works in their system. Look at the specific programs used to achieve the task and verify that the data elements required to achieve the task are present. Do not allow the software vendor to sidestep your questions by retreating into obfuscating technical jargon.

SOFTWARE IMPLEMENTATION

As with the selection process, ERP software implementation may also require outside assistance. Whether you use consultants from the software vendor, a business partner, or an independent firm, the implementation plan will likely be the same. It is very important to listen to consultants and be prepared to dedicate the resources outlined in the implementation plan. A common mistake made by health care entities going through their first major implementation is to underestimate the complexity of their operations, the extent of system setup and testing, and the impact the implementation will have on their operation. Here is an outline of a common scenario in single-hospital ERP implementations:

1. The consultants warn of the consequences of not dedicating adequate resources.
2. Management publicly agrees but privately thinks the consultants are crying wolf.
3. Implementation fails or goes poorly.
4. Management claims "how could we have known?"

Do not let this be you. The only thing to assume about the implementation is that it will be much more difficult than expected, it will take longer than you expected, and it will cost more than expected.

Like most other projects, the success of a software implementation will be based upon the skill of the people involved, training, planning, and the effort put forth. Plan to have the most knowledgeable employees heavily involved in the system setup and testing.

Adequate time should be dedicated to make sure every aspect of every process is thoroughly tested. An example of a detailed testing program is listed below

1. Does the PO receipt screen have all the information needed to perform the receipt such as vendor item number, item description, and unit of measure?
2. What happens when we receive more than the PO quantity?
3. What happens when we receive less than the PO quantity?
4. What happens when we enter multiple receipts against the same line?
5. What happens if someone tries to change the PO quantity after we have entered a receipt?
6. What happens if one changes the PO quantity at the same time we are entering a receipt?

7. What happens when we reverse a receipt?
8. What happens when we reverse a receipt after it has been paid?
9. What happens if the ordered unit of measure is different from the stocking unit of measure?
10. What happens when we receive an early shipment?
11. What happens when we try to receive against a cancelled PO?
12. What happens when we change the receipt location?

After the system has been thoroughly tested, employee training begins. Remember, dealing with unexpected issues is the norm; you do not also need to be training employees after the system is supposed to be operating.

The training should consist of hands-on training and include written procedures for the tasks performed. For most positions, make sure that each employee has entered the equivalent of at least a full day's transactions during the training. Using an actual day's transactions is a good way to make sure that the variety of transactions an employee is likely to encounter have been experienced. The most common mistake made in training is a lack of adequate repetition. Just because someone was able to perform the task once during a training session on a Saturday, 3 weeks prior to "going-live," does not mean that they will be able to perform the task with system start-up. If they have repeated the task many times over a series of training sessions, they are much more likely to remember how to do it.

Watch the data. During and immediately after the implementation, it is incredibly important to watch the data and make sure everything is working as planned. Monitor the status of orders, POs (like pharmacy), and delivery orders, paying specific attention to "stuck orders" or other exceptions. Conduct some aggressive cycle counting of fast-moving items to make sure transactions are working correctly [7].

POST-IMPLEMENTATION FUNCTIONALITY

Do not let it end with the initial implementation. A new system likely has additional functionality that can improve business processes. Once comfortable with a new system, go back to the system documentation and start reviewing detailed functionality. Review all business processes to determine opportunities for improvement. This should be a continuous process. It is very unlikely that initial implementation truly optimized the system for the health care organization.

In the end, the success or failure of any software selection/implementation project is directly related to the efforts put into it. Information systems are a critical part of managing health care operations, so do not shortchange the process.

INTERNET BROWSER–BASED APPLICATIONS

During the past few years, Web-based business applications have evolved using a Software-as-a-Service or cloud model. The ability to access software from any location that has Internet access is certainly attractive, but unfortunately, the downside to this approach seems to be that most systems suffer from cumbersome user interfaces and slow response times. Anyone that shops online should be familiar with using a program within a browser to place an online order. If you have been annoyed with having to go through three or more screens to place your order (and the delay as you wait for each page to load), just imagine conducting all your business activities this way.

In addition, these applications tend to be built around drop-down selection lists and mouse clicks. These can be extremely cumbersome when trying to execute high-volume data entry tasks of small items like pharmaceuticals. This is a problem that also plagues most graphical user interfaces (Windows-based software). Others include Chrome, Chrome [+] Linux, Unix, Macintosh, or open-source interfaces. While these programs are attractive and easy to learn, they are still far less productive than the older character-based mainframe applications where data entry was accomplished with keystrokes and navigation was accomplished with function keys.

CONCLUSIONS

HMMIS and EOQ strategies are not a panacea that solves all SCIM inventory cost problems or easily add to bottom line profits. There is much to consider before adopting an EOQ policy for all DME across an entire health care enterprise. Nonetheless, it is a good SCIM tool to consider when evaluating what ordering policy is best used for a DME-intensive health care organization.

CASE MODEL 12.1: INVENTORY SWITCHING AT THE ABC MEDICAL CENTER

The new administrator for the ABC Medical Clinic understood that all inventory costing methods were acceptable to use in his durable medical equipment (DME) department. Last-in first-out (LIFO), first-in first-out (FIFO), specific identification, and the average cost method are all attractive methods under different circumstances in the business cycle, and companies may use the method that best fits their circumstances.

For example, if ABC wished to reduce corporate income taxes in a period of inflation and rising prices, it would use LIFO. If matching DME sales revenue with the current cost of DME goods sold was desired, LIFO would also be used. Unfortunately, LIFO may charge against DME revenue the cost of DME not actually sold, and LIFO may allow the ABC Medical Clinic to manipulate net income by varying the time periods it makes additional DME purchases. On the other hand, FIFO and specific identification method allows a more precise matching of ABC revenue with historic DME costs. However, FIFO too, can promote "paperless-phantom profits," while specific identification can promote possible income manipulation. It is only under FIFO that net income manipulation is not possible.

"Let's go with FIFO," the new administrator said to his chief financial officer, Bert. "The profits will make us look good to the home office and we can always switch back to LIFO if inflation starts back-up again, right Bert?" he mused.

However, Bert was not amused because freedom of choice does not include changing DME inventory methods every few years, especially if only to report higher income. "The switching of methods violates the basic tenet of consistency, which requires the use of the same inventory cost and accounting methods in preparing financial reports and statements," Bert emphatically stated.

KEY ISSUES:

1. Is this sort of inventory costing and maneuvering permissible?
2. What is its justification?
3. How is it notated in financial reports?
4. Is this sort of thing ethical?

RESOLUTION

Companies may occasionally make changes in spite of the principle of accounting consistency if improved financial reporting is the justification for change. The company must make a full disclosure, usually in a footnote to its financial statements (see example below). This includes the reason(s) for change, descriptions of the changes, and potential effects on corporate net income. This "switch" in inventory methods is ethical, but should be done with the best interests of the organization in mind, and you should make full disclosure of any change in your financial statements.

SAMPLE FOOTNOTE

Note G: Changes in inventory accounting and costing methods: Effective with the year ending December 31, 2005, the ABC Medical Center changed its method of calculating DME inventory costs from the lower of average costs (or market) methods to the FIFO method for substantially all DME inventory. Management believes that FIFO more accurately reflects income by providing a closer match of current DME costs, against current DME revenues.

CHECKLIST 1: Inventory Management	YES	NO
If you are a manager of central supplies, director of durable medical equipment, or an inventory control specialist in a health care organization, are you aware of these basic inventory management requirements for economic order quantity (EOQ) costing?		
Do I recognize EOQ costing as a key parameter of supply chain inventory management?	o	o
Do I determine the correct amount and delivery time for inventory orders and supplied items?	o	o
Do I understand the balancing act between too much inventory (holding and opportunity costs) and too little inventory (stock outs and repurchasing costs)?	o	o
Do I determine which inventory items to ignore and which items to manage?	o	o
Is my annual inventory demand:		
Fixed for each item?	o	o
Variable for each item?	o	o
Constant for each item?	o	o
Is inventory waste occurring through repeated orders?	o	o
Do I know my re-order point for each inventory item?	o	o
Am I aware of my lead time for each inventory item?	o	o
Is there a minimum quantity of each inventory item identified?	o	o
Do I use the "rule of common sense" (e.g., do not spend $100,000 to avoid $10,000 of opportunity cost) in my inventory management duties?	o	o
Is there a supplier purchaser in place for the facility?	o	o
Is a purchase order system in place?	o	o
Is a single facility, or centralized department, in place for multiple entity inventory supplies?	o	o
Have I developed a plan to work with just-in-time suppliers or vendors and delivery schedules?	o	o
Have vendor prices been checked recently?	o	o
Are inventory order quantity discounts given?	o	o
Is competitive bidding an option by vendors?	o	o

CHECKLIST 2: Inventory Dos and Don'ts	YES	NO
If you are a manager of central supplies, director of durable medical equipment (DME), or an inventory control specialist in a health care organization, you must monitor purchasing activities to ensure that the correct amount of inventory is ordered at the appropriate time for maximum financial efficiency:		
Am I a manager of supply chain inventory control or central supplies and DME?	o	o
Do I use last-in first-out costing?	o	o
Do I use first-in first-out costing?	o	o
Do I use specific identification costing?	o	o
Do I use average cost methods?	o	o
Do I use just-in-time (JIT) costing?	o	o
Do I use economic order quantity (EOQ) costing?	o	o
Do I understand JIT purchasing?	o	o
Do I understand the implications of the above costing methods in periods of rising or declining inflation rates and inventory prices?	o	o

	YES	NO
Do I understand the inventory flow process?	o	o
Do I recognize inventory revenues or inventory depletion rates?	o	o
Are inventory revenue and/or depletion rates constant?	o	o
Do I know the annual carrying costs per each unit of inventory?	o	o
Do I know the annual use or percentage of use for each unit of inventory?	o	o
Do I know the costs per order for each inventory segment or item?	o	o
Are the costs per order stable?	o	o
If not, can I obtain stability from vendors and suppliers?	o	o
If so, does the company's board of directors have a supply chain inventory management (SCIM) or DME purchasing individual, manager, or committee?	o	o
Do I understand how JIT delivery allows the placement of orders so that new orders arrive when inventory approaches zero?	o	o
Do I use EOQ costing?	o	o
Do I know when to order DME inventory?	o	o
Do I know how much DME inventory to order?	o	o
Do I have a budget for supply chain management activities?	o	o
Is the inventory budget fixed?	o	o
Is the inventory budget variable?	o	o
Do I have discretion over the inventory budget?	o	o
Does it satisfy requirements for independence, authority, and economic DME resources?	o	o
Does it provide appropriate economic oversight during inventory audits?	o	o
Does it contain at least one inventory, SCIM, or EOQ costing financial expert input?	o	o

---

CHECKLIST 3: Health Care Materials Management Information System Software Selection and Functionality Review

	YES	NO
As a central supply or health facility inventory manager, never assume a software package "must" be capable of handling something you consider a standard function.		
Is the software program, or Software-as-a-Service (SaaS) application, under consideration capable of the following functions?		
Multi-facility demand planning	o	o
Postponement and configure-to-order functionality	o	o
Back-order processing	o	o
Forecasting and demand planning	o	o
Forward pick location replenishment	o	o
Lot or serial number tracking	o	o
Batch or wave order picking	o	o
Returns processing	o	o
Back-flushing durable medical equipment inventory	o	o
Co-product processing	o	o
Outsourcing specific operations	o	o
Multiple stocking units of measure	o	o
Product substitutions	o	o
Blanket orders	o	o
Shipment consolidation	o	o
Multi-carrier rate shopping and manifesting	o	o
First-in first-out processing	o	o
Is the software application under consideration CD-ROM based?	o	o
Is the software application under consideration Internet based?	o	o

	YES	NO
If Internet delivered, is it secure and compliant under the Health Insurance Portability and Accountability Act of 1996 (HIPAA)?	o	o
Is the software application under consideration delivered by a SaaS model?	o	o
If SaaS delivered, is it secure, "always-on" and HIPAA compliant?	o	o
Do I have a budget for the Hospital Materials Management Information System (HMMIS) software?	o	o
Is the HMMIS budget fixed?	o	o
Is the HMMIS budget variable?	o	o

CHECKLIST 4: Using Automated Data Collection Technologies for Inventory	**YES**	**NO**
As a central supply or health facility inventory manager, am I familiar with these hospital automated data collection technologies?		
Bar codes	o	o
Bar-code scanners	o	o
Are you familiar with these subtypes?	o	o
Laser or charge-coupe device scanners	o	o
Autodiscrimination scanners	o	o
Keyboard-wedge scanners	o	o
Fixed-position scanners		
Portable computers	o	o
Hand-held devices	o	o
Vehicle-mounted devices	o	o
Wearable systems	o	o
Voice recognition technology	o	o
Optical character recognition	o	o
Light systems	o	o
Electronic product codes	o	o

REFERENCES

1. Deeter, K. and Zimmerman, J. 2011. Developing and implementing pull systems in the Intensive Care Unit. In: *Leading the Lean Healthcare Journal*, edited by J. Wellman and P. Hagan. New York: Productivity Press.
2. Greene, J.H. 1996. *American Production and Inventory Control Society. Production and Inventory Control Handbook*. New York: McGraw-Hill.
3. Marcinko, D.E. and Hetico, H.R. 2008. *Dictionary of Health Information Technology and Security*. New York: Springer Publishing.
4. Piasecki, D. Optimizing Economic Order Quantity (EOQ). *Solutions Magazine* (January 2001). Also available online at: www.inventoryops.com/economic_order_quantity.htm.
5. Piasecki, D.J. 2003. *Inventory Accuracy: People, Processes & Technology*. Madison, WI: Ops Publishing.
6. Shim, J.K. and Siegel, J.G. 2000. *Modern Cost Management and Analysis*. New York: Barron's.
7. Wanaka, S. and Marquardt, B. 2011. Balancing the line in out-patient pharmacy. In: *Leading the Lean Healthcare Journal*, edited by J. Wellman and P. Hagan. New York: Productivity Press.

13 Lean Six Sigma Applications for Health Care Delivery Improvement

Gaining and Maintaining a Competitive Edge

Mark Mathews

CONTENTS

There is absolutely no question that the health care industry is facing significant challenges in this twenty-first century. We are being asked to cut costs, to guarantee top quality through public reporting, and to implement efficiencies in operations like never before. Therefore, gaining and maintaining a competitive edge or just surviving in today's health care environment will demand razor-sharp managerial skills and an innovative organizational culture devoted to cutting-edge thinking.

All stakeholders in the health care arena, from patients to physicians to hospital board members, are searching for higher quality and flawless service delivery, leading to greater patient satisfaction at an affordable cost. They want improved reimbursement, operational efficiencies, retention of labor, medical and pharmaceutical error reduction, and above all, minimal expenditures. Achieving these lofty goals requires looking beyond the borders of one's own industry for management initiatives that drive both quality and low cost while serving the customer in his or her own best interest. The health care industry's holy grail of providing quality while minimizing cost is often thought of as extremely difficult, if not impossible, to attain, until now.

What is now standard in the manufacturing and non-health care service industries provides a valuable lesson for health care managers and providers to stay competitive. The hottest management improvement initiative sweeping many industries is the one approach with the most visible success above all improvement methods thus far. It is not a new fad or passing fancy, but rather, a flexible system built on the best of past management ideas and proven practices of the business world's most successful companies. This philosophy is designed to markedly improve an organization's performance and management leadership. Today's top technology is Lean Six Sigma.

INTRODUCTION

Lean Six Sigma is a powerful and clearly validated technology that marries two distinct, but complimentary methodologies utilized for performance improvement in all but a handful of top countries around the entire globe.

The Lean methodology, first introduced in Japan within the Toyota Production System, was one of the first to call attention to identifying and removing waste within a process. It can be defined as a methodology that is used to accelerate the speed and reduce the cost of any process by removing waste (or non-value-added [NVA] activity). Simply put, this methodology allows one to "do more with less."

Six Sigma, imported from Japan by Motorola and made famous by Jack Welch, the former CEO of General Electric Corporation (GE), has attained widespread appeal in all business industries because of its wholesome concept of data-driven process improvement to drive quality and minimize costs. When problems and solutions are quantified, the numbers do not lie. Decisions are made from a more concrete and tangible viewpoint. Welch even calls Six Sigma the "code that changes corporate DNA." The Six Sigma approach to a process improvement problem reveals the underlying "physics" of the process. There are no assumptions or innuendos about whether things get better or not, it is about how much and in which direction.

Health care providers are beginning to incorporate the culture changing philosophy of Lean Six Sigma to integrate with or even replace current quality initiatives they already have in place.

The goal of this chapter is to help the health care executive better understand what Lean Six Sigma is, how it can help to improve performance, and why the provider needs to take a closer look at the potential benefits to their organization, particularly in comparison to previous process improvement programs. Because the two components of Lean and Six Sigma provide distinctly different perspectives, we will examine each technique individually to allow a greater understanding. We will then provide the framework for integrating these approaches to provide a "whole that is greater than the sum of the parts"—Lean Six Sigma.

STORY OF LEAN

CONCEPT OF LEAN THINKING

In their highly acclaimed book entitled *Lean Thinking*, James Womack and Daniel Jones are often quoted in their description of Lean thinking as "a way to do more and more with less and less—less human effort, less equipment, less time, and less space—while coming closer and closer to providing customers with exactly what they want" [1]. Indeed, this methodology is based squarely on the philosophy of meeting our patient's requirements of quality and precision in the most efficient manner possible. The hallmarks of this philosophy center on four concepts that were defined by one of Toyota Motor Corporation's pioneers of the Toyota Production System, Taiich Ohno:

1. We need to re-examine the way we think about waste.
2. Waste can be difficult to recognize.
3. We need to make waste obvious to everyone.
4. Lean is the first step toward attaining efficiency in any process.*

Thus, the "central theorem" of Lean thinking revolves around hitting the performance goal *every time* while avoiding wasteful activities. This concept can be visualized as the desire to hit a target's bull's eye, which represents the goal, while avoiding the peripheral regions of the target, which represent waste. Waste is sometimes referred to as "Muda" which is the Japanese term for waste. There are two forms of Muda. Type 1 represents "necessary" waste, which does not add value, but cannot be avoided, as with regulation or infrastructure limitations. Type 2 Muda is "unnecessary" waste, which should be identified and removed if at all possible.

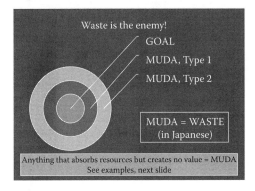

The goals of a Lean undertaking in any context are

1. To satisfy our customers
2. To improve production through higher quality and lower costs
3. To sustain gains after they have been achieved
4. To do more with less
5. To eliminate waste

---

* Stamps, Beatriz, MD, MBA, Creative Healthcare, Scottsdale, AZ (personal communication).

6. To follow the basic tenets of Lean production:
   a. Stable processes and environments (less waste)
   b. Continuous flow of resources (no batching)
   c. Pull systems (replenish supplies only when customers demand)
   d. Standard work (repeatable and reliable processes)
   e. Level production (to deal with regular fluctuations in demand)

FIVE PRINCIPLES OF LEAN THINKING

The five accepted principles of Lean thinking are value, value stream, flow, pull, and perfection.

Value

A producer of certain services may create value, but the "customer" is the only person who can define value as it applies to them. Frequently, we assume that we know what the "customer" wants, but we are also frequently incorrect in those assumptions. This leads to an inaccurate assessment of process defects from the customer's perspective and faulty design or re-design. It is important to note that most health care entities will have different "customers" for the entire set of their processes. For example, the process of admitting a patient to the emergency room has as its customer the patient, but the medical records process of completing charts through physician review and signatures has as its customers the many physicians on their medical staff. Processes on a patient floor may have nursing personnel as their customers as processes at the administrative level may have administrators as their customers.

Value Stream

This is defined as the set of all the actions required to complete a process. Processes are defined as a systematic series of actions that are directed to some end goal. An easy way to think about this is to identify "verb" statements that describe a particular action. Examples might include testing a sample of blood for electrolytes or delivering the proper medications to each patient on a particular inpatient unit. Value stream analysis shows the value of each process step that unambiguously creates value (value added or VA) as opposed to no value (non-value added or NVA).

A typical value stream map is illustrated below

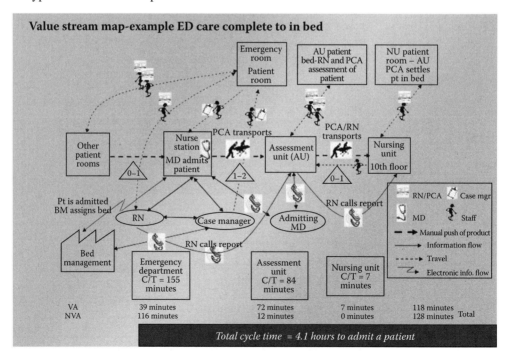

Value stream map-example ED care complete to in bed

Flow

When a process "flows," the entire process (or value stream) moves in a continuous fashion with no stoppages, slowdowns, or need to "rework" a particular step. Although counter-intuitive, flow processing is much more efficient than our typical style of "batch and queue" processing. "Batch and queue" refers to our typical manner of gathering items for processing and then handling them all at once. An example of this can be seen with the processing of physician orders where the unit assistant will stack all new charts with orders until a sufficient number of them are gathered, after which he will then process each individual one. This practice is not only inefficient but can potentially lead to delays in patient care. A common metric used to quantify a flowing process is "cycle time." Cycle time can be defined as the total time it takes for a process (all process steps added together) *plus* any delays inherent in the process.

Pull

This principle deals with the dynamics of the supply chain. It can be characterized by the following general traits:

1. No supplier should produce a good or service until the customer downstream asks for it.
2. The customer should "tell" you what they need instead of you trying to "sell" them something you already have.
3. Demands of customers become much more stable when they can get what they want when they want it.

A "pull" system is the exact opposite of a "push" system. A pull system will utilize a cue to alert one to the fact that more of a particular item is needed, but only when the customer requests it. In contrast, a "push" system exists when there is no particular relationship between demand and supply of a particular item, and those items are frequently stocked without regard to usage. A common symptom of this situation can be seen when hospital employees hoard a particular item because they have experienced fluctuations in its availability. Most hospitals used to stock surgical scrubs on open shelves, but with poor inventory management, soon discovered that shortages occurred and certain scrubs were prone to "disappear." This is because employees and physicians experienced a time when they could not find their size and so put a few away in their locker for the next time that might occur. This cascaded into increased supply costs due to replacement fees. The Pyxis system was adopted to eliminate hoarding and provide a stable supply of scrubs.

Perfection

This principle holds that perfection is achieved with the complete elimination of waste so that all activities along the value stream create value. It is understood that transparency along the entire value stream is a prerequisite for perfection to occur. The continuous pursuit of perfection is sometimes referred to as "continuous quality improvement" (CQI) and is characterized by ongoing strategies like Lean in an effort to remove waste and increase speed.

STEPS IN LEAN PROCESS IMPROVEMENT

Many organizations will utilize a variant of the DMAIC framework (traditionally used in the Six Sigma methodology) in applying the Lean methodology to problem solving. This leads to the following steps in Lean process improvement:

1. Define the "current state" or actual process performance as it exists today.
2. Define the "future state" or desired process performance.

3. Gather and analyze data to identify root causes.
4. Revise the process to remove root causes in a pilot format.
5. Institute process changes on a permanent basis to sustain the gains observed.
6. Standardize.

LEAN TOOLS AND TECHNIQUES

A few tools and techniques are unique to the world of Lean process improvement and include

1. Kaizen events
2. 5S technique
3. Standard work
4. Visual controls and human factors engineering.

KAIZEN EVENTS

Kaizen is one of the most powerful tools in the Lean methodology. These events involve intense work sessions aimed at making concrete decisions in a short time period without the need for much data collection. Kaizen events are fairly narrow in scope, ideally concentrating on making one or two decisions at the most. For example, there may be competing improvement ideas that require more exploration. Using a kaizen event can provide the necessary structure to make the decision needed to move forward with implementation. The steps in a typical kaizen event often include

1. Determine and define the objectives.
2. Determine the current state of the process.
3. Determine the requirements of the process.
4. Create a plan for implementation.
5. Implement the improvements.
6. Check the effectiveness of the improvements.
7. Document and standardize the improved process.
8. Continue the cycle.

5S TECHNIQUE

This technique was developed to allow employees to visually control their work area around visual management techniques. The principles involved in visual management include

1. Improving workspace efficiency and productivity
2. Helping people share workstations by providing standard layouts
3. Reducing the time required to look for needed supplies or tools
4. Improving the work environment

Each "S" in 5S stands for a step in the process:

1. Sort—Classify every item in the designated area as either needed or not needed.
2. Set (Straighten)—Put "everything in its place."
3. Shine (Sweep)—Clean all work environments for order and organization.
4. Standardize—Document what goes where, who will clean, and who will inspect and on what schedule.

5. Sustain—Design a system for monitoring process, providing feedback, and rewarding good outcomes.

Prior to conducting a 5S event, a significant amount of planning is vital. It is important to scope the target area as something that is manageable, draw a physical map of the area under consideration, and assemble a list of current items in that area. This is usually accomplished by taking photographs (both before and after) of the area.

STANDARD WORK

Standard work is a concept for producing stable and reliable processes in any environment. It involves choosing the best way to perform a current process while allowing for worker input and flexibility to change as the environment changes. Standard work is best implemented as written documentation of the way in which each step in a process should be performed. Primary tools that serve as elements of the standard work concept include

1. 5S approach—A form of visual control; this concept was described previously.
2. Takt time—Measures the "speed" with which customers must be served to satisfy the demand for that particular service. In health care, a useful example is calculating how many emergency department (ED) physician hours are available in a day to meet the needs of the patient demand for that day. For example:
   a. If there are eight physicians who work for 12 hours per day and the patient volume for that ED is 100 patients per day, the takt time = $(5 \times 12)/100$ or 0.6 physician hours per patient = 36 minutes per patient.
   b. This can be contrasted with throughput time—the time a process requires to complete from start to finish. The ultimate goal is to balance throughput with takt time so that no delays occur.
3. Lead time—Represents the relationship between waiting customers (queue), throughput time of the process, and waiting time for each customer. As an example, in health care, the waiting time of a patient (lead time) to be registered can be determined from the number of patients ahead of her multiplied by the process throughput time. If there are 10 people ahead of her and the registration clerk is taking 5 minutes per patient for the registration process, her lead time is approximately 50 minutes.
4. Work sequence—By standardizing a processes sequence, variability is reduced and the process becomes more efficient.
5. Work layout—By standardizing the "environment" in which work is performed, variability is reduced and the process is again made more efficient.
6. In-process stock—This refers to having enough supply available to meet the average demand, assuming that the range of demand is narrow (a Lean characterization as well). In health care, this would mean having sufficient instruments available for all the cases in an operating room on a given day, allowing for the typical number of emergency cases as well.

VISUAL CONTROLS AND HUMAN FACTORS ENGINEERING

Visual management centers on the goal of creating a visual workplace where the environment is self-explanatory and defects can be immediately recognized. Visual controls and human factors engineering can assist with better visual management. By providing visual cues to the work involved, errors are concomitantly reduced. Examples include universal signs, color-coding, outlines of items, and charts and graphs.

EIGHT TYPES OF WASTE IN HEALTH CARE

Waste in health care processes can be classified into eight different subtypes:

1. *Overproduction*—This term refers to the performance of redundant work. Examples include duplicate charting, multiple forms with the same information, copies of reports being sent automatically, and multiple caregivers asking the patient for the same information.
2. *Motion*—This term refers to the extra steps taken by employees in order to complete a task (part or all of a process). People working in health care facilities or offices often spend a large part of their day moving around the environment searching for people or information, gathering supplies, moving items, dropping off records, etc.
3. *Waiting*—This is epidemic in most health care settings and is often referred to as "queuing." Waiting for items like medical records or radiographs, or a patient waiting for providers is simply inactive time with no value content at all.
4. *Transport*—The unnecessary movement of patients, supplies, or materials that are necessary for, involved in, or produced by a process. Examples include delivery of medication from a distant central pharmacy, procurement of an unexpected surgical pack to the operating room, staff needing to travel a great distance to retrieve supplies, or transporting patients large distances from the emergency room to obtain diagnostic tests. This movement adds time to a process and contains no value.
5. *Overprocessing*—Excess processes that do not add value from the patient's perspective. The most prevalent example of this in health care is the processing of regulatory paperwork or the inclusion of extra steps merely to satisfy a regulatory condition. Also included are activities like order clarification due to poor handwriting or erroneous abbreviations, missing medications from a pharmacy area leading to a delay in treatment, and redundant charting or paperwork.
6. *Inventory waste*—This is seen when too much product is acquired ahead of actual demand. This leads to a risk that items may become outdated or expired, leading to waste and excess cost. This is most often seen in health care in association with poor inventory management. Inspection of the average hospital storeroom will yield many items that will not be needed for months to years ahead. In addition, catering to the individual needs of all surgeons in the operating room leads to the accumulation of multiple trays and costly instruments that are used infrequently.
7. *Rework*—This term refers to work that contains errors or defects that require correction. In health care, this is seen in coding and billing errors requiring reprocessing, medication errors requiring additional reconciliation, patient mishaps requiring reporting and perhaps additional treatment, and surgical errors requiring re-operation.
8. *Not using people to their full potential capabilities*—This is often referred to as the "eight forms of waste" because it was described after the original seven forms of waste related to manufacturing were defined. It refers to a mismatch of a particular task to the skill set of the person assigned to perform that task. It is common to see significant variation in the ways different people will perform the same task. This often arises when there is an unclear expectation set forth by management or a lack of standard processes. Matching tasks to skill sets can lead to improved quality of work, employee satisfaction, and employee loyalty.

EXAMPLE OF A LEAN PROJECT IN HEALTH CARE

TIMELY RECEIPT OF ADMISSIONS ORDERS IN AN ED

In a certain community hospital located in California, it was discovered that the average time for receipt of admission orders for a patient being admitted from their ED was 6 hours against a standard goal of 3 hours. This performance was clearly unacceptable and was sure to be influencing overall throughput in the ED. A Lean project team was assembled to evaluate the process and make recommendations for improvement.

Lean Project Charter
Project Name: Timely Receipt of Admission Orders

Champion/ Sponsor	xxxxxx	**Sponsor**	xxxxxx
Project Leader	xxxxxx	**Team Member**	xxxxxx
Business Case	The Emergency Department provides 69% of all Hospital admissions. Patient throughput is one of the most common measures of hospital performance and increases patient satisfaction. One way of measuring patient satisfaction is analyzing their length of stay. The ED averages about 1.5 patients every hour per day. So for every hour in excess of 3 hours waiting for admission orders, the hospital loses 1.5 potential ED patients per hour being seen. That's a 1.5 patient loss opportunity without accounting for multiple admissions with extended hold times. So looking at this extremely conservatively, this delay causes an extended length of stay and a lost opportunity of $124,000 of revenue per month of $1,500,000 for the year assuming just 1.5 patients per day with an extended wait time. Therefore, it is essential to plan and implement an effective admission order process.		
Problem Statement	In the last 6 months there was an average of a 6 hour delay in receiving admission orders vs. 3 hours per hospital policy. We have experienced ED closures, an increase in patients leaving without being seen (LWBS), an increased length of stay, excessive waiting to be seen times, and decreased patient satisfaction.		
Performance Goal	Reduce time of receipt of admission orders from an average of 6 hours to 1 hour. Once approved, this process to be implemented within one month.		
Secondary Success Criteria	Improvement in the first response time when consulting the admitting MD. Improvement in the average overall turnaround time for the ED patient who is being admitted.		
Support Required	Policy change, Physician leaders, Pre-admit order set.		

The Project Charter, shown above, was centered on the business case for improving patient throughput. It was also noted that, based on current volumes, a 1-hour delay for 1.5 patients per day for an entire month led to a loss of revenue of $228,000, or $2.7 million annualized. The project goal was to reduce the time for receipt of admission orders to 1 hour, starting from when the admission decision was made.

After carefully defining the scope of the project, a workflow diagram was constructed to define the "current state" of the process. Once completed, a major problem was identified—there were multiple and redundant calls to the admitting physicians in an attempt to finalize the orders.

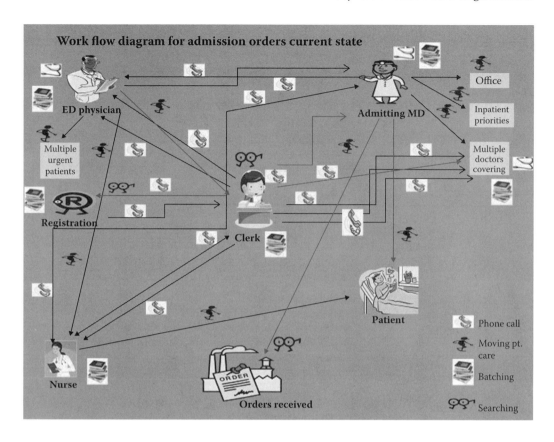

Work flow diagram for admission orders current state

During the measure phase of the project, the time for receipt of admission orders and overall cycle time for a patient in the ED who was being admitted were documented. Receipt of admission orders averaged 6 hours and the length of stay 5 hours.

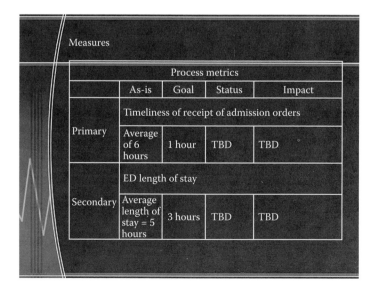

Measures				
	Process metrics			
	As-is	Goal	Status	Impact
Primary	Timeliness of receipt of admission orders			
	Average of 6 hours	1 hour	TBD	TBD
Secondary	ED length of stay			
	Average length of stay = 5 hours	3 hours	TBD	TBD

In addition, it was documented that, on average, it took four calls to reach the correct MD for admission orders. It was also noted that the time required to reach that physician was, on average, 2–4 hours.

Measures

		Process metrics			
		As-is	Goal	Status	Impact
Primary Phase 1	Number of calls to the consulting physician				
		4	1	TBD	TBD
Secondary Phase 1	Timeliness of first response time when consulting an MD about the order				
		2–4 h	30 min	TBD	TBD

A full value stream map was then prepared, illustrating the VA and NVA steps in the detailed process.

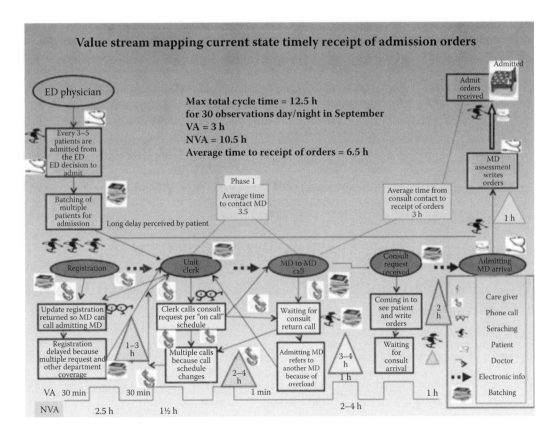

In addition to all of the confounding issues within the process, such as multiple players, multiple patients, and batch processes, the following were observed:

1. The average overall process cycle time from the time the physician decides to admit to the time the orders are received is 12.5 hours.
2. The average amount of time that the unit clerk calls the physician to the time he/she returns the call is 3.5 hours.
3. The average amount of time from the unit clerk contacting the physician to the time the MD order is written is 3 hours.
4. The amount of calls, on average, to locate the admitting physician was 4.

After examining the detailed process map, it was decided that, due to the problem of multiple phone calls being required to reach the admitting physician, focus was needed on a subprocess map to clarify that issue further. That process map revealed the multitude of steps involved in contacting the appropriate physician to obtain admission orders. Suggested changes to the process were made and implemented. Those changes included

1. Development of a One Call System for consultation request
2. Utilization of pre-admission orders to expedite transfer of patient to ward
3. Tender a request for Medical Staffing Support to assist with MD accountability issues, timely updates of on-call lists, and policy changes to implement the above changes

A pilot program was instituted to test these changes and to provide a template for a full rollout, if successful. The results of this successful pilot are noted below.

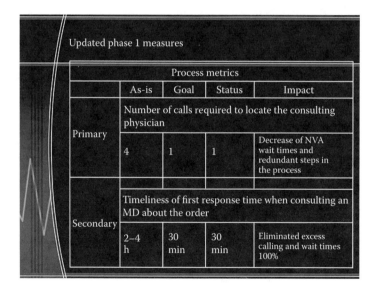

Updated phase 1 measures

| | Process metrics | | | |
	As-is	Goal	Status	Impact
Primary	Number of calls required to locate the consulting physician			
	4	1	1	Decrease of NVA wait times and redundant steps in the process
Secondary	Timeliness of first response time when consulting an MD about the order			
	2–4 h	30 min	30 min	Eliminated excess calling and wait times 100%

STORY OF SIX SIGMA

The concepts of process improvement and total quality management (TQM) emerged after World War II, when the Japanese auto and electronics industries, in a quest to capture the U.S. marketplace, virtually re-coined the term "Made in Japan" from a trademark of inferiority to a worldwide stigmata of quality and endurance. Toyota Motor Corporation soon became the ideal model to emulate by U.S. companies such as Ford, Motorola, and later, GE. The Deming model and subsequent total quality improvement/continuous improvement management initiatives, copied from Japan, evolved with a passion when brought to America. The search for best practices led to the popularity of accolades such as The Malcolm Baldrige Quality Award; an award that became Olympic gold to a company's marketing campaign.

The quality envelope was pushed further during the 80s when Motorola Corporation augmented traditional improvement tools with a systematic problem-solving method based on rigorous statistical analysis. This evolution of a process-oriented problem-solving approach soon became the genesis of what is now known as the Six Sigma methodology. The ultimate goal of the Six Sigma model is to find the root causes of variation in the processes of a business, find the problems that created the variations, determine ways to measure them, and control (or eliminate) those variations. The overriding goal of this improvement effort is to produce a new process that has long-term sustainability. The achievement of quality to its greatest extent is measured in the quantifiable metric of "sigma." The greater the sigma level reached, the more efficient the process.

In reaching the Six Sigma level, there is almost no variation in a process, thus demonstrating the most efficient way of doing things. Is this ultimate goal of perfection too ambitious a goal for health care? Perhaps. For service industries and the health care industry, the goal of virtual perfection may be impossible by virtue of the significant number of variables involved. However, one must consider the implications of a less than almost perfect system, as illustrated in Figure 13.1.

Sigma is the 18th letter of the Greek alphabet and represents the statistical symbol for standard deviation. In statistics, with a standard bell-shaped normal population distribution, one sigma represents one standard deviation from the mean to the nearest specification level; two sigma represents an even greater variance, and so on.

In Six Sigma vernacular, the bell-shaped curve becomes a representation of variation itself; in other words, achieving a "Six Sigma" process means virtual perfection in the upper standard limits of being 99.99966% good, as shown in Figure 13.2.

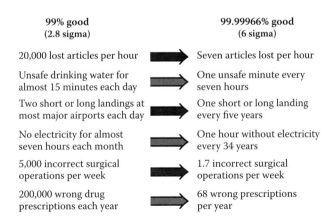

99% good (2.8 sigma)		99.99966% good (6 sigma)
20,000 lost articles per hour	→	Seven articles lost per hour
Unsafe drinking water for almost 15 minutes each day	→	One unsafe minute every seven hours
Two short or long landings at most major airports each day	→	One short or long landing every five years
No electricity for almost seven hours each month	→	One hour without electricity every 34 years
5,000 incorrect surgical operations per week	→	1.7 incorrect surgical operations per week
200,000 wrong drug prescriptions each year	→	68 wrong prescriptions per year

FIGURE 13.1 Is 99% good enough? (Butter, K. and Lazarus, I., The promise of Six Sigma, *Managed Healthcare Executives*, October, 2001, p. 2.)

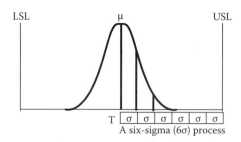

FIGURE 13.2   A "Six Sigma" process. (Butter, K. and Lazarus, I., The promise of Six Sigma, *Managed Healthcare Executives*, October, 2001, p. 2.)

Cost of Quality

The cost of quality actually goes up when the variation and error rate of a process goes up. For example, the costs of pharmaceutical errors alone, in terms of lives and money, are huge. Consider the legal implications of incorrect procedures to an institution. Coding errors that lead to variability in reimbursements represent loss of income to hospital, physicians, and other providers. Think also of the cost of additional safeguards, such as inspectors, that must be put into place to oversee defective processes. When a process is improved, the cost of quality goes down. There are fewer costs due to redundancy, lost time, and lost labor.

The concept of looking at variation in a process is analogous to the process of teaching a child to ride a bicycle for the first time. The child will be wobbly when he or she gets on the bicycle at first and may even fall several times. As long as you are watching closely, to help the child back on the bicycle, help steer a little, and provide encouragement, the child soon learns to ride smoothly and it appears all so natural. The child soon learns to balance from the feedback gained from you and the internal feedback from the environment. After studying the learning process closer, you may find the child to be more successful learning on a set of training wheels or on a bicycle a little smaller in size. Regardless, the closed-loop feedback, analysis, and monitoring by a teacher or process "champion," keeps the child from wobbling too much and to stay on a straight and narrow course.

Businesses also wobble in their processes and, in Six Sigma terminology, this wobbling is the variation that needs continual feedback to help correct and stabilize. Unlike riding a bike, where when once learned it becomes natural and smooth, businesses continue to wobble in their processes and may fall without ever being able to get back up. The institution of Six Sigma methodology is a closed feedback loop to prevent instability in processes.

Virtual perfection may not be easily attainable in a service industry as with computer chips coming off an assembly line, and the health care industry certainly has its share of "wobbliness." It is, nonetheless, this desire to constantly improve operations, perfect the way business is carried out, and become attuned to what the customer needs that separates this improvement method from those that have come before. Moreover, the benefits of setting higher performance goals is a strategic decision to accelerate improvement, promote continual learning, and reach sustainable efforts to succeed. It is truly a cultural change in mind-set to attain quality at its highest level.

Example of Process Variation in a Health Care Institution

The potential for Six Sigma to yield significant cost savings or new revenue is significant. Figure 13.3 below illustrates the wide potential when Six Sigma is applied to the health care industry.

The radiology department at the University of Texas MD Anderson Cancer Center (MDACC) in Houston, TX had goals of increasing its capacity, reduce patient waiting time, eliminate errors, and improve morale in the department.

Project	Validated savings ($)	Long term savings ($)
Supply chain management	163,410	841,540
"Captain of the ship"	519,000	790,000
Dentals	232,637	425,000
Results reporting	367,621	341,000
Medication safety	31,774	242,777
ED wait time	100,000	202,428
HR recruitment	32,000	124,430
Physician satisfaction	39,780	66,000

FIGURE 13.3 Six Sigma project potential. One hospital's experience. (Stamps, B. and Lazarus, I., The promise of Six Sigma, Part I, *Managed Healthcare Executives*, January, 2002, p. 4.)

At first glance, and where most expansion efforts have previously failed, the inclination is for most organizations to hire more staff, minimize hardware limitations by adding more CT scanners, and add more physical space. In essence, they would be duplicating the current process to meet demands.

Six Sigma consultants hired by MDACC looked at the entire process of patient CT throughput, or CT cycle time, and using Six Sigma tools, identified where the greatest variations in the process occurred. They found that the greatest variation and, therefore, the greatest opportunities for improvement were in the flow of patients and time management of the radiologist; not important were the scanning speed or number of CT scanners. In fact, the rate-limiting factors for CT cycle time were discovered to be in the transcription and interpretation of CT films. Innovative solutions included hiring facilitators to handle clinician phone calls and providing indexing of radiology studies, allowing for faster interpretations by radiologists. Future MDACC changes will involve voice recognition technology to improve transcription cycle time.

The cultural lexicon of Six Sigma defines quality as a reduction in variation or number of "defects" in a process given a million opportunities of occurrence. This is referred to as "defects per million opportunities" or DPMO. Each incremental increase in sigma level achieved is a significant reduction in defects, as in Figure 13.4.

The Six Sigma movement gained its greatest notoriety and acceptance by major industry in the 1990s when Jack Welch of GE wanted to empower his employees and challenge them to participate in the decision-making process. The company had reached a plateau of growth, and Welch knew that staying there meant death by stagnation.

Welch wanted GE to constantly change and improve, becoming an even more dynamic organization. He elicited the advice of Honeywell's CEO Larry Bossidy, and soon the largest, most ambitious management initiative ever undertaken at GE began. The results have been nothing short of impressive over the course of 5 years—over $3 billion in savings and consistent annual productivity increases in the double digits. The impact of Six Sigma on bottom-line improvements on costs, return on investment (ROI), and profitability caught the attention of every industry from

Sigma Level	Defects per million opportunities
1.5	500,000
2	308,537
3	66,807
4	6,210
5	233
6	3.4

FIGURE 13.4 Six Sigma and DPMOs. (Cherry, J. and Seshadri, S., Six Sigma: Using statistics to reduce process variability and costs in radiology, *Radiology Management*, Nov/Dec, 2001, p. 1.)

merchandising to hospitality services. This interest also prompted a company, like GE, to begin taking the Six Sigma methodology to its customers, including those in health care. The impact on early adopters in the medical industry has been impressive and continued to grow steadily over the years.

Six Sigma Health Care Pioneers

Example 1

One of these earliest health care adopters of Six Sigma was the Mount Carmel Health System in Columbus, Ohio. The organization was barely breaking even in the summer of 2000 when competition from surrounding providers made things worse. Employee layoffs added fuel to an already all-time low employee morale.

CEO Joe Calvaruso was determined to stem the bleeding, break the cycle of poor financial performance, and return the hospital system to profitability. He sought the potential benefits of Six Sigma and began a full deployment of its methodology. The plan was a bold move, as the organization ensured that no one would be terminated as a result of a Six Sigma project having eliminated his or her previous duties. These employees would be offered an alternative position in a different department. Moreover, top personnel were asked to leave their current positions to be trained and work full time as Six Sigma expert practitioners who would oversee project deployment while their positions were backfilled.

The Six Sigma deployment was the right decision. More than 50 projects were initiated with significant success. An example of an early Mount Carmel success story is the dramatic improvement in their Medicare + Choice product reimbursements, previously written off as uncollectible accounts. These accounts were often denied by the CMS due to coding of those patients as "working aged." Since the treatment process status often changed in these patients, CMS often rejected claims or lessened reimbursement amounts, effectively making coding a difficult and elusive problem. The employment of the Six Sigma process fixed the problem, resulting in a real gain of $857,000 to the organization. The spillover of this methodology to other coding parameters also has dramatically boosted revenue collection.

Example 2

With the help of GE, Commonwealth Health Corporation of Bowling Green, Kentucky realized nearly $1 million in annualized billing improvement savings and reduced radiology expenses. These savings came from recognizing specific opportunities in patient throughput, resulting in increases of 25%. These changes also resulted in a reduction of cost per procedure by 21.5%, although fewer resources were utilized.

Commonwealth's CEO, John Desmarais, became a passionate believer of the impact Six Sigma had on his company and publicly remarked, "It's the single most important thing we have done in the history of our organization."

Example 3

Scottsdale Healthcare in Arizona used consultants from Creative Healthcare to analyze its problem of ED diversions. Diversions occur when EDs are too full in capacity to handle acute emergencies and a decision is made to close its doors to patients, diverting ambulances elsewhere. The issue of closed and diverted emergency rooms is a growing nationwide problem because of fewer EDs and a growing aged and uninsured population. The consultants, using Six Sigma principles, mapped the ED process and found multiple bottlenecks that had a direct effect on the probability of evoking a "diversionary" status in the emergency room.

One bottleneck process deemed "out of control" was the issue of bed control. A process is considered "in control" when operating within acceptable specification limits. It was found that the average transfer time for a patient admitted to a hospital bed from the ED was 80 minutes, even when half of the time, a bed was available. The process was a significant "waste of time" and, moreover, complicated by an administrative nurse "inspector" locating beds on different floors. Two tenements of Six Sigma were violated: one, inspection is a correction for an inefficient process and two, the more

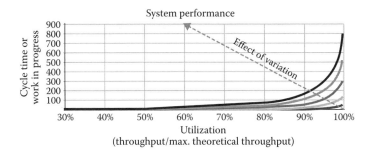

FIGURE 13.5 Expansion of commercial delivery systems. (Butter, K. and Lazarus, I. The promise of Six Sigma, *Managed Healthcare Executives*, October, 2001, p. 4)

steps involved, the less the potential yield of a process. Through this revelation, the hospital reassigned the administrative nurse, reduced cycle time by 10% in bed control, and improved ED throughput with greater turnover, thereby improving revenue by nearly $600,000 annually.

The addition of a nurse inspector and waiting patients in a busy ED is an example of "Little's Law," sometimes referred to as the first fundamental law of system behavior. When more and more inputs are put into a system, such as more ED patients and an additional nurse employee, and when there is variation in their arrival time (no control over patient arrivals) or process variation (different people doing the same things differently), there results an exponential rise in "cycle time." Productivity of the system begins to fall and inefficiency and variation creeps in, as seen in Figure 13.5.

Example 4

The Charleston Area Medical Center (CAMC) in Charleston, West Virginia chose to implement Six Sigma techniques in its supply chain management. The initial savings from a just-in-time (JIT) inventory management system totaled $163,410, with projected long-term savings expected to be over $800,000. The Six Sigma staff of CAMC moved to additional projects and produced remarkable results, as exemplified below

> *Medical error reduction*
>   1. Reducing patient falls
>   2. Reducing medication errors
>   3. Improving pharmacy turnaround times.
> *Business operations*
>   1. Improving the revenue cycle
>   2. Improving human resource recruiting and retention
>   3. Improving OR scheduling and throughput.
> *Patient case management*
>   1. Decreasing length of stay
>   2. Reducing ED diversions
>   3. Improving radiology scheduling, operational flow, and resource maximization patient satisfaction.

ROADMAP TO SUCCESS

Six Sigma is a rigorous systematic discipline that demands the use of various problem-solving tools and a particular methodology to drive process improvement. While the approach is best known for its basis in the quantitative metrics of quality, it is the approach to improving quality and reducing variation that separates Six Sigma from other quality campaign methods. In fact, many organizations use the measurable feedback data provided by Six Sigma to augment existing quality initiatives such as TQM or the balanced scorecard. By validating the impact of defects and improvements, as well as the use of small-scale experiments, reaching the optimal solution to a problem makes implementing a change more believable to the organization. One chief of staff of a major metropolitan hospital has stated that the medical staff respects the statistical rigor of the Six Sigma methodology. Data and evidence gathered by stakeholders get their attention. Root causes to variation suddenly emerge as a result of the problem-solving discipline. Many times, according to practitioners, the real problem is not what you originally deduced after looking at the data.

At the heart of the Six Sigma management philosophy is the scientific approach known by the acronym DMAIC:

(D) Define. This is the first phase of the Six Sigma process. The team in charge of the project must clearly define the problem and the factors critical to quality (CTQ) that are important to the customer. Six Sigma's alignment with the goals of health care is demonstrated by what it regards as CTQ from the vantage point of any customer—delivery consistent with expectations, with a desired quality outcome, and at a fair price. Health care professionals will quickly recognize this as paralleling with our industry goals of "access, quality and cost," in what has become the three pillars of health care delivery. Six Sigma projects begin with a clear and unambiguous declaration of customer expectations in each of these categories. An examination of the business process through mapping techniques correlates those CTQ factors with gaps where the process falls short. An example of the delivery of patient test kits to a hospital by a laboratory illustrates the approach.

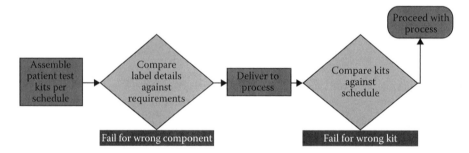

Most process maps fail to account for all potential—and potentially frequent—process failures. The assembly of patient test kits may involve a multitude of component activities, all of which may introduce variables of error into the process, leading to a cycle of error management. In further defining the process, these hidden factors add to the cost of quality including mistakes in kit components, handling, or delivery. Compounding the problems with traditional maps is the focus on the end result—potentially at the expense of failures that occur along the way. For example, it is not uncommon for management to focus on the "final test yield," such as the number of acceptable kits (or appointments, surgeries, discharges, etc.) produced at the end of the process, rather than the "rolled throughput yield" which accommodates the impact of any rework incurred within the process.

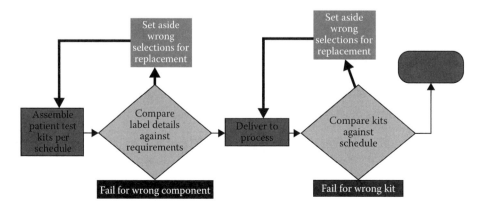

A more detailed "Process Flow Diagram" can flush out those process failures not intended by the design of the process, but compromising the overall efficiency and yield from the process. It has been estimated that "rework" can represent up to 25% of an organization's total gross revenues.

In the theoretical situation described above, it is conceivable that the final test yield of kit preparation is 92%, indicating that 92% of the kits were acceptable upon delivery. When incorporating the rework required to achieve this yield, however, we may find that 20% of kits were set aside for wrong components or other defects (80% of kits are acceptable on this measure). The rolled throughput yield of this process is determined by the cumulative probabilities of successful movement through the process *the first time*, determined by the product $(0.92)(0.80) = 0.74$. *Just as in this theoretical scenario, it has been estimated that "rework" can represent up to 25% of an organization's total gross revenues.* Six Sigma's use of rolled throughput yield produces a more robust measure of performance that can also help to identify that part of the process most in need of improvement. Once a process is mapped, the Six Sigma practitioner then begins isolating all the variables that enter into the fulfillment and delivery of patient care kits. Sometimes, the "low hanging" fruit of simple error correction is revealed by the basic process map.

The concept of the "hidden hospital" refers to hidden processes that require rework, due to errors during the initial process steps. The "hidden hospital," therefore, becomes all the redundant factors that do not add true value to the patient care delivery system.

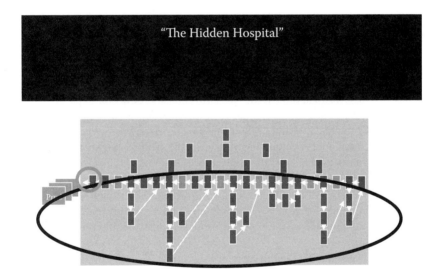

"The Hidden Hospital"

The diagram above illustrates all the "hidden" or NVA side steps a process may incur along its main path. Examples are redundant paperwork, a technician having to go find supplies not readily available, or a physician having to re-dictate a lost case history.

(M) Measure. The objective of the measure phase of a Six Sigma project is to establish the reliability of internal data and what these data suggest about process performance. How do you know if you have an effective process? Six Sigma provides both the formula and, ultimately, the answer. The process of establishing data integrity is perhaps one of the most unique aspects of Six Sigma. All too often, organizations place far too much trust in their own internal data systems. Management decisions made on unreliable data may have disastrous effects. Industries are replete with examples of performance improvement initiatives that had the opposite effect because they were based upon data that misrepresented what was really happening in the underlying process. Other managers have become so skeptical of their own data that they may only provide "lip service" to departmental reports and become ambivalent when management tries to make improvements based upon what they know to be unreliable information.

Six Sigma provides an extensive toolset of "reliability studies" (also known as "Gage R&R") to establish whether data are reliable and where improvements are needed. After this rigorous stage is complete, everyone in the organization should become confident that downstream decisions are based on sound data sources.

Once the baseline of the process has been established, with reliable data, the measure phase moves into a determination of process capability. How do you know if a process is "capable?" Looking at performance averages falls far short of answering this question, and understanding the range of variation gets us only halfway to the answer. Process capability is a function of expectations, driven by the voice of the customer (VOC). Only our customers can define expectations, according to the tenets of Six Sigma. When we compare the voice of the process (VOP) with the VOC, we have established the true process capability, expressed as the sigma level of the process.

(A) Analyze. Before Six Sigma came to enlighten many different industries, process analysis came in many forms. Unfortunately, many organizations suffer from "analysis paralysis." Worse than this, they may collect a team of individuals to brainstorm root causes, "round up the usual suspects," then send each team member off to devote time and resources to possible root causes with no regard for the impact one root cause may have on the other. Much of the waste in industry may be tied to performance improvement efforts focused on the wrong performance issue or the wrong root causes. These resources are too precious to waste, and the outcome of their efforts often does more harm than good.

Six Sigma suggests that a different philosophy is needed with respect to process analysis. Because Six Sigma focuses on the "critical Xs" or key drivers of process performance, it compels the practitioner to apply a disciplined methodology to statistically validate these critical inputs. In the view of Six Sigma, it is only the critical inputs that matter; all others are incidental. Of course, Six Sigma reveals much "low hanging fruit" as it proceeds down the path of identifying the functional characteristics of $y = f(x)$, and these are often inventoried for action in parallel with the main focus of the project. In the end, a thorough analysis is able to identify all variables that impact process performance and a relative ranking of their impact.

Here is where Six Sigma tools become the most valuable. The Six Sigma practitioner will apply a variety of hypothesis tests to challenge the conventional wisdom with respect to the process being analyzed. The operative question asked is "Does this input matter?" with respect to performance and, if so, how much? A series of hypothesis tests will reveal those critical Xs that are often buried deep in the process and taken for granted. When finally tallied and presented to management and medical staff for analysis, they have the power of statistical tests behind them to defend their relevance and importance.

Typical problems investigated in health care projects might include

1. Does time of day impact the likelihood that we will invoke diversionary status in the ED?
2. Do multiple blood draws impact cycle time for lab tests?
3. Which has a greater impact on surgery delays—surgeon or room availability?
4. Does the timing of antibiotic administration impact surgical infection rates?
5. Does the lead time between pre-op testing and surgery impact cancellation rates?
6. What duration of ventilator use and weaning time produce the ideal recovery rate?

(I) Improve. At this stage in our project, the Six Sigma practitioner will employ the benefit of the preceding statistical examination and a series of brainstorming techniques to identify various small-scale experiments aimed at process improvement.

One particular technique, the "failure modes and effects analysis (FMEA)," has become so ubiquitous in health care that it is now a core requirement for accreditation by JCAHO or JC. The FMEA is an inventory of process "failure modes" that will include a series of possible initiatives designed to mitigate or avoid the potential for failure. The FMEA is a useful brainstorming technique in the absence of useful data. Unlike typical applications of the FMEA, however, Six Sigma will always validate the FMEA with findings from the Measure and Analyze phases of the project.

Armed with these powerful data, the project leader will typically train trial and control groups to work in parallel and to test the impact of the process changes. This is an important step to overcome any downstream claims that improvements were found as a result of "random chance." This also avoids committing the organization to a large-scale implementation that has not yet been proven in the target environment.

At the conclusion of the trial, statistical tests are again employed to validate any improvements found as a result of the trial. A comparison of the trial and control groups will be made, with the operative question being "Did we make a difference?" It is possible that many different improvements were tested over time and that a series of permanent changes will be recommended at the close of the trial.

At the close of the trial, the organization is now provided with evidence of improvement that has been validated statistically. Skeptics have the compelling results needed to overcome any concerns they may have had originally. More importantly, however, the Six Sigma practitioner is able to demonstrate the true potential and results that might be expected when the improvements are made on a larger scale. There should be no surprises after this stage and the organization can move forward with confidence that the problem has been solved, *for the last time.*

(C) Control. A common pitfall of performance improvement efforts is that the organizations will experience a temporary gain in performance from the process being altered, only to find performance regress once again to its original baseline. These initiatives often relied upon controlling human behavior through incentives or punitive measures, and they lacked the control mechanisms or breakthrough improvement that would have been possible from a more rigorous examination of the underlying process.

Six Sigma, again, takes a decidedly different approach. Within any Six Sigma project, it is likely that human factors will be found to be "statistically significant"; however, it is *unlikely* that a reliance on only behavioral measures will be recommended. Six Sigma aims to fundamentally alter the way a process works so that *it is impossible to regress back to where it was before.*

Once a solution is implemented, ongoing measures are put into place to ensure that the process is monitored and that the appropriate "alarms" will be activated if each subprocess should divert from established expectations of performance. The control plan summarizes responsibility for future data collection and analysis, the frequency of analysis, and the point at which intervention might be necessary. Control plans, combined with the finalized FMEA, may also lead to the identification of future projects with regard to those parts of the process that were originally "out of scope" for the project now completed.

CULTURAL SEA-CHANGE

Successful implementation of Lean Six Sigma involves changing the very nature of an organization. This cultural shift is essential for sustainability and maximal success. If an organization can make this transition in the way it "thinks" about eradicating waste and defects, CQI will become a "permanent way of life."

Our traditional philosophy regarding quality tends to center around meeting specifications between two limits. If our results fall somewhere in between these "spec limits," then we have succeeded. The Japanese engineer, Genicihi Taguchi, suggested a paradigm shift function to describe the loss to society of not having reached a more exact specification target. In his model, any deviation of a single target results in that loss and should be addressed. Consider the financial and social implications in pharmaceutical errors incurred by institutions alone. This is one issue of quality in which vigilant focus on minimal variation is truly warranted.

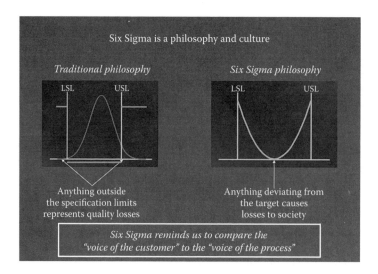

In order to accomplish this cultural sea-change, the organization must give Six Sigma projects the momentum and support it needs through the proper alignment of its organization. Without the proper environment for cultivating change, initiatives never develop the momentum needed to reach critical mass. A supportive critical mass, or a guiding powerful coalition, is necessary for an organization to gain wide acceptance and belief. Leadership must be the biggest supporter of Six Sigma projects through a top down quality agenda. They must create the vision, communicate it, and encourage a sense of urgency to "get it done." Management must reward those employees who are diverted from their usual duties to become Six Sigma trained. These employees will bring a skill set needed to reinforce Six Sigma at the process level, and to drive and sustain quality improvement.

Six Sigma projects must support also the strategic goals of the organization, and quantitative metrics must reflect the achievement of those goals. In health care, Six Sigma aligns patient goals with strategic goals, as illustrated in Figure 13.6.

A project such as ED throughput makes sense because patient satisfaction, and the perception of quality as well, is known to be directly related to patient waiting time as seen in many patient surveys. Improving ED throughput decreases patient waiting time, but increases satisfaction, optimizes revenue generation, and minimizes diversion time.

FIGURE 13.6   Six Sigma aligns patient goals with strategic plans. Six Sigma applies customer-driver measures to process improvement; customers can be patients, physicians, and employees. (Stamps, B. and Lazarus, I., The promise of Six Sigma, Part II, *Managed Healthcare Executives*, January, 2003, p. 6.)

HOW LEAN SIX SIGMA IS EMPLOYED IN A HEALTH CARE SETTING

Health care executives considering Six Sigma have a variety of options regarding implementation, but it fundamentally comes down to a make/buy decision. Those not quite ready to subject their organization to the rigors of Six Sigma or unsure of the organization's resolve can simply "buy" the time of Six Sigma practitioners and consultants to solve persistent process performance challenges. Over time, more projects may be undertaken until greater confidence exists to bring such capabilities in-house. Those that truly wish to "make" the institution a Six Sigma organization will "deploy" the program through training, coaching, and certification of employees. The infrastructure of a Six Sigma organization will include "Blackbelts" and "Greenbelts" designating different levels of expertise in the methodologies.

The first step for an organization, before it decides to employ Six Sigma, is to define its strategic objectives and set forth its goals. The organization must have a clear vision of where it wants to go, what kind of organization it wants to be (preferably world class), and whether satisfying the customer as well as the stakeholders involved in the process is the key to long-term success. The continuous pursuit of excellence is the ever-present hallmark of Six Sigma companies.

The incorporation of Six Sigma into an organization is not about a one-time effort to right the ship; it is about a strategic decision to be always customer focused, constantly vigilant, and developing the agility to stay on top of the marketplace. In essence, Six Sigma becomes a cultural change in philosophy and mind-set. It is a vigilant focus on what the customer wants. The traditional philosophy of ensuring that operations stay within lower and upper specification limits or "goalpost mentality" is replaced with customer-driven measures to achieve specific target goals. Any deviation from the target becomes a loss to the organization and, ultimately, a loss to society.

Keys to Making Lean Six Sigma Work

The key elements necessary for successful implementation of Six Sigma methodologies were summarized by Jerome Blakeslee Jr. in *Quality Progress, July 1999*. The article names several key principles for organizations to reap the most benefits from their investment in Six Sigma:

1. *Committed leaders must drive implementation efforts.* Leaders must be willing to go against the grain in recommending unpopular or unconventional management ideas. Their hands-on leadership and personal responsibility for driving Six Sigma efforts should leave little room for delegation to others.
2. *Six Sigma efforts must be integrated with current quality, management, and strategic initiatives.* This is good news to those who thought Six Sigma would have to replace the investment in existing management techniques. On the contrary, the quantitative metrics of Six Sigma enhances TQI, CQ, or more recently, balanced scorecard measures with feedback data that extend beyond assumptions.
3. *Process thinking is the supporting framework for success with Six Sigma efforts.* The organization must be rigorous in mapping existing business processes to see where they fall short of meeting customer expectations and market demand. This must be combined with accurate information to compare the VOC to the current VOP. In short, organizations must discipline themselves to follow the formula for process improvement set forth by the Six Sigma teachings. They work.
4. *The organization must be relentless in intelligence gathering on what the market and the customer wants.* This means figuring out what metrics reflect customer satisfaction or loyalty. A closed feedback loop ensures the maximization of company output to match customer requirements. In the words of one hospital administrator, "If we stay focused on becoming the gold standard for health care, the patients and profits will follow."

Of course, Six Sigma projects should also be designed to produce real savings and ROI. Short-term "quick hit" projects are designed to engage Six Sigma principles quickly, engender belief in the system, and establish a foundation for long-term Six Sigma success. Long-term payoffs are often the result of incremental short-term benefits, as well as long-term design.

LEAN SIX SIGMA COMPARED TO TQM

Many organizations have quality initiatives in place and are seeking to improve or replace current organizational improvement methods. To better understand where Lean Six Sigma might fit in, a summary comparison of several key differences in the quality initiatives of TQM versus Six Sigma helps us to improve our understanding of where TQM measures have fallen short and where Six Sigma initiatives may succeed in picking up where it left off.

Customer Focus

TQM

1. The early mantra of TQM policies and mission statements was to "meet or exceed customer requirements."
2. If customers were happy before, let us keep it that way.
3. Unfortunately, customers have dynamic and ever-changing requirements that often were measured on a one-time, or sporadic, if not ongoing, basis.
4. No one took the time to truly understand the customer needs and to adjust the process to constantly fit that need.
5. Lack of control mechanisms to sustain change.
6. Quality meant that as long as the customer was happy, the process was fine with less regard to the possibility of making it more efficient and less costly.

Six Sigma

1. The customer focus is top priority.
2. The goal is to truly understand the customer.
3. Before defining the problem, the customers of the process and their requirements must be fully understood. This is important, particularly in designing a controllable and sustained improvement with the appropriate metrics that allow the organization to stay on top of customer developments and unmet needs.
4. The solutions are dynamic and ever-changing in order to achieve Six Sigma level qualities.
5. Control mechanisms of a process are designed to be sustaining, but constant monitoring signals are needed for adaptation.

Goals

TQM

1. The achievement of quality was a fuzzy concept with a specific quality department focused on "quality control" or "quality assurance."
2. The emphasis was on stabilization rather than improvement of existing processes.
3. The answers to improvement were, at times, based on assumptions and hypotheses. No real hard data.
4. Not having the tools to understand customer needs meant the possibility of an "open-loop system."
5. The quality initiatives were often separated from management objectives and strategic goals.

Six Sigma

1. Solutions are data driven and fact driven with evidence-based improvement. For the first time, questions are being asked as to what measurements are needed to gauge the performance of business processes.
2. The difference is that managers are now asking what essential information is needed and how can this information be used to optimize results?
3. The integration of Six Sigma, employing its tools and practices, requires a proactive management philosophy.
4. In order to cultivate support for improvement changes, process owners must build buy-in at all levels, from top down and across departments.
5. Management is constantly aware of improvements and, therefore, process ownership and accountability.
6. In a culture of continual adaptation to a changing environment, management must stay on top of its business practices in order to achieve its ambitious goals.
7. The "closed loop" of a Six Sigma system allows organizations to track customer needs and adjust accordingly.

Organization

TQM

1. Inconsistent integration of quality policies, reforms, and decisions across the organization
2. Managers were sometimes left out of the circle while "quality councils" made changes
3. Leadership apathy, possibly as a result of above
4. Little attention paid to process ownership, acceptance, and accountability
5. Incremental changes
6. Ineffective training

Six Sigma

1. Clear, consistent, and focused emphasis on customer requirements, process improvement, and management.
2. Implementation of Six Sigma methodology begins with the top leadership where the vision to drive cultural change is derived. The passion for constant reinvention of the business is essential for survival.
3. Training is in-depth and ongoing. Mentoring and coaching nurtures the infrastructure for sustainable change.
4. Incremental exponential change.

CONCLUSIONS

Critics of Lean Six Sigma have called it "the flavor of the month," in spite of the fact that it is based on centuries of proven statistical techniques. Moreover, Lean Six Sigma was initially introduced in health care in the late 1990s; but today, hundreds of health care organizations are successfully applying the leaner principles. The reason for any current misunderstanding is that the differences between Lean Six Sigma and traditional methodologies are not well understood. Furthermore, while success stories of TQM/CQI abound, and these initiatives provided the fertile impetus for today's Lean Six Sigma, previous failures of half-hearted TQM implementation have left some with a bad taste for quality improvement programs. These opinions have left many to be skeptical of Lean Six Sigma's quality focus and methods.

The misconceptions of TQM/CQI, and possibly failings, have had more to do with ambivalent management of these ideals than an actual failure of the system itself. These errors in implementation could also be repeated by organizations wanting to adopt Lean Six Sigma as well. That is why an organization must take the time and make the commitment to truly educate itself on the successful ways of implementing Lean Six Sigma into its culture. It is surely not for everyone, but there are clearly many impressive success stories among those that decide to take a quantum leap forward in competitive edge thinking.

Future challenges of lowered reimbursement, increased competition, workforce shortages, and increased demands to improve and maintain safe care might leave the management resigned to choose between quality care and fiscal solvency. Fortunately, it does not have to be this way. Physicians and health care executives are in a better position to make good decisions when presented with credible, measurable, and controllable results. Buy-in for improvement within Lean Six Sigma organizations is higher because of the collaboration required from multiple stakeholders in different departments. Process improvement becomes more robust and decisive rather than intuitive, and second-guessing quickly disappears, as it is no longer necessary. Six Sigma improvement methodologies are the competitive edge an organization needs to sustain long-term results.

CASE MODEL 13.1: SIX SIGMA AND LEAN COMBINATION PROJECT—PATIENT THROUGHPUT IN EMERGENCY DEPARTMENT

DEFINING THE LEAN SIGMA PROJECT

- Environmental assessment
- Business case and project scope
- Initial process map

LEAN SIGMA ED PATIENT THROUGHPUT PROJECT: PROJECT CHARTER

Problem Statement: Delays in patient throughput have grown significantly in the hospital's emergency department (ED), and walkouts (patients leaving without being seen) have grown to 302 patients for the 8-month period ending in May 2002, a 272% increase over the same period 1 year ago. Diversion hours are also on the increase, a direct consequence of throughput problems, and up 74% from 1 year ago. Delays in treatment cause patient and provider dissatisfaction and threaten to erode the quality of care rendered when such delays affect patient safety.

Who Are the Customers?
ED patients, nurses, physicians, etc.

What Is Critical to their Satisfaction?
Timely treatment and admission when appropriate

What Is the Cost of Poor Quality?
Treatment delays, physician and patient dissatisfaction, potential impact on morbidity and mortality, and revenue shortfalls

Defect Definition: Disposition to discharge or admit in excess of 90 minutes

Project Specification: TAT of 90 minutes or less
Project Metric: Time from disposition to discharge or admission
Project Objective: 100% compliance with spec

This particular project began with no further direction than "go fix patient throughput." The original scope, therefore, ran from the point a patient presented for treatment until a disposition was rendered, and he or she was admitted or discharged. Such a scope can challenge the most talented Lean Sigma practitioner, but by breaking the process down, attention was drawn to the process of admitting a patient once a disposition was rendered; more on that finding later.

Building the Business Case for the ED Project:

Q: What are the obstacles to achieving a 70% reduction in walkouts and diversions? (Refer to the following table.)

Obstacle	Score
Getting patients out of the department (especially inpatients)	80
No plan for backup/overflow	53
Faster cycle time on lab and X-ray	49
Lack of quick registration	38
Need universal guidelines for decision making	28
Better utilization of resources (esp. inpatient)	23
Not enough personnel	22
Poor physical layout	19
Lack of professional staff	17
Too many people involved in too many steps	17
Not enough trauma resources	13
Better cooperation with MDs	13
Dependence on multiple departments	12
Fluctuating staff and MD resources	10
Do not pay for performance	9
Poor communication with other departments	7

From the perspective of the management, the most expedient solution to this problem was to build a larger ED. However, building capacity is expensive, and reducing variation is a less expensive alternative that can accomplish the same thing. Indeed, when a brainstorming session was conducted with the ED personnel, issues related to the need for more resources and space were far down the list of priorities. More important, they said, was making better use of the resources they had.

At the 10,000-ft. level, the ED process map appeared complex, but not much more than any other ED. Certain steps drew the suspicion of the Lean Sigma practitioner, who produced a separate map to illustrate it (see the following figure).

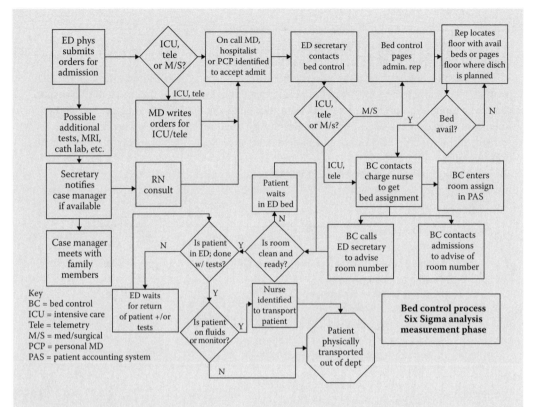

This is the process that began if and when a physician had determined that the patient would be admitted to the hospital, from the ED. Note the number of diamonds in this PFD, setting forth the decision rules about whether this process would move forward or not. Diamonds in a PFD signify a level of complexity. Moreover, the steps in the upper right corner (in red) looked as if it represented a process of inspection, something Lean Sigma considers fundamentally unproductive. This process became the complete focus of the project going forward, and ultimately represented the greatest opportunity for improvement.

MEASURE PHASE

- Establishing baseline performance
- Ensuring data integrity
- Establishing capability

Simply to get a baseline measure and to help the hospital to understand the quality of their process, the ED cycle time was determined using a "Box Cox Transformation." Box Cox is frequently used with non-normal data to assist in converting the data so that it can be analyzed more effectively (Box Cox is typically taught at the blackbelt level and is not generally necessary other than to serve as a useful illustration for management). The average cycle time for the entire process ("door to discharge") is about 3.5 hours. By allowing very generous specification limits of 2–6 hours from door to discharge, the hospital enjoys a sigma level of 3.91. However, such a cursory analysis can create a false sense of security. For one thing, nobody in the hospital felt that a 6-hour cycle time was acceptable.

MEASURING BED CONTROL CYCLE TIME

The purpose of "bed control" is to provide a disciplined process to move patients from the ED to an inpatient unit, once the presiding ED physician has deemed that such an admission is necessary for the benefit of the patient. Three steps are involved as illustrated in the figure below. Because the focus of the project turned early on to bed control, further measurement of this subprocess was necessary.

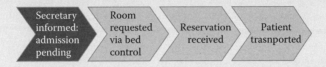

SAMPLING PLAN—SAMPLES TAKEN AT TWO INTERVALS: DEC 2000 ($N = 100$) AND JUNE 2001 ($N = 300$)

An interesting thing happened once the process of data gathering was initiated: management revealed that the process was actually improved after the timeframe we designated for analysis (December—a month selected because it would be one of the busiest of the year). Therefore, the Lean Sigma practitioner collected data again, this time in June. Can you guess what happened? In spite of the well-intentioned efforts of management to improve the process, performance actually *deteriorated*. Unfortunately, nobody was aware of the erosion in performance because this part of the process was not subject to much analysis before the project had begun.

ANALYSIS PHASE

- "Rounding up the usual suspects"
- Hypothesis testing
- Identification of Critical Xs

ANALYZING RESULTS: BED CONTROL CYCLE TIME

It was time now to validate our suspicion that the performance of bed control represented a key driver of overall process performance. First, the process was measured once data integrity issues were resolved. The bed control process alone takes an average of 1.33 hours. Even more significant is the variation in the process, with a standard deviation of 0.73 (three-quarters of an hour). When a process exhibits variation that is over half the total cycle time, it is indicative of a process that is decidedly "out of control." Management was of the general opinion that bed control should take no longer than 90 minutes. On that measure, the hospital did not perform very well. At this point, the sigma level is about 1.0. When compared with the cycle time of the entire process, 38% of the time spent with patients is focused on getting them out of the department.

When conducting a thorough data analysis, a Lean Sigma practitioner will likely walk down many "blind alleys," which result in no significant findings. Just as often, they might stumble on low hanging fruit. An important skill is not only how to distinguish between the two, but to know when to look beyond such findings to find the most significant drivers of process performance. Clearly, "bed control" was the process needing improvement. However, the analysis also revealed that cycle time for bed control was a function of the type of bed requested—telemetry, observation, and neurology beds were in short supply. Management used this finding to reallocate beds, yielding a small improvement in the process. However, the Lean Sigma analysis moved on to seek more significant improvements.

IMPROVE PHASE

- FMEA initiation
- Brainstorming solutions
- Fundamentally changing the process

A failure modes and effects analysis (FMEA) is a useful tool in the absence of data, although a Lean Sigma practitioner can also populate the FMEA with reliable data as well. A FMEA prepared for this project confirmed the bed control process needed to be treated as the highest priority for improvement.

IMPROVEMENT RECOMMENDATIONS

- Process violates two fundamental "rules" of Lean Sigma:
  - o Inspection is unproductive.
  - o Interim process steps reduce potential productivity.
- Recommended process streamlining techniques:
  - o Redeploy administrative representative position.
  - o Revise reporting relationship directly to nursing administration.
  - o Implement use of IT application for housekeeping.
- Recommended repeat measurements to test hypothesis:
  - o Null hypothesis—No impact from improvements.
  - o Alternative—Improvements significantly reduce cycle time.

The Lean Sigma Team ultimately made three recommendations:

1. To redeploy an administrative nurse whose purpose at that time was to "inspect" beds in a well-intentioned effort to identify those ready to accept a new patient. With workforce shortages in most hospitals, the opportunity to redeploy a valued asset like this was welcome news.
2. Often, the simple step of revising a reporting relationship can have a dramatic effect, so long as it is not done for trivial reasons. In this case, it was perceived that Nursing Administration could align bed control cycle time objectives with their existing strategic initiatives, yielding an improvement from the realignment of responsibilities and goals.
3. Finally, the hospital used a software application in the housekeeping department to facilitate workflow in that department and to identify rooms needing to be prepared for new patients. Expanding access to the application was viewed as a means to spread more timely information to staff that needed it.

IMPROVEMENT PHASE: VALIDATING THE SOLUTION

The bed control cycle time was reduced to approximately 1 hour. More impressive than the reduction in cycle time was the improvement in the processes predictability, measured by its variation. Variation was reduced from three-quarters of an hour (0.73 hours) to a little over one-half of an hour (0.55 hours). Although the illustration in the following figure is not drawn precisely to scale, it demonstrates the "home run" effect a Lean Sigma practitioner hopes to see as a result of their project. The bed control project resulted in both a faster process, and a more predictable one. We tightened the bell curve and made it happen faster. Almost time to celebrate.

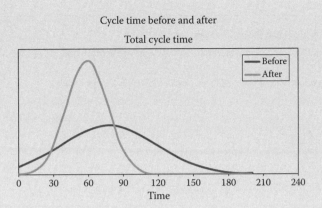

Cycle time before and after

Total cycle time

CONTROL PHASE

- Celebrating success
- Holding the gains

PRACTICAL INTERPRETATION OF IMPROVEMENT PHASE

- Results of hypothesis test:
  o 9.9% improvement in productivity
  o 50% reduction in diversion hours: 14.06 vs. 27.12 YTD
- Savings estimate:
  o Improved productivity from 5.20 pts/h to 5.29 pts/h
  o Improved contribution to profits: $591,116
  o Does not include redeployed salary
  o Does not include impact of accelerating inpatient revenue

An important part of the control phase is the interpretation of results, validation that results are sustained, and development of a control plan. In this particular case, the improvement in productivity for an operation that operates 24 × 7, 365 days per year, was significant, even though only those patients ultimately admitted to the hospital experienced the benefit. An important byproduct of the improvement was also the dramatic reduction in diversion hours recorded, and the department manager reported a positive budget variance for her department for the first time in her memory (she had worked at the hospital for over 12 years).

This project came on the heels of a previous "management reengineering" effort undertaken by the hospital that was focused purely on cost cutting. Needless to say, the environment was skeptical. However, the "soft benefits" cited here relate to the respect the team developed for the process, the use of data to make decisions, and the empowerment of the team to make the improvements on their own.

Where "the rubber meets the road" is ultimately how the process performs long after improvements have been implemented. On that measure, the process looks much better than before. Today, the process is more stable, centered around the faster mean, and with virtually no statistical violations indicative of a process out of control.

CHECKLIST 1: Lean Six Sigma Basic Concepts	YES	NO
Value, Value Stream, Flow, Push, and Perfection—Are these the five accepted principles of Lean thinking?	o	o
Are waiting and overprocessing considered types of waste in the health care industry?	o	o
In order to reach the Six Sigma level, there can still be a significant amount of variation in a particular process.	o	o
Is Six Sigma about efficiencies, and Lean methodology about defects?	o	o
In health care, is it important that Six Sigma aligns patients' goals with the strategic goals of the hospital?		
For Six Sigma to be successful, a proactive management is not required; however, process owners must build buy-in across all levels (top down and across departments)	o	o

CHECKLIST 2: Lean Six Sigma Readiness	YES	NO
Do we use understand the principles of Lean thinking?	o	o
Do we recognize and appreciate kaizen events in our health care entity?	o	o
Do we understand 5S techniques and how they are applied to health care organizations?	o	o
Do we strive to avoid the eight types of waste in health care today?	o	o
Do we understand the concept of "variation" and how it impacts our health care setting?	o	o
Do we know and use the quality improvement process of DMAIC?	o	o
Do we know what enterprise-wide departments are most amenable to a Six Sigma revolution?	o	o
Do we understand the differences between Six Sigma and the various other quality initiatives and reporting processes?	o	o
Are we willing to become a patient-focused and patient-centered health care entity?	o	o
Is a Six Sigma expert or trainer available to our organization—either in-house or out-sourced?	o	o
Is executive management willing to promote, champion, and lead a conceptual cultural revolution in order to implement Six Sigma?	o	o
Is our institutional leadership and governance willing to fund Six Sigma initiatives?	o	o

ACKNOWLEDGMENTS

To Daniel Gee, MD, MBA, of Creative Healthcare, Scottsdale, Arizona, and Hope Rachel Hetico, RN, MHA CMP™, of the Institute of Medical Business Advisors Inc., Atlanta, Georgia.

REFERENCE

1. Womack, J.P. and Jones, D.T. 1996. *Lean Thinking: Banish Waste and Create Wealth in Your Corporation.* New York: Simon & Schuster.

BIBLIOGRAPHY

Arnold, J. Six Sigma Reveals Astounding Results. Page 4 of reprint from www.GEHealthcare.com.
Arthur, J. 2011. *Lean Six Sigma for Hospitals: Simple Steps to Fast, Affordable, Flawless Healthcare.* Milwaukee, WI: ASQ Quality Press.
Arthur, J. 2011. *Lean Six Sigma for Hospitals: Simple Steps to Fast, Affordable, and Flawless Healthcare.* New York: McGraw-Hill.

Barry, R., Murcko, A., and Brubaker, C. 2002. *The Six Sigma Book for Healthcare: Improving Outcomes by Reducing Errors (ACHE Management Series)*. Chicago, IL: Health Administration Press.

Black, J.R. 2008. *The Toyota Way to Healthcare Excellence: Increase Efficiency and Improve Quality with Lean (ACHE Management Series)*. Chicago, IL: Health Administration Press, Seattle, WA.

Blakeslee, J., Jr. 1999. Implementing the Six Sigma Solution. *Quality Progress*, 75–85.

Butler, G., Caldwell, C., and Poston, N. 2009. *Lean-Six Sigma for Healthcare, Second Edition: A Senior Leader Guide to Improving Cost and Throughput*. Milwaukee, WI: ASQ Quality Press.

Butler, K. and Lazarus, I. 2001. The promise of Six Sigma. *Managed Healthcare Executives*, 2.

Butler, K. and Lazarus, I. 2001. The promise of Six Sigma. *Managed Healthcare Executives*, 4.

Caldwell, C., Butler, G., and Poston, N. 2011. *Lean-Six Sigma for Healthcare, Second Edition: A Senior Leader Guide to Improving Cost and Throughput*. Milwaukee, WI: ASQ Quality Press.

Cherry, J. and Seshadri, S. 2001. Six sigma: Using statistics to reduce process variability and costs in radiology. *Radiology Management*, 1.

Cherry, J. and Seshadri, S. 2000. Six Sigma: Using Statistics to Reduce Variability and Costs in Radiology. *Radiology Management*, 3: 44–46.

Ettinger, W. 2001. Six Sigma: Adopting GE's lesson to healthcare. *Trustee*, 9: 4.

Graban, M. 2009. *Lean Hospitals: Improving Quality, Patient Safety, and Employee Satisfaction*. New York: Productivity Press, Taylor & Francis Group.

Hastings, G.R. 2009. *Our Journey to Performance Excellence*. Milwaukee, WI: ASQ Quality Press.

Lazarus, I.R. and Andell, J. 2006. Providers, payers and IT suppliers learn it pays to get Lean. *Managed Healthcare Executive*, 16(2): 1–4.

Owens, T.L. 2011. *Six Sigma Green Belt, Round 2: Making Your Next Project Better than the Last One*. Milwaukee, WI: ASQ Quality Press.

Pande, P., Neuman, R., and Cavanagh, R. 2000. The Six Sigma Way: How GE, Motorola and Other Top Companies Are Honing Their Performance, pp. 11–13. New York: McGraw-Hill Publishing.

Scalese, D. 2001. Six Sigma: The quest for quality. *Hospital and Health Networks*, 77(5): 57–62, 2.

Stamatis, D.H. *Essentials for the Improvement of Healthcare Using Lean & Six Sigma*. New York: Productivity Press, Taylor & Francis Group.

Stamps, B. and Lazarus, I. 2002. Primer on Six Sigma for healthcare providers. *Managed Healthcare Executive*, 12(1): 27–30.

Stamps, B. and Lazarus, I. 2003. The promise of Six Sigma, Part I. *Managed Healthcare Executives*, 6.

Stamps, B. and Lazarus, I. 2003. The promise of Six Sigma, Part II. *Managed Healthcare Executives*, 4.

Suneja, A. and Suneja, C. 2011. *Lean Doctors: A Bold and Practical Guide to Using Lean Principles to Transform Healthcare Systems, One Doctor at a Time*. Milwaukee, WI: ASQ Quality Press.

Venable, S. and Silverman, P. 2000. Six sigma methodology. Applying a corporate model to radiology enabled MDACC to boost CT capacity. *Journal of Imaging and Technology Management*, 13: 7.

14 Hospital Flow-Through Efficiency, Operations, and Logistics

Achieving Leaner and Faster Organizations with Sustainable Improvements

Denice Soyring Higman, Adam Higman, and Dragana Gough

CONTENTS

With two-thirds of all U.S. hospitals looking for ways to improve the functionality and quality of their organizations, it is imperative that hospital leadership addresses these efficiency challenges and work to prioritize and systematically reduce weaknesses. Like exercise, process improvement is a discipline and a habit. Day-to-day time limitations often sidetrack managers from reviewing clinical and administrative processes, but improvement is crucial for long-term viability. New thinking about employee productivity, case management, lean processes, and policies can dramatically affect patient flow in a health care facility. With some guidance, hospital leaders can make over their organizations into leaner, faster, and overall better organizations with sustainable improvements.

DOES MY DEPARTMENT/FACILITY HAVE A PATIENT FLOW PROBLEM?

If you suspect that your department or unit may be facing patient flow challenges, do not wait. Assess where things stand by asking these questions:[1]

1. What is my hospital's methodology to efficient and effective patient flow? Is the approach comprehensive and well organized?
2. Who is responsible for the processes and procedures related to patient flow? Are they successful at taking the initiative when it comes to bed management?
3. Are physicians aware of the need to maximize patient flow efforts?
4. Is staff motivated to admit, treat, and transfer/discharge patients in a timely manner?
5. Is the staff aggressively participating in hospital initiatives for improvement?

As you may have gathered from the questions above, it takes all hands on deck to truly have an impact on patient flow. Departments and staff must work together through the entire patient flow process of admitting, treating, and discharging, and if a single department or process is not functioning up to par with the others, this one single threat can be detrimental to patient safety, patient satisfaction, quality of care, and financial performance.[1]

AN OVERVIEW OF PATIENT FLOW

Evaluating staff, processes and procedures, techniques, and technology will help determine the course of action your facility/department should take. A review of the following will assist in prioritizing those departments most in need of a patient flow assessment:[2]

- The departments' use of available resources
  - Consistent methods and communication practices
  - Anticipating demand for services
  - Prioritizing tasks
  - Allocating staff during busier shifts
- The timeliness of their patient transfers
  - Constant access of bed status and availability
  - Performing timely rounds and processing of orders
  - Timeliness of test results
- Steady, high-quality patient care
  - Good communication and organization among case managers, physicians, and nursing staff
  - Daily department/unit meetings to ensure consistent quality care
  - Educating patient and their family

When reviewing patient flow from a facility standpoint, it is important to ensure that you touch on all the clinical departments/areas that most impact your length of stay (LOS). A diagram is provided below as a starting point:

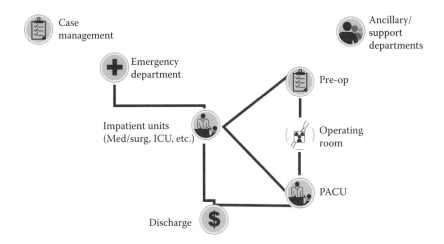

ORGANIZING YOUR PATIENT FLOW EFFORTS

CASE MANAGEMENT/ADMISSIONS/BED PLACEMENT

Admission/bed placement and/or case managers have the daunting task of putting "the right patient in the right bed at the right time." Facilities are increasingly permanently stationing case managers in their emergency departments (EDs) to determine if patients are meeting criteria for admission, to coordinate patient transfers to other facilities, and to assist with discharge planning efforts prior to admission.[3]

Unsuccessful bed management leads to capacity constraints that can impede hospitals' ability to develop new markets, grow service lines, and generate new revenue streams. When patient flow is poor, hospitals may be too full with patients for whom they cannot get full reimbursement to accept new admissions. Management can stay alert to potential problems with patient flow by monitoring patient census, ED diversions, LOS, and other relevant metrics as detailed in monthly progress reports.[3]

EMERGENCY DEPARTMENT

Hospitals typically see greater than 50% of their admissions from patients first seen in the ED, making it the unofficial "front door" of the hospital. The impression you give at your front door is critical in establishing your reputation in the community and ensuring that you continue to attract patients.

LOS is the biggest indicator of not only your department's efficiency, but also patient perception of your hospital. Patients are asking themselves how long it takes to get seen, get treated, and get out. LOS is also a critical factor in patient satisfaction and quality of care.[8]

Breaking down the overall LOS within an ED into time stamps will aid in discovering the root cause for increases in LOS and help answer the "how am I doing" question. The following are the key time stamps to track:

- Door to triage
- Triage to bed (without immediate bedding in place)

- Door to physician
- Bed to physician
- Bed to nurse
- Bed to decision
- Door to admission/discharge/transfer

Tracking these time stamps is critical in reducing LOS and improving patient satisfaction. Once you know where you stand, it is time to look at ways to improve your LOS.

BETTER ED LOS IN 5 STEPS

Once the critical points are identified within the LOS continuum, leadership within the ED can address these issues.

Step One: Better Bedding

Two processes to help improve door-to-bed time include immediate bedding and the use of a separate area for low-acuity patients. Immediate bedding allows for triage to occur at the bedside, as opposed to a specific area. Triage is a process, not a place, and fast patient throughput is the biggest contributor to patient satisfaction as well as the most effective solution to decreasing LOS. Some areas to look at during the triage process include communication from staff to patients during the wait process, length of documentation, and initiation of physician-approved protocols by triage registered nurses.

Diversion

To avoid increasing LOS at your facility, you must involve any and all ED personnel capable of providing patient care or support. If diversion is due to bed availability, develop a team with ED and inpatient personnel to resolve the underlying issues. The team should evaluate the bed availability system, determine which patients are to be transferred out of critical care areas, and open additional beds.

Patient Room Assignments

When making bed assignments, use acuity indicators to determine placement and consider the distribution of nurse workloads. Rooms can be assigned at triage with input from the charge nurse.

Patient Discharge and Additional Considerations

Encourage staff to resolve any patient complaints before they leave the ED. Leadership needs to observe in the department and evaluate patient flow by assessing the immediate bedding process, the number of patients in the waiting room, and any test result delays.[3]

Step Two: Scheduling

With scheduling, the key is to evaluate your volume trends and mirror your staffing to those trends by day/time/season to prevent labor shortages. Another consideration is ensuring that staff assignments are effective in relation to the care needed by patients, which plays a pivotal role in reducing LOS.

Step 3: Diagnostic Testing

Test results are a key factor in improving the time from bed to decision. Utilizing standard protocols for clinical care pathways will help get speedy results by standardizing tests for common complaints. Also, having a strong working relationship with ancillary departments that provide these tests is critical for timely delivery.

Step Four: Notification

Diagnostic testing is being processed quickly and efficiently, now what? Updates between nursing and physicians are critical in LOS. The use of communication devices to keep key team members in the loop enables staff to know immediately when results have been received and whether follow-up is needed.

Step Five: Troubleshooting

To improve bed-to-admission/transfer/discharge, case management can play a positive role in the appropriate decision for each patient. Get case management or bed placement personnel involved early and often when patients fall outside of your normal LOS and require better coordination between other departments.

Better Prep, Execution, and Discharge in the Operating Room

Preoperative

The operating room (OR) should run like a well-oiled machine with patients moving through each stage seamlessly as the slightest factor can have lasting negative effects. As with most things, the process of improvement must start at the beginning with preadmission preparation. Ensuring that patient files have an up-to-date history and physical (H&P) and laboratory and radiology reports as well as financial clearance will aid in the improvement process.

One of the keys to improving preoperative performance is involving physicians. Assess where things stand by asking these questions:

- Are anesthesia staff involved in team decision making?
- Are medical staff taking an active role in throughput?
- Is your anesthesia staff reviewing patient charts for the next day?
  - Anesthesia staff should assess a scheduled patient when the health history suggests potential problems

Holding Area or Not?

It depends. Most hospitals do not use holding areas for all patients, even though the areas may exist. Typical uses for holding areas include inpatient surgery patients and anesthesia services for line insertions, and so forth. For smoother transitions in the OR, you should consider elimination of multiple stops for outpatients.

Operative

Operative throughput should start with an assessment of your instrument and supplies. This begins with a review of your case cart readiness, including the number of trays and instruments, both used and unused. The goal of this review is to eliminate any additional unneeded instrument counting/processing. To avoid case delays, ensure that all materials and supplies pulled for the case are correct and your preference cards are updated. As with any procedure, make sure that the equipment is functioning correctly and that all personnel are fully trained for the job. Perform proper maintenance checks ahead of time and review storage and organization procedures to ensure that the equipment is readily available for the next case start time. Unreliable items that frequently break/malfunction can have a huge effect on turnover.

Team Approach to Room Turnover

It is imperative that the OR staff be ready to start on time and every person in surgery should have a part of the turnover process. Surgeons can set the stage for expectations, especially if they are present during turnover/setup. Do not let them perform a disappearing act. Work with surgeon's office staff on scheduling issues if there continues to be a problem. For anesthesia, scrub, and circulator staff, create buy-in for quick turnover time, utilize specialty teams, if possible, publicize turnover results (monthly), and celebrate improvements. Anesthesia staff can help transport patients from holding/day surgery to OR and housekeeping needs to be readily available to assist with cleanup. Nursing staff can assist with cleanup of rooms and patient transport. The bottom line, everyone needs to pitch in whether it is in their "job description" or not.

POSTOPERATIVE

To continue the momentum, make strides in postoperative procedures starting with discharging from the post-anesthesia care unit (PACU). Acute care facilities should consider discharging select, low-acuity patients directly from PACU.

PACU Overload, Dealing with Inpatients

Are there inpatients in your PACU delaying surgical starts? You have two options. First, the easiest solution: deal with it. Have alternative staffing available, either a staffing agency or float pool, to stage inpatients in a dedicated part of PACU. This solution assumes that there are PACU beds available for this function. Also, train PACU nurses to care for their inpatients. Second, the harder solution: fix it. Fixing it will require not only a larger discussion with the affected inpatient departments but also ways on how to improve LOS for inpatient units.

Protocols for Discharge and LOS

For a smooth, seamless transition through the discharge process, ensure that Anesthesia staff is using the appropriate, up-to-date medications to reduce postoperative LOS. Adhering to protocols in PACU and Day Surgery, the nursing staff will be able to discharge in a timelier basis.

INPATIENT UNIT BED MANAGEMENT

Long waits for inpatient bed assignments affect a hospital's revenue and play a part in the facility's safety record, reputation, and satisfaction scores. The three main actions for improvement include addressing work flow, aligning volume with demand, and leveling out variation. The use of hospitalists has shown to improve the flow of units. During rounds, hospitalists should check on their patients as well as other patients that are awaiting possible discharge or transfer orders to another department as a way of speeding up the process.[4]

Coordinating the flow of bed management is also a factor to improve patient flow. It is vital that a system be set in place and run by a well-organized team of individuals since they need to follow all movements of patients within the hospital. Having regular communication and updates from each department regarding current census, anticipated admissions, discharges, transfers, rooms waiting to be cleaned, preoperative and postoperative patients, and any additional information will help smooth the patient flow process.[4]

To further improve bed management, discharge planning needs to be part of the admission process. Upon each patient's admission, pathways to discharge should be developed with prediction for LOS based on current known facts about the patient's condition. Staff members need to have an awareness of where their patients are in the discharge process. They can then provide input to medical staff and/or case managers in order to remove obstacles in the discharge planning process of each patient. Ultimately, frontline patient care staff and the immediate nursing leadership (charge nurses) are in the best position for frequent reviews of patients' conditions and to use this information to decrease LOS.

PATIENT FLOW VARIABILITY IN CRITICAL CARE UNITS

Clinicians generally assume that the LOS of individual patients is unpredictable. Intensivists are expected to be able to roughly predict LOS, but the accuracy of this prediction depends largely on the intensivist's experience. Studies suggest that if comprehensive evaluations comparing diagnosis, prognostic variables, and LOS translated into known discharge models, then these models might be able to predict LOS with greater accuracy.

A substantial portion of a health care facility's budget goes to intensive care units (ICUs) due to the increasing cost of newer, more up-to-date treatments. Hospitals typically experience capacity problems within the ICU as studies have determined "high rates of refusal to admit because of lack of empty beds."[5,6] In addition, "the need to serve the 'greying' population is likely to increase demand for ICU beds further, exacerbating the current strain on ICU capacity."[7] As a result, the higher demand for intensive care beds and higher rates of refusal to admit other critically ill patients may lead to more cancelled surgeries.[6,8]

Patient planning depends importantly on reliable and adequate management information. Key elements in the ICU setting are the patient's expected LOS in the ICU at admission and possible changes in expected LOS resulting from later treatment. Starting from the admission date and expected LOS, the planner will be able to pinpoint the anticipated date at which an ICU bed will once again become available. This information, along with subsequent changes in a patient's expected LOS, is needed to schedule the next OR patient who requires postoperative intensive care or to reserve emergency patient capacity in the ICU.

Emerging studies classify ICU patient flow delays in several areas.[9] Three major areas are institutional, medical, and social.

Institutional

Major teaching hospitals have longer LOS for patients with similar admission diagnosis and similar dispositions than LOS of similar patients in non-teaching hospitals or minor teaching hospitals. Furthermore, presence of a full-time ICU physician who does daily rounds has been associated with reducing the likelihood of prolonged LOS and reduced complications for high-risk patients.[9]

Medical Factors

A recently conducted study revealed that "for patients in a medical surgical ICU requiring stays longer than 14 days, the most common reasons for admission were neuromuscular weakness, pneumonia, multiple trauma, and septic shock, in that order. Respiratory arrest, postoperative mechanical ventilator, congestive heart failure, cardiac arrest, airway protection or obstruction and exacerbation of chronic obstructive pulmonary disease were the next most common indications for ICU admission in these patients."[8]

SOCIAL FACTORS

Miscommunication among patient families and hospital staff is likely to lead to impractical expectations and longer time spent in the ICU. This has shown to be a recurring obstacle in ICUs and the results can cause delays in the treatment process.[9]

New Admits and Discharges

An important factor in improving critical care patient flow is ensuring that the workload-to-nursing staff ratio is appropriate, particularly related to the extra time required for discharges and admits. A backlog of discharges can develop and reduce bed availability for new admits. Assigning staff to specifically assist with the admitting and discharging of patients based on times and days when discharges and admits are most frequent helps improve overall flow. Analyzing the data below for your facility will help you make appropriate staffing decisions.

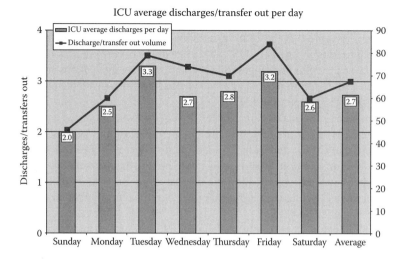

ICU average discharges/transfer out per day

SUPPORT DEPARTMENTS/ANCILLARY DEPARTMENTS

Your clinical departments are dependent on well-run efficient ancillary departments. You can evaluate a well-run ancillary department by assessing its interrelationship with clinical departments and staff.

To help you make this evaluation, assess this quick checklist:

1. Have you tasked your department leaders with measuring the effectiveness of their staff? Department leaders can use their knowledge of benchmarking characteristics to measure the effectiveness of their staff in the department. Each support department has unique workload characteristics that flex based on inpatient or outpatient activity. Recognition and knowledge of this workload and ability to adjust staffing based on changes in workload are characteristics of a thriving support department.

2. Do these departments regularly exhibit their flexibility? It is important that the department be able to overcome obstacles and create work-arounds while simultaneously producing good results. More often than not, support departments have not been at the top of the list for updates, expansions, and new equipment. Support departments' ability to work with older equipment and space constraints, while still producing good results, is a good indicator that the department is being managed effectively.

3. Have you evaluated your departments' coverage to determine the most appropriate schedules? Hospitals often struggle with providing coverage and resort to using costly callback offers. Ancillary departments such as radiology offer valuable services outside of regular work hours.

To best improve the position of the support department, evaluate the need to provide services outside of regular hours, assess the hours and days to provide such services, and determine the costs of those services. It is not unusual to find that a realignment of offered services and the scheduled or on-call staff is needed. This realignment can be done in various ways depending on the facility. The biggest mistake is providing the same level of staffing/service for all days of the week and/or disregarding the proximity of a sister hospital that is offering the same services.

4. Has management communicated expected standards? Building department-wide awareness of the professional organizations, certifications, and standards that have an effect on regulations, protocols, and reporting of outcomes for each

department is an important way to ensure that departments can self-identify compliance and safety issues. Support department management should have a clear communication plan for the myriad of standards that apply to their employees. This communication about standards helps to bring to the forefront any areas where you may be out of compliance.

5. Are your departments creating satisfied "customers"?

Perhaps the most important measure of success for support departments is the satisfaction of the clinical departments, or "customers," they serve. Support departments' leadership and its staff should strive to build strong relationships with clinical departments by consistently meeting with clinical leadership and surveying clinical department satisfaction and outcomes. When such a relationship exists, problems can be brought to the forefront, addressed, and solved quickly. Ultimately, these strong working relationships result in meeting not only the departments' but also the patients' needs efficiently and effectively.

A CLOSER LOOK AT LABORATORY/RADIOLOGY

A strong approach to radiology and laboratory work, in particular, enhances hospital patient flow. Making advances in ancillary departments will encompass teamwork and cooperation with other units and departments. The majority of the information on a patient's chart is laboratory information. Delayed laboratory results can lead to delays in diagnosis and treatment. Waiting for test results have a direct relationship with wait times and patient flow, impacting quality of care and thus overall patient satisfaction.[10]

To speed up this process, track cycle times and set benchmarks for the departments. Once the staff recognizes where they stand and where they need to be, things can start progressing. Communication is key if you want to improve turnaround times. Prioritize test requests by working closely with the departments you service and case management will bring you a step closer to improved patient flow.[10]

You can further enhance your patient flow by setting up teams to track and monitor process improvement and workflow adjustments. To sustain newly improved processes as a result of the team's work, make the tools available for managers to continue to monitor and enhance processes.

Examples may include the following:

- Balanced scorecards to monitor process effectiveness (quality, customer satisfaction, operational processes, and financial metrics)
- Staffing plans based on volume data by time of day, day of week, and seasonal variations from your laboratory and radiology test data systems
- Productivity comparison database to monitor and trend productivity daily and biweekly

A GLIMPSE AT EQUIPMENT AND MATERIALS HANDLING

Hospitals should look at the success of their inventory management process as another way to enhance patient flow. The materials your facility uses on a day-to-day basis have greater impact on patient flow than people may realize. It is not uncommon for patient flow to be held up due to ineffective or unavailable materials and equipment.

One key area to look at when reviewing the unavailability of equipment is the hospital property records. These are often overlooked and underutilized as equipment, furniture, and instrumentation no longer in use are regularly found disorganized in storage areas. With simple, effective management of the facility's property, lifetime use of equipment can be extended while decreasing repair and operating costs. Maintaining up-to-date property records improves management of these resources and allows for potential cost savings from supply standardization, product/equipment change, process improvement, and increased utilization.

When establishing a process that ensures that equipment is effectively managed, keep the following in mind:

- Identify property/equipment by department
- Determine lifetime use and depreciation date to verify if replacement is required
- Ensure routine monitoring for patient items/furniture
- Regularly perform preventive maintenance
- Remove obsolete/old items that are no longer in use

When reviewing the inventory management process, it is important to look at the following factors:

- The inventory management budget
- Days of inventory on hand
- Turnovers for a specified period of time
- Utilization and accuracy of your inventory management system
- Satisfaction of "customers" or departments served

Above all, keep the patient in mind when recommending changes for patient products and equipment. While the goal is to optimize patient flow in the hospital, you do not want to sacrifice high-quality patient care.

CONCLUSION

Any health care facility's ability to consistently deliver high-quality patient care and receive high patient satisfaction rates is constantly being tested against the efficiency of patient flow. While many instances and patient flow problems may seem outside the facility's control, the truth is that taking the initiative to alleviate the challenges can lead to positive, lasting effects that will improve not only department-specific but also hospital-wide difficulties. The sooner the hospital recognizes and identifies its setbacks, the better off the facility will be.

Improving patient flow takes effort and action from all employees. Staff must be willing to work together to move along each phase of the patient flow process. Without the cooperation among staff and department leaders, a single slowdown can create long-term negative effects on overall satisfaction and finances. Policies and procedures, case management, and staff morale are all factors that, when managed efficiently, will improve patient flow.

CASE MODEL 14.1: ED THROUGHPUT—IMPROVING PATIENT SATISFACTION

BACKGROUND

A 250+ bed hospital with 20+ emergent beds located in a middle income neighborhood in the South with a fast-track system and chest pain and primary stroke center.

Patients were not being seen by triage in a timely manner and those awaiting admission/discharge/transfer caused an increase in length of stay, patients who have left without being seen, and patients leaving against medical advice. Immediate bedding was not happening, and as a result, patient satisfaction was decreasing significantly. Diversion, slow laboratory test results, length of documentation, and lack of bedside registration were causing major holdups throughout the department. Interdepartmental communication between staff and physicians needed to improve as it was causing patient care to suffer.

KEY ISSUES

1. LOS for psych patients
2. Slow laboratory test results
3. Interdepartmental communications
4. Admission process
5. Orientation process
6. Teamwork and employee morale

SOLUTIONS/OUTCOMES

To resolve the hospital's difficulties, the first step was to track and monitor the department's patient flow by volume and time stamps. After analysis, a process was developed to decrease patients left without being seen and against medical advice. By involving all ED personnel capable of providing patient care or support, LWBS (leave without being seen) patients were decreased by 4.23% and diversion was reduced to zero.

Lagging test results from low-quality laboratory draws was addressed and corrected. A close working relationship with admitting departments was established to open up the lines of communication between physicians and department staff in order to speed up the discharge and transfer processes.

Immediate bedding was instituted, which allowed patients to go straight to a bed, if available, and begin bedside triage. Establishing a collaborative working relationship between registrars and the registration department led to 100% of patient registration being completed at the bedside after the medical screening exam for EMTALA (Emergency Medical Treatment and Active Labor Act) compliance.

For low-acuity patients, the department utilized mid-level practitioners. This allowed for additional patient care providers at a lower cost and within the budget. The use of acuity indicators in patient room placement as well as the assigning of rooms at triage with input from the charge nurse helped alleviate some of the pressure in regard to patient room assignments. Permanently stationing a case manager within the ED allowed for smoother coordination of patient transfers to other facilities and assistance with discharge planning efforts prior to admission.

Staff was educated to keep physicians better informed and aware of patients awaiting possible discharge/transfer. Laboratory turnaround times were dramatically reduced due to the success of higher-quality laboratory draws.

The current orientation process was evaluated and found to be disorganized. Competency checklists were created to improve the quality of the program and the on-boarding process for employees.

To improve teamwork and employee morale, steps were taken to involve the team during process changes as a way of increasing buy-in and facilitating communication related to breakdowns in processes.

RESULTS

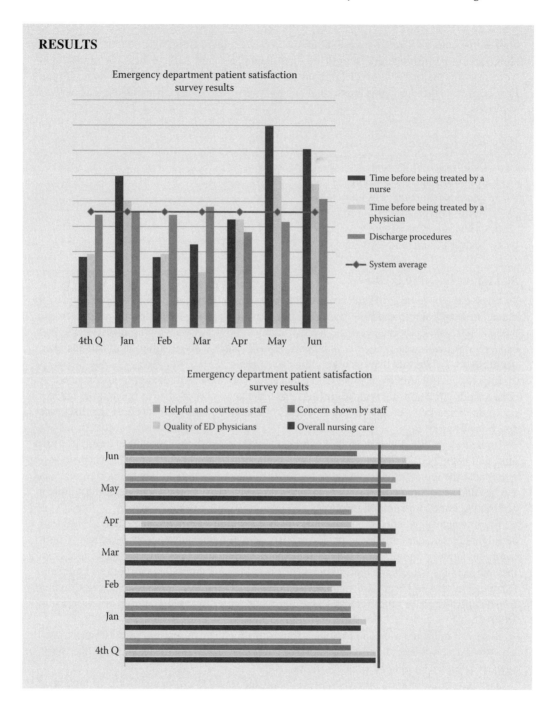

Emergency department patient satisfaction
survey results

- Time before being treated by a nurse
- Time before being treated by a physician
- Discharge procedures
- System average

4th Q   Jan   Feb   Mar   Apr   May   Jun

Emergency department patient satisfaction
survey results

- Helpful and courteous staff
- Quality of ED physicians
- Concern shown by staff
- Overall nursing care

Jun

May

Apr

Mar

Feb

Jan

4th Q

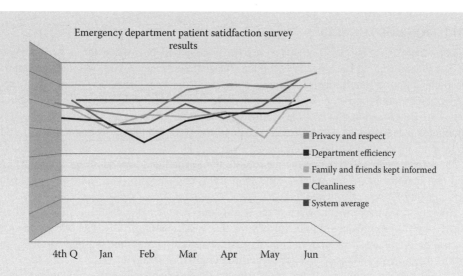

Emergency department patient satidfaction survey results

- Privacy and respect
- Department efficiency
- Family and friends kept informed
- Cleanliness
- System average

4th Q   Jan   Feb   Mar   Apr   May   Jun

CASE MODEL 14.2: OR THROUGHPUT—BETTER PREP, EXECUTION, AND DISCHARGE IN THE OR

BACKGROUND

A 600+ bed hospital with 14+ ORs in the main operating room and a tertiary referral center, located in a middle income neighborhood in the South with a large pediatric and adult population.

Patient flow was frequently backed-up in the PACU and OR due to inadequate case readiness. Checklists were not completed prior to start times, charts were not organized, and there was no NPO compliance. Incomplete case carts, preference cards, stock-outs, and storage locations and time wasted searching for patient care equipment caused major delays in the OR.

Within pre-admission testing (PAT), only 60% of patients were being processed through PAT. Patients were experiencing long wait times, anesthesia staff was not participating in pre-surgical assessments as they did not see abnormal test results until the day of surgery, and H&P information was not getting sent to the hospital from physician offices. The flow of communication among physician offices, hospital, and patients was problematic as incorrect information was getting passed along.

A backlog of patients awaiting admission to the PACU was caused by a lack of inpatient beds and by the staff being prohibited from transferring patients to nursing units at the change of shift (1.5-hour window).

KEY ISSUES

- Patient and materials flow
- Utilization and productivity
- Turnover between cases
- Clinical practice
- Interpersonal relations

SOLUTIONS/OUTCOMES

A goal—that 95% of surgical patients were to be preassessed and all anesthesia variances and abnormal tests were to be assessed by an anesthesia practitioner (a certified registered nurse anesthetist or nurse practitioner) in order to avoid delays in case start times—was established.

For better communication, PAT packets with testing information, directions, and instructions were developed and to be given to the patient in the physician's office. They were also to include the H&P and consent forms that can be completed in the office and hand carried to the hospital by the patient during PAT.

All patients were to be called the day before their scheduled procedure for questions and final instructions and/or reminders, NPO guidelines, and so forth. The "no transfer" during shift change rule was eliminated.

Operational improvements were made within the department, resulting in a 15-minute reduction (30% improvement) in turnover time. Daily review of the OR schedule for the next day was to be reviewed by materials management, central processing, equipment techs, and the OR manager to anticipate and get everything ready for the day.

The processes to reduce patient arrival time to 1 hour prior to the procedure as well as the patient discharge process were streamlined. The discharge process was reduced to 45 minutes or less on average in same day surgery. A goal was established to reduce OP average LOS to 5 hours within 6 months with the ultimate goal being 4 hours.

Full-time equivalent requirements and daily staffing plans were assessed and redesigned for a new block schedule. The plan provided for the staffing level necessary for the peak hours and has significantly reduced overtime. Equipment records were reviewed to determine instrumentation shortages and increased instrumentation to more effectively meet increased workloads.

RESULTS

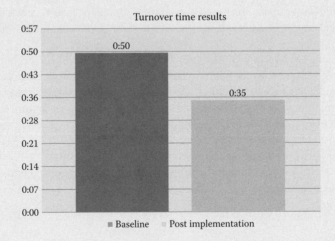

Turnover time results

- Baseline
- Post implementation

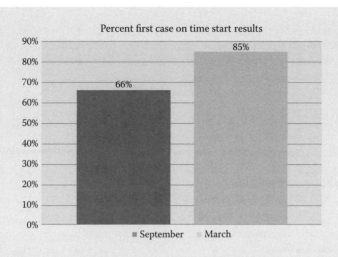

Percent first case on time start results

CHECKLIST 1: Does My Department/Unit Have a Patient Flow Problem? YES NO

What is my department's approach to efficiently and effectively manage patient flow? o o

Is the approach comprehensive and well organized? o o

Who is in charge of processes and procedures related to patient flow? o o

Is there one person or multiple managers in charge of patient flow? o o

Do physicians recognize our facility's need to optimize bed placement more productively? o o

Is our staff motivated to treat patients in a timely manner, including the discharging process? o o
Why/why not?

Are our nurses and medical staff actively participating in the hospital's initiatives for improving o o
patient flow and decreasing LOS?

Is your department/unit utilizing the available resources to optimize patient flow? o o

CHECKLIST 2: Emergency Department YES NO

Are time stamps being tracked to determine LOS? o o
What are the time stamps?

Does the ED experience diversion? o o
    How often?
    What is the percentage?
Do ED volume trends mirror your staffing? o o

Is ED staff communicating all information in a timely manner?   o   o
Are holdups in the ED negatively affecting the flow of communication and causing an increase   o   o
  in LOS?
    Where are the holdups?

_____

_____

_____

_____

CHECKLIST 3: Perioperative Department	YES	NO
Is anesthesia staff involved in team decision making?	o	o
Is medical staff taking an active role in throughput?	o	o
Is your anesthesia staff reviewing patient charts for the next day?	o	o
Is there a holding area for patients?	o	o
Are there inpatients in your PACU delaying surgical starts?	o	o
Are all materials and supplies pulled for surgical cases correct?	o	o
Are preference cards kept up-to-date?	o	o

CHECKLIST 4: Inpatient Units	YES	NO
Are transfers and discharges happening in a timely manner?	o	o
Are physicians and nurses performing timely rounds and processing orders?	o	o
Is there a system in place that allows for organized bed placement/movement of patients?	o	o
Does the department receive regular updates regarding current census, anticipated admissions, discharges, transfers, rooms waiting to be cleaned, preoperative and postoperative patients, etc., that will aid in the patient flow decision process?	o	o
Are there discharge procedures within the admission process that will allow for a timelier discharge of patients?	o	o

CHECKLIST 5: Critical Care Units	YES	NO
Is there a reliable and adequate flow of patient information within the unit?	o	o
Does the unit estimate patients' LOS and anticipate their discharge to free up ICU beds?	o	o
Are physicians and nurses educating patients and their family members regarding the stay of the patient?	o	o
Do patients' family members feel informed and understand the information relayed to them?	o	o
Is the workload-to-nursing staff ratio appropriate?	o	o
Is there staff specifically assigned to assist with the admitting and discharging of patients?	o	o

CHECKLIST 6: Support and Ancillary Departments	YES	NO
Have you tasked your department leaders with measuring the effectiveness of their staff?	o	o
Do these departments regularly exhibit their flexibility?	o	o
Have you evaluated your departments' coverage to determine the most appropriate schedules?	o	o
Has management communicated expected standards?	o	o
Are your departments creating satisfied "customers"?	o	o

CHECKLIST 7: Laboratory and Radiology	YES	NO
Does the department have balanced scorecards to monitor process effectiveness (quality, customer satisfaction, operational processes, and financial metrics)?	o	o
How is the department staffed?	o	o
Is staffing based on volume data by time of day, day of week, and seasonal variations from your laboratory and radiology test data systems?	o	o
Does your department monitor and track test cycle times and productivity? What is the process?	o	o
Is there a delay in test results that is slowing the diagnosis and treatment of patients?	o	o

CHECKLIST 8: Equipment and Materials Handling	YES	NO
Do you know the location of all of your facilities equipment?	o	o
Is there a readily available maintenance log for all equipment?	o	o
Do you know the remaining life on all of your equipment?	o	o
Does your inventory management budget consistently rise?	o	o
Is this attributable to a rise in volume or change in physician preference?	o	o
Do you have a goal for days of inventory on hand? If so, are you meeting that goal?	o	o
Do you have a goal for inventory turnover? If so, are you meeting that goal?	o	o
Are you using all the functions of your inventory management system?	o	o
Is your inventory management system consistently updated?	o	o
Is your inventory management system integrated with clinical systems at point of use?	o	o
Do you measure the satisfaction of the departments you serve?	o	o
Are you meeting your satisfaction goals?	o	o

ACKNOWLEDGMENTS

We thank Kristin Spenik, of Soyring Consulting, for assistance in the preparation of this chapter.

REFERENCES

1. Freedman, Barry, Susan Bernini, Robert W. Champion, and Kathleen Lennon. Enhancing Patient Flow. *Trustee Magazine*. Health Forum, Inc., Dec. 2009. Web. http://www.trusteemag.com/trusteemag_app/jsp/articledisplay.jsp?dcrpath=TRUSTEEMAG/PubsNewsArticleGen/data/2005/0506TRU_DEPT_Above_Board
2. Pate, David C., and Michael Puffe. Improving Patient Flow. Rep. *The Physician Executive*, May–June 2007. Web. http://net.acpe.org/Resources/PEJ/2007/May_June/Pate.pdf
3. Meeting Patient Flow Demands with Creative Case Management. *RNCaseManagers.com*. Case Management Professional Staffing Solutions, Inc., September 8, 2007. Web. July 25, 2011. http://www.rncase manager.com/articles/MeetingPatientFlow.asp
4. Gesensway, Deborah. Today's hospitalist. *Today's Hospitalist Magazine*. Today's Hospitalist, Oct. 2009. Web. http://todayshospitalist.com/index.php?b=articles_read
5. Duke, G. J. 2004. Metropolitan audit of appropriate referrals refused admission to intensive care. *Anaesth. Intensive Care* 32: 702–706.
6. Garrouste-Org, M., L. Montuclard, J. F. Timsit, J. Reignier, T. Desmettre, P. Karoubi et al. 2005. Predictors of intensive care unit refusal in French intensive care units: A multiple-center study. *Crit. Care Med.* 33: 750–755.
7. Van Houdenhoven, Mark, Duy-Tien Nguyen, Marinus J. Eijkemans, Ewout W. Steyerberg, Hugo W. Tilanus, Diederik Gommers, Gerhard Wullink, Jan Bakker, and Geert Kazemier. 2007. Optimizing intensive care capacity using individual length-of-stay prediction models. *Critical Care* 11: R42.

8. Wong, D. T., M. Gemez, G. P. McGuire, and B. Kavanaugh. 1999. Utilization of intensive care unit days in a Canadian medical–surgical intensive care unit. *Crit. Care Med.* 27: 1319–1324.

9. Gruenberg, D. A., Wayne Shelton, Susannah L. Rose, Ann E. Rutter, Sophia Socaris, and Glenn McGee. 2006. Factors influencing length of stay in the intensive care unit: Results. *American Journal of Critical Care* 15(5): 502–509.

10. *Leading Practices in Emergency Department Patient Experience.* Rep. Ontario Hospital Association. InfoFinders, 2011. Web. http://www.oha.com/KnowledgeCentre/Library/Documents/Leading%20Practices%20in%20Emergency%20Department%20Patient%20Experience.pdf

15 Medical Career Leadership and Development

Transformational Strategies for the Next Generation of Physician Executives

Eugene Schmuckler, David Edward Marcinko, and Hope Rachel Hetico

CONTENTS

A plethora of educational materials have been published on professional career development and leadership skills; far fewer for physicians of course, but the basics remain the same. Why such a proliferation on this topic? Perhaps it is due to the fact that health care leadership today is now considered very different from the leadership style of yesterday. Every aspect of leadership has been under intense scrutiny, by employees, industry experts, physician executives, and business management gurus. Much like [health, the Internet, and 2.0] today, the very form of leadership is in a state of evolution—changing, modifying, and redefining core values. Many leadership theories or models have been developed, revised, reviewed, and assessed by the experts. What is needed, therefore, is an integration of several models specifically appropriate for today's health care business environment and modern health care executive [1].

YESTERDAY'S DEATH KNOLL FOR MEDICINE?

Replication of the leadership skills of yesterday is the death knoll for business today; especially for the business of health care. Leadership is no longer based on managing, directing, or supervising (top-down or command and control model). As stated by James S. Doyle in his book, *The Business Coach* (A Game Plan for the New Work Environment):

> Today's employees…do not respond well to bosses. Quite simply, they have plenty of other options where they will be treated as full members of a team. Societal norms, generational beliefs and expanding diversity in health care are, in part, contributing to the new business environment. Likewise, medical leaders are required to respond, react and re-direct in the moment.

Without an appreciation of this new philosophy and cultural sea-change, the result can be career disillusionment, burnout, depression, emotional distress, and more [2].

SCENARIO

Jimmy's mother called out to him at seven in the morning, "Jimmy, get up. It's time for school." There was no answer. She called again, this time more loudly, "Jimmy, get up! It's time for school!" Once more there was no more answer. Exasperated, she went to his room and shook him saying, "Jimmy, it's time to get ready for school."

He answered, "Mother, I'm not going to school. There are fifteen hundred kids at that school and every one of them hates me. I'm not going to school."

"Get to school!" she replied sharply.

"But, Mother, all the teachers hate me, too. I saw three of them talking the other day and one of them was pointing his finger at me. I know they all hate me so I'm not going to school," Jimmy answered.

"Get to school!" his mother demanded again.

"But mother, I don't understand it. Why would you want to put me through all of that torture and suffering?" he protested.

"Jimmy, for two good reasons," she fired back. "First, you're forty-two years old. Secondly, you're the principal."

Many of us have had conversations with medical colleagues at which time sentiments of those expressed by Jimmy have been voiced. The career choice that was made many years ago is now, for some reason, no longer as exciting, interesting, and enjoyable as it was when we first began in the field. The career that was undertaken with great anticipation is now something to dread.

The reason for this occurrence is not that difficult to understand. Two of the most important decisions individuals are asked to make are ones for which the least amount of training is offered—choice of spouse and choice of career. How many college students receive a degree in the field they identified when they first enrolled at the college or university? In fact, how many entering freshmen list their choice of major as undecided? It is only during the sophomore year when a major must be declared is the choice actually made. Therefore, career choices made at the age of 19 years might be due to having taken a course that was interesting or easy, appeared to have many entry-level jobs, did not require additional educational or professional training requirements, or was a form of the "family business." Now, as an adult, the individual is functioning in a career field that was selected for him or her by an 18-year-old.

JUDGING CAREER SUCCESS

How do we judge career success? A career represents more than just the job or sequence of jobs we hold in a lifetime. The typical standard for a successful career is by judging how high the individual goes in the organization, how much money is earned, or one's standing attained in the profession. Career success actually needs to be judged on several dimensions. Career adaptability refers to the willingness and capacity to change occupations and/or the work setting to maintain a standard of career progress. Many of you did not anticipate the changes in your chosen medical profession, or specialty, when you began your training.

A second factor is career attitudes. These are your own attitudes about the work itself, our place of work, your level of achievement, and the relationship between work and other parts of your life.

Career identity is that part of your life related to occupational and organizational activities. This is the unique way in which we believe that we fit into the world. Our career is only one part of our being. We play many roles in life, each of which combine to make up our totality. At any point in time, one role may be more important than another. The importance of the roles will generally change over time. Thus, at some point, you may choose to identify more with your career, and at other times, with your family.

A final factor is career performance—a function of both the level of objective career success and the level of psychological success. How much you earn and your reputation factor into, and reflect, objective career success. To be recognized as a "leader" in a field and asked to submit chapters for inclusion in books such as this may be a more important indicator of career success than money.

Psychological success is the second measure of career performance. It is achieved when your self-esteem, the value you place on yourself, increases. As you can see, there is a direct relationship between psychological success and objective success. It may increase as you advance in pay and status at work or decrease with job disappointment and failure. Self-esteem may also increase as one begins to sense personal worth in other ways such as family involvement or developing confidence and competence in a particular field, such as consistently shooting par on the golf course. At that point, objective career success may be secondary in your life. This is why many persons choose to become active in their church or in politics. Even though some may have slowed down on the job, or in their professional career, they can be extremely content with their life.

Consider the following situation. You are traveling on business. Although you are on a direct flight, you have a one-hour layover before the second leg of the flight and your final destination. Leaving the plane, after having placed the "occupied" card on your seat, you walk down the concourse. On the way, you encounter a friend that you knew in high school. The two of you sit to have a cup of coffee and then you realize that your departure time is rapidly approaching. In fact, you will be cutting it quite close. Running down the concourse, you return to the gate only to find that the door has been closed, the Jetway is being retracted, and the plane is being backed away from the gate. You stare out the window watching the plane go to the end of the runway and then begin its takeoff. Something goes horribly wrong and the plane crashes on takeoff, bursting into flames. It is apparent that there will be no survivors. To the world, you are on that plane (remember the occupied card). Traveling on business, your generous insurance policy will be activated. In anticipation of being in a location where they may not have automated teller machines, you have a good deal of cash, sufficient for at least a month. The question for you to consider is: What do you do? For many of you, this will be a good indicator of your career as well as personal success [3].

MEDICAL CAREER PATHS

In retrospect, how many persons are truly aware of their own interests, values, strengths, and weaknesses during their teen years? As with much of human behavior, career choices actually go through a series of stages. Psychologists have for years identified stages of human development. Kohlberg discussed stages of moral development.

In the 1970s, Daniel Levinson published *The Seasons of a Man's Life*, a project he undertook when he began to look inward and tried to understand his behaviors, values, and attitudes toward work. Discussions with his university colleagues indicated that what he was experiencing was not unique to him.

For many years, the prevailing thought was that the correct way to function in the labor market was to gain employment with a company progressing through the years until such time as you were eligible to receive the "gold watch," the symbol of retirement. If you entered a professional discipline such as medicine or law, you did that for the rest of your life.

Today, there are still individuals who follow these traditional patterns, but there are other career paths that may be taken.

The most traditional career route follows a linear path, one that most of you have rejected. This entails gaining employment in a large, bureaucratic organization with a tall pyramidal structure. It involves a series of upward (hopefully) moves in the organization until the career limit is reached. As the individual progresses upward in the organization, he or she may work in different functional departments such as marketing, finance, and production. Organizations having these paths seek employees who tend to be highly oriented toward success defined in organizational terms and exhibit "leadership" skills. In general, these people demonstrate a strong commitment to the workplace. A person with this type of orientation (organizationalist) exhibits the following tendencies:

1. A strong identification with the organization; seeking organization rewards and advancement that are important measures of success and organizational status
2. High morale and job satisfaction
3. A low tolerance for ambiguity about work goals and assignments
4. Identification with superiors, showing deference toward them, conforming and complying out of a desire to advance; maintains the chain of command and compliance, and views respect for authority as the way to succeed
5. Emphasis on organizational goals of efficiency and effectiveness, avoiding controversy and showing concern for threats to organizational success

As readers of this book, you have followed the expert career path, building a career on the basis of personal competence, or the development of a profession (professionals). As you are so painfully aware, you invest heavily, personally, and financially in acquiring a particular skill and then you spend the major portion of your life following that skill.

Unlike the pyramidal structure of the linear path, career paths are found in organizations that tend to be relatively flat, have departments in which there is a functional emphasis, emphasize quality and reliability, and have reward systems containing a strong recognition component.

Medical professionals are persons who are job centered—not organization centered—viewing the demands of the organization as a nuisance that they seek to avoid. However, that avoidance is impossible because the professional must have an organization in which to work. This is even more prevalent in today's era of managed health care. At work, professionals experience more role conflict and are more alienated. Medical professionals exhibit these four tendencies:

1. An experience of occupational socialization that instills high standards of performance in the chosen field; highly ideological about work values.
2. Sees organizational authority as nonrational when there is pressure to act in ways that are not professionally acceptable.
3. Tends to feel that their skills are not fully utilized in organizations; self-esteem may be threatened when they do not have the opportunity to do those things for which they have been trained.

4. Seeks recognition from other professionals outside the organization, and refuses to play the organizational status game except as it reflects their worth relative to others in the organization. Professionals are very concerned with personal achievement and doing well in their chosen field. Organizational rewards serve to reflect the professional's importance relative to others in the system. This recognition may be extremely fulfilling, especially when he or she is accorded higher status and pay than others. In the absence of organizational rewards, the professional may use material objects (large homes, expensive cars) as a way of reflecting status and accomplishment.

Medical professionals are of the opinion that successful performance, not compliance with authority, is more reinforcing. With this mindset, it is not surprising why many medical practitioners balk at working in the managed health care environment. Many professionally oriented people come from the middle class and have become successful through a higher level of education or by other efforts to acquire competence.

Those on the spiral career path make periodic moves from one occupation to another. Individuals who follow this career path tend to have high personal growth motives and are relatively creative. These changes usually come after you have developed competence in the occupation you are working in and you think it is time to change what you do. The ideal spiral career path is to move from one occupation to an area related to it. This enables you to use some of the basic knowledge that you developed in your past work and to transfer it to your new occupation. The difference between this path and the linear path discussed above is that in this case, the mobility pattern is lateral, not upward.

People who take the transitory career path cannot seem to, and perhaps do not want to, settle down. The pattern is one of consistent inconsistency in their work. These are individuals who may find a great deal of satisfaction working as consultants.

The work style is marked by an ability to do many things reasonably well. They value independence and variety, and they work best in relatively loose and unstructured organizations that tolerate the type of freedom they demand in their work.

We have so far discussed the four types of career paths and two career orientations. A final form of career orientation is that of the indifferents—those who simply work for a paycheck. These are individuals who do their work well, but they are not highly committed to their job or the organization. Some characteristics of indifferents are

1. More oriented toward leisure, not the work ethic ("Is it Friday yet?"); separates work from more meaningful aspects of life and seeks higher order need satisfaction outside the work organization
2. Tends to be alienated from work and not committed to the organization
3. Rejects status symbols in organizations
4. Withdraws psychologically from work and organizations when possible

Indifferents are not necessarily born that way; some are actually a product of their work experiences. People who once had an organizational orientation and were highly loyal may no longer follow orders without question. For example, you may have had an officer manager who very early in his or her career was extremely committed to you and your organization. He or she may seek rewards and want to advance. However, in later career life, after having been passed over several times for promotion, the person seeks rewards elsewhere. Thus, it is possible that through office practices, your organization may turn highly committed organizationalists (or professionals) into indifferents.

MEDICAL CAREER EVALUATION

Studs Turkel, in his outstanding book *Working*, makes the comment that work is the mechanism by which many of us get our daily bread and our daily purpose. If this is to be the case, then the workplace needs to offer us something more than a paycheck. The Wilson Learning Corporation surveyed 1500 people asking "If you had enough money to live comfortably for the rest of your life, would you continue to work?" Seventy percent said that they would continue to work, but 60% of those said they would change jobs and seek "more satisfying" work.

Each of us has in fact been put in charge of our own careers. Our personal career management is a lifelong process. Our task is to be able to discover our place in the world where we will be able to enjoy a high level of wellness. This requires us to now assess our career, not from the eyes of the 16-year-old that initially chose the career. The career you are now pursuing needs to be compatible with your own unique skills, knowledge, personality, and interests. It is important to keep in mind that no one is married to his or her job. When it comes to the workplace, most of us are in dating relationships.

As part of your examining your current medical career, answer the following questions: Why do you work? What does work mean to you? What do you want from work?

Research shows that most people work for three major reasons. The first of these is money. Not only is this necessary for our most basic needs; it also serves as a means of determining our self-image. A second reason is to be with other people. Being at work enables us to belong, to be part of something beyond ourselves. We become part of a team. Some offices consider co-workers to be part of an extended family. The work setting affords us the opportunity for receiving feedback, recognition, and support. The third most often given reason is that work validates us as people if we consider what we do as having meaning. "I chose the medical profession so as to make a difference." Individuals with career success have a sense of purpose—a feeling that their work has meaning and contributes to a worthwhile cause. This is not a trick question. How well does what you do in your office every day meet your needs for money, affiliation, and meaning?

Without a sense of purpose on the job, the chances are that your performance, while adequate, will not place you in the excellent category. Therefore, it is necessary for each and every one of us to be able to succinctly answer the question, "What is the purpose of your job?" That is a tough question to answer. As a medical professional, you may have seen what you considered to be the purpose of your job radically changed due to changes in the way services are now delivered. While we cannot bring back the past, we can work around the present. Think about this for a moment, "If you want something to happen make a space for it" [4]. What this means is that whether you remain in your current profession or move elsewhere, there is a need for you to establish long-range, medium-range, short-range, mini-, and micro-goals.

Long-range goals are those concerned with the overall style of life that you wish to live. Regardless of your current age, these goals are necessary. Long-range goals do not need to be too detailed, because like the federal budget surplus, changes will come along. Just as the government is making projections into the future, you too need to be making projections, including but not limited to retirement.

Medium-range goals are goals covering the next 5 years or so. These are the goals that include the next step in your career. These are goals over which we have control and we are able to monitor them and see whether we are on track to accomplish them and modify our efforts accordingly.

Short-range goals generally cover a period of time about 1 month to 1 year from now. These are goals that can be set quite realistically and we are able to see fairly quickly whether or not we are on track to reaching them. We do not want to set these goals at impossible levels, but we do want to stretch ourselves. After all, that is the reason you are probably reading this chapter.

Mini-goals are those goals covering from about 1 day to 1 month. Obviously, we have much greater control over these goals than you do over those of a longer term. By thinking in small blocks of time, there is much more control over each individual unit.

Micro-goals are goals covering the next 15 minutes to an hour. These are the only goals over which you have direct control. Because of this direct control, micro-goals, even though modest in impact, are extraordinarily important, for it is only through these micro-goals that you can attain your larger goals. If you do not take steps toward your long-range goals in the next 15 minutes, when will you? The following 15 minutes? The 15 minutes after that? Sooner or later, you have to pick 15 minutes and get going. At some point, procrastination has to be put aside.

PERSONAL ASSETS EVALUATION

In thinking of your goals, it now becomes necessary to evaluate your personal assets. Conducting this personal inventory requires you to identify your assets as well as your shortcomings. First, look at a time in your life when you were performing at your best. What were your thoughts and feelings? How did you behave? What were you doing? Now look at the reverse when you were doing poorly. What were your thoughts and feelings at that time? How did you behave? What were you doing?

If you are like others when you were at your best, you described yourself as being confident, enthusiastic, organized, relaxed, focused, in control, friendly, and decisive. The flip side, when at your worst you were fearful, apathetic, messy, anxious, lacking direction, out of control, argumentative, and frustrated.

As you can see, the emotions when we are at our best are all positive. This leads to the conclusion that it is to our advantage to be at our best as much as possible. Being at our best derives from working in those areas where we contribute our talents to something we believe in. As we continue our own personal inventory, we need to look at our special abilities. That is, what are you good at and find easy to do. Think of the following questions. It is not necessary to write down your answers; just think about them.

1. How would you like to be remembered?
2. What have you always dreamed of contributing to the world?
3. Looking back on your life, what are some of your major contributions?
4. When people think of you, what might they say are your most outstanding characteristics?
5. What do you really want from your life and your work?
6. In what way may you still feel limited by the past? If so, by what?
7. What will it take to let go of what has happened, no matter how good or bad? Are you willing to let go?
8. How might the rut of conformity or comfort be limiting you? Why?
9. How different do you really want life to be? Why?
10. Have you ever stated what it is you truly desire? If no, why not?

Thinking about remaining in your present career or moving into another one is not easy. You are at the edge of a cliff and need to decide if you are going to turn back or to trust in yourself to successfully make it down to the bottom. People who are afraid of the dark lose their fear with just the slightest of a light in the room. As you have been going through this chapter, you have been shining a light, however dim it may appear to you. You can see all of the items around you. The obstacles are there, but with your advanced knowledge, you can anticipate ways to avoid them.

Having looked at and possibly re-evaluated your plans, you can now do a thorough analysis of your assets. The assets requiring the most scrutiny are the following:

1. Your talents and skills
2. Your intelligence
3. Your motivation
4. Your friends
5. Your education
6. Your family

Your talents and skills are more than likely what has gotten you to the point you are at in your present career. For purposes of definition, talents are innate, whereas skills are acquired. Some have talent in interpersonal relations and some in artistic pursuits. Skills may be selected to complement the already present talents. It is skills that are necessary for expanding your options. As you seek out new skill areas, ask yourself these questions: Do the skills provide occupational relevance? Might you be able to get others to pay you to teach them the skill? Will the skill be useful throughout life? Will the skill help you conquer new environments and gain new experiences? In addition, of course, is it something you like to do?

Intelligence is considered to be the ability of the individual to cope with the world. Originally, intelligence focused primarily in the area of cognitive skills. Recently, attention has been directed to what is called emotional intelligence, a concept that directs attention to social skills. Whether you were able to breeze through your courses in college or you truly had to work hard, earning your degrees demonstrates a better than average amount of cognitive intellectual ability. In order to maximize your brainpower, challenge yourself regularly.

Motivation looks at how hard you are willing to work, your level of persistence, and the degree to which you want to do well. Different things motivate each of us and our personal motivators can vary from day to day. How many times have you had people say that they could not do your job? What are the activities that are attractive to you? More than likely, an important motivator for you is to do something worthwhile. It has also been found that we tend to perform at about the same level as those people who are close to us. What this means is that those people with whom you work are going to have a substantial impact on your motivation.

Friends of course are invaluable assets. We use our friends as models for our own behavior. Those persons we consider friends share many of our attitudes, actions, and opinions. With time, we will change to be like our friends, and they will change to become like us. Associating with those like us tends to temper our behavior. We try not to associate with the "wrong crowd" lest we become like them.

Education needs to be ongoing. Recently, it was reported that "all careers and businesses will be transformed by new technologies in often unpredictable ways. The era of the entrepreneur will make 'boutique' businesses more competitive with the behemoths, as mid-sized institutions get squeezed out. And medical breakthroughs and the ongoing health movement will enhance—and extend—people's lives." The implication of these changes is that new technologies often require a higher level of education and training to use them effectively, and new biotechnology jobs will open up. The authors state that all the technological knowledge we work with today will represent only 1% of the knowledge that will be available in 2050. The half-life of an engineer's knowledge today is only 5 years; in 10 years, 90% of what an engineer knows will be available on the computer. In electronics, fully half of what a student learns as a freshman is obsolete by his or her senior year. The implication here is that all of us must get used to the idea of lifelong learning.

Family influences who and what we are and do. They can be a support group or they can be a deterrent to your goals. It is incumbent on every individual reading this chapter to consult with immediate family members at all stages of your career planning process.

WHAT MAKES A LEADER?

In a prominent Harvard Business Review publication, *What Makes a Leader*, and book *Primal Leadership: Learning to Lead with Emotional Intelligence*, author Daniel Goleman, PhD, suggested that the desired traits most often cited were intelligence, toughness, determination, and vision. A sufficient level of technical and analytical ability is even more essential now that we have moved into the Health 2.0 era. However, the leadership skills of this era are placing much more emphasis on the so-called 'soft skills' or 'emotional intelligence' and this may very well be the key attribute that distinguishes outstanding health care leaders, and successful physician executives, from those who are merely adequate [4].

CHANGING HEALTH 2.0 PARADIGMS

In the health care space, the fundamental shift for physicians and public health professionals occurred in the landmark 2003 Institute of Medicine (OPM) report from Academic Press—*Who*

Will Keep the Public Healthy? (Educating Public Health Professionals for the 21st Century). A key recommendation was to work on integrating leadership skills and related training within medical, nursing, and all allied health care programs.

MULTIGENERATIONS

Today, it is common to have three generations represented in any health care organization. We have the Baby Boomers, Gen X (generation following the baby boom [especially Americans and Canadians born in the 1960s and 1970s]), and now, Gen Y (Millennial Generation, Echo Boomers, or the Trophy Generation). This newest generation of physicians has grown up with Facebook and Google, with Twitter and YouTube, and with Sermo.com and the MedicalExecutivePost.com. They "get" the technology, but do not always understand how its use affects their efforts to forge identities as medical professionals.

Generations X and Y have a very strong work ethic, but seek balance and satisfaction in their work and professional lives. Moreover, this is applicable to both men and women. Bruce Tuglan, a consultant who works with younger generations, opines that Gen X and Y are going to be

> The most high-performing civic-minded workforce in the history of the world, but they are also going to be the most high-maintenance workforce in the history of the world.

Gen Y is completely unchained and comfortable with Health 2.0 initiatives. They have been using technology for years now. Therefore, rather than trying to get them to conform to traditional health care models, and society membership, they should be empowered to lead the way themselves into the future.

On the other hand, the Baby Boomer generation is saying with some sadness, "Medicine sure isn't what it used to be!", while Generation X is saying "It's about time things changed!" and the latest generation to enter the medical workforce, Gen Y's, are saying "Ready or not, we're here, get used to it."

Each generation is extraordinarily complex, bringing various skills, expertise, and expectations to the medical work environment. Determining the best methods to unite such diverse thinking is one of the many challenges faced by health care leaders. Is it any wonder that many leaders in the Baby Boomer generation find themselves at a loss? The days of functional leadership are gone and, suddenly, no one cares about the expertise of the Baby Boomers or how they climbed the corporate ladder, in medicine, or elsewhere. The concept of 'paying your dues' is as foreign to the younger generations as is life without email, wikis, or social networks. Still not convinced? Just think about the election of Barack H. Obama as 44th president of the United States. Leadership in the era of Health 2.0 is no longer about controlling or dictating with intense focus on the bottom line; it is about collaboration, empowerment, and communication.

LEADERSHIP VERSUS MANAGEMENT

Many times, individuals will use the terms management and leadership synonymously. In actuality the terms have significantly different meanings. Warren Bennis describes the difference between managers and leaders as "Managers do thing right, Leaders the right thing."

Managers are those individuals who have been managing, as their primary function, a team of people and their activities. In effect, managers are those who have been given their authority by the nature of their role and ensure that the work gets done by focusing on day-to-day tasks and their activities. On the other hand, a leader's approach is generally innate in its approach. Good leadership skills are difficult to learn because they are far more behavioral in nature than those skills needed for management. Leaders are also very focused on change, recognizing that continual improvement can be achieved in their people and their activities can be a great step toward continued success.

Perhaps some of the best training grounds for the development of leaders are the military. The Marine Corps slogan is "A Few Good Men" and the military academies at Annapolis (Navy), New

London, Connecticut (Coast Guard), Colorado Springs (Air Force), and West Point (Army) all have as their main mission, the development of leaders. This is done by a number of different techniques. At graduation, the new officers, regardless of the branch of service, have been taught, and more importantly, have internalized the following—communicate the missions, sensitivity matters, real respect is earned, and trust and challenge your soldiers. It is due to these lessons that many graduates of the military academies go on to positions of leadership in the private sector as well as in the government. Communicating the mission refers to conveying to those who work with us what our practice is hoping to accomplish and the role of each employee in achieving that goal. Given an understanding and awareness of the mission, when confronted with a barrier, employees are able to face hard problems when there is no well-defined approach by which to deal with them.

Sensitivity does matter—A leader treats each employee with respect and dignity, regardless of race, gender, cultural background, or particular role they actually perform in the practice. Consider how many legal suits are filed against any type of organization, whether it is a medical practice or a large manufacturing facility due to perceived disparate treatment toward the employee based on race, religion, gender, sexual preference, or other non-work-related issues.

Real respect is earned—Having initials after one's name and the wearing of a lab coat does not automatically entitle an individual to respect. Formal authority has been found to be one of the least effective forms of influence. Only by earning the respect of your staff as well as your patients can you be sure that your intent will be carried out when you are not present. Setting the example in performance and conduct, rather than "do as I say, not as I do," level of activity enables one to exert influence far greater than titles.

Trust and challenge your employees—How many times have practices sought to hire the best and brightest, only to second guess the employee. Eric Schmidt, the former CEO of Google, describes his management philosophy as having "…an employee base in which everybody is doing exactly what they want every day." Obviously, there are certain policies and procedures, but at the same time, the leader enables decision making to the lowest possible level. This also enables employees to question why certain policies and procedures are still being followed when more effective and efficient methods are available.[*]

The phrase "Physician, heal thyself" (Luke 4:23, King James Version) means that we have to attend to our own faults, in preference to pointing out the faults of others. The phrase alludes to the readiness of physicians to heal sickness in others while sometimes not being able or willing to heal themselves. By the same token, it now is necessary for us to learn how to manage ourselves. It suggests that physicians, while often being able to help the sick, cannot always do so, and when sick themselves are no better placed than anyone else.[†]

"We will have to learn how to develop ourselves. We will have to place ourselves outside the boundaries where we can make the greatest contribution. And we will have to stay mentally alert and engaged during a 50-year working life, which means knowing how and when to change the work we do."[‡] Although one's IQ and certain personality characteristics are more or less innate and appear to remain stable over time, there are individual capabilities that enable leadership and can be developed. Enhancement of these capabilities can lead to the individual being able to carry out the leadership tasks of setting direction, gaining commitment, and creating alignment. These capabilities include self-management capabilities, social capabilities, and work facilitation capabilities.

Without question, while it is possible to cram for a test and graduate at the top of one's class, that does not assure leadership ability. We all know at least one person who scores at the highest levels on cognitive measures, but would be incapable of pouring liquid out of a boot if the instructions were written on the heel [5].

---

[*] Raymond, D. How the army prepared me to work at Google. *Harvard Business Review*, June 16, 2009. Available at http://blogs.hbr.org/frontline-leadership/2009/06/how-the-army-prepared-me-to-wo.html.

[†] Martin, G. Physician, heal thyself. *The Phrase Finder*. 2010. Available at http://www.phrases.org.uk/meanings/281850.html.

[‡] Drucker, P. Managing oneself. Harvard Business Review (January 2005): 100–109.

New Rules of Physician Executive Leadership

There are more than 950,000 physicians in the United States. Yet, the brutal supply and demand, and demographic calculus of the matter is that there are just too many aging patients chasing too few doctors. Compensation and reimbursement is plummeting as Uncle Sam becomes the payer-of-choice for more than 52% of us. Furthermore, in recent years, many large health care corporations, hospitals, and clinical and medical practices have not been market responsive to this change. Some physicians with top-down business models did not recognize the changing health care ecosystem or participatory medicine climate. Change is not inherent in the DNA of traditionalists. These entities and practitioners represented a rigid or "used-to-be" mentality, not a flexible or "want-to-be" mindset. Yet today's physicians and emerging Health 2.0 initiatives must possess a market nimbleness that cannot be recreated in a command-controlled or collectivist environment.

Going forward, it is not difficult to imagine the following rules for the new virtual medical culture, and physician executive leader.

Rule 1

Forget about large office suites, surgery centers, fancy equipment, larger hospitals, and the bricks and mortar that comprised traditional medical practices. One doctor with a great idea, good bedside manners, or competitive advantage can outfox a slew of insurance companies, CPAs, or the AMA, while still serving patients and making money. It is now a unit-of-one economy where "ME Inc." is the standard. Physicians must maneuver for advantages that boost their standing and credibility among patients, peers, and payers. Examples include patient satisfaction surveys, outcomes research analysis, evidence-based-medicine, direct reimbursement compensation, physician economic credentialing, and true patient-centric medicine.

For example, physicians should realize the power of networking, vertical integration, and the establishment of virtual offices that come together to treat a patient and then disband when a successful outcome is achieved. Job security is *earned* with more successful outcomes, not a magnificent office suite or onsite presence.

Rule 2

Challenge conventional wisdom, think outside the traditional box, recapture your dreams and ambitions, disregard conventional gurus, and work harder than you have ever worked before. Remember the old saying, "if everyone is thinking alike, then nobody is thinking." Do traditionalists or collective health care reform advocates react rationally or irrationally?

For example, some health care competition and career thought-leaders, such as Shirley Svorny, PhD, a professor of economics and chair of the Department of Economics at California State University, Northridge, wonder if a medical degree is a barrier—rather than enabler—of affordable health care. An expert on the regulation of health care professionals, including medical professional licensing, she has participated in health policy summits organized by Cato and the Texas Public Policy Foundation. She argues that licensure not only fails to protect consumers from incompetent physicians, but, by raising barriers to entry, makes health care more expensive and less accessible. Institutional oversight and a sophisticated network of private accrediting and certification organizations, all motivated by the need to protect reputations and avoid legal liability, offer whatever consumer protections exist today.

Rule 3

Differentiate yourself among your health care peers. Do or learn something new and unknown by your competitors. Market your accomplishments and let the world know. Be a non-conformist. Conformity is an operational standard and a straitjacket on creativity. Doctors must create and innovate, not blindly follow entrenched medical societies into oblivion.

For example, the establishment of virtual medical schools and hospitals, where students, nurses, and doctors learn and practice their art on cyber entities that look and feel like real patients, can be generated electronically through the wonders of virtual reality units.

Rule 4

Realize that the present situation is not necessarily the future. Attempt to see the future and discern your place in it. Master the art of quick change with fast, but informed decision making. Do what you love, disregard what you do not, and let the fates have their way with you. Then, decide for yourself if you are of this ilk—and adhere to the above rules. In other words, *get fly!*

Or, become an employed, or government doctor. Just remember that the entity that can give you a job, can also take it away.

ASSESSMENT

Popular health care CEOs and their leadership blogs:

1. Paul Levy, President/CEO of Beth Israel Deaconess Medical Center in Boston
2. Bill Roper, CEO of University of North Carolina Health Care System
3. Bruce Bullen, CEO of Harvard Pilgrim Health Care
4. Dr. Bill Atkinson, CEO of WakeMed Health & Hospitals in Raleigh
5. Marty Bonick, CEO of Jewish Hospital in Louisville
6. Rob Colones, CEO of McLeod Health in South Carolina
7. Scott Kashman, CEO of St. Joseph Medical Center
8. Todd Linden, CEO of Grinnell Regional Medical Center
9. Tom Quinn, CEO of Community General Hospital
10. Francine R. Gaillour MD, physician leadership coach

CONCLUSIONS

This chapter has presented an overview of initial career selection, career pathing and development, career change, and leadership in order to help you determine what you truly want to be when you grow up. As we wrote it, we could not help but reflect on an anecdote shared by a colleague. An individual came to see him expressing concern that at 40 years of age he still had not reached a satisfactory point in his life. Our colleague then asked him where he wanted to be. The response was "I don't know" to which he responded in unison, "Congratulations, you've arrived. Too many times we encounter physicians and medical practitioners who express the same statements. Unhappy with what they are doing they have no idea as to what it is they would like to be doing" [6].

Victor Frankl, MD, a psychiatrist who was a Holocaust survivor, created an entire school of psychotherapy based upon his experiences in the German concentration camps. In his book, *Man's Search for Meaning*, he makes reference to the fact that it became possible for him to determine when a fellow prisoner was going to die simply by that person's behavior—giving up. Frankl writes, "Evermore people today have the means to live, but no meaning to live for."

CASE MODEL 15.1: SEEKING A CHIEF MEDICAL DIRECTOR FOR A MISSISSIPPI HEALTH MAINTENANCE ORGANIZATION

Centene Corporation is seeking a Chief Medical Director (CMD) for Magnolia Health Plan (Magnolia), a wholly owned subsidiary and Health Maintenance Organization for the state of Mississippi. The regional headquarters for Magnolia are located in Jackson, MS.

ABOUT CENTENE

A Fortune 500 company, Centene is a national leader in low-cost solutions for high-quality health care services for uninsured and underinsured patients. Centene's subsidiary health plans bring better health outcomes to their 1.5 million members. Centene's core philosophy is that quality health care is best delivered locally. This local approach enables them to provide accessible, high-quality, and culturally sensitive health care services to their members in their own communities.

VISIONARY LEADER NEEDED

The CMD will establish the strategic vision and attendant policies and procedures for Magnolia Health Plan. The CMD will provide leadership and direction to the medical management, quality improvement, and credentialing functions for Magnolia Health Plan based on, and in support of, the company's strategic plan. The CMD will review analyses of activities, costs, operations, and forecast data to determine progress toward stated goals and objectives. Also within the purview of CMD will be oversight for compliance with National Committee on Quality Assurance and/or Joint Commission on Accreditation of Health Care Organization standards as determined for accreditation of the health plan.

IDEAL PHYSICIAN CANDIDATES

Successful candidates will be physician leaders with thorough knowledge of quality improvement practices and familiarity with medical information systems, medical claims payment processing, and coding. Knowledge of managed care, Medicaid, and case management programs are also essential. Board certification in a recognized medical specialty and an active medical license are required.

We welcome your interest, or nominations, for this highly visible role.

SEARCH FIRM CONTACT

Cejka Executive Search
4 CityPlace Dr., Ste. 300
St. Louis, MO 63141
314.236.4478 Office
mwohldmann@cejkasearch.com
http://www.cejkaexecutivesearch.com

CHECKLIST 1: Leadership and Career Development	YES	NO
Review leadership qualities at your facility[ies].		
Could the operations managers do a better job of communicating the capabilities and limitations of the operations management function to managers of other functional areas?	o	o
Would increased involvement of physicians and other stakeholders in the strategic planning process improve performance?	o	o
Could operations managers benefit by increasing their knowledge of clinical areas?	o	o
Do operations managers have the necessary communication skills to collaborate with other functional and clinical areas?	o	o
Could board composition be improved by adding representatives from the community who are concerned with community health status?	o	o
Could the level of participation in reporting and monitoring of community health be increased?	o	o

CHECKLIST 2: Human Resources	YES	NO
Determine your human resources development needs.		
Would training in service-encounter management improve the perception of quality by patients?	o	o
Could training in the operation of equipment or software improve utilization of facilities?	o	o
Could an infusion of personnel from other organizations bring in new skills and attitudes to existing personnel?	o	o
Could training and development aid in the implementation of patient-focused health care?	o	o
Could training and development aid in the implementation of consumer-driven health care?	o	o
Could training and development aid in the development of a safety culture?	o	o

ACKNOWLEDGMENTS

Modified and updated with permission from Schmuckler, E., Relinquishing the leadership role of physicians, *The Business of Medical Practice*, edited by D.E. Marcinko, Springer Publishing, New York, NY, 2000.

REFERENCES

1. Avansino, J., Gow, K., and Migita, D. 2011. Transforming doctors into change agents. In: *Leading the Lean Health Care Journal*, edited by J. Wellman and P. Hagan. New York: Productivity Press.
2. Brousseau, K.R., Driver, M.J., Eneroth, K., and Larson, R. 1996. Career pandemonium: Realigning organizations and individuals. *Academy of Management Executive* 10 (4), 52–66.
3. Campbell, D. 1974. If You Don't Know Where You Are Going You'll Probably End Up Somewhere Else. Niles, IL: Argus Communications.
4. Hagan, P. and Bailey, C. 2011. What we need most—We can't buy: Leadership and cultural change engaging everyone in a patient-focused culture. In: *Leading the Lean Health Care Journal*, edited by J. Wellman and P. Hagan. New York: Productivity Press.
5. McNally, D. 1991. *Even Eagles Need A Push*. New York: Delacorte Press.
6. Presthus, R. 2001. *The Organizational Society*. New York: St. Martin's Press.

BIBLIOGRAPHY

Bauer, J.C. 2009. Mastering Relentless Progress in Medical Science and Technology Realities of Health Reform: New Strategies for Survival and Growth. The Governance Institute (Leadership Conference), Naples, FL, January.

Doyle, J.S. 1999. *The Business Coach*. New York: Wiley.

Gardner, K., 2009. *The Excellent Board II: Practical Solutions for Health Care Trustees and CEOs*. Washington, DC: AHA Press.

Gardner, K. 2008. *Better CEO Board Relations*. Washington, DC: AHA Press.

Goldsmith, J. 2003. *Digital Medicine: Implications for Health Care Leaders*. Bozeman, MT: Second River Health Care Press.

Goleman, D. 2004. *Primal Leadership: Learning to Lead with Emotional Intelligence*. Boston: Harvard Business School.

Irelan, C. and Irelan, J. 2008. *It's Not Rocket Surgery: How to be a Star Leader at Every Level*. Bozeman, MT: Second River Health Care Press.

Kenagy, J. 2010. *Designed to Adapt: Leading Health Care in Challenging Times*. Tampa, FL: Health Administration Press.

Lauer, C.S. 2009. *Decency*. Bozeman, MT: Second River Health Care Press.

Leebov, W. 2008. *Essentials for Great Personal Leadership*. Washington, DC: AHA Press.

Leebov, W. 2009. *Great Personal Leadership*. Chicago, IL: AHA Press.

Marcinko, D.E. 2003. *The Status of Physician and Medical Unions. Financial Planning for Health Care Professionals*. New York: Aspen Publishers.

Pointer, D.D. 2002. *Getting to Great: Principles of Health Care Organization Governance*. New York: Jossey-Bass.

Scott, M., Kaiser, L., and Baltus, R. 2009. *Courage to Be First*. Bozeman, MT: Second River Health Care Press.

Schipman, C. and Kay, K. 2009. Womenomics: Write your own Rules for Success. New York: Harper Business.

Schmuckler, E. 2011. Physician leadership and self branding. In: *The Business of Medical Practice*, 3rd edition, edited by D.E. Marcinko. New York: Springer.

Svorny, S. 2008. Medical Licensing: An Obstacle to Affordable Medical Care. Policy Analysis No. 621. CATO Institute, September (CATO.org).

Tamura, G. and Migita, D. 2011. Delivering compassionate care through clinical work on rounds. In: Leading the Lean Health Care Journal, edited by J. Wellman and P. Hagan. New York: Productivity Press.

Tuglan, B. 2007. *It's Okay to be the Boss*. New York, NY: Collins Business.

Tuglan, B. 2009. *Not Everyone Gets a Trophy*. Hoboken, NJ: Jossey-Bass.

INTERNET RESOURCES

http://executivephysician.blogspot.com/
http://www.rainmakerthinking.com/
http://www.EntrepreneurialMD.com/
http://www.MedicalExecutivePost.com

Index